T0399448

OXFORD THEORETICAL PERSPECTIVES IN LAW

Series Editor

ALEXANDER TSESIS
*Professor and D'Alemberte Chair in Constitutional Law, Florida State
University College of Law*

Aligning Election Law

OXFORD THEORETICAL PERSPECTIVES IN LAW

The *Oxford Theoretical Perspectives in Law* series publishes works that explore a diversity of topics pertinent to jurisprudence, statutory review, constitutional principles, substantive entitlements, procedural justice, legal history, and policymaking. The series is committed to intellectual diversity.

Books in this series parse, critique, expand, and elaborate theoretical approaches to broad ranges of legal topics. Authors' works explain the principles, priorities, sensibilities, perspectives, traditions, or social conditions that drive evolution of law. Authors write of how sovereignty, wealth, connection, privilege, culture, and popular discourse influence legal concepts, rules of decision, procedural justice, and substantive fairness. The series further examines how law impacts sociology, politics, traditions, and culture and, in turn, how they impact precedents, policy priorities, administrative tactics, separation of powers, and representative governance.

Oxford Theoretical Perspectives in Law offers a forum for pursuit of contested matters in legal theory that impact contemporary society. Approaches range from empirical, to normative, to positivist. The basic concept may be said to articulate core, rule-of-law principles in subjects that range from constitutional law to property law.

Authors in the series advance fields of knowledge by elaborating, parsing, analyzing, and criticizing text, history, norms, doctrines, and structure. They thereby provide readers with substantive and structural frameworks to be used in research and teaching. Comprehensive studies enable authors and readers to explore challenges facing a variety of current affairs. A dive into legal theory, ultimately and perhaps idealistically, seeks to evaluate and effectuate fairness and justice.

Aligning Election Law

NICHOLAS O. STEPHANOPOULOS

Kirkland and Ellis Professor of Law, Harvard Law School, USA

OXFORD
UNIVERSITY PRESS

OXFORD
UNIVERSITY PRESS

Oxford University Press is a department of the University of Oxford.
It furthers the University's objective of excellence in research, scholarship,
and education by publishing worldwide. Oxford is a registered trade mark of
Oxford University Press in the UK and in certain other countries.

Published in the United States of America by Oxford University Press
198 Madison Avenue, New York, NY 10016, United States of America.

© Nicholas O. Stephanopoulos 2024

Library of Congress Cataloging-in-Publication Data
Names: Stephanopoulos, Nicholas O., author.
Title: Aligning election law / Nicholas O. Stephanopoulos.
Description: New York : Oxford University Press, [2024] | Series: Theoretical perspectives in
law series | Includes bibliographical references and index. |
Identifiers: LCCN 2024024238 | ISBN 9780197662151 (hardback) | ISBN 9780197662175 (epub) |
ISBN 9780197662168 (updf) | ISBN 9780197662182 (online)
Subjects: LCSH: Presidents—Wisconsin—Election. | Election districts—Wisconsin. |
Election law—Wisconsin. | Election law—United States—States.
Classification: LCC KFW2820 .S74 2024 | DDC 342.775/07—dc23/eng/20240604
LC record available at https://lccn.loc.gov/2024024238

DOI: 10.1093/9780197662182.001.0001

Pod

Note to Readers
This publication is designed to provide accurate and authoritative information in regard to the
subject matter covered. It is based upon sources believed to be accurate and reliable and is intended
to be current as of the time it was written. It is sold with the understanding that the publisher is not
engaged in rendering legal, accounting, or other professional services. If legal advice or other expert
assistance is required, the services of a competent professional person should be sought. Also, to
confirm that the information has not been affected or changed by recent developments, traditional
legal research techniques should be used, including checking primary sources where appropriate.

(Based on the Declaration of Principles jointly adopted by a Committee of the
American Bar Association and a Committee of Publishers and Associations.)

You may order this or any other Oxford University Press publication
by visiting the Oxford University Press website at www.oup.com.

Contents

Acknowledgments

The first flicker of the idea that eventually became this book arose during a conversation I had with Eric Posner early in my stint as an assistant professor at the University of Chicago Law School. Eric noted that economists and political scientists often use a left-right spatial model to assess politicians and policies. Do election law scholars rely on a similar model, Eric asked? No they don't, I answered, but they could. Governmental outputs and popular preferences could be plotted on the same axis (or axes). Electoral regulations could then be analyzed to determine if they bring what the government does closer to, or further from, what the people want it to do. With this information in hand, courts and other institutions could look sympathetically at aligning electoral rules and skeptically at misaligning ones. This insight remains the core of the alignment theory of election law that I develop in the book. I'm grateful to Eric for helping to plant the seed that grew into this theory.

A good deal of the book builds on articles I previously published. The book as a whole is a (much) expanded version of *Elections and Alignment*, 114 COLUM. L. REV. 283 (2014), in which I first introduced the alignment approach. The empirical findings about how different electoral regulations affect alignment in *The Realities of Electoral Reform*, 68 VAND. L. REV. 761 (2015) (with Eric M. McGhee and Steven Rogers), also pepper the book. Chapter 9: "Campaign Finance" is based closely on *Aligning Campaign Finance Law*, 101 VA. L. REV. 1425 (2015). Chapter 11: "The Anti-Alignment Court" borrows considerably from *The Anti-Carolene Court*, 2019 SUP. CT. REV. 111. And the first half of Chapter 12: "Aligning Alternatives" is derived from *The Sweep of the Electoral Power*, 36 CONST. COMMENT. 1 (2021).

The book benefited from conversations with, and comments from, many colleagues and friends. These include Abhay Aneja, Yochai Benkler, Adam Bonica, Richard Briffault, Jessica Bulman-Pozen, Josh Chafetz, Guy-Uriel Charles, Yasmin Dawood, Rosalind Dixon, Michael Dorf, Joshua Douglas, Justin Driver, Christopher Elmendorf, Joseph Fishkin, Edward Foley, David Fontana, Charles Fried, James Gardner, John Goldberg, Jonathan Gould, Richard Hasen, Deborah Hellman, Aziz Huq, Samuel Issacharoff, Howell Jackson, Vicki Jackson, Michael Kang, Louis Kaplow, Ellen Katz, Tarunabh Khaitan, Michael Klarman, Lawrence Lessig, Daryl Levinson, Justin Levitt, Saul Levmore, Michael Morley, Michael Morse, Jennifer Nou, Nicholas Papaspyrou, Nathaniel Persily, Richard Pildes, David Pozen, Jonathan Rodden, Andrew Sabl, Benjamin Sachs, David

Schleicher, Naomi Schoenbaum, Larry Schwartztol, Miriam Seifter, Larry Solum, Geoffrey Stone, David Strauss, Chris Tausanovitch, Franita Tolson, Alexander Tsesis, Mark Tushnet, Christopher Warshaw, Laura Weinrib, and Robert Yablon. I deeply appreciate your engagement and encouragement.

I had the opportunity to present part or all of the book at numerous conferences, seminars, and workshops. These included events at Cornell Law School, DePaul University College of Law, George Washington University Law School, Harvard Law School, Harvard University, Loyola University Chicago School of Law, UC Irvine School of Law, University of Athens, University of Chicago Law School, University of Michigan, University of New South Wales Law School, University of Oklahoma College of Law, University of Pittsburgh School of Law, Valparaiso University Law School, University of Wisconsin Law School, Washington University School of Law, and Yale Law School. I'm thankful to the participants for their helpful comments and questions.

Finally, I'm indebted to my children, Adrian and Iliana, and my wife, Ruth. Ruth is my academic muse, my collaborator in myriad litigation and policy projects, and my life partner. Without you, neither this book nor anything else would have been possible.

Introduction

What's Wrong with Wisconsin?

Here's a question that divides judges and scholars of election law: What—if anything—is wrong with Wisconsin's political system? Over the last decade, Wisconsin's statewide elections have been exceptionally competitive. Its last two presidential races (2016 and 2020) were decided by less than a percentage point. The margin of victory in its last senatorial race (2022) was exactly one point. On the other hand, Wisconsin's districted elections haven't been nearly so close. Just a single congressional seat, and a handful of state legislative seats, changed hands over the last ten years. At both electoral levels, the average margin of victory hovered around thirty points, close to the national mean.

Wisconsin's record with respect to voter participation is similarly ambiguous. Its turnout has long been among the highest in the country. In the 2020 general election, for example, more than 70 percent of Wisconsinites over eighteen cast ballots—compared to a share nationwide just above 60 percent. However, after Republicans took control of the state government in 2011, they enacted a series of voting restrictions. These limits included a photo ID requirement for voting, a proof-of-citizenship requirement for college students registering to vote, a cutback to early voting locations and hours, and a ban on certain modes of sending absentee ballots. Underlying these policies, according to a federal district court, was "the intent to suppress Democratic voters to gain a partisan advantage."[1]

The unified Republican government that made it harder to vote also aggressively gerrymandered Wisconsin's district maps in 2011. Over the ensuing five state house elections, Republican candidates managed to earn a majority of the statewide vote only twice. Yet thanks to artfully drawn districts, they controlled no fewer than *sixty* of the chamber's ninety-nine seats during this period.[2]

---

[1] One Wisconsin Inst., Inc. v. Thomsen, 198 F. Supp. 3d 896, 927 (W.D. Wis. 2016), *rev'd*, 963 F.3d 665 (7th Cir. 2020).

[2] This ruthless gerrymander-spawned litigation, in which I was an attorney, culminating in the Supreme Court decision of *Gill v. Whitford*, 138 S. Ct. 1916 (2018). This gerrymander also endured into the 2020 redistricting cycle after, in the face of deadlock by the elected branches, the Wisconsin Supreme Court eventually approved the legislature's state house and state senate maps. *See* Johnson v. Wis. Elections Comm'n, 972 N.W.2d 559 (Wis. 2022). However, the Wisconsin Supreme Court later invalidated these maps because of their many noncontiguous districts, thus finally ending the gerrymander's distortion of the state's politics. *See* Clarke v. Wis. Elections Comm'n, 998 N.W.2d 370 (Wis. 2023).

Aligning Election Law. Nicholas O. Stephanopoulos, Oxford University Press. © Nicholas O. Stephanopoulos 2024.
DOI: 10.1093/9780197662182.001.0001

Almost all the members of the Republican supermajority compiled conservative voting records in the legislature. They supported the aforementioned voting
restrictions, tax cuts, limits on collective bargaining rights, limits on abortions,
environmental deregulation, gun deregulation, and so on.[3] Since Wisconsin's
governor from 2011 to 2019 was also a conservative Republican, most of these
right-wing bills became law. One of America's purplest states thus amassed one
of the nation's reddest sets of policies.[4]

These outcomes were out of step with the views of most Wisconsin residents—
but very much *in* line with the preferences of Republicans' financial backers.
At the wealthier end of the spectrum, conservative billionaires like Diane
Hendricks and Dick Uihlein, as well as cash-rich groups like the Chamber of
Commerce and the Club for Growth, made huge outlays on behalf of Republican
candidates.[5] Scores of less affluent, but equally right-wing, individual donors
contributed smaller sums, too.[6] (By the same token, Wisconsin Democrats' financial backers were quite liberal. The ideological extremism of campaign
funders is a bipartisan phenomenon.)

With this snapshot in mind, let's go back to my question. Federal courts would
say—in fact, they *did* say—that nothing much is wrong with Wisconsin's political system. Simplifying somewhat, federal courts approach electoral disputes
by weighing individual rights against countervailing state interests. The courts
value rights like voting, running for office, associating with other people, and
speaking (including by giving or spending money). But the courts also recognize that these rights aren't absolutes: that they can be limited to achieve important state goals like preventing fraud, avoiding corruption, and running orderly
elections. The dominant theme of election law jurisprudence is thus *balancing*—
burdening individual freedoms no more than is necessary to advance substantial
state interests.

From this perspective, Wisconsin's political system can seem benign. The
state's new voting restrictions don't make it *that* difficult to vote (at least, not
for most people). The interest supposedly served by the measures, thwarting
fraud, is also a legitimate one. For these reasons, a federal court upheld most
of the restrictions against a constitutional challenge.[7] Similarly, partisan

---

[3] In recent years, Wisconsin's state legislature has been among the most ideologically polarized in
the country. *See* Boris Shor & Nolan McCarty, *The Ideological Mapping of American Legislatures*, 105
AM. POL. SCI. REV. 530, 546 (2011).

[4] Scholars have recently calculated summary scores for the overall liberalism or conservatism of
states' policies. *See* Devin Caughey & Christopher Warshaw, *The Dynamics of State Policy Liberalism,
1936-2014*, 60 AM. J. POL. SCI. 899 (2016). Measured by these scores, Wisconsin experienced the
biggest right-wing policy shift in its history from 2010 to 2014.

[5] For a representative account, see Lincoln Caplan, *Scott Walker's Wisconsin and the End of
Campaign-Finance Law*, NEW YORKER, July 21, 2015.

[6] On the ideological extremism of individual donors, see, for example, Adam Bonica et al., *Why
Hasn't Democracy Slowed Rising Inequality?*, 27 J. ECON. PERSP. 103, 115 (2013).

[7] *See* Luft v. Evers, 963 F.3d 665 (7th Cir. 2020).

gerrymandering doesn't directly infringe any individual right. It doesn't bar anyone from casting a ballot, becoming a candidate, or speaking or associating about political issues. Consequently, the Supreme Court approved Wisconsin's state house map, and later held that *no* gerrymandering claim can *ever* succeed under the U.S. Constitution.[8] As for the vast pools of money sloshing around Wisconsin's elections, they constitute core political speech, in the eyes of federal judges—something to be celebrated, not criticized. A legal problem could arise only if Wisconsin tried to curb the activities of campaign funders.

Some academics agree with the courts that election law should focus on comparing rights burdens with countervailing interests. Most of these scholars, though, would strike a different balance than the courts. They would invalidate voting restrictions like Wisconsin's on the ground that the state's interests aren't compelling enough, and aren't sufficiently furthered, to justify limiting the franchise. They would also uphold stringent campaign finance regulations (were Wisconsin to pass any) because these checks promote equality among candidates and people. But these are distinctions in application, not conception. This strand of academic thinking essentially accepts the courts' doctrinal framework and argues within it for different results.

In contrast, other election law scholars disagree more fundamentally with the courts. They believe the courts' emphasis on individual rights is misplaced. The real action in electoral disputes, these writers contend, is *structural*—how the rules governing elections advance, or undermine, *system-wide* democratic values. Among these values, the most commonly invoked is competition: how hotly contested a jurisdiction's elections tend to be. Competition-oriented structuralists would have mixed feelings about Wisconsin's political system. They would applaud its razor-close statewide elections, which, they would hope, foster accountability and responsiveness. But they would worry about its overly safe districts, which, they would fear, allow politicians to break free from popular control. To address this situation, these structuralists would favor judicial intervention to redraw Wisconsin's districts and make them more competitive.[9]

Other structuralists prioritize a different democratic value: political participation. Voter turnout is the most obvious aspect of participation. But it also includes activities like canvassing, attending meetings, volunteering for campaigns, contacting representatives, and donating money. From this angle, too, Wisconsin's recent record is equivocal. Its high turnout (by American standards) is commendable. However, its efforts to discourage voting by certain

---

[8] *See* Gill v. Whitford, 138 S. Ct. 1916 (2018) (upholding Wisconsin's state house map); Rucho v. Common Cause, 139 S. Ct. 2484 (2019) (holding that partisan gerrymandering claims are nonjusticiable).

[9] *See, e.g.,* Samuel Issacharoff, *Gerrymandering and Political Cartels*, 116 HARV. L. REV. 593 (2002).

people—poor and minority individuals who lean Democratic—are distressing. To participation-oriented structuralists, these franchise restrictions are the cardinal sin of Wisconsin's political system.

I count myself as a structuralist—but a dissatisfied one. Like my peers in the structuralist camp, I object to "the stagnant discourse of individual rights and competing state interests" that characterizes election law jurisprudence.[10] But I also think something vital is missing from the competition- and participation-oriented accounts, something close to the heart of what it means to be a democracy. Recall that most Wisconsin politicians are more ideologically extreme than their constituents; that Wisconsin's legislature is dominated by conservative Republicans even though the state's electorate is evenly divided between the parties; and that Wisconsin's enacted policies over the last decade are far more right-wing than the state's residents. (And note that the same patterns hold nationwide. Virtually everywhere in America, people are comparatively centrist, politicians are closer to the ideological fringes, and policy outcomes are more liberal or conservative than most people would like.[11])

This pervasive *misalignment* between governmental outputs and popular preferences matters. When severe and durable enough, it conflicts with the most basic definition of democracy: government (krátos) by and for the people (dêmos). The people *don't* truly rule if their views are systematically ignored by both their elected representatives and the laws that shape their lives. Under these conditions, even if the people are able to speak, assemble, and vote, their voices are politically silent. Their government operates in defiance of their wishes.

Yet the courts are blind to misalignment. No plaintiff can sue on this basis because misalignment doesn't impose a burden on any cognizable right. And misalignment is equally invisible to the competition- and participation-oriented theories of election law. Conceptually, competition and participation are distinct from alignment. Congruence between the government's acts and the people's wishes isn't the same as elections' closeness or people's political engagement. Functionally, competition and participation aren't even the main drivers of alignment. Take Wisconsin again, where statewide races couldn't be tighter and voter turnout is near its American apex. Misalignment is nevertheless rampant—in districts and statewide, and in terms of partisanship, representation, and policy alike.

My aim in this book, then, is to develop a theory of election law that revolves around alignment. This account is structuralist because alignment, like competition and participation, is a systemic property of an entire political order. This

---

[10] Samuel Issacharoff & Richard H. Pildes, *Politics as Markets: Partisan Lockups of the Democratic Process*, 50 STAN. L. REV. 643, 717 (1998).

[11] For an example of a study reaching these conclusions (at the state level), see Jeffrey R. Lax & Justin H. Phillips, *The Democratic Deficit in the States*, 56 AM. J. POL. SCI. 148 (2012).

account is also a theory of judicial review. Courts persuaded that alignment is a core democratic and constitutional tenet could strike down misaligning policies and uphold aligning ones against attacks on other grounds. But this account isn't only (or even primarily) a theory of judicial review. Alignment provides a useful lens through which scholars, journalists, activists, and concerned individuals can analyze electoral regulations. Alignment constitutes a critical objective, too, for nonjudicial policymakers to pursue. These efforts outside the courts are at least as likely to be impactful as any litigation strategy.

Alignment

I've already hinted that alignment can be conceptualized in different ways. These varieties are attributable to the facts that (1) people are aggregated into political units at multiple levels, (2) people's preferences can be summarized through simpler or more complex methods, and (3) government wears several faces, all of which ought to be aligned with public opinion. Each of these points represents an axis along which alignment can be defined. Start with the political units into which people are aggregated: most notably, electoral districts and whole jurisdictions (which can be municipalities, states, or the country in its entirety). *District-specific* alignment can exist (or not) between people in a particular district and their representative. Similarly, *jurisdiction-wide* alignment is present (or absent) between the population and the government of a whole municipality, state, or nation.

Next, consider two ways in which the views of a group of people can be summarized. One approach is to report the preferences of the median individual: the person in the middle of the ideological distribution. Congruence with this figure's opinions—*majoritarian* alignment—usually guarantees that the wishes of the majority are heeded. Another, more demanding method is to determine the opinions of all relevant people and then to measure how near or far some governmental output is from all these preferences. The most congruent outcome—the one that maximizes *collective* alignment—minimizes the average gap between that result and each person's viewpoint.

Lastly, think of three important things that governments (or their subparts) do. Elected officials belong to parties. So we can speak of *partisan* alignment between people's partisan preferences and officeholders' party affiliations. Elected officials also take ideological positions, quintessentially by voting on bills in the legislature. Accordingly, *representational* alignment refers to the distance between people's ideological views and officeholders' ideological stances. And then through some combination of voting in the legislature and decision-making by the executive, public policy is eventually formed. *Policy* alignment captures the extent to which these enacted laws reflect people's policy preferences.

This typology might be complicated but the democratic appeal of alignment isn't. As I alluded above, when governmental outputs (officeholders' party affiliations, officeholders' policy positions, or actual policy outcomes) are congruent with the views of the people (a majority or all of them) within a given political unit (a district or a jurisdiction), the people can genuinely be said to rule. But the more government diverges *from* the people, the less it can claim to be government *by* and *for* the people. Precisely because alignment is such an intuitive value, it overlaps with several theories of representation and democracy. Take the delegate model of representation: the idea that a legislator should abide by the preferences of her constituents. In the terminology I just introduced, this is a prescription for district-specific representational alignment.

Likewise, the pluralist theory that dominated political thought both at the Framing and for much of the twentieth century sees public policy as emerging from the continuous interplay of myriad groups. This unending cycle of making and breaking alliances is supposed to yield outcomes that, in the long run and over many issues, coincide reasonably well with most groups' wishes. I'd call this aspiration jurisdiction-wide, collective, policy alignment. That's also how I'd label the ultimate goal of the deliberative theory that's prominent in contemporary debates about democracy. Deliberative democrats want people to engage in extensive, open-minded dialogue before undertaking any official action, as a result of which their original views may well change. Once enough discussion has taken place, though, people's refined opinions must be translated accurately into policy. Otherwise all their deliberation will have been in vain.

Lest I be misunderstood, I want to make two concessions about alignment right from the start. The first is that alignment isn't the only democratic value that should matter to courts, policymakers, and political observers. I've already mentioned the tenets prized by other structuralist scholars: competition and participation. I agree that these are important elements of a vibrant democracy. So are, among others, freedom to speak and associate, rational deliberation, political equality, minority representation, and impartial election administration. If any of these was missing from a regime—even one that featured high levels of alignment—we'd rightly question its democratic legitimacy. The pursuit of alignment, then, is perfectly capable of coexistence with other election law approaches. It offers judges, politicians, and people *one* reason to back certain policies and oppose other ones. But it doesn't purport to occupy the field, to deny the validity of other ways of thinking about democracy.

The second caveat is that alignment isn't always desirable. People sometimes have poorly informed preferences, reflecting insufficient knowledge or interest. Congruence with these (non)opinions could result in inefficient, incoherent public policy. People also sometimes have malignant views, espousing discrimination against members of groups other than their own. Allowing these attitudes to become law would yield immoral, not just incompetent, outcomes.

People's inchoate preferences with respect to particular issues mean it's better to assess alignment in the aggregate, in terms of people's overall ideologies. It's reasonable to discount public opinion on specific, technical matters as to which most people haven't given much thought. But it's not defensible (from a democratic perspective) to disregard people's overarching liberalism or conservatism—the sets of beliefs they use to make sense of their political world. These general philosophies are entitled to respect as the will of the people about the society they're supposed to rule. As for the problem of invidious views, the classic solution is to exclude from the domain where alignment is sought policies that discriminate against disfavored groups or violate fundamental rights. This is typically done through constitutional provisions that render certain outcomes unavailable through the ordinary political process. I have no quarrel with these safeguards because, again, I don't see alignment as an imperialist principle striving to supplant all other values.

Legal Status

This is all well and good, you might say, but what does it have to do with *law*? Democratic theorists might support alignment, but why should public lawyers? In fact, several modalities of constitutional interpretation indicate that alignment isn't alien to our legal order. These analytic modes certainly don't compel the recognition of alignment, but they do make its embrace plausible. Consider the constitutional text. "We the People," the Preamble proclaims, "establish this Constitution" in order to "promote the general Welfare."[12] Jurisdiction-wide, collective, policy alignment isn't the only possible definition of the general welfare, but it's at least a reasonable one. "The House of Representatives shall be [elected] by the People," Article I continues.[13] Popular election isn't synonymous with representational alignment, but the two concepts do dovetail nicely. And Article IV "guarantee[s] to every State . . . a Republican Form of Government."[14] Popular sovereignty—government by the people—is the essence of republicanism, and it's the core of alignment, too.[15]

---

[12] U.S. Const. preamb.

[13] *Id.* art. I, § 2.

[14] *Id.* art. IV, § 4.

[15] A well-known article equating republicanism with popular sovereignty is Akhil Reed Amar, *The Central Meaning of the Republican Government: Popular Sovereignty, Majority Rule, and the Denominator Problem*, 65 U. Colo. L. Rev. 749 (1994).

Or take the intentions of the Constitution's drafters. James Madison wrote that "[p]ublic opinion sets bounds to every government" and "must be obeyed by the government."[16] This is a more unequivocal endorsement of congruence between public policy and public opinion than you'll find in this book. John Bingham, the primary author of the Fourteenth Amendment, similarly declared, "If there is anything settled under the American Constitution . . . it is the absolute, unquestioned, unchallenged right of a majority of American [eligible] citizens . . . to control [a state's] entire political power."[17] This embrace of majoritarian alignment underpins the provision he penned, the fountainhead of modern election law.

The most common method of constitutional interpretation, the analysis of precedent, further strengthens alignment's legal pedigree. In the 1960s decision that established the courts' approach to voting restrictions, Chief Justice Earl Warren wrote that heightened scrutiny is warranted when a plaintiff mounts "a challenge [to] this basic assumption" that "the institutions of state government are structured so as to represent fairly all the people."[18] In my vocabulary, this is a call for more stringent review when the crux of a lawsuit is jurisdiction-wide, collective, representational misalignment. In the 1960s case that launched the reapportionment revolution, Chief Justice Warren added that, because "legislatures are responsible for enacting laws by which all citizens are to be governed, they should be bodies which are collectively responsive to the popular will."[19] This is another acknowledgment of jurisdiction-wide alignment as a normative—and constitutional—ideal.

If the courts were to recognize alignment as a legal principle, it could function as either a sword or a shield. As a sword, a plaintiff would attack an electoral policy on the ground that it's misaligning: that it causes a divergence between popular preferences and governmental outputs. Depending on how the courts structured the doctrine, a showing of substantial misalignment might be enough to invalidate a regulation. Or, less aggressively, such a showing might shift the burden to the state, giving it an opportunity to justify the misaligning measure based on its contribution to the state's legitimate interests. Whatever the doctrinal details, the upshot is that a new cause of action would exist, under which litigants could directly challenge electoral rules because of their misaligning effects.

As a shield, alignment (not misalignment) would be asserted by the state (not the plaintiff) in response to some other legal grievance (like a claim that a policy burdens voting or speech). The state would argue that its disputed regulation is aligning—that it shrinks the gap between popular preferences and governmental

---

[16]   14 THE PAPERS OF JAMES MADISON 170 (Robert A. Rutland et al. eds., 1983).
[17]   CONG. GLOBE, 39TH CONG., 2D SESS. 450 (1867).
[18]   Kramer v. Union Free Sch. Dist. No. 15, 395 U.S. 621, 628 (1969).
[19]   Reynolds v. Sims, 377 U.S. 533, 565 (1964).

outputs—and should be upheld for that reason. Alignment would thus operate as a state interest that, if actually advanced by a measure, could save it from judicial nullification. Plainly, this is a more conventional, less disruptive role for alignment. As a shield, alignment doesn't require the courts to create a new cause of action. It merely asks them to accept one more governmental interest (and only when it's cited by the state).

A few points should be flagged about the judicial implementation of alignment. First, it would rely heavily on empirical evidence. If misalignment was wielded as a sword, the plaintiff would need social scientific proof that the allegedly unlawful policy, in fact, makes governmental outputs less congruent with popular preferences. Likewise, if alignment was brandished as a shield, the state would have to demonstrate that its challenged regulation genuinely has an aligning impact. Such dependence on empirical evidence is unusual in constitutional law writ large. But it's more common in election law, where experts routinely testify about malapportionment, racial polarization in voting, the effects of voting restrictions, and a host of other quantitative issues. As one scholar has commented, "Law and social science are perhaps nowhere more mutually dependent than in the voting-rights field."[20]

Second, judicial recognition of alignment wouldn't necessarily entail a great deal of judicial intervention. As will become clear in the pages ahead, many electoral policies aren't particularly misaligning—including many measures that are often *thought* to be misaligning. Efforts to strike down these regulations, on this basis, would therefore be unavailing. On the other hand, some electoral policies do boost alignment. These measures would generally be sustained against suits charging other kinds of legal violations. In that case, the result would again be that the courts hold their fire and democratically enacted laws remain in force.

Lastly, this discussion focuses on litigation but it mostly applies to nonjudicial policymaking, too. Outside the courts, the democratic value of alignment can be deployed both to criticize misaligning regulations (so as a sword) and to laud provisions that tighten the congruence between popular preferences and governmental outputs (so as a shield). Also outside the courts, empirical evidence is vital because it's the only way to know whether a proposed policy change will exert an aligning or a misaligning influence. Outside the courts, as well, the pursuit of alignment doesn't threaten large swathes of the status quo: those electoral measures that either align or don't much misalign. This close relationship between judicial and nonjudicial analysis is a theme of the book. Alignment is a theory of judicial review *and* regulatory design—not just a prescription for the courts.

---

[20] Richard H. Pildes, *Is Voting-Rights Law at War with Itself? Social Science and Voting Rights in the 2000s*, 80 N.C. L. Rev. 1517, 1518 (2002).

Applications

But let's get down to brass tacks. If alignment was operationalized (by judicial and/or nonjudicial actors), what would be the implications for particular electoral policies? I address two important types of laws here: district maps crafted to benefit the line-drawing party and restrictions on individual campaign donations. These aren't random examples; rather, they're the best illustrations of how misalignment could function as a sword (partisan gerrymandering) and alignment as a shield (individual contribution limits). The book also goes through several more areas: burdens on voting, regulations of political parties, the pursuit of minority representation through the Voting Rights Act, and even *non*electoral measures (like labor law) with aligning or misaligning impacts. In some of these fields, alignment would be inert in that it would be of little use to plaintiffs or defendants. In other domains, alignment would have considerable, but more contestable, consequences. Nowhere else are there cases as clean as partisan gerrymandering and individual contribution limits.

Starting with gerrymandering, then, its essence is winning additional seats for the line-drawing party through clever district design. This is typically done by cracking the opposing party's voters among many districts where their preferred candidates lose by relatively narrow margins and by packing those voters in a few districts where their candidates of choice win by inefficiently large margins. Properly executed, a gerrymander can produce jurisdiction-wide partisan misalignment—sometimes even a median voter who backs one party paired with a median legislator who affiliates with the other party. And increasingly, gerrymanders *are* properly executed. There exist several quantitative measures of jurisdiction-wide partisan misalignment, all of which indicate that parties in control of redistricting now usually manage to generate biases in their favor.[21]

Partisan misalignment doesn't necessarily result in *representational* misalignment; it all depends on how legislators behave. In an era like ours of severe legislative polarization, though, we'd expect partisan skews to turn into representational skews since the extra legislators a party secures through gerrymandering generally compile ideologically extreme voting records. And in fact, that's exactly what happens. Partisan misalignment in a party's favor due to districting is a powerful driver of representational misalignment in the same ideological direction.[22] *Representational* misalignment, in turn, may or may not yield *policy* misalignment; it depends on whether the skewed legislative chamber is able to enact its preferences into law. But here as well, since unified government is

---

[21] *See, e.g.,* Nicholas O. Stephanopoulos, *The Causes and Consequences of Gerrymandering,* 59 WM. & MARY L. REV. 2115, 2131–40 (2018).

[22] *See, e.g.,* Devin Caughey et al., *Partisan Gerrymandering and the Political Process: Effects on Roll-Call Voting and State Policies,* 16 ELECTION L.J. 453, 461–64 (2017).

now the norm at the state level, we'd anticipate a close correspondence between representational and policy distortion. And we'd be right. Policy outcomes, just like legislators' voting records, veer ideologically toward the gerrymandering party—and away from the will of the electorate.[23]

Based on this evidence, many district maps drawn by a single party would be vulnerable if alignment was legally cognizable. Quite often, a plaintiff would be able to show that a plan would produce significant partisan misalignment, which would subsequently translate into significant representational and policy misalignment. As noted earlier, such a demonstration might be enough to invalidate a map. Or, less dramatically, it might shift the burden to the state to justify its plan on legitimate, nonpartisan grounds. This burden might not sound onerous but it typically would be. For any given state, there exist innumerable district maps that satisfy all nonpartisan criteria: equal population, compactness, respect for political subdivisions, compliance with the Voting Rights Act, and so on. Among these myriad maps, there are almost always some that are less biased in the line-drawing party's favor than the enacted plan. In that case, though, the enacted plan is legally unjustifiable. The state could have achieved all its nonpartisan goals without tilting the map so far in the line-drawing party's direction.

Turn next to individual contribution limits. Plaintiffs unhappy with them have no reason to invoke misalignment. There's no evidence these restrictions lead to any kind of noncongruence between popular preferences and governmental outputs. Plaintiffs can also make a more familiar claim that has succeeded many times before: that the limits violate their First Amendment rights of speech and association. For alignment to play a role in the campaign finance context, then, it must be the state that brings it into the litigation. Specifically, the state must present alignment as a compelling interest that's furthered by its restrictions on individual donations and that therefore rescues the limits from judicial nullification.

Helpfully, even after decades of hostile jurisprudence, alignment remains doctrinally available as a rationale for campaign finance regulations. Almost half a century ago, the Supreme Court held that money in politics can't be curbed because a jurisdiction wants to equalize candidates' resources or people's political influence.[24] Alignment, however, is distinct from any form of equalization. It doesn't necessarily (or even probably) follow from dueling candidates with identically sized war chests. Nor does it require that every person have the same political sway. In fact, alignment with the median individual is possible only if there's misalignment with people at all other points in the ideological distribution. More recently, the Court has ruled out the distortion of electoral outcomes

---

[23] *See, e.g., id.* at 464–65.
[24] *See* Buckley v. Valeo, 424 U.S. 1, 48–49 (1976).

as a justification for campaign finance regulations.[25] But again, electoral distortion is a separate concept from misalignment. Under the former, it's *voters* whose judgments are distorted by overly influential expenditures. Under the latter, in contrast, it's *elected officials* who become misaligned with their constituents as a result of the funding the politicians receive.

A jurisdiction trying to defend its individual contribution limits couldn't just wave alignment like a wand, though. Instead, it would have to prove that its restrictions in fact have an aligning effect. This proof would generally come in two steps. First, the jurisdiction would need to show that, when their activities are unchecked (or less checked), individual donors are a source of misalignment. According to extensive research, they are. Individual donors (large and small) tend to be ideologically extreme. Their money leads politicians to take extreme stances, too, to keep the contributions flowing.[26] Second, the jurisdiction would have to establish that curbs on individual donors are aligning. Additional studies document this impact. Tighter individual contribution limits induce politicians to shift their positions toward the ideological center: the home of most voters (but few donors).[27] District-specific representational alignment, then, isn't just a doctrinally available rationale for campaign finance reform. It's also a justification backed by everything we know about donors, politicians, and the relationships among them.

To be clear, my argument isn't that every district map devised by a single party would be invalid if alignment could be invoked in court, or that every individual contribution limit (let alone every campaign finance regulation) would be upheld. Some district maps exhibit low levels of partisan misalignment. They cause little, if any, representational or policy misalignment. The ecosystem of electoral money is complex, too. Some campaign funders are actually quite moderate, so if their donations were restricted, the outcome could well be *less* representational alignment. The point, in other words, is that the details matter. Generalizations are difficult about how different policies affect the congruence between governmental outputs and popular preferences. There's no alternative to scrutinizing the particular facts presented by each case using the best available empirical techniques.

It's also worth reiterating, in light of these examples, that alignment isn't only a judicial theory. Yes, the courts should strike down misaligning district plans. But mapmakers shouldn't create these plans in the first place, and federal or

---

[25] *See* Citizens United v. FEC, 558 U.S. 310, 349–56 (2010).

[26] For a very recent study finding a causal link between donors' extreme preferences and U.S. House members' voting records, see Brandice Canes-Wrone & Kenneth M. Miller, *Out-of-District Donors and Representation in the U.S. House*, 47 LEGIS. STUD. Q. 361 (2022).

[27] *See, e.g.,* Michael J. Barber, *Ideological Donors, Contribution Limits, and the Polarization of American Legislatures*, 78 J. POL. 296 (2016).

state legislation should bar undue misalignment due to districting. Similarly, the courts should sustain individual contribution limits when litigants attack them. But political actors of every stripe—members of Congress, state legislators, the people themselves through voter initiatives—should enact these limits because of their potent aligning influence. Again, the courts are one useful agent of alignment. But that's all they are: one agent among many, not necessarily the most important, and not due the attention that's lavished on them by the legal literature.

Judicial Obstacles

If I'm being frank, my emphasis on nonjudicial means of promoting alignment has two bases. One is my conviction that most of America's aligning milestones have been the product of constitutional amendment, federal or state legislation, or direct democracy. The Reconstruction Amendments, the Voting Rights Act, the Federal Election Campaign Act, independent redistricting commissions, public financing for campaigns—they were all accomplishments of nonjudicial actors. The other reason is the record of the current Supreme Court. Under the leadership of Chief Justice John Roberts, the Court has exhibited unrelenting hostility to the judicial pursuit of alignment. Over and over, the Roberts Court has refused to intervene when confronted with misaligning electoral policies. Even worse, the Court *has* aggressively moved to prevent other institutions from better aligning governmental outputs with popular preferences.

Partisan gerrymandering presents the most egregious case of judicial passivity where aligning judicial action was urgently needed. As explained above, gerrymandering can be highly misaligning—likely the most misaligning electoral regulation a modern government can adopt. In a pivotal 2019 decision, the Roberts Court agreed with this assessment. Gerrymandering, the Court conceded, "violates the core principle of our republican government . . . namely, that the voters should choose their representatives, not the other way around."[28] The Court nevertheless declined to invalidate the grossly gerrymandered North Carolina congressional plan before it. Going further, the Court held that *no* gerrymandering plaintiff can *ever* prevail in federal court. Partisan gerrymandering is categorically nonjusticiable, that is, beyond the federal judiciary's power to rebuke or remedy.

The story is much the same with voting restrictions. Photo ID requirements for voting, cutbacks to early voting, purges of voter rolls, and the like have proliferated in recent years. The motive for these limits is unquestionably

---

[28] Rucho v. Common Cause, 139 S. Ct. 2484, 2506 (2019) (internal quotation marks and alterations omitted).

misaligning: preventing certain people (mainly racial minorities and the poor) from voting and thereby causing the *actual* electorate to diverge from the *eligible* electorate. Whether voting restrictions in fact achieve this goal is more ambiguous. Studies are divided on whether they reduce turnout, change the partisan balance of power, or make public policy less congruent with public opinion. In the face of certainty about these policies' aims, but lack of clarity about their effects, the Roberts Court has refused to lift a finger against them. Among others, it has upheld Indiana's photo ID requirement for voting, Ohio's purge of its voter registration list, and Wisconsin's strict absentee voting deadlines.[29] Over its entire history, this Court has *never* ruled in favor of a plaintiff disputing a voting restriction.

This might seem like judicial restraint (even when a more robust judicial role would have been advisable) but it isn't. When addressing *aligning* measures enacted by other actors, the Roberts Court has been all too happy to intercede. Consider individual contribution limits, which, again, are among the few provisions known to improve representational alignment. The Court struck down Vermont's especially low (and thus especially effective) donation cap.[30] The Court also nullified the aggregate federal ceiling on contributions to all candidates and political committees.[31] And the Court's jurisprudence led to an (unappealed) lower-court ruling that individuals must be free to give as much as they want to Super PACs, which in turn must be free to spend as much as they want.[32] These cases reveal many things, none of which is judicial reluctance to meddle in politics.

Or take the Voting Rights Act, which significantly boosted minority participation and representation in the decades after its 1965 passage. Thanks to these gains, the collective alignment of American governments surged as minority residents became full members of the political community. Yet the Roberts Court knocked out one of the Act's two pillars in a major 2013 decision, arguing that "things have changed in the South" in that minority residents no longer face serious attempts to deny or dilute their votes.[33] The Court also imposed a series of constraints on the Act's key remaining section, hindering plaintiffs' ability to prosecute many cases.[34] Again, this isn't a principled record of political noninterference. What it most resembles is a dogged judicial campaign against alignment, whether sought through the courts or other bodies.

---

[29] *See* Democratic Nat'l Comm. v. Bostelmann, 141 S. Ct. 28 (2020); Husted v. A. Philip Randolph Inst., 138 S. Ct. 1833 (2018); Crawford v. Marion Cnty. Elections Bd., 553 U.S. 181 (2008).

[30] *See* Randall v. Sorrell, 548 U.S. 230 (2006).

[31] *See* McCutcheon v. FEC, 572 U.S. 185 (2014).

[32] *See* SpeechNow.org v. FEC, 599 F.3d 686 (D.C. Cir. 2010).

[33] Shelby Cnty. v. Holder, 570 U.S. 529, 540 (2013) (internal quotation marks and alterations omitted).

[34] *See, e.g.,* Brnovich v. Democratic Nat'l Comm., 141 S. Ct. 2321, 2339 (2021).

At present, then, the Supreme Court is among the last places where reformers enamored with alignment should look for help. The Court *could* do a great deal to align governmental outputs with popular preferences. In fact, an earlier Court (the Warren Court) *did* do a great deal. But as long as the Court is headed by Chief Justice Roberts, and dominated by a like-minded majority, it's highly unlikely to heed this book's recommendations of invalidating misaligning policies and upholding aligning ones. Instead, the Court is more apt to be an obstacle to aligning efforts pursued through other institutions—so not a supporter of alignment, or even a disinterested bystander, but rather an outright antagonist.

Aligning Alternatives

Fortunately, this foe is far from omnipotent. Many of the aligning initiatives that might be undertaken outside the federal courts would likely (if grudgingly) be approved by the Roberts Court if they were challenged. Think of congressional legislation. Congress could do many things to bolster alignment. It could require states to use independent redistricting commissions, thereby ending partisan gerrymandering. It could forbid states from engaging in voter suppression. It could dilute the impact of private campaign contributions by flooding elections with public financing. It could revive the portion of the Voting Rights Act neutered by the Court and undo the Court's curbs on the rest of the Act, too. And these aligning ideas aren't just hypothetical. All of them were recently embraced by the U.S. House even though they ultimately foundered on the U.S. Senate's filibuster.[35]

If these policies were enacted, the Roberts Court's precedents suggest they would be sustained. Critically, the Court has taken an expansive view of Article I's Elections Clause, under which Congress can regulate the "times, places and manner" of congressional elections.[36] "The Clause's substantive scope is broad," the Court has commented, adding that the provision enables Congress, if it wishes, to "provide a complete code for congressional elections."[37] This extensive a code would reach even further than Congress has yet contemplated. Additionally, the Court has noted in dicta that Congress could mandate the use of independent redistricting commissions,[38] establish public financing for elections,[39] and revise the Voting Rights Act.[40] These steps amount to much of

---

[35] *See* For the People Act of 2021, H.R. 1, 117th Cong. (2021); Voting Rights Advancement Act of 2019, H.R. 4, 116th Cong. (2019).

[36] U.S. CONST. art. I, § 4.

[37] Arizona v. Inter Tribal Council of Ariz., 570 U.S. 1, 8–9 (2013) (internal quotation marks omitted).

[38] *See* Rucho v. Common Cause, 139 S. Ct. 2484, 2508 (2019).

[39] *See* Ariz. Free Enter. Club's Freedom Club PAC v. Bennett, 564 U.S. 721, 753–54 (2011).

[40] *See* Shelby Cnty. v. Holder, 570 U.S. 529, 556–57 (2013).

the federal electoral reform agenda—and would launch an aligning revolution if adopted.

At the state level, likewise, a variety of actors could promote (and have promoted) alignment. State legislatures, first, may seem like unlikely progenitors of policies that threaten to disrupt the misaligned status quo. But as voting has become a more partisan issue, state legislatures under the sway of the pro-voting camp have passed many laws facilitating access to the polls.[41] Voter initiatives, next, are a tool uniquely suited to circumventing politicians who benefit from misalignment and refuse to fight it. Direct democracy has been deployed, among other things, to create independent redistricting commissions, ease voting burdens, institute public financing, and experiment with new kinds of party primaries. State courts, lastly, aren't bound by the crabbed justiciability doctrines of the federal judiciary. State courts also enforce state constitutions that typically recognize democratic values more explicitly than the U.S. Constitution. Consequently, state courts have often ventured where the federal judiciary fears to tread, striking down franchise restrictions, partisan gerrymanders, and other misaligning measures.

The bulk of this state-level activity is lawful as well—even in the eyes of the Roberts Court. The Court conceives of state legislatures as the default regulators of both state and federal elections.[42] So there's virtually no aligning electoral policy that's beyond the scope of state legislative authority. The Court also continues to acknowledge the ability of other state actors, including voters through ballot initiatives and courts via state constitutional interpretation, to set electoral rules. This capacity is unquestioned with respect to state elections. It's more contested, but still present in most circumstances, with respect to federal elections.[43] Under current precedent, then, the harnessing of direct democracy and state constitutional litigation to pursue alignment is largely unrestricted.

Moreover, the harnessing of *private* aligning activity is completely free of legal limits. On their own, without any governmental involvement, private actors can induce better representational alignment in several ways. For instance, they can simply reach out to their elected officials. Studies show that when legislators are contacted by a more representative slice of their constituents, their votes become more congruent with their constituents' preferences.[44] Further, a nonprofit group, academic center, or other institution could report the public's views on policy matters by state or district. Techniques for converting national polling

---

[41] *See Voting Laws Roundup 2020*, BRENNAN CTR. FOR JUSTICE (Dec. 8, 2020), https://www.brennancenter.org/our-work/research-reports/voting-laws-roundup-2020-0.

[42] *See, e.g., Shelby Cnty.*, 570 U.S. at 543.

[43] *See* Moore v. Harper, 143 S. Ct. 2065 (2023).

[44] *See, e.g.*, David E. Broockman & Christopher Skovron, *Bias in Perceptions of Public Opinion Among Political Elites*, 112 AM. POL. SCI. REV. 542, 558 (2018).

into accurate estimates of local opinion have recently been developed. Emerging research suggests that when these estimates are shared with legislators—allowing them to *know* what their constituents think about different issues—their votes more closely track their constituents' wishes.[45] Of course, both these aligning ideas are perfectly legal. Not only does the U.S. Constitution not constrain private political activity, the First Amendment affirmatively protects it.

Thanks to these and other options, the battle for alignment is far from hopeless. It's true (and deeply unfortunate) that the Roberts Court is an adversary in this struggle, not the ally it could and should be. But even a Court intent on misalignment (in its preferred ideological direction) can only do so much. Without reversing its precedents and inventing new doctrines out of whole cloth, the Court can't thwart most federal, state, and private efforts to achieve a more congruent political system. The futility of constructive federal litigation, at least for now, is therefore no cause for despair. Rather, it's an invitation, to lawyers and legal scholars in particular, to be more receptive to aligning mechanisms that operate outside the federal courts.

Plan of the Book

The book's structure tracks the discussion to this point. The first four chapters address alignment in general, without delving into specific doctrinal areas. Chapter 1 critically describes the rights-structure debate that has dominated election law over the last generation. This debate has grown stagnant, failing to incorporate a range of new findings about American politics. Chapter 2, the book's conceptual core, introduces the democratic value of alignment. Alignment can be defined in different ways; it overlaps with most existing models of representation and democracy; and it's most compelling when analyzed jurisdiction-wide and with respect to enacted policies. Chapter 3 presents what's known about the alignment of modern American governments. They're generally quite misaligned, at every electoral level, in favor of the wealthy and the ideologically extreme. And Chapter 4 comments on the law of alignment. It enjoys some (though not unequivocal) support from conventional legal sources, and it could function in litigation as either a sword or a shield.

The next six chapters apply alignment to a series of subjects: burdens on voting, regulations of political parties, district plans, the Voting Rights Act, money in politics, and nonelectoral policies like labor law. Each chapter explains how alignment would work legally and politically in that context. Each chapter

---

[45] *See, e.g.,* Christopher S. Elmendorf & Abby K. Wood, *Elite Political Ignorance: Law, Data, and the Representation of (Mis)perceived Electorates,* 52 U.C. Davis L. Rev. 571, 628–30 (2018).

also surveys the empirical literature to determine, provisionally, whether the measures at issue actually align or misalign. These chapters further explore questions including: What's the relevant population with whose preferences governmental outputs should align? Should parties' positions be congruent with the views of their members? What relationship is there, if any, between district-specific and jurisdiction-wide alignment? And under the U.S. Constitution, is alignment a proscribed, a permissible, or even a compelling state interest?

The last two chapters then consider institutions with the capacity to make governmental outputs more congruent with people's views. Chapter 11 focuses on the Supreme Court. The Roberts Court, alas, has shown itself to be the anti-alignment Court. It has consistently declined to intervene when given the opportunity to strike down misaligning policies. On several occasions, it has also stepped in to impede the aligning efforts of other bodies. Chapter 12 examines actors beyond the federal courts. Congress, state legislatures, state executives, state courts, state electorates, and even private groups and individuals can all take steps to promote alignment. What's more, most of these initiatives are entirely lawful, even under our current judicial regime. The road to alignment therefore isn't blocked. At present, it just doesn't run through the federal courts.

* * *

Some readers may find it odd that I haven't yet mentioned the aftermath of the 2020 election, when American democracy endured its most trying test in generations. A sitting President refused to accept his electoral defeat. Incited by his rhetoric, a mob stormed and occupied the Capitol. After a new President was finally sworn in, states across the country passed laws restricting the franchise and politicizing election administration. Thanks to these laws, the next attempt to steal an election may well succeed.

I've been quiet about these developments for two reasons. First, this book is about all of election law, not just the field's most alarming incidents. I don't want the book's broader contributions to be overshadowed by the events that followed the 2020 election. Second, those events amount to such an easy case for alignment as to be intellectually uninteresting. A majority of voters nationwide—including a majority of voters in states constituting an Electoral College majority—preferred Joe Biden to Donald Trump. So if Trump's lawsuits, political maneuvers, and mob violence had somehow allowed him to stay in office, the resulting misalignment couldn't have been more glaring. The will of the electorate would plainly have been defied. My limited commentary on the 2020 election, then, isn't indicative of any shortcoming in the principle of alignment. The principle has no trouble identifying, and denouncing, an assault on democracy itself.

1

The Rights-Structure Debate

Introduction

Legal fields are defined by their debates. Clashes between different theories, methods, and values demonstrate that legal issues can be analyzed from multiple perspectives. The choice among perspectives is itself interesting, implicating questions about legal legitimacy, normative appeal, and institutional role. Which framework is adopted also often has important practical consequences, resulting in some practices being struck down instead of others, laws being interpreted one way rather than a different way, liability attaching in certain cases but not elsewhere, and so on. Just think of the struggles between originalism and living constitutionalism in constitutional law, between textualism and purposivism in legislation, and between political accountability and technical expertise in administrative law (to cite three other public law fields). Scholars argue endlessly about the merits of these approaches. And they do so not just because these thrusts and ripostes are intellectually stimulating, but also because it matters which view prevails—for the outcomes of particular disputes, for what the state can and can't do, and ultimately for the content of the rules that govern American society.

Within election law, the *rights-structure debate* has been a major academic cleavage for at least a generation. On one side of this divide are the *balancers*. They're highly attentive to individual rights like voting and speaking. But they also recognize that the government sometimes has good reasons for restricting these rights. So the balancers weigh the rights burdens imposed by electoral regulations against the government's rationales for the regulations, focusing on the strength of the state's interests and the extent to which they're furthered by the regulations. This careful weighing determines whether the policies at issue should be invalidated or upheld. Most Supreme Court Justices are balancers (at least most of the time). So are a minority of contemporary election law scholars.

On the other side of the fault line are the *structuralists*, who now count among their ranks most election law academics. They think the courts' emphasis on individual rights is myopic. What are really at stake in many electoral disputes, they argue, are structural, system-wide values like competition and participation. Some electoral practices aim to (and do) suppress competition or participation, often in order to entrench incumbent politicians in power. Other measures

Aligning Election Law. Nicholas O. Stephanopoulos, Oxford University Press. © Nicholas O. Stephanopoulos 2024.
DOI: 10.1093/9780197662182.003.0001

(commonly opposed by incumbents) make elections more competitive or people more likely to engage in politics. All these regulations should be analyzed in these terms, according to the structuralists, based on their implications for key democratic values. To fixate on the rights burdens levied by electoral policies is to miss the forest for the trees, to go for the capillaries instead of the jugular.

I describe the rights-structure debate in some detail in this chapter. Understanding it is helpful to grasping how alignment fits into existing election law doctrine and scholarship. I also articulate several reasons why I'm dissatisfied with the present shape of the debate. First, because its battle lines have been fixed for more than a decade, it hasn't incorporated important political and empirical developments. These include the deepening polarization of politicians and policies, the growing clout of the wealthy, and a rush of new methods and studies illuminating the effects of different electoral practices. Second, both the balancers and the structuralists have asked, above all, what courts should do in electoral cases. But courts aren't the only (or even the primary) decision makers about American democracy, and other actors' roles, incentives, and options should also be considered. Lastly, until now, the rights-structure debate has overlooked what I (and others) see as maybe the most fundamental democratic value of all: alignment. The balancers can't conceive of claims rooted not in rights violations but rather in noncongruence between governmental outputs and popular preferences. The ascendant structural values of competition and participation are also distinct from, and not even closely linked to, alignment.

The Judicial Method

As I noted a moment ago, courts deciding electoral cases generally balance burdens on individual rights against countervailing state interests. In the early days of judicial intervention in this area, courts applied a particular form of balancing—strict scrutiny—that's tilted heavily in plaintiffs' favor. Courts reasoned that the right to vote is vital and that when it's abridged, the legitimacy of governmental action can no longer be taken for granted. As the Supreme Court put it in the 1969 case of *Kramer v. Union Free School District No. 15*, "the right to exercise the franchise in a free and unimpaired manner is preservative of other basic civil and political rights."[1] When a plaintiff alleges that this right has been infringed, the usual "assumption that the institutions of state government are structured so as to represent fairly all the people" becomes inoperative.[2]

---

[1] 395 U.S. 621, 626 (1969) (internal quotation marks omitted).
[2] *Id.* at 628.

Given these postulates of an essential right whose limitation threatens democracy, courts naturally turned to strict scrutiny. In *Kramer*, the Court repeatedly stressed the rigor of its inquiry. Burdens on voting warranted "careful examination," "close scrutiny," "exacting judicial scrutiny," and "close judicial examination."[3] To survive such demanding review, voting restrictions had to be "necessary to promote a compelling state interest."[4] This test, the most stringent known to constitutional law, typically results in the nullification of challenged policies. Not many state interests qualify as compelling. And even when the government has a persuasive reason for curbing voting, it could often realize its objective in other, less intrusive ways.[5]

Modern courts, however, no longer apply strict scrutiny to all regulations that make it harder to vote.[6] Instead, they use a doctrine unique to election law, *sliding-scale scrutiny*, under which the intensity of judicial review varies in tandem with the severity of the burden imposed on voting. Sliding-scale scrutiny, also known as *Anderson-Burdick* balancing, originated in the 1983 case of *Anderson v. Celebrezze*[7] and the 1992 case of *Burdick v. Takushi*.[8] In *Anderson*, the less significant of these decisions, the Court abandoned the classic formulation of strict scrutiny: the requirement that a measure be the least restrictive means of achieving a compelling state interest. In place of that formulation, the Court described the appropriate judicial inquiry in more general, less rigorous terms. A reviewing court "must first consider the character and magnitude of the asserted injury to the rights protected by the First and Fourteenth Amendments."[9] The court "then must identify and evaluate the precise interests put forward by the State as justifications for the burden imposed by its rule."[10] "[T]he legitimacy and strength of each of those interests" is relevant to the court's ruling, as is "the extent to which those interests make it necessary to burden the plaintiff's rights."[11]

---

[3] *Id.* at 626, 628, 629.

[4] *Id.* at 627. *Kramer* echoed the earlier Warren Court case of *Harper v. Virginia State Bd. of Elections*, 383 U.S. 663 (1966), where the Court stated that burdens on voting "must be closely scrutinized and carefully confined." *Id.* at 670.

[5] For a thoughtful analysis of strict scrutiny, see Richard H. Fallon Jr., *Strict Judicial Scrutiny*, 54 UCLA L. REV. 1267 (2007).

[6] It's not clear that *Kramer*-style strict scrutiny was ever the operative rule for all voting burdens. In 1970s cases like *Storer v. Brown*, 415 U.S. 724 (1974), the Court stated that its doctrine doesn't "automatically invalidate[] every substantial restriction on the right to vote or to associate." *Id.* at 729; *see also, e.g.*, Ill. State Bd. of Elections v. Socialist Workers Party, 440 U.S. 173, 193 (1979) (examining "the character of the classification in question, the importance of the individual interests at stake, and the state interests asserted in support of the classification" instead of applying strict scrutiny).

[7] 460 U.S. 780 (1983).

[8] 504 U.S. 428 (1992).

[9] *Anderson*, 460 U.S. at 789.

[10] *Id.*

[11] *Id.*

Almost a decade later, as Justice Antonin Scalia once observed, "*Burdick* forged *Anderson's* amorphous 'flexible standard' into something resembling an administrable rule."[12] Under *Burdick*, the critical initial question is how severely a policy impairs voting. The answer to that question determines how stringently a court will examine the measure. In the Court's words, "the rigorousness of our inquiry into the propriety of a state election law depends upon the extent to which a challenged regulation burdens First and Fourteenth Amendment rights."[13] If "those rights are subjected to severe restrictions," then "the regulation must be narrowly drawn to advance a state interest of compelling importance."[14] The regulation, that is, must survive traditional strict scrutiny. On the other hand, if "a state election law provision imposes only reasonable, nondiscriminatory restrictions," then "the State's important regulatory interests are generally sufficient to justify the restrictions."[15] Less severe voting burdens therefore trigger less aggressive judicial review.

Why did the Court dilute *Kramer's* strict scrutiny into *Anderson* and *Burdick's* sliding-scale scrutiny? Most likely because strict scrutiny threatens too many electoral policies. Most rules about elections—even benign ones—make it at least somewhat harder for some people to vote. If any impediment to voting brought down the hammer of strict scrutiny, then these otherwise unobjectionable laws would frequently be invalid. Consider a poll closing time of 9 p.m. (the latest of any state).[16] This deadline for voting presumably serves the government's interests in conserving resources and counting ballots expeditiously. But it's not clear these are compelling interests; some cases have suggested they aren't.[17] And even if they are weighty enough, less restrictive ways to save money (e.g., pay election officials less) and quickly tally ballots (e.g., use faster tabulation machines) can readily be imagined. Strict scrutiny would thus doom a 9 p.m.— and maybe any—poll closing time.

Highly deferential rational basis review, though, is equally unsatisfying as an across-the-board solution. Some electoral regulations disenfranchise large numbers of people; others insulate officeholders from challenges to their rule. It would be foolish for courts to sustain these laws just because some legitimate interest can be conceived that the laws might plausibly further. Sliding-scale scrutiny, then, occupies the middle ground between the unworkable extremes

---

[12] Crawford v. Marion Cnty. Election Bd., 553 U.S. 181, 205 (2008) (Scalia, J., concurring in the judgment).

[13] *Burdick*, 504 U.S. at 434.

[14] *Id.* (internal quotation marks omitted).

[15] *Id.* (internal quotation marks omitted).

[16] See *State Poll Opening and Closing Times (2021)*, BALLOTPEDIA, https://ballotpedia.org/State_Poll_Opening_and_Closing_Times_(2021) (last visited Feb. 1, 2024).

[17] *See, e.g.,* Tashjian v. Republican Party of Conn., 479 U.S. 208, 218 (1986) (rejecting "the cost of administering the election system" and "administrative convenience" as rationales for burdening political party members' right of association).

of strict scrutiny and rational basis review. It directs courts to approve most electoral policies but to approach with rising skepticism rules that are more burdensome or discriminatory—and so more likely to be the product of something other than impartial election administration. Justice Sandra Day O'Connor once defended sliding-scale scrutiny on exactly this basis. "As [voting] restrictions become more severe . . . and particularly where they have discriminatory effects," she wrote, "there is increasing cause for concern that those in power may be using electoral rules to erect barriers."[18] Under these circumstances, "applying heightened scrutiny helps to ensure that such limitations are truly justified and that the State's asserted interests are not merely a pretext."[19]

In the same opinion, Justice O'Connor also characterized sliding-scale scrutiny as balancing. Under that doctrine, "[w]e have sought to balance the . . . interests of parties and voters against the States' regulatory interests."[20] Other Justices, too, have referred to *Anderson* and *Burdick*'s "balancing approach,"[21] "balancing analysis,"[22] and "open-ended balancing test."[23] What these jurists seem to mean by balancing is achieving an optimal (or at least a satisfactory) combination of individual rights protection and state interest promotion. Justice O'Connor and her ilk value rights like voting, speaking, and associating. But they also acknowledge the force of a variety of state interests—running elections efficiently, preserving electoral integrity, preventing voter confusion, and so on—that sometimes require these rights to be encumbered. Faced with pressing concerns on both sides of the ledger, these jurists strive to limit rights as little as possible while advancing the government's ends as much as possible. They therefore uphold electoral policies when their policy benefits appear to outweigh their rights costs, and strike them down otherwise. Their implicit philosophy is that judicial intervention is justified in the electoral domain to ensure an acceptable balance between rights and interests.

This framework unquestionably governs the areas of franchise restriction, ballot access, and party regulation. When laws make it harder for people to vote,[24] block candidates from being listed on ballots,[25] and interfere with parties' internal affairs,[26] courts dutifully quote *Anderson* and (especially) *Burdick* and

---

[18] Clingman v. Beaver, 544 U.S. 581, 603 (2005) (O'Connor, J., concurring in the judgment).
[19] *Id.*
[20] *Id.*
[21] Crawford v. Marion Cnty. Election Bd., 553 U.S. 181, 190 (2008) (plurality opinion).
[22] *Id.* at 210 (Souter, J., dissenting).
[23] Democratic Nat'l Comm. v. Wis. State Legis., 141 S. Ct. 28, 35 (2020) (Kavanaugh, J., concurring in denial of application to vacate stay).
[24] *See, e.g., id.* at 35–40; *Crawford*, 553 U.S. at 189–203 (plurality opinion).
[25] *See, e.g.*, Timmons v. Twin Cities Area New Party, 520 U.S. 351, 357–70 (1997).
[26] *See, e.g.*, Wash. State Grange v. Wash. State Republican Party, 552 U.S. 442, 451–59 (2008); Clingman v. Beaver, 544 U.S. 581, 586–97 (2005); Cal. Democratic Party v. Jones, 530 U.S. 567, 572–86 (2000).

apply sliding-scale scrutiny. A wholesale version of *Anderson-Burdick* balancing is also the operative test in the campaign finance context.[27] Here, courts don't evaluate the burdens on speech and association imposed by curbs on money in politics on a case-by-case basis.[28] Instead, they've decided, more or less categorically, that expenditure limits heavily burden First Amendment rights and thus warrant strict scrutiny, while contribution caps only moderately impair speech and association and so are subject to intermediate scrutiny. As the Court reasoned in the foundational 1976 campaign finance case of *Buckley v. Valeo*, "expenditure ceilings impose significantly more severe restrictions on protected freedoms of political expression and association than do . . . limitations on financial contributions."[29] Consequently, "restrictions on contributions require less compelling justification than restrictions on independent spending."[30]

Courts even weigh rights against interests in certain redistricting cases. For instance, the Court has held that each resident of a state has a right, "individual and personal in nature," to be placed in an electoral district with about the same population as any other district.[31] However, this right can be burdened—and malapportionment permitted to some extent—to satisfy legitimate redistricting criteria like compactness, respect for county and municipality boundaries, and respect for communities of interest.[32] Similarly, under the Court's racial gerrymandering jurisprudence, each citizen has a "personal" right not to be "subjected to a racial classification" by being assigned to a district that was drawn for a predominantly racial reason.[33] Again, though, this right can be limited if necessary for the government to remedy past discrimination or to comply with the Voting Rights Act.[34]

An important point about rights-interests balancing is that it mirrors the Court's approach in many *nonelectoral* constitutional cases. Across fields as diverse as free speech, equal protection, and substantive due process, the Court also analyzes the strength of state interests and the degree to which they're served

---

[27] For an article-length analysis of how rights-interests balancing is applied in the voting and campaign finance contexts, see Robert Yablon, *Voting, Spending, and the Right to Participate*, 111 Nw. U. L. Rev. 655 (2017).

[28] *See, e.g.*, McCutcheon v. FEC, 572 U.S. 185, 206 (2014) (rejecting the "ad hoc balancing of relative social costs and benefits" in the campaign finance context).

[29] 424 U.S. 1, 23 (1976).

[30] FEC v. Mass. Citizens for Life, Inc., 479 U.S. 238, 259–60 (1986).

[31] Reynolds v. Sims, 377 U.S. 533, 561 (1964). An alternative, structuralist account of the one-person, one-vote rule would emphasize the systemic democratic harms of malapportionment.

[32] *See, e.g.*, Karcher v. Daggett, 462 U.S. 725, 740 (1983) (countenancing "population deviations" that are "necessary to achieve some legitimate state objective").

[33] Alabama v. Ala. Legis. Black Caucus, 575 U.S. 254, 263 (2015) (internal quotation marks and alterations omitted). Again, it's debatable whether a genuine individual right (as opposed to a structuralist objection to the expression of certain racial messages) is really the core of racial gerrymandering doctrine.

[34] *See, e.g.*, Miller v. Johnson, 515 U.S. 900, 920–27 (1995).

by policies that burden individual rights.[35] The Court's dominant election law methodology is therefore "conventional," as several scholars have observed, "because it imports into the law of democracy the same doctrinal tools, legal tests, and ways of framing the issues from more fully developed areas of constitutional law."[36] Precisely because of its conventionality, the Court's election law doctrine lacks any explicit role for structural democratic values like competition, participation, and alignment. A plaintiff can't bring a claim on the ground that the government is subverting these values. At best, a defendant can present a democratic principle as a state interest that justifies a given regulation (though, in practice, this rarely happens). Law originating in nonelectoral contexts simply has no special place for the tenets that undergird democracy.[37]

That said, there *are* structural undercurrents in the Court's election law jurisprudence. I just noted Justice O'Connor's account of sliding-scale scrutiny as a technique for intensifying judicial review when it's more likely that electoral regulation is anticompetitive or misaligning. On this view, rights-interests balancing itself ultimately promotes systemic democratic values. Later, in Chapter 4, I go through a number of additional passages—some penned by individual Justices, others the product of Court majorities—that express some sympathy for alignment as a legal principle. These snippets are glimpses of an alternative doctrinal universe, one where courts decide electoral cases overtly on the basis of structural democratic values. That universe isn't currently our universe. But it's conceivable that, one day, it could be. The structural seeds now scattered across the Court's opinions could, in time, flower into a new analytic approach for electoral disputes.

A final comment about rights-interests balancing is that it's often done inconsistently. Courts, that is, commonly exhibit biases in how rigorously they review different kinds of electoral policies. The Roberts Court, in particular, has been extremely deferential toward restrictions of the right to vote, *never* nullifying such a limit over nearly two decades. But the same Court has been relentlessly skeptical of regulations of the right to give and spend money in political campaigns, striking

---

[35] For an insightful discussion of this methodology, see RICHARD H. FALLON JR., THE NATURE OF CONSTITUTIONAL RIGHTS: THE INVENTION AND LOGIC OF STRICT JUDICIAL SCRUTINY (2019). However, sliding-scale scrutiny has no exact analogue outside election law.

[36] Richard H. Pildes, *Competitive, Deliberative, and Rights-Oriented Democracy*, 3 ELECTION L.J. 685, 687 (2004); *see also, e.g.*, James A. Gardner, *Partitioning and Rights: The Supreme Court's Accidental Jurisprudence of Democratic Process*, 42 FLA. ST. U. L. REV. 61, 65 (2014) ("[T]he Court unthinkingly imported an antidiscrimination approach . . . into a large number of disputes dealing with democratic process . . . ."); Nathaniel Persily, *The Search for Comprehensive Descriptions and Prescriptions in Election Law*, 35 CONN. L. REV. 1509, 1515 (2003) ("The Court's jurisprudence in 'democracy' cases often flows logically from or fits comfortably within larger constitutional doctrines.").

[37] *See, e.g.*, Samuel Issacharoff & Richard H. Pildes, *Politics as Markets: Partisan Lockups of the Democratic Process*, 50 STAN. L. REV. 643, 646 (1998) ("[T]he Court's electoral jurisprudence lacks any underlying vision of democratic politics that is normatively robust or realistically sophisticated about actual political practices.").

down one such check after another.[38] The formal structure of rights-interests balancing would never predict this pattern. How could burdens on voting always be lawful (in recent years) while restraints on funding campaigns are nearly always invalid? Instead, as I suggest in Chapter 11, the likely explanation for the Roberts Court's set of decisions is ideological. The Court seems suspicious, even hostile, toward measures that would yield a political system more reflective of popular preferences. But this survey of the case law lies down the road. For now, the upshot is just that a nominally neutral doctrine like rights-interests balancing can be—and has been—applied in decidedly non-neutral ways.

Academic Balancers

Shifting gears from the judiciary to the academy, several election law scholars agree with the Court's usual method. Balancing impairments of individual rights against countervailing state interests, they concur, is the right way to decide electoral cases. For example, Richard Hasen argues in a major book that courts should "balance infringements on individual and group core political equality rights with other government interests, such as the interest in preventing voter confusion."[39] "[T]here is no obvious escape from the balancing of individual rights and state interests in election law cases."[40] Likewise, Daniel Lowenstein asserts that "liberty interests have to be weighed and balanced" against the government's rationales for electoral regulation.[41] "In [his] personal opinion," he adds, "the Supreme Court has drawn the balance wisely in the ballot access cases," at least.[42]

Nathaniel Persily also favors "thinking about election law controversies as battles between state interests and individual, associational, or group rights."[43] Any "jurisprudential shift away from rights-based analysis," causing "the judicial role [to] morph from rights protector" to something else, would be imprudent,

[38] See, e.g., Yablon, supra note 27, at 677 (noting "the strikingly different positions that the Supreme Court has taken in its recent voting and spending cases").

[39] RICHARD L. HASEN, THE SUPREME COURT AND ELECTION LAW: JUDGING EQUALITY FROM BAKER V. CARR TO BUSH V. GORE 138 (2003).

[40] Richard L. Hasen, The "Political Market" Metaphor and Election Law: A Comment on Issacharoff and Pildes, 50 STAN. L. REV. 719, 727 (1998).

[41] Daniel H. Lowenstein, Competition and Competitiveness in American Elections, 6 ELECTION L.J. 278, 282 (2007).

[42] Id.

[43] Nathaniel Persily, The Place of Competition in American Election Law, in THE MARKETPLACE OF DEMOCRACY 171, 193 (Michael P. McDonald & John Samples eds., 2007).

in his view.[44] Bruce Cain, too, endorses a "framework that balances the state's interests in enacting a law against the impact of that law on individuals' constitutional rights."[45] "[T]he courts [should] balance those laws against the rights of voters, candidates, parties, and groups to determine whether they are constitutionally permissible."[46]

To be clear, these scholars don't necessarily support the courts' *applications* of rights-interests balancing. For the most part, they would be more likely than the Roberts Court to condemn voting restrictions and to approve campaign finance regulations.[47] Hasen also espouses an "antiplutocracy" principle that he describes as egalitarian but that could equally be deemed a systemic democratic value.[48] To that extent, his position isn't so different from that of the structuralists I discuss next. And Persily is primarily a critic of centering election law on competition. His commitment to rights-interest balancing isn't as strong as his objection to competitive structuralism.[49] But now we're straying into the academic weeds. The point here is that the Court's standard election law methodology is not without its high-profile defenders.

Academic Structuralists

Nor is it without its detractors—the structuralists.[50] This group comprises a wide range of scholars including Justice Stephen Breyer,[51] Christopher

[44] Nathaniel Persily, *In Defense of Foxes Guarding Henhouses: The Case for Judicial Acquiescence to Incumbent-Protecting Gerrymanders*, 116 HARV. L. REV. 649, 651, 667 (2002).

[45] Bruce E. Cain, *Garrett's Temptation*, 85 VA. L. REV. 1589, 1603 (1999).

[46] *Id.*

[47] For example, voting restrictions tend to violate Hasen's "essential political rights" principle, while campaign finance regulations usually further his "antiplutocracy" principle. *See* HASEN, *supra* note 39, at 82–88.

[48] *See id.* at 86–88.

[49] Note the less than emphatic language of the above quotes from his work. *See supra* notes 43–44 and accompanying text.

[50] Still other scholars try to bridge the divide between the balancers and the structuralists. *See, e.g.*, Guy-Uriel Charles, *Judging the Law of Politics*, 103 MICH. L. REV. 1099, 1102 (2005) (advocating "a dualistic understanding of the relationship between rights and structure"); Daniel A. Farber, *Implementing Equality*, 3 ELECTION L.J. 371, 377 (2004) (recommending an approach that "lies somewhere between structuralism and the traditional conception of individual rights"); Joseph Fishkin, *Equal Citizenship and the Individual Right to Vote*, 86 IND. L.J. 1289, 1297 (2011) (endorsing "'election law pluralism': the proposition that there are multiple, irreducibly distinct interests at stake in voting controversies").

[51] *See, e.g.*, STEPHEN BREYER, ACTIVE LIBERTY: INTERPRETING OUR DEMOCRATIC CONSTITUTION 28 (2005) ("[W]e can find in the Constitution's structural complexity an effort to produce a form of democracy . . . that could produce legislation that would match the needs of the nation.").

Elmendorf,[52] James Gardner,[53] Heather   Gerken,[54] Samuel Issacharoff,[55] Michael Kang,[56] Pamela Karlan,[57] Michael Klarman,[58] Daniel Ortiz,[59] Spencer Overton,[60] Richard Pildes,[61] David Schleicher,[62] and Robert Yablon.[63] The essential structuralist claim is that the courts' rights-interests balancing fails to capture what's truly at stake in election law cases. What's at stake, on this view, is irreducibly structural: the relationships among candidates, groups, and parties; the allocation of power among different political actors; and the operation of the political system as a whole. These structural factors, summarized by Pildes as "the interlocking relationships of the institutions . . . that organize the democratic system,"[64] explain why much election law litigation is launched in the first place. These factors can also be bolstered or undercut by the outcomes of the litigation. They should therefore be the focus of the courts' analysis—not rights and interests linked only tenuously to underlying functional realities.

---

[52] See, e.g., Christopher S. Elmendorf, *Undue Burdens on Voter Participation: New Pressures for a Structural Theory of the Right to Vote?*, 35 HASTINGS CONST. L.Q. 643, 644 (2008) ("[C]ourts would have an easier time developing judicially manageable rules for decision if they adopted an expressly structural understanding of the right to vote . . . .").

[53] See, e.g., Gardner, *supra* note 36, at 94 ("There is no reason why the Court cannot derive . . . an account of the nature and appropriate processes of representative democracy.").

[54] See, e.g., Heather K. Gerken, *Lost in the Political Thicket: The Court, Election Law, and the Doctrinal Interregnum*, 153 U. PA. L. REV. 503, 519 (2004) ("Should the Court . . . choose to remain in the political thicket, it could try to get a better map by adopting an explicitly structural approach.").

[55] For a representative article, see Samuel Issacharoff, *Gerrymandering and Political Cartels*, 116 HARV. L. REV. 593 (2002).

[56] See, e.g., Michael S. Kang, *When Courts Won't Make Law: Partisan Gerrymandering and a Structural Approach to the Law of Democracy*, 68 OHIO ST. L.J. 1097, 1099 (2007) ("Structural understanding is a necessary predicate to developing the law of democracy . . . .").

[57] For a representative article, see Pamela S. Karlan, *Nothing Personal: The Evolution of the Newest Equal Protection from Shaw v. Reno to Bush v. Gore*, 79 N.C. L. REV. 1345 (2001).

[58] See, e.g., Michael J. Klarman, *Majoritarian Judicial Review: The Entrenchment Problem*, 85 GEO. L.J. 491, 528–39 (1997) (critiquing the Court's election law doctrine from an "anti-entrenchment," majoritarian perspective).

[59] See, e.g., Daniel R. Ortiz, *From Rights to Arrangements*, 32 LOY. L.A. L. REV. 1217, 1218 (1999) (arguing that election law has improved by shifting to "a more pragmatic and structural view of politics as a matter of institutional arrangements").

[60] See, e.g., Spencer Overton, *Voter Identification*, 105 MICH. L. REV. 631, 674 (2007) ("Judges should not ignore questions of democratic structure and skewed results . . . .").

[61] For a representative article, see Richard H. Pildes, *The Theory of Political Competition*, 85 VA. L. REV. 1605 (1999).

[62] See, e.g., David Schleicher, *"Politics as Markets" Reconsidered: Natural Monopolies, Competitive Democratic Philosophy and Primary Ballot Access in American Elections*, 14 SUP. CT. ECON. REV. 163, 167 (2006) ("[Structuralist] theory has become the most important idea in the study of law and democracy and rightfully so.").

[63] See, e.g., Yablon, *supra* note 27, at 713 (arguing that courts should "take greater account of structural values in at least a subset of election law cases").

[64] Richard H. Pildes, *Foreword: The Constitutionalization of Democratic Politics*, 118 HARV. L. REV. 28, 41 (2004).

Out of the set of democratic values, most structuralists prioritize competition.[65] As Issacharoff and Pildes write in a seminal article, "[o]ur aim is to read into the Constitution an indispensable commitment to the preservation of an appropriately competitive political order."[66] Competition, of course, can mean many things.[67] It can refer to the closeness of elections, measured by the average margin of victory. It can indicate the contestedness of elections, that is, how often candidates run practically or actually unopposed. It can be equated with the level of turnover of particular positions or legislative chambers. Or it can denote whether one, two, or multiple parties typically vie for office. Competitive structuralists don't appear to have a favorite among these conceptions. They laud competition generally without zeroing in on a specific aspect of this broad value.

Competitive structuralists also prize competition for its putative effects as much as for its own sake. One of these effects is greater responsiveness: governmental outputs that change more quickly in response to shifts in popular preferences. "Only through an appropriately competitive partisan environment," assert Issacharoff and Pildes, can "the policy outcomes of the political process be responsive to the interests and views of citizens."[68] Another alleged consequence of competitive elections is more accountability: a higher likelihood that elected officials will be punished for poor performance (by being ousted from office) and rewarded for a positive record (by being reelected). "[P]artisan competition," avers Issacharoff, "serves as the locus of accountability of the governors to the governed."[69]

A different democratic value stressed by a second school of structuralists is participation. By participation these scholars mostly mean voter turnout: the fraction of citizens (or eligible voters) who cast ballots. "The aggregate pattern of voter participation," opines Elmendorf, "is a proper object of constitutional concern."[70] But participation further entails deliberating with fellow citizens,

---

[65] For examples beyond Issacharoff and Pildes, see Michael S. Kang, *Race and Democratic Contestation*, 117 YALE L.J. 734, 738 (2008) (defining and arguing for "democratic contestation"); Klarman, *supra* note 58, at 497–98 (defining and arguing for "antientrenchment"); and Daniel R. Ortiz, *Got Theory?*, 153 U. PA. L. REV. 459, 485–90 (2004) (discussing the anticompetitive effects of partisan gerrymandering).

[66] Issacharoff & Pildes, *supra* note 37, at 716.

[67] *See, e.g.*, Kang, *supra* note 65, at 761 (noting the "many manifestations" of democratic contestation); Yen-Tu Su, *Retracing Political Antitrust: A Genealogy and Its Lessons*, 27 J.L. & POL. 1, 44 (2011) (listing several "[c]ommon measures of electoral competition").

[68] Issacharoff & Pildes, *supra* note 37, at 646; *see also, e.g.*, Issacharoff, *supra* note 55, at 615 ("[C]ompetition [is] critical to the ability of voters to ensure the responsiveness of elected officials to the voters' interests . . . .").

[69] Samuel Issacharoff, *Private Parties with Public Purposes: Political Parties, Associational Freedoms, and Partisan Competition*, 101 COLUM. L. REV. 274, 276 (2001); *see also, e.g.*, Pildes, *supra* note 64, at 43 ("[E]lectoral accountability can exist only when effective political competition generates genuine political choices.").

[70] Elmendorf, *supra* note 52, at 653; *see also, e.g.*, Overton, *supra* note 60, at 636 (emphasizing "the value of widespread participation").

organizing political activities, and contacting elected officials—fully engaging in the process of self-government—especially in the work of Justice Breyer.[71] Moreover, like competition, participation is not just an intrinsic but also an instrumental value: a principle that's attractive due to both its supposed implications and its own normative pull. According to Overton, these implications include "fully informed decisions" by officeholders, "democratic legitimacy," "a redistribution of government resources and priorities," and "self-fulfillment and self-definition of individual citizens."[72]

Under both the competitive and the participatory versions of structuralism, courts would no longer balance rights against interests. Instead, when presented with a challenge to a given electoral policy, they would assess how that policy, in fact, affects electoral competition or civic participation. Courts would usually strike down anticompetitive or antiparticipatory measures: laws that threaten the democratic values at the heart of the theories. By the same token, courts would normally uphold procompetitive or proparticipatory provisions that advance the theories' underlying goals. Here's how Pildes, a prominent competitive structuralist, sums up the proper judicial role: "[C]ourts should attempt to recognize the structural and organizational implications of [their] decisions,"[73] and in particular they "ought to focus on . . . ensuring competition and, through it, electoral accountability."[74] Similarly, this is how Elmendorf, a leading participatory structuralist, argues that courts should approach voting regulations: "[C]ourts would ask whether the requirements cause the number or distribution of participating voters to deteriorate by more than a given amount ($x\%$)."[75] "If so, the requirements would be deemed presumptively impermissible," but "[i]f not, the requirements would be . . . reviewed very leniently."[76]

As I mentioned earlier, the fundamental structuralist critique of rights-interests balancing is that it ignores core democratic values like competition and participation. For their part, the balancers have a number of objections to structuralism, most of them specific to the competitive variant that dominates the literature. One of these charges is that no ideal or optimal level of competition exists.[77] *Maximally* competitive elections, notably—races as close to fifty-fifty as

---

[71] See BREYER, *supra* note 51, at 15–16 (discussing the concept of active liberty).

[72] Overton, *supra* note 60, at 657; *see also, e.g.*, Elmendorf, *supra* note 52, at 677 (arguing that participation enhances "the legitimacy of the political order" and serves the "electoral ideal in which public officials are chosen by and accountable to the normative electorate as a whole").

[73] Pildes, *supra* note 61, at 1611.

[74] Pildes, *supra* note 36, at 688.

[75] Elmendorf, *supra* note 52, at 675.

[76] *Id.*

[77] *See, e.g.*, HASEN, *supra* note 39, at 145 ("Missing from the initial political markets model was a theory of appropriate political competition."); Nathaniel Persily & Bruce E. Cain, *The Legal Status of Political Parties: A Reassessment of Competing Paradigms*, 100 COLUM. L. REV. 775, 790 n.55 (2000) ("The central question—what level of political competition is appropriate—is impossible to answer.").

possible—are undesirable because they lead to many disappointed voters and huge shifts in outcomes in response to small changes in public opinion. Second, precisely because the right amount of competition is uncertain, courts would have little objective guidance in determining when a policy is so anticompetitive that it should be judicially nullified. Competitive structuralism thus "offers no real limits on judicial intervention"[78] when "judges [face] the awesome task of measuring whether the array of political choices offered to voters is sufficiently anemic to deserve a judicial remedy."[79]

Third, from a certain vantage point, American elections aren't that uncompetitive. Substantial shares of legislators turn over after each election; so too do numerous state legislatures flip from one party's control to the other's; and jurisdictions whose general elections are free of suspense sometimes have hotly contested primary elections.[80] Accordingly, competitive structuralism may be a solution (procompetitive judicial review) in search of a problem (lack of competition). And fourth, standard modalities of constitutional interpretation don't support competitive structuralism. The theory is "completely disconnected from the text of the Constitution."[81] It also can't easily be linked to the Constitution's original understanding, its overarching principles, or the Supreme Court's election law jurisprudence.

Unsurprisingly, the structuralists have parries to these attacks. Their response to the first criticism—that it's impossible to specify the ideal level of competition—is that, even if so, it *is* usually possible to know when an electoral system is *highly* uncompetitive. "In theory and in doctrine, we can often identify what is troublingly unfair, unequal, or wrong without a precise standard of what is optimally fair, equal, or right."[82] Second, the structuralists maintain that their approach wouldn't result in excessive or overly intrusive judicial intervention. After all, few electoral regulations are very anticompetitive (and some are actually procompetitive). Structuralism therefore "is not an expansive invitation to more aggressive judicial action across the board as much as it is an effort to make the target of that action more focused and better justified."[83]

Third, the structuralists point to different evidence suggesting that American elections are quite uncompetitive. For instance, congressional and state legislative incumbents almost always win reelection; they frequently run without any opposition at all; and most districts are safe seats decided by more than

---

[78] HASEN, *supra* note 39, at 150.

[79] Nathaniel Persily, *Toward a Functional Defense of Political Party Autonomy*, 76 N.Y.U. L. REV. 750, 794 n.179 (2001).

[80] *See* Persily, *supra* note 44, at 653–64 (summarizing this evidence).

[81] *Id.* at 652.

[82] Pildes, *supra* note 61, at 1612.

[83] *Id.* at 1619; *see also, e.g.*, Issacharoff & Pildes, *supra* note 37, at 717 (explaining that their theory "is not a plea for more activist constitutionalism across the board").

20 percentage points.[84] This picture is said to be one of "incumbent entrench-ment and the erosion of political competition."[85] Lastly, the structuralists typi-cally concede that "[t]here is no narrow textual justification" for their theory.[86] But, they continue, standard constitutional modalities are equally unsupportive of the courts' rights-interests balancing. "The Court has built [that] regulatory edifice on the Equal Protection Clause," even though that provision, as originally understood, "conspicuously excluded such political rights as voting."[87] Existing election law doctrine, then, is just as textually unmoored as the structuralists' proposal for reform.

A Stagnant Debate

I want to make a few observations about the rights-structure debate whose contours I just sketched. To put my cards on the table, I'm a structuralist.[88] The democratic value I defend in this book, alignment, is a systemic interest just like competition and participation, one that can't be framed in terms of individual rights. Nevertheless, I'll express some skepticism about the competitive and the participatory strands of structuralism. That's why I called myself a dissatisfied structuralist in the introduction—and why I'm taking the trouble to develop a new kind of structuralism that highlights a different democratic principle.

To begin with, the balancers' objections to competitive structuralism lose much of their force with respect to the aligning structuralism I favor. Consider the argument that there's no ideal level of competition. In contrast, there *is* an ideal level of alignment: *complete* congruence between popular preferences and governmental outputs.[89] Better alignment is democratically preferable to worse alignment (even if its advantage in nondemocratic terms is uncertain). Put an-other way, competition is a Goldilocks value, at its best when there's neither too little nor too much of it. Alignment, on the other hand, is a normal good. More of it beats less. This makes things easier conceptually, and it also simplifies matters for courts. They wouldn't have to consider possibilities like unwise procompetitive policies or desirable anticompetitive measures (in situations

---

[84] *See, e.g.*, Issacharoff, *supra* note 55, at 623–26 (presenting this evidence); Ortiz, *supra* note 65, at 476–90 (same).

[85] Issacharoff, *supra* note 55, at 642.

[86] Samuel Issacharoff, *Surreply: Why Elections?*, 116 Harv. L. Rev. 684, 687 (2002).

[87] *Id.*

[88] However, as I explain in Chapter 4, I'm not opposed to balancing per se. I object only to bal-ancing in election law cases that excludes structural democratic values like alignment from the weighing process. I affirmatively favor balancing the promotion of alignment against other goods.

[89] With the qualifications I identify in the next chapter: most importantly, that alignment is assessed in the aggregate, across many issues and over many points in time.

where there's already too much competition). Instead, they could take it for granted that aligning regulations make the political system more democratic and misaligning rules less so.

Or take the mixed evidence about the competitiveness of contemporary American elections. The evidence about the alignment of modern American institutions is more unambiguous. As I discuss in Chapter 3, misalignment is rampant at every political level, whether noncongruence is measured with respect to the median individual or all people, and whether it's analyzed in terms of partisanship, representation, or policy. Consequently, no one could say with a straight face that aligning structuralism is a solution in search of a problem. The problem of misalignment is obvious and urgent.

Remember, too, the competitive structuralists' concession that their approach is unsupported by standard constitutional modalities. Aligning structuralism need not be so modest. I explain in Chapter 4 that alignment is a latent value in the constitutional text itself. Alignment plays a more explicit role in the history of the ratification of the original Constitution and the Reconstruction Amendments. And alignment is still more salient in several Warren Court decisions and opinions by individual Justices. To be sure, these sources in no way *compel* alignment's constitutionalization. But they do make alignment as legally plausible as other extratextual principles the Court has recognized over the years.

A second aspect of the rights-structure debate I want to underscore is its sheer age. Issacharoff and Pildes's pioneering article introducing competitive structuralism was published in 1998.[90] Hasen's major defense of balancing was unveiled in 2003.[91] That same period is when the most important works on participatory structuralism,[92] as well as the key critiques of competitive structuralism,[93] hit the presses. Since about 2010, the rights-structure debate has been essentially frozen in place. The debate's protagonists have made no new moves or countermoves. In fact, they've added virtually nothing to the positions they previously articulated.

The debate's age arguably shows itself in the values prioritized by the competitive and the participatory structuralists. Congressional elections in the late 1990s and early 2000s were unusually uncompetitive and resulted in very few seats changing hands by historical standards.[94] Given this political context, it's

---

[90] *See* Issacharoff & Pildes, *supra* note 37.

[91] *See* HASEN, *supra* note 39.

[92] *See, e.g.*, BREYER, *supra* note 51 (2005); Elmendorf, *supra* note 52 (2008); Overton, *supra* note 60 (2007).

[93] *See, e.g.*, Cain, *supra* note 45; Persily, *supra* note 44 (2002).

[94] *See, e.g., Party Divisions of the House of Representatives, 1789 to Present*, U.S. HOUSE OF REPRESENTATIVES, https://history. house.gov/Institution/Party-Divisions/Party-Divisions (last visited Feb. 1, 2024) (showing that Democratic House seats varied only from 201 to 212 between 1995 and 2007).

easy to see how scholars could have concluded that lack of competition was the central threat faced by American democracy. Likewise, voter turnout was anomalously low in this era, reaching its modern presidential election nadir in 1996.[95] Depressed turnout was the impetus for the National Voter Registration Act of 1993, which enables citizens to register to vote when they interact with motor vehicle agencies.[96] Depressed turnout might also have spurred scholars to construct theories aimed above all at promoting greater participation.

The datedness of the rights-structure debate further manifests itself in the political developments that *aren't* incorporated into the structuralists' accounts. One of these developments is the polarization of governmental outputs. Democratic and Republican legislators in Congress have grown more ideologically unlike than ever before in American history.[97] State legislators have also sorted ideologically by party, in some states to a greater extent than in Congress.[98] State policy outcomes are sharply bimodal, as well, in that states with unified Democratic (or Republican) governments now enact consistently liberal (or conservative) sets of policies.[99] Yet all these aspects of polarization play no role in competitive or participatory structuralism. Severe polarization is plainly different from lack of competition or participation. Severe polarization isn't even driven, to any significant degree, by lack of competition or participation.[100] So one of the most striking features of our political age goes unnoticed by the existing structuralist models, triggering neither heightened judicial review nor any sense that something is amiss.[101]

The story is the same with another defining characteristic of modern American politics: the clout of the wealthy. When the views of the rich deviate from those of the less affluent, federal and state legislators tend to do the bidding of the rich.[102] Under these conditions of preference divergence by wealth,

---

[95] *See, e.g., National General Election VEP Turnout Rates, 1789-Present*, U.S. ELECTIONS PROJECT, http://www.electproject. org/national-1789-present (last visited Feb. 1, 2024) (showing that presidential election turnout in 1996 was the lowest since the 1920s).

[96] *See* 52 U.S.C. §§ 20501–11 (2018).

[97] *See, e.g.*, Jeff Lewis, *Polarization in Congress*, VOTEVIEW.COM (June 4, 2020), https://www.voteview.com/articles/party_polarization.

[98] *See, e.g.*, Boris Shor & Nolan McCarty, *The Ideological Mapping of American Legislatures*, 105 AM. POL. SCI. REV. 530, 546 (2011).

[99] *See, e.g.*, Jeffrey R. Lax & Justin H. Phillips, *The Democratic Deficit in the States*, 56 AM. J. POL. SCI. 148, 155 (2012).

[100] *See, e.g.*, Nolan McCarty et al., *Does Gerrymandering Cause Polarization?*, 53 AM. J. POL. SCI. 666 (2009) (finding that the creation of uncompetitive districts has no substantial impact on the level of legislative polarization).

[101] To be fair, one leading competitive structuralist, Pildes, has written a major article about polarization, albeit not through the lens of competitive structuralism. *See* Richard H. Pildes, *Why the Center Does Not Hold: The Causes of Hyperpolarized Democracy in America*, 99 CALIF. L. REV. 273 (2011).

[102] I previously summarized the relevant findings in Nicholas O. Stephanopoulos, *Aligning Campaign Finance Law*, 101 VA. L. REV. 1425, 1468–74 (2015).

federal and state policy outcomes also track the opinions of the rich more closely than those of anybody else.[103] Again, though, competitive and participatory structuralism have nothing to say about this seeming descent into plutocracy. Government for the affluent isn't synonymous with, or even much related to, lack of competition or participation. It's simply orthogonal to the concerns that animate the current structuralist theories.[104]

I continue this discussion of polarization and plutocracy in Chapter 3: my survey of what we know about the (mis)alignment of American institutions. In Chapters 5 through 10, I further describe an array of findings about the aligning or misaligning effects of different (mostly electoral) regulations. The emerging empirical literature that has generated these findings is the last major development that postdates the introduction of competitive and participatory structuralism. Because these accounts were set forth at a relatively early date, they're conspicuously unempirical. Yes, the structuralists cite data about the lack of competition or participation in contemporary American elections. But when the rubber meets the road—when the question turns to how particular policies *influence* competition or participation, and thus to how courts and other actors should resolve actual disputes—the structuralists generally engage in speculation. They hypothesize that this or that law will enhance or dampen competition or participation, but they point to no studies backing their intuitions.[105] For the most part, this is because the relevant works hadn't yet been written. It's only in the last few years that political scientists have managed to quantify democratic values and rigorously probe how they're advanced or undermined by different measures. Theorizing before this empirical revolution, the structuralists had no choice but to resort to impressionistic, qualitative analysis.

My third objection to the rights-structure debate is its juriscentrism. This point applies equally to the balancers and to the structuralists, both of whom fixate on how the courts (especially the Supreme Court) should decide electoral cases.[106] Of course, this issue is important. From the balancers' perspective, the courts can reach a good or a bad equilibrium between individual rights and

---

[103] I previously summarized the relevant findings in Nicholas O. Stephanopoulos, *Political Powerlessness*, 90 N.Y.U. L. REV. 1527, 1577–79 (2015).

[104] However, government for the affluent is exactly what Hasen hopes to forestall through his antiplutocracy principle. *See supra* note 48 and accompanying text.

[105] In their initial presentation of competitive structuralism, for example, Issacharoff and Pildes cite no political science studies on the pro- or anti-competitive effects of primary regulations, ballot access restrictions, or campaign finance regulations. *See* Issacharoff & Pildes, *supra* note 37, at 652–90. Overton similarly stresses the "need [for] better data regarding the impact of [voting] requirements on participation by legitimate voters"—data that didn't exist in 2007 but now very much does. Overton, *supra* note 60, at 657.

[106] For instance, Hasen's major book on balancing is titled *The Supreme Court and Election Law*. *See* HASEN, *supra* note 39. Likewise, Issacharoff and Pildes note their "principal focus on the failure of the institution best positioned to destabilize these lockups, the United States Supreme Court, to develop a [suitable] theoretical framework." Issacharoff & Pildes, *supra* note 37, at 644. *But see* Pildes,

countervailing interests. Either way, the content of this rights-interests compromise is noteworthy. Similarly, from a structuralist angle, the courts have the capacity to push elections in more or less competitive or participatory directions. The courts, that is, can impact the democratic values that structuralism seeks to vindicate.

But the courts aren't the only, or even the most effective, actors that can play these roles. Consider balancing. Elected officials, unelected administrators, and the people themselves (through direct democracy) can also weigh individual rights against countervailing interests. In fact, these figures do this weighing all the time, producing huge quantities of electoral regulation the vast majority of which is never litigated. Or take structuralism. Competition and participation are relevant considerations for legislators, bureaucrats, and ordinary citizens. In sum, the decisions these actors make—the policies governing the electoral process on which the courts never opine—dramatically affect how hotly elections are contested and how vigorously people participate in their democracy.

My quarrel, then, is with the presentations of balancing and of structuralism as theories of judicial review. To be clear, they *are* that. But they're potentially so much more: guides to how officeholders, election officials, and all of us should think about the rules that structure politics. These broader conceptions might be called theories of democratic design—blueprints for the architecture of self-government. Because that's what's really at stake in the rights-structure debate. Not how the courts should resolve electoral disputes but how we the people should organize our political system. Judicial review is just a facet of this larger, more interesting, question.

The Missing Structural Value

My final and weightiest complaint about the rights-structure debate—the only one that warrants its own section—is that both the balancers and the structuralists overlook the vital democratic value of alignment. I devote much of the next chapter to explaining what exactly alignment is and why it's appealing. For now this working definition should suffice: Alignment means congruence between governmental outputs (like officeholders' party affiliations, legislators' votes, or policy outcomes) and popular preferences (captured by the views of the median person or of all people) within a given political unit (either an individual district or an entire jurisdiction). My claim is that alignment is more or less invisible to the balancers, the competitive structuralists, and the participatory structuralists alike.

This point should be uncontroversial with respect to the balancers. Misalignment plainly isn't equivalent to a burden on a constitutionally protected

supra note 61, at 1611 (observing that anticompetitive behavior by political actors could also be checked by "independent electoral commissions" or "statutorily adopted regulatory frameworks").

right like voting, speaking, or associating. In fact, misalignment can't easily be portrayed as an impediment to the exercise of any individual right at all (whether in or out of the Constitution).[107] This is because misalignment is a property of a political system, not a personal freedom that some other actor could abridge. As a result, no cause of action (or nonlegal grievance) for misalignment does or could exist under rights-interests balancing. The only protests recognized by rights-interests balancing are for rights infringements, which misalignment doesn't and couldn't cause.

But what about the "interests" half of rights-interests balancing? It's true that a jurisdiction could offer alignment as a justification for a law challenged on some other basis. The jurisdiction's argument would be that alignment is a sufficiently important interest furthered well enough by its law. This use of alignment, though, is quite rare. Out of the dozens of cases decided by the Supreme Court by balancing rights against interests, only a handful (all flagged in Chapter 4) involve assertions of alignment as a rationale for a disputed regulation. Moreover, this use of alignment only allows courts to uphold (or other institutions to defend) *aligning* policies. It doesn't enable them to object to *misaligning* measures that *widen* the gap between governmental outputs and popular preferences. Put differently, the "interests" half of rights-interests balancing is the defendant's half. As long as alignment is confined to that side of the doctrine, it's useless for any plaintiff (or other actor) who wants to curb misalignment.

Proceeding to the structuralists and their favorite democratic value, competition, it's meaningfully different from alignment. To reiterate, competition can refer to elections' closeness, contestedness, turnover, or range of choices. None of these meanings is the same as the congruence between the work of the government and the will of the people. In fact, competition and alignment are properties of different things. *Elections* are (or aren't) competitive. But *whole political systems* are (or aren't) aligned. The governmental outputs and popular preferences that must be examined to determine the level of alignment aren't features of elections. They may influence, and be influenced by, elections, but they're not themselves electoral.

These potential links between elections, governmental outputs, and popular preferences raise another possibility: Even if competition isn't synonymous with alignment, could competition always or usually lead to alignment? The Wisconsin anecdote with which I began the book suggests the answer is no. Again, Wisconsin may currently be the most competitive state in the country. Yet during the eight recent years when Republicans enjoyed full control of Wisconsin's government (2011–19), their policies hardly aligned with the

---

[107] With some difficulty, alignment could be portrayed as a *collective* right enjoyed by the people as a whole—to a government that reflects their aggregate preferences.

moderate views of the state's electorate. To the contrary, Republicans passed one archconservative law after another, typically in defiance of voters' wishes. Intense competition thus failed utterly to yield alignment. Instead, Wisconsin simultaneously experienced razor-close elections and yawning misalignment.

The Wisconsin story turns out to be the norm, not the exception. If competitive races induce legislators to align their positions with their constituents' views, then we should observe a strong relationship between legislators' voting records and their districts' makeups. Specifically, we should see legislators from more competitive districts adopting more moderate stances than legislators from safer seats. But we don't see this pattern at all. Anthony Fowler and Andrew Hall examine how the likelihood that a legislator votes conservatively is linked to the legislator's vote share in the previous election, for members of the U.S. House, the U.S. Senate, state houses, and state senates.[108] As shown in Figure 1.1, these scholars find no connection whatsoever. Legislators from even the most competitive districts compile voting records indistinguishable from those of legislators from the safest seats. *Party affiliation* has a massive effect on representation, as Democratic (or Republican) legislators generally cast liberal (or conservative) votes. But competition has no discernible impact. Among legislators from the same party, the correlation between voting record and district composition is essentially zero.[109]

Why are competition and alignment so weakly related? One explanation might be that, while competition is an aligning force, it's dwarfed by the misaligning influences in modern American politics. These include politicians' own ideologies as well as the pressures they face from party leaders, activists, and donors. Competition might not be able to offset all the factors pushing in the opposite direction. Another intriguing answer comes from work by a team of political scientists probing the ideological distributions of voters in more and less competitive districts.[110] On average, more competitive districts *don't* have

[108] *See* Anthony Fowler & Andrew B. Hall, *Long-Term Consequences of Election Results*, 47 BRIT. J. POL. SCI. 351, 358 (2015).

[109] *See id.* Devin Caughey and Christopher Warshaw replicate this finding for governors and for state house members over a longer timeframe. *See* DEVIN CAUGHEY & CHRISTOPHER WARSHAW, DYNAMIC DEMOCRACY: PUBLIC OPINION, ELECTIONS, AND POLICYMAKING IN THE AMERICAN STATES 67–68 (2022). They also show that *median* state house members compile voting records that are barely responsive to the closeness of *legislative chambers. See id.; see also, e.g.,* David S. Lee et al., *Do Voters Affect or Elect Policies?: Evidence from the U.S. House*, 119 Q.J. ECON. 807, 826–46 (2004) (finding close to no relationship between U.S. House members' voting records and their districts' makeups); John G. Matsusaka, When Do Legislators Follow Constituent Opinion? Evidence from Matched Roll-Call and Referendum Votes 18–20 (Feb. 2021) (finding close to no relationship between state legislators' margins of victory and their congruence with views expressed by their constituents in referenda).

[110] *See* Nolan McCarty et al., *Geography, Uncertainty, and Polarization*, 7 POL. SCI. RSCH. & METHODS 775 (2019).

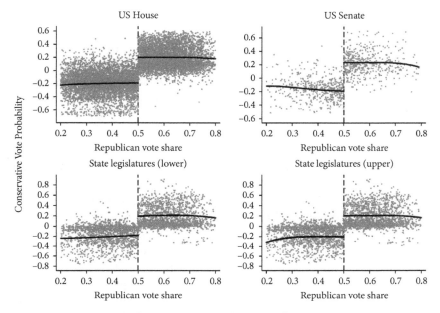

FIGURE 1.1 LEGISLATOR BEHAVIOR VERSUS DISTRICT COMPOSITION

Figure 1.1 is reproduced with permission from Anthony Fowler & Andrew B. Hall, *Long-Term Consequences of Election Results*, 47 BRIT. J. POL. SCI. 351, 358 (2015). Copyright © 2010 by Cambridge University Press.

more moderate voters. Rather, they have more evenly sized groups of liberal and conservative voters—that is, greater ideological heterogeneity.[111] Faced with this landscape of scarce moderates and abundant extremists, politicians have little incentive to adopt centrist positions. There are few votes to be won in the ideological middle, and many activists, donors, and primary constituents clamoring from the ideological fringes. A plausible pathway thus exists between more competition and *less* alignment. More competition usually means greater ideological heterogeneity; and when their voters are more ideologically divided, politicians reflect their views less accurately.[112]

The competitive theorists might reply that I'm forgetting their belief that competition is an instrumental, not an intrinsic, value.[113] Even if competition itself doesn't encompass alignment, the democratic goods to which competition

[111] *See id.* at 780.
[112] *See id.* at 788; *see also, e.g.,* Girish J. Gulati, *Revisiting the Link between Electoral Competition and Policy Extremism in the U.S. Congress,* 32 AM. POL. RSCH. 495, 506–10 (2004) (finding that U.S. senators are more misaligned with the midpoint of state public opinion in more competitive states).
[113] *See supra* note 68 and accompanying text.

allegedly[114] leads might do so. Responsiveness is the more relevant of the goods that's said to flow from competition. To repeat, responsiveness is the rate at which governmental outputs change in response to shifts in popular preferences. Responsiveness can be conceived both cross-sectionally and temporally.[115] Cross-sectionally, it tells us how quickly governmental outputs move as public opinion varies from one political unit to another (e.g., state to state). Temporally, responsiveness denotes the rate at which governmental outputs change as popular preferences shift over time (e.g., year to year).

Responsiveness certainly bears a resemblance to alignment in that it, too, involves the relationship between governmental outputs and popular preferences.[116] However, responsiveness *divides* the *change* in outputs by the *change* in preferences (across units or over time). In contrast, alignment *subtracts* the *level* of outputs from the *level* of preferences (at a single point in time).[117] To grasp how these concepts can conflict, think of the recent political history of another state: Virginia. Before 2020, Virginia looked much like Wisconsin. It was a highly competitive state in which Republicans nevertheless managed to enact very conservative policies during their period of unified government in 2012–13. In 2020, though, Democrats won control of Virginia's governorship and both chambers of the state legislature. Over the next two years, they proceeded to pass a series of unabashedly liberal measures: legalized marijuana, the abolition of the death penalty, a minimum wage hike, gun control, greater abortion availability, and so on.[118] These laws amounted to off-the-charts temporal responsiveness. A small shift in public opinion (just enough to flip Virginia from red to blue) led to a wholesale transformation in public policy. On the other hand, the picture was more ambiguous in terms of alignment. Before the Democrats'

---

[114] Competition does seem to be linked positively to accountability. *See, e.g.,* Philip Edward Jones, *The Effect of Political Competition on Democratic Accountability,* 35 POL. BEHAVIOR 481, 501–09 (2013) (finding that voters in more competitive states are more likely to vote against senators with whose views they disagree). However, the evidence is mixed with respect to the relationship between competition and responsiveness. *Compare, e.g.,* John D. Griffin, *Electoral Competition and Democratic Responsiveness: A Defense of the Marginality Hypothesis,* 68 J. POL. 911, 915–19 (2006) (finding a positive connection), *with* Elisabeth R. Gerber & Jeffrey B. Lewis, *Beyond the Median: Voter Preferences, District Heterogeneity, and Political Representation,* 112 J. POL. ECON. 1364, 1374–78 (2004) (finding a negative connection).

[115] For rare examples of work analyzing responsiveness in both its cross-sectional and temporal forms, see CAUGHEY & WARSHAW, *supra* note 109, at 97–112; and Griffin, *supra* note 114, at 915–19.

[116] For this reason, I don't want to overstate the differences between responsiveness and alignment. I'd be quite content if readers concluded that (1) alignment is similar to responsiveness; and (2) responsiveness is a normatively and legally appealing value.

[117] For other scholars drawing this distinction, see CAUGHEY & WARSHAW, *supra* note 109, at 97; Christopher H. Achen, *Measuring Representation,* 22 AM. J. POL. SCI. 475, 481–87, 490–94 (1978); Daniela Beyer & Miriam Hänni, *Two Sides of the Same Coin? Congruence and Responsiveness as Representative Democracy's Currencies,* 46 POL'Y STUD. J. S13, S18–19 (2018); and Lax & Phillips, *supra* note 99, at 148.

[118] *See, e.g.,* David Smith, *'We're Making Our Way': How Virginia Became the Most Progressive Southern State,* GUARDIAN, Mar. 8, 2021.

ascendance, Virginia's laws were much more conservative than its citizens. For a time after the Democrats took control, the state enjoyed excellent alignment. And then as the Democrats continued enacting left-wing policies, misalignment may have arisen anew, only this time in a liberal direction.[119]

This uncertain, contingent link between responsiveness and alignment is confirmed by more comprehensive analysis. In an earlier project, I collaborated with political scientists Eric McGhee and Steven Rogers to calculate the responsiveness and the alignment of median state house members from 1992 to 2012.[120] For responsiveness we determined the rate of change of the median legislator's voting record in response to swings over time in statewide public opinion.[121] For alignment we computed the ideological distance between the median legislator and the median voter.[122] As illustrated by Figure 1.2, state house chambers' responsiveness and alignment scores were essentially uncorrelated over this period.[123] Some chambers with high positive responsiveness (like Michigan) exhibited severe misalignment. Some chambers with high negative responsiveness (like Georgia) evinced exemplary alignment. Some chambers with average responsiveness (like Ohio) were misaligned to the right while others (like California) were misaligned to the left. On the whole, there was no consistent pattern in the data, no clear connection between the two variables.[124]

The other good to which competition is said to lead is accountability: rewarding (or punishing) officeholders for strong (or weak) records. This good can be dealt with briskly. You can imagine voters reelecting aligned representatives and ousting from office misaligned ones. In fact, there's evidence that aligned legislators fare somewhat better electorally than misaligned legislators at both the federal[125] and state[126] levels. But the fact that alignment (or its absence)

---

[119] More quantitatively, using Caughey and Warshaw's estimates of state-level public policy and public opinion, Virginia's policies shifted from roughly the eighty-fifth to the forty-fifth percentile in conservatism over this period—one of the biggest liberal swings ever. The views of Virginia's residents, however, barely budged.

[120] See Nicholas O. Stephanopoulos et al., *The Realities of Electoral Reform*, 68 VAND. L. REV. 761 (2015).

[121] See id. at 792.

[122] See id. at 791–92.

[123] See id. at 800.

[124] See also John G. Matsusaka, "Responsiveness" as a Measure of Representation 9–10 (June 2015) (finding that the congruence of state legislators' votes with the views of their constituents, as expressed in referenda, is unrelated to the responsiveness of state legislators' votes to the views of their constituents).

[125] See, e.g., Brandice Canes-Wrone et al., *Out of Step, Out of Office: Electoral Accountability and House Members' Voting*, 96 AM. POL. SCI. REV. 127, 134 (2002) (finding that a one-standard-deviation increase in a House member's ideological misalignment results in a vote share drop of about 2 percentage points).

[126] See, e.g., Steven Rogers, *Electoral Accountability for State Legislative Roll Calls and Ideological Representation*, 111 AM. POL. SCI. REV. 555, 559 (2017) (finding that a one-standard-deviation increase in a state legislator's ideological misalignment results in a vote share drop of about 1 percentage point).

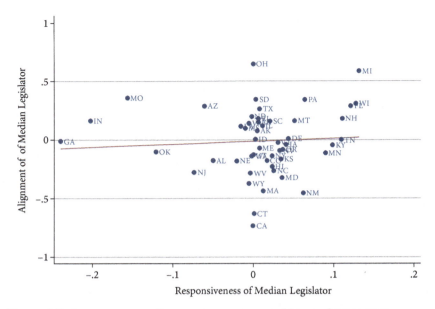

FIGURE 1.2 ALIGNMENT AND RESPONSIVENESS OF THE MEDIAN LEGISLATOR
Figure 1.2 is derived from data used in Nicholas O. Stephanopoulos et al., *The Realities of Electoral Reform*, 68 VAND. L. REV. 761, 800 (2015).

is one potential basis for accountability hardly means the two concepts are equiv-alent. Voters can hold officeholders accountable for many things other than their level of alignment: the state of the economy on their watch, their constituent service, their character, and so on. As an empirical matter, the impact of align-ment on accountability is also statistically detectable but practically modest.[127] And fundamentally, this tie between the values merely establishes that they're (weakly) connected—not that they're different ways of saying the same thing.

This logic holds as well for voter turnout, the darling of the participatory theorists. Higher turnout might result in better alignment (if representatives pay more attention to mobilized constituents). Alternatively, better alignment might yield higher turnout (if voters are more engaged when representatives reflect their views). These hypotheses are perfectly plausible despite never having been tested. But for present purposes, the hypotheses are also irrelevant. Say there is, in fact, a link between turnout and alignment. A link isn't an identity; it's just some sort of relation. Concepts are linked all the time without thereby becoming interchangeable.

[127] *See supra* notes 125–26.

As for the goods that participation allegedly fosters, they're undoubtedly important—and undoubtedly different from alignment. These goods include more informed governmental decision-making, enhanced governmental legitimacy, the redistribution of governmental resources, and individual self-fulfillment.[128] None of these should be slighted. And none should be equated with the congruence between governmental outputs and popular preferences. Alignment is simply a separate idea from informedness, legitimacy, redistribution, or fulfillment. As always, alignment might be connected to these values, but even if so, that's the extent of its affinity.

* * *

How should courts decide electoral cases? Most judges and some scholars advocate balancing burdens on individual rights against countervailing state interests. However, most contemporary election law academics object to balancing on the ground that it neglects the system-wide democratic values that are furthered, or frustrated, by electoral regulations. Among these values, competition and participation are the favorites of the structuralists. Courts should directly examine whether policies serve or set back competition or participation, according to this group of scholars.

I have a number of concerns about this rights-structure debate. It's dated, having barely budged since roughly 2010. It's juriscentric, paying little heed to the role of nonjudicial institutions in our political system. And most relevant here, both the balancers and the structuralists are blind to the democratic value of alignment. Because it infringes no rights, misalignment can't set into motion the machinery of rights-interests balancing. Alignment also isn't tantamount to any of the goods prized by the structuralists: not competition, nor participation, nor any of their supposed by-products.

But enough about what alignment isn't. In the next chapter I explore what this concept is and why we should care about it. To preview the argument, alignment can be defined in different ways depending on which governmental outputs, popular preferences, and political units we have in mind. However it's specified, alignment is close to the core of what it means to be a democracy—a society where the people actually rule. This proximity to the beating heart of self-government is why courts should prioritize alignment when they resolve electoral disputes. It's why nonjudicial actors, too, should craft rules that bring the work of the government and the will of the people closer together.

---

[128] *See, e.g.,* Overton, *supra* note 60, at 657.

2

The Concept of Alignment

Introduction

Political theorist Andrew Sabl recently criticized empirical political scientists for embracing an unsupported, unappealing conception of democracy. Most empiricists, according to Sabl, back a "normative model of democracy whereby democratic majorities are to get whatever they want, on every issue, and in short order."[1] However, this vision of a perfectly congruent democratic order is shared by essentially no theorists. "Political theorists do not, and never have, regarded responsiveness as the central measure of democratic quality."[2] Beyond its lack of academic grounding, universal, instantaneous congruence is undesirable on the merits. "When [theorists] have imagined a perfectly responsive regime, they have judged that this would be a bad thing."[3]

One goal of mine in this chapter is to show that alignment, properly defined and contextualized, isn't vulnerable to this critique. The most normatively attractive form of alignment—the version I defend here—aims for congruence with people's overarching ideologies, not their views on each individual issue. This model of alignment also incorporates time, objecting more to durable than to transient noncongruence. And this model acknowledges that alignment isn't the only relevant value, meaning that it can be subordinated or even disregarded in some cases. So understood, alignment does overlap with several prominent families of democratic theory. And with these qualifications, alignment is indeed an appealing, even invaluable, aspect of democracy. The people only rule—we only have a kratos of the dêmos—if what the people want is a major driver of what the government does. If the government persistently defies the broad direction of public opinion, its democratic legitimacy is sharply undermined.

---

[1] Andrew Sabl, *The Two Cultures of Democratic Theory: Responsiveness, Democratic Quality, and the Empirical-Normative Divide*, 13 PERSP. POL. 345, 346 (2015).

[2] *Id.*

[3] *Id.* For similar observations, see Jane Mansbridge, *Rethinking Representation*, 97 AM. POL. SCI. REV. 515, 525 (2003) ("In the field of United States legislative studies, the democratic norms regarding representation have often been reduced to one criterion: Does the elected legislator pursue policies that conform to the preferences of voters in the legislator's district?"); and Andrew Rehfeld, *Representation Rethought: On Trustees, Delegates, and Gyroscopes in the Study of Political Representation and Democracy*, 103 AM. POL. SCI. REV. 214, 216 (2009) ("[E]mpirical scholars by and large tend to treat representation with artificial precision, reducing 'representation' to the idea of 'responsiveness' or 'correspondence' itself.").

Aligning Election Law. Nicholas O. Stephanopoulos, Oxford University Press. © Nicholas O. Stephanopoulos 2024.
DOI: 10.1093/9780197662182.003.0002

I begin by identifying three key axes of alignment: (1) the applicable political unit (a specific district or an entire jurisdiction); (2) the method by which popular preferences are summarized (majoritarian or collective); and (3) the type of governmental output (partisanship, representation, or policy). These axes give rise to multiple variants of alignment, of which the most desirable, in my opinion, is jurisdiction-wide, collective, policy alignment. Next, I address a number of questions about alignment: Should it be sought with respect to people's overall ideologies or their positions on each issue? (I say overall ideologies.) Should it be conceived dynamically or statically? (Dynamically, I think.) And precisely *whose* preferences should be summarized? (It depends, but practically it doesn't matter much.) I then explore the mechanisms that can either generate or thwart alignment. Some of these are electoral, like voters' selection of certain candidates over others and officeholders' adaptation in anticipation of voters' future behavior. Several other mechanisms are unrelated to elections themselves, like the political geography of jurisdictions and how the elected branches actually make policy.

With this conceptual work out of the way, I return to Sabl's challenge. I argue that this refined form of alignment plays a role in the delegate model of representation, pluralism, and (maybe most surprisingly) deliberative democracy. Among these theories, at least, there's agreement about the need for, and importance of, alignment. Lastly, I grapple with a pair of additional attacks on alignment. The first is that people's preferences are so uninformed and incoherent that they can't serve as a meaningful benchmark for comparison with governmental outputs. This concern is rebutted by empirical work finding that most people's views are captured by a single, stable ideological dimension. The second critique is that no democratic value, not even alignment, should always take precedence over every other consideration. I concede this point. I support sacrificing some alignment, for example, to protect individual freedoms through a bill of rights and to enact sound policies on technical matters through expert agencies.

The Axes of Alignment

I mentioned that one of my objectives in this chapter is to offer a normative defense of alignment. Another, antecedent aim is to carefully examine the concept of alignment: to identify its constituent pieces, show how they can be assembled in different ways, and answer some initial questions about this democratic value. I start with this essentially taxonomic project because it's difficult to argue *for* alignment before it's clear what alignment *is*. Moreover, subsequent chapters frequently cite one or another form of alignment. So again, it's worth elaborating on these forms at some length before attempting to advocate for any of them.

In a sentence, then, alignment means congruence between governmental outputs and popular preferences within a given political unit.[4] Each term in this definition—a given political unit, popular preferences, and governmental outputs—constitutes a dimension along which alignment can productively be analyzed. To be sure, more axes of alignment are imaginable. As I discuss below, we could distinguish between alignment with respect to overarching ideologies or individual issues, or between dynamic or static alignment, or between alignment with all people, all citizens, all voters, or some other population. In my judgment, though, the three dimensions that derive from the very definition of alignment are sufficient for most purposes. Together, they encompass most senses in which I (and other scholars) use alignment (and related concepts like responsiveness).

Beginning with the relevant political unit, it can be either a particular district or a whole jurisdiction. For a particular district, *district-specific* (also known as *dyadic*) alignment refers to congruence between the district's residents[5] and their representative.[6] Note that this is a many-to-one relationship in the case of a single-member district, the norm in the United States. In a multimember district, it's a relationship between many residents and multiple legislators. Note also that a representative in America usually lacks the authority to set policy, on her own, for her district.[7] For this reason, while it's possible to speak of district-specific policy alignment, this is rarely a useful category.

The other level at which alignment can be analyzed is that of the entire jurisdiction: the city, county, state, or nation. *Jurisdiction-wide* alignment denotes congruence between the jurisdiction's residents and some facet of their government.[8] At the jurisdictional level, there are again many residents. But there are many representatives as well: all the members of the legislature. A many-to-many relationship thus applies to a jurisdiction's residents and legislators. (In contrast, a many-to-one relationship typically applies to a jurisdiction's residents and executive.[9]) Unlike a district, moreover, a jurisdiction always wields at least some

---

[4] This is a good place to note that I'm not wedded to the term "alignment." Throughout the book I use (what I consider to be) synonyms like "congruence," "correspondence," "reflection," "mirroring," and so on.

[5] Bracket for now whether the relevant population is residents or some other group.

[6] For a classic work on dyadic representation, see Robert Weissberg, *Collective vs. Dyadic Representation in Congress*, 72 AM. POL. SCI. REV. 535 (1978).

[7] Chicago aldermen are a well-known exception to this rule. *See, e.g.*, Christopher Thale, *Aldermanic Privilege*, ENCYCLOPEDIA OF CHICAGO, http://www.encyclopedia.chicagohistory.org/pages/2197.html (last visited Feb. 1, 2024) (discussing "the power of Chicago city council members (aldermen) to initiate or block city council or city government actions concerning their own wards").

[8] Weissberg calls this "collective" representation in his prominent study, *see* Weissberg, *supra* note 6, but I reserve that term for one way in which popular preferences can be summarized.

[9] *But see* Christopher R. Berry & Jacob E. Gersen, *The Unbundled Executive*, 75 U. CHI. L. REV. 1385 (2008) (discussing the plural executive officers of many states).

policymaking power. Jurisdiction-wide policy alignment is therefore not just a conceivable category but also a practically significant one.[10]

Turning to popular preferences, there are (at least) two ways to summarize them. The simpler and more common approach is to determine the position of the median person—the person at the midpoint of the popular distribution.[11] This position could be the median person's view on a particular issue, or it could be the median person's overall ideology on a left-right axis. What's so special about the median opinion? Under reasonable assumptions, it's the only stance that's favored by a popular majority over any other option.[12] Alignment with the median opinion, then, comes as close as possible to *majoritarian* alignment. As important as the median is, though, it fails to communicate any information about the shape of a distribution or the preferences of people not at the distribution's center.[13] As a result, majoritarian alignment is perfectly consistent with misalignment with many people's desires.

The more complex and rarer method for summarizing popular preferences tries to solve these problems with relying on the median.[14] Under this approach, the entire distribution of public opinion is plotted, revealing its tails and spread in addition to its midpoint. The distance between each person's position and one or more governmental outputs is then computed. *Collective* alignment is maximized when the sum of these distances is as small as possible (in more sophisticated versions, adjusting for the dispersion of the opinion distribution).[15] This form of alignment takes into account all people's views (not just the median person's). It also incorporates the shape of the opinion distribution. But it requires a good deal of data: more than many surveys produce. This lack of necessary information likely explains why collective alignment is estimated less often than majoritarian alignment.[16]

[10] *See, e.g.,* STUART N. SOROKA & CHRISTOPHER WLEZIEN, DEGREES OF DEMOCRACY: POLITICS, PUBLIC OPINION, AND POLICY 13 (2010) ("Policy outputs are necessarily an aggregate, or system-level, outcome.").

[11] Major works analyzing alignment using the views of the median person as a summary of public opinion include MICHAEL D. MCDONALD & IAN BUDGE, ELECTIONS, PARTIES, DEMOCRACY: CONFERRING THE MEDIAN MANDATE (2005), and G. BINGHAM POWELL, JR., ELECTIONS AS INSTRUMENTS OF DEMOCRACY: MAJORITARIAN AND PROPORTIONAL VISIONS (2000).

[12] These assumptions are a single-issue dimension and a distribution with a single peak. *See, e.g.,* POWELL, *supra* note 11, at 163.

[13] *See, e.g.,* Matt Golder & Jacek Stramski, *Ideological Congruence and Electoral Institutions,* 54 AM. J. POL. SCI. 90, 93 (2010) (observing that the median "ignores all information about the distribution of citizen preferences").

[14] *See, e.g., id.* ("To our knowledge . . . only two [prior] studies in the American and comparative literatures on congruence have [analyzed collective alignment].").

[15] *See, e.g.,* Daniela Beyer & Miriam Hänni, *Two Sides of the Same Coin? Congruence and Responsiveness as Representative Democracy's Currencies,* 46 POL'Y STUD. J. S13, S17–18 (2018); Golder & Stramski, *supra* note 13, at 93–95.

[16] *See, e.g.,* Hee-Min Kim & Richard C. Fording, *Extending Party Estimates to Governments and Electors, in* MAPPING POLICY PREFERENCES: ESTIMATES FOR PARTIES, ELECTORS, AND

A diagram may be helpful at this point. Figure 2.1, borrowed from Matt Golder and Jacek Stramski's pioneering work on collective alignment, displays three kinds of relationships between popular preferences and governmental outputs. The first is between a citizen and a representative in a district along a single opinion dimension. If the citizen is the median citizen, the distance between the citizen and the representative indicates the level of majoritarian misalignment.[17] The second panel plots the distribution of citizens' views in a district along with the representative's position. Collective alignment would be maximized at X^*, the spot that minimizes the sum of citizens' distances from their representative. The gap between X^* and R (the representative's actual position) is thus the extent of collective misalignment.[18] And the third panel shows the distributions of citizens' and representatives' preferences in a jurisdiction as a whole. At this jurisdictional level, the space between these distributions denotes the degree of collective misalignment.[19]

This leaves only the third axis of alignment: the governmental outputs that are (or aren't) congruent with popular preferences. I've already alluded to this axis in my references to policy enactment and the distance between constituents and legislators. But I'll now address this dimension more systematically. Officeholders' party affiliations, then, are one governmental output that can be aligned (or not) with people's partisan preferences. In a district, there's *partisan* alignment if the representative affiliates with the party favored by the median person.[20] At the jurisdictional level, partisan alignment is present if the median legislator and the median person both back the same party.[21] Of course, these

GOVERNMENTS 1945–1998, at 157, 159 (Ian Budge et al. eds., 2001) (noting that often "it is not feasible to describe the exact shape of the voter distribution on an ideological dimension").

[17] Majoritarian alignment can also be analyzed at the jurisdictional level, between the median person in the jurisdiction and the median legislator or some policy output.
[18] Many-to-one collective alignment can be analyzed at the jurisdictional level, too, between all persons in the jurisdiction and the median legislator or some policy output.
[19] Many-to-many collective alignment is only a sensible concept at the jurisdictional level, though the governmental outputs could be a set of policies instead of legislators' positions. For somewhat different approaches to measuring the space between people's and legislators' opinion distributions, compare Golder & Stramski, *supra* note 13, at 96–98 (examining the gap between people's and legislators' cumulative distribution functions), with Noam Lupu et al., *A New Measure of Congruence: The Earth Mover's Distance*, 25 POL. ANAL. 95, 100–04 (2017) (introducing the earth mover's distance as a new many-to-many congruence metric).
[20] Partisan *mis*alignment in a district can arise in several ways. In a race with more than two candidates competing under a plurality winner rule, the candidate preferred by the median voter might not be elected. Even if the elected candidate is the choice of the median *voter*, she might not be the favorite of the median *person* who *would* have voted but for voter suppression. And outright fraud can render meaningless even the preference of the median voter in a two-candidate race. *See, e.g.,* G. Bingham Powell & Georg S. Vanberg, *Election Laws, Disproportionality, and Median Correspondence: Implications for Two Visions of Democracy*, 30 BRIT. J. POL. SCI. 383, 399 (2000) (flagging the first of these scenarios).
[21] *See, e.g.,* Miriam Seifter, *Countermajoritarian Legislatures*, 121 COLUM. L. REV. 1733, 1737 (2021) (focusing on jurisdiction-wide partisan alignment).

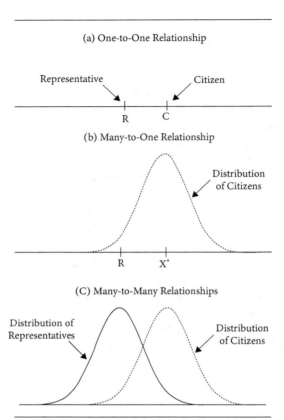

(a) One-to-One Relationship

Representative   Citizen

R   C

(b) Many-to-One Relationship

Distribution
of Citizens

R   X*

(C) Many-to-Many Relationships

Distribution of
Representatives

Distribution
of Citizens

Note: X^* is the position that minimizes the distance between all
the citizens.

FIGURE 2.1   MAJORITARIAN AND COLLECTIVE ALIGNMENT

Figure 2.1 is reproduced with permission from Matt Golder & Jacek Stramski, *Ideological Congruence and Electoral Institutions*, 54 AM. J. POL. SCI. 90, 91 (2010). Copyright © 2010 by Wiley.

are majoritarian notions. Collective versions of jurisdiction-wide partisan align-ment also exist, focusing on the links between parties' statewide seat and vote shares. I cover several of these measures when I discuss partisan gerrymandering in Chapter 7.[22]

Officeholders' policy positions are another governmental output that can be more or less congruent with people's policy preferences. Legislators

---

[22] *See also* REIN TAAGEPERA, PREDICTING PARTY SIZES: THE LOGIC OF SIMPLE ELECTORAL SYSTEMS 65–82 (2007) (discussing analogous measures applicable to proportional representation systems).

characteristically express their policy positions through legislative votes: up-or-down decisions on the bills presented to them. But legislators can also (and executives can only) articulate their policy stances through campaign platforms, speeches, press releases, and the like.[23] Conceptually, *representational* alignment works much like partisan alignment. In a district, there's majoritarian (or collective) representational alignment if the legislator's policy position is shared by the median person (or minimizes the sum of the legislator's distances from all people). At the jurisdictional level, majoritarian (or collective) representational alignment is present if the median legislator and the median person both hold the same policy views (or if the gap between legislators' and people's opinion distributions is minimized).[24]

Enacted policies are the last governmental output that can be tied more or less tightly to people's policy preferences. For legislators, the bills passed by the legislature and then signed into law are the most prominent enacted policies. For executives, enacted policies include executive orders, agency regulations, law enforcement activities, and (at the federal level) foreign policy decisions. As I noted earlier, *policy* alignment at the district level is a trivial category since electoral districts generally lack independent policymaking authority. In a jurisdiction, majoritarian policy alignment refers to the congruence between a given policy (or set of policies) and the views of the median person. In turn, collective policy alignment denotes the congruence between one or more policies and all people's opinions.

Together, these three axes of alignment generate twelve possible combinations: two political units (the district and the jurisdiction) times two methods for summarizing popular preferences (majoritarian and collective) times three governmental outputs (partisanship, representation, and policy). I think all these forms of alignment are meaningful and desirable (except for district-specific policy alignment). To tip my normative hand, though, the *most* compelling version, in my view, is jurisdiction-wide, collective, policy alignment.[25] A jurisdiction-wide focus seems apt because (to reiterate) jurisdictions,

---

[23] Heinz Eulau and Paul Karps famously identify "four possible components" of legislative representation: the policy positions taken by legislators, their "service" to their constituents, their "allocation" of governmental spending to their districts, and their "symbolic" stances through their public gestures. Heinz Eulau & Paul D. Karps, *The Puzzle of Representation: Specifying Components of Responsiveness*, 3 LEG. STUD. Q. 233, 241 (1977). While I use the term "policy" here, this framework applies equally to service, allocation, and symbolic representation.

[24] With respect to the executive of a jurisdiction (typically a single figure), there's majoritarian (or collective) representational alignment if the executive's policy position is shared by the median person in the jurisdiction (or minimizes the sum of the executive's distances from all people in the jurisdiction).

[25] To complement my normative intuitions, it would be extremely helpful for a survey to poll people about how appealing they find different forms of alignment. To my knowledge, though, no such survey has ever been conducted.

not districts, enact policies in our system. I prefer describing popular preferences collectively in order to register all people's opinions, not just the stances of the median person. And enacted policies are the government's most critical products—the ones that ultimately shape people's lives. Accordingly, in the book's empirical sections, I prioritize evidence about jurisdiction-wide, collective, policy alignment. But when this information is unavailable (as is often the case), I don't hesitate to present data about other kinds of alignment.

The typology of alignment also raises the question: Along each axis, how are the different classifications related? First, there's no necessary link between district-specific and jurisdiction-wide alignment. Districts that exhibit excellent partisan and representational alignment might add up to a legislature that's highly aligned in these respects. Or they might not. The point of partisan gerrymandering, in particular, is to disrupt the connection between district-specific and jurisdiction-wide assessments. To illustrate, suppose a jurisdiction has 300 persons of whom 170 are conservative Republicans and 130 are liberal Democrats.[26] Further assume the jurisdiction is divided into three 100-person districts, one with 80 Republicans and 20 Democrats, two each with 45 Republicans and 55 Democrats. Posit, too, that the former district is represented by a conservative Republican and the latter two by liberal Democrats. In this unexceptional scenario, superb district-specific alignment cumulates to glaring jurisdiction-wide misalignment. Across the jurisdiction, the median person is a conservative Republican but, thanks to the district configuration, the median legislator is a liberal Democrat.[27]

Second, for any district in isolation, majoritarian alignment and collective alignment are identical. The median person's preference *is* the spot that minimizes the sum of the distances from all people. A legislator who adopts the median person's preference therefore maximizes both majoritarian and collective alignment.[28] However, this identity collapses when multiple districts are compared. To adapt an example from Golder and Stramski,[29] imagine two

---

[26] To simplify the example, also suppose all 300 persons are voters.

[27] *See, e.g.,* John G. Matsusaka, *Popular Control of Public Policy: A Quantitative Approach,* 5 Q.J. POL. SCI. 133, 153–54 (2010) ("Even if districts are [drawn] so that each legislator ends up representing the district's median voter, district lines can be gerrymandered so that the median legislator is not congruent with the median voter in the population."). One team of scholars actually finds that district-specific and jurisdiction-wide alignment are *negatively* correlated. "[O]ver most of American political history, the quality of collective representation of Americans' political preferences by the House of Representatives . . . has generally been inversely related to the degree of responsiveness of individual members of Congress to the preferences of their own constituents." Larry M. Bartels et al., *Representation, in* THE OXFORD HANDBOOK OF AMERICAN POLITICAL DEVELOPMENT 399, 400 (Richard Valelly et al. eds., 2016).

[28] *See* Golder & Stramski, *supra* note 13, at 93 ("For any single constituency, absolute citizen congruence is highest when the representative is located at the ideological position of the median citizen.").

[29] *See id.* at 92.

districts with normal, bell-curve-shaped distributions of public opinion and medians of 50 on a 1–100 scale. But say this distribution varies from 1 to 100 in the former district and only from 40 to 60 in the latter. Then from the perspective of majoritarian alignment, legislators in both districts are equally (and perfectly) aligned if they locate themselves at the midpoint of public opinion. From the point of view of collective alignment, in contrast, the legislator from the former district is more misaligned. Because of the greater dispersion of popular preferences in her district, she's more distant from her constituents, on average, despite being as close to them as she can be.[30]

Lastly, partisan alignment doesn't always lead to representational alignment, which itself doesn't always lead to policy alignment. As I explain in Chapter 3, most contemporary officeholders are quite liberal or conservative while most people today remain relatively moderate. This stylized fact means that partisan alignment is no guarantee of representational alignment. It's common for a legislator (or legislature) to reflect popular partisan preferences but nevertheless to be more politically extreme than most people would like. As for representational alignment and policy alignment, they're sometimes at odds because the laws that are enacted are driven by many factors beyond the median, or even the overall shape, of a legislative chamber's opinion distribution. These include the composition of legislative committees, the use of agenda control by legislative leaders, supermajority voting rules, and the need for the assent of another chamber as well as the executive. Due to these factors, a chamber that faithfully mirrors people's views may be unable to produce policy that does so, too.

Another diagram concludes this section. Figure 2.2 displays the three dimensions of alignment: the applicable political unit, the method by which popular preferences are summarized, and the type of governmental output. Figure 2.2 also shows the possible classifications along each axis. The dotted arrows between these classifications—district-specific and jurisdiction-wide alignment; majoritarian and collective alignment; and partisan, representational, and policy alignment—represent their ambiguous relationships. Together, these dimensions and classifications are the building blocks of the concept of alignment. I return to them often in the pages ahead.

Issues and Ideologies

In the discussion to this point, I've avoided specifying what *kinds* of popular policy preferences should be congruent with officeholders' policy positions

---

[30] As Golder and Stramski show, majoritarian alignment and collective alignment remain distinct across districts even if an adjustment is made for the dispersion of public opinion. *See id.* at 95.

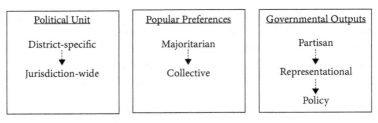

FIGURE 2.2 DIMENSIONS AND CLASSIFICATIONS OF ALIGNMENT

(in the case of representational alignment) or enacted policies (in the case of policy alignment). One option is to conceive of people's policy preferences as their views on a long series of individual issues. For instance, suppose there are a hundred issues that constitute the policy agenda in some period. Then to evaluate representational alignment, we might ask in what fraction of those hundred matters are a legislator's (or legislature's) policy stances consistent with the opinions of her (or their) constituents. Likewise, to gauge policy alignment, the question would be in what share of the hundred matters do enacted policies reflect the public's views.[31]

Another approach is to *collapse* popular policy preferences and governmental outputs into summary ideological scores before comparing them.[32] To continue the above example, techniques like factor analysis and item-response-theory modeling can convert people's opinions on the hundred separate issues into ideal points on a single, or at most a handful of, ideological axes.[33] These methods can also transform legislators' votes and policy outcomes on those issues into ideal points on the same ideological scale(s). After this preliminary data reduction is complete, it's straightforward to determine representational alignment and policy alignment. People's ideal points simply have to be compared to those of legislators to calculate representational alignment, and to those of enacted policies to compute policy alignment.

---

[31] For a vigorous defense of this approach to conceptualizing people's policy preferences, see David E. Broockman, *Approaches to Studying Policy Representation*, 41 LEG. STUD. Q. 181, 185 (2016) ("[W]e should prefer the answers issue-by-issue approaches yield . . . .").

[32] It should be obvious that "ideologies" identified through these empirical methods aren't necessarily coherent political worldviews. Rather, they're positions on political issues that *do* go together *in fact*, whether or not they *should* go together *in theory*.

[33] For a prominent study using factor analysis to analyze people's policy preferences, see Stephen Ansolabehere et al., *The Strength of Issues: Using Multiple Measures to Gauge Preference Stability, Ideological Constraint, and Issue Voting*, 102 AM. POL. SCI. REV. 215, 219–20 (2008). For a major study using item-response-theory modeling, see Chris Tausanovitch & Christopher Warshaw, *Measuring Constituent Policy Preferences in Congress, State Legislatures, and Cities*, 75 J. POL. 330, 333 (2013).

I don't have a favorite between these options. Each has been employed in path-breaking recent studies.[34] And each has its pros and cons.[35] Use of an array of individual issues to analyze alignment provides more detail and requires less data manipulation. On the other hand, any given set of issues is somewhat arbitrary, and people's views on particular matters are notoriously subject to measurement error. In turn, summary ideological scores make for easier comparisons between popular policy preferences and governmental outputs, reduce the impact of measurement error, and link different jurisdictions and periods with the same metrics. But methodological controversy persists over how to generate these scores, and they necessarily discard some relevant information in their pursuit of simplification. In the end, my judgment resembles that of Devin Caughey and Christopher Warshaw, the authors of the best work yet on state-level alignment: Each approach "has advantages of its own," rendering impossible a definitive choice between them.[36]

But I can take a stand on—in opposition to—another way of thinking about the connection between popular policy preferences and governmental outputs. This strategy is to discern people's views on a certain issue, and then to demand that representation and policy mirror public opinion on that matter. The strategy then repeats for each additional issue, insisting on alignment in every case. One problem with this approach is its excessive ambition. Officeholders don't even know all the policies their constituents want. Without this knowledge, it's unrealistic to ask politicians somehow to achieve alignment on every matter. Moreover, the mechanisms that intermittently push toward alignment, which I examine later in this chapter, are relatively crude forces. Even when working well, they can't be expected to give rise to perfect representational and policy congruence.

The aspiration of across-the-board alignment also runs headlong into the shortcomings of popular policy preferences (another topic to which I return below). People lack informed, coherent views on certain subjects. The opinions they do firmly hold are sometimes malicious. Alignment in these circumstances might be democratic in the sense that people get what they wish for. But it isn't otherwise desirable. Representation and policy that reflect ignorant, illogical preferences are no better than those deficient views. The faithful transmission

[34] *See, e.g.,* Devin Caughey & Christopher Warshaw, Dynamic Democracy: Public Opinion, Elections, and Policymaking in the American States 113–29 (2022) (using both a set of individual issues and ideological summarization to study alignment); Jeffrey R. Lax & Justin H. Phillips, *The Democratic Deficit in the States,* 56 Am. J. Pol. Sci. 148, 150–64 (2012) (using a set of individual issues).
[35] For other discussions of these pros and cons, see Caughey & Warshaw, *supra* note 34, at 12, and Broockman, *supra* note 31, at 186–96.
[36] Caughey & Warshaw, *supra* note 34, at 12. Importantly, similar substantive conclusions follow whether preferences are analyzed issue by issue or using ideological scales. This is why I don't need to take a position on which approach is preferable.

of invidious opinions into governmental outputs is equally troubling. Alignment therefore becomes less attractive when it's sought in all cases, including when people's views are less worthy of respect.[37]

The aggregation of popular policy preferences, either across many issues or into summary ideological scores, mitigates these concerns. It's less ambitious to ask that representation and policy be consistent with public opinion on a substantial share of matters—not all matters—or reasonably proximate to people's ideal points. It's also more plausible to expect the mechanisms of alignment, when they're running smoothly, to generate this sort of rough congruence. Furthermore, when people's views are aggregated, their uninformed, incoherent, or malicious attitudes become easier to discount. Even if representation and policy are misaligned with these flawed preferences, they can still match people's sounder opinions on other subjects. The flawed preferences are also combined with the sounder ones when they're converted into summary ideological scores. Representation and policy can often come close to these ideal points without embracing the worst aspects of public opinion.[38]

Dynamic Alignment

Another issue I've bracketed until now is the role of *time* in analyzing alignment. Alignment can certainly be understood statically. On this view, it's congruence between governmental outputs and popular preferences within a given political unit and at a given moment in time. But I think a dynamic perspective on alignment—one that explicitly incorporates time—is more realistic and so preferable. In particular, time is relevant to the conceptualization and calculation of alignment in (at least) three ways.

First, and most obviously, people's opinions can change from one point in time to another. People can support Democrats (or liberalism) at t1 and Republicans (or conservatism) at t2.[39] For governmental outputs to remain

---

[37] This is part of why I place a low priority on whether any given electoral regulation is itself popular. Any regulation is just one of many issues, and alignment on any individual issue is relatively unimportant. Additionally, unlike most other policies, an electoral regulation has the capacity to affect alignment with respect to many other issues—if the regulation has a significant aligning or misaligning impact. This potential influence on alignment across the board outweighs whether the regulation itself is or isn't congruent with public opinion.

[38] *Cf.* Ansolabehere et al., *supra* note 33, at 222–23 (finding that when numerous issue positions are used to calculate ideal points, the addition of each incremental item has little impact). In this chapter's final section, I discuss another available response to the shortcomings of popular policy preferences: excluding certain areas from alignment's domain through bureaucratization or judicialization.

[39] *See, e.g.,* Cass R. Sunstein, *Preferences and Politics*, 20 PHIL. & PUB. AFF. 3, 5 (1991) (observing that "preferences are not fixed and stable, but are instead adaptive to a wide range of factors").

aligned with popular preferences, in the face of such shifts, the outputs must vary as well. Here, officeholders' party affiliations must switch from Democratic to Republican, and representation and policy must swing from liberal to conservative. This simple point connects to the discussion of alignment and responsiveness in the last chapter. Temporal responsiveness, again, is the rate at which governmental outputs change as popular preferences shift over time. *Some* responsiveness is necessary to maintain alignment when people's views vary temporally.[40] But if there's too little responsiveness, governmental outputs lag behind popular preferences that have changed to a greater degree. And if there's too much, governmental outputs overshoot popular preferences, shifting even further than public opinion.[41]

Second, it necessarily takes time for governmental outputs to move much. Officeholders rarely vary their party affiliations or ideologies. In fact, there's a saying in political science that legislators "die with their ideological boots on," refusing to change their positions even in their last terms in office, when their electoral incentives have disappeared.[42] Consequently, for officeholders' partisanship and representation to shift significantly, they must often be replaced by other politicians. But replacement is itself slow and difficult, owing to the time between elections (as much as six years) and the fact that most incumbents who run again are reelected. Moreover, policymaking is a gradual process, too. There are many veto gates at all levels of American government (in Washington above all). Coalitions with the power to enact new laws also have limited space on their agendas, limited time, and limited political capital. As a result, observe Caughey and Warshaw, "it often takes years or even decades for the force of public opinion to filter through the political process."[43]

Because of this lag, it's unwise to measure alignment only at a given moment in time. People's views could have changed shortly before any particular snapshot was taken, in which case governmental outputs wouldn't have had enough time to adjust. The better approach, I think, is to measure alignment *continuously*—at regular intervals over time—and then to average the resulting scores.[44] This sort of aggregation across years is the temporal analogue to the aggregation across

---

[40] *See, e.g.,* Beyer & Hänni, *supra* note 15, at S19 ("Responsiveness does not necessarily lead to congruence but congruence can be a result of responsiveness.").

[41] *See, e.g.,* Lax & Phillips, *supra* note 34, at 164 (discussing how state policy outcomes are often "[o]verresponsive to [popular] ideology" and therefore noncongruent).

[42] KEITH T. POOLE & HOWARD ROSENTHAL, CONGRESS: A POLITICAL-ECONOMIC HISTORY OF ROLL CALL VOTING 8 (1997).

[43] CAUGHEY & WARSHAW, *supra* note 34, at 4.

[44] *See, e.g.,* Daniel C. Lewis & Matthew L. Jacobsmeier, *Evaluating Policy Representation with Dynamic MRP Estimates,* 17 ST. POL. & POL'Y Q. 441, 456 (2017) (employing this approach with respect to state-level policy alignment on the issue of same-sex marriage). Alternatively, we could identify when an issue emerges on the policy agenda and track alignment at regular intervals after that date. *See, e.g.,* CAUGHEY & WARSHAW, *supra* note 34, at 115–20, 123–24 (employing this approach).

issues I recommended above. And it confers the same advantages: It's less ambitious to ask for alignment over a longer period, during which governmental outputs have had more time to move, than at a specific moment. It's more realistic that the mechanisms of alignment could yield satisfactory congruence when they're given years to churn away. And if people's opinions are uninformed, incoherent, or malicious, it's possible they could improve over time. In that fortuitous event, alignment with flawed preferences wouldn't even be democratic for very long. It would eventually turn into misalignment with sounder views.

The last point about time is that it isn't only governmental outputs that can shift to achieve congruence. Alignment can also ensue from temporal variation in public opinion. Imagine that policy in a jurisdiction is quite conservative while people's ideologies are quite liberal. From this starting point, the more familiar way to get to alignment is for policy to move in a liberal direction. But an equally effective route is for people's ideologies to become more conservative. Put another way, the concept of alignment has two components: governmental outputs and popular preferences. Over time, either piece can change in ways that either enhance or undermine alignment.[45]

Furthermore, alignment's two parts aren't independent of each other. Most of this book deals with how governmental outputs can be tethered more tightly to popular preferences. But popular preferences are themselves shaped, in part, by governmental outputs. In particular, under the well-known "thermostatic" model of public opinion, people's policy views tend to shift in the opposite direction from that in which public policy is moving.[46] At both the federal and state levels, more liberal enacted policies give rise to more conservative mass sentiment, and vice versa.[47] The implication is that the dance of alignment never ends. Popular preferences go one way and governmental outputs hopefully follow (in due time). But when the outputs finally converge with the preferences, the match is fleeting. The preferences soon swing the other way, starting the whole cycle anew.

---

[45] *See, e.g.,* Lewis & Jacobsmeier, *supra* note 44, at 456 ("[P]olicy congruence can be achieved either by the state acting to bring policy in line with public opinion or by public opinion shifting to reflect state policy. Similarly, policy incongruence can result either from state action or through changes in public opinion.").

[46] The term was coined by Christopher Wlezien, *The Public as Thermostat: Dynamics of Preferences for Spending*, 39 AM. J. POL. SCI. 981 (1995).

[47] Wlezien identified this thermostatic pattern with respect to Americans' preferences for federal spending. *See id.* For a similar finding at the state level, Julianna Pacheco, *The Thermostatic Model of Responsiveness in the American States*, 13 ST. POL. & POL'Y Q. 306 (2013).

Defining the Dêmos

The final issue on which I've reserved comment so far is *with whom* there should be alignment. I've referred in general terms to "people" without identifying exactly which individuals I have in mind. One aspect of this question is comparatively easy. With respect to district-specific alignment, most would agree that it's people in the district whose opinions are relevant. For jurisdiction-wide alignment, similarly, people in the jurisdiction are presumably the ones whose views matter. True, there are some complications at the margins: recent arrivals in a district or jurisdiction, people who live in one place but work in another, American citizens located abroad, and so on. By and large, though, it's not too controversial that people outside a district or jurisdiction aren't members of the applicable political community. They therefore have no claim that governmental outputs be congruent with their preferences.[48]

The more difficult dilemma is which people within a district or jurisdiction count for purposes of alignment. All residents? Just citizens? Those who are eligible or registered to vote? Those who actually vote? Those who would have voted but for voting restrictions? Unfortunately, democratic theory isn't very helpful here. The models of democracy I discuss later in this chapter have much to say about how the members of a given dêmos should govern themselves. But they're mostly silent as to the antecedent matter of how the dêmos should be defined—which people it should include and exclude. This muteness is attributable to the fact that standard democratic procedures (majoritarian voting, deliberation, and the like) can't be used to determine the boundaries of the dêmos. Those processes are available only when it's clear who's entitled to participate in them. But of course, that's the very issue in dispute here: Who's part of the political community with whose opinions alignment should be sought, and who isn't? Democracy can't specify its own membership criteria.[49]

---

[48] *See, e.g.*, Reiner Bauböck, *Political Membership and Democratic Boundaries, in* THE OXFORD HANDBOOK OF CITIZENSHIP 60, 63 (Ayelet Shachar et al. eds., 2017) (noting that the standard approach "justif[ies] the inclusion of all current residents in a polity and only these"); Frederick G. Whelan, *Prologue: Democratic Theory and the Boundary Problem*, 25 NOMOS 13, 18 (1983) (discussing the "usual resort to the territorial principle," under which "authoritative institutions . . . are responsive to the collective preferences of the people residing in[] geographically bounded territories").

[49] Political theorists call this the democratic boundary problem. In Whelan's words, "democracy, which is a method for group decision-making or self-governance, cannot be brought to bear on the logically prior matter of the constitution of the group itself, the existence of which it presupposes." Whelan, *supra* note 48, at 40; *see also, e.g.*, ROBERT A. DAHL, A PREFACE TO DEMOCRATIC THEORY 54 (1956) ("[T]he theory of . . . democracy does not provide any satisfactory criteria for deciding who should be included in the system."). Unsurprisingly, some political theorists have thought deeply about the democratic boundary problem. *See, e.g.*, MARGARET CANOVAN, THE PEOPLE (2005); ELIZABETH F. COHEN, SEMI-CITIZENSHIP IN DEMOCRATIC POLITICS (2010). My point isn't that *political theorists* have nothing to say about this issue; it's that the issue is largely unaddressed by the *models of democracy* I discuss later in the chapter. A related constitutional

One response to this problem is that, however the relevant population is de-cided, alignment is then a powerful tool for analyzing whether that population's preferences are satisfied. This response necessarily concedes that alignment (like much of democratic theory) has no bearing on the political community's borders. Those limits have to be set some other way: by tradition, via normative reflection, through an authoritative statement by some governmental institution, and so on. But *once* the limits are set, alignment springs into motion. It offers a thorough, compelling framework for ascertaining whether, and to what extent, the government is doing what the people deemed pertinent want. This frame-work can be used to assess the status quo, to compare it to other jurisdictions and periods, and to examine the effects of a host of electoral and nonelectoral rules. These are substantial contributions even if they don't extend to the definition of the dêmos itself.

Another response is that, in practice, it often makes little difference which population is used to measure alignment. Consider partisan alignment. A long line of political science studies find that voters' partisan preferences aren't too divergent from those of eligible voters who choose not to cast ballots. In partic-ular, nonvoters aren't (as is sometimes asserted) significantly more likely than voters to support Democratic candidates.[50] Accordingly, officeholders' levels of partisan alignment with actual voters and with eligible voters are usually similar. It's rare for politicians to reflect the partisan views of the actual electorate but to flout those of the eligible electorate.

Or take representational alignment and policy alignment. They both hinge on people's policy preferences—and people's policy preferences don't vary much whether they're residents, eligible voters, or actual voters. The ideolog-ical distributions of residents and actual voters resemble each other; in both cases, most survey respondents are moderates and relatively few hold extreme opinions.[51] Likewise, the mean ideologies of actual voters and eligible nonvoters

question is, for purposes of the one-person, one-vote rule, who exactly should be equalized among districts—all people, eligible voters, or some other population? Just as democratic models don't specify who should be included in a democracy, the Supreme Court declined to say whose equal rep-resentation the one-person, one-vote rule is meant to achieve. *See* Evenwel v. Abbott, 136 S. Ct. 1120, 1133 (2016) ("[W]e need not and do not resolve whether . . . States may draw districts to equalize voter-eligible population rather than total population.").

[50]   The most famous work in this literature is RAYMOND E. WOLFINGER & STEVEN J. ROSENSTONE, WHO VOTES? (1980). For a representative study about two decades later, see Bernard Grofman et al., *Rethinking the Partisan Effects of Higher Turnout: So What's the Question*, 99 PUB. CHOICE 357 (1999). And for recent analyses again confirming the minor partisan differences between voters and nonvoters, see KNIGHT FOUND., THE 100 MILLION PROJECT: THE UNTOLD STORY OF AMERICAN NON-VOTERS 21, 24–25, 28 (2020), and DARON R. SHAW & JOHN R. PETROCIK, THE TURNOUT MYTH: VOTING RATES AND PARTISAN OUTCOMES IN AMERICAN NATIONAL ELECTIONS (2020).

[51]   *See, e.g.*, Stephen Ansolabehere et al., *Purple America*, 20 J. ECON. PERSPECTIVES 97, 102 (2006) (plotting the ideological distribution of residents based on the General Social Survey and noting that the "[t]he American National Election Study," which surveys voters, "produce[s] almost the same

are quite close: typically no further apart than one or two tenths of a point on a seven-point scale.[52] Based on this data we might surmise that enacted policies are about equally congruent with people's views no matter which people we mean. This hypothesis turns out to be correct. According to work by John Matsusaka, essentially identical fractions of state policy outcomes are aligned with residents' and with actual voters' preferences.[53]

Before moving on from the definition of the dêmos, there's one more question to consider: Should alignment be conceptualized only with respect to the *whole* population (whichever population that is) or also vis-à-vis *groups* of people? Unfortunately, American society is riven by cleavages including wealth, race, and gender. These cleavages give rise to groups that sometimes have quite different attitudes from the population in its entirety: the poor, middle class, and rich; African Americans, Hispanics, Asian Americans, and Whites; women and men. Alignment could certainly be calculated with respect to each of these groups. It would then indicate congruence between governmental outputs and the preferences of a particular group's members within a given political unit.

Group-specific alignment has much to commend it. It can shed light on the power relations of American society. It can show, for instance, that historically disadvantaged groups like the poor, Blacks, and women continue to be handicapped in the translation of their views into governmental outputs. Group-specific alignment can also help explain why alignment is or isn't present with respect to the whole population (however defined). Say the rich are a minority in a jurisdiction, with partisan and policy preferences that diverge from those of the less affluent majority. Then if there's close alignment with the opinions of the rich, there must be considerable misalignment with everyone else's views. Alignment with the rich, in other words, is a driver of misalignment with the population in its entirety.

Despite these selling points, group-specific alignment is largely unsupported by democratic theory. Models of democracy commonly maintain that most or all people's preferences, maybe after refinement through deliberation, should at least be heeded by the government, if not necessarily instantiated. In contrast, no prominent school of thought holds that members of a numerical minority

picture"); Anthony Fowler et al., *Moderates*, 117 AM. POL. SCI. REV. 643, 654 (2023) (replicating and confirming the analysis of Ansolabehere et al. with different survey data).

[52] *See, e.g.*, JAN E. LEIGHLEY & JONATHAN NAGLER, WHO VOTES NOW? DEMOGRAPHICS, ISSUES, INEQUALITY, AND TURNOUT IN THE UNITED STATES 166 (2013) (presenting this data at the national level); John D. Griffin & Brian Newman, *Are Voters Better Represented?*, 67 J. POL. 1206, 1214 (2005) (presenting this data state by state).
[53] *See* Matsusaka, *supra* note 27, at 142. *But see* Griffin & Newman, *supra* note 52, at 1215–18 (finding that senators' voting records are more responsive to voter ideology than to nonvoter ideology, though not examining alignment).

should be able to consistently prevail in the struggle over the state's outputs.[54] Not even pluralism, the perspective that recognizes the biggest role for groups, makes this audacious claim. As I elaborate below, the pluralist hope is that from the continuous interplay of many groups over many issues, there eventually emerges public policy that's consistent with the public interest and reasonably satisfactory to most groups. This might be a prescription for jurisdiction-wide, collective, policy alignment. It surely isn't a call for group-specific alignment.

For these reasons, I focus throughout the book on alignment with the whole population. I do present some data in Chapter 3 on group-specific alignment, for groups classified by wealth, race, and gender. But even there, I do so because group-specific alignment is sometimes a factor that influences population-level alignment. I don't mean to suggest that group-specific alignment is democratically appealing for its own sake.

Aligning Mechanisms

I just noted that group-specific alignment can be a driver of population-level alignment. Of course, many other things can affect alignment, too. I now turn to the array of potentially aligning or misaligning mechanisms, with two caveats I flag at the outset. First, while the causes of alignment are ultimately an empirical topic, my discussion here is largely nonempirical. I survey what's known about the impact of several factors in Chapters 5 through 10 and 12. At this stage, though, my aim is only to identify a series of hypotheses about alignment's origins without trying to confirm or reject any of the explanations. Second, I emphasize *electoral* mechanisms that might promote or impede alignment. This is a book mostly about *election* law, so electoral forces, especially ones that can be legally regulated, are my primary interest. That said, both here and later in the book, I do touch on nonelectoral drivers of alignment.

So which electoral mechanisms might be aligning? One possibility is *selection*: the choices voters make among candidates. The potential link between selection and partisan alignment is clear, at least in a two-candidate race. If voters have partisan preferences and candidates have party affiliations, and if voters cast their ballots on a partisan basis, then partisan alignment ensues between the victorious candidate and the median voter.[55] But selection can also foster representational alignment and policy alignment. Suppose voters have unidimensional

---

[54] As Justice Thomas once quipped, "in a majoritarian system, numerical minorities lose elections." Holder v. Hall, 512 U.S. 874, 901 (1994) (Thomas, J., concurring in the judgment).

[55] As noted above, even in this scenario, partisan alignment doesn't necessarily ensue between the victorious candidate and other populations, like eligible voters who did vote *or would have voted* in the absence of voter suppression. *See supra* note 20.

policy preferences, candidates have unidimensional policy positions, and each voter casts her ballot for the ideologically closest candidate. Then the elected candidate (again in a two-candidate race) provides better representational alignment than the defeated, more ideologically distant candidate would have offered. To the extent the elected candidate has influence over policymaking (high for most executives, low for most legislators), better representational alignment leads to better policy alignment as well. Not necessarily *good* policy alignment, but better than if the defeated, more ideologically distant candidate had pursued her policy agenda instead.[56]

Another potentially aligning electoral mechanism is *adaptation*: officeholders' adjustments of their party affiliations, policy positions, or enacted policies in anticipation of voters' future judgments. The usual impetus for adaptation is a politician's sense that she's out of step with her constituents: identifying with the wrong party, taking overly liberal or conservative stances, or adopting unpopular policies. The politician must also believe that these misaligned outputs will matter at the next election—that voters will make their decisions at least partly on these grounds. Under these conditions, adaptation is a plausible political strategy, one that might raise the politician's odds of being reelected. And in this scenario, adaptation results in better alignment without the politician's replacement by another candidate. The officeholder stays the same, but her party, ideology, or policies shift in the direction of popular preferences.[57]

Importantly, selection and adaptation both require a certain kind of voter behavior to be effective. For these mechanisms to generate better representational alignment and policy alignment, voters have to vote *spatially*, for the candidate who's ideologically nearest them.[58] As more voters vote for more nonspatial reasons—say, due to the state of the economy or for the more charismatic candidate—selection and adaptation become less aligning. Additionally, while selection and adaptation both rely on spatial voting, the temporal orientation of voter behavior varies between them. With selection, voters examine candidates' *current* policy positions to determine what they'll do in the *future*, if they're elected. With adaptation, on the other hand, officeholders expect voters to vote *retrospectively*, based on how aligned politicians' *prior* outputs were with voters' preferences.[59]

---

[56] For good discussions of the selection mechanism, see CAUGHEY & WARSHAW, *supra* note 34, at 81–82; and Bernard Manin et al., *Elections and Representation*, *in* DEMOCRACY, ACCOUNTABILITY, AND REPRESENTATION 29, 30–40 (Adam Przeworski et al. eds., 1999).

[57] Again, for good discussions of the adaptation mechanism, see CAUGHEY & WARSHAW, *supra* note 34, at 87–88; and Manin et al., *supra* note 56, at 40–44.

[58] Analogously, for selection and adaptation to generate partisan alignment, they require partisan voting.

[59] Of course, selection and adaptation can be deployed simultaneously. Voters can cast ballots based on the ideological proximity of both candidates' current policy positions and officeholders'

Nonspatial voting is one explanation why selection and adaptation might fail to yield much alignment.[60] Another involves the candidates with whom voters are presented. Imagine that almost all candidates are extremists, ideologically distant from most voters, who then try to implement their extreme agendas in office. Then even exemplary spatial voting wouldn't be very aligning. With selection, the ideologically closest candidate would still be quite ideologically far from most voters. Electing her over her opponent would thus produce only a small gain in alignment. With adaptation, retrospective voting would be a Sisyphean task in a world of extreme officeholders. Voters could reject one incumbent on account of her misaligned outputs, only to be confronted by another, and another, with no end in sight.

A last point about selection and adaptation: While they're typically conceived in candidate-specific terms, the mechanisms can also apply to parties. Party-based selection means that voters choose one party (including all its candidates) over other parties. If voters make this choice for spatial reasons, because one party's policy platform is ideologically nearer to their views, then better representational alignment and policy alignment can result. Similarly, party-based adaptation means that officeholders sharing the same party label collectively revise their outputs in anticipation of voters' retrospective voting. If voters' retrospective voting is spatial, rewarding or punishing a party due to its prior alignment or misalignment, then again, better representational alignment and policy alignment can be the consequence. Notably, individual politicians disappear from these party-based versions of selection and adaptation. On these accounts, candidates have no ability to distinguish their policy positions from those of their party, and officeholders can't compile distinct personal records. A party's politicians all rise or fall together.[61]

As potent as selection and adaptation can be, they hardly exhaust the universe of aligning and misaligning mechanisms. I'll now describe several more such forces, albeit in much less detail. I'll also categorize these factors by where (and if) I address them more extensively in the book. Certain mechanisms, then, fall squarely within election law since they involve the legal regulation of elections. Voting restrictions, first, can't affect alignment with *actual* voters (who manage to vote despite the limits). But they can cause misalignment with other normatively appealing populations, like eligible voters who did vote *or would*

---

prior records. *See, e.g.,* BERNARD MANIN, THE PRINCIPLES OF REPRESENTATIVE GOVERNMENT 177 (1997) ("Obviously, these two types of preferences may be combined in varying proportions.").

[60] I mean representational alignment and policy alignment here, not partisan alignment.

[61] For works noting the possibility of party-based selection and adaptation, see James M. Snyder, Jr. & Michael M. Ring, *Roll Calls, Party Labels, and Elections,* 11 POL. ANALYSIS 419, 422–23 (2003); and Chris Tausanovitch & Christopher Warshaw, *Does the Ideological Proximity Between Candidates and Voters Affect Voting in U.S. House Elections,* 40 POL. BEHAV. 223, 226–29 (2018).

have voted in the absence of the restrictions. I discuss limits on the franchise in Chapter 5. Next, the type of primary election might be aligning if it induces candidates to espouse policies that are popular with general election voters. Or it might be misaligning if it leads candidates to take stands that please primary but not general election voters. Party regulations are the subject of Chapter 6.

In turn, how districts are aggregated into district plans can have large effects on jurisdiction-wide alignment. Partisan gerrymanders, the focus of Chapter 7, harness the power of aggregation to produce legislatures whose partisan and ideological makeups diverge from public opinion. Chapter 8 analyzes the common argument that efforts to design districts in which minority citizens can elect their preferred candidates, often to comply with the Voting Rights Act, can skew maps in a conservative Republican direction. Lastly, campaign finance can shift the views of both voters (if they're influenced by the advertising bought with the money) and politicians (who want the funds to keep flowing). In the former case, there's the possibility of misalignment with voters' attitudes before they were changed by the advertising. In the latter, misalignment can arise as officeholders' positions veer away from their constituents and toward their funders. These dynamics are explored in Chapter 9.

Another set of mechanisms implicate nonelectoral bodies of law. Labor law, for example, concerns itself with regulations that can raise or lower the clout of unions. Powerful unions can impact alignment by increasing the political knowledge of union members, inducing them to vote, and pressuring elected officials. Likewise, the field of legislation studies the laws and rules of legislative procedure. Legislative procedure—how committees work, who controls the agenda, whether majority or supermajority support is needed, and the like—has major repercussions for which bills are actually passed. And First Amendment doctrine, communications law, and antitrust enforcement are all relevant to the vibrancy of the news media. More vigorous media coverage can make it more likely that public policy in a given area will reflect public opinion. Chapter 10 spans these and other areas of nonelectoral law.

Still other mechanisms are less amenable to legal control but can still be initiated by private activity. One of these is mass outreach to elected officials. If officeholders are contacted by a large and representative slice of the public, they might perceive their constituents' attitudes more accurately—and update their behavior accordingly. One more approach that operates by improving the information available to politicians is simply telling them what polls show about the views of their constituents. Surprisingly, politicians tend to lack this data and to err in their assessments of public opinion—but these are, in principle, correctable issues. And since money in politics can be misaligning, but current precedent precludes many governmental actions that would curb it, private individuals can take matters into their own hands. They can lobby candidates not to accept certain funds, protest corporate and wealthy individual funders, pool resources to offset misaligning funding sources, and so on. I consider these and other nonlegal strategies in Chapter 12.

Finally, a few factors are beyond the scope of this project because they're virtually impossible to change, legally or nonlegally, at least in the short to medium term. Take jurisdictions' political geography, in particular, how Democratic and Republican voters are spatially distributed. These geographic patterns significantly affect how districts are aggregated into district plans, and thus the degree of jurisdiction-wide alignment. But these patterns also can't be altered quickly, by public or private actors, barring interventions that would be unthinkable in modern American politics. The same is true for the many complicated features of American government, especially the separation of powers, federalism, the administrative state, and localism. This complexity undermines retrospective voting by making it unclear who's responsible for any development, positive or negative. But this complexity is also baked into the system, impervious to subconstitutional reform. And the usual American electoral rules—single-member districts in which victory requires a plurality of the vote—are often blamed for various kinds of misalignment. In fact, an empirical literature concludes that proportional representation leads to greater representational congruence than U.S.-style winner-take-all elections.[62] Again, though, the only way to adopt true proportional representation, at the level of the nation as a whole, is a constitutional revolution.[63]

Democratic Theory

To sum up, alignment can be specified along three axes: the applicable political unit, the method by which popular preferences are summarized, and the type of governmental output. Alignment is most attractive with respect to an aggregate of many different issues or, alternatively, people's overarching ideologies. Alignment is also best understood dynamically, as the typical congruence between governmental outputs and popular preferences as those parameters both vary over time. Alignment can be evaluated for any population, though the choice among plausible categories of individuals is seldom critical. And many mechanisms can generate alignment or misalignment, most fundamentally how voters select candidates and how officeholders adapt in anticipation of voters' verdicts.

---

[62] *See, e.g.,* Golder & Stramski, *supra* note 13, at 103–04.
[63] As I discuss in Chapter 6, proportional representation could be adopted at the state or local level without any constitutional change.

So conceived, does alignment fall victim to the critique by Sabl with which I began the chapter? Recall that Sabl attacks the "normative model of democracy whereby democratic majorities are to get whatever they want, on every issue, and in short order" on two grounds.[64] First, this perspective is foreign to democratic theory, espoused by essentially no thinkers. Second, universal, instantaneous congruence is an undesirable goal, one that has no place in a compelling account of democracy. Unsurprisingly, I think both charges miss the mark if they're redirected at the refined version of alignment I've presented here.

Start with whether different schools of democratic theorists value alignment. I don't have the space (or the expertise) to address this issue comprehensively. At a relatively high level, though, alignment does play a substantial role in several perspectives on democracy. Consider the delegate model of representation. The delegate model sees legislators as agents of their constituents, obligated to identify their constituents' preferences and then to follow them faithfully. In the words of Hanna Pitkin, the author of a seminal book on representation, a delegate "must do what his principal would do, must act as if the principal himself were acting . . . must vote as a majority of his constituents would."[65] However, even a delegate doesn't have to pretend that people's views are set in stone, unmovable by new information or arguments. A delegate can wait to act until people have given more thought to a matter. A delegate can also participate in that reflective process by sharing facts or reasons. Once constituents have reached their conclusions, though, a delegate must heed those judgments even if they seem unwise.[66]

The overlap between the delegate model and alignment is considerable. A legislator who's supposed to abide by constituents' preferences is, ipso facto, supposed to achieve district-specific representational alignment. The theory's normative ideal *is* a type of alignment. If anything, the delegate model is more consistent with a cruder version of alignment under which people's opinions on specific issues are to be respected (once those opinions have solidified). The distinction I drew earlier between alignment on individual matters and alignment across many issues or ideologies isn't generally recognized by delegate

---

[64] Sabl, *supra* note 1, at 346.

[65] HANNA FENICHEL PITKIN, THE CONCEPT OF REPRESENTATION 144–45 (1967); *see also, e.g.,* Donald J. McCrone & James H. Kuklinski, *The Delegate Theory of Representation,* 23 AM. J. POL. SCI. 278, 278 (1979) ("The delegate theory of representation . . . posits that the representative ought to reflect purposively the preferences of his constituents."). To be sure, Pitkin herself doesn't endorse the delegate model.

[66] *See, e.g.,* Lisa Disch, *Toward a Mobilization Conception of Democratic Representation,* 105 AM. POL. SCI. REV. 100, 111 (2011) (recognizing that a delegate's representation can be "iterative, involving a dynamic movement between authoritative acts and opinion in process"); Mansbridge, *supra* note 3, at 526 ("[O]ne would expect constituents to have moved both toward and with the representative's positions and the representative to have moved similarly both toward and with the constituents.").

theorists.[67] However, the delegate model does incorporate the dynamic approach I favor, at least in some of its iterations.[68] To allow a legislator to wait before mirroring people's views, until those views have coalesced, is to sanction temporal lags in representation.

Another democratic theory that includes a place for alignment is pluralism.[69] As I've already alluded, pluralists maintain that the population is divided into many groups by an array of crosscutting and overlapping cleavages. These groups pursue their policy aims through every tool at their disposal: the ballot box, lobbying, campaign spending, grass-roots organizing, and the like. The groups also continuously compete and bargain with one another to advance their respective interests. From this endless back-and-forth, public policy eventually emerges. No single group always prevails since the makeup of the winning coalition shifts from issue to issue. But nor are most groups perennial losers, left in the cold time after time. Instead, across matters and over the years, the sum of public policy is reasonably (if imperfectly) compatible with most groups' preferences, especially on the subjects that mean the most to them. As pluralist theorist Nicholas Miller puts it, "[p]olitical outcomes probably please and displease nobody all the time; rather they please almost everybody some of the time."[70]

Again, the convergence between pluralism and alignment is notable. Take the pluralist aspiration that public policy, in the aggregate, be reasonably consistent with most groups' views.[71] Among them, most groups comprise most people. Public policy is also a key governmental output, and reasonable consistency is equivalent to reasonable congruence. The pluralist hope is therefore a species of alignment, specifically, jurisdiction-wide, collective, policy alignment. Observe, too, that pluralists stress the need to analyze multiple issues—really, all matters of public policy—over a prolonged period. It's the sum of policy outcomes over the years that's supposed to be reasonably in line with most groups'

---

[67] *See, e.g.*, Rehfeld, *supra* note 3, at 227 (characterizing the archetypal delegate as one who does "exactly what [her constituents] want on every issue when voting in the legislature").

[68] *See supra* note 66 and accompanying text (discussing versions of the delegate model that allow for preference change over time).

[69] Classic pluralist accounts include ARTHUR F. BENTLEY, THE PROCESS OF GOVERNMENT (Peter H. Odegard ed., 1967), and DAVID B. TRUMAN, THE GOVERNMENTAL PROCESS: POLITICAL INTERESTS AND PUBLIC OPINION (1951).

[70] Nicholas R. Miller, *Pluralism and Social Choice*, 77 AM. POL. SCI. REV. 734, 737 (1983); *see also, e.g.*, FRANK R. BAUMGARTNER & BETH L. LEECH, BASIC INTERESTS: THE IMPORTANCE OF GROUPS IN POLITICS AND IN POLITICAL SCIENCE 54 (1998) ("[T]he end result [of pluralism] would be a set of [policies] accurately reflecting the needs and desires of the population."); Earl Latham, *The Group Basis of Politics: Notes for a Theory*, 46 AM. POL. SCI. REV. 376, 390 (1952) (arguing that, under pluralism, public policy corresponds to "the balance of power among the contending groups," "the equilibrium reached in the group struggle").

[71] Of course, the pluralist aspiration may be unrealistic for the reasons identified by public choice scholars, *see generally* MANCUR OLSON, THE LOGIC OF COLLECTIVE ACTION: PUBLIC GOODS AND THE THEORY OF GROUPS (rev. ed. 1971), but that's a practical objection, not a normative one.

preferences.[72] These are exactly the points I previously made about alignment: It's best conceptualized across issues and over time.

One more theory that intersects with alignment is deliberative democracy.[73] As their name suggests, deliberative democrats prize the deliberation that precedes a policy decision. They want decision makers (be they legislators, bureaucrats, or ordinary citizens) to give reasons for their views. Those engaging in discussion must also be open to changing their minds as they're exposed to new arguments and information. The dialogue must be inclusive as well— accepting of all who wish to participate, not dominated by any speaker or viewpoint. And in the end, the deliberation must culminate in a decision. People's opinions, potentially reshaped by their exchange of ideas, must be converted into action. "The *point* of deliberative democracy," writes deliberative theorist Joshua Cohen, "is not for people to reflect on their preferences, but to decide, in light of reasons, what to do."[74]

It's this last aspect of deliberative democracy that links it to alignment. Deliberation itself doesn't have much to do with alignment; it involves the evolution of people's views through thoughtful discussion, not their translation into governmental outputs.[75] But the decision that follows all the dialogue brings alignment into the picture. That decision is typically about policy and so at the jurisdictional level. That decision is also meant to reflect the (updated) opinions of as many people as possible—ideally, all of them.[76] These are precisely the elements of jurisdiction-wide, collective, policy alignment, which I thus see as the ultimate objective of deliberative democracy. What about my points that alignment is best defined across issues and over time? Like the delegate model, deliberative democracy most naturally applies to matters one by one: A single issue is the subject first of deliberation and then of action. But also

---

[72] On the need to analyze multiple issues, see NELSON W. POLSBY, COMMUNITY POWER AND POLITICAL THEORY 115 (1963) (discussing how pluralism is "tied to issues," which "can be fleeting or persistent, provoking coalitions . . . ranging in their duration from momentary to semi-permanent"). On the need for an extended time horizon, see Latham, *supra* note 70, at 391 ("The entire process is dynamic, not static; fluid, not fixed.").

[73] For useful sets of essays on the vast field of deliberative democracy, see DEBATING DELIBERATIVE DEMOCRACY (James S. Fishkin & Peter Laslett eds., 2003); and DELIBERATIVE DEMOCRACY (Jon Elster ed., 1998).

[74] Joshua Cohen, *Deliberative Democracy, in* DELIBERATION, PARTICIPATION AND DEMOCRACY: CAN THE PEOPLE GOVERN? 219, 222 (Shawn W. Rosenberg ed., 2007); *see also, e.g.,* Dennis F. Thompson, *Deliberative Democratic Theory and Empirical Political Science*, 11 ANN. REV. POL. SCI. 497, 502 (2008) (arguing that deliberative democracy's "essential aim is to reach a binding decision").

[75] This is precisely the basis of James Gardner's critique of deliberation when done solely for its own sake. "Citizens can talk all they want, but their talk ultimately disappears into a black hole." James A. Gardner, *Shut Up and Vote: A Critique of Deliberative Democracy and the Life of Talk*, 63 TENN. L. REV. 421, 438 (1996).

[76] *See, e.g., id.* at 430 (noting the "commitment to consensus" of some deliberative democrats). Note that I'm referring here to deliberation by ordinary people—not by legislators, bureaucrats, or other elite policymakers.

like the delegate model, deliberative democracy has a temporal dimension. In fact, the possibility that people's preferences might shift as they learn more is the crux of the entire theory.

At least three accounts of democracy, then, acknowledge, respect, even emphasize alignment. This refutes the claim that alignment is alien to democratic theory. It actually plays a nontrivial role in several models of democracy. And this isn't just my idiosyncratic appraisal. Leading theorist Robert Dahl comments that, "at a minimum ... democratic theory is concerned with processes by which ordinary citizens exert a relatively high degree of control over leaders."[77] That considerable level of control is the essence of alignment. Noted scholar of representation Jane Mansbridge adds that "constituent-representative congruence"— what I'd call district-specific representational alignment—"is a factor in each of the forms of representation" that she describes in an important article.[78] Another expert on representation, Andrew Rehfeld, concurs that "[a]ny comprehensive account of democracy" must share the "presumption" that "there be a close correspondence between the laws of a nation and the preferences of citizens."[79] In my terminology, that correspondence is jurisdiction-wide policy alignment.

But I want to be careful here. There might be agreement about the desirability of alignment among *some* perspectives on democracy, but this consensus isn't universal. Think of the trustee model of representation, the great historical rival of the delegate model.[80] A trustee is supposed to follow her own considered judgment as to what's in the best interest of not just her district but also her whole jurisdiction. She's not meant to investigate her constituents' preferences and then to adhere to them. It should be plain that a trustee doesn't necessarily seek or achieve alignment. Alignment only arises if, coincidentally, a trustee's assessment of the best course of action happens to coincide with the views of her constituents.[81]

---

[77] DAHL, *supra* note 49, at 3; *see also, e.g.,* ROBERT A. DAHL, POLYARCHY: PARTICIPATION AND OPPOSITION 1 (1971) ("[A] key characteristic of a democracy is the continuing responsiveness of the government to the preferences of its citizens . . . .").

[78] Mansbridge, *supra* note 3, at 526.

[79] Rehfeld, *supra* note 3, at 214; *see also, e.g.,* SOROKA & WLEZIEN, *supra* note 10, at 2 ("This opinion-policy relationship is central not just in everyday politics, but in the theoretical literature on democracy and representation as well . . . ."); Archon Fung, *Democratic Theory and Political Science: A Pragmatic Method of Constructive Engagement,* 101 AM. POL. SCI. REV. 443, 44 (2007) ("Every conception of democracy must . . . . relate collective decisions and actions to the interests and views of the individuals who compose a collectivity.").

[80] For more on the trustee model, see PITKIN, *supra* note 65, at 127; and Rehfeld, *supra* note 3, at 215.

[81] Or maybe not so coincidentally. Pitkin argues that, "[n]ormally, the conflict between what [the representative] thinks best (for them) and what they want (as best for themselves) simply should not arise." PITKIN, *supra* note 65, at 165.

Minimalist democracy, too, bears little relation to alignment.[82] Minimalists strip down democracy to a single, bare-bones criterion: whether free and fair elections are held in which it's at least possible the incumbent government will be replaced. Minimalists take no position on how voters should cast their ballots or what politicians should do after being elected. Again, alignment *could* develop in a minimalist democracy if voters decide to vote spatially or officeholders choose to heed popular preferences.[83] But these would be acts the theory neither endorses nor condemns. It's simply silent on matters beyond the holding of legitimate elections.

And if thin conceptions of democracy are mute about alignment, thick conceptions can even require its rejection.[84] The hallmark of thick models is that they incorporate substantive values into their definitions of democracy. A democracy must respect a series of individual rights, for instance, or a democracy demands social and economic equality among its participants. Alignment is certainly compatible with this approach *if* people actually want inviolable rights or egalitarian relations. If they don't, though, conflict ensues. Thick conceptions must insist on misalignment with public opinion to protect their favored rights and implement their social and economic objectives. Misalignment becomes the price of a substantively appealing society.

Accordingly, my relatively modest response to Sabl's first objection is that several theories of democracy do appreciate and aim for alignment. I don't make the more aggressive assertion that alignment is prized by most, let alone all, schools of democratic thought. What about Sabl's second complaint—that alignment (or at least a caricatured version of it) is normatively unattractive? The sheer fact that alignment is embedded in multiple accounts of democracy begins to answer this grievance. The delegate model of representation, pluralism, and deliberative democracy are prominent theories with long pedigrees still championed by many thinkers today. To the extent these theories are compelling, so must be alignment. The theories' merit has to reach one of their important components. Alignment can't be separated from perspectives of which it's a major part.

Another point in favor of alignment, as I've presented it, is that it evades the usual critiques of cruder forms of congruence. John Ferejohn, for example, claims that "popular responsiveness is not so attractive" with respect to issues

---

[82] Important minimalist works include JOSEPH SCHUMPETER, CAPITALISM, SOCIALISM, AND DEMOCRACY (1942), and Adam Przeworski, *Minimalist Conception of Democracy: A Defense*, in DEMOCRACY'S VALUE 12 (Ian Shapiro & Casiano Hacker-Cordon eds., 1999).

[83] Some minimalists think this is a likely scenario. *See, e.g.,* RICHARD A. POSNER, LAW, PRAGMATISM, AND DEMOCRACY 165 (2003) ("[Minimalist] democracy tends to align the behavior of politicians and officials with the people's interests as the people perceive them.").

[84] For a favorable perspective on thick conceptions of democracy, see CHRISTOPHER EISGRUBER, CONSTITUTIONAL SELF-GOVERNMENT (2001). For a skeptical view, see James Allan, *Thin Beats Fat Yet Again: Conceptions of Democracy*, 25 LAW & PHIL. 533 (2006).

like "the dispensing of justice" and "managing monetary policy."[85] These are areas where we might want governmental outputs to be based on adjudication and technical evaluation, respectively, not public opinion. As I explained above, I agree that alignment on each individual matter is an unsound ambition. Aggregating across many issues or into overall ideologies is one way to eliminate the need to match governmental outputs to popular preferences on any particular topic. Another strategy, which I explore below, is to exclude certain areas entirely from the domain in which alignment is sought. Either way, Ferejohn's concern is addressed: Under the approach I urge, people's views on legal and technocratic matters don't necessarily have to be followed.

To Sabl, analogously, the most problematic feature of a "simple responsiveness criterion" is that it mandates immediate congruence with public opinion.[86] Instead, Sabl contends, scholars should "embrace ... [a] 'damped' responsiveness standard" under which "policy typically adapts ... to public preferences—but ... with a lag."[87] Again, I concur. To reiterate earlier points, instantaneous alignment in the face of varying popular attitudes is neither feasible nor desirable. It's better to measure alignment at regular intervals, giving both governmental outputs and people's views time to adjust, and to reach conclusions based on an average of these readings. That way, alignment incorporates the reality that public policy, especially, is usually slow to change. Additionally, as Sabl observes, this dynamic method "ensures that shifts in the status quo reflect durable shifts in public opinion rather than ones that the median voter will soon regret."[88]

But these are ancillary arguments, not the main event. The essential reason alignment is appealing isn't that it plays a role in certain theories or that it dodges certain authors' attacks on cruder concepts. Rather, alignment's allure stems from its connection to democracy itself. Put aside the sophisticated democratic models I've been discussing and focus on the word, democracy, in isolation. It literally means *government* (krátos) by and for the *people* (dêmos).[89] We might also translate democracy as self-rule or popular sovereignty—a system where the people are responsible for taking collective actions on their own behalf. Alignment is either equivalent to this fundamental idea or, at least, quite similar

---

[85] John Ferejohn, *Accountability and Authority: Toward a Theory of Political Accountability, in* DEMOCRACY, ACCOUNTABILITY, AND REPRESENTATION 131, 132 (Adam Przeworski et al. eds., 1999).

[86] Sabl, *supra* note 1, at 347.

[87] *Id.* at 353.

[88] *Id.*

[89] *See, e.g.,* Steven Klein, *Democracy Requires Organized Collective Power,* 29 J. POL. PHIL 26, 37 (2022) ("[D]emocracy originally meant something like the power (*kratos*), in the sense of an organized capacity to act together, wielded by the people (*demos*)."); Josiah Ober, *The Original Meaning of "Democracy": Capacity to Do Things, Not Majority Rule,* 15 CONSTELLATIONS 3, 7 (2008) ("*Demokratia* ... refers to a *demos*' collective capacity to do things in the public realm, to make things happen.").

to it.[90] Remember that, in all its formulations, alignment denotes congruence between popular preferences, on the one hand, and governmental outputs, on the other. Popular preferences are alignment's link to the dêmos. They capture what the dêmos wants, people's partisan and policy views, their opinions on the future of their polity.

In turn, governmental outputs tie alignment to the krátos. Officeholders in the krátos have partisan and policy stances of their own. As a whole, the krátos enacts policies. These are precisely the products of the government (and of governmental officials) that I've highlighted throughout this chapter. And then, just as democracy bonds the dêmos and the krátos, so too does alignment bring together popular preferences and governmental outputs. Democracy means the krátos reflects the will of the dêmos.[91] Likewise, alignment means governmental outputs reflect popular preferences. Both democracy and alignment fuse the same two entities—the people and the government—and insist that the work of the latter correspond to the wishes of the former.[92]

This etymological reasoning, of course, won't persuade everyone. *Nonliteral* democracy—democracy as we use the term today, not as it was originally defined in ancient Athens—is an archetype of an essentially contested concept.[93] This is a complex, multifaceted idea about which reasonable people can disagree, debate indefinitely, and ultimately fail to reach consensus.[94] As an essentially contested concept, democracy has no single meaning, not alignment nor anything else. That absence of a single meaning is what it means for an idea to be essentially contested.

But even if alignment isn't the one true theory of democracy, it does seem to be people's *preferred* theory. That's my final normative point in favor of alignment: Just as it prizes popular preferences, popular preferences reciprocally prize alignment. One line of relevant scholarship simply asks people whether

---

[90] If there's a gap between the literal meaning of democracy and alignment, it arises in the connotation of democracy that government be *by* the people, *composed* of them. Alignment is agnostic as to *who* selects governmental outputs as long as those outputs are consistent with popular preferences. In contrast, the connotation of democracy that government be *for* the people, reflecting their will, is nearly indistinguishable from alignment.

[91] As noted above, democracy also suggests that the krátos is constituted by the dêmos. Again, alignment isn't identical to this connotation of democracy. *See supra* note 90.

[92] For a scholar sharing this view, see John D. May, *Defining Democracy: A Bid for Coherence and Consensus*, 26 Pol. Stud. 1, 3 (1978) ("A regime is democratic relative to another regime in so far as its arrangements yield closer correspondence between its governmental acts and the preferences of the persons who are affected by those acts."). However, alignment *alone* may be necessary, but it plainly isn't sufficient, for a system to qualify as genuinely democratic. Alignment must at least be supplemented by free and fair elections where voters can, if they choose, replace their current rulers.

[93] *See, e.g.,* Dan M. Kahan, *Democracy Schmemocracy*, 20 Cardozo L. Rev. 795, 795 (1999) ("[D]emocracy is an essentially contested concept: there is not just one, but rather a plurality of competing conceptions of democracy ....").

[94] *See, e.g.,* W.B. Gallie, *Essentially Contested Concepts*, 56 Proceedings of Aristotelian Soc'y 167, 171–72 (1956) (introducing and defining the idea of essentially contested concepts).

they want their representatives and governments to respond to public opinion or to do what they think is best regardless of popular attitudes. These studies generally find that people favor the first form of democracy.[95] The studies characterize this result as a popular preference for the delegate model of representation over the trustee model. I'd frame it as a popular preference for both district-specific and jurisdiction-wide alignment, with respect to both representation and policy.

Another strand in the literature investigates whether better alignment with people's policy views leads to their greater satisfaction with the performance of democracy. Again, the verdict is unambiguous: Alignment is, in fact, a driver of democratic satisfaction. This is true if alignment is measured with respect to governmental policy positions (i.e., jurisdiction-wide representational alignment).[96] It's also the case if alignment is conceived in terms of *parties'* policy positions (a kind of congruence I haven't yet considered, and to which I return in Chapter 6).[97] Theorists, then, will no doubt continue to clash about the meaning of democracy far into the future. Among the public, though, this issue appears to be more settled. When asked, people say they prefer alignment even to misalignment that's best for the polity. And when their level of alignment is calculated, it's linked to their satisfaction with democracy. This mass support certainly adds legitimacy to alignment, though I'll be the first to concede that an idea's popularity is only a facet of its normative appeal.

Popular Preferences

I want to stay on the subject of popular preferences but switch from a theoretical to an empirical lens.[98] Another potential critique of alignment is that people's policy views are so ill-formed that they can't provide a useful benchmark for

[95] *See, e.g.,* Shaun Bowler, *Trustees, Delegates, and Responsiveness in Comparative Perspective,* 50 COMP. POL. STUD. 766, 772 (2017) (finding that "a clear majority [of respondents] support the delegate model" with respect to governmental policy); Jan Rosset et al., *I the People? Self-Interest and Demand for Government Responsiveness,* 50 COMP. POL. STUD. 794, 805 (2017) (same); Christopher Jan Carman, *Assessing Preferences for Political Representation in the U.S.,* 17 J. ELECTIONS, PUB. OPINION & PARTIES 1, 10 (2007) (finding support for the delegate model with respect to legislator behavior).

[96] *See, e.g.,* Quinton Mayne & Armen Hakhverdian, *Ideological Congruence and Citizen Satisfaction: Evidence from 25 Advanced Democracies,* 50 COMP. POL. STUD. 822, 832–38 (2017); Christian Stecker & Markus Tausendpfund, *Multidimensional Government-Citizen Congruence and Satisfaction with Democracy,* 55 EUR. J. POL. RSCH. 492, 499–506 (2016).

[97] *See, e.g.,* Lawrence Ezrow & Georgios Xezonakis, *Citizen Satisfaction with Democracy and Parties' Policy Offerings,* 44 COMP. POL. STUD. 1152, 1162–69 (2011).

[98] Dwelling on theory for another moment, my focus on people's *actual* preferences differs from Rousseau's general will because it's supposed to capture the views that people would *rationally* hold *if* they sought to further the common good rather than their individual interests. *See generally* JEAN-JACQUES ROUSSEAU, ON THE SOCIAL CONTRACT (Donald A. Cress trans., Hackett 2d ed. 2019) (1762).

assessing governmental outputs. Call this the Conversian position after its most famous exponent, political scientist Philip Converse.[99] Converse and his followers argue that people's policy views are highly unstable, frequently flipping from one stance to another when they're asked the same question at different times. Additionally, the Conversian position continues, people's policy views generally lack a clear structure. They're not the product of a coherent, intelligible ideology. And because of their volatility and disorganization, Converse and his cohort maintain, people's policy views are prone to cycling. People often prefer Policy A to Policy B and Policy B to Policy C—but, in violation of the transitive property, Policy C to Policy A.[100]

If the Conversian position was correct, the consequences for alignment would be devastating.[101] Alignment needs popular preferences to be meaningful so they can serve as the reference point for representation and policy. If people's attitudes are actually as erratic and confused as Converse and his backers claim, then there's a gaping void where alignment requires a sturdy anchor. There's no real public opinion to which governmental outputs can correspond or fail to correspond. Fortunately, the Conversian position appears to be wrong, or at least exaggerated, based on my reading of the empirical evidence. People's policy views may not be models of sophistication, but they're reliable enough for alignment to be a tenable goal.

Start with the supposed instability of people's responses to survey questions about policy matters. It's true enough that if you ask an *individual* person about an *individual* issue, you may well get different answers at different times. But much of this seeming volatility disappears when either issues or people are aggregated. As to issues, Stephen Ansolabehere and his coauthors repeat some of Converse's earlier analysis but for issue scales, created from multiple survey questions, rather than individual survey items. They find that "[i]ssue scales are much more highly correlated over time than are individual items."[102] In fact, the average temporal consistency of issue scales is equivalent to that of people's party

[99] *See* Philip E. Converse, *The Nature of Belief Systems in Mass Publics*, 18 CRITICAL REV. 1 (1964). For other well-known works in the Conversian tradition, see DONALD R. KINDER & NATHAN P. KALMOE, NEITHER LIBERAL NOR CONSERVATIVE: IDEOLOGICAL INNOCENCE IN THE AMERICAN PUBLIC (2017); and JOHN R. ZALLER, THE NATURE AND ORIGINS OF MASS OPINION (1992).

[100] The cycling point is more associated with William Riker than with Converse. *See generally* WILLIAM H. RIKER, LIBERALISM AGAINST POPULISM: A CONFRONTATION BETWEEN THE THEORY OF DEMOCRACY AND THE THEORY OF SOCIAL CHOICE (1982).

[101] At least, the consequences for *representational* and *policy* alignment would be devastating. Even Converse agrees that people's *partisan* preferences are quite stable. *See generally* ANGUS CAMPBELL ET AL., THE AMERICAN VOTER (1960) (coauthored by Converse and stressing the durability of party affiliation). So the Conversian position, even if correct, leaves unscathed the aspiration of partisan alignment.

[102] Ansolabehere et al., *supra* note 33, at 220; *see also* Sean Freeder et al., *The Importance of Knowing "What Goes with What": Reinterpreting the Evidence on Policy Attitude Stability*, 81 J. POL. 274, 277–78 (2018) (confirming Ansolabehere et al.'s results).

affiliations.[103] Partisanship, according to Converse himself, is the "unmoved mover" of voter behavior, the foundation on which all else is built.[104] Yet it turns out that when people's policy views are examined in tandem, not one by one, they're roughly as durable.

Aggregation across people (instead of issues) tells a similar story. Even with respect to a single policy, the proportion of a large group of people (like the American public) supporting or opposing it tends to be fairly stable over time.[105] Moreover, when mass opinion shifts, it usually does so for an understandable reason: a particular event that prompts people to rethink their stances, overall economic conditions, generational replacement, and the like.[106] How can the collective public be so rational, as Benjamin Page and Robert Shapiro put it, when individual people are anything but? Thank the magic of large numbers. When (up to) hundreds of thousands of survey respondents' views are combined, much of the noise cancels out. Some respondents randomly swing one way, other respondents happen to veer another way, and the net result is often temporal consistency.[107] Likewise, when something happens in the world to jolt people's attitudes, only a fraction of respondents respond to that stimulus. But that responsive fraction, when paired with the bulk of people whose preferences keep varying haphazardly (or remaining constant), still causes mass opinion to move in a sensible direction.[108]

Next, consider the Conversian assertion that most people's policy views lack a coherent ideological structure. One way to test this claim is to ask survey respondents about dozens or hundreds of policy matters and then to use statistical techniques to try to collapse their answers into fewer dimensions.[109] If this attempt at simplification failed, or yielded a large number of dimensions, that would support the Conversian position. On the other hand, if this process returned just one or two dimensions, that would indicate that popular policy preferences are actually quite well-organized. And so they are, at least in contemporary America. The most recent work, by Anthony Fowler and a team of collaborators, explicitly investigates whether most Americans are "Conversians" (holding policy opinions that can't be captured by a single axis) or "Downsians"

---

[103] Ansolabehere et al., *supra* note 33, at 220.

[104] *See generally* CAMPBELL ET AL., *supra* note 101.

[105] *See generally* BENJAMIN I. PAGE & ROBERT Y. SHAPIRO, THE RATIONAL PUBLIC: FIFTY YEARS OF TRENDS IN AMERICANS' POLICY PREFERENCES (1992).

[106] *See generally id.*

[107] *See, e.g.,* ROBERT S. ERIKSON ET AL., THE MACRO POLITY 5–6 (2002); James N. Druckman & Thomas J. Leeper, *Is Public Opinion Stable? Resolving the Micro/Macro Disconnect in Studies of Public Opinion*, 141 DAEDALUS 50, 55 (2012).

[108] *See, e.g., id.*

[109] *See supra* note 33 and accompanying text (noting two of these techniques, factor analysis and item-response-theory modeling).

(whose policy views mostly fall along a single dimension).[110] According to this paper, only one-fifth of Americans are Conversians while almost three-fourths are Downsians.[111] Many other studies don't distinguish between Conversians and Downsians but rather explore how many dimensions are necessary to account for most of the variation in people's policy stances. Most of this literature concludes that a single axis is sufficient: At present, policy disagreement in America largely maps onto the classic liberal-conservative continuum.[112]

Interestingly, this wasn't always the case. Caughey and his coauthors separately analyze people's economic, racial, and social attitudes from the 1950s to the present. Between the 1950s and the 1980s, people's opinions in these areas were only loosely correlated with one another. But this correlation across domains rose dramatically between the 1980s and the 2010s and is now close to perfect. So people today who are economically liberal (or conservative) are also very likely to be racially and socially liberal (or conservative).[113] This work adds some nuance to my rebuttal of the Conversian position. When Converse himself was writing in the 1960s, Americans' policy preferences were indeed reasonably complex, spanning three fairly distinct dimensions. But over the half century that followed, this intricate ideological lattice dissolved, leaving behind only one all-consuming left-right axis. *That* ideological structure—*our* ideological structure—couldn't be simpler.

As for the last Conversian point, about the alleged frequency of cycles among different policy options, it's undermined by the research I just cited. Cycling is possible only if people's views are either multidimensional or multipeaked along a single axis.[114] Most contemporary Americans' policy stances, however, are unidimensional. They're unimodal as well, in that when they're plotted as a histogram, there's generally a single peak corresponding to ideological moderation.[115]

---

[110] "Downsians" is a reference to economist Anthony Downs, whose famous spatial model of voting assumes a single political dimension. *See* ANTHONY DOWNS, AN ECONOMIC THEORY OF DEMOCRACY (1957).

[111] *See* Fowler et al., *supra* note 51, at 653. The remainder of respondents are inattentive, answering survey questions more or less randomly. *See id.*

[112] *See, e.g.*, Devin Caughey et al., *The Ideological Nationalization of Partisan Subconstituencies in the American States*, 176 PUB. CHOICE 133, 146 (2018); Stephen A. Jessee, *Spatial Voting in the 2004 Presidential Election*, 103 AM. POL. SCI. REV. 59, 65 (2009); Tausanovitch & Warshaw, *supra* note 33, at 333. A few studies find that two dimensions—still not many—are needed to capture most variation in public opinion. *See, e.g.*, Robert N. Lupton et al., *Political Sophistication and the Dimensionality of Elite and Mass Attitudes, 1980-2004*, 77 J. POL. 368, 373 (2015); Shawn Treier & D. Sunshine Hillygus, *The Nature of Political Ideology in the Contemporary Electorate*, 73 PUB. OP. Q. 679, 687 (2009).

[113] *See* Caughey et al., *supra* note 112, at 144–46 (conducting this analysis for Democrats and Republicans in each state); *see also* CAUGHEY & WARSHAW, *supra* note 34, at 44–50 (conducting a similar analysis focusing on the rising explanatory power of party affiliation in predicting people's economic, racial, and social attitudes).

[114] *See, e.g.*, Jack Knight & James Johnson, *Aggregation and Deliberation: On the Possibility of Democratic Legitimacy*, 22 POL. THEORY 277, 283 (1994) ("[I]f relevant voters have single-peaked preferences, there will be no cycling when choice ranges over only one dimension.").

[115] *See, e.g.*, Fowler et al., *supra* note 51, at 654.

Under these conditions, cycling should be quite rare. And in fact it is quite rare, not just today but also historically. Gerry Mackie scrutinizes nearly every cycle claimed by Converse and his allies: a school desegregation bill in the 1950s, Abraham Lincoln's election in 1860, the constitutional convention of 1787, and many more.[116] "[A]lmost every alleged cycle identified in the social choice literature," Mackie determines, is "based on faulty data or otherwise spurious."[117]

But I want to note a caveat here. Based on the above scholarship, I believe most Americans have meaningful policy preferences. But I don't think most Americans are particularly *knowledgeable* about most policy matters. I actually think the opposite is true for a wide swath of the public.[118] How can valid policy preferences exist in the absence of much policy information? Part of the answer is that most people are able to state policy stances even when they haven't deeply studied issues. A vast majority of survey respondents, one article finds, "did articulate their own preferences on salient roll-call votes, even though most did not say they followed closely or cared about public affairs."[119] The rest of the story is our friend, the miracle of aggregation. When issue scales are constructed for less knowledgeable individuals, they exhibit considerable stability over time (if less than for more informed individuals).[120] Similarly, when the policy views of less knowledgeable individuals are combined to generate mass opinion, collective rationality often emerges from personal ignorance—a group signal out of the individual noise.

That's all I have to say about the Conversian position. I'd like to add a few words, though, about another argument about popular policy preferences: that their relative *intensity* should be incorporated into calculations of alignment. On this account, people's policy stances shouldn't all be weighted equally. Instead, some people's views should be amplified (because they're felt more strongly) and other people's views should be discounted (because they're held less deeply). Thanks to this upweighting and downweighting, the minority perspective on some issues should serve as the benchmark for representation and

---

[116] *See* GERRY MACKIE, DEMOCRACY DEFENDED 197–377 (2003).

[117] IAN SHAPIRO, THE STATE OF DEMOCRATIC THEORY 15 (2003) (summarizing Mackie's conclusions); *see also, e.g.,* WILLIAM V. GEHRLEIN & DOMINIQUE LEPELLEY, VOTING PARADOXES AND GROUP COHERENCE: THE CONDORCET EFFICIENCY OF VOTING RULES 21 (2011) (showing through simulations that fewer than 10 percent of preference distributions result in cycles). A further response to the cycling point is that democracies may sometimes *want* to rotate through different policy options. *See* Richard H. Pildes & Elizabeth S. Anderson, *Slinging Arrows at Democracy: Social Choice Theory, Value Pluralism, and Democratic Politics,* 90 COLUM. L. REV. 2121, 2171 (1990) ("Democracies might wish to express the view that none of the values at stake ought to be subordinated to any others; cycling can provide a means for so doing.").

[118] And I've said so in prior work. *See* Nicholas O. Stephanopoulos, *Accountability Claims in Constitutional Law,* 112 Nw. U. L. REV. 989, 1022–24, 1032–34, 1040–41 (2018).

[119] Stephen Ansolabehere & Philip Edward Jones, *Constituents' Responses to Congressional Roll-Call Voting,* 54 AM. J. POL. SCI. 583, 586 (2010).

[120] *See, e.g.,* Ansolabehere et al., *supra* note 33, at 224–26; Jessee, *supra* note 112, at 72–75.

policy. Specifically, when a smaller number of people have sufficiently more intense preferences about a given matter than a larger number of people, utility is maximized by allowing the minority to prevail.[121]

In principle, I have no objection to calibrating the weight placed on people's views based on how strongly those views are held. In practice, though, is where the complications lurk. One difficulty is simply measuring the intensity of popular policy preferences. Few surveys ask people how passionately they feel about different issues. Even if more surveys included these questions, it would be hard to know what to make of the answers. Suppose Respondent A (says she) feels "extremely strongly" about some matter while Respondent B (says he) feels "somewhat strongly." With no way of probing these persons' internal mental states, we can't be sure that Respondent A's "extremely strongly" is actually more intense than Respondent B's "somewhat strongly." It might be that Respondent A selects a higher level of intensity for a policy attitude that, if it could be observed, is no more or even less deeply held than that of Respondent B. It's precisely for this reason that Dahl despairs of including preference intensity in a workable theory of democracy. "[W]e cannot hope to establish any political rules to deal with problems of sensate intensity, ethically desirable as such rules possibly might be."[122]

Another concern is that certain people might (say they) feel very strongly about issue after issue. If preference intensity is taken into account matter by matter, these people's views would be amplified across the board. By the same token, the opinions of other people—those who don't profess fervor about every policy—would be systematically discounted. You can imagine responses to this problem. Perhaps each survey respondent should be allocated the same number of "intensity points," which the respondent could then distribute among different issues.[123] But ideas like this haven't been tried before, they're barely feasible in the polling context, and they're almost certainly fanciful in the real world of politics. And yet without some sort of mechanism for equalizing total preference intensity, any attention to the strength of people's attitudes would violate the norm of political equality that underpins most democratic models. As political theorist

---

[121] Prominent recent expositions of this argument include Eric A. Posner & Glen Weyl, Radical Markets: Uprooting Capitalism and Democracy for a Just Society (2018) and Seth J. Hill, Frustrated Majorities: How Issue Intensity Enables Smaller Groups of Voters to Get What They Want (2022).

[122] Dahl, *supra* note 49, at 118; *see also, e.g.,* Hill, *supra* note 121, at 48, 52, 101 (observing that voters with low preference intensities have an incentive to convince politicians that they have high preference intensities); Saul Levmore, *Voting with Intensity*, 53 Stan. L. Rev. 111, 145 (2000) ("[A] problem with trying to take intensities into account is that we find it difficult to compare different voters' reports of the sentiments they hold, even if these voters are trying to be perfectly honest.").

[123] *Cf.* Eric A. Posner & Nicholas O. Stephanopoulos, *Quadratic Election Law*, 172 Pub. Choice 265 (2017) (proposing a similar system for voting in elections).

Elaine Spitz writes, "the introduction of an intensity dimension attacks political equality in ways not permissible within the context of democratic theory."[124]

A last point about preference intensity is that incorporating it into alignment might make little practical difference. In a study I've already mentioned, Matsusaka estimates the congruence of state policy outcomes with the views of all people and with the views of those who (say they) hold their opinions "strongly." He finds essentially no difference between these groups: Statewide policy alignment is about the same for all people as for strong preference holders.[125] Also suggestive is work by Chris Tausanovitch determining that people with relatively *extreme* stances on issues like guns, taxes, and immigration don't have more *intense* attitudes. To the contrary, preference intensity seems to be distributed fairly evenly across the policy spectrum.[126] In that case, intensity-adjusted public opinion must be similar to raw public opinion, and alignment with the former can't stray too far from alignment with the latter.

Alignment's Domain

I hope the above discussion helps allay a number of worries about popular preferences: that they're too unstable, lack structure, frequently cycle, and require weighting based on their intensity. What about fears that people's views on particular matters may be ignorant or invidious?[127] To repeat, one powerful response to this possibility is aggregation. If alignment is assessed across many issues, then reasonable overall congruence can be achieved notwithstanding noncongruence in areas where people's opinions are less worthy of respect. Likewise, if alignment is conceived ideologically, then people's uninformed or malicious stances don't have to be directly confronted. Instead, they're folded into summary ideological scores along with all of people's other policy attitudes.

Another approach—my focus here—is to exclude entirely from the domain in which alignment is sought those topics as to which most people's views are

---

[124] ELAINE SPITZ, MAJORITY RULE 30 (1984).

[125] *See* Matsusaka, *supra* note 27, at 143; *see also* POWELL, *supra* note 11, at 167 (finding no difference in his conclusions about alignment if it's calculated using mean rather than median public opinion).

[126] *See* Chris Tausanovitch, *Measuring the Intensity of Policy Preferences* 10–11 (Feb. 2019); *see also* MARTIN GILENS, AFFLUENCE AND INFLUENCE: ECONOMIC INEQUALITY AND POLITICAL POWER IN AMERICA 91 (2012) (finding insignificant differences among poor, middle-class, and rich respondents in their propensity to say they "strongly" favor or oppose a given policy).

[127] We could add here other epithets that render people's views less worthy of respect. Lack of knowledge and malice toward others, though, are quintessential reasons why we might not want to pursue alignment in certain areas. *See, e.g.,* LAWRENCE R. JACOBS & ROBERT Y. SHAPIRO, POLITICIANS DON'T PANDER: POLITICAL MANIPULATION AND THE LOSS OF DEMOCRATIC RESPONSIVENESS 304 (2000) (arguing that responsiveness shouldn't be sought with respect to issues "the public neither cares nor knows about" or that involve "the rights of minorities").

likely to be ignorant or invidious. For instance, say most people have no relevant knowledge about where thresholds for pollutant emissions should be set. Then this matter could simply be omitted from calculations and evaluations of alignment.[128] Or assume that most people are intolerant of transgender individuals. Again, alignment could be gauged without considering at all the extent to which representation and policy reflect this anti-transgender bias. In case it isn't obvious, notice how this strategy of exclusion differs from aggregation. Aggregation *dilutes* people's uninformed or malicious opinions by examining them alongside other stances or transforming them into overarching ideologies. In contrast, exclusion, well, excludes. Objectionable preferences are kept out of the alignment analysis altogether. For this purpose, it's as if these attitudes don't exist.[129]

Two common forms of exclusion are bureaucratization and judicialization. Administrative agencies are responsible for regulating many technical subjects about which people tend to know little. Similarly, courts have jurisdiction over many issues as to which people are prone to prejudice, sometimes thanks to bills of rights that expressly authorize judicial review in these fields. Importantly, public opinion plays little to no role in most accounts of bureaucratization and judicialization. As to agencies, scholars disagree over whether they should prioritize their own expert judgments or the desires of the executive or the legislature, but virtually no one contends that they should try to comply with popular preferences.[130] As to courts, not only is the mass appeal of a given position not a familiar genre of constitutional interpretation, it may well be an "antimodality"—a form of reasoning deemed categorically out of bounds.[131] Put differently, bureaucratization and judicialization are moves well-suited to excluding alignment because they rely on regulators and judges with no electoral incentive to pursue alignment. And in practice, that's exactly how these moves have worked, as effective secessions from alignment's domain.

Not just effective but also appropriate. I value alignment as much as anyone. I think it's a concept at the core of what it means to be a democracy. Yet even I'm

---

[128] However, the antecedent issue of *whether* thresholds for pollutant emissions should be set likely isn't one that should be withdrawn from alignment's domain. *Cf.* ROBERT A. DAHL, DEMOCRACY AND ITS CRITICS 68 (1989) (distinguishing between "moral questions" about nuclear weapons, to which most people can provide answers, and "extraordinarily complex" implementation issues "far beyond the reach of ordinary citizens").

[129] *See, e.g.*, GILENS, *supra* note 126, at 60 (excluding from his landmark analysis of policy alignment "proposed policy changes that would require a constitutional amendment or Supreme Court ruling").

[130] *See, e.g.*, Sabl, *supra* note 1, at 350 (noting that "theorists [who] defend administrative expertise" do so "at the cost of some responsiveness").

[131] *See* David E. Pozen & Adam M. Samaha, *Anti-Modalities*, 119 MICH. L. REV. 729, 760–63 (2021) (characterizing "popularity arguments" as a constitutional antimodality). Note the distinction between courts trying to adopt popular positions *themselves*—arguably an antimodality—and courts trying to ensure that *other* governmental branches' decisions fairly reflect public opinion. That latter strategy is my subject in Chapter 4.

willing to abandon alignment in certain contexts, if its realization would yield representation or policy as troubling as people's ignorant or invidious views. I'm ready to make this concession because, to quote Dahl, "no one, except perhaps a fanatic, wishes to maximize [one goal] at the expense of all others,"[132] and I'm not a fanatic. I believe deeply in the significance of alignment. But I also believe in other things, like technically sound policy in areas where people are uninformed and the protection of vulnerable minorities from malicious majorities. Sometimes—when popular attitudes are worthy of respect—there's no tension between alignment and these other aims. Regrettably, though, there are occasions when we can have congruent *or* competent governmental outputs, congruent *or* ethical outcomes, but not both. In these cases, I think it's entirely proper for alignment to cede to other principles that are locally more compelling.

But I still want to flag the democratic cost that's incurred whenever territory is removed from alignment's domain. Each such carveout creates a setting in which the krátos might not reflect the will of the dêmos, in which the people might not genuinely rule themselves.[133] To lessen this cost, agencies and courts should take jurisdiction over issues when it's likely that most people's preferences are ignorant or invidious. In general, agencies and courts should avoid settling matters as to which public opinion is creditable—even if, on balance, the regulators and the judges see things differently from the populace.[134] Of course, this claim raises the question: How do we *know* when most people's stances are uninformed or malicious enough that alignment should be dropped as an aspiration? Unfortunately, this is another version of the boundary problem with which I grappled earlier. There, the trouble was that the concept of alignment sheds no light on the population with whose views governmental outputs should be congruent. Here, analogously, the stumbling block is that alignment itself doesn't tell us when alignment ceases to be a normatively attractive objective. That's a determination that can only be made based on other factors—data and intuitions about popular attitudes—about which alignment is mute.[135]

---

[132] DAHL, *supra* note 49, at 50; *see also, e.g.*, Gerry Mackie, *Schumpeter's Leadership Democracy*, 37 POL. THEORY 128, 140 (2009) ("[W]hy can't an allegiance to democracy be strong but qualified by allegiance to liberal values?").

[133] *See, e.g.*, Maria Paula Saffon & Nadia Urbinati, *Procedural Democracy, the Bulwark of Equal Liberty*, 41 POL. THEORY 441, 462 (2013) ("If, despite the formal operation of democracy, the most relevant decisions of society are taken outside of it, democracy becomes trivial.").

[134] Or, less strongly, agencies and courts should avoid settling these matters unless (1) the public wants them to do so or (2) these bodies aim for alignment in their decisions.

[135] To illustrate the point, a plausible hypothesis is that the political process can't be trusted—and alignment shouldn't be sought—when there's widespread "prejudice against discrete and insular minorities." United States v. Carolene Prods. Co., 304 U.S. 144, 152 n.4 (1938). But on its own, the concept of alignment doesn't explain when such prejudice is common enough to warrant exclusion or even why such prejudice renders popular preferences discreditable. So the *Carolene* hypothesis must be accepted or rejected on grounds external to alignment itself.

I'm equally agnostic about another way in which alignment's sails can be trimmed. Suppose we're firmly inside what I've been calling alignment's domain, the conceptual zone where public opinion is worthy of respect because it isn't ignorant or invidious. Even here, alignment doesn't occupy the field; it's not the only democratic principle we might want to take into account. Other democratic values include competition and participation (the favorites of the structuralist theorists I surveyed in Chapter 1), freedom to speak and associate, rational deliberation, political equality, minority representation, and impartial election administration. Unsurprisingly, I think alignment is closer to the essence of democracy than these ideas. But I recognize that others may disagree, and I also appreciate democratic principles beyond alignment myself. I therefore see nothing wrong with alignment being weighed alongside other democratic values, even within alignment's domain.[136]

This weighing may often lead to the same conclusions that would have been reached based on alignment alone. As I noted in Chapter 1, competition and participation are potential drivers of alignment. The same is true for freedom to speak and associate. To the extent these causal links are confirmed, conflict should rarely arise between these democratic principles. Steps that make elections more competitive, more participatory, or freer should typically produce better alignment as well. Likewise, alignment is entwined with rational deliberation, political equality, and impartial election administration. Deliberation is meant to yield refined popular preferences, which in turn are meant to be enacted into law. Alignment also presupposes that all members of the dêmos are equal, their views counting the same regardless of race, gender, wealth, or any other attribute. And alignment requires elections to be run properly so that the voice of the electorate can be discerned accurately. So again, these democratic values are unlikely to point in different directions.

Unlikely, though, doesn't mean impossible. Reconsider competition. It's conceivable for an electoral policy, like a district plan in which the same party wins every seat by a narrow margin, to foster competition while thwarting jurisdiction-wide alignment. The reverse scenario is just as imaginable: a series of exceedingly safe districts that nevertheless elect a legislature that mirrors aggregate public opinion. Or take minority representation. Redistricting is also the context in which it might clash with alignment. Designing more districts in which minority voters are able to elect candidates of their choice could entail

---

[136] For other scholars sharing this view, see, for example, Guy-Uriel Charles, *Constitutional Pluralism and Democratic Politics: Reflections on the Interpretive Approach of Baker v. Carr*, 80 N.C. L. REV. 1103, 1106 (2002) (arguing that "judicial review of democratic politics must be evaluated from a multidimensional continuum," including "majoritarianism, responsiveness, substantial equality, and interest representation"); and Jonathan S. Gould, *The Law of Legislative Representation*, 107 VA. L. REV. 765, 784 n.68 (2021) (arguing that representation "implicates multiple values that are not reducible either to each other or to any single supervalue").

creating fewer total districts won by minority voters' favored party, thus biasing the district map. Even freedom to speak and associate may not always dovetail with alignment. If you believe (like the current Supreme Court) that campaign finance restrictions burden this liberty, and if limits on money in politics result in closer representational congruence, then in this area at least, less freedom means more alignment, and vice versa.

In these situations where democratic principles diverge, the boundary problem rears its head one last time. Alignment can tell us a great deal about the congruence of governmental outputs with popular preferences and how various regulations affect the quality of this match. But alignment can't help us decide what to do when it suggests one course of action but other values distinct from alignment advise a different route. We have to make that choice without alignment's guidance. To be sure, we're not rudderless in the face of discord among democratic values. We can ask which value is more important to us, both generally and in the case at hand. We can also compare the costs and benefits along the dueling democratic dimensions. If we're lucky, we'll find a large cost (or benefit) on one axis paired with a small benefit (or cost) on another axis. As sensible as these tactics are, however, the key point here is that they're unrelated to alignment itself. Only considerations beyond alignment can resolve disputes among alignment and other aspects of democracy.

* * *

In this chapter, I laid the theoretical foundation for the rest of the book. I divided alignment into its three constituent pieces: the applicable political unit, the method by which popular preferences are summarized, and the type of governmental output. I clarified several points about this framework: Alignment should be analyzed in the aggregate, not issue by issue. Alignment should be conceived dynamically, not statically. And the relevant dêmos must be selected based on factors other than alignment. I described the range of mechanisms that can further or frustrate alignment, some electoral, others unrelated to elections. I argued that alignment is both supported by several models of democracy and normatively appealing in its own right. I explained that popular preferences are sufficiently meaningful to serve as the benchmark for representation and policy. And I allowed that alignment need not be sought at all times since it hardly exhausts societies' pragmatic and democratic objectives.

In the next chapter I turn from the theory to the empirics of alignment. I review what we know about the extent of alignment in modern American politics. The news, in short, isn't good. Within districts, legislators routinely espouse positions very different from those held by their constituents. At the jurisdictional level, partisan, representational, and policy misalignment are all rampant.

This assessment holds for federal, state, and local governments alike. What's more, the beneficiaries of misalignment are far from random. Ideologically extreme individuals are one winning group. The wealthy, especially those who fund politicians' campaigns, also enjoy closer congruence with their views. So do people who favor maintaining rather than disrupting the status quo. Taken as a whole, this record strikes me as quite dismal. It aptly justifies the next chapter's title, "Misaligned America."

3
Misaligned America

Introduction

If I'd written this chapter a generation ago, my perspective on alignment in America would have been quite different. In 1993, Robert Erikson, Gerald Wright, and John McIver published their book, *Statehouse Democracy*, on the link between public opinion and public policy at the state level.[1] "The awesome strength of the opinion-policy correlation" was their key finding.[2] States with more liberal publics systematically enacted more liberal policies, and vice versa.[3] Then in 2002, Erikson teamed up with Michael MacKuen and James Stimson to write *The Macro Polity* about the responsiveness of the *federal* government to public opinion *nationwide*.[4] Again, the degree of responsiveness they discerned was exceptional. When public opinion swung to the left or right, so, in short order, did roll call votes in Congress, the President's policy stances, and even the rulings of the Supreme Court.[5] Based on these landmark studies, I'd have thought that governmental outputs in America are highly sensitive to popular preferences.[6]

An initial concern with this account, though, is that it pertains only to responsiveness. *Statehouse Democracy* demonstrated the *cross-sectional* responsiveness (across jurisdictions) of state policies. Likewise, *The Macro Polity* established the *temporal* responsiveness (across years) of federal activities. As I've previously explained, however, alignment is conceptually and empirically distinct from responsiveness. In particular, it's possible for governmental outputs to be quite responsive to—but still quite misaligned from—popular preferences. Suppose that as the public's preferred minimum wage increases by a dollar from one state to another, the actual minimum wage rises by sixty cents. Imagine, also, that no matter what the public's preferred minimum wage is, the actual minimum wage

---

[1] ROBERT S. ERIKSON ET AL., STATEHOUSE DEMOCRACY: PUBLIC OPINION AND POLICY IN THE AMERICAN STATES (1993).
[2] *Id.* at 80.
[3] *See id.* at 79.
[4] ROBERT S. ERIKSON ET AL., THE MACRO POLICY (2002).
[5] *See id.* at 304–16.
[6] For other scholars acknowledging the influence of these studies, see DEVIN CAUGHEY & CHRISTOPHER WARSHAW, DYNAMIC DEMOCRACY: PUBLIC OPINION, ELECTIONS, AND POLICYMAKING IN THE AMERICAN STATES 2 (2022); and Jeffrey R. Lax & Justin H. Phillips, *The Democratic Deficit in the States*, 56 AM. J. POL. SCI. 148, 149 (2011).

Aligning Election Law. Nicholas O. Stephanopoulos, Oxford University Press. © Nicholas O. Stephanopoulos 2024.
DOI: 10.1093/9780197662182.003.0003

is two dollars lower. Then we'd have considerable cross-sectional responsiveness: a sixty-cent change in actual policy for each one-dollar shift in preferred policy. But we'd have significant misalignment as well: actual policy diverging by two dollars from preferred policy. (And, in fact, that's what we *do* have, according to a recent article: "responsiveness [that] coexists with a substantively large ... policy bias" in states' minimum wage laws.[7])

Another worry about the narrative of *Statehouse Democracy* and *The Macro Polity* stems from the books' age. *Statehouse Democracy* covered state public opinion and public policy from the mid-1970s to the late 1980s.[8] *The Macro Polity* analyzed nationwide data from the mid-1950s to the mid-1990s.[9] That era, the second half of the twentieth century, was very different from the American present. Back then, congressional polarization was near its historical nadir thanks to the prevalence of conservative southern Democrats and liberal northeastern Republicans.[10] People were also far less ideologically sorted than they are today, in that many conservatives were Democrats and many liberals were Republicans.[11] The second half of the twentieth century further predates modern developments like more aggressive partisan gerrymandering, greater spending on elections, and renewed efforts to restrict voting. You might reasonably suspect, then, that the rosy conclusions of decades-old works are no longer applicable.

And you'd be right to have this hunch. As I show in this chapter, a major theme of contemporary American politics is misalignment. Enacted state policies, the subject of *Statehouse Democracy*, are frequently noncongruent with people's policy views. The same is true for roll call votes in Congress and the President's policy stances, the outputs of the elected branches examined in *The Macro Polity*.[12] And the list goes on: Federal policy outcomes often fail to reflect public opinion. Individual officeholders' ideologies are usually out of step with those of their constituents. District maps commonly distort the translation of parties' statewide votes into legislative seats. Everywhere you look, it can

---

[7] Gabor Simonovits, *Responsiveness Without Representation: Evidence from Minimum Wage Laws in U.S. States*, 63 AM. J. POL. SCI. 401, 402 (2019).

[8] *See* ERIKSON ET AL., *supra* note 1, at 12.

[9] *See* ERIKSON ET AL., *supra* note 4, at 294–301.

[10] *See, e.g.*, Jeff Lewis, *Polarization in Congress*, VOTEVIEW.COM (June 4, 2020), https://www.votev iew.com/articles/party_polarization.

[11] *See, e.g.*, MATTHEW LEVENDUSKY, THE PARTISAN SORT: HOW LIBERALS BECAME DEMOCRATS AND CONSERVATIVES BECAME REPUBLICANS (2009).

[12] Unlike the authors of *The Macro Polity*, I don't consider the rulings of federal judges because they have no electoral incentive to pursue alignment. But the inclusion of the Supreme Court would be unlikely to change this chapter's narrative. *See, e.g.*, Stephen Jessee & Neil Malhotra, *The Chart That Shows the Supreme Court Will Be out of Step with the Country*, N.Y. TIMES, July 12, 2018 (showing that, since the retirement of Justice Kennedy, the median Supreme Court justice has been more conservative than roughly 80 percent of Americans).

sometimes seem, another case appears of American government not doing what the American public wants.

To give some structure to this discussion, I rely on the axes of alignment I introduced in the previous chapter. I start with policy alignment: the correspondence between enacted policies and popular policy preferences. Next, I consider representational alignment: the fit between officeholders' and their constituents' policy positions. And last I address partisan alignment: the match between officeholders' and their constituents' party affiliations. Within each category, I first comment on the (rare) studies that capture public opinion by incorporating all people's preferences. I then turn to the (more abundant) works that use the median person's stances to represent public opinion. Also within each category, I proceed from jurisdiction-wide to (where relevant) district-specific alignment. And with respect to jurisdiction-wide alignment, I march in descending order through the levels of American government: federal, state, and local.

Throughout this chapter (and this book), I focus on alignment with the whole population of a jurisdiction or district. But I also describe here, albeit more briefly, what's known about various kinds of group-specific alignment. Stark misalignment with the population in its entirety, it turns out, typically coincides with much better alignment with the preferences of certain favored groups. These winners of the political process include the wealthy, campaign donors, ideological extremists, conservatives, and proponents of the status quo. Congruence with their views is a likely driver of noncongruence with the opinions of the general public. And that's exactly why I include group-specific alignment in this survey—because it helps explain the striking pattern of population-level misalignment.

One last point before diving into the literature. Prominent political scientists like Brandice Canes-Wrone,[13] Robert Shapiro,[14] and Christopher Wlezien[15] have previously reviewed the many studies of public opinion and its connection to public policy. But those treatments have mostly been limited to responsiveness. This chapter is the first to hone in on alignment in all its forms, to put in one place much of what we know about the correspondence between governmental outputs and popular preferences. So I hope the chapter is of interest not just to legal scholars (who may be unaware of the recent summaries of responsiveness) but also to political scientists (who may be informed about responsiveness but not alignment).

---

[13] *See* Brandice Canes-Wrone, *From Mass Preferences to Policy*, 18 ANN. REV. POL. SCI. 147 (2015).

[14] *See* Robert Y. Shapiro, *Public Opinion and American Democracy*, 75 PUB. OPINION Q. 982 (2011).

[15] *See* Christopher Wlezien, *Public Opinion and Policy Representation: On Conceptualization, Measurement, and Interpretation*, 45 POL'Y STUD. J. 561 (2017).

Policy Alignment

The starting point for our tour of alignment is policy alignment at the federal level. No work on this topic explicitly estimates the gaps between federal policy outcomes and all people's policy preferences. Instead, most studies analyze majoritarian alignment: whether the preferences of a popular majority are reflected in federal policy outcomes, either at the time of the poll or subsequently.[16] In this vein, the most notable recent contribution is Martin Gilens's book, *Affluence and Influence*. Gilens compiles roughly two thousand survey questions from 1981 to 2006, all asking respondents if they supported or opposed a specific change in federal policy.[17] He then determines if each change was, in fact, implemented during the four years after the date of the poll.[18] With this data in hand on people's policy views and ensuing policy outcomes, the calculation of alignment is straightforward.

As displayed in Figure 3.1, Gilens finds that when a bare majority of respondents backed a policy change, that change actually occurred less than 30 percent of the time.[19] In other words, federal policy from the 1980s to the 2000s was misaligned with the views of the median respondent more than 70 percent of the time, at least when that respondent was part of a narrow majority and wanted policy to shift, not to stay the same. Remarkably, this misalignment persisted even when the proportion of respondents favoring a policy change rose far beyond a mere majority. Not until about *90 percent* of respondents supported a different policy was that new measure more likely than not to be enacted—and the preference of the median respondent more likely than not to be heeded.[20]

You might object that Gilens ignores cases where the median respondent wanted policy to remain constant, not to vary. Using his data, I can determine the overall level of majoritarian alignment across all two thousand or so survey questions.[21] In sum, when a majority of respondents backed a given policy— either the status quo or an alternative to it—the majority's preference was realized over the next four years about 54 percent of the time. This is a significantly higher figure than the sub-30-percent likelihood that a bare majority's desire for policy

[16]   *See, e.g.,* MARTIN GILENS, AFFLUENCE AND INFLUENCE: ECONOMIC INEQUALITY AND POLITICAL POWER IN AMERICA 66 (2012) (noting that most of these studies "have relied . . . on consistency between majority opinion and policy outcome").

[17]   *See id.* at 57–60. An important caveat about work on alignment that relies on surveys, like Gilens's book, is that the issues addressed by surveys aren't necessarily representative of all issues that could have been addressed. So Gilens's book, for example, estimates the extent of policy noncongruence only for a certain set of issues—mostly higher-profile ones at particular political moments—not for all possible issues.

[18]   *See id.* at 60.

[19]   *See id.* at 73.

[20]   *See id.*

[21]   I'm grateful to Gilens for making his data available to me.

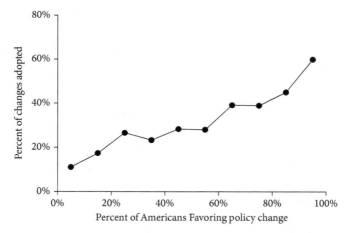

FIGURE 3.1 LIKELIHOOD OF FEDERAL POLICY ADOPTION VERSUS POPULAR SUPPORT FOR POLICY

Figure 3.1 is reproduced with permission from MARTIN GILENS, AFFLUENCE AND INFLUENCE: ECONOMIC INEQUALITY AND POLITICAL POWER IN AMERICA 73 (2012). Copyright © 2012 by Princeton University Press.

change was subsequently followed. But 54 percent is still far from an impressive rate of alignment. Barely more often than a coin flip, from the 1980s to the 2000s, did federal policy align with the median respondent's views.[22]

You might also wonder about the degree of *collective* policy alignment at the federal level—as noted above, an issue no scholar has previously investigated. Using Gilens's data, I can incorporate all respondents' preferences by calculating, for each survey question and ensuing policy outcome, the fraction of respondents who agreed or disagreed with that outcome.[23] For example, if 70 percent of respondents favored a policy change, and that change in fact occurred, the level of agreement would be 70 percent. If the change didn't materialize, the level of agreement would be 30 percent. Under this approach, the

---

[22] *See also* PAUL BURSTEIN, AMERICAN PUBLIC OPINION, ADVOCACY, AND POLICY IN CONGRESS: WHAT THE PUBLIC WANTS AND WHAT IT GETS 56–59 (2014) (finding a majoritarian policy alignment rate of about 50 percent for a random sample of bills considered by Congress in 1989–90). In contrast, the rate of majoritarian policy alignment is about 10 percentage points higher in European countries. *See* Anne Rasmussen et al., *The Opinion-Policy Nexus in Europe and the Role of Political Institutions*, 58 EUR. J. POL. RSCH. 412, 423 (2019). This comparative finding indicates that it's plausible to expect better policy alignment from a political system than that currently exhibited by the United States.

[23] *See* CAUGHEY & WARSHAW, *supra* note 6, at 123 (introducing this measure of agreement). With a series of individual survey questions—as opposed to ideal points for respondents and federal policy—it isn't possible to compute the ideological distances between respondents and federal policy.

average level of agreement with federal policy from the 1980s to the 2000s was 52 percent. Again, this is an underwhelming figure. Over this period, federal policy earned the support of slightly more than half of respondents—and the opposition of almost as many.

The reference to this period begs the question: What was federal policy alignment like in other eras? Unfortunately, no one has extended Gilens's dataset to the present. In a study of federal policy from 1960 to 1979, though, Alan Monroe finds an overall rate of majoritarian alignment of 63 percent.[24] That is, the preference of a majority of respondents (whether for policy change or for policy stasis) was realized over the next four years close to two-thirds of the time. Also using this methodology, Benjamin Page and Robert Shapiro cover the period from 1935—the dawn of opinion polling—to 1979. They discern an even higher rate of majoritarian alignment: 68 percent.[25] Based on this work, the alignment of federal policy with the median respondent's views appears to have declined substantially over time. From a rate of near (or even more than) two-thirds from the 1930s to the 1970s, federal policy alignment has fallen to a level almost indistinguishable from random chance.[26]

Turning from the federal government to the states, Devin Caughey and Christopher Warshaw are the authors of by far the most comprehensive work on state policy alignment. Caughey and Warshaw analyze dozens of issues and hundreds of surveys from 1935 to 2020.[27] They also compute both collective policy alignment (the share of respondents who agree with a given policy outcome) and majoritarian policy alignment (whether a policy outcome is congruent with the median respondent's preference).[28] With respect to collective policy alignment, they find that, on average, state policy matches the views of 55 percent of respondents.[29] With respect to majoritarian policy alignment, the average figure is slightly higher: a 59 percent rate of congruence with the median respondent's preference.[30] These statistics modestly exceed my calculations using Gilens's data for the 1981–2006 period. But they're lower than Monroe,

---

[24] See Alan D. Monroe, *Public Opinion and Public Policy, 1980-1993*, 62 Pub. Opinion Q. 6, 13 (1998). He also finds a rate of majoritarian alignment of 55 percent from 1980 to 1993—extremely close to the rate of 54 percent I calculated for the 1981–2006 period.

[25] See Benjamin I. Page & Robert Y. Shapiro, *Effects of Public Opinion on Policy*, 77 Am. Pol. Sci. Rev. 175, 179 (1983).

[26] See Monroe, *supra* note 24, at 12–13 (also observing this decline); Shapiro, *supra* note 14, at 992 (same); *see also* Matt Grossman, Artists of the Possible: Governing Networks and American Policy Change Since 1945 (2014) (arguing based on more qualitative evidence that federal policy rarely and indirectly reflects public opinion).

[27] See Caughey & Warshaw, *supra* note 6, at 14–23.

[28] See *id.* at 123–24. Note that, unlike the scholars of federal policy alignment, Caughey and Warshaw consider public opinion and public policy *contemporaneously*. They don't give public policy a four-year window to match public opinion.

[29] See *id.* at 124.

[30] See *id.* at 114.

Page, and Shapiro's estimates for the pre-1979 era. On the whole, a reasonable conclusion is that state policy alignment is about the same—about as poor—as federal policy alignment.[31]

A sunnier picture emerges, though, from Caughey and Warshaw's examination of how state policy alignment changes over time.[32] For the most recent year in which data is available, they determine the proportion of states in which the outcome on each issue is congruent with the median respondent's views. They then plot this proportion against how long the issue has been on the policy agenda—that is, how many years have elapsed since the issue was first polled. As shown in Figure 3.2, majoritarian policy alignment is abysmal for newly emerging issues. In the first few years after an issue becomes salient, only about 40 percent of states' policies are congruent with the median respondent's preferences.[33] But this fraction rises steadily for roughly forty years before finally leveling off. For issues that have been on the policy agenda for several decades, alignment with the median respondent's views is achieved in around 70 percent of states.[34] Accordingly, the aligning mechanisms I described in the previous chapter do seem to work with some efficacy *if* they're given many years to operate. Eventually, state public policy tends to reflect public opinion, though only over a time horizon that's likely to frustrate all but the most patient observers of the political process.[35]

Lastly, there are no studies of policy alignment at the local level.[36] It's possible (if laborious) to compile information about municipalities' enacted policies. But no polls exist asking people if they support or oppose those policies. However, several scholars have analyzed cross-sectional local policy *responsiveness*—the extent to which policies vary from one municipality to another as overall public opinion becomes more liberal or conservative. These academics agree that municipal spending,[37] municipal

---

[31] Earlier, less exhaustive studies of state policy alignment reach verdicts similar to (or more pessimistic than) those of Caughey and Warshaw. *See* Christopher Hare & James E. Monogan III, *The Democratic Deficit on Salient Issues: Immigration and Healthcare in the States*, 40 J. Pub. Pol'y 116, 127 (2020) (finding an average rate of majoritarian policy alignment of 52 percent across seven issues in 2014); Lax & Phillips, *supra* note 6, at 153 (48 percent across thirty-nine issues in the 2000s); John G. Matsusaka, *Popular Control of Public Policy: A Quantitative Approach*, 5 Q.J. Pol. Sci. 133, 142 (2010) (57 percent across ten issues in the 1990s).

[32] *See* Caughey & Warshaw, *supra* note 6, at 125–28.

[33] *See id.* at 125–26.

[34] *See id.* at 126.

[35] For other studies finding some improvement in state policy alignment for more established issues, see Hare & Monogan, *supra* note 31, at 127 (showing a 10-percentage-point increase from 2008 to 2014); Lax & Phillips, *supra* note 6, at 157 (4-percentage-point increase for issues that entered the policy agenda more than ten years earlier).

[36] *See* Chris Tausanovitch & Christopher Warshaw, *Representation in Municipal Government*, 108 Am. Pol. Sci. Rev. 605, 615 n.13 (2014) (noting that "[f]uture work might try to [determine] the congruence between public opinion and city policy conservatism").

[37] *See* Katherine Levine Epstein & Vladimir Kogan, *Pushing the City Limits: Policy Responsiveness in Municipal Government*, 52 Urb. Aff. Rev. 3, 14–17 (2016); Christine Kelleher Palus,

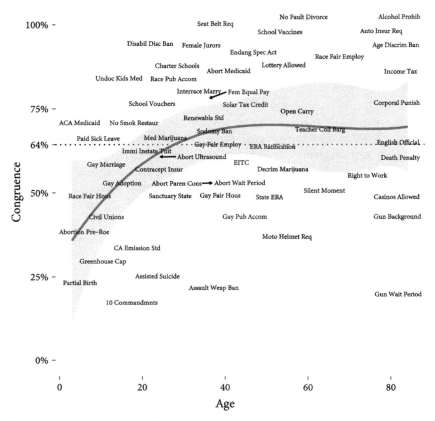

FIGURE 3.2 PROPORTION OF STATES WITH MAJORITARIAN POLICY ALIGNMENT ON
ISSUE VERSUS AGE OF ISSUE

Figure 3.2 is reproduced with permission from DEVIN CAUGHEY & CHRISTOPHER WARSHAW,
DYNAMIC DEMOCRACY: PUBLIC OPINION, ELECTIONS, AND POLICYMAKING IN THE AMERICAN
STATES 126 (2022). Copyright © 2022 by University of Chicago Press.

taxation,[38] and an aggregate of dozens of nonfiscal municipal policies[39] are all
responsive to people's ideologies. Let me repeat my earlier caution, though, that
responsiveness is distinct from alignment. Federal and state policies are also

Responsiveness in American Local Governments, 42 ST. & LOCAL GOV'T REV. 133, 142–44 (2010);
Tausanovitch & Warshaw, *supra* note 36, at 612; Bryant J. Moy, Responsiveness in the Patchwork of
Local Government 20–25 (Nov. 19, 2021).

[38] *See* Tausanovitch & Warshaw, *supra* note 36, at 612; Moy, *supra* note 37, at 20–25.
[39] *See* BRIAN F. SCHAFFNER ET AL., HOMETOWN INEQUALITY: RACE, CLASS, AND REPRESENTATION
IN AMERICAN LOCAL POLITICS 124–25 (2020); Tausanovitch & Warshaw, *supra* note 36, at 612.

responsive to people's ideologies, yet as I just explained, they're frequently misaligned with public opinion. Moreover, Warshaw finds that municipal spending, economic policies, and social policies are all *less* responsive to people's ideologies than those same outputs at the state level.[40] There's no reason to think, then, that local policy alignment is superior to its state analogue. If anything, given Warshaw's results, you might hypothesize that it's inferior.

So policy alignment at the federal, state, and (probably) local level is mediocre. With whose preferences *are* policies aligned when they're noncongruent with the views of the general public? I've already hinted at one answer: people who favor the status quo. In Gilens's dataset, a popular majority's desire for federal policy change is realized within four years at a rate of just 39 percent. In contrast, when a popular majority wants federal policy to stay the same, it prevails at a rate of 75 percent.[41] Similarly, Caughey and Warshaw show that when the status quo for a given state issue is liberal (or conservative), and a bare majority prefers a conservative (or liberal) outcome, the likelihood of the majority getting its way in a given year is close to zero.[42] Even an enormous majority in favor of change (more than three-fourths of the public) succeeds at a rate of less than 5 percent per year.[43]

Another group that benefits from policy misalignment in its favor is the one that accounts for the title of Gilens's book, *Affluence and Influence*. In the book, Gilens demonstrates that, when the preferences of middle-income and high-income respondents diverge by at least 10 percentage points, the probability of federal policy change is highly responsive to the views of the wealthy.[44] On the other hand, this probability is entirely nonresponsive to the views of the middle class—despite their much greater number.[45] In later work, responding to the familiar critique that responsiveness is different from alignment, Gilens extends his analysis to policy congruence. When the preferences of middle-income and high-income respondents diverge, and more than three-fourths of rich respondents support or oppose a policy, alignment with those respondents' views ensues at a rate of 66 percent.[46] But when more than three-fourths of the

[40] *See* Christopher Warshaw, *Local Elections and Representation in the United States*, 22 ANN. REV. POL. SCI. 461, 473 (2019).
[41] These are my calculations using Gilens's data. *See also* Jarron Bowman, *Do the Affluent Override Average Americans? Measuring Policy Disagreement and Unequal Influence*, 101 SOC. SCI. Q. 1018, 1023–24, 1031–33 (2020) (discussing the status quo bias evident in Gilens's data).
[42] *See* CAUGHEY & WARSHAW, *supra* note 6, at 121–22.
[43] *See id.* at 122. Of course, these annual probabilities cumulate over time and result in the gradually improving policy alignment that I previously noted. *See supra* notes 32–35 and accompanying text.
[44] *See* GILENS, *supra* note 16, at 80.
[45] *See id.*
[46] *See* Martin Gilens, *The Insufficiency of "Democracy by Coincidence": A Response to Peter K. Enns*, 13 PERSP. POL. 1065, 1066 (2015). Note that this method (which I also use below) doesn't take into account whether respondents from a group are especially likely to oppose the status quo, in which case the frustration of their preferences might be attributable to the status quo bias of federal policymaking—not the group's political weakness.

middle class back or object to a policy, their views are subsequently heeded at a rate of just 34 percent.[47]

At the state level, preferences on specific policies by income group are rarely available, so there's no equivalent to Gilens's contribution.[48] However, a handful of scholars have investigated the cross-sectional responsiveness of state policies to the overall ideologies of the wealthy, the middle class, and the poor. Their results aren't as stark as Gilens's but do generally indicate greater responsiveness to the rich than to any other income group, especially with respect to social (as opposed to economic) policies and in less (rather than more) affluent states.[49] One political scientist, Patrick Flavin, has also managed to track down views by income group on a few hot-button issues like abortion, gun control, and the death penalty. He, too, finds greater state policy responsiveness to the rich in most cases.[50] To reiterate, these are all studies of responsiveness, not alignment. But they're largely consistent with Gilens's conclusions and certainly don't suggest that middle-income Americans fare significantly better in state than in federal policy formulation.

Returning to Gilens's data, he only uses it to evaluate federal policy congruence by income group. However, the data also includes respondents' race and gender. Thanks to this information, I can compute federal policy congruence with the preferences of White, Black, and Hispanic respondents, as well as with those of men and women, following Gilens's methodology. I observe a modest advantage for White respondents over Black and Hispanic respondents. Specifically, when racial groups' views diverge and most White respondents support or oppose

---

[47] *See id.*; *see also* Bowman, *supra* note 41, at 1027–33 (largely confirming Gilens's findings); Matt Grossman et al., *Political Parties, Interest Groups, and Unequal Class Influence in American Policy*, 83 J. POL. 1706, 1714–16 (2021) (same); *cf.* Martin Gilens & Benjamin I. Page, *Testing Theories of American Politics: Elites, Interest Groups, and Average Citizens*, 12 PERSP. POL. 564, 571–75 (2014) (showing that federal policy is also highly responsive to the preferences of business interest groups).

   Some scholars disagree with Gilens on the ground that different income groups' policy preferences don't actually diverge very much. In that case, policy alignment and responsiveness can't vary significantly by income stratum. *See, e.g.*, Yosef Bhatti & Robert S. Erikson, *How Poorly Are the Poor Represented in the U.S. Senate?*, *in* WHO GETS REPRESENTED 223, 233 (Peter K. Enns & Christopher Wlezien eds., 2011); Stuart N. Soroka & Christopher Wlezien, *On the Limits to Inequality in Representation*, 2 PS: POL. SCI. & POL. 319, 325 (2008). However, these scholars rely on relatively crude measures of people's views like their ideological self-placements, *see* Bhatti & Erikson, *supra*, at 233, or their opinions on governmental spending by issue area, *see* Soroka & Wlezien, *supra*, at 321. Using Gilens's more fine-grained data, differential alignment and responsiveness by income group are indeed evident. *See* Bowman, *supra* note 41, at 1025–26 (confirming this result using twenty-two different definitions of preference divergence between income groups).

[48] *See, e.g.*, Devin Caughey & Christopher Warshaw, Dynamic Democracy: Citizens, Politicians, and Policymaking in the American States 173 (Aug. 30, 2020) ("[W]e lack consistent survey data that breaks public opinion down by income.").

[49] *See* Patrick Flavin, *Income Inequality and Policy Representation in the American States*, 40 AM. POL. RSCH. 29, 41–45 (2012); Elizabeth Rigby & Gerald C. Wright, *Whose Statehouse Democracy? Policy Responsiveness to Poor Versus Rich Constituents in Poor Versus Rich States*, *in* WHO GETS REPRESENTED, *supra* note 47, at 195, 206–17.

[50] *See* Flavin, *supra* note 49, at 44–45.

a policy, they prevail at a rate of 56–57 percent.[51] In contrast, when there's racial disagreement and most Black or Hispanic respondents back or object to a policy, they get their way around 50 percent of the time.[52] This small White edge in federal policy alignment mirrors Caughey and Warshaw's result at the state level.[53] With respect to gender, I find a large male advantage, albeit in a limited number of cases. In the rare situations when men and women's preferences diverge and most men support or oppose a policy, their policy alignment rate is 80 percent.[54] Conversely, in the face of gendered disagreement and strong female views, women's policy alignment rate is just 40 percent.

I'm not the only one to have mined Gilens's data for additional insights. Alexander Branham and his coauthors,[55] as well as Matt Grossman and his team,[56] code whether each proposed policy change in Gilens's data was ideologically liberal or conservative. Both groups determine that federal policy is more likely to shift in a conservative direction.[57] Using Gilens's data, I can confirm that conservative and Republican respondents enjoy a congruence advantage over liberal and Democratic respondents, respectively, on the order of 10 percentage points.[58] At the state level, likewise, Caughey and Warshaw identify a pronounced conservative bias in policy adoption. When a bare majority favors a liberal outcome, the actual policy result is conservative about three-fourths of the time.[59] Not until support for a liberal outcome reaches about three-fourths is the actual policy result as likely as not to be liberal.[60]

---

[51] To be precise, 57 percent when paired against Black respondents, and 56 percent when paired against Hispanic respondents.

[52] This is coincidentally the figure for both Black and Hispanic policy congruence when paired against White respondents.

[53] See Caughey & Warshaw, *supra* note 48, at 173 (finding an 8-percentage-point congruence advantage for Whites over Blacks in the 1950–70 period and a 1-percentage-point advantage in the 2010–20 period). My result is also consistent with work examining White, Black, and Hispanic respondents' "win rates" with respect to federal spending in different areas. This work, too, finds a modest advantage for White respondents. See JOHN D. GRIFFIN & BRIAN NEWMAN, MINORITY REPORT: EVALUATING POLITICAL EQUALITY IN AMERICA 64–69 (2008); ZOLTAN L. HAJNAL, DANGEROUSLY DIVIDED: HOW RACE AND CLASS SHAPE WINNING AND LOSING IN AMERICAN POLITICS 125–39 (2020).

[54] Only 10 cases meet these criteria, compared to 147 when men and women's preferences diverge by more than 10 percentage points and more than three-fourths of *women* support or oppose a policy.

[55] See J. Alexander Branham et al., *When Do the Rich Win?*, 132 POL. SCI. Q. 43, 52 (2017).

[56] See Grossman et al., *supra* note 47, at 1709–10.

[57] See Branham et al., *supra* note 55, at 53–54; Grossman et al., *supra* note 47, at 1714, 1717.

[58] Specifically, when there's ideological or partisan disagreement and most conservative or Republican respondents support or oppose a policy, their policy alignment rates are 54 percent and 57 percent, respectively. The corresponding rates for liberal or Democratic respondents in these situations are 44 percent and 45 percent, respectively.

[59] See CAUGHEY & WARSHAW, *supra* note 6, at 121.

[60] See id. However, much of this effect is attributable to the policy status quo usually being conservative. See id. at 189–92; see also Lax & Phillips, *supra* note 6, at 157 (also finding a conservative advantage in state policy congruence); Matsusaka, *supra* note 31, at 143 (same).

A final form of group-specific policy misalignment has been documented only at the state level.[61] Jeffrey Lax and Justin Phillips show that, in sum, state policies are more congruent with the preferences of ideologically extreme respondents— conservative *and* liberal—than with those of ideological moderates.[62] This pattern is attributable to the polarization of state policy. Across the roughly forty issues that Lax and Phillips examine, state publics generally favor the liberal policy outcome in fifteen to twenty-five cases.[63] Yet in a majority of states, there are actually fewer than fifteen, or more than twenty-five, liberal policy results.[64] "[B]lue states tend to go 'too far' in adopting liberal policies and the red states go 'too far' in the other direction."[65] As we'll see next, representation in America is polarized in exactly the same way as state policy.

Representational Alignment

As with policy alignment, I start my summary of representational alignment with its collective variant and at the federal level. In recent years, scholars including Joseph Bafumi and Michael Herron,[66] Michael Barber,[67] Seth Hill and Chris Tausanovitch,[68] and Boris Shor[69] have calculated ideal points—overall ideological positions—for voters[70] and members of Congress on the same scale. These academics' approach has been to ask questions of voters on which

[61] At the federal level, where the major parties commonly rotate in power, policy misalignment in either ideological direction may be less troubling. If, say, a conservative government goes "too far" in a conservative direction, this skew may be offset in the future when a liberal government overshoots public opinion to the left.

[62] This refers to the overall national pattern. *Within* a given state, it's typically conservatives *or* liberals—not both—who enjoy better policy congruence with their views.

[63] *See* Lax & Phillips, *supra* note 6, at 157.

[64] *See id.*

[65] *Id.; see also* Jacob M. Grumbach, *From Backwaters to Major Policymakers: Policy Polarization in the States, 1970-2014*, 16 PERS. POL. 416, 419 (2018) (showing that the polarization of state policy has increased over time). *But see* MATT GROSSMAN, RED STATE BLUES: HOW THE CONSERVATIVE REVOLUTION STALLED IN THE STATES (2019) (arguing that state policy has remained relatively liberal even as Republicans have made electoral gains).

[66] *See* Joseph Bafumi & Michael C. Herron, *Leapfrog Representation and Extremism: A Study of American Voters and Their Members in Congress*, 104 AM. POL. SCI. REV. 519, 522–26 (2010).

[67] *See* Michael J. Barber, *Representing the Preferences of Donors, Partisans, and Voters in the U.S. Senate*, 80 PUB. OP. Q. 225, 233–35 (2016).

[68] *See* Seth J. Hill & Chris Tausanovitch, *A Disconnect in Representation? Comparison of Trends in Congressional and Public Polarization*, 77 J. POL. 1058, 1061–65 (2015) (analyzing trends in voters' and legislators' ideologies separately).

[69] *See* Boris Shor, All Together Now: Putting Congress, State Legislatures, and Individuals in a Common Ideological Space to Assess Representation at the Macro and Micro Levels 4–12 (Apr. 25, 2011).

[70] Most, though not all, of the literature on representational alignment analyzes voters as opposed to persons, citizens, registered voters, or some other population. I typically use voters as shorthand throughout this section, even when particular studies examine some other group.

members of Congress have already expressed their opinions by casting roll call votes. The voters' responses and the politicians' roll call votes can then be used to determine their respective ideal points along the same ideological dimension. As indicated by Figure 3.3, this literature finds that the ideal points of representatives and senators are sharply bimodal. Almost all members of Congress are liberals or conservatives while very few are moderates.[71] The literature further finds that voters' ideal points could hardly be more different. In stark contrast to members of Congress, most voters are moderates while smaller fractions are liberals or conservatives.[72] The space between the polarized ideological distribution of members of Congress and the more normal ideological distribution of voters, then, represents the extent of collective representational misalignment. The sheer size of that space reveals just how misaligned Congress collectively is with the preferences of the American public.[73]

This picture of extreme politicians and more moderate voters recurs at the state legislative level. Raymond La Raja and Brian Schaffner compile the estimated ideologies of state legislators and voters from Catalist, a leading voter file vendor.[74] (Catalist uses a proprietary formula to produce an ideology score for each of the nearly two hundred million registered voters in its database.) Again, most state legislators are liberals (if they're Democrats) or conservatives (if they're Republicans).[75] And again, the ideological distribution of voters is very different: a bell curve with its peak close to the center of the ideological distribution.[76] Collective representational misalignment is therefore almost as severe for state legislatures as for Congress. At both levels, voters at the ideological fringes are overrepresented while voters in the ideological middle experience inferior representation.[77]

Collective representational misalignment even extends to (but isn't as acute at) the local level. Schaffner, Jesse Rhodes, and La Raja pull Catalist's ideology scores for city council members across the country.[78] The ideological

---

[71] See, e.g., Bafumi & Herron, supra note 66, at 528–38; Barber, supra note 67, at 235–41; Hill & Tausanovitch, supra note 68, at 1067; Shor, supra note 69, at 21–28.

[72] See, e.g., id.

[73] David Broockman argues that ideal point calculations overestimate the extremism of politicians, and underestimate that of voters, because they're driven by the *consistency* of policy views (which is often high for politicians and low for voters). See David E. Broockman, *Approaches to Studying Policy Representation*, 41 Leg. Stud. Q. 181, 186–201 (2016). However, recent work responding to Broockman's critique shows that the ideological distribution of voters is indeed normal and centered on the middle of the ideological spectrum. See Anthony Fowler et al., *Moderates*, 117 Am. Pol. Sci. Rev. 643, 654 (2023). *But see* David E. Broockman & Benjamin E. Lauderdale, "Moderates" (Oct. 17, 2023) (critiquing the study by Fowler and his coauthors).

[74] See Raymond J. La Raja & Brian F. Schaffner, Campaign Finance and Political Polarization: When Purists Prevail 94 (2015).

[75] See id.

[76] See id.

[77] See also Shor, supra note 69, at 26, 29 (also showing that state legislators are sharply polarized compared to the general public).

[78] See Schaffner et al., supra note 39, at 42–44, 47–50.

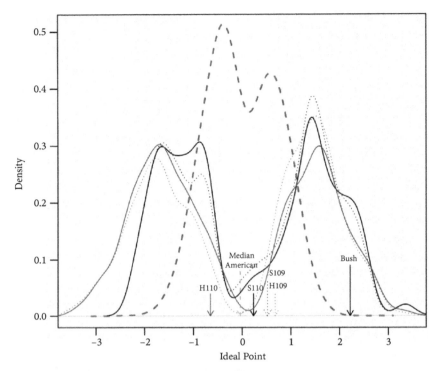

Notes: The dashed grey density line describes the distribution of voter ideal points; the dotted (solid) black density line describes the distribution of senator ideal points in the 109th (110th) Congress, whereas the dotted (solid) gray density line shows this distribution for representatives in the 109th (110th) Congress. Senate and House medians are denoted "S" and "H," respectively, with a Congress number appended. The ideal point of President George W. Bush is denoted with "Bush."

FIGURE 3.3 IDEAL POINT DISTRIBUTIONS OF VOTERS AND MEMBERS OF CONGRESS

Figure 3.3 is reproduced with permission from Joseph Bafumi & Michael C. Herron, *Leapfrog Representation and Extremism: A Study of American Voters and Their Members in Congress*, 104 AM. POL. SCI. REV. 519, 536 (2010). Copyright © 2010 by Cambridge University Press.

distribution of these local elected officials *is* bimodal but isn't *as* bimodal as the corresponding histograms for members of Congress and state legislators.[79] There are quite a few moderate city council members, in other words, even though they're outnumbered by liberal and conservative city council members. Consequently, the degree of collective representational misalignment is somewhat lower at the local level. Ideologically extreme voters aren't quite as overrepresented and moderates' underrepresentation isn't quite as glaring.

[79] *See id.* at 101.

This data on *collective* misalignment implies significant *majoritarian* misalignment, too. Since legislators are highly polarized ideologically, but voters aren't, we should expect the median legislator in a chamber generally to be more liberal or conservative than the median voter in a jurisdiction. In particular, the median legislator should be more liberal than the median voter when Democrats comprise a legislative majority, and more conservative when Republicans control a chamber. Figure 3.3 largely validates this hypothesis. The median member of the U.S. House was more conservative than the median American voter during the 109th Congress from 2005 to 2007 (under a Republican majority). The median House member was then more liberal than the median American voter during the 110th Congress from 2007 to 2009 (under Democratic control).[80] However, the median senator remained misaligned to the right during both Congresses because even though Democrats controlled the Senate from 2007 to 2009, by the slimmest of margins, their majority depended on a handful of conservative Democrats (a rare breed then and even rarer now).

Of course, the 2005–09 period is just a single short era in American political history. Unfortunately, no one has systematically compared the median member of Congress to the median American voter over a longer time horizon, probably because of the difficulty of calculating ideal points on the same scale in earlier years. As displayed in Figure 3.4, though, Voteview tracks the ideal point of the median member of Congress from the Founding all the way to the present.[81] The 2005–09 pattern of liberal medians during Democratic majorities and conservative medians under Republican control clearly applies to the entire period from the mid-1990s to the present. There being no reason to think the median American voter's ideology oscillates this rapidly, it's safe to conclude that majoritarian representational misalignment has been widespread in Congress in recent decades.[82]

And not just in Congress. Shor relies on ideal points derived from state legislators' roll call votes and voters' survey responses to show that the median state legislator is usually well to the left or right of the median voter in the state.[83]

---

[80] Bafumi and Herron dub this pattern of the median legislator jumping ideologically from one side to the other of the median voter "leapfrog representation." *See* Bafumi & Herron, *supra* note 66 at 519.

[81] *See Parties Overview*, VOTEVIEW.COM, https://voteview.com/parties/all (last visited Feb. 1, 2024).

[82] *See also* Larry M. Bartels et al., *Representation*, *in* THE OXFORD HANDBOOK OF AMERICAN POLITICAL DEVELOPMENT 399, 412–14 (Richard Valelly et al. eds., 2016) (displaying a similar chart and concluding that "the House median … is almost always higher (more conservative) than national opinion when the Republicans are in the majority, and almost always lower (more liberal) when the Democrats are in the majority"). Interestingly, the congressional median was much steadier from roughly the 1940s to the 1990s. This, of course, was the anomalous era of a less polarized Congress. Less congressional polarization means less variation in the congressional median when party control changes.

[83] *See* Shor, *supra* note 69, at 26.

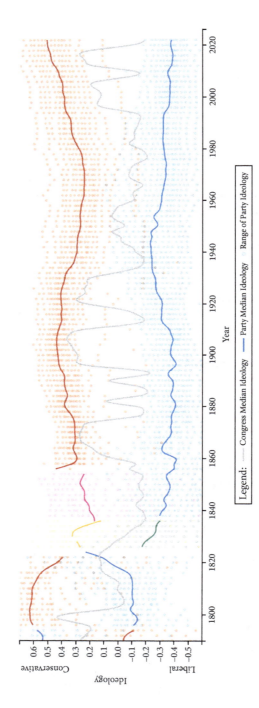

FIGURE 3.4 CONGRESSIONAL AND PARTY MEDIAN IDEAL POINTS OVER TIME

Figure 3.4 is reproduced with permission from *Parties Overview*, VOTEVIEW.COM, https://voteview.com/parties/all (last visited Feb. 1, 2024). Copyright (c) 2024 by UCLA Department of Political Science.

In fact, it's common for the median state legislator to be more liberal or conservative than not just a majority but fully 90 percent of the electorate.[84] Adam Bonica arrives at a similar result using ideal points computed a completely different way—based on records of who donates money to which candidates.[85] Again, the median state legislator is typically quite liberal if a Democrat and quite conservative if a Republican.[86] At the local level as well, La Raja and his coauthors determine that the median city council member tends to have a substantially more liberal or conservative Catalist ideology score than the median voter.[87] Interestingly, this representational bias is pro-conservative much more often than it's pro-liberal.[88]

Just as collective misalignment implies majoritarian misalignment, so too does *jurisdiction-wide* misalignment suggest *district-specific* misalignment. Since legislators as a group hold policy positions that are more polarized than those of voters, individual legislators should also be more liberal or conservative than most of their constituents. Bafumi and Herron confirm this expectation for members of Congress. Figure 3.5, for instance, plots the ideal points of states' senators, median voters, and median Democratic and Republican voters.[89] In virtually every case, Democratic senators are more liberal than states' median voters and even states' median Democratic voters. The converse is true for Republican senators; they're almost always more conservative than both their median constituents and their median co-partisans. District-specific representational misalignment, in the direction of the ideological extremes, is thus ubiquitous in Congress.[90]

Once more, the story is similar in state legislatures—at least in California, the one state for which scholars have analyzed representational alignment within districts. Seth Masket and Hans Noel take advantage of the fact that California voters commonly voice their opinions in referenda on exactly the same issues on which California state legislators have previously voted.[91] As a result, it's possible to calculate voters' and state legislators' ideal points using directly comparable policy preferences—which themselves are legally binding, not merely responses to surveys. Masket and Noel show that Democrats in the California Assembly

[84] *See id.*
[85] *See* Adam Bonica, *Mapping the Ideological Marketplace*, 58 AM. J. POL. SCI. 367, 369–73 (2014).
[86] *See id.* at 378.
[87] *See* SCHAFFNER ET AL., *supra* note 39, at 115.
[88] *See id.*
[89] *See* Bafumi & Herron, *supra* note 66, at 531.
[90] *See also id.* at 529 (reporting similar results for House members); Barber, *supra* note 67, at 239 (reporting similar results for senators); Anthony Fowler & Andrew B. Hall, *The Elusive Quest for Convergence*, 11 Q.J. POL. SCI. 131, 143 (2016) (showing the divergence in how Democratic and Republican House members represent districts in eight issue areas).
[91] *See* Seth E. Masket & Hans Noel, *Serving Two Masters: Using Referenda to Assess Partisan Versus Dyadic Legislative Representation*, 65 POL. RSCH. Q. 104, 106–09 (2012).

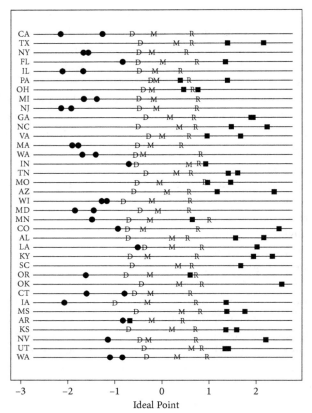

Notes: This figure describes the locations senators (black circles for Democrats and black squares for Republicans), state median voters (M), statewide Democratic median voters (D), and statewide Republican median voters (R). States are ordered by the number of voters in them, and all states listed have at least forty voters.

FIGURE 3.5 IDEAL POINTS OF SENATORS, MEDIAN VOTERS, AND MEDIAN DEMOCRATIC AND REPUBLICAN VOTERS

Figure 3.5 is reproduced with permission from Joseph Bafumi & Michael C. Herron, *Leapfrog Representation and Extremism: A Study of American Voters and Their Members in Congress*, 104 AM. POL. SCI. REV. 519, 531 (2010). Copyright © 2010 by Cambridge University Press.

are almost always more liberal, and Republicans more conservative, than their districts' median voters.[92] However, this district-specific representational misalignment isn't quite as extreme as at the congressional level. Also unlike Congress, it's Republican state legislators in California who are a bit closer ideologically to

---

[92] *See id.* at 109–15.

their constituents, maybe because their minority status incentivizes them to provide better representation.[93]

You may have noticed that I haven't said a word yet about *executive* branch officials. How congruent are presidents' policy positions, then, with those of most Americans? What about the stances of governors and other state-level officeholders? With respect to presidents, Figure 3.3 contains the beginning of an answer. It indicates that President Bush's ideal point was much more conservative than that of the median American voter from 2005 to 2009.[94] Other scholars have extended this finding both backward and forward in time using presidents' positions on issues voted on by Congress. From at least the 1950s to the present, Democratic presidents have been quite liberal, and Republican presidents quite conservative. Moreover, recent Republican presidents have deviated about twice as far to the right of the ideological center as recent Democratic presidents have to the left.[95]

It's true that these results hinge on the relatively few bills on which presidents take explicit stances. But Shawn Treier determines that even if presidents are assumed to back all bills they sign into law—even if they never say so—their ideal points remain liberal (if they're Democrats) or conservative (if they're Republicans).[96] It's also true that presidents take positions on many policies never voted on by Congress. In this vein, Jeffrey Cohen studies the rhetorical liberalism of State of the Union addresses. In these speeches, Democratic presidents generally express preferences more left-wing than those of the median American, while Republican presidents state more right-wing views.[97] Dan Wood extends Cohen's work to *all* public utterances by presidents that happen to be recorded. Again, Democratic presidents are more rhetorically liberal than most of the American public, while Republican presidents are more rhetorically

---

[93] *See id.* at 116. At least, this was the case in 2003–06 when the California Assembly was under Democratic control. Democratic state legislators were somewhat closer ideologically to their constituents in 1995–96, a brief window of Republican control. *See id.* For another useful California study, see Thad Kousser et al., *Reform and Representation: A New Method Applied to Recent Electoral Changes*, 6 POL. SCI. RSCH. & METHODS 809, 821 (2018) (finding that California Democrats and Republicans in *Congress* are more liberal and conservative, respectively, than their districts' median voters).

[94] *See* Bafumi & Herron, *supra* note 66, at 536.

[95] *See* Michael A. Bailey, *Comparable Preference Estimates Across Time and Institutions for the Court, Congress, and Presidency*, 51 AM. J. POL. SCI. 433, 444 (2007); Nolan M. McCarty & Keith T. Poole, *Veto Power and Legislation: An Empirical Analysis of Executive and Legislative Bargaining from 1961 to 1986*, 11 J.L., ECON. & ORG. 282, 304 (1995); Keith T. Poole et al., *The Presidential Square Wave Through the 113th Congress*, VOTEVIEW BLOG (Aug. 4, 2016), https://voteviewblog.com/2016/08/04/the-presidential-square-wave-through-the-113th-congress/.

[96] *See* Shawn Treier, *Where Does the President Stand? Measuring Presidential Ideology*, 18 POL. ANAL. 124, 129–30 (2010).

[97] *See* JEFFREY E. COHEN, PRESIDENTIAL RESPONSIVENESS AND PUBLIC POLICYMAKING: THE PUBLIC AND THE POLICIES THAT PRESIDENTS CHOOSE 103 (1999).

conservative. What's more, the ideology of presidential remarks is either insensitive or *negatively* related to the public's ideological mood.[98]

As for state-level officeholders, Bonica estimates their ideal points based on the identities of their campaign donors. Governors, attorneys general, and secretaries of state all have highly polarized ideological distributions.[99] In fact, more than two-thirds of these officials have more extreme ideal points than the average state legislator from their party.[100] Each party's average state legislator already tends to be much more liberal or conservative than the state's median voter— yet the representational misalignment of state-level officeholders is even worse. This noncongruence reaches its apogee for secretaries of state, the officials who administer states' elections. Their ideological polarization exceeds even that of members of Congress.[101]

This discussion should make unmistakably clear one group whose members enjoy highly congruent representation: voters at the ideological fringes. However representational alignment is analyzed—for all voters or the median voter, for the whole jurisdiction or individual districts, for Congress, state legislatures, city councils, or executive branch officials—the same theme emerges. In modern American politics, Democratic officeholders take more liberal stances than do most of their constituents, while Republican politicians hold more conservative positions. This is bad news for most voters, who are ideologically moderate yet consigned to liberal or conservative representation depending on officeholders' party affiliations. But it's wonderful news for the smaller fractions of voters who are themselves staunch liberals or conservatives. As long as their preferred party is in power, the extreme representation they get is the extreme representation they want.

Who are these voters at the ideological fringes in whose favor politicians' policy stances are so skewed? Like Walt Whitman, they contain multitudes,[102] but among their ranks they count most campaign donors. Campaign donors, the small group of Americans who give money to candidates for political office, have a highly polarized ideological distribution. However their ideal points are calculated, most donors are liberals or conservatives while very few are moderates.[103]

---

[98] *See* B. Dan Wood, The Myth of Presidential Representation 84 (2009).

[99] *See* Bonica, *supra* note 86, at 376–78.

[100] *See id.* at 376.

[101] *See id.* at 377.

[102] *See* Fowler et al., *supra* note 73, at 656 (showing that ideological extremism is linked to political interest and knowledge, making campaign contributions, and being white, old, rich, and college-educated).

[103] *See, e.g.*, Bafumi & Herron, *supra* note 66, at 536–37; Barber, *supra* note 67, at 235–41; Adam Bonica, *Avenues of Influence: On the Political Expenditures of Corporations and Their Directors and Executives*, 18 Bus. & Pol. 367, 385 (2016); Jesse H. Rhodes & Brian F. Schaffner, *Economic Inequality and Representation in the U.S. House: A New Approach Using Population-Level Data* 34–36 (Apr. 7, 2013).

This pattern looks nothing like the more normal ideological distribution of the entire American public. But it's virtually identical to the polarization of members of Congress, presidents, state legislators, governors, and so on. Of the array of scholars to make this point,[104] Barber shares the most arresting results. Democratic (or Republican) senators are more liberal (or conservative) than both the median voter in their state and the median voter from their party. But the ideal points of senators are almost exactly the same as those of their median donors. The distribution of donor-senator representational alignment peaks at zero—that is, no ideological gap at all.[105]

Most donors are wealthy, of course, but most of the rich don't contribute money to politicians. Whether high-income individuals generally (as opposed to donors specifically) are better represented than middle- and low-income individuals has been a major research question in political science in recent years. Unfortunately, most of the relevant work has investigated differential *responsiveness* by income group.[106] A few scholars, though, have examined representational alignment with the wealthy, the middle class, and the poor. At the federal level, the best study is by Lax, Phillips, and Adam Zelizer. They show that senators' votes over the last two decades are somewhat more congruent with the preferences of the wealthy than with those of the middle class and the poor—2 and 5 percentage points, respectively.[107] But much of this effect is mediated by party. Republican senators' votes are 7 and 18 percentage points better aligned with the views of the rich than with those of the middle class and the poor, respectively.[108] In contrast, Democratic senators' votes are most congruent with the desires of the poor and least congruent with those of the rich (though the gaps are modest).[109]

As far as I know, no analogous study exists at the state legislative level. The smaller populations of state legislative districts make it hard to segment intra-district public opinion by income group, at least if public opinion is derived from polling. However, it should be possible for scholars to tackle this issue using

---

[104] *See id.*; *see also* Brandice Canes-Wrone & Kenneth M. Miller, *Out-of-District Donors and Representation in the U.S. House*, 47 LEGIS. STUD. Q. 361, 373 (2022) (finding that when national donor opinion diverges from district opinion, members of Congress side with national donor opinion about four-fifths of the time).

[105] *See* Barber, *supra* note 67, at 235–41.

[106] For a discussion of this literature, see Nicholas O. Stephanopoulos, *Aligning Campaign Finance Law*, 101 VA. L. REV. 1425, 1468–74 (2015).

[107] *See* Jeffrey R. Lax et al., *The Party or the Purse? Unequal Representation in the US Senate*, 113 AM. POL. SCI. REV. 917, 930 (2019).

[108] *See id.*

[109] *See id.*; *see also* Christopher Ellis, *Understanding Economic Biases in Representation: Income, Resources, and Policy Representation in the 110th House*, 65 POL. RSCH. Q. 938, 944 (2012) (reporting similar results for House members over a smaller number of bills); Cory Maks-Solomon & Elizabeth Rigby, *Are Democrats Really the Party of the Poor? Partisanship, Class, and Representation in the U.S. Senate*, 73 POL. RSCH. Q. 848, 853 (2020) (reporting similar results for senators).

ideology scores from voter file vendors since those scores are available for all registered voters, not just a sample of them. In fact, Schaffner, Rhodes, and La Raja *have* taken this approach at the local level, where most municipalities are even smaller than state legislative districts. Using data from Catalist, they find that residents in the highest income tercile are somewhat closer ideologically to their local elected officials than are residents in the middle and lowest income terciles.[110] The representational advantage of the rich thus extends to local politics as well.

While no other cleavage has been scrutinized to the same extent as wealth, scholars have looked into representational alignment by race, gender, education, and age. Members of Congress vote consistently with the preferences of White respondents more often than with those of Black and Hispanic respondents.[111] White residents are also closer ideologically to their local elected officials than are Black and Hispanic residents.[112] At both the federal and local levels, these racial gaps in representation are larger than the corresponding differences by income group.[113] Similarly, the votes of members of Congress more closely match the views of men than of women, of better-educated than of worse-educated respondents, and of old than of young respondents.[114] However, these variations in representational alignment generally aren't as large as the gaps for different racial and income groups.[115] Nor has the literature on the role of gender, education, and age in representation yet ventured from the federal to lower governmental levels.

Partisan Alignment

The last stop on our tour is partisan alignment: the fit between officeholders' party affiliations and their constituents' partisan preferences. I consider the collective and the majoritarian forms of partisan alignment at the jurisdictional level. But I don't address district-specific partisan alignment. Partisan *misalignment* at the district level is certainly possible. It can occur if a third-party candidate siphons off votes that would have gone to a major-party candidate, resulting in a winner who isn't backed by the median voter.[116] Partisan misalignment with the median

---

[110] *See* SCHAFFNER ET AL., *supra* note 39, at 176.

[111] *See* Ellis, *supra* note 111, at 944; John D. Griffin & Brian Newman, *The Unequal Representation of Latinos and Whites*, 69 J. POL. 1032, 1038 (2007).

[112] *See* SCHAFFNER ET AL., *supra* note 39, at 117–18.

[113] *See id.* at 176; Ellis, *supra* note 111, at 944; Griffin & Newman, *supra* note 113, at 1038.

[114] *See* Ellis, *supra* note 111, at 944; John D. Griffin et al., *A Gender Gap in Policy Representation in the U.S. Congress?*, 37 LEGIS. STUD. Q. 35, 48 (2012); Griffin & Newman, *supra* note 113, at 1038.

[115] *See id.*

[116] Assuming, that is, an election using a plurality winner rule, not an alternative like ranked-choice voting.

eligible voter can also arise if voting restrictions prevent certain people entitled to vote from actually casting ballots. And outright fraud—the subtraction of lawfully cast ballots or the addition of counterfeit ballots—can yield a winner who isn't the choice of the public in any sense. However, systematic data on these varieties of district-specific partisan misalignment is entirely lacking. I therefore bracket them for present purposes while noting the need for further research.

Beginning with collective partisan alignment, it can be measured in several ways. A number of metrics exist that use parties' votes and seats to determine their overall levels of advantage or disadvantage in a legislative chamber. For both ease of exposition and substantive reasons that are extraneous here,[117] I focus on a single measure of partisan bias known as the efficiency gap. The efficiency gap is based on the insight that both cracking and packing—the two fundamental means of partisan gerrymandering—operate by "wasting" votes for the targeted party's candidates. In the case of cracking (dispersing the targeted party's supporters among many districts where they constitute minorities of the electorate), votes for losing candidates are wasted. In the case of packing (concentrating the targeted party's backers in a few districts where they make up overwhelming majorities), votes for winning candidates in excess of the threshold for victory are wasted. The efficiency gap simply totals each party's wasted votes across all districts in a plan, subtracts one sum from the other, and divides that difference by the number of votes cast in the election. The metric reveals which party is the net beneficiary of a plan's cracking and packing choices—that is, which party is better able to translate its popular support into legislative representation.[118]

Figure 3.6 plots the *absolute* efficiency gap and the *net* efficiency gap for the U.S. House, the U.S. Senate, state houses, and state senates from 1972 to the present.[119] The absolute efficiency gap is the absolute value of the efficiency gap. It indicates the *size* of a legislative chamber's partisan bias but not its partisan *direction*. For the U.S. House, the trend of the absolute efficiency gap is roughly U-shaped. The chamber's partisan skew was relatively large in the 1970s and 1980s,

---

[117] *See* Nicholas O. Stephanopoulos & Eric M. McGhee, *The Measure of a Metric: The Debate Over Quantifying Partisan Gerrymandering*, 70 STAN. L. REV. 1503, 1516–36 (2018) (explaining why the efficiency gap is generally preferable to certain other measures of partisan bias in districting).

[118] *See generally* Nicholas O. Stephanopoulos & Eric M. McGhee, *Partisan Gerrymandering and the Efficiency Gap*, 82 U. CHI. L. REV. 831 (2015).

[119] Data for the U.S. Senate aggregates the results of the three most recent elections and begins with 1980. Data for state senates aggregates the results of the two most recent elections, where necessary, and begins with 1974. For similar plots of efficiency gaps from 1972 to 2012, see Stephanopoulos & McGhee, *supra* note 120, at 873. For longitudinal studies of partisan bias by other scholars, see ANTHONY J. MCGANN ET AL., GERRYMANDERING IN AMERICA: THE HOUSE OF REPRESENTATIVES, THE SUPREME COURT, AND THE FUTURE OF POPULAR SOVEREIGNTY 88–89, 92 (2016); Andrew Gelman & Gary King, *Enhancing Democracy Through Legislative Redistricting*, 88 AM. POL. SCI. REV. 541, 556–57 (1994); and Gregory S. Warrington, *Quantifying Gerrymandering Using the Vote Distribution*, 17 ELECTION L.J. 39, 44–48 (2018).

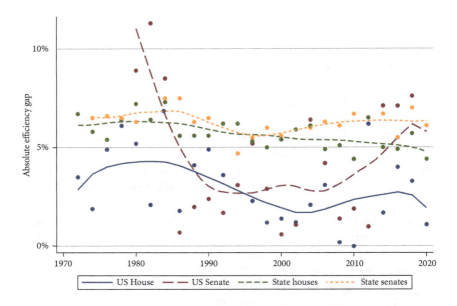

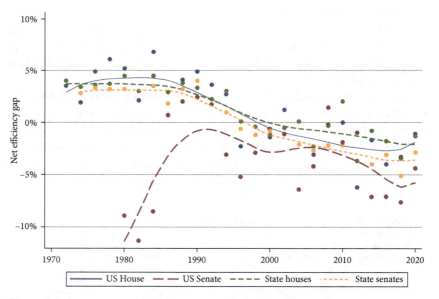

Figure 3.6 ABSOLUTE AND NET EFFICIENCY GAPS OVER TIME

Figure 3.6 was created using efficiency gaps calculated by Christopher Warshaw for the PlanScore website, *see* PLANSCORE, https://planscore.org (last visited Feb. 1, 2024), as well as U.S. Senate results compiled by Ari Goldbloom-Helzner.

indicating substantial collective partisan misalignment. The chamber's absolute efficiency gap then shrank in the 1990s and remained small through the 2000s. Over the last decade, the U.S. House's partisan skew has grown again, albeit not to the size of the 1970s and 1980s.[120]

The pattern for the U.S. Senate is an exaggerated version of the U.S. House's U-shape.[121] The chamber's absolute efficiency gap was very large in the early 1980s, denoting severe collective partisan misalignment. The chamber's partisan skew then improved significantly in the late 1980s and stayed at this moderate level through the 2000s. Lately, the U.S. Senate's partisan skew has worsened again, though not to the extent of the early 1980s. And at the state legislative level, no U-shape is evident in the data. For both state houses and state senates, the average absolute efficiency gap has been more or less constant over the last half-century.[122] For both sets of chambers, the average absolute efficiency gap has also been quite large—always bigger than the U.S. House's partisan skew and usually bigger than of the U.S. Senate, too. Collective partisan misalignment, then, has been both more uniform and more acute at the state legislative level in recent decades.

The net efficiency gap, in turn, is the raw, unadjusted value of the efficiency gap. It tells us *which* party benefits from a legislative chamber's partisan bias (and to what extent). The story here is virtually identical for the U.S. House, state houses, and state senates.[123] In all these chambers, Democrats enjoyed a steady and significant advantage in how efficiently their votes translated into seats in the 1970s and 1980s. This Democratic edge then evaporated in the 1990s, leaving Republicans in a slightly superior position. Since about 2000, the net efficiency gap has gradually moved further in a Republican direction, especially in the U.S. House and state senates.[124] In contrast, the trend for the U.S. Senate is sharply different, at least before the early 1990s. In the early 1980s, the chamber was heavily skewed in *Republicans'* favor. This pro-Republican tilt almost disappeared over the next decade. Since the early 1990s, the U.S. Senate's net efficiency gap has

[120] And most recently, the U.S. House's partisan skew has declined again, likely because of court decisions striking down a number of highly biased congressional maps.
[121] Of course, the pattern for the U.S. Senate is driven in part by states' unequal populations—and *isn't* the result of redistricting.
[122] The average absolute efficiency gap is the mean of all available chambers' absolute efficiency gaps in a given year.
[123] Note that I'm comparing the net efficiency gap of the U.S. House to the *average* net efficiency gaps of state houses and state senates. Note also that, by convention, positive efficiency gaps are pro-Democratic and negative efficiency gaps are pro-Republican.
[124] For a book-length argument that the U.S. House's partisan bias has shifted from pro-Democratic to pro-Republican over the last half-century, see KYLE KONDIK, THE LONG RED THREAD: HOW DEMOCRATIC DOMINANCE GAVE WAY TO REPUBLICAN ADVANTAGE IN U.S. HOUSE ELECTIONS (2021).

again become more pro-Republican, moving roughly in tandem with the biases of the other chambers.

Next, majoritarian partisan alignment is a simpler concept than collective partisan alignment. Majoritarian partisan alignment exists in a legislative chamber when the party favored by the median voter is also the party to which the median legislator belongs. There's majoritarian partisan *mis*alignment, on the other hand, when the party that earns the most votes fails to win the most seats as well. Political scientists sometimes call this scenario a "manufactured majority"—a majority made possible by how votes happen to be converted into seats.[125]

In the U.S. House, there have been three cases of majoritarian partisan misalignment over the last half-century, all benefiting Republicans. In 1998, 2000, and 2012, Democratic candidates received 50.1 percent, 50.1 percent, and 51.2 percent of the nationwide two-party vote, respectively. Yet in those elections, Democrats obtained 49.0 percent, 48.8 percent, and 46.2 percent of U.S. House seats, respectively. In the U.S. Senate, there have been *eleven* instances of majoritarian partisan misalignment since 1980, again all in Republicans' favor. In 1980, 1982, 1984, 1994, 1996, 2000, 2002, 2004, 2014, 2016, and 2018, Democratic candidates received more than 50 percent of the nationwide two-party vote over the three elections that shaped the chamber's composition. After each of those elections, though, Republicans controlled the U.S. Senate. Only once since 1980, in 1998, did Republicans win a U.S. Senate majority after also earning a majority of the nationwide two-party vote over the three determinative elections.

Cases of majoritarian partisan misalignment have been even more common in state legislatures. Figure 3.7 displays the numbers of pro-Democratic and pro-Republican manufactured majorities in state legislatures (including state houses and state senates) from 1972 to 2020.[126] Every election in this period led to at least one manufactured majority. Five elections (1994, 1996, 1998, 2000, and 2004) yielded ten or more. In sum, the majority party in the electorate failed to become the majority party in the state legislative chamber 169 times over the last half-century.[127] Seventy of these misfires benefited Democrats and ninety-nine were in Republicans' favor. Pro-Republican majoritarian partisan misalignment has also been more frequent lately, accounting for twenty-eight of thirty-six cases over the last decade.

* * *

---

[125] *See* Miriam Seifter, *Countermajoritarian Legislatures*, 121 COLUM. L. REV. 1733, 1762 (2021).

[126] For a similar analysis by another scholar (albeit without imputing results for uncontested races), see *id.* at 1764.

[127] These 169 cases of majoritarian partisan misalignment represent about 10 percent of the state legislative elections for which data is available.

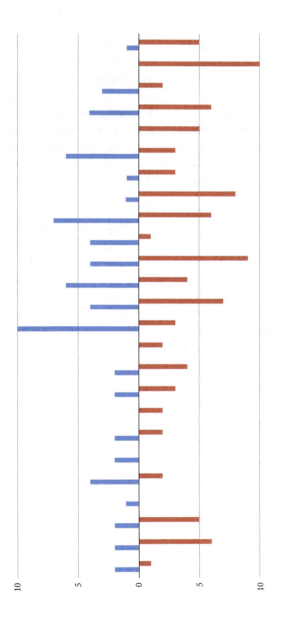

FIGURE 3.7 CASES OF MAJORITARIAN PARTISAN MISALIGNMENT IN STATE LEGISLATURES OVER TIME

This chart was created using data compiled by Christopher Warshaw for the PlanScore website. *See* PLANSCORE, https://planscore.org (last visited Feb. 1, 2024).

The bulk of this chapter has been a literature review, a genre known for its dryness. But I hope the findings I've described—some original to this project—have prompted more gasps than yawns. The alignment of governmental outputs with popular preferences is a core democratic value. That value, though, is honored in the breach more than in the observance in contemporary American politics. Misalignment is widespread with respect to each governmental output I've examined: officeholders' partisanship, officeholders' representation, and policy outcomes themselves. Pervasive misalignment is also evident whether all people's views are taken into account or just those of the median individual. And misalignment persists at every governmental level: in congressional and state legislative districts as well as in jurisdictions spanning municipalities, states, and the federal government as a whole. Once upon a time, de Tocqueville could write about democracy in America. Today, a more apt moniker would be misalignment in America.

An obvious question at this point is why misalignment matters to the law (as opposed to democratic theory or empirical political science). I tackle this issue in the next chapter. I argue that a variety of legal materials—constitutional text, ratification history, and judicial precedent, both federal and state-specific—support the recognition of alignment as a legal principle. These sources certainly don't *require* inscribing alignment into the law, but they make this move as reasonable as many other judicial choices. Courts already enforce extratextual values like federalism and the separation of powers. It would take no great leap for them to incorporate alignment, too, into their jurisprudence.

4

The Law of Alignment

Introduction

Structuralist election law scholars sometimes state that their approaches can't be grounded in conventional forms of constitutional argument. Only democratic theory, untethered from the Constitution, they say, can justify their views. In their landmark article introducing their model of competitive structuralism, for example, Samuel Issacharoff and Richard Pildes lament that "the Constitution offers little textual or historical guidance on this framework."[1] Issacharoff and Pildes therefore "read into the Constitution an indispensable commitment to the preservation of an appropriately competitive political order" based on nothing more than the normative appeal of electoral competition.[2] Writing alone, Issacharoff is even blunter. "So, let's be candid."[3] "[T]he answers to the questions of how to make democracy work are [not] compelled by vague [constitutional] terms . . . ."[4] "Sometimes it is simply best to tell poor Virginia the sad truth: sorry, there really is no Santa Claus."[5] Michael Klarman concurs. "A majoritarian theory of judicial review can be persuasively grounded only in democratic principle, not in the Constitution."[6]

I think these concessions are too quick. In fact, a reasonable case can be made, using standard modes of constitutional interpretation, that courts should recognize structural democratic values like competition, participation, and, in particular, alignment.[7] Consider the text of the Constitution. As amended, it stipulates that both chambers of Congress must be chosen "by the People."[8] Each state must also adopt a "Republican Form of Government."[9] And these republican

---

[1] Samuel Issacharoff & Richard H. Pildes, *Politics as Markets: Partisan Lockups of the Democratic Process*, 50 STAN. L. REV. 643, 713 (1998).

[2] *Id.* at 716.

[3] Samuel Issacharoff, *Surreply, Why Elections?*, 116 HARV. L. REV. 684, 687 (2002).

[4] *Id.* at 688.

[5] *Id.*

[6] Michael J. Klarman, *Majoritarian Judicial Review: The Entrenchment Problem*, 85 GEO. L.J. 491, 499 (1997).

[7] I don't present the cases here for recognizing competition or participation as federal constitutional values, leaving these projects for other scholars. Additionally, many of the materials I cite are general enough to evoke not just alignment but also related concepts like representation, responsiveness, and accountability. These materials should therefore be understood as plausibly supporting the recognition of a cluster of kindred ideas.

[8] *See* U.S. CONST. art. I, § 2; *id.* amend. XVII.

[9] *Id.* art. IV, § 4.

Aligning Election Law. Nicholas O. Stephanopoulos, Oxford University Press. © Nicholas O. Stephanopoulos 2024.
DOI: 10.1093/9780197662182.003.0004

governments must enact unbiased policies that don't "deny to any person . . . the equal protection of the laws."[10] Squinting a bit, this is a plausible description of an aligned political system, both in Washington, DC and in each state.

Or take the intentions of the Constitution's drafters. One of the tenets of James Madison's philosophy was that public opinion should guide the actions of the new federal government. Of course, politicians could (and should) try to shape people's preferences. But once fixed, public opinion should be followed.[11] Similarly, the primary author of the Fourteenth Amendment, John Bingham, stressed the right of the majority in each state to exert political power. Minoritarian political control—misalignment in favor of a minority—was intolerable. A crucial aim of the Fourteenth Amendment was to authorize Congress and the federal courts to intervene against state-level minoritarian rule.[12]

The most extensive support for alignment as a constitutional principle, though, comes from the most common form of constitutional argument: reasoning based on precedent. A substantial number of Supreme Court decisions have treated alignment as a value of constitutional magnitude. Some of these rulings have wielded alignment as a sword—to strike down misaligning electoral practices. Other cases have brandished alignment as a shield—to uphold aligning policies against attacks on other grounds. These invocations of alignment were most prevalent in the Warren Court, when they helped inspire John Hart Ely's political process theory.[13] But even in more recent years, Court majorities (occasionally) and individual Justices (more frequently) have lauded alignment. Moreover, paeans to alignment span the entire domain of election law. Among others, they appear in cases about the right to vote, the regulation of political parties, redistricting, and campaign finance.

I want to acknowledge up front that these materials don't *require* the constitutionalization of alignment. There's no Alignment Clause making it indisputable that the achievement of alignment is a constitutional objective. Alignment thus differs from the age prerequisites for federal officeholders, say, or the allocation of two senators per state: provisions written with such specificity, at such a low level of generality, that their meaning is agreed on by essentially all observers. However, very few constitutional rulings or doctrines are actually compelled. The vast majority of courts' constitutional choices, at least in difficult cases, are permissible but not inevitable. They find some backing in interpretive modes like text, history, and precedent, but also some inconsistent

[10]   *Id.* amend. XIV, § 1.

[11]   *See generally, e.g.,* COLLEEN A. SHEEHAN, JAMES MADISON AND THE SPIRIT OF REPUBLICAN SELF-GOVERNMENT (2009).

[12]   *See generally, e.g.,* William W. van Alstyne, *The Fourteenth Amendment, the "Right" to Vote, and the Understanding of the Thirty-Ninth Congress,* 1965 SUP. CT. REV. 33.

[13]   *See generally* JOHN HART ELY, DEMOCRACY AND DISTRUST: A THEORY OF JUDICIAL REVIEW (1980).

evidence. Alignment fits comfortably into this heartland of constitutional law in which courts must exercise discretion to reach their conclusions. Specifically, alignment resembles other broad principles like federalism and the separation of powers that are never named by the Constitution—but that nevertheless reflect a reasonable reading of its language, its drafters' thinking, and courts' decisions over the years. Federalism and the separation of powers follow contingently, but not necessarily, from ordinary legal sources. So does alignment.[14]

It's true as well that the current Supreme Court is exceptionally unlikely to embrace alignment. Over a series of dismaying rulings, the Roberts Court has exhibited open hostility to the use of alignment as a legal sword or shield. That's why I dub this Court, in Chapter 11, the anti-alignment Court. But the fact that *this* Court won't constitutionalize alignment hardly means that *no* Court will. An earlier Court, the Warren Court, *did* incorporate alignment into its constitutional doctrine in a variety of ways. A future Court could easily go further. The legal materials that make plausible alignment's adoption will still be there down the road, even though they're discounted by the Justices currently responsible for the Constitution's interpretation.

As this discussion indicates, this chapter's focus is federal constitutional law. However, state constitutional law recognizes the importance of alignment even more clearly than does its federal counterpart. State constitutions typically codify popular sovereignty, majority rule, and political equality—all facets of alignment. Construing these provisions, state courts often declare that alignment is an essential aim of state charters. I'm indifferent whether alignment is judicially implemented on the basis of federal or state constitutional law. I'm also happy for courts to be instructed by legislatures to pursue alignment—that is, for alignment to be judicially implemented thanks to statutory rather than constitutional law. As I explain in Chapter 12, I further support aligning policies enacted, and then enforced, by nonjudicial actors. *This* chapter's focus is federal constitutional law, then, but that's certainly not the limit of this book's project.

So how would alignment work if it was integrated into federal (or state) constitutional (or statutory) law? As my references to swords and shields suggest, there are two main options. First, a *plaintiff* could cite alignment as a basis for *invalidating* a *misaligning* electoral practice. Significant misalignment, if empirically established, might be enough to doom the challenged practice. Alternatively, significant misalignment might trigger another doctrinal inquiry like scrutiny of whether, and how well, the practice furthers a legitimate governmental interest. Alignment would therefore constitute a new, offensive cause of action.

---

[14] *See, e.g.,* Jack M. Balkin, *Republicanism and the Constitution of Opportunity,* 94 Tex. L. Rev. 1427, 1428 (2016) (naming federalism, the separation of powers, and democracy as "underlying principles that are not directly stated but that we infer from constitutional text and structure").

Second, a *defendant* could cite alignment as a basis for *sustaining* an *aligning* electoral policy. The policy would presumably be disputed on some other ground, like infringement of speech, association, or another constitutional right. In response, the defendant would offer the promotion of alignment as a justification for the policy. If the policy, in fact, substantially improved alignment, then it would be upheld for that reason. Alignment would thus operate as a new, defensive state interest. In Chapters 5 through 10, I show how these models— alignment as sword and alignment as shield—would work in a range of specific contexts. Here, I describe the models in more general terms, bracketing for now their substantive applications.

Text and Intent

Federal constitutional law typically starts with the federal constitutional text. A series of provisions in the Constitution and its amendments make it plausible for courts to recognize alignment as a constitutional value. Again, these provisions in no way mandate the constitutionalizion of alignment. But they render this a reasonable judicial move, comparably controversial to many other judicial choices over the years.

Beginning, well, at the beginning, the Preamble declares that "We the People" enact the Constitution, among other things, to "promote the general Welfare."[15] The general Welfare could be advanced by policies that are good for We the People, even if We the People don't actually want those policies or think they're good. On this reading, the Preamble wouldn't identify alignment as a justification for the Constitution's adoption. However, the general Welfare could also be furthered by policies that We the People prefer, precisely because we prefer them. On this view, the Preamble *would* refer to alignment as a rationale for writing and ratifying the Constitution. Specifically, the Preamble would articulate an aspiration of jurisdiction-wide, collective, policy alignment.[16]

Turning to Congress, Article I, Section 2 states that members of the House of Representatives shall be "chosen . . . by the People."[17] The Seventeenth Amendment echoes this language, providing that senators, too, shall be "elected by the people."[18] Of course, there are several reasons why popular election might be used to determine who serves in Congress. One of these reasons, though, is the achievement of alignment. Popular election is the quintessential aligning

---

[15] U.S. CONST. prmbl.
[16] *See, e.g.,* Akhil Reed Amar, *The Document and the Doctrine,* 114 HARV. L. REV. 26, 60 (2000) (discussing the "broad democratic language of the Preamble").
[17] U.S. CONST. art. I, § 2.
[18] *Id.* amend. XVII.

THE LAW OF ALIGNMENT 101

mechanism. As I elaborated in Chapter 2, voters can *select* candidates whose positions are better aligned with their views. Faced with the prospect of such selection, officeholders can also *adapt* so that their stances better match those of their constituents. Nor is this perspective on popular election some idiosyncratic, ahistorical take. In *The Federalist No. 52*, Madison writes that the House "should have an immediate dependence on, and an intimate sympathy with, the people."[19] How is this representational alignment to be attained? Through elections. "[E]lections are unquestionably the only policy by which this dependence and sympathy can be effectually secured."[20]

The Constitution arguably addresses state-level alignment as well. Article IV, Section 4 "guarantee[s] to every State in this Union a Republican Form of Government."[21] Republicanism is (and was) synonymous with popular sovereignty: government by and for the people, in whom all political power is ultimately vested. "The central pillar of Republican Government," concludes one important study of the topic, "is popular sovereignty."[22] In turn, popular sovereignty is typically operationalized through majority rule. Quoting Madison again, this time in *The Federalist No. 10*, "the republican principle" is that "the majority [can] defeat [a minority's] sinister views by regular vote."[23] Or in Alexander Hamilton's words, in *The Federalist No. 22*, "the fundamental maxim of republican government [is] that the sense of the majority should prevail."[24] An almost mathematical set of relations thus connects the state-level republicanism safeguarded by the Guarantee Clause to alignment. Republicanism is equivalent to popular sovereignty. Popular sovereignty operates through majority rule. And majority rule is another way of saying majoritarian alignment.

The Fourteenth Amendment can be read as continuing the Guarantee Clause's pursuit of state-level alignment. Its first section prohibits states from "abridg[ing] the privileges or immunities of citizens of the United States."[25] These privileges or immunities of federal citizenship include the rights, embodied in Article I, Section 2 and the Seventeenth Amendment, respectively, to participate in House and Senate elections. These privileges or immunities also include

---

[19] THE FEDERALIST NO. 52 (James Madison).

[20] *Id.; see also, e.g.*, Christopher S. Elmendorf, *Refining the Democracy Canon*, 95 CORNELL L. REV. 1051, 1078 (2010) ("I submit that Article I and the Seventeenth Amendment should be understood to incorporate [a democratic] norm vis-à-vis congressional elections . . . .").

[21] U.S. CONST. art. IV, § 4.

[22] Akhil Reed Amar, *The Central Meaning of Republican Government: Popular Sovereignty, Majority Rule, and the Denominator Problem*, 65 U. COLO. L. REV. 749, 749 (1994); *see also, e.g.*, Fred O. Smith, Jr., *Awakening the People's Giant: Sovereign Immunity and the Constitution's Republican Commitment*, 80 FORDHAM L. REV. 1941, 1949 (2012) ("The 'republican principle' is the cardinal and indispensable axiom that the ultimate sovereignty . . . rests in the hands of the governed, not persons who happen to govern.").

[23] THE FEDERALIST NO. 10 (James Madison).

[24] THE FEDERALIST NO. 22 (Alexander Hamilton).

[25] U.S. CONST. amend. XIV, § 1.

the right under the Guarantee Clause to live in a state with a republican government. Accordingly, the Privileges or Immunities Clause bolsters the commitment to alignment already exhibited by those other provisions. It adds to those provisions an explicit ban on certain state actions, enforceable by both Congress and the courts.

The Fourteenth Amendment further forbids states from "deny[ing] to any person . . . the equal protection of the laws."[26] Collective alignment is one connotation of the equal protection of the laws. When governmental outputs are as close as they possibly can be to all people's preferences, all people can be said to be equally protected by the laws (or, at least, as equally protected as they feasibly can be). By the same token, collective *mis*alignment is a related concept to the *un*equal protection of the laws. Suppose governmental outputs are sharply skewed in favor of the rich, or the ideologically extreme, or the politically conservative. Then you might reasonably conclude that the rich and the poor, extremists and moderates, conservatives and liberals, aren't equally protected by the laws. Rather, in each pairing, one group's members enjoy greater protection than do the other's.

Lastly, the Constitution's right-to-vote amendments (the Fifteenth, Nineteenth, Twenty-Fourth, and Twenty-Sixth Amendments) are linked to alignment in much the same way as Article I, Section 2 and the Seventeenth Amendment. Recall that the achievement of alignment is a classic rationale for popular election. Likewise, that goal justifies prohibiting the denial or abridgement of the franchise on the basis of race (per the Fifteenth Amendment), sex (per the Nineteenth), failure to pay a tax (per the Twenty-Fourth), and age if over eighteen (per the Twenty-Sixth).[27] Without these bans, significant misalignment could ensue. Racial vote suppression, for example, could result in glaring noncongruence with the targeted racial group's views. To be sure, unobstructed access to the franchise might not preclude misalignment along the lines of race, sex, wealth, and age. But it's at least a major aligning step, a necessary if not sufficient condition for avoiding these troubling types of bias.

Unsurprisingly, I'm far from the first scholar to argue that the Constitution, read as a whole, endorses democratic principles like alignment. This is also one of Ely's central points in his famous 1980 book, *Democracy and Distrust*. Surveying many of the same provisions I've cited, Ely maintains that courts "should pursue . . . '[democratic] values' . . . since those are the 'values' . . . with which our Constitution has preeminently and most successfully concerned itself."[28] "On [his] more expansive days," indeed, Ely is "tempted to claim that

---

[26] U.S. Const. amend. XIV, § 1.
[27] See id. amends. XV, XIX, XXIV, XXVI.
[28] Ely, *supra* note 13, at 76.

[pro-democratic] judicial review . . . represents the ultimate [textualism]."[29] Akhil Amar similarly lauds "the deep democratic social structure implied by the Philadelphia Constitution."[30] "The document promises a democratic republic,"[31] a nation founded on "the right of the people to ordain and establish government," "their right to alter or abolish it," and "the centrality of popular majority rule."[32] This form of reasoning even extends to the Supreme Court. "[A] fundamental principle," according to Justice Stephen Breyer, is that "We the People . . . sought to create and to protect a workable form of government that is in its principles, structure, and whole mass, basically democratic."[33]

You might object that these are the views of modern commentators—not the leaders who penned the Constitution and its amendments. Key constitutional drafters, however, expressed at least as much enthusiasm for alignment as contemporary observers like Ely, Amar, and Justice Breyer.[34] I've already quoted Madison's position that the House of Representatives should reflect the will of the people,[35] as well as his equation of republicanism with majority rule.[36] More such statements fill the pages of *The Federalist*. Here's Madison on the House again, this time in *The Federalist No. 57*. House members should be "bound to fidelity and sympathy with the great mass of the people."[37] A "communion of interests and sympathy of sentiments" should connect House members to their constituents.[38] Here's another passage by Madison about republicanism, drawn from *The Federalist No. 58*. "[T]he fundamental principle of free government would be reversed" if "the majority [could not] rule" and "power [were] transferred to the minority."[39] And here's Madison in *The Federalist No. 46* summarizing the new constitutional system in its entirety. "The federal and State governments are in fact but different agents . . . of the people."[40] Different agents with the same mission of discerning and following the people's wishes.

Madison advocates alignment still more emphatically in a set of essays that postdate *The Federalist* by a few years. In these essays, Madison states repeatedly

---

[29] *Id.* at 87–88.
[30] Amar, *supra* note 16, at 60.
[31] *Id.*
[32] Amar, *supra* note 22, at 762.
[33] Vieth v. Jubelirer, 541 U.S. 267, 356 (2004) (Breyer, J., dissenting) (internal quotation marks omitted); *see also generally* STEPHEN BREYER, ACTIVE LIBERTY: INTERPRETING OUR DEMOCRATIC CONSTITUTION (2005).
[34] In the interest of space, I address only Madison and Bingham here—the most important drafters of the original Constitution and the Fourteenth Amendment, respectively. For a discussion of the similar views of other Framers, see GORDON S. WOOD, THE CREATION OF THE AMERICAN REPUBLIC, 1776-1787, at 532–36 (rev. ed. 1998).
[35] *See supra* notes 19–20 and accompanying text.
[36] *See supra* note 23 and accompanying text.
[37] THE FEDERALIST NO. 57 (James Madison).
[38] *Id.*
[39] THE FEDERALIST NO. 58 (James Madison).
[40] THE FEDERALIST NO. 46 (James Madison).

that governmental outputs must reflect popular preferences. "Public opinion sets bounds to every government . . . ."[41] "[P]ublic opinion must be obeyed by the government . . . ."[42] The government's "will must be made subordinate to, or rather the same with, the will of the community."[43] True, people's views are sometimes open to persuasion. "[W]here not being fixed," public opinion "may be influenced by the government."[44] But once people have considered an issue and made up their minds, the government must heed their judgment. Based on these essays, Larry Kramer contends that "Madison's first principle" is that "public opinion not only would, but *should* control the course of government."[45] Colleen Sheehan reaches the same verdict: Madison's "central philosophical idea" is "the fundamental authority of the people and the sovereignty of public opinion in free government."[46]

Jumping ahead to Reconstruction, remember my argument that the Privileges or Immunities Clause of the Fourteenth Amendment redeems the aligning promises of Article I, Section 2 and the Guarantee Clause. Bingham, the architect of the Fourteenth Amendment, also advances this position.[47] Article I, Section 2 is an "express guarantee" that "the majority of the . . . citizens . . . in each State . . . shall forever exercise the political power of the State."[48] Likewise, "a republican form of government" is one that respects the "absolute, unquestioned, unchallenged right of a majority of American . . . citizens . . . within [a State] to control its entire political power, both State and national."[49] According to Bingham, the Privileges or Immunities Clause enforces these commitments to majoritarian alignment in the original Constitution. "[T]his principle [of majority rule] has been affirmed . . . in the solemn ratification of [the Fourteenth Amendment] . . . ."[50] The Privileges or Immunities Clause "conform[s] exactly to the spirit of the Constitution" by enabling "the majority of . . . citizens in every State . . . to control . . . the future power of their States and the future power of the Republic."[51]

---

[41]   14 THE PAPERS OF JAMES MADISON 170 (Robert A. Rutland et al. eds., 1983).

[42]   *Id.*

[43]   *Id.* at 207.

[44]   *Id.* at 170.

[45]   Larry D. Kramer, *"The Interest of the Man": James Madison, Popular Constitutionalism, and the Theory of Deliberative Democracy,* 41 VAL. U. L. REV. 697, 718 (2006).

[46]   SHEEHAN, *supra* note 11, at 9; *see also generally* Colleen A. Sheehan, *Madison v. Hamilton: The Battle Over Republicanism and the Role of Public Opinion,* 98 AM. POL. SCI. REV. 405 (2004). *But see generally* MICHAEL J. KLARMAN, THE FRAMERS' COUP: THE MAKING OF THE UNITED STATES CONSTITUTION (2016) (portraying Madison and other constitutional drafters in much less democratic terms).

[47]   For another scholar noting this stance of Bingham's, see Earl A. Maltz, *The Concept of Equal Protection of the Laws—A Historical Inquiry,* 22 SAN DIEGO L. REV. 499, 521 (1985).

[48]   CONG. GLOBE, 39TH CONG., 1ST SESS. 431 (1866).

[49]   CONG. GLOBE, 39TH CONG., 2ND SESS. 450 (1867).

[50]   *Id.*

[51]   CONG. GLOBE, 39TH CONG., 1ST SESS. 430 (1866).

Bingham further refutes the claim, still heard today,[52] that Section 1 of the Fourteenth Amendment doesn't protect "political" rights like voting. The Privileges or Immunities Clause doesn't protect the franchise *directly* since the original Constitution doesn't identify voting, *in general*, as a right of American citizens. But when franchise restrictions threaten the majority rule recognized by Article I, Section 2 and the Guarantee Clause, the Privileges or Immunities Clause absolutely applies. As Bingham puts it, under Section 1 of the Fourteenth Amendment, "suffrage *is* subjected to congressional law" when "the right in the people of each State to a republican government and to choose their Representatives in Congress" is undermined.[53] "[B]y this amendment a remedy might be given directly" when politicians "change a State government from a republican to a despotic government and thereby deny suffrage to the people."[54] Put differently, the Privileges or Immunities Clause isn't a plenary grant of federal power over elections. But it does authorize Congress and the courts to intervene against majoritarian misalignment in the states.

Let me reiterate that this evidence doesn't definitively establish alignment as a constitutional value. Madison, Bingham, and other constitutional drafters are intellectually complex, even contradictory. So are the Constitution and its amendments. These inconsistent materials would pose a grave problem if my thesis was that federal constitutional law *commands* the recognition of alignment. But, to be clear, that's not my argument. My more modest claim, rather, is that federal constitutional law *permits* the recognition of alignment. I think the constitutional provisions I've discussed, along with the writings I've excerpted from Madison and Bingham, amply support this more limited proposition. As I show next, further backing for alignment as a plausible constitutional principle comes from Supreme Court precedent.

Precedent

Owing to the number of relevant Court decisions, an organizational scheme is essential. I first sort cases by category: voting, redistricting, political parties, and campaign finance. The reason for this order is that it lets me address alignment initially as a sword and then as a shield. In the Court's doctrine, misalignment is sometimes a basis for striking down voting restrictions and district plans.

---

[52] *See, e.g.,* John Harrison, *Reconstructing the Privileges or Immunities Clause*, 101 YALE L.J. 1385, 1455 (1992) ("[P]rivileges or immunities as understood in 1866 probably did not include political rights.").

[53] CONG. GLOBE, 39TH CONG., 1ST SESS. 2542 (1866) (emphasis added).

[54] *Id.; see also, e.g.,* van Alstyne, *supra* note 12, at 41 (noting Bingham's belief that "Congress derived some authority from [the Privileges or Immunities Clause] to invalidate state suffrage disqualifications that violated a republican form of government").

Conversely, alignment is sometimes a rationale for upholding regulations of political parties and money in politics. I next sort cases by year. As will become evident, the modern Court can be divided, roughly but still usefully, into two eras. The Warren Court took alignment quite seriously, in a few cases even treating it as the lodestar of its election law jurisprudence. In contrast, reliance on alignment by subsequent Courts has been more sporadic (though still noteworthy).

A few more preliminaries: First, I only describe the role of alignment in the Court's election law cases. Alignment does appear in other areas, such as First Amendment law, where its promotion is a common justification for protecting political speech.[55] But I bracket those other contexts for now because my primary aim in this book is to orient election law—not all of public law—around alignment.[56] Second, in the interest of space, I focus on major decisions by Court majorities (or, occasionally, pluralities). I relegate less significant rulings, as well as opinions by individual Justices, to the footnotes. Landmark Court decisions, it goes without saying, enjoy a privileged position in argument based on precedent. Third, my commentary in this chapter is restricted to Court cases that support the recognition of alignment as a constitutional principle. As I noted at the outset, I grapple with the anti-alignment record of the Roberts Court in Chapter 11. Lastly, I always flag the type of alignment to which the Court refers. I did so above in my analysis of constitutional text and drafters' intent, and I continue to be attentive to the taxonomy of alignment below.

With that throat clearing out of the way, a suitable entry point into the doctrine is the Warren Court's 1965 decision in *Carrington v. Rash*.[57] The Texas Constitution used to prohibit members of the military from voting in any elections in the state.[58] The Court invalidated this provision partly because of how it threatened to skew policy outcomes away from the preferences of all Texas residents (including military members). The Court observed that military members might "oppose local police administration or teaching [certain] policies in local schools."[59] If military members were sufficiently numerous and able to vote, "[l]ocal bond issues [might thus] fail, and property taxes [stay] at low levels."[60] But the opposite laws might be adopted as long as military members were disenfranchised, causing policy misalignment with at least their views and possibly those of a majority of residents. Such "'fencing out' from the franchise

---

[55] *See, e.g.*, Stromberg v. California, 283 U.S. 359, 369 (1931) ("The maintenance of the opportunity for free political discussion [serves] the end that government may be responsive to the will of the people....").

[56] I return to the Court's nonelectoral references to alignment in Chapter 10, where I explore the promotion of alignment through nonelectoral means.

[57] 380 U.S. 89 (1965).

[58] *See id.* at 89.

[59] *Id.* at 93.

[60] *Id.*

a sector of the population because of the way they may vote," the Court held, "is constitutionally impermissible."[61] It risks biasing policy outcomes against the preferences of the excluded individuals.

The Warren Court's 1969 decision in *Kramer v. Union Free School District No. 15*[62]—one of the last opinions written by the great Chief Justice—brought alignment even deeper into the Court's voting jurisprudence. A New York law allowed only parents and property owners to vote in school district elections.[63] This law, the Court announced, had to be subjected to strict scrutiny because its disenfranchisement of certain residents could lead to representational misalignment. Normally, the Court explained, a "presumption of constitutionality" is appropriate thanks to the "assumption that the institutions of state government are structured so as to represent fairly all the people."[64] But when the presence of representational alignment is disputed—"when the challenge to the statute is in effect a challenge of this basic assumption"—then "the assumption can no longer serve as the basis for presuming constitutionality."[65] Strict scrutiny therefore applies when voting restrictions are alleged to yield distorted representation.

As I pointed out in Chapter 1, *Kramer*'s rule of strict scrutiny for voting limits didn't stick. Instead, courts now evaluate these laws using the doctrine of sliding-scale scrutiny, under which the intensity of judicial review varies in tandem with the severity of the voting burden. *Kramer* was also the last time a Court majority expounded about alignment in a case involving the right to vote.[66] Subsequent Court decisions about voting restrictions—even decisions striking down restrictions—have emphasized the policies' effects on individual citizens, not their potential misaligning impact. However, as soon as we broaden our perspective beyond the voting context, *Kramer* (and *Carrington*) appear less unusual. In the redistricting realm, in particular, both the Warren Court and its successors grounded their interventions in the prevention of misalignment.

The Warren Court first referred obliquely to alignment in the 1963 case of *Gray v. Sanders*.[67] Georgia used a county unit system for the nominations of statewide officeholders. Under this system, the candidate who won each county

---

[61] *Id.* at 94.

[62] 395 U.S. 621 (1969).

[63] *See id.* at 622.

[64] *Id.* at 628.

[65] *Id.*

[66] For a recent (albeit implicit) reference to alignment by a dissenter in a voting case, see *Democratic Nat'l Comm. v. Wis. St. Legis.*, 141 S. Ct. 28, 43 (2020) (Kagan, J., dissenting) (arguing for heightened scrutiny of voting restrictions "whenever suppressing votes benefits the lawmakers who make the rules").

[67] 372 U.S. 368 (1963). Note that *Gray* wasn't technically a redistricting case even though it's typically discussed along with the Warren Court's reapportionment decisions. A year before *Gray*, Justice Clark commented on the majoritarian misalignment that malapportionment can cause. Thanks to Tennessee's grossly malapportioned state legislative map, "[t]he majority of the voters have been caught up in a legislative strait jacket." Baker v. Carr, 369 U.S. 186, 259 (1962) (Clark, J., concurring).

received all the county's nominating votes, which were equal to double the county's state house members.[68] In this era, (just) prior to the reapportionment revolution, rural Georgia counties were hugely overrepresented in the state legislature relative to urban ones.[69] The county unit system thus resulted in severe jurisdiction-wide misalignment in favor of rural areas and to the detriment of cities. As the Court put it, the system "weights the rural vote more heavily than the urban vote."[70] "[O]ne person [is] given twice or 10 times the voting power of another person ... merely because he lives in a rural area ...."[71] This pro-rural skew helps explain why the Court invalidated the county unit system.

Gray's nod to alignment turned into a vigorous embrace in the 1964 case of Reynolds v. Sims,[72] the most important of the Warren Court's malapportionment decisions. The Court held in Reynolds that the one-person, one-vote rule applies to state legislative districts, requiring them to have roughly the same population. How come? Among other reasons, because malapportionment can cause jurisdiction-wide majoritarian misalignment—a majority of legislators elected by a minority of voters. "Logically, in a society grounded on representative government ... a majority of the people of a State [should] elect a majority of that State's legislators."[73] As a result of majoritarianism, state legislatures "should be bodies which are collectively responsive to," that is, aligned with, "the popular will."[74] However, malapportionment can lead to "minority control of state legislative bodies."[75] When some districts are overpopulated and others are underpopulated, the consequence can be "frustration of the majority will through minority veto,"[76] or even "a minority stranglehold on the State Legislature."[77] The Court's action was necessary to avoid such misalignment.[78]

Obviously, countermajoritarian outcomes can be caused by not just malapportionment but also partisan gerrymandering. Districts that crack and pack a targeted party's supporters can prevent that party's candidates from winning a legislative majority even if they command majority support

[68] See Gray, 372 U.S. at 370–71.
[69] See id. at 371–73.
[70] Id. at 379.
[71] Id.
[72] 377 U.S. 533 (1964).
[73] Id. at 565.
[74] Id.
[75] Id.
[76] Id. at 576.
[77] Id. at 570.
[78] Even one of the Warren Court's skeptics about judicial intervention agreed that malapportionment is unconstitutional where it "permit[s] the systematic frustration of the will of a majority of the electorate of the State." Lucas v. Forty-Fourth Gen. Assembly of State of Colo., 377 U.S. 713, 753–54 (1964) (Stewart, J., dissenting); cf. Whitcomb v. Chavis, 403 U.S. 124, 167 (1971) (opinion of Harlan, J.) (observing that the Warren Court's malapportionment decisions "can best be understood ... as reflections of deep personal commitments by some members of the Court to the principles of pure majoritarian democracy").

from the electorate. Appreciating this possibility, in the 1986 case of *Davis v. Bandemer*,[79] a plurality of the Court made jurisdiction-wide, majoritarian, partisan misalignment an element of the new cause of action it created for partisan gerrymandering. "In this context . . . a finding of unconstitutionality must be supported by evidence of continued frustration of the will of a majority of the voters."[80] In other words, a district plan must "consign the [victimized party] to a minority status."[81] This "preference" that "majorities are not consigned to minority status," the plurality continued, is hardly new.[82] Rather, it's an "extrapolation from our general majoritarian ethic . . . recognized in *Reynolds*."[83]

Today, *Bandemer* represents a road (mostly[84]) not taken. In the decades after the decision, no federal court ultimately found in favor of a partisan gerrymandering plaintiff. And in 2019, the Court officially overruled *Bandemer*, holding that partisan gerrymandering claims are nonjusticiable.[85] Nevertheless, the idea that partisan gerrymanders are highly misaligning—and should be struck down for that reason—has continued to appear in dissenting Justices' opinions, some of which I quote below the line.[86] Unlike a majority of the Court, these Justices have remained committed to using misalignment as a sword to curb redistricting abuses.

Now shift your attention from swords to shields, and from redistricting to political parties. On a few occasions, the Court has recognized a state interest in restricting minor party candidates' access to the ballot in order to prevent these candidates from playing the role of "spoiler." A spoiler is a minor party candidate running in an election held under a plurality winner rule[87] who receives enough votes not to prevail but rather to change what the election's outcome would have been had only two candidates competed.[88] When a minor party candidate is a

---

[79] 478 U.S. 109 (1986).

[80] *Id.* at 133 (plurality opinion).

[81] *Id.* at 135.

[82] *Id.* at 125 n.9.

[83] *Id.*

[84] As I discuss below, some *state* courts have gone down this road, nullifying partisan gerrymanders based on state constitutional provisions.

[85] *See* Rucho v. Common Cause, 139 S. Ct. 2484 (2019).

[86] *See, e.g., Rucho*, 139 S. Ct. at 2512 (Kagan, J., dissenting) (thanks to gerrymandering, "a party in office at the right time can entrench itself there for a decade or more, no matter what the voters would prefer"); Gill v. Whitford, 138 S. Ct. 1916, 1940 (2018) (Kagan, J., concurring) (through gerrymandering, "legislators can entrench themselves in office despite the people's will"); League of United Latin Am. Citizens v. Perry, 548 U.S. 399, 466–67 (2006) (Stevens, J., concurring in part and dissenting in part) (discussing a quantitative measure of collective partisan misalignment); Vieth v. Jubelirer, 541 U.S. 267, 361 (2004) (Breyer, J., dissenting) ("[G]errymandering that so entrenches a minority party in power violates basic democratic norms and lacks countervailing justification.").

[87] Other election rules, like ranked-choice voting, eliminate the possibility of spoilers—as well as any state interest in restricting minor party ballot access to prevent spoilers.

[88] *See, e.g.,* Michael C. Herron & Jeffrey B. Lewis, *Did Ralph Nader Spoil Al Gore's Presidential Bid? A Ballot-Level Study of Green and Reform Party Voters in the 2000 Presidential Election*, 2 Q.J. POL. SCI. 205, 206 (2007).

spoiler, majoritarian misalignment ensues. The choice of a majority of voters, had they been allowed to pick between just two candidates, fails to win office.

The Warren Court acknowledged a state interest in avoiding spoilers in the 1968 case of *Williams v. Rhodes*.[89] "[T]he State does have an interest," the Court declared, "in attempting to see that the election winner be the choice of a majority of its voters."[90] It would be concerning "if three or more parties [were] on the ballot . . . and the runner-up might have been preferred to the plurality winner by a majority of the voters."[91] The Court confirmed majoritarian alignment as an available justification for ballot access limits in the 1972 case of *Bullock v. Carter*.[92] "[T]he State understandably and properly seeks to . . . assure that the winner is the choice of a majority . . . of those voting . . . ."[93] True, the Court rejected the specific policies challenged in *Williams* and in *Bullock* because of their stringency and lack of necessity. In *Bullock*, in particular, Texas already required a runoff election in the event that no candidate cleared the 50 percent threshold, rendering superfluous the state's hefty filing fee as a means of preventing spoilers.[94] Still, *Williams* and *Bullock* at least establish that less onerous and better tailored ballot access restrictions *could* be upheld based on their aligning effects.

Another party regulation context in which individual Justices (though not a Court majority) have endorsed alignment as a state interest is the selection of primary type. States that use primary elections to determine general election nominees (i.e., almost all states) must decide what *kind* of primary to hold: one open to all voters, or to voters registered with a given party and independents, or just to voters registered with a given party. A recurring fact pattern in litigation is that a state chooses a more open primary and a party then sues because it would prefer a more restricted primary. In turn, a common refrain among individual Justices, when these cases reach the Court, is that the more open primary should be upheld because it promotes representational alignment. A candidate who prevails in a primary whose voters more closely resemble the general electorate, the argument goes, is more likely to hold views that resonate with voters as a whole. I cite several Justices' claims to this effect below the line.[95]

---

[89] 393 U.S. 23 (1968).
[90] *Id.* at 32.
[91] *Id.*
[92] 405 U.S. 134 (1972).
[93] *Id.* at 145.
[94] *See id.* at 145 n.22.
[95] *See, e.g.,* Cal. Democratic Party v. Jones, 530 U.S. 567, 600 (2000) (Stevens, J., dissenting) (deeming "substantial, indeed compelling" California's justification for its blanket primary, which was "fostering democratic government by increasing the representativeness of elected officials" (internal quotation marks omitted)); Democratic Party of U.S. v. Wisconsin ex rel. La Follette, 450 U.S. 107, 133 (1981) (Powell, J., dissenting) ("By attracting participation by relatively independent-minded voters, [Wisconsin's open primary] arguably may enlarge the support for a party at the general election."); *cf.* Tashjian v. Republican Party of Conn., 479 U.S. 208, 221 (1986) (ruling in favor

If these Justices' remarks are underwhelming as a precedential matter, the statements of the full Court about alignment, in the campaign finance arena, are more impressive. Time and again, the Court has said that the prevention of representational misalignment is a valid rationale for limits on money in politics. As usual, the Warren Court was the pioneer. In the 1957 case of *United States v. Automobile Workers*,[96] the Court observed that the purpose of the federal prohibition on corporate campaign expenditures was "to prevent . . . the great aggregations of wealth from using their corporate funds . . . to send members of the legislature . . . to vote for their protection and the advancement of their interests as against those of the public."[97] The law's purpose, in other words, was to avoid misalignment in favor of powerful corporations. The Court added that, when corporations spend heavily on politics, they "receive consideration by the beneficiaries . . . which not infrequently is harmful to the general public interest."[98] Put another way, corporations obtain governmental activity that reflects their preferences but not those of the people.

Automobile Workers' notion of alignment as a justification for campaign finance restrictions occasionally resurfaced in individual Justices' opinions in the decades after the decision.[99] This idea came to full flower, though, in two holdings of the Court in the early 2000s. First, in the 2000 case of *Nixon v. Shrink Missouri Government PAC*,[100] the Court described the problem that individual contribution limits are meant to solve as the "broader threat from politicians too compliant with the wishes of large contributors."[101] Politicians too compliant with the wishes of contributors, of course, are not compliant enough with those of voters. The Court also noted that outsized checks can foster the "cynical assumption that large donors call the tune."[102] This is a point about the appearance rather than the reality of pro-donor bias, but it sounds in a similar register.

Second, in the 2003 case of *McConnell v. FEC*,[103] the Court used language even more evocative of alignment to uphold the Bipartisan Campaign Reform Act's soft money ban.[104] The Court described how soft money donors received special

---

of a party challenging a *closed* primary because the *open* primary preferred by the party would "produce the candidate and platform most likely to achieve that goal" of "most effectively appeal[ing] to the independent voter").

[96] 352 U.S. 567 (1957).
[97] *Id.* at 571 (internal quotation marks omitted).
[98] *Id.* at 576.
[99] *See, e.g.*, FEC v. Nat'l Conservative Pol. Action Comm., 470 U.S. 480, 497 (1985) (White, J., dissenting) ("The candidate may be forced to please the spenders rather than the voters, and the two groups are not identical.").
[100] 528 U.S. 377 (2000).
[101] *Id.* at 389.
[102] *Id.* at 390.
[103] 540 U.S. 93 (2003).
[104] "Soft money" refers to previously unregulated funds that were donated to political parties to pay for activities other than express advocacy for or against candidates. *See id.* at 122–24.

access to officeholders, which then metastasized into undue influence over their decisions. "Implicit . . . in the sale of access is the suggestion that money buys influence."[105] The Court further catalogued numerous cases in which soft money donors managed to thwart the passage of popular bills. "The evidence connects soft money to manipulations of the legislative calendar, leading to Congress' failure to enact, among other things, generic drug legislation, tort reform, and tobacco legislation."[106] And in its clearest articulation of alignment as a weighty interest, the Court announced, "Just as troubling to a functioning democracy . . . is the danger that officeholders will decide issues not on . . . the desires of their constituencies, but according to the wishes of those who have made large financial contributions valued by the officeholder."[107] This prioritization of donors' over constituents' preferences is archetypal misalignment.

McConnell was decided shortly before John Roberts's elevation to the Court. Under his leadership, as I discuss in Chapter 11, the Court has retreated from *McConnell*'s reasoning and reversed some of its rulings.[108] However, even Chief Justice Roberts once authored a campaign finance opinion that can fairly be read as a tribute to alignment. "For the past 40 years," he wrote for a plurality in the 2014 case of *McCutcheon v. FEC*,[109] "our campaign finance jurisprudence has focused on the need to [avoid] compromising *the political responsiveness* at the heart of the democratic process."[110] Such responsiveness, the plurality went on, is required by democratic theory. "As Edmund Burke explained . . . a representative owes constituents . . . judgment informed by the strictest union, the closest correspondence, and the most unreserved communication with his constituents."[111] Summing up its views, the plurality concluded, "Representatives are not to follow constituent orders, but can be expected to be cognizant of *and responsive to* those concerns."[112] "*Such responsiveness*"—representational alignment in my terminology—"is key to the very concept of self-governance through elected officials."[113]

---

[105] *Id.* at 154.
[106] *Id.* at 150.
[107] *Id.* at 153.
[108] In this era, consequently, the torch of alignment has been carried mainly by campaign finance dissenters. *See, e.g.,* Ariz. Free Enter. Club's Freedom Club PAC v. Bennett, 564 U.S. 721, 757 (2011) (Kagan, J., dissenting) ("If an officeholder owes his election to wealthy contributors, he may act for their benefit alone, rather than on behalf of all the people."); Citizens United v. FEC, 558 U.S. 310, 455 (2010) (Stevens, J., dissenting) ("[C]orporations with large war chests to deploy on electioneering . . . find democratically elected bodies becoming much more attuned to their interests."); FEC v. Wis. Right to Life, Inc., 551 U.S. 449, 507–508 (2007) (Souter, J., dissenting) ("[T]he purchase of influence . . . threaten[s] . . . the responsiveness of its law to the interests of citizens").
[109] 572 U.S. 185 (2014) (plurality opinion).
[110] *Id.* at 227 (emphasis added).
[111] *Id.* (internal quotation marks omitted).
[112] *Id.* (emphasis added).
[113] *Id.* (emphasis added).

Before you can object, let me jump in with some caveats. As to *McCutcheon*, Chief Justice Roberts may have had in mind officeholders' responsiveness to *donors*, not to *constituents* (though that certainly isn't what he said). In that case, the Court also nullified the aggregate federal limits on campaign contributions despite their likely aligning effects. More generally, alignment plainly isn't the dominant theme of the Court's election law jurisprudence. That distinction, as I stressed in Chapter 1, unquestionably belongs to the balancing of individual rights against countervailing state interests. And *McCutcheon* aside, the Roberts Court has come closer to categorically rejecting alignment than to heeding its prescriptions. In recent years, as I lament in Chapter 11, the theme of alignment has quieted to little more than a whisper.

A whisper, though, is still a sound. It's still capable of being heard, repeated, and, one day, amplified into a song. That's my ultimate point about alignment. Switching metaphors, it's not the most salient strand in the tapestry of the Court's election law doctrine. But it *is* undeniably a strand. A future weaver could therefore notice it, approve of it, and begin using it in more stitches and knots. True, this approach would be *different* from what came before. But it would still be *true* to the earlier work. It would rely on the same doctrinal threads, just braided into a new combination.

State Constitutional Law

What if there was a body of law that already championed alignment? That is, what if there was an area that didn't require a future weaver to alter the legal tapestry because alignment was already a highly salient strand? Perhaps surprisingly, there is such an area: state constitutional law. The usual modes of constitutional interpretation—text, history, precedent, and so on—indicate that alignment is a vital, arguably *the* vital, principle of state constitutional law. In this domain, then, the judicial recognition of alignment wouldn't represent a merely acceptable reading of ordinary legal sources. Rather, it could well be their *best* reading.

Jessica Bulman-Pozen and Miriam Seifter make this argument at length in a recent article. They contend that state constitutions exhibit "a powerful democratic commitment, a composite of constitutional text, history, and structure [they] term the *democracy principle* as a shorthand."[114] This democracy

---

[114] Jessica Bulman-Pozen & Miriam Seifter, *The Democracy Principle in State Constitutions*, 119 MICH. L. REV. 859, 862 (2021). For other scholars making similar claims, see Daniel J. Elazar, *The Principles and Traditions Underlying State Constitutions*, PUBLIUS (Winter 1982) 11, 12 (noting state constitutions' "emphasis on direct, continuing consent of political majorities"), and G. Alan Tarr, *For the People: Direct Democracy in the State Constitutional Tradition*, in DEMOCRACY: HOW DIRECT?

principle, in turn, is based on three pillars. "Popular sovereignty" is the first one, the idea that "all government power resides in the people," who can exercise their authority through elections for representatives, direct democracy, and even the revision or replacement of their state constitution.[115] The second pillar is majority rule. "[S]tate constitutions treat the unmediated majority as the best approximation of the people and indicate that the preference of the majority is to prevail in the face of political disagreement."[116] And the third component of the democracy principle is political equality. "These constitutions propose that all members of the political community share in the power to influence government and further seek to foreclose forms of special treatment by government . . . ."[117]

In Bulman-Pozen and Seifter's view, popular sovereignty, majority rule, and political equality amount to a model of democracy. I'd add that these concepts are closely linked to alignment. Popular sovereignty is the key to alignment's normative appeal. It's because *the people* rule that governmental outputs should embody *their* preferences—not those of the wealthy, the well born, or any other group. Similarly, majority rule is synonymous with majoritarian alignment. When a popular majority prevails in an election, or with respect to a policy, the views of the median person are necessarily heeded.[118] And at least within a given district or jurisdiction, political equality helps justify majority rule.[119] As I observed in Chapter 2, the position that minimizes the sum of the ideological distances between all people's preferences and a governmental output is the median position. In other words, the most equal possible treatment of all people requires the adoption of the one stance that a majority would favor over any other.

To avoid retreading too much of Bulman-Pozen and Seifter's ground, let me highlight just a few of the state constitutional provisions and judicial precedents they cite in support of the democracy principle (which is to say alignment). Almost all state constitutions proclaim that the people are sovereign and the source of governmental power.[120] "All power resid[es] originally in the people," states the constitution of my home state, Massachusetts, for example, "and [is]

87, 89 (Elliott Abrams ed., 2002) (observing that the primary threat to democracy contemplated by state constitutions is "minority faction—power wielded by the wealthy or well-connected few").

[115] Bulman-Pozen & Seifter, *supra* note 114, at 864.
[116] *Id.* at 864.
[117] *Id.*
[118] More precisely, the views of the median person are necessarily heeded when there are *two* candidate or policy choices and a popular majority prevails. The story becomes more complex with multiple choices.
[119] *Across* multiple districts or jurisdictions, collective alignment (which is also tied to political equality) may diverge from majoritarian alignment. *See generally* Matt Golder & Jacek Stramski, *Ideological Congruence and Electoral Institutions*, 54 AM. J. POL. SCI. 90 (2010).
[120] *See* Bulman-Pozen & Seifter, *supra* note 114, at 881.

derived from them."[121] State constitutions also endorse majority rule for most governmental actions.[122] In Massachusetts, that's the decision-making procedure for, among other things, the election of legislators[123] and executive officers,[124] the enactment of legislation,[125] and the amendment of the state constitution.[126] State constitutions further embrace political equality and disavow disparities in political influence.[127] "All men are born free and equal," avers the first article of the Massachusetts Constitution.[128] Representation in the state legislature is "founded upon the principle of equality."[129] In general, "[g]overnment is instituted for the common good"—"not for the profit, honor, or private interest of any one man, family, or class of men."[130]

These provisions refer almost verbatim to the pillars of Bulman-Pozen and Seifter's democracy principle. Other provisions go in slightly different directions but are still entirely consistent with both the democracy principle and alignment. For instance, all state constitutions affirmatively confer the right to vote.[131] As I argued above, the achievement of alignment is one (if not the only) reason to grant the franchise.[132] A narrow majority of state constitutions also stipulate that elections must be "free," "free and equal," or "free and open."[133] Less restricted, more egalitarian elections are better tools for identifying the will of the electorate, the input that governmental outputs must match to attain alignment. Another half or so of state constitutions provide for voter initiatives.[134] When voters pass laws or amend constitutions themselves, without the intercession of their representatives, congruence between enacted policies and voters' preferences is virtually assured. And a large minority of state constitutions allow voters to recall officeholders before their terms are up.[135] An intuitive (if not exclusive) basis for recalling politicians is their disregard for—their misalignment with—public opinion.

Turning to precedent, I'll limit my discussion to a pair of recent state court decisions striking down partisan gerrymanders on state constitutional grounds.

---

[121] MASS. CONST. pt. I, art. V.
[122] See Bulman-Pozen & Seifter, *supra* note 114, at 887.
[123] See MASS. CONST. pt. II, ch. I, § II, art. IV.
[124] See id. pt. II, ch. II, § I, art. III.
[125] See id. pt. II, ch. I, § I, art. II.
[126] See id. amend. art. IX (requiring majority support from state senators and voters but two-thirds support from state house members).
[127] See Bulman-Pozen & Seifter, *supra* note 114, at 890.
[128] MASS. CONST. pt. I, art. I.
[129] Id. pt. II, ch. I, § III, art. I.
[130] Id. pt. I, art. VII.
[131] See Bulman-Pozen & Seifter, *supra* note 114, at 870; *see also* Joshua A. Douglas, *The Right to Vote Under State Constitutions*, 67 VAND. L. REV. 89, 144–49 (2014).
[132] See *supra* notes 19–20 and accompanying text.
[133] See Bulman-Pozen & Seifter, *supra* note 114, at 871.
[134] See id. at 876.
[135] See id. at 878.

Partisan gerrymandering is conspicuous in that its misaligning impact is palpable yet federal courts have utterly failed to thwart it. State courts, on the other hand, haven't been so feckless. Relying on what Bulman-Pozen and Seifter would call the democracy principle, and I'd term alignment, they've nullified extreme gerrymanders precisely because of their pernicious effects. Here's how the Supreme Court of Pennsylvania explained its invalidation of a highly biased congressional plan. The Pennsylvania Constitution is meant to "form a government more directly responsive to the needs of the people."[136] Under that charter, "each voter [should] have an equally effective power to select the representative of his or her choice."[137] Gerrymandering, however, frustrates these democratic and aligning objectives. It "thwart[s] the will of the people."[138] It "artificially entrench[es] representative power."[139] Because "all voters do not have an equal opportunity to translate their votes into representation," the practice represents "the antithesis of a healthy representative democracy."[140]

The North Carolina Supreme Court justified its intervention against severely skewed congressional and state legislative plans in analogous terms. Under the North Carolina Constitution, "this is a government . . . founded upon the will of the people, and in which the will of the people . . . must control."[141] This is because the state charter embraces "the core democratic principle," namely, "the revolutionary faith in popular sovereignty."[142] But "[i]f through [gerrymandering] the ruling party chokes off the channels of political change on an unequal basis, then government ceases to derive its power from the people."[143] In that case, "elections are not free and do not serve to effectively ascertain the will of the people."[144] In Bulman-Pozen and Seifter's terminology, the court thus held that the plans violated the democracy principle recognized by the North Carolina Constitution. In my lexicon, the court applied the state constitutional value of alignment, striking down the plans because of their misaligning impact.

As promising as the Pennsylvania and North Carolina rulings were, they didn't incorporate alignment into a particular doctrinal framework. They clearly *invoked* alignment and acknowledged its legal significance. But they didn't lay out a doctrinal approach that courts could use in subsequent cases to determine if electoral practices are impermissibly misaligning. This point holds for all of

---

[136] League of Women Voters v. Commonwealth, 178 A.3d 737, 806 (Pa. 2018).

[137] *Id.* at 809.

[138] *Id.* at 806.

[139] *Id.* at 814.

[140] *Id.*

[141] Harper v. Hall, 868 S.E.2d 499, 539 (N.C. 2022), *overruled in later appeal*, 886 S.E.2d 393 (N.C. 2023) (cleaned up).

[142] *Id.* at 538 (internal quotation marks omitted).

[143] *Id.* at 539 (internal quotation marks omitted).

[144] *Id.* at 542.

state constitutional law.[145] Alignment is one of its foundational tenets, not just in Pennsylvania and North Carolina but throughout the country. But state constitutional law has not yet developed rules for evaluating either offensive claims that policies are misaligning or defensive claims, in cases brought on other grounds, that policies actually align. Next, I consider how state or federal constitutional law (the type of constitution is irrelevant for present purposes) might do so.

Doctrinal Implementation

Starting with offensive claims—alignment as a sword—an aggressive approach would be for courts to hold that sufficiently misaligning electoral policies are categorically or presumptively unlawful.[146] Chapter 3 made clear that alignment can generally be measured empirically. A high enough level of misalignment, if causally linked to a particular measure, could therefore be enough to strike down that measure, or at least to create a presumption of its illegality. I'm unaware of any existing effects-based doctrines that automatically invalidate laws whose impact exceeds a certain threshold. Under the one-person, one-vote rule, though, district plans with sufficiently high population deviations (10 percent at the state legislative level,[147] 0 percent at the congressional level[148]) are presumptively unconstitutional. These plans can be upheld only if their population deviations are necessary to achieve a compelling state interest—that is, if their population deviations can survive strict scrutiny. A high-profile precedent thus exists for making sufficient misalignment a presumptive, if not a categorical, condition for a legal violation.

My aim here isn't definitively to endorse or reject any doctrinal option. Still, I worry that the one-person, one-vote rule (let alone an across-the-board ban on sufficiently misaligning practices) is too draconian a model. One person, one vote is frequently (and fairly) criticized for prioritizing population equality over all the other legitimate redistricting goals that jurisdictions might want to achieve.[149] Jurisdictions can't achieve those other goals unless they can prove

---

[145] It also holds for prior work by structuralist election law scholars: They haven't clearly laid out how they think courts should incorporate competition or participation into election law doctrine. *See, e.g.,* Yasmin Dawood, *The Antidomination Model and the Judicial Oversight of Democracy,* 96 GEO. L.J. 1411, 1424 (2008) ("[T]he competition model does not provide much guidance on how it would be operationalized in practice. What exactly would courts do in their opinions were they to implement a structural solution, and which standards would they employ?").

[146] An even blunter strategy would be to strike down *all* misaligning practices, no matter how slight their misaligning impact.

[147] *See* White v. Register, 412 U.S. 755, 764 (1973).

[148] *See* Kirkpatrick v. Preisler, 394 U.S. 526, 530–32 (1969).

[149] I'm one of these critics. *See* Nicholas O. Stephanopoulos, *Our Electoral Exceptionalism,* 80 U. CHI. L. REV. 769, 808–10 (2013) (discussing the stringency of the American one-person, one-vote rule in comparative perspective).

that the goals' attainment *requires* a level of population inequality above the constitutional floor—a very high hurdle. A doctrine that made sufficient misalignment presumptively unlawful would be vulnerable to the same objection. Recall my description in Chapter 2 of all the values beyond alignment that electoral systems may hope to realize: competition, participation, deliberation, minority representation, freedom to speak and associate, and so on. Electoral systems wouldn't be able to further those values if doing so gave rise to misalignment above the legal threshold, unless that misalignment was necessary to the values' advancement. That necessity, in turn, would be very difficult to demonstrate in most cases. Strict scrutiny is called strict for a reason.

If not as a categorical or presumptive condition of illegality, how else could alignment be implemented (as a sword)? Another possibility is a variant of the sliding-scale scrutiny that already applies to most election law claims. Remember that, under this doctrine, the initial issue is how severely the challenged policy burdens a right like speaking or associating. The intensity of judicial review then varies in tandem with the severity of the burden. To fit this model to alignment, the first question would become *how misaligning* the disputed practice is. A highly misaligning practice would then be subject to strict scrutiny, a moderately misaligning practice to intermediate scrutiny, and so on. Unlike strict scrutiny for all sufficiently misaligning laws, this approach wouldn't always rank alignment above other democratic values. It *would* do so when misalignment is extreme—when the principle that governmental outputs should reflect popular preferences is most threatened. In other circumstances, though, this approach would allow alignment to be balanced against other valid objectives. Considerable misalignment could sometimes be excused if it furthered another proper end.

Don't structuralist election law scholars (like me) object to sliding-scale scrutiny because it ignores structural democratic values? Yes, we do. But this concern obviously doesn't apply to the revised version of sliding-scale scrutiny I just outlined. If the first stage of the analysis was how misaligning a challenged policy is—not how severely it burdens some individual right—then the structural democratic value of alignment wouldn't be overlooked. It would be front and center, rather, the critical determinant of how closely courts would scrutinize a disputed practice. Put another way, there's no intrinsic reason why sliding-scale scrutiny can't accommodate alignment or other comparable principles. It's a flexible doctrine that can calibrate the intensity of judicial review on any basis, be it a burden on a right, a threat to a structural democratic value, or some other legal harm.[150]

---

[150] For other proposals seeking to extend sliding-scale scrutiny to new electoral contexts, see Nicholas O. Stephanopoulos, *The New Vote Dilution*, 96 N.Y.U. L. Rev. 1179, 1206–1209 (2021) (claims of vote dilution through election fraud), and Daniel P. Tokaji, *Gerrymandering and Association*, 59 Wm. & Mary L. Rev. 2159 (2018) (partisan gerrymandering claims).

One more option for operationalizing alignment (again as a sword) is a permutation of the burden-shifting framework that governs disparate impact claims under Title VII of the Civil Rights Act, the Fair Housing Act (FHA), and other civil rights laws.[151] Under this framework, the plaintiff must first prove that a particular policy causes a statistically and practically significant racial disparity. The burden then shifts to the defendant to show that the policy substantially advances an important interest. Lastly, the burden returns to the plaintiff to demonstrate that the defendant's interest could be equally furthered by another, less discriminatory measure. As with sliding-scale scrutiny, the adjustment that would incorporate alignment into the burden-shifting framework would apply to the doctrine's initial inquiry. That inquiry would become whether a particular practice causes statistically and practically significant *misalignment*. If so, the defendant would next have an opportunity to justify the misaligning practice, and if that justification was successful, the plaintiff would have a final chance to establish an equally effective, less misaligning alternative. Like the variant of sliding-scale scrutiny I introduced above, this approach would avoid exalting alignment above other values and enable it to be balanced against competing considerations.

It's worth noting here that disagreement persists over the crucial second step of the burden-shifting framework—the point at which the defendant tries to justify the challenged policy. Title VII uses the language of both strict scrutiny ("consistent with business *necessity*") and more relaxed review ("job *related* for the position in question").[152] The FHA formerly relied on strict scrutiny ("*necessary* to achieve . . . *substantial* . . . interests") but now employs a less rigorous standard ("*advances* a *valid* interest").[153] For its part, the Supreme Court has waffled between more[154] and less[155] demanding formulations of what the defendant must show. Unsurprisingly, if the framework's second step requires strict scrutiny, I'd find it less appealing. In that case, the second step would overvalue alignment (assuming it's misalignment that's now the crux of the first step) and underweight other objectives. Conversely, if the second step imposes something more like intermediate scrutiny, I'd deem it perfectly acceptable—a reasonable way of balancing alignment against other aims.

---

[151] For more on this framework, see Nicholas O. Stephanopoulos, *Disparate Impact, Unified Law*, 128 YALE L.J. 1566, 1596–1600 (2019).

[152] 42 U.S.C. § 2000e-2(k)(1)(A)(i) (2018) (emphasis added).

[153] The FHA's new formulation is codified at 24 C.F.R. § 100.500(c)(2), as previously was its old formulation.

[154] *See, e.g.*, Griggs v. Duke Power Co., 401 U.S. 424, 431 (1971) ("The touchstone is business necessity.").

[155] *See, e.g.*, Wards Cove Packing Co. v. Atonio, 490 U.S. 642, 659 (1989) ("[T]he dispositive issue is whether a challenged practice serves . . . the legitimate employment goals of the employer.").

Switching military devices, there's no need to amend existing doctrines to implement alignment as a shield. Most election law theories already permit a jurisdiction, when sued over an electoral practice, to assert a state interest that the practice allegedly promotes. That's what the second stage of sliding-scale scrutiny is all about: determining how strong a jurisdiction's proffered interest is and how well it's furthered by the policy at issue (with the requisite showings varying along with the intensity of judicial review). Conventional strict scrutiny, the rule that applies to district plans with population deviations above the constitutional floor as well as many campaign finance regulations, similarly asks whether a jurisdiction's interest is compelling and whether the disputed practice is narrowly tailored to achieve it. The Voting Rights Act, too, includes as a relevant factor the force and fit of a jurisdiction's rationale for a policy.[156]

In all these areas, then, a jurisdiction could argue that alignment is its interest. Alignment is what's served by its ballot access restriction, primary type, district plan, campaign finance limit, and so on. To validate this interest, courts wouldn't have to resort to any doctrinal creativity. They would simply have to agree that alignment is a weighty enough interest, when actually advanced by a practice, to justify some sacrifice of another legal value. This shouldn't be a heavy lift. Courts already recognize as sufficiently important interests the avoidance of administrative inconvenience,[157] the prevention of voter confusion,[158] the simplification of the ballot,[159] the dissemination of political information,[160] the assurance of political stability,[161] and many other goals. At the very least, alignment is as pressing a governmental objective as these already acknowledged interests. Quite plausibly, as a principle at the very core of what it means to be a democracy, alignment is *more* vital and so *more* deserving of the status of legitimate state interest that a jurisdiction may freely assert.

It should be evident that alignment as a shield would be more doctrinally familiar—less legally disruptive—than alignment as a sword. As a shield, alignment would be just one more available state interest, one more rationale a jurisdiction might (or might not) offer for a challenged policy. No legal theory would have to be modified to accommodate alignment in this form. Instead, alignment would slot neatly into the analysis of interests' weight and tailoring that most election law doctrines already prescribe. In contrast, alignment as a sword would

---

[156] *See, e.g.,* Brnovich v. Democratic Nat'l Comm., 141 S. Ct. 2321, 2339 (2021) ("[T]he strength of the state interests served by a challenged voting rule is also an important factor that must be taken into account."); *id.* at 2343 (electoral practices should "reasonably pursue important state interests").

[157] *See, e.g.,* Democratic Nat'l Comm. v. Wis. State Legis., 141 S. Ct. 28, 31 (2020) (Kavanaugh, J., concurring in denial of application to vacate stay).

[158] *See, e.g.,* Purcell v. Gonzalez, 549 U.S. 1, 4–5 (2006).

[159] *See, e.g.,* Munro v. Socialist Workers Party, 479 U.S. 189, 194–95 (1986).

[160] *See, e.g.,* Buckley v. Valeo, 424 U.S. 1, 66–67 (1976).

[161] *See, e.g.,* Timmons v. Twin Cities Area New Party, 520 U.S. 351, 366–67 (1997).

be a genuinely new cause of action, a new claim for plaintiffs to bring against misaligning practices. A new legal structure would therefore have to be built for this form of alignment—maybe based on sliding-scale scrutiny or the burden-shifting framework, or maybe modeled on no existing theory. Unlike alignment as a shield, alignment as a sword would also threaten policies whose lawfulness is currently unquestioned but whose misaligning impact could be established. Of course, I think this would be *positive* change, an improvement on the status quo with its pervasive misalignment. But it would indeed be change.

Another point, applicable to both offensive and defensive uses of alignment, is that they would hinge on empirical evidence. A plaintiff wielding alignment as a sword would have to prove that the disputed practice is, in fact, responsible for misalignment. Likewise, a defendant brandishing alignment as a shield would have to show that its policy, attacked on other grounds, is actually aligning. In both these scenarios, academic studies and testimony from social scientists would be essential. Without this information, the aligning or misaligning effects of different measures couldn't be demonstrated. To this point in the book, I haven't addressed these effects in any detail. Major portions of the next six chapters, though, summarize what we know about the consequences for alignment of a wide range of electoral (and even some nonelectoral) practices. In a legal world where alignment was an accepted theory, these findings would heavily influence whether its use was *plausible* in any given context, not just *possible*.

I also want to stress here that courts' recognition of alignment wouldn't be a blueprint for extensive judicial intervention. Critics of structuralist election law theories sometimes claim they would "require great intrusion by the judiciary into the political processes"—a "misguided and dangerous" prospect.[162] Alignment as a shield, however, would entail judicial passivity, not aggression. If a defendant established that its challenged policy led to better alignment, a court would uphold that policy, thereby refraining from intruding into the political sphere. As for alignment as a sword, its thrust would be repelled in the many cases where misaligning impact couldn't be empirically proven. The next six chapters reveal that these cases are abundant, probably more common than the cases where practices do cause misalignment. Offensive uses of alignment would fail, too, wherever jurisdictions could justify misaligning measures on non-alignment grounds. Notably, my two preferred models for alignment as a sword, sliding-scale scrutiny and the burden-shifting framework, both include explicit justification stages.[163]

---

[162] Richard L. Hasen, The Supreme Court and Election Law: Judging Equality from Baker v. Carr to Bush v. Gore 139 (2003).

[163] Moreover, courts hardly balk at intervention under the nonstructuralist status quo. They intrude into the political sphere all the time, just for different (and arguably worse) reasons. *See, e.g.,* Richard H. Pildes, *The Theory of Political Competition*, 85 Va. L. Rev. 1605, 1619 (1999) (describing his theory of competitive structuralism as "not an expansive invitation to more aggressive judicial

Lastly, while I've concentrated on courts in this chapter, much of the discussion is applicable to nonjudicial actors. Like courts, elected officials, election administrators, policy entrepreneurs, and concerned citizens should carefully evaluate the aligning and misaligning effects of different electoral practices. Always balancing these effects against the implications for values beyond alignment, nonjudicial actors should generally try to adopt aligning provisions and avoid (or repeal) misaligning ones. Why is the political function of alignment so similar to its legal role? Fundamentally, because alignment is both a constitutional principle and a tenet of a normatively appealing democracy. Alignment's constitutional roots mean that courts could and should operationalize it. By the same token, its democratic provenance makes it a proper basis for statutory, administrative, and direct popular action.

* * *

Contrary to the concessions of some structuralist election law scholars, the usual modes of interpretation permit the judicial recognition of alignment as a constitutional value. The constitutional text repeatedly (albeit implicitly) refers to alignment. Prominent drafters like Madison and Bingham believed that the document they shaped embraced alignment. Alignment arises over and over in the Supreme Court's case law, especially in the decisions of the Warren Court. And if anything, all these arguments for alignment's constitutionalization are stronger at the state level. To implement doctrinally alignment as a shield, courts would hardly have to lift a finger. They would just have to acknowledge alignment as a valid interest if and when a jurisdiction asserted it. On the other hand, a new legal theory would be necessary for alignment to work as a sword. That theory should incorporate both the empirically demonstrable effects of challenged policies and the extent to which the policies serve other legitimate goals.

If you've been wondering about alignment's upshot for different laws—voting restrictions, district plans, campaign finance regulations, and the like—take heart. That's the subject of the half-dozen chapters that follow this one. These chapters survey the social scientific evidence about how these measures impact alignment: positively, negatively, or not at all. The chapters further explore a number of legal and theoretical subtleties that haven't yet surfaced. In sum, the chapters make clear that alignment is a concept capable of rigorous real-world application. It might seem abstract, when framed as a constitutional and democratic principle, but it can be tethered to legal and political practice.

action across the board," but rather "an effort to make the target of that action more focused and better justified").

5

Voting

Introduction

Voting is the logical place to begin to consider how alignment would work as a legal and political principle. Voting is the foundational activity of democracy: the key practice through which voters express their preferences, reward or punish the politicians who seek their approval, and influence how their society will be governed. That's why every election law course covers voting first, and why the Supreme Court long ago described voting as "preservative of all [other] rights."[1] In this chapter, accordingly, I analyze both restrictions and expansions of the franchise through the lens of alignment. I construe these regulations broadly so as to include qualifications for voting, voter registration, convenience voting, voter identification, and the time and place of elections.

Before discussing these measures, though, I respond to the argument, associated with Joseph Fishkin, that structural goals like alignment are inapplicable to voting.[2] On this view, when the state regulates voting, it either affirms or denies the equal status of all its citizens. The state's respect for the value of equal citizenship (or the lack thereof) should therefore be the focus of judges and scholars. My answer, which follows from my catholic attitude toward other election law theories, is that there's no need to choose between equal citizenship and alignment. It's important for the state to see all its citizens as equals, fully entitled to participate in the political process. It's also important for voting rules not to skew governmental outputs away from, but instead to align them closer to, people's preferences. The latter, structural objective is perfectly compatible with the former, egalitarian aim.

Next, I revisit a vexing conceptual question from Chapter 2: *With whose* preferences should governmental outputs be aligned? One notable point is that voting regulations can't affect (positively or negatively) alignment with the views of actual voters. That's because actual voters necessarily manage to comply with voting rules, so their preferences are a meaningless benchmark for measuring rules' aligning or misaligning effects. Since actual voters' views are inapt here, I suggest that the more useful baseline is the opinion distribution of the

---

[1] Yick Wo v. Hopkins, 118 U.S. 356, 370 (1886).
[2] *See generally* Joseph Fishkin, *Equal Citizenship and the Individual Right to Vote*, 86 IND. L.J. 1289 (2011).

Aligning Election Law. Nicholas O. Stephanopoulos, Oxford University Press. © Nicholas O. Stephanopoulos 2024.
DOI: 10.1093/9780197662182.003.0005

population on which a given voting regulation operates. In most cases, this population is comprised of eligible voters: people legally entitled to vote, whose participation may be induced or inhibited by the regulation at issue. With respect to voting qualifications, however, the relevant population is made up of all people, since it's this entire universe that qualifications narrow into the eligible electorate.

I then dive into the empirics of voting rules. While the political science literature on their impacts is vast and rich, the crucial takeaway is simple: Most modern restrictions and expansions of the franchise *don't* cause alignment to change significantly. Voting regulations typically don't much alter the partisan composition of the electorate, meaning that they don't much influence partisan alignment. Representational and policy alignment are less commonly studied in this area, but they too seem mostly impervious to how easy or hard it is to vote. This absence of a relationship is primarily attributable to the fact that, for most eligible voters today, cognitive (not institutional) factors are the main drivers of why they do or don't vote. The lack of a link also indicates that alignment would have limited purchase here as a sword or as a shield. As a sword, there simply are few misaligning voting regulations that aggrieved parties could attack. As a shield, likewise, most voting policies don't improve alignment and so couldn't be defended on that basis.

But the insensitivity of alignment to most *contemporary* voting rules doesn't imply that the value would have been equally immovable *historically*. Past voting restrictions like poll taxes, literacy tests, and the introduction of voter registration indeed transformed the partisan composition of the electorate. This partisan distortion was then reversed when (some of) these measures were repealed. Even today, certain regulations of the time and place of elections have substantial implications for alignment. In particular, elections that are held off-cycle (on different dates than national, especially presidential, elections) cause turnout to plummet—and disproportionately so for Democratic and liberal constituents, who experience less congruent representation as a result. One of the more prosaic aspects of election administration, where polling places are located, also turns out to shift turnout significantly, and in ways that can enhance or undermine alignment. Even if alignment isn't generally an effective sword or shield with respect to voting regulations, then, there do exist cases where the principle is more potent.

Applicability of Alignment

Most critics of structuralist election law theories oppose them across the board. They don't want courts (or other actors) prioritizing competition, participation, or alignment in any area. So Fishkin is unusual in that he doesn't generally object to structuralist approaches (and explicitly favors them in the redistricting context).[3] Yet Fishkin argues that these methods have no place in the domain of voting. Here, "a purely structural approach . . . is the wrong set of tools for adjudicating the new vote denial."[4]

What distinguishes voting from other areas where structuralist theories are applicable? According to Fishkin, the harm that ensues when the government restricts the franchise. That harm is "exclu[sion] from the circle of full and equal citizens,"[5] being unable to exercise a right—voting—that's "partly constitutive of what it means to be a full citizen."[6] That harm, Fishkin continues, is invisible to structuralist approaches. Those approaches "direct our attention away from questions of individual right and toward structural features of the democracy as a whole."[7] None of those structural features "is the same as an individual voter's interest in being able to cast a ballot and have it counted."[8] Structuralism is therefore unsuitable for the voting domain because it fails to capture the connection between the franchise and full and equal citizenship.

I have no quarrel with Fishkin's premises—only his conclusion. The right to vote is surely an aspect of citizenship. The government should surely treat its citizens equally. And yes, such equal treatment is distinct from the concerns of structuralist theories.[9] But from none of these points does it follow that structuralism doesn't *also* have a role to play when the state regulates voting. As Fishkin contends, voting restrictions can offend the principle of equal treatment of all citizens. However, voting restrictions can also cause misalignment when they alter the composition of the electorate, disproportionately preventing people with certain partisan and ideological preferences from casting ballots. This misalignment matters, too, no less and no more than if it was the product of a regulation of an activity other than voting. That this misalignment differs from the harm identified by Fishkin in no way lessens its significance. Put another way, Fishkin may be right that structuralism shouldn't occupy the voting field because it doesn't recognize the problem of unequal treatment of citizens. By the same token, though, Fishkin's model has no claim to exclusivity either, because it's equally unaware of the structuralist threats that voting restrictions can pose.

---

[3] *See* Joseph Fishkin, *Weightless Votes*, 121 YALE L.J. 1888, 1893 (2012) ("[I]n one person, one vote cases, in contrast to vote denial cases, the real action is not in the domain of individual rights, but rather in structural questions about the allocation of group political power.").

[4] Fishkin, *supra* note 2, at 1293.

[5] *Id.* at 1322.

[6] *Id.* at 1333.

[7] *Id.* at 1294.

[8] *Id.* at 1307.

[9] Though not entirely distinct. As I've argued throughout the book, the achievement of collective alignment entails treating all people as equally as possible—adopting governmental outputs that minimize the aggregate ideological distance between those outputs and all people's preferences.

To be fair, Fishkin sometimes suggests that he doesn't mind structuralism operating *alongside* his egalitarian theory. "[T]he individual right to vote matters," he writes, "for reasons that are not entirely reducible to the structural interests of the polity as a whole."[10] The inference is that the polity's structural interests *do* carry weight—just not *all* the weight. Fishkin similarly defends what he calls "election law pluralism," "the proposition that there are multiple, irreducibly distinct interests at stake in voting controversies."[11] Again, the implication is that egalitarianism and structuralism are both relevant to voting disputes, since they both embody significant and separate interests. To the extent Fishkin is an election law pluralist, then, not an egalitarian maximalist, there's no conflict between his position and mine. Voting cases can be resolved based on both egalitarianism and structuralism.

Why would it be helpful for voting cases to consider both these approaches? One answer is that each model highlights a different troubling aspect of certain voting restrictions. Take the infamous voting limits of the Jim Crow era—poll taxes, literacy tests, and the like—about which I say more later in the chapter. From an egalitarian perspective, these policies are objectionable because they treated African Americans (and poor Whites) as second-class citizens not entitled to participate in the political process. From the standpoint of alignment, the problem with the policies is that they excluded Blacks (and poor Whites) from the electorate, thereby ensuring that governmental outputs wouldn't reflect their preferences. The key point is that both these views are accurate. Jim Crow curbs on voting were deplorable because of both their unequal treatment of citizens and the misalignment they generated. Recognition of egalitarianism and structuralism helps us see both faces of the evil of Jim Crow.

Another rationale for applying both theories is that sometimes they *don't* point in the same direction. In these cases, one theory might spotlight a harm that the other theory is unable to perceive. Imagine a law that discarded every hundredth ballot turned in to an election official.[12] This measure wouldn't affect alignment because it would randomly, proportionately shrink the electorate. It wouldn't change the relative size of any group of voters. But the provision would still be alarming because of its disrespect for certain citizens, its trashing of their ballots for no good reason. The egalitarian model would thus throw a flag in a scenario where alignment was untouched by a voting restriction. And that's a good thing, I'm happy to say as a staunch advocate of alignment. Misalignment

---

[10] *Id.* at 1293.

[11] *Id.* at 1297.

[12] Fishkin also uses this example (albeit to make a different point). *See id.* at 1318. The opposite scenario—misalignment in the absence of an egalitarian injury—arises with respect to some of the policies discussed in this chapter's final section. For instance, off-cycle local elections are quite misaligning yet don't plausibly indicate disrespect for any citizens.

isn't the only injury that franchise limits can inflict, and a sensible approach should be attentive to other ills.

One more of these ills is *intentional* voter suppression—enacting voting restrictions with the *goal* of making it more difficult for certain people to vote. Lisa Manheim and Elizabeth Porter zero in on suppressive intent and argue that it should be the linchpin of legal analysis in the voting context.[13] The right to vote is a constitutional right, they point out, even if it's partly inferred by precedent rather than announced by the Constitution's text.[14] A tenet of constitutional law, Manheim and Porter continue, is that jurisdictions are generally barred from acting with the aim of undermining a constitutional right.[15] Consequently, intentional voter suppression is unconstitutional. Note that this logic is different from Fishkin's. Suppressive intent may often go hand in hand with unequal treatment of citizens, but the concepts aren't synonymous. Note also that suppressive intent is a quintessentially nonstructural idea. It pertains to the mental state of policymakers, not the extent to which democratic values are realized or sacrificed.[16]

I have the same response to Manheim and Porter's proposal as to Fishkin's. Namely, that it's possible to probe for suppressive intent *and* to examine whether voting restrictions cause misalignment. There's no need to choose between these methods, which are capable of peaceful coexistence. Now, like most structuralists, I'm fonder of effect- than intent-based tests. Suppressive motives don't greatly trouble me if they fail to yield actual suppression. But this isn't a fight I want to have. I recognize that other keen observers are disturbed by deliberate (even if unsuccessful) efforts to stop people from voting. I also appreciate that the law might better reflect common intuitions if it condemned both purposeful voter suppression and suppression that biases governmental outputs away from popular preferences. So I say to Manheim and Porter what I said to Fishkin: This isn't an either/or issue. It's a matter of both/and. Multiple theories of the harm of voting restrictions can operate concurrently.[17]

One last point about the applicability of alignment in the area of voting: The most obvious use of the principle is as a sword swung at misaligning voting limits

---

[13] *See* Lisa Marshall Manheim & Elizabeth G. Porter, *The Elephant in the Room: Intentional Voter Suppression*, 2018 SUP. CT. REV. 213, 237–54 (2018).

[14] *See id.* at 240–42.

[15] *See id.* at 242–43.

[16] Note, too, that preventing Democratic and minority citizens from voting does seem to be a ubiquitous motive for recently enacted voting restrictions. *See, e.g.*, Keith G. Bentele & Erin E. O'Brien, *Jim Crow 2.0? Why States Consider and Adopt Restrictive Voter Access Policies*, 11 PERSP. POL. 1088 (2013); Daniel R. Biggers & Michael J. Hanmer, *Understanding the Adoption of Voter Identification Laws in the United States*, 45 AM. POL. RSCH. 560 (2017).

[17] Moreover, any inquiry into the justifications for a misaligning voting regulation—an inquiry I supported in Chapter 4—would implicate issues of illicit intent. To the extent illicit intent is admitted or proven, other legitimate rationales for the challenged rule would become less plausible.

(like the curbs of the Jim Crow era). But this isn't the only way alignment can be deployed here. One more use is as a *shield* for voting *expansions* that *promote* alignment. To the extent such measures exist (an empirical question I address below), their aligning impact is a reason to uphold, or to enact, them in the face of criticisms on other grounds. These criticisms, however, are rarely very powerful. In litigation, in particular, there are few plausible bases for challenging the legality of election day registration, early voting, absentee voting, and the like. Accordingly, alignment as a shield for voting expansions is a category that's unlikely to arise frequently, simply because voting expansions usually don't need shields.

Even less probable uses of alignment are conceivable, and so worth mentioning here for the sake of analytic thoroughness. Consider a voting expansion that's *misaligning*, maybe because it authorizes an additional mode of voting that's disproportionately exploited by wealthier, better educated citizens. That misalignment could support an attack on the policy—even though the attack might ultimately fail because the policy is sufficiently related to a strong enough state interest. (Recall my argument in Chapter 4 that misalignment should lead to heightened scrutiny, not per se invalidation.) Conversely, suppose a voting restriction is *aligning*, maybe because it repeals a mode of voting that's disproportionately used by a certain slice of citizens. That alignment could help justify the measure if objections are raised on other grounds, like those articulated by Fishkin, Manheim, and Porter.

The underlying point is that alignment is conceptually distinct from electoral participation. *In general*, greater participation likely leads to an electorate that's more representative of the pool of eligible voters, and thus to better alignment. That's why alignment typically functions as a sword against laws that make it harder to vote, and as a shield for laws that facilitate voting. However, greater participation *could* produce a less representative electorate (if the higher turnout is concentrated in certain groups of citizens). Likewise, reduced participation *could* result in a more representative electorate (if turnout becomes lower, but more even, across different groups). That's why the categories of alignment as a sword against voting expansions and alignment as a shield for voting restrictions aren't null sets. In theory, if probably not in practice, voting expansions could be misaligning and voting restrictions aligning.

Identifying the Benchmark

The above discussion assumed that—but didn't explain why—the preferences of *eligible voters* are a useful benchmark for determining the impact of most voting regulations on alignment. I now try to defend this assumption. Remember the two lessons from Chapter 2 about specifying the population with whose views governmental outputs should be congruent. The first is that alignment specifically, and democratic theory generally, can't help with this choice. The baseline population has to be selected based on other factors. The second lesson is that, in many circumstances, which benchmark is used has limited substantive implications. That's because different plausible baseline populations (residents, citizens, eligible voters, actual voters, etc.) tend to have similar partisan and policy preferences.

The first point means there's no "correct" or "proper" benchmark in the voting context (or in any other area).[18] There are only baselines that are more or less helpful or illuminating for different purposes. However, the second point is inapt here in the sense that one particular benchmark for measuring alignment—the views of actual voters—*does* have clear substantive implications. If that baseline is used, then no voting regulation can have any effect on alignment. By necessity, the aligning or misaligning impact of any voting rule must be zero.

To see why, note that there's just one way in which a voting restriction or expansion can influence alignment: by changing who votes. A voting regulation doesn't affect the aggregation of votes into legislative seats. It doesn't involve the nomination of candidates, the procedures of policymaking bodies, or money in politics. All a voting rule can potentially vary is the composition of the electorate. That composition, in turn, has to be compared to something, to some benchmark of who votes (and for whom). If that benchmark is anything other than the actual electorate, then the comparison is meaningful. The actual electorate can be analyzed relative to the hypothetical electorate that serves as the baseline. If the benchmark *is* the actual electorate, on the other hand, the comparison becomes pointless. In that case, both sides of the equation are the same. The preferences of the actual electorate are judged against the preferences of the actual electorate, and always the twain shall meet.

The upshot isn't that actual voters' views are a "wrong" baseline. Again, that's not a verdict that alignment specifically, or democratic theory generally, can reach. Instead, actual voters' views are simply an *uninteresting* baseline in the voting context, one that returns the same null result for every voting regulation's effect on alignment.[19] What's a more useful benchmark capable of saying different things about different voting rules? For most rules, I favor the preferences of eligible voters as a reference point. The views of actual voters—those who

---

[18] At least, not from the perspective of alignment or democratic theory. There might be a right benchmark for other reasons.

[19] In contrast, actual voters' views are an interesting and appealing baseline in most other contexts. In the redistricting domain, for instance, they can be compared to the representation and policy that ensue after voters are sorted into districts. In the campaign finance arena, similarly, actual voters' views can be compared to those of officeholders influenced by funders with quite different preferences.

manage to cast ballots in spite of, or thanks to, a voting policy—should thus be compared to the views of eligible voters—those entitled to cast ballots in a jurisdiction, whether they do so or not. For the subset of voting laws that amount to voting qualifications, though, I prefer the baseline of *all* people's preferences. Voting qualifications are criteria for voting eligibility like citizenship, residence, and age. For these regulations, the views of actual voters should be compared to the views of all persons.

Once more, I can't ground this approach in alignment specifically or democratic theory generally. The basis for the approach, rather, is the observation that every voting regulation operates on a certain population. Every voting regulation, that is, authorizes or encourages members of some population to vote, or discourages or prohibits them from doing so. A corollary of this observation is that the preferences of the population on whom a voting rule directly acts are a helpful benchmark for determining alignment. That population bears the brunt, or reaps the benefit, of the rule. That population's members are the ones whose odds of voting may be affected by the rule. Consequently, comparing those members' views to the views of actual voters is interesting and meaningful. Doing so reveals whether and how the rule skews the actual electorate relative to the baseline population.

Under this approach, eligible voters are plainly the baseline population for most voting regulations. Most voting regulations, after all, make it harder or easier for eligible voters to cast ballots. Eligible voters bear the brunt, or reap the benefit, of most voting regulations. They're the ones whose odds of voting may be affected by the policies. To illustrate, think of a high-profile voting restriction, like a photo identification requirement for voting, or a salient voting expansion, like universal vote by mail. Who are unable to vote if they lack photo IDs, but able to cast ballots if they possess them? Eligible voters. Similarly, who might be more likely to vote if they received their ballots in the mail? Again, eligible voters. That's why the preferences of eligible voters are an intuitive benchmark for measuring alignment in most cases—because they're the population directly acted on by most voting rules.

By most voting rules, but not by all of them. Voting qualifications *don't* make it harder or easier for eligible voters to cast ballots. Instead, voting qualifications determine who's eligible to cast ballots in the first place. Take a residency requirement, a nearly universal voting qualification in the contemporary United States. A resident in a jurisdiction might vote if she's otherwise eligible and able and willing to comply with any applicable voting regulations. In contrast, a nonresident simply can't vote. It doesn't matter how eager she is to cast a ballot or how easily she could satisfy any relevant voting rules. As this example shows, voting qualifications operate not on eligible voters but rather on all people. Voting qualifications transform the entire population into the eligible electorate, whose members then vote if they want to do so and follow all germane voting rules. The entire population is therefore the baseline population for ascertaining the aligning or misaligning impact of voting qualifications.[20]

Specifying the baseline population is obviously important. It provides a normative target for the actual electorate—a point at which, if the actual electorate is perfectly representative of the baseline population, voting regulations have done all they can to achieve alignment. To isolate the effect of any particular rule on alignment, however, we need one more piece of information: the preferences of the relevant individuals (eligible voters or all people) who *would* have voted in the *absence* of the rule. Together with the views of actual voters and of the baseline population, this last bit of data lets us say whether the policy at issue is aligning or misaligning (or neither). First, we compare the preferences of actual voters to the preferences of the relevant individuals who would have voted but for the rule. Second, we ask whether the preference distribution of actual voters is closer to, or farther from, the preference distribution of the baseline population than is the preference distribution of the relevant individuals who would have voted but for the rule. If the preference distribution of actual voters is closer, the regulation is aligning. If the preference distribution of actual voters is farther away, it's misaligning.

For example, suppose that after the implementation of *Policy* (which could be a voting restriction or a voting expansion), the actual electorate is 45 percent Democratic. Also suppose that, in the absence of *Policy*, the hypothetical electorate would have supported Democratic candidates at a 50 percent rate. And last, suppose that the entire pool of relevant individuals (whether or not they cast ballots) is 55 percent Democratic. (These predicates are plotted in Figure 5.1.) Then we can conclude that *Policy* worsens partisan misalignment. Without *Policy*, the hypothetical electorate would be 5 percentage points less Democratic than the baseline population (50 percent versus 55 percent). *With Policy* in effect, the actual electorate is *10* percentage points less Democratic than the baseline population (45 percent versus 55 percent). *Policy* thus increases the partisan mismatch between the actual electorate and the baseline population by 5 percentage points. It makes the actual electorate that much more unrepresentative of the baseline population.

One final conceptual point: I've been talking about comparing the *views* of different groups of people (the actual electorate, the hypothetical electorate

---

[20] Since voting qualifications transform the entire population into the eligible electorate, one could measure the alignment, or lack thereof, between those groups' preferences. However, this approach would sever from the concept of alignment one of its constituent pieces: the outputs of the government. *Eligible* voters don't necessarily vote. *Actual* voters do. *Actual* voters elect politicians, who then go on to represent them and make policy. Accordingly, the most useful comparison for voting qualifications is between the views of all persons and the views of actual (not eligible) voters.

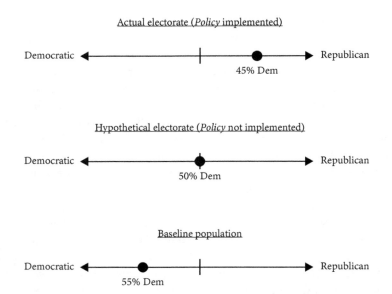

FIGURE 5.1 PARTISAN PREFERENCES OF DIFFERENT POPULATIONS

but for a regulation, and the baseline population). As in the above example, we need to know these groups' views in order to identify the impact of a voting rule on partisan alignment. To determine how a rule influences *representational* or *policy* alignment, though, the analysis is subtly different. Recall that the governmental outputs aren't actual voters' choices at the polls for these forms of alignment.[21] Instead, the governmental outputs are how officeholders represent their constituents or what policies officeholders enact. The first question thus becomes how actual representation or policy compares to the representation or policy that would have arisen but for a given regulation. The second question is then which of these outputs—the actual or the hypothetical one—is more proximate to the representation or policy that would have ensued if all relevant individuals voted. If actual representation or policy is more proximate, the rule improves representational or policy alignment. If actual representation or policy is more distant, the rule is misaligning.

---

[21] Technically speaking, the governmental outputs aren't actual voters' choices at the polls for partisan alignment either. They're officeholders' party affiliations. But officeholders' party affiliations are more or less determined by actual voters' choices at the polls. And the translation between actual voters' choices at the polls and officeholders' party affiliations is the same no matter what voting regulations actual voters have to satisfy.

Null Results

Having explained what studies of the impact of voting regulations on alignment should do, I'm now in a position to survey studies that do just that. I only address pieces that shed light on partisan, representational, or policy alignment. So I mostly avoid the even larger literature about how voting policies affect voter turnout. As I noted earlier, voter turnout is theoretically distinct from (even if it may be practically correlated with) alignment. I also don't cover work that investigates differences in compliance with voting rules by race, wealth, education, age, or any other nonpartisan cleavage. I argued in Chapter 2 that alignment is a population-level concept—even if there's disagreement as to *which* population matters—not a group-specific idea. How voting laws influence group-specific alignment is therefore beyond this book's scope.[22]

I further deal with the sheer variety of voting regulations by sorting them by the stage of the voting process to which they apply. The voting process can be segmented, roughly chronologically, into five stages. First, a person must be eligible to vote because she satisfies all voting qualifications. Second, an eligible voter must register to vote. Third, a registered voter may vote before election day through a form of convenience voting. Fourth, especially on election day, a registered voter may have to show identification to vote. And fifth, the time and place of elections are themselves set by the government. I go through these stages in this order in this section and the next.[23]

One last organizational matter: I only comment on voting regulations that *don't* significantly affect alignment in this section (hence its title). This lack of a major aligning or misaligning impact turns out to be a theme of the empirical literature. Most modern voting rules don't cause officeholders' party affiliations, officeholders' policy positions, or enacted policies to become substantially more or less congruent with popular preferences. In most cases involving voting rules, alignment would thus be ineffective as a sword or as a shield. However, there do exist some policies about voting, certainly historically and even today, that considerably influence alignment. Those more potent (but less common) policies are the subject of the next section.

Starting with voting qualifications, then, the aligning implications of only one contemporary condition for voting eligibility have been examined in any

---

[22] Since voting regulations mostly don't affect the partisan or ideological composition of the actual electorate, though, it would be surprising if they significantly altered its makeup along other dimensions. For a finding that a range of voting rules don't much affect the racial composition of the actual electorate, see BERNARD L. FRAGA, THE TURNOUT GAP: RACE, ETHNICITY, AND POLITICAL INEQUALITY IN A DIVERSIFYING AMERICA 171–94 (2018).

[23] However, I discuss the fifth stage—the time and place of elections—only in the next section.

depth: the lack of a prior felony conviction.[24] Some early contributions to this literature claimed that the disenfranchisement of ex-felons significantly skews the partisan composition of the actual electorate in a Republican direction.[25] More recent (and methodologically sound) studies, though, typically find that ex-felon disenfranchisement has a marginal partisan effect. The ex-felons made ineligible to vote by these laws *would* have voted, *had* they been eligible, at very low rates—on the order of 10 percent in presidential elections.[26] Contrary to the conventional wisdom, the members of this disenfranchised population also aren't overwhelmingly Democratic. They do prefer Democratic candidates, but only by a ratio of about two-to-one, a figure comparable, for example, to the support of Hispanic voters for Democrats.[27] In combination, these results ensure a muted partisan impact. Excluding relatively few people from the eligible electorate who otherwise would have voted, and whose partisan preferences would have been mixed had they cast ballots, entails little partisan misalignment.[28]

To illustrate with more specificity, take Florida, which used to disenfranchise ex-felons for life, and which continues to disenfranchise them as long as they can't pay all their fines and fees. There are about 1.5 million ex-felons in Florida, seemingly a population large enough to sway many elections in this famously competitive state.[29] But the best estimate is that, if they were eligible to vote, only around 11 percent of these ex-felons would cast ballots in presidential elections.[30] That's the proportion of ex-felons who *did* cast ballots after a 2007 reform

---

[24] In contrast, there's little or no work on the aligning implications of citizenship, residence, or age conditions for voting eligibility. *Cf.* Steven J. Rosenstone & Raymond E. Wolfinger, *The Effect of Registration Laws on Voter Turnout*, 72 AM. POL. SCI. REV. 22, 33–34 (1978) (finding that residence requirements have statistically insignificant effects on voter turnout, and thus likely on partisan alignment); *see also* Thomas R. Gray & Jeffery A. Jenkins, Estimating Disenfranchisement in U.S. Elections, 1870–1970, at 17 (2022) (finding that the enfranchisement of women through the Nineteenth Amendment had a statistically insignificant impact on partisan alignment).

[25] *See, e.g.*, JEFF MANZA & CHRISTOPHER UGGEN, LOCKED OUT: FELON DISENFRANCHISEMENT AND AMERICAN DEMOCRACY (2008); Christopher Uggen & Jeff Manza, *Democratic Contraction? Political Consequences of Felon Disenfranchisement in the United States*, 67 AM. SOC. REV. 777 (2002).

[26] *See, e.g.*, Marc Meredith & Michael Morse, *Do Voting Rights Notification Laws Increase Ex-Felon Turnout?*, 651 ANNALS AM. ACAD. POL. & SOC. SCI. 220, 222 (2014) (finding turnout rates of about 10 percent for ex-felons eligible to vote in New Mexico, New York, and North Carolina); Marc Meredith & Michael Morse, *The Politics of the Restoration of Ex-Felon Voting Rights: The Case of Iowa*, 10 Q.J. POL. SCI. 41, 71 (2015) (finding a turnout rate of 13 percent for ex-felons eligible to vote in Iowa).

[27] *See, e.g.*, Traci Burch, *Turnout and Party Registration Among Criminal Offenders in the 2008 General Election*, 45 L. & SOC'Y REV. 699, 720–21 (2011) (reporting results for Florida and North Carolina); Michael Morse, *The Future of Felon Disenfranchisement Reform: Evidence from the Campaign to Restore Voting Rights in Florida*, 109 CALIF. L. REV. 1141, 1175–76 (2021) (reporting results for Florida).

[28] *See also* Nicholas O. Stephanopoulos et al., *The Realities of Electoral Reform*, 68 VAND. L. REV. 761, 805 (2015) (finding that ex-felon disenfranchisement has a statistically significant effect on neither district- nor chamber-level representational alignment).

[29] *See* Morse, *supra* note 27, at 1180.

[30] *See id.* at 1179.

restored the franchise to roughly 150,000 people.[31] Moreover, less than two-thirds of Florida ex-felons favor Democratic candidates, while more than one-third back Republicans.[32] It thus takes three ex-felons voting to net Democrats slightly less than one vote. Put these findings together, and Democrats would earn just 20,000 to 60,000 more votes statewide if every Florida ex-felon was eligible to vote.[33] As Michael Morse wryly remarks, "[t]he estimated Democratic gain from a more inclusive democracy is equal to roughly one half of one percent of all ballots cast."[34]

Next, states employ several policies to increase, or sometimes to decrease, the number of registered voters. Online voter registration enables eligible voters to register from their computers or smartphones, without mailing forms or traveling to registration sites. More ambitiously, automatic voter registration causes eligible voters to be registered when they interact with state agencies, unless they take affirmative steps to prevent their registration. On the other hand, voter purges remove eligible voters from the registration rolls, typically on the grounds of not voting and not responding to mailings. These policies, too, seem to have at most a minor impact on alignment. "Seem" is the right word here because the relevant scholarship is both thin and focused on voter turnout. The minor impact on alignment can be inferred from the failure of registration laws to change turnout very much.

The availability of online voter registration, for instance, doesn't perceptibly vary the likelihood that eligible voters cast ballots—or even register to vote.[35] In the absence of such effects, a major impact on alignment is hard to imagine. Automatic voter registration, likewise, is a statistically significant driver of neither voter turnout nor even voter registration.[36] Accordingly, it doesn't increase the turnout of registered Democrats, as some might suspect.[37] And at least one

[31] See id. at 1178.
[32] See id. at 1175 (reporting the party registrations of Amendment 4 registrants).
[33] See id. at 1180.
[34] Id. at 1181; see also Justin Grimmer & Eitan Hersh, How Election Rules Affect Who Wins 28 (June 29, 2023) (estimating that the enfranchisement of ex-felons would change the parties' presidential vote shares by no more than 0.1 percentage points in each state).
[35] See Holly Ann Garnett, Registration Innovation: The Impact of Online Registration and Automatic Voter Registration in the United States, 21 ELECTION L.J. 34, 40–41 (2022); see also Jinhai Yu, Does State Online Voter Registration Increase Voter Turnout?, 100 Soc. Sci. Q. 620, 629 (2019) (finding that online voter registration only statistically significantly increases the youngest eligible voters' likelihood of voting).
[36] See Garnett, supra note 35, at 41; cf. JAN E. LEIGHLEY & JONATHAN NAGLER, WHO VOTES NOW? DEMOGRAPHICS, ISSUES, INEQUALITY, AND TURNOUT IN THE UNITED STATES 96 (2013) (reviewing the literature on the National Voter Registration Act, which enables people to register to vote when they interact with government agencies, and concluding that the law "did not increase turnout substantially"). But see Justin Grimmer & Jonathan Rodden, Changing the Default: The Impact of Motor-Voter Reform in Colorado (Jan. 2022) (finding that the aggressive implementation of automatic voter registration in Colorado did increase voter registration).
[37] See Seo-Young Silvia Kim, Automatic Voter Reregistration as a Housewarming Gift: Quantifying Causal Effects on Turnout Using Movers, 117 AM. POL. SCI. REV. 1137, 1141 (2023) (examining Orange County, California).

voter purge (the only one studied in such detail) had a low error rate in the sense that it removed few people from the registration rolls who still lived at their old addresses and intended to vote.[38] With that small an affected population, that voter purge couldn't have substantially influenced alignment. Thanks to results like these, a literature review concludes that "today's registration laws appear to have much smaller partisan effects" than some of their predecessors in earlier times.[39] "Scholars have investigated the partisan implications of changing registration laws and consistently found little, if any, noticeable effects."[40]

Turning from voter registration to voting itself, maybe the most important development of the last generation is the rise of convenience voting. Most states now allow eligible voters to cast their ballots early—prior to election day—at local polling places. About half the states authorize no-excuse absentee voting: returning ballots by mail instead of in person. A handful of mostly western states even conduct all-mail elections in which all registered voters are sent ballots that they may then mail in or drop off at designated sites. Unlike the voter registration laws discussed above, these forms of convenience voting *do* considerably increase voter turnout. A meta-analysis of studies of early voting and no-excuse absentee voting finds that these policies raise turnout by 2 to 5 percentage points.[41] Similarly, the most comprehensive examination of all-mail elections shows that they boost turnout by 4 to 6 percentage points.[42]

Despite enhancing participation, though, convenience voting doesn't significantly influence alignment. Early voting and no-excuse absentee voting are among the reforms covered by Devin Caughey and Christopher Warshaw in their invaluable book on policy alignment at the state level. Neither voting liberalization has any discernible effect on how congruent state policies are with popular policy preferences.[43] Nor, according to the meta-analysis I just mentioned, does early voting or no-excuse absentee voting have a substantial impact on partisan alignment. "In terms of the partisan composition of the electorate, [these] reforms seem neither to help nor to hurt political parties."[44] As for all-mail

---

[38] *See* Gregory A. Huber et al., *The Racial Burden of Voter List Maintenance Errors: Evidence from Wisconsin's Supplemental Movers Poll Books*, SCI. ADVANCES, Feb. 17, 2021, at 5 (reporting a 3.5 percent error rate affecting about 9,000 individuals for a 2018 voter purge in Wisconsin).

[39] Benjamin Highton, *Voter Registration and Turnout in the United States*, 2 PERSP. POL. 507, 510 (2004).

[40] *Id.*

[41] *See* Paul Gronke et al., *Convenience Voting*, 11 ANN. REV. POL. SCI. 437, 443 (2008).

[42] *See* Eric McGhee et al., Vote-by-Mail Policy and the 2020 Presidential Election 11 (Aug. 4, 2021) (reporting a 4-point rise prior to 2020 and a 6-point rise in the 2020 election).

[43] *See* DEVIN CAUGHEY & CHRISTOPHER WARSHAW, DYNAMIC DEMOCRACY: PUBLIC OPINION, ELECTIONS, AND POLICYMAKING IN THE AMERICAN STATES 158–59 (2022); *see also* Stephanopoulos et al., *supra* note 28, at 805 (finding that early voting has no effect on chamber-level representational alignment).

[44] *See* Gronke et al., *supra* note 41, at 444–45. However, a few studies disagree with this consensus with respect to early voting—though these studies themselves disagree as to which party early voting supposedly benefits. *Compare* Barry C. Burden et al., *The Complicated Partisan Effects of State*

elections—the target of so much of President Trump's ire in 2020—they fail to change the partisan calculus as well. Mailing ballots to all registered voters in California, Utah, and Washington,[45] in Colorado,[46] in Washington and Utah,[47] and in all states where this approach has been tried,[48] benefits neither Democrats (as President Trump feared) nor Republicans.

How can these measures improve participation but not alignment? By bringing in new voters with about the same partisan and policy preferences as existing voters. It's a truism of American politics that voters are different from nonvoters: wealthier, better educated, and more politically knowledgeable. These descriptions also apply to the users of convenience voting. They too are socioeconomically advantaged and politically informed relative to eligible voters who choose not to cast ballots.[49] Incorporating the users of convenience voting into the actual electorate therefore doesn't much change the composition of the actual electorate. Doing so increases the *size* of the actual electorate. But actual voters' partisan and ideological distributions remain roughly the same as before the adoption of these reforms.

Lastly, if convenience voting is the most salient voting expansion of the last generation, voter identification is the highest-profile restriction. A growing number of states require each eligible, registered voter to show an ID before being allowed to cast a ballot. The most onerous of these provisions mandate that the ID be government-issued, nonexpired, and photographic. Once more, though, even strict photo ID requirements don't significantly affect alignment. In Caughey and Warshaw's analysis of policy alignment, they don't cause state policy outcomes to be less (or more) congruent with popular policy preferences.[50] Nor, according to the most thorough study of strict photo ID laws' partisan implications, do they meaningfully alter the partisan composition of

Election Laws, 70 POL. RSCH. Q. 564 (2017) (arguing that early voting helps Republicans), *with* Ethan Kaplan & Haishan Yuan, *Early Voting Laws, Voter Turnout, and Partisan Vote Composition: Evidence from Ohio*, 12 AM. ECON. J: APP. ECON. 32 (2020) (arguing that early voting helps Democrats).

[45] *See* Daniel M. Thompson et al., *Universal Vote-by-Mail Has No Impact on Partisan Turnout or Vote Share*, 117 PROC. NAT'L ACAD. SCI. 14052, 14054 (2020).

[46] *See* Adam Bonica et al., *All-Mail Voting in Colorado Increases Turnout and Reduces Turnout Inequality*, 72 ELECTORAL STUD. 1, 4 (2021).

[47] *See* Michael Barber & John B Holbein, *The Participatory and Partisan Impacts of Mandatory Vote-by-Mail*, SCI. ADV., Aug. 26, 2020, at 5.

[48] *See* McGhee et al., *supra* note 42, at 15.

[49] *See, e.g.*, Adam J. Berinsky, *The Perverse Consequences of Electoral Reform in the United States*, 33 AM. POL. RSCH. 471, 482 (2005) (noting that the users of convenience voting are "more politically engaged and interested," "better educated," and "have higher incomes"); Gronke et al., *supra* note 41, at 444 ("Voters who use convenience voting are more politically aware, more partisan, and more ideologically extreme.").

[50] *See* CAUGHEY & WARSHAW, *supra* note 43, at 158–59; *see also* Stephanopoulos et al., *supra* note 28, at 805 (finding that different identification requirements have ambiguous effects on representational alignment).

the actual electorate. This study relies on individual-level data about essentially all eligible voters in the United States from 2008 to 2018—the period when most strict photo ID laws went into effect.[51] These laws' implementation, it turns out, has no impact on the parties' relative fortunes. "[S]trict ID laws do not affect the relative vote share of Democratic and Republican candidates."[52]

The explanation for strict photo ID laws' minimal consequences isn't that virtually all eligible voters possess valid IDs. A sizable fraction of U.S. citizens over eighteen—on the order of 10 percent—lack government-issued, nonexpired photo IDs.[53] The reason for the minimal consequences, rather, is that very few of these eligible voters without valid IDs *do* vote (in states without stringent ID requirements) or *would* vote (if states with stringent ID requirements rescinded them). Several recent studies document the startlingly low participation of eligible voters without valid IDs using administrative records from states that request, but don't require, showing an ID to vote. In Florida, a trivial 0.02 percent of voters in federal and state elections lack valid IDs.[54] In Michigan, this proportion is about 0.3 percent, a bit larger but still tiny.[55] In North Carolina, the share of voters without valid IDs is close to 0.1 percent,[56] and in Texas it's around 0.2 percent.[57] Plainly, these figures are too small to cause alignment to budge. If the actual electorate with strict photo ID laws is virtually identical to the actual electorate without them—as Figure 5.2 indicates—then the laws can't have a material misaligning (or aligning) effect.

Generalizing from these cases, voting regulations must satisfy two conditions to significantly influence alignment.[58] First, they must prevent from voting a substantial number of people who otherwise would have voted (if they're

[51] *See* Enrico Cantoni & Vincent Pons, *Strict ID Laws Don't Stop Voters: Evidence from a U.S. Nationwide Panel, 2008-2018,* 136 Q.J. ECON. 2615, 2628 (2021).

[52] *Id.* at 2618; *see also, e.g.,* Zoltan Hajnal et al., *Voter Identification Laws and the Suppression of Minority Votes,* 79 J. POL. 363, 372 (2016) ("[A]t least during general elections, Democrats and liberals are not more affected than Republicans or conservatives by the presence of strict voter ID laws."); Emily Rong Zhang, *Questioning Questions in the Law of Democracy: What the Debate Over Voter ID Laws' Effects Teaches About Asking the Right Questions,* 69 UCLA L. REV. 1028, 1040 (2022) ("If we give more weight to better studies, the answer from the social scientific community on the effects of voter ID laws appears to be: they have none.").

[53] *See, e.g.,* BRENNAN CTR. FOR JUSTICE, CITIZENS WITHOUT PROOF: A SURVEY OF AMERICANS' POSSESSION OF DOCUMENTARY PROOF OF CITIZENSHIP AND PHOTO IDENTIFICATION 3 (Nov. 2006).

[54] *See* Mark Hoekstra & Vijetha Koppa, *Strict Voter Identification Laws, Turnout, and Election Outcomes* 19 (Nat'l Bureau of Econ. Rsch., Working Paper No. 26206, 2019).

[55] *See id.; see also* Phoebe Henninger et al., *Who Votes Without Identification? Using Individual-Level Administrative Data to Measure the Burden of Strict Voter ID Laws,* 18 J. EMPIRICAL LEGAL STUD. 256, 258 (2021) (reporting a figure of 0.45 percent for Michigan).

[56] *See* Justin Grimmer & Jesse Yoder, *The Durable Differential Deterrent Effects of Strict Photo Identification Laws,* 10 POL. SCI. RSCH. & METHODS 453, 465–66 (2022).

[57] *See* Bernard L. Fraga & Michael G. Miller, *Who Do Voter ID Laws Keep from Voting?,* 84 J. POL. 1091, 1103 (2022).

[58] These conditions are necessary and sufficient to influence partisan alignment; they're merely necessary to influence representational and policy alignment.

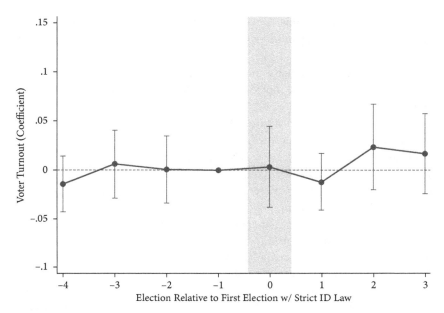

FIGURE 5.2 VOTER TURNOUT BEFORE AND AFTER REQUIRING PHOTO
IDENTIFICATION TO VOTE

Figure 5.2 is reproduced with permission from Enrico Cantoni & Vincent Pons, *Strict ID Laws Don't Stop Voters: Evidence from a U.S. Nationwide Panel, 2008-2018*, 136 Q.J. ECON. 2615, 2640 (2021). Copyright © 2021 by Oxford University Press.

voting restrictions), or they must induce to vote a substantial number of people who otherwise wouldn't have voted (if they're voting expansions). Second, the people prevented from voting by voting restrictions, or induced to vote by voting expansions, must have distinctive partisan and/or policy preferences. Unless both these conditions are met, voting regulations can't change the composition of the actual electorate, and so can't skew it relative to any benchmark.[59] This framework makes clear why the policies addressed in this section aren't highly aligning or misaligning: They fail to satisfy one or both of the conditions. Felon disenfranchisement laws stop relatively few people, with relatively nondistinct preferences, from voting. Voter registration laws neither bring into the actual electorate, nor kick out of it, many people at all. Convenience voting *does* bring a considerable number of new voters into the actual electorate, but their partisan

---

[59] For other scholars identifying these two conditions, see Grimmer & Hersh, *supra* note 34, at 2; and Highton, *supra* note 39, at 510 ("The partisan impact of a [voting] law depends on two factors: the number of people affected by a law and their political distinctiveness."). Note that, even if these conditions aren't met, a voting regulation can have a decisive impact in a particular election that happens to be very close.

and policy views largely mirror those of existing voters. And even strict photo ID requirements bar only miniscule shares of people who otherwise would have voted from casting ballots.

These results, though, leave unanswered a deeper question: *Why* do most modern voting regulations not directly affect many people, in the sense of causing them to, or not to, vote?[60] The explanation likely involves the costs of voting, which can be divided into categories: institutional costs related to the rules that govern the voting process, and cognitive costs stemming from people's political knowledge and interest (or the lack thereof).[61] People then vote if their combined institutional and cognitive costs are smaller than the benefits they perceive from voting. A fair inference from the scholarship I've surveyed in this section is that most contemporary voting policies *don't* significantly vary the institutional costs of voting. Most people find these costs to be about the same when voting restrictions are imposed, because the restrictions don't apply to other modes of voting that remain available. Likewise, the institutional costs of voting stay roughly constant when voting expansions are enacted, because it was already easy enough for most people to vote without the expansions. Of course, the point isn't that voting regulations can never materially vary the institutional costs of voting. The next section shows that they do have this capability. Instead, the point is that, under modern American electoral conditions, the institutional costs of voting are mostly fixed. Voting rules (of the kind I've covered so far) therefore have little ability to move turnout or alignment. They pale compared to cognitive factors beyond their reach, which do dramatically affect who votes.[62]

Moving the Needle

In theory, given this discussion, some voting policies could significantly influence alignment. Under the framework of the two conditions for impacting alignment, some policies could satisfy both requirements. That is, they could draw into the actual electorate, or exclude from it, a substantial number of people with distinctive preferences. Under the rubric of the institutional and cognitive costs of voting, similarly, some policies could meaningfully vary the institutional

---

[60] I'm *not* speaking here of convenience voting, which *does* cause more people to vote.

[61] *See, e.g.*, Berinsky, *supra* note 49, at 472 (distinguishing between "the direct costs of registration and getting to the ballot box" and "the cognitive costs of becoming engaged with and informed about the political world").

[62] *See, e.g., id.* at 473 ("Political information and interest, not the high tangible costs of the act of voting, are the real barriers to a truly democratic voting public."); Paul Gronke et al., *Early Voting and Turnout*, 40 PS: POL. SCI. & POL. 639, 644 (2007) (commenting that convenience voting "pal[es] in significance to such effects as citizen empowerment, interest in and concern about the election, and political mobilization by parties, candidates, and other political organizations").

costs. They could make voting easier or harder enough that the calculation of whether voting's combined institutional and cognitive costs exceed its benefits comes out differently for a considerable volume of people. What in theory *could* happen turns out in practice *to* occur for a small set of voting regulations. These atypical rules, some relics of the past, others still in operation today, do significantly influence alignment. The regulatory impotence that was the refrain of the previous section therefore isn't universal. On occasion, voting laws are subject to criticism because they misalign, or to praise because they bring governmental outputs and popular preferences closer together.

The infamous voting restrictions of the Jim Crow South—poll taxes, literacy tests, grandfather clauses, good character requirements, and so on—illustrate the misalignment that voting regulations can sometimes cause. These measures decimated Black (and poor White) turnout after they were adopted in the decades after Reconstruction. To take one representative example, the proportion of African American adults who were registered to vote in Louisiana plummeted from around 90 percent in the 1870s and 1880s to below 5 percent from the 1890s through the 1940s.[63] Moreover, the Black population excluded from political participation in the Jim Crow South was highly distinctive in partisan and ideological terms. Above all, African Americans tended to be Republicans while the vast majority of southern Whites affiliated with the Democratic Party (in this era).[64] African Americans were also more liberal than southern Whites, especially with respect (but hardly limited) to civil rights issues.[65] The Jim Crow voting limits thus produced an actual electorate much more Democratic and conservative than the population that would have voted in the absence of the limits. In turn, this distorted actual electorate gave rise to the Solid South: a conservative Democratic stronghold in a region where many, sometimes even most, people were anything but conservative Democrats.[66]

---

[63] *See* KHALILAH BROWN-DEAN ET AL., 50 YEARS OF THE VOTING RIGHTS ACT: THE STATE OF RACE IN POLITICS 9 (2015); *see also, e.g.,* James E. Alt, *Race and Voter Registration in the South, in* CLASSIFYING BY RACE 313, 316 (Paul E. Peterson ed., 2015) (showing that, as late as 1950, the White registration rate in southern states was three to seven times higher than the Black registration rate).

[64] *See generally* BORIS HEERSINK & JEFFERY A. JENKINS, REPUBLICAN PARTY POLITICS AND THE AMERICAN SOUTH, 1865–1968 (2020).

[65] *See, e.g.,* CAUGHEY & WARSHAW, *supra* note 43, at 162 (describing how "Southern states disenfranchised many of their more economically liberal citizens, including nearly all of their Black citizens").

[66] *See, e.g., id.* at 212 (showing that policy alignment was significantly lower in the South than in the North prior to the enactment of the Voting Rights Act); Gray & Jenkins, *supra* note 24, at 17 (finding that the poll tax and the literacy test both significantly reduced Republican vote share in the South); Michael P. Olson, "Restoration" and Representation: Legislative Consequences of Black Disfranchisement in the American South, 1879-1916, at 2 (May 1, 2023) (finding that "formal disfranchisement of African Americans substantially changed patterns of roll call voting, led to the election of more Democrats, and played a central role in creating the 'Solid South'").

If the Jim Crow voting regime was highly misaligning, did its repeal undo (some of) this noncongruence? It certainly did. In the wake of Congress's and the Supreme Court's interventions in the 1960s, Black registration and turnout soared in the South.[67] Today, African Americans register and vote at close to the same rates as Whites in ex-Confederate states.[68] Consequently, the actual electorate in the South is no longer significantly racially distorted relative to the eligible electorate (though other biases remain). Furthermore, as Caughey and Warshaw show, the alignment of state policies with the preferences of African Americans in the South has risen steadily from the mid-twentieth century to the present.[69] Southern state policy alignment with the views of White respondents has increased, too, over this period.[70] It's therefore clear that overall state policy alignment in the South, taking into account both Black and White respondents' opinions, is now significantly higher than in the Jim Crow era.[71]

Of course, poll taxes, literacy tests, and the like have been consigned to history's ash heap. But another voting regulation adopted at about the same time as the Jim Crow voting curbs—the need to register to vote by a deadline prior to election day—remains in force in most states. I explained earlier that several contemporary registration policies have little effect on alignment. When voter registration *itself* was instituted in the decades around 1900, however, its impact *was* misaligning. First, voter registration excluded a substantial number of people who would otherwise have voted from the actual electorate. In the North (where the Jim Crow voting barriers didn't exist), voter turnout fell by over 15 percentage points after eligible voters were required to register.[72] Some of this decline was due to other factors (like diminished competition), but about 5 percentage points of the drop was attributable to voter registration.[73] Second, the people prevented from voting by voter registration were politically unrepresentative. They were more likely to be immigrants, to live in urban areas, and to

---

[67] *See, e.g.,* KHALILAH BROWN-DEAN ET AL., *supra* note 63, at 9–10.

[68] *See id.; see also, e.g.,* Shelby Cnty. v. Holder, 570 U.S. 529, 547 (2013) (noting that Black "voter turnout and registration rates now approach parity" in the South (internal quotation marks omitted)).

[69] *See* CAUGHEY & WARSHAW, *supra* note 43, at 134–35.

[70] *See id.*

[71] *Cf.* Elizabeth U. Cascio & Ebonya Washington, *Valuing the Vote: The Redistribution of Voting Rights and State Funds Following the Voting Rights Act of 1965,* 129 Q.J. ECON. 379, 395–423 (2014) (finding that the elimination of the literacy test led to more redistributive transfers to areas with larger Black populations).

[72] *See* STEVEN J. ROSENSTONE & JOHN MARK HANSEN, MOBILIZATION, PARTICIPATION, AND DEMOCRACY IN AMERICA 206 (2003).

[73] *See, e.g.,* Stephen Ansolabehere & David M. Konisky, *The Introduction of Voter Registration and Its Effect on Turnout,* 14 POL. ANAL. 83, 90–97 (2006); Vanessa M. Perez, *America's First Voter Identification Laws: The Effects of Personal Registration and Declining Party Competition on Presidential Election Turnout, 1880-1916,* 69 ELECTORAL STUD. 1, 9–10 (2021).

be Catholic.[74] At the turn of the twentieth century, these were all characteristics linked in the North to affiliation with the Democratic Party. The introduction of voter registration thus caused partisan misalignment in a Republican direction.

By the same token, the effective *elimination* of voter registration reverses this noncongruence. In recent years, a number of states have allowed eligible voters to register at the same time that they cast ballots, during either the early voting period (same-day registration), election day itself (election day registration), or both. Under these policies, voter registration ceases to be an independent requirement for voting since it can be done concurrently with going to the polls. Unlike other registration regulations, election day registration does significantly increase voter turnout. A literature review estimates this boost to be roughly 5 percentage points—close to the drop in turnout caused a century ago by the adoption of voter registration.[75] Also unlike most other voting expansions, election day registration doesn't bring into the actual electorate new voters who strongly resemble existing voters. Rather, the beneficiaries of election day registration tend to be younger, more mobile, and less politically aware people.[76] This is a highly Democratic voting bloc in modern American politics. Accordingly, election day registration considerably raises the vote share of Democratic candidates, at least in presidential elections.[77] That is, it negates the pro-Republican partisan misalignment typically produced by voter registration.

Next, remember the five stages of the voting process I mentioned above. I haven't said anything yet about regulations of the final stage: the time and place of elections. Some temporal and spatial voting rules, though, are among the few voting laws that significantly influence alignment. With respect to time, when an election is held turns out to be an important variable. Specifically, when an election is held "off-cycle"—not in the November of a federal election year, possibly even on a non-November date in an odd-numbered year—voter turnout falls precipitously. At the municipal level, turnout in off-cycle elections is about *half* the turnout in on-cycle elections—a plunge in voter participation on par with those caused by the voting restrictions of Jim Crow.[78] Additionally, the people

[74] *See, e.g.*, Paul Kleppner & Stephen C. Baker, *The Impact of Voter Registration Requirements on Electoral Turnout, 1900-16*, 8 J. POL. & MIL. SOC. 205, 216–20 (1980); Vanessa Melinda Perez, The Effects of Voter Registration and Declining Political Party Competition on Turnout in the United States of America, 1880-1916, at 116–17 (2014).

[75] *See* Highton, *supra* note 39, at 509; *see also, e.g.*, LEIGHLEY & NAGLER, *supra* note 36, at 100–01; Greg Vonnahme, *Registration Deadlines and Turnout in Context*, 34 POL. BEHAVIOR 765, 774 (2012).

[76] *See, e.g.*, MICHAEL J. HANMER, DISCOUNT VOTING: VOTER REGISTRATION REFORMS AND THEIR EFFECTS 152–57 (2009); LEIGHLEY & NAGLER, *supra* note 36, at 101–07; Highton, *supra* note 39, at 509–10.

[77] *See, e.g.*, Burden et al., *supra* note 44, at 567–73; Ikuma Ogura, Does Election Day Registration Make a Difference? Evidence from Illinois 13–19 (2018). However, this improvement in partisan alignment isn't accompanied by a significant rise in state policy alignment. *See* CAUGHEY & WARSHAW, *supra* note 43, at 156–59.

[78] *See, e.g.*, Zoltan L. Hajnal et al., *Who Votes: City Election Timing and Voter Composition*, 116 AM. POL. SCI. REV. 374, 374 (2022) (summarizing this literature).

who don't vote off-cycle (but would vote on-cycle) are politically distinctive. Most relevant here, they're more likely to affiliate with the Democratic Party and to hold liberal policy views.[79] Their exclusion from the off-cycle actual electorate therefore skews that population in Republicans' and conservatives' favor. That bias subsequently turns into jurisdiction-wide representational misalignment. As shown in Figure 5.3, members of city councils[80] and school boards[81] elected off-cycle are more ideologically noncongruent with their constituents than are local politicians chosen on-cycle.

Off-cycle elections are interesting not just because of their misaligning impact but also because of how they bring it about. Like all the other voting regulations I've covered, off-cycle elections involve the institutional costs of voting in that they specify what people must do to cast valid ballots. Unlike the other voting rules, though, off-cycle elections implicate the *cognitive* costs of voting as well. In particular, off-cycle elections capitalize on people's lower knowledge of, and lower interest in, races that don't take place in the November of a presidential election year. Thanks to this reduced political attention, the cognitive costs of voting off-cycle are generally higher. It takes more mental effort to find out who's running, to learn about their positions, and to go to the trouble of voting. Moreover, the cognitive costs of voting off-cycle are *disproportionately* higher for certain groups of people: less politically aware, lower-propensity voters, who in modern American politics are more apt to be Democrats and liberals. Off-cycle elections thus present a rare example of voting regulations operating mainly through psychological mechanisms. Off-cycle elections' potent misaligning effect may be attributable precisely to this reliance on psychological forces—which, I previously suggested, dominate institutional drivers of voting in present-day America.

With respect to place, a (seemingly) mundane aspect of election administration is that voting sites must be, well, sited. *Where* they're located ends up having aligning implications. As always, the initial issue in the alignment analysis is whether a voting policy influences voter turnout. Placing voting sites farther from people does make them less likely to vote, by about 2 percentage points for each standard deviation increase in distance.[82] Moving people's voting sites

---

[79] *See, e.g., id.* at 378–79; Vladimir Kogan et al., *Election Timing, Electorate Composition, and Policy Outcomes: Evidence from School Districts,* 62 AM. J. POL. SCI. 637, 645 (2018).

[80] *See* BRIAN F. SCHAFFNER ET AL., HOMETOWN INEQUALITY: RACE, CLASS, AND REPRESENTATION IN AMERICAN LOCAL POLITICS 203 (2020); *cf.* Adam M. Dynes et al., *Off-Cycle and Off Center: Election Timing and Representation in Municipal Government,* 115 AM. POL. SCI. REV. 1097 (2021) (finding that city policies are less responsive to residents' preferences when city elections are held off-cycle).

[81] *See* Michael T. Hartney & Sam D. Hayes, *Off-Cycle and Out of Sync: How Election Timing Influences Political Representation,* 22 ST. POL. & POL'Y Q. 335, 342–50 (2021).

[82] *See, e.g.,* Enrico Cantoni, *A Precinct Too Far: Turnout and Voting Costs,* 12 AM. ECON. J: APP. ECON. 61, 63 (2020); Elliot B. Fullmer, *Early Voting: Do More Sites Lead to Higher Turnout?,* 14 ELECTION L.J. 81, 91 (2015) (finding that each additional *early* voting site per thousand people raises voter turnout by about 2 percentage points).

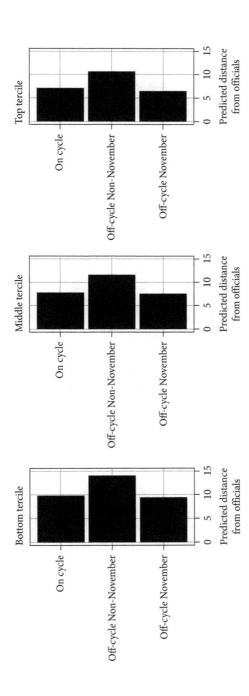

FIGURE 5.3 IDEOLOGICAL DISTANCE BETWEEN CONSTITUENTS AND CITY COUNCIL MEMBERS BY ELECTION TIMING AND INCOME GROUP

Figure 5.3 is reproduced with permission from BRIAN F. SCHAFFNER ET AL., HOMETOWN INEQUALITY: RACE, CLASS, AND REPRESENTATION IN AMERICAN LOCAL POLITICS 207 (2020). Copyright © 2020 by Cambridge University Press.

reduces their turnout, too, by an analogous 2-point margin.[83] The next question is whether this change in turnout is unequal across different groups. It is when distance to people's voting sites goes up: Greater distance reduces turnout more in heavily minority, Democratic-leaning areas, and less in Whiter, more Republican precincts.[84] Likewise, turnout drops by about half a percentage point more for registered Democratic voters than for registered Republicans when their voting sites are moved.[85] Consequently, both building blocks are present for voting sites' locations to affect alignment: nontrivial and unrepresentative shifts in turnout.

These building blocks, at first glance, might not seem too sturdy. If all people's voting sites were moved farther away, voter turnout would decline by a few percentage points. But the partisan differences in how much turnout would fall would be too small to cause significant partisan misalignment. The rationale for including voting sites' locations in this section rather than the last one, then, is the possibility of *targeted* manipulation of the geography of elections. Imagine a partial administrator who shuffled and eliminated voting sites in one party's stronghold while leaving intact existing and abundant voting sites in the other party's more supportive areas.[86] Then turnout would only drop in the victimized party's stronghold, and if that party was the Democratic Party, the decline would be exacerbated by the greater vulnerability of Democrats to relocated and more distant voting sites. This scenario is why I say that voting sites' locations can substantially influence alignment. If these locations are set on partisan instead of good government grounds, considerable partisan distortion of the actual electorate can be the result.

Let me repeat here an important point from Chapter 4. That a given voting regulation is misaligning doesn't necessarily mean that a court should strike it down, or that a nonjudicial actor should repeal or decline to enact it.[87] There might be compelling justifications for the regulation that outweigh its misaligning

---

[83] *See, e.g.*, Henry E. Brady & John E. McNulty, *Turning Out to Vote: The Costs of Finding and Getting to the Polling Place*, 105 Am. Pol. Sci. Rev. 115, 116 (2011); Jesse Yoder, How Polling Place Changes Reduce Turnout: Evidence from Administrative Data in North Carolina 10–14 (May 30, 2018).

[84] *See, e.g.*, Cantoni, *supra* note 82, at 79–81.

[85] *See, e.g.*, Brady & McNulty, *supra* note 83, at 127–28.

[86] This isn't a fanciful scenario. *See, e.g.*, Elliott B. Fullmer, *The Site Gap: Racial Inequalities in Early Voting Access*, 43 Am. Pol. Rsch. 283, 293–96 (2015) (areas with larger Black populations are allotted fewer early voting sites per capita); Markie McBrayer et al., *Local Officials as Partisan Operatives: The Effect of County Officials on Early Voting Administration*, 101 Soc. Sci. Q. 1475, 1482–84 (2020) (Republican-majority counties create fewer early voting sites). In addition, a partial administrator might try to restrict a mode of voting predominantly used by voters with a particular party affiliation—in recent years, mail-in voting in the case of Democrats, and in-person voting on election day in the case of Republicans.

[87] Likewise, not every aligning voting rule is necessarily desirable.

impact. Think of orderly election administration as a reason to register voters before election day, or focusing local races on local issues as a basis for off-cycle elections. I don't want to endorse these rationales (in fact, I'm skeptical of them), but they obviously carry weight for some reasonable observers. So my argument in this section isn't that we should get rid of all misaligning voting rules (though I do think we should *stay* rid of some misaligning voting rules, like those of the Jim Crow South). Rather, my claim is that we should subject misaligning voting rules to closer inspection. We should consider whether justifications we'd otherwise accept remain persuasive when they entail subversion of the democratic value of alignment. We should analyze whether modest changes to misaligning voting rules could significantly lessen their negative effects. In other words, we should treat misalignment caused by voting rules as a trigger for scrutiny—not a ground for abolition.

*　*　*

Voting is a critical act in elections—and in election law. As befits an overarching election law value, alignment is fully applicable to regulations of the voting process. Other principles may also be applicable, like Fishkin's notion of equal treatment of all citizens, but there's no need to choose a single victor among these ideas. In the voting context, the trickiest issue about alignment is which benchmark to use to measure congruence with popular preferences. Actual voters' views are an uninteresting baseline here, but the views of the population directly acted on by a voting rule are a more promising reference point. In most cases, this population is comprised of eligible voters, though all people are directly acted on by voting qualifications. On the merits, maybe surprisingly, few modern voting policies significantly affect alignment. The disenfranchisement of ex-felons, automatic voter registration, early and absentee voting, photo ID requirements for voting—none of these controversial laws moves the alignment needle much. Historically, however, the Jim Crow voting restrictions and the introduction of voter registration were highly misaligning. Even today, the effective elimination of voter registration, the use of off-cycle elections, and the manipulation of voting sites' locations considerably influence alignment. So there remain some voting measures as to which alignment would be a potent sword or shield.

If voting is a key act in elections (and in election law), political parties are key actors. They take policy stands, command the allegiance of voters and politicians, and compete for (and, if successful, exercise) the authority of the state. "Modern democracy," political scientist E. E. Schattschneider thus quips, "is unthinkable save in terms of parties."[88] The regulation of these vital institutions is the

---

[88] E. E. SCHATTSCHNEIDER, PARTY GOVERNMENT 1 (1942).

subject of the next chapter. Parties' access to the ballot is sometimes restricted. So is their ability to freely choose their general election nominees. Even the structure of the electoral system can be understood as a party regulation. I explore the aligning effects of these and other policies that arguably impinge on party autonomy. I also consider whether *intraparty* alignment—congruence between *party* outputs and *party* members' preferences—is normatively appealing.

6

Political Parties

Introduction

A single question dominates the jurisprudence and the legal literature on political parties: What *are* these institutions? Are they private organizations with public goals, akin to the American Civil Liberties Union or the National Rifle Association? In that case, under standard First Amendment doctrine, governmental regulation of their internal activities should be highly disfavored.[1] Or are parties effectively arms of the state because of their entanglement with the political process? On that view, governmental regulation of parties is innocuous and parties' own decisions have to satisfy the criteria applicable to state action.[2] Or, as some scholars have recently argued, is the true nature of parties more complex, dynamic, and contingent? If a party is "a loose coalition of diverse entities . . . organized around a popular national brand,"[3] or "a loose collection of political relationships . . . among a diverse set of actors and institutions . . . in furtherance of a common general agenda,"[4] then party regulability is likely to vary from one context to another.

I don't take sides in this debate here, at least not overtly. Instead, I *assume* that parties can be regulated, and I then ask which party regulations align, which ones misalign, and which exert no significant influence on the congruence between governmental outputs and popular preferences. Put differently, my interest in this chapter is the impact of party regulations, not their permissibility. But note that this approach intersects the legal debate in interesting ways. With respect to aligning regulations, that positive effect is a good reason to approve them, even in the face of claims that they burden parties' associational rights. With respect to misaligning policies, conversely, there's no democratic interest to offset any perceived interference with party autonomy. In fact, these laws should

---

[1] *See, e.g.,* Cal. Democratic Party v. Jones, 530 U.S. 567, 582–83 (2000) (analogizing political parties to a veterans' group organizing a St. Patrick's Day Parade); Bruce E. Cain, *Party Autonomy and Two-Party Electoral Competition,* 149 U. PA. L. REV. 793 (2001).

[2] *See, e.g., Jones,* 530 U.S. at 594 n.5 (Stevens, J., dissenting) ("[P]rimaries—as integral parts of the election process by which the people select their government—are state affairs, not internal party affairs."); Samuel Issacharoff, *Private Parties with Public Purposes: Political Parties, Associational Freedoms, and Partisan Competition,* 101 COLUM. L. REV. 274 (2001).

[3] Joseph Fishkin & Heather K. Gerken, *The Party's Over: McCutcheon, Shadow Parties, and the Future of the Party System,* 2014 SUP. CT. REV. 175, 187.

[4] Michael S. Kang, *The Hydraulics and Politics of Party Regulation,* 91 IOWA L. REV. 131, 133 (2005).

Aligning Election Law. Nicholas O. Stephanopoulos, Oxford University Press. © Nicholas O. Stephanopoulos 2024.
DOI: 10.1093/9780197662182.003.0006

be suspect even if parties don't object to them. And as to measures that neither align nor misalign, I make no intervention in the legal debate. These provisions can be defended or criticized only on grounds external to this project.

Before probing the impact of party regulations, I address an antecedent issue. Until now, I've conceived of alignment in terms of *governmental* outputs and *popular* preferences. Should this notion of alignment be supplemented (or even replaced) by *intraparty* alignment—congruence between *party* outputs and *party* members' preferences? Some Justices and scholars think so, but I disagree. As important as parties are, they're not the polity itself. They're not the entity that engages in self-government to exercise the authority of the state. Whether parties are internally aligned or misaligned is therefore irrelevant from a democratic perspective (vital though it is from parties' own standpoints). Moreover, intraparty alignment can be a potent driver of polity-wide misalignment. If an internally aligned party has members whose preferences diverge from those of the general public, and if that party manages to win control of the government, then representation and policy are likely to follow the party line, not popular opinion. Intraparty alignment is thus a threat to—not an aspect of—democracy.

Turning to the core of this chapter, party regulations can be sorted into three categories. First, some laws relate to how parties choose their general election nominees. Strikingly, the type of primary election that a state holds has little to no effect on representational alignment. At the district level, individual legislators are about as ideologically distant from their constituents whether the primary is limited to registered party members or open to all comers. At the jurisdictional level, the same is true for how well (or not) legislators collectively reflect the views of all people in the state or country. One explanation for these results is the insensitivity of primary turnout to primary type. Roughly the same share of voters, with roughly the same attitudes, go to the polls in the primary no matter what kind of primary it is. Another reason is voter ignorance. If voters can't reliably distinguish between extreme and moderate candidates, it doesn't particularly matter which voters are entitled to participate in the primary.

Second, other party regulations pertain to ballot access. They can make it difficult for certain candidates, especially minor party nominees and independents, to secure places on the general election ballot. These ballot access restrictions are aligning—but only weakly so, and only if a plurality winner rule is in effect. One mechanism through which these measures promote alignment is the prevention of wrong-winner outcomes: scenarios where the victor in a multicandidate field is opposed by a majority of voters. Wrong-winner outcomes are impossible if ballot access restrictions limit the number of general election choices to two. Another aligning mechanism is the inducement of convergence on the middle of the ideological spectrum, where most people are located. This convergence can be disrupted by the emergence of a moderate minor party. Ballot access restrictions can thwart this emergence, thereby allowing the converging dynamic to operate. But the caveats I flagged above—only weakly so, and only if a plurality winner rule is in effect—are noteworthy. Ballot access restrictions aren't strongly aligning because the forms of misalignment they avoid are rare in modern American politics. These laws are also unnecessary to achieve alignment under alternatives to plurality rule.

Alternatives to plurality rule, then, are the last category of party regulations I cover in this chapter. In an election for a single position, these options include a runoff election, instant-runoff voting, and pairwise voting. All these policies regulate parties in the sense that they shape the political environment in which parties compete. And all these policies are aligning because they make wrong-winner outcomes under multicandidate fields unlikely or even impossible. More ambitiously, in an election for *multiple* seats, proportional representation is the great alternative to plurality rule. Proportional representation can be attained in several ways: through the single transferable vote, via party lists, and by supplementing legislators from districts with a pool of at-large members. Again, all these variants are aligning. They yield excellent partisan alignment as long as the number of seats is reasonably large. A sizable comparative literature also shows that collective representational alignment is superior under proportional representation than under single-member districts with plurality rule.

Intraparty Alignment

I identified the axes of alignment in Chapter 2: the dimensions that provide the intellectual scaffolding for this democratic value. Much of this conceptual work is applicable to intraparty alignment—congruence within a political party—but not all. One distinction is that party outputs are different from governmental outputs. Party outputs include the identities of general election nominees, the positions taken by these nominees (as well as their intraparty competitors), and the platform set forth by the party itself. But party outputs *don't* include enacted policies because the party, unlike the state, lacks the authority to convert policy stances into binding laws. Policy alignment therefore has no role in the intraparty context.

Another distinction is that it's unclear whose preferences count for purposes of intraparty alignment. All voters registered with the party? All voters who back the party in the general election? Activists who devote their time and energy to the party's cause? Donors who give their money to the party and its candidates? The party's officeholders and/or organizational leaders? Some combination of these groups? The difficulty is that the party comprises many constituencies, whose size and influence are constantly changing. So neither in theory nor in practice is it possible to pinpoint the population whose views should constitute the benchmark relative to which party outputs should be assessed. Determining this population requires a fixed understanding of the party's internal organization, but the point about party structure is that it's always in flux.[5]

Despite these conceptual issues,[6] Justice Antonin Scalia lauded intraparty alignment in a 2000 case. "[A] political party," he argued, should be able to "select[] a standard bearer who best represents the party's ideologies and preferences."[7] "[N]ominees of parties" should reflect the "policy views . . . of the party faithful."[8] Still more vigorously, Justice Scalia objected to regulatory efforts to undermine intraparty alignment. He could "think of no heavier burden on a political party[]" than requiring it to have its "nominees, and hence their positions, determined by" the preferences of nonparty members.[9] He also warned that "encourag[ing] candidates—and officeholders who hope to be renominated—to curry favor with persons who views are [different] than those of the party base" might "severely transform" or even "destroy the party."[10]

Several scholars echo Justice Scalia's praise for intraparty alignment. Joseph Fishkin and Heather Gerken explicitly argue that "parties are valuable because they serve as *democratic arenas*."[11] Within these arenas, parties' "voters are the real principals, and the party officials and the party-in-government are merely their agents."[12] In other words, parties' leaders should align their positions with those of parties' rank and file. More subtly, Bruce Cain and Nathaniel Persily contend that American elections are already centripetal enough thanks to the plurality winner rule they usually employ. Internally aligned parties—aligned at a point *away* from the political center—are thus "a countermajoritarian check on a system highly skewed toward representation of the median voter," in Persily's words.[13] Or as Cain puts it, internally aligned (and noncentrist) parties offset the "strong centripetal forces" and "non-ideological and centrist candidates" that supposedly characterize American politics.[14]

---

[5] This can be understood as a more acute form of the democratic boundary problem. At least in the usual context of the polity as a whole, the structure of the polity isn't constantly changing and there's widespread (if not universal) agreement that all persons meeting some membership criterion (residence, citizenship, voting, etc.) constitute the dêmos.

[6] Note how, in the quotes from *Jones*, Justice Scalia refers to the "party faithful" and the "party base" without nailing down whom these groups include.

[7] *Jones*, 530 U.S. at 575 (internal quotation marks omitted).

[8] *Id.* at 578.

[9] *Id.* at 577, 582.

[10] *Id.* at 579–80.

[11] Fishkin & Gerken, *supra* note 3, at 199. Fishkin and Gerken ultimately embrace a hybrid model that also gives elites a role in setting parties' agendas. *See id.* at 203.

[12] *Id.* at 199.

[13] Nathaniel Persily, *Toward a Functional Defense of Political Party Autonomy*, 76 N.Y.U. L. REV. 750, 807 (2001).

[14] Bruce E. Cain, *Party Autonomy and Two-Party Electoral Competition*, 149 U. PA. L. REV. 793, 809 (2001).

You won't be surprised that I have a factual disagreement with Cain and Persily. They think that, thanks to plurality rule, American governmental outputs are reasonably congruent with the preferences of the American public. In contrast, as I explained in Chapter 3, I see misalignment with the views of most Americans at every turn. The partisan compositions of legislatures and their electorates often sharply differ. Most officeholders are conservative or liberal while most Americans are moderate. Policy outcomes, too, are skewed in favor of the wealthy, the ideologically extreme, and the defenders of the status quo. If this is the true picture of American politics, then internally aligned (and noncentrist) parties aren't a modest counterweight within an otherwise well-aligned system. The system *isn't* well-aligned, meaning that such parties exacerbate the system's centrifugal (rather than mitigate its centripetal) tendencies.

My skepticism of intraparty alignment, though, has deeper roots than my reading of the empirical literature on modern American politics. Fundamentally, a political party isn't a polity. No matter how broadly they're construed, a party's members aren't coextensive with the population of the jurisdiction. Instead, a party's members are necessarily a smaller set, limited to individuals who support the party in some fashion. Likewise, no matter how interlocked a party may be with the machinery of government, it's not equivalent to the state. A party attempts to influence how governmental power is used, but it doesn't wield governmental power itself. Consequently, a party lacks both of the constituent elements of democracy: a dêmos comprising the membership of the polity, and a kratos exercising authority on the polity's behalf. In the absence of these elements, intraparty alignment may be of great interest to a party's members, but it has no direct democratic significance. Democracy, that is, isn't necessarily enhanced (or eroded) by the fact that a party is (or isn't) internally aligned.

The same conclusion follows from the array of democratic theories I discussed in Chapter 2. The delegate and trustee models of representation, pluralism, deliberative democracy, minimalist democracy, and thick democracy—these accounts agree on very little. But one point on which they do see eye to eye is that intraparty alignment is irrelevant per se.[15] Neither the delegate nor the trustee model advocates that an officeholder toe the party line. (In fact, party loyalty could prevent an elected official from being an effective delegate or trustee.) From a pluralist perspective, parties are just a few of the interest groups from whose conflict and compromise public policy is meant to emerge. So a party's

---

[15] *See, e.g.,* Ingrid van Biezen & Michael Saward, *Democratic Theorists and Party Scholars: Why They Don't Talk to Each Other, and Why They Should,* 6 PERSP. POL. 21, 24 (2008) (observing, albeit critically, that "the theory of democracy [is] detached from analysis of the character and roles of political parties"); Russell Muirhead & Nancy L. Rosenblum, *The Political Theory of Parties and Partisanship: Catching Up,* 23 ANN. REV. POL. SCI. 95, 96 (2020) (also complaining that parties are "largely absent from agonistic, liberal, deliberative, and participatory democratic theories").

internal alignment is of no more importance than that of any other organization. For their part, deliberative democrats want the *public* to argue and learn about *governmental* decisions. These theorists don't care how thoughtful *party* members are in their reflection about *party* choices. And both thin and thick conceptions of democracy identify polity-level desiderata: free and fair elections, in the former case, substantive human rights and socioeconomic equality, in the latter. On this list of goals, intraparty alignment is nowhere to be found.

Of course, intraparty alignment could have implications for—even though it's not synonymous with—democratic values. But these potential effects only add to my concerns about it. Suppose a party's members (however defined) have policy preferences distinct from those of the polity's entire population. Also say the party is internally aligned in that its candidates and officeholders, their policy stances, and the party-wide platform all reflect the views of the party's members. Then what would happen if this party managed to win control of the government? Significant representational and policy *misalignment* with the preferences of the polity's whole population. The government's outputs would now match the views of the party's members—but those views, by stipulation, are different from those of the general public. Intraparty alignment, in this scenario, would therefore be the cause of polity-wide misalignment. If you're persuaded that polity-wide misalignment is a democratic injury, intraparty alignment would be the cause of that harm.[16]

That harm could be avoided, moreover, if the party *wasn't* internally aligned. Imagine that the party's outputs were out of line with the preferences of the party's members—but *in* line with those of the polity's entire population. Typically, this would entail the party's politicians and policy positions being more moderate than the party's membership would like. Then if this internally misaligned party took power, representational and policy alignment with the views of the general public would ensue. The party base would protest but the work of the government would mirror the will of the people. Intraparty misalignment would be responsible for successful democracy.

I want to acknowledge that some party members fervently desire intraparty alignment (as well as polity-wide misalignment in their preferred ideological direction). These activists, donors, and interest groups devote enormous energy to persuading their fellow party members, policing candidates and their policy stances, and pressuring the party to follow through on its commitments when

---

[16] *See, e.g.,* Daniel R. Ortiz, *Duopoly Versus Autonomy: How the Two-Party System Harms the Major Parties,* 100 COLUM. L. REV. 753, 772 (2000) ("[T]he greatest prize to a party is being able to leverage the will of [its members] into the 'will' of all."); Nathaniel Persily & Bruce E. Cain, *The Legal Status of Political Parties: A Reassessment of Competing Paradigms,* 100 COLUM. L. REV. 775, 786 (2000) (noting that, from a Progressive perspective, "parties remain obstructive forces for the realization of the general will of the electorate").

it holds the reins of power. Nor are these "intense policy demanders" a minor party constituency. Rather, to a growing number of political scientists, they're the heart and soul of the party, even more central than the party's officeholders. "[P]arties in the United States," write one group of scholars, "are best understood as coalitions of interest groups and activists seeking to capture and use government for their particular goals."[17] These "energized segments of the population" continuously "attempt to pull government policy toward their own preferences."[18]

As badly as intense policy demanders want intraparty alignment, though, the rest of us don't have to pay them any heed. That's my underlying argument here. From a polity-wide (as opposed to an internal party) angle, intraparty alignment holds no intrinsic appeal. Its achievement advances no democratic principles, vindicates no democratic values. In fact, intraparty alignment can be positively harmful to the extent it enables polity-wide misalignment. In that case, intraparty alignment exacts an affirmative democratic toll. Translating these points into the language of doctrine, the state has no interest in helping parties to be better internally aligned. If anything, the state should have the opposite aim: thwarting intraparty alignment so that if a party captures the machinery of government, polity-wide misalignment isn't the result.[19]

Primary Type

Moving from the theory to the practice of party regulation, there are three main types of laws that bear on political parties.[20] First, certain measures shape the processes by which parties choose their general election nominees. Second, other provisions determine whether those nominees are able to appear on the general election ballot. And third, still other laws establish the overall electoral structure in which parties compete. I tackle these sets of party rules in this order.

[17] Kathleen Bawn et al., *A Theory of Political Parties: Groups, Policy Demands and Nominations in American Politics*, 10 PERSP. POL. 571, 571 (2012).
[18] MARTY COHEN ET AL., THE PARTY DECIDES: PRESIDENTIAL NOMINATIONS BEFORE AND AFTER REFORM 7 (2008).
[19] Of course, a *party* might have a constitutional interest in intraparty alignment, even if the state doesn't. That's precisely the position the Court took in *Jones*, finding in the First Amendment a party associational right that was burdened when the state selected a primary type that, the party believed, hindered the party's pursuit of internal alignment.
[20] Independent of the laws that affect their operation, parties (and partisanship) help to shape people's policy preferences. I don't directly address this endogenous role that parties play in influencing public opinion.

(And I defer until Chapter 9 my discussion of a fourth category of party regulation: limits on parties' ability to raise and spend money.[21])

Beginning with the selection of parties' general election nominees, all states now rely on primary elections for nonpresidential offices. These are governmentally administered elections in which some or all registered voters can participate. In a closed primary, only people registered with the relevant party can cast ballots. In a semi-closed primary, party registrants and independents can vote (but people registered with another party can't). All registered voters can take part in an open primary. The same is true in a semi-open primary, with the caveat that people must state publicly in which party's primary they intend to vote. Lastly, in a nonpartisan or top-two primary, all candidates from all parties are listed together, and all registered voters choose among them. The two candidates for each position with the most votes then advance to the general election.[22]

In the popular media, more exclusive (i.e., closed or semi-closed) primaries are often blamed for representational misalignment. By the same token, more inclusive (i.e., open, semi-open, or top-two) primaries are common proposals for improving alignment. The logic underlying these claims goes like this: Party registrants tend to hold ideologically extreme views. If only (or mostly) party registrants are allowed to participate in primaries, then candidates sharing their liberal or conservative preferences will typically win parties' nominations. When these nominees are ultimately elected, their stances will be noncongruent with those of their constituents—who obviously aren't restricted to party registrants. Conversely, if all (or most) registered voters can take part in primaries, then the ideological distribution of the primary electorate will be more centrist, more like that of the general electorate. This ideological distribution will help more moderate candidates to win parties' nominations. In turn, when these nominees are ultimately elected, their positions will be a better match for those of (all of) their constituents.[23]

Despite its plausibility, this dynamic turns out not to hold. A robust political science literature establishes that primary type has little effect on politicians'

---

[21] Moreover, I don't discuss regulations of parties' internal affairs because these rules are generally unconstitutional, *see, e.g.,* Eu v. San Francisco Cnty. Democratic Cent. Comm., 489 U.S. 214 (1989), and their implications for alignment are unclear.

[22] For a good discussion of these types of primary elections, see Eric McGhee et al., *A Primary Cause of Partisanship? Nomination Systems and Legislator Ideology,* 58 AM. J. POL. SCI. 337, 339–41 (2014). For information on primary type by state, see *State Primary Election Types,* NAT'L CONF. ST. LEGIS. (Jan. 5, 2021), https://www.ncsl.org/research/elections-and-campaigns/primary-types.aspx.

[23] Innumerable pundits and reformers make arguments along these lines. For a few examples drawn from the month before I wrote this chapter, see Katherine M. Gehl, *It's Time to Get Rid of Party Primaries,* CNN (Mar. 12, 2021), https://www.cnn.com/2021/03/12/opinions/reform-american-political-primaries-gehl/index.html, and Nick Troiano, *Party Primaries Must Go,* THE ATLANTIC (Mar. 30, 2021), https://www.theatlantic.com/ideas/archive/2021/03/party-primaries-must-go/618428/.

ideologies—meaning it also has little effect on representational alignment.[24] In the best-known study in this genre, Eric McGhee and his coauthors examine how the ideal points of Democratic and Republican state legislators vary based on the kind of primary in which they run.[25] As Figure 6.1 illustrates, these ideal points *don't* materially vary by primary type. Levels of legislative polarization (and collective representational misalignment) are about the same whether the primary is more inclusive or exclusive.[26] Other studies extend this finding to all candidates competing in primaries as well as to candidates who win in primaries but subsequently lose in general elections. Again, no consistent relationship appears between candidate ideology and primary type.[27] Still other studies zero in on the top-two primary—a favorite of reformers—and even the very use of primaries to nominate candidates instead of caucuses or conventions. Once more, the top-two primary doesn't produce substantially more moderate, better aligned politicians,[28] and primaries themselves, when they were first adopted, didn't cause the opposite outcomes.[29]

What accounts for these null results? One explanation is that the ideological distribution of the primary electorate is roughly constant no matter what sort of primary is used. At both the congressional[30] and presidential[31] levels, the mean and the variance of primary voters' ideologies don't change much based on whether the primary is more inclusive or exclusive. This fact falsifies one of the assumptions of the argument for why more inclusive primaries should lead to improved representational alignment: that more inclusive primaries should attract different, ideologically more moderate voters. More inclusive primaries actually draw more or less the same voters as more exclusive primaries. Apparently,

[24] *See, e.g.,* R. Michael Alvarez & J. Andrew Sinclair, Nonpartisan Primary Election Reform: Mitigating Mischief 195 (2015) (noting "the current 'conventional wisdom' . . . that primary laws have little or no effect on political outcomes").

[25] *See* Eric McGhee et al., *A Primary Cause of Partisanship? Nomination Systems and Legislator Ideology*, 58 Am. J. Pol. Sci. 337, 342–47 (2014).

[26] *See id.*

[27] *See* Lindsay Nielson & Neil Visalvanich, *Primaries and Candidates: Examining the Influence of Primary Electorates on Candidate Ideology*, 5 Pol. Sci. Rsch. & Methods 397, 401–02 (2017); Jon C. Rogowski & Stephanie Langella, *Primary Systems and Candidate Ideology: Evidence from Federal and State Legislative Elections*, 43 Am. Pol. Rsch. 846, 856–63 (2015); Nicholas O. Stephanopoulos et al., *The Realities of Electoral Reform*, 68 Vand. L. Rev. 761, 806–09 (2015).

[28] *See, e.g.,* Douglas J. Ahler et al., *Do Open Primaries Improve Representation? An Experimental Test of California's 2012 Top-Two Primary*, 41 Legis. Stud. Q. 237, 247–50 (2016); Thad Kousser et al., *Reform and Representation: A New Method Applied to Recent Electoral Changes*, 6 Pol. Sci. Rsch. & Methods 809, 818–24 (2018).

[29] *See* Shigeo Hirano et al., *Primary Elections and Partisan Polarization in the U.S. Congress*, 5 Q.J. Pol. Sci. 169, 173–75 (2010).

[30] *See* Seth J. Hill, *Institution of Nomination and the Policy Ideology of Primary Electorates*, 10 Q.J. Pol. Sci. 461, 471–74 (2015); John Sides et al., *On the Representativeness of Primary Electorates*, 50 Brit. J. Pol. Sci. 677, 683 (2020).

[31] *See* Barbara Norrander & Jay Wendland, *Open Versus Closed Primaries and the Ideological Composition of Presidential Primary Electorates*, 42 Electoral Stud. 229, 232–35 (2016).

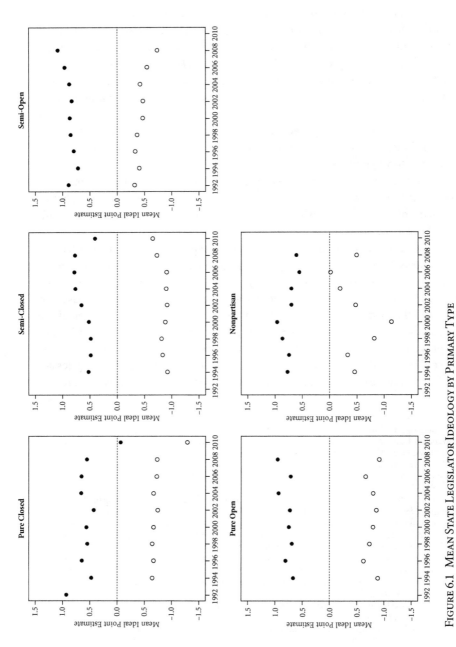

FIGURE 6.1 MEAN STATE LEGISLATOR IDEOLOGY BY PRIMARY TYPE

Figure 6.1 is reproduced with permission from Eric McGhee et al., *A Primary Cause of Partisanship? Nomination Systems and Legislator Ideology*, 58 AM. J. POL. SCI. 337, 343 (2014). Copyright © 2014 by Wiley.

few individuals registered with a given party, or as independents, choose to participate in a different party's primary when presented with that opportunity.

Voter ignorance is another reason for the absence of strong relationship between primary type and representational alignment. Even if more moderate voters *did* participate in more inclusive primaries, their ballots could only affect candidates' ideologies if they could *distinguish* between more and less extreme candidates. Many primary voters, however, lack this capability. In the aggregate, their perceptions of candidates' ideologies are almost wholly untethered to candidates' actual liberalism or conservatism. This is true in both Democratic and Republican primaries, and as to both incumbent and non-incumbent candidates.[32] "In perhaps the most striking example," voters in California's top-two primary "failed to view Abel Maldonado, the moderate Republican who spearheaded the top-two reform, as appreciably more centrist than his Tea Party opponent."[33] Instead, voters "placed the two candidates at almost the same position on the ideological continuum."[34]

Of course, even if the kinds of primaries currently used in the United States don't materially affect representational alignment, other policies might do so. For a brief period in the late 1990s, for instance, California relied on the so-called blanket primary, in which voters choose race by race in which party's primary to participate. "Virtually every study" that examined the impact of the blanket primary "found a small but notable increase in moderation during that time."[35] More dramatically, for most of the first half of the twentieth century, California allowed candidates to run in multiple parties' primaries without identifying their party affiliations. Under this system of "cross-filing," legislators compiled strikingly moderate voting records, resulting in impressive representational alignment at both the district and jurisdictional levels.[36] Legislators behaved this way because, "[i]f one wishes to run as both a Democrat and a Republican, one cannot make a record that is too blatantly partisan in either direction."[37] "Middle-of-the-road politics—or what seems middle-of-the-road in one's own district—is the safest route."[38]

---

[32] *See* Ahler et al., *supra* note 28, at 242–45.

[33] *Id.* at 243.

[34] *Id.* But note that in primaries where voters choose among candidates from *different* parties, like top-two or top-four primaries, candidates' party affiliations make possible more informed voting.

[35] Eric McGhee & Boris Shor, *Has the Top Two Primary Elected More Moderates?*, 15 PERSP. POL. 1053, 1056 (2017); *see, e.g.*, Will Bullock & Joshua D. Clinton, *More a Molehill than a Mountain: The Effects of the Blanket Primary on Elected Officials' Behavior from California*, 73 J. POL. 915, 919–27 (2011).

[36] *See* Seth E. Masket, *It Takes an Outsider: Extralegislative Organization and Partisanship in the California Assembly, 1849-2006*, 51 AM. J. POL. SCI. 482, 485–94 (2007).

[37] *Id.* at 489.

[38] *Id.* Among the primary systems currently in use in the United States, maybe the most aligning is Alaska's top-four regime, under which the top four candidates in the primary election, regardless of their party affiliations, advance to the general election, which is held using ranked-choice voting. There's emerging evidence that this system is aligning because it increases the likelihood that

Putting aside these historical curiosities, the upshot is clear for the sorts of primaries now used across America. They neither improve nor worsen alignment to any significant extent. This conclusion continues a theme from the last chapter: that numerous electoral regulations commonly thought to be highly aligning or misaligning are, in fact, much less impactful. This conclusion also means that, legally and politically, alignment should be peripheral to debates about primary type. More inclusive primaries shouldn't be defended on the ground that they encourage more congruent representation when they're attacked on other bases, like the burdens they allegedly impose on parties that would rather choose their nominees a different way. To reiterate, more inclusive primaries don't actually cause officeholders to better reflect their constituents' views. By the same token, more exclusive primaries shouldn't be criticized for driving a wedge between constituents and the politicians who represent them. That wedge, intuitive though it may seem, isn't corroborated by empirical analysis.

Ballot Access

Even after a party has chosen its nominee, there remains the question of whether that standard-bearer will be able to secure a spot on the general election ballot.[39] This is rarely a serious concern for major party nominees, whose ballot access is ensured, or at least greatly facilitated, by their parties' previous electoral success. Minor party nominees and independent candidates, however, often face an array of hurdles to appear on the general election ballot. They must typically compile a substantial number of signatures by a deadline months before the election. They're sometimes banned from launching write-in candidacies. They're also sometimes barred from the general election ballot if they previously ran and lost in any party's primary election. And in most states, anti-"fusion" laws forbid a minor party from nominating a candidate already selected by a major party.[40]

---

moderate candidates will make it to the general election (rather than being winnowed out at the primary stage). *See, e.g.,* David Lublin & Benjamin Reilly, *Encouraging Cooperation and Responsibility, in* APSA PRESIDENTIAL TASK FORCE ON POLITICAL PARTIES, MORE THAN RED AND BLUE: POLITICAL PARTIES AND AMERICAN DEMOCRACY 138 (2023).

[39] Another question is whether a *defeated* primary election candidate can access the general election ballot. In most states, a "sore loser" law means the answer is no. In an intriguing study, Barry Burden and his coauthors find that sore loser laws worsen legislative polarization (and thus representational misalignment) within both individual districts and whole chambers. Sore loser laws do so directly by preventing losing centrist politicians from continuing their candidacies, and indirectly by increasing the leverage of party activists whose approval candidates must generally win to advance to the general election. *See generally* Barry C. Burden et al., *Sore Loser Laws and Congressional Polarization,* 39 LEGIS. STUD. Q. 299 (2014).

[40] The definitive guide to ballot access rules is Richard Winger's *Ballot Access News,* http://ballot-access.org/ (last visited Feb. 1, 2024).

To some structuralist scholars, ballot access restrictions are canonical examples of antidemocratic measures that courts should strike down. To take a prominent pair, Samuel Issacharoff and Richard Pildes contend that these policies are "the worst kind of anticompetitive practices."[41] By excluding minor party candidates from the general election ballot, they "insulate the dominant parties from those few possible sources of competitive pressure that do potentially remain."[42] Because I emphasize alignment instead of competition, my perspective is quite different. It's the *presence* of minor party candidates on the general election ballot that's misaligning in some circumstances. Ballot access restrictions are therefore desirable to the extent they prevent misalignment due to multiple general election candidates from arising. But this extent is limited in modern American politics, rendering my endorsement of these laws partial rather than full-throated.

Why are multiple (i.e., more than two) general election candidates potentially misaligning? The more obvious reason is that, if a plurality winner rule is in effect, multiple candidates make it possible for a "spoiler" to emerge. As I noted in Chapter 4, a spoiler is a minor party candidate who fails to win but who *does* receive enough votes to change what the election's outcome would have been had only two candidates competed.[43] When a minor party candidate plays the role of spoiler, partisan misalignment is guaranteed and representational misalignment is a virtual certainty, too. Think of a race in a right-leaning district between a liberal Democrat, a conservative Republican, and an anti-government Libertarian. Also suppose the Democrat earns 45 percent of the vote, the Republican takes 40 percent, and the Libertarian musters 15 percent—all of which would have gone to the Republican if the Libertarian hadn't been on the ballot. Then an electorate that prefers Republican to Democratic representation is saddled with a Democrat instead. And since the Democrat is a liberal while the district is right-leaning, this partisan misalignment leads to representational misalignment as well.

Plainly, ballot access restrictions could stop this spoiler scenario from taking place. If onerous enough, the policies could make it impossible for the Libertarian to qualify for the general election ballot. In that case, the ballot would include only two candidates, the Democrat and the Republican, and the Republican would win by a margin of 55 percent to 45 percent. This victory would avoid the partisan and representational misalignment caused by a liberal

[41] Samuel Issacharoff & Richard H. Pildes, *Politics as Markets: Partisan Lockups of the Democratic Process*, 50 STAN. L. REV. 643, 668 (1998).

[42] *Id.* at 676.

[43] *See, e.g.,* Michael C. Herron & Jeffrey B. Lewis, *Did Ralph Nader Spoil Al Gore's Presidential Bid? A Ballot-Level Study of Green and Reform Party Voters in the 2000 Presidential Election*, 2 Q.J. POL. SCI. 205, 206 (2007).

Democratic triumph in a three-way race. This logic explains why I favor ballot access restrictions, albeit weakly. There exist plausible situations in which these laws promote alignment by thwarting would-be spoilers.

The caveats to my support, though, are significant. Together, they make me unenthused about trying to keep minor party candidates off the general election ballot. First, there simply aren't many spoilers in contemporary American elections. Out of more than 10,000 federal and state races in 2020, for instance, there were just seventy-seven—less than 1 percent—in which minor party candidates received more votes than the margin of victory between the major party candidates.[44] In 2018, this figure was a similarly small ninety-nine.[45] Moreover, even in these exceptional races, it's merely possible that minor party candidates changed the outcomes. It's also possible that their votes were drawn evenly enough from the major party candidates that the results would have been the same had they not been on the ballot. Notwithstanding high-profile cases like Florida's 2000 presidential election, then, misalignment stemming from minor party spoilers is a rare occurrence. The limited scale of the problem reduces the appeal of measures that might solve it.

Second, the main American ballot access restrictions *don't* solve the problem of multiple general election candidates potentially leading to misalignment. The most widespread of these policies are signature requirements and previous vote requirements. Unsurprisingly, these laws reduce the *number* of candidates on the general election ballot.[46] But they don't materially affect the *total vote share* of minor party candidates, because minor party candidates capable of attracting nontrivial popular support are also generally able to satisfy the criteria for qualifying for the general election ballot.[47] Figure 6.2, drawn from a study by Bernard Tamas and Matthew Hindman, makes this point historically. The first panel shows signature requirements and previous vote requirements for appearing on U.S. House general election ballots steadily rising over the last century. The second panel plots the total vote share of minor party U.S. House candidates over the same period. The two data series have very little in common. In particular, the total vote share of minor party candidates swings wildly in the early twentieth century, then stays low for several decades, and then begins to edge upward—all while ballot access requirements grow ever stricter. These

[44] *See* Dave Beaudoin, *77 Third-Party Candidates Received More Votes than the Winner's Margin of Victory in 2020*, BALLOTPEDIA NEWS (Jan. 29, 2021), https://news.ballotpedia.org/2021/01/29/77-third-party-candidates-received-more-votes-than-the-winners-margin-of-victory-in-2020/.

[45] *See id.*

[46] *See* Barry C. Burden, *Ballot Regulations and Multiparty Politics in the States*, 49 PS: POL. SCI. & POL. 669, 671 (2007); Bernard Tamas & Matthew Dean Hindman, *Ballot Access Laws and the Decline of American Third Parties*, 13 ELECTION L.J. 260, 269 (2014).

[47] *See* Stephen Ansolabehere & Alan Gerber, *The Effects of Filing Fees and Petition Requirements on U.S. House Elections*, 21 LEGIS. STUD. Q. 249, 256–58 (1996); Burden, *supra* note 46, at 671; Tamas & Hindman, *supra* note 46, at 269.

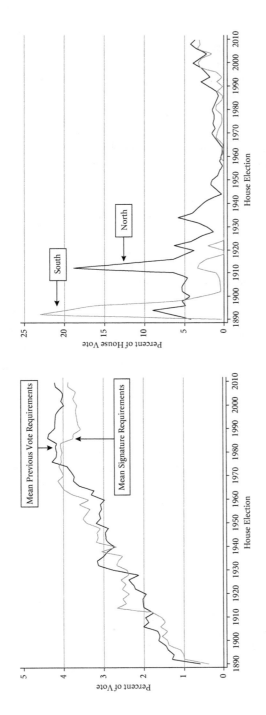

FIGURE 6.2 U.S. HOUSE BALLOT ACCESS REQUIREMENTS AND TOTAL MINOR PARTY VOTE SHARE

Figure 6.2 is reproduced with permission from Bernard Tamas & Matthew Dean Hindman, *Ballot Access Laws and the Decline of American Third Parties*, 13 ELECTION L.J. 260, 264, 267 (2014). Copyright © 2014 by Mary Ann Liebert, Inc.

trends confirm that the popular support of minor party candidates is driven by political, not legal, factors. Legal interventions of the sort that states have historically undertaken thus can't effectively suppress the total vote share of minor party candidates.[48] For that reason, these measures also can't prevent much misalignment due to minor party spoilers.

Third, another common kind of ballot access restriction, a ban on fusion candidacies, is positively perverse (not just ineffective) in stopping misalignment from spoilers. Again, fusion candidacies are those in which a major party and a minor party both nominate the same person. Votes cast for the minor party then accrue to the fusion candidate just as do votes cast for the major party. Crucially, when a minor party uses the fusion tactic, its nominee can no longer be a spoiler since she no longer siphons off votes from the major parties' candidates.[49] Consequently, when states prohibit fusion, they outlaw a practice that has at least some capacity to avoid spoilers.[50] They force minor parties to put forward their own distinct nominees, who under the right (i.e., wrong) circumstances can cause elections to come out differently than if they had been two-candidate races.

Lastly, and most importantly, spoilers are only possible under a plurality winner rule—if a candidate necessarily prevails when she receives the most votes. Under certain other systems, which I discuss in the next section, minor party candidates can run without any risk that their bids might change elections' outcomes. My support for ballot access restrictions is therefore hesitant to begin with, but entirely nonexistent if plurality rule isn't presumed. Under plurality rule, misalignment due to minor party spoilers can occur (even if rarely), and ballot access restrictions (even if not signature requirements, previous vote requirements, or bans on fusion candidacies) can prevent it. Reject the predicate of plurality rule, though, and this case for keeping minor party candidates off the general election ballot collapses. Under proper alternatives to plurality rule, no curbs on minor party candidacies are needed to lower to zero the likelihood of misalignment from spoilers.

Recall my earlier comment that misalignment from spoilers is the more obvious kind of noncongruence that can be caused by multiple parties on the

---

[48] Of course, more drastic interventions like limiting the number of general election candidates to two could obviously drive the total vote share of minor party candidates to zero.

[49] See, e.g., Bernard Tamas, *Does Fusion Undermine American Third Parties? An Analysis of House Elections from 1870 to 2016*, 39 New Pol. Sci. 609, 612 (2017) ("Fusion makes it possible for voters to show support for a ... minor party without risking accidentally helping the less liked major party win another seat.").

[50] See, e.g., Benjamin R. Kantack, *Fusion and Electoral Performance in New York Congressional Elections*, 70 Pol. Rsch. Q. 291, 296 (2017) (identifying twenty-eight races in New York, the most important state that permits fusion candidacies, in which such candidacies *did* avoid wrong-winner outcomes).

general election ballot. A subtler form can arise when a minor party candidate *doesn't* play the role of spoiler but *does* enable the major party candidates to take more extreme positions that are more distant from the views of most voters. To grasp this dynamic, first imagine there are just two candidates on the general election ballot, each the nominee of a major party. These candidates have an electoral incentive to shift their stances toward the center of the electorate's ideological distribution, because that's the strategy that maximizes their vote shares if voters vote spatially. But now suppose a moderate minor party candidate is also on the ballot. This candidate's presence in the race reduces the electoral penalty incurred by the major party candidates if they take more liberal or conservative stands. True, those stands may still cost them the support of more centrist voters. But those voters may now cast their ballots for the moderate minor party candidate, not the opposing major party nominee. Put arithmetically, an extreme stance in a two-candidate race might decrease a candidate's vote margin by *two*—one vote lost by that candidate, one vote gained by her opponent. But that same stance in a race that also features a moderate minor party alternative might only cut that candidate's vote margin by *one*—the vote she loses, which then doesn't go to her chief rival.[51]

Does this dynamic play out in the real world? It does in Britain, where a centrist minor party, the Liberal Democratic Party, has contested a varying number of parliamentary seats over the last few decades. The more races that have included a Liberal Democratic candidate, the more ideologically divergent the Labour and the Conservative Parties' platforms have been. Greater Liberal Democratic participation, that is, has resulted in worse representational misalignment as more extreme Labour and Conservative politicians have taken office.[52] In the United States, similarly, Ross Perot was a centrist, quirky, and unusually successful candidate in the 1992 and 1996 presidential elections. In U.S. House districts in which Perot performed particularly well, Democratic and Republican congressional candidates exhibited greater ideological divergence. Mere *anticipation* of the entry of a minor party congressional candidate in the Perot mold was enough to induce Democrats to take more liberal, and (especially) Republicans more conservative, positions.[53]

Despite this evidence, misalignment due to moderate minor party candidates likely isn't more concerning than misalignment due to minor party spoilers. The reason is that, in modern American politics, minor party centrists like Perot are

---

[51] For an in-depth discussion of this dynamic, see James Adams & Samuel Merrill, III, *Why Small, Centrist Third Parties Motivate Policy Divergence by Major Parties*, 100 AM. POL. SCI. REV. 403, 403–10 (2006).

[52] *See id.* at 411–13.

[53] *See* Daniel J. Lee, *Anticipating Entry: Major Party Positioning and Third Party Threat*, 65 POL. RSCH. Q. 138, 143–44 (2012).

the exception and minor party extremists are the rule. In recent years, the minor parties whose candidates have received by far the most votes are the Libertarian Party and the Green Party.[54] The Libertarian Party is on the right side of the ideological spectrum and the Green Party is on the left. Neither resembles Britain's Liberal Democrats in slotting ideologically between the major parties. Critically, minor party candidates who outflank the major party candidates don't engender the same polarization as minor party moderates. Instead, they induce *both* major party candidates to move in the opposite ideological direction from the extreme minor party candidate (i.e., to the left in the case of a Libertarian candidate, to the right in the case of a Green).[55] This movement can produce either better or worse representational alignment depending on the ideology of the minor party candidate and the affiliation of the winning major party candidate. Accordingly, minor party candidates on the ideological fringes don't pose a consistent misaligning threat.

Furthermore, my points about the lack of fit between ballot access restrictions and misalignment from spoilers also apply to misalignment from minor party centrists. Since signature requirements and previous vote requirements don't reduce the total vote share of minor party candidates, they don't dampen the forces that push toward greater major party divergence in the presence of minor party moderates. Likewise, anti-fusion laws are affirmatively harmful here to the extent they cause minor parties to advance their own centrist nominees instead of endorsing major party candidates. And again, the dynamic of minor party moderates leading to worse representational misalignment is particular to the plurality winner rule. Under proper alternatives to plurality rule, this mechanism ceases to operate. For all these reasons, I'm as tepid a backer of ballot access restrictions to prevent misalignment from minor party centrists as to stop misalignment from spoilers.

Electoral System

I've been alluding to, without yet elucidating, electoral systems other than plurality rule that promise to avoid some of its misaligning effects. These alternatives can be grouped into less and more radical categories. The less radical policies still select a single winner in a race, just not based on which candidate receives

---

[54] *See, e.g., Third Party and Independent Candidates for the 2020 United States Presidential Election*, Wikipedia, https://en.wikipedia.org/wiki/Third_party_and_independent_candidates_for_the_2020_United_States_presidential_election (last visited Feb. 1, 2024) (showing that the Libertarian Party and Green Party candidates received far more votes than all other minor party candidates in the 2020 presidential election).

[55] *See* Adams & Merrill, *supra* note 51, at 414 (discussing this scenario).

the most votes. The policies that would represent a more dramatic break with American political history abandon *both* plurality rule *and* the requirement of a single winner. I consider these categories in this order. And I do so in this chapter about political parties because the electoral system influences the terrain on which parties compete more than any other factor. The electoral system affects how many viable parties there are, how they position themselves ideologically, and how much governmental power they ultimately wield. Moreover, while the electoral system isn't a classic party regulation that parties can challenge in court, this is also true for certain primary types. The top-two primary, in particular, doesn't tell parties how to choose their nominees, and so doesn't burden their associational rights.[56] Since the top-two primary is typically analyzed alongside conventional party regulations, it's reasonable for the underlying electoral system to be part of the same discussion.

Starting with the less disruptive policies that still pick a single winner, just not on the basis of plurality rule, they comprise a large set. In the interest of space, I'll therefore mention only three of them: two already in use in some American jurisdictions, and a third approach that's the favorite of many academics because of its distinctive properties. A runoff election, first, is a conditional election held only if no candidate receives a majority of the vote in the general election. The two candidates receiving the most votes in the general election advance to the runoff election, in which it's certain one of them will muster majority support.[57] Under instant-runoff voting, second, voters rank candidates in their order of preference. If no candidate gets a majority of first-place votes, the candidate with the fewest first-place votes is eliminated, and each ballot ranking that candidate first is reallocated to the next candidate on the voter's list. This process repeats until a candidate compiles more than half the votes.[58] And third, under pairwise voting, the ballot can be the same as under instant-runoff voting, or it can ask voters to state their preference between each pair of candidates. Either way, each candidate's record is assessed across all possible pairings. The winner is then the candidate with the best record, that is, the candidate who prevails one-on-one against the most other candidates. In the event of a tie, several tiebreakers are available, maybe most intuitively, each candidate's aggregate vote margin against all other candidates.[59]

The appeal of these policies is that they sharply reduce the likelihood of minor party spoilers. In most cases, they thus avert the partisan and representational

---

[56] *See* Wash. State Grange v. Wash. State Republican Party, 552 U.S. 442, 453 (2008).

[57] *See, e.g., States Using Runoffs for Statewide or Federal Office,* FAIRVOTE, http://archive.fairvote.org/?page=2293 (last visited Feb. 1, 2024).

[58] *See, e.g., Details About Ranked Choice Voting,* FAIRVOTE, https://www.fairvote.org/rcv#where_is_ranked_choice_voting_used (last visited Feb. 1, 2024).

[59] *See, e.g.,* Edward B. Foley, *Tournament Elections with Round-Robin Primaries: A Sports Analogy for Electoral Reform,* 2021 WIS. L. REV. 1187, 1194–1205.

misalignment that spoilers tend to cause. To see how, return to the toy example of the liberal Democratic candidate receiving 45 percent of the vote, the conservative Republican earning 40 percent, and the anti-government Libertarian getting 15 percent. Also assume all Democratic voters prefer the Republican candidate to the Libertarian, all Republican voters prefer the Libertarian candidate to the Democrat, and all Libertarian voters prefer the Republican candidate to the Democrat. These are plausible rankings if voters mostly vote spatially, the Libertarian candidate is to the right of the Republican, and the Republican is ideologically closer to the Libertarian than to the Democrat.

In this scenario, a runoff election prevents the Democratic candidate from winning and the Libertarian from playing the role of spoiler. As the top two candidates in the general election, the Democrat and the Republican advance to the runoff election, in which the Republican triumphs by a margin of 55 percent to 45 percent. Instant-runoff voting also produces this outcome. As the candidate with the fewest first-place votes, the Libertarian is eliminated first. When the ballots ranking the Libertarian first are reallocated to those voters' second choice, the Republican, that candidate again wins with 55 percent of the vote. Under pairwise voting as well, the Republican candidate has the best head-to-head record against the other candidates, and so is elected. The Republican is preferred to the Democrat, 55 percent to 45 percent, and to the Libertarian, 85 percent to 15 percent. (The Democrat and the Libertarian each lose to the Republican, and between them, the Libertarian is preferred, 55 percent to 45 percent.)

Of course, this is just one example. (Though it's a common one, with an extremist minor party candidate outflanking the two major party candidates.) In other cases, these alternatives to plurality rule *don't* yield the same result. When the electoral systems diverge, moreover, the outcome under pairwise voting is the best one from the perspective of maximizing alignment. To illustrate, suppose a liberal Democratic candidate still receives 45 percent of the vote and a conservative Republican still earns 40 percent. But now say a *center-right* Independent candidate gets the remaining 15 percent of the vote. And also say all Democratic voters prefer the Independent candidate to the Republican, all Republican voters prefer the Independent candidate to the Democrat, and all Independent voters prefer the Republican candidate to the Democrat.

In this scenario, the Democratic candidate still wins under plurality rule. And this victory still leads to stark partisan and representational misalignment since most voters don't want to be represented by a Democrat or by a liberal. Using either a runoff election or instant-runoff voting, in contrast, the Republican candidate wins. As in the prior example, the Republican either beats the Democrat in a runoff election or crosses the 50 percent threshold after the ballots ranking the Independent first are reallocated to the Republican. But unlike in the prior example, this result isn't maximally aligning. Voters favor the moderate

Independent candidate over the conservative Republican by a margin of 60 percent to 40 percent, but this preference is thwarted. Lastly, this preference *isn't* thwarted under pairwise voting. As just noted, the Independent candidate is favored over the Republican, 60 percent to 40 percent, and the Independent is also favored over the Democrat, 55 percent to 45 percent. So the Independent prevails since she has the best head-to-head record of the three candidates.

A candidate like the Independent in this scenario (or the Republican in the last one) is known as a "Condorcet winner." Voters prefer a Condorcet winner to each other candidate in a head-to-head matchup. That is, a Condorcet winner would beat each other candidate in a runoff election.[60] From the standpoint of maximizing majoritarian alignment, a Condorcet winner is superior to any alternative. By definition, a Condorcet winner is favored by a majority of voters over each of her rivals. If any of those rivals takes office instead, the preferences of an electoral majority are necessarily frustrated.[61] The question thus becomes: Which electoral system is most likely to identify a Condorcet winner? If this query has a unique answer, that policy is the most aligning possible choice.

This query, it turns out, does have a unique answer. If a Condorcet winner exists (which isn't always the case), pairwise voting is the electoral system most likely to identify her. In fact, pairwise voting is *certain* to identify a Condorcet winner, if there is one. This claim is proven mathematically by Partha Dasgupta and Eric Maskin, who also establish that pairwise voting dominates every other policy in terms of finding Condorcet winners. Specifically, if some other policy identifies a Condorcet winner in some scenario, pairwise voting will also lead to that candidate prevailing. Additionally, with respect to every other policy, there exist certain situations in which it fails to identify a Condorcet winner but pairwise voting succeeds in doing so.[62] The upshot is unusually simple and satisfying for the purpose of promoting majoritarian alignment. Pairwise voting is the most aligning available policy if a single winner is to be selected.

While they're not the *most* aligning electoral systems, though, a runoff election and instant-runoff voting are *more* aligning than plurality rule. Thanks to examples like the ones above, plurality rule is "spectacularly vulnerable to spoilers" when more than two general election candidates draw substantial support.[63] A runoff election and instant-runoff voting, on the other hand, perform

---

[60] *See, e.g.*, Amartya Sen, *Majority Decisions and Condorcet Winners*, 54 Soc. Choice & Welfare 211, 211 (2020).

[61] *See, e.g.*, Foley, *supra* note 59, at 1209 n.60 (a Condorcet winner "is more majoritarian than any other candidate in the field"). But note that a different voting rule, the Borda count, best captures the preferences of the mean (as opposed to the median) voter.

[62] *See* Partha Dasgupta & Eric Maskin, *On the Robustness of Majority Rule*, 6 J. Eur. Econ. Ass'n 949, 953 (2008); Partha Dasgupta & Eric Maskin, Elections and Strategic Voting: Condorcet and Borda 6, 8 (Nov. 2019).

[63] Eric Maskin, *The Arrow Impossibility Theorem: Where Do We Go from Here?*, in The Arrow Impossibility Theorem 43, 48 (Eric Maskin & Amartya Sen eds., 2014).

"far better on that score."[64] Notably, in recent elections in the United States and the United Kingdom using instant-runoff voting, there seem to be very few cases in which a Condorcet winner failed to be elected.[65] Accordingly, if a jurisdiction would like to improve alignment but is unwilling to adopt pairwise voting for some reason, a runoff election and instant-runoff voting are worthy alternatives. They promise considerable, even if not maximal, aligning benefits relative to the status quo of plurality rule.[66]

These aligning benefits from alternative single-winner systems are nothing to sneeze at. But even if they were fully realized, the gains wouldn't reach much of the noncongruence that characterizes modern American politics. Most American officeholders are already Condorcet winners, even under plurality rule.[67] They nevertheless take positions at odds with those of their constituents with alarming regularity. Moreover, single-winner systems say nothing about how districts are aggregated into legislatures; that's not their job. But how this aggregation is done has enormous implications for jurisdiction-wide alignment. For exactly these reasons, the adoption of instant-runoff voting has no measurable effect on the ideological composition of city councils or the policies they enact.[68] Instant-runoff voting mostly (if not perfectly) solves the problem of non-Condorcet winners taking office—but since that issue isn't the driver of most misalignment, resolving it leaves most misalignment intact.

For electoral systems to be more aligning, then, they have to reject the premise of single-winner races. That is, they have to provide for the election of *multiple* legislators from each district. The most notable policies specifying how multiple legislators per district are to be chosen are forms of proportional representation, of which I'll cite three.[69] First, the single transferable vote is a

---

[64] Eric Maskin & Amartya Sen, *The Rules of the Game: A New Electoral System*, N.Y. Rev. of Books (Jan. 19, 2017).

[65] *See, e.g.*, Marc D. Kilgour et al., *The Prevalence and Consequences of Ballot Truncation in Ranked-Choice Elections*, 184 Pub. Choice 197, 201–02 (2020) (discussing the 2009 mayoral race in Burlington, Vermont). However, such misfires are significantly more common in *simulations* of races held under instant-runoff voting. *See id.* at 207–09; *see also* Nathan Atkinson et al., *Beyond the Spoiler Effect: Can Ranked-Choice Voting Solve the Problem of Political Polarization*, 2023 U. Ill. L. Rev. (forthcoming 2023) (manuscript at 19–29) (showing that the winners selected by instant-runoff voting are more polarized, and less representative of the median voter, than the winners selected by pairwise voting).

[66] Some scholars also claim that instant-runoff voting has other benefits over pairwise voting, like inducing candidates to run less negative campaigns. *See generally* G. Michael Parsons et al., Against Condorcet: Election Reform and Election Subversion (Nov. 8, 2022).

[67] I'm referring here only to general election candidates. If defeated primary election candidates are also taken into account, it's less clear that most officeholders are Condorcet winners.

[68] *See* Arjun Vishwanath, Electoral Institutions and Substantive Representation in Local Politics: The Effects of Ranked Choice Voting 18–31 (Dec. 6, 2021).

[69] Also worth mentioning, briefly, are at-large elections for multiple seats, in which the majority party typically wins every seat. Because of this winner-take-all property, this is the most misaligning electoral system of which I'm aware. *See, e.g.*, Anthony Bertelli & Lilliard E. Richardson Jr., *Ideological Extremism and Electoral Design: Multimember Versus Single Member Districts*, 137 Pub. Choice 347, 362–65 (2008) (finding worse collective representational alignment under multimember

variant of instant-runoff voting for the multiple-winner context. Voters again rank candidates in their order of preference. Each candidate with more first-place votes than the relevant threshold is then elected, and "surplus" votes for that candidate are subsequently reallocated to voters' next choices. This process continues until either enough candidates are elected or no more candidates surpass the threshold for election. In the latter case, the remaining candidate in last place is eliminated, and votes for that candidate are reallocated to voters' next choices. Further rounds of elimination take place until enough candidates clear the threshold and so win office.[70]

Second, party-list proportional representation assigns seats to each party in proportion to its share of the district vote. For instance, a party that receives 40 percent of the vote in a district with ten seats is entitled to four seats. Party lists can be closed, meaning each party sets the order in which its candidates are elected. Or party lists can be open, in which case voters vote for a candidate rather than a party, and more popular candidates from a party are elected before their less popular co-partisans.[71] And third, mixed-member proportional representation is a hybrid of single-member districts and party-list proportional representation. As in most American jurisdictions, districts elect individual legislators (through plurality rule or some alternative to it). These legislators are then supplemented by additional members selected through party-list proportional representation and allocated in the necessary numbers to ensure jurisdiction-wide proportionality. For example, a party that wins thirty single-member districts out of fifty, as well as 40 percent of the party-list vote, in a jurisdiction with a hundred total seats, is entitled to ten supplemental seats.[72]

Compared to single-member districts under plurality rule, you should expect proportional representation to yield better jurisdiction-wide, collective, partisan alignment. As I discuss in the next chapter, single-member districts under plurality rule are notoriously susceptible to both intentional gerrymandering and accidental seat-vote skews caused by electoral waves, candidate quality, and political geography. In contrast, the whole point of proportional representation is that it results in, well, proportional representation—seats for each party in proportion to its popular support, and thus a legislature whose partisan makeup

at-large elections); Isaac Hale, *Candidate Extremism and Electoral Design in U.S. State Legislative Elections*, 101 Soc. Sci. Q. 861, 874 (2020) (multimember at-large elections "may be the worst of both worlds: increased legislative polarization without an increase in proportional representation").

[70] *See, e.g., Proportional Ranked Choice Voting Example*, FairVote, https://www.fairvote.org/multi_winner_rcv_example (last visited Feb. 1, 2024).

[71] *See, e.g., Variations of Party List Proportional Systems: Closed List, Open List and Free List*, FairVote, http://archive.fairvote.org/factshts/partylst.htm (last visited Feb. 1, 2024).

[72] *See, e.g., Mixed Member Systems*, FairVote, http://archive.fairvote.org/?page=2046 (last visited Feb. 1, 2024).

mirrors that of the electorate. Sure enough, when scholars calculate indices of aggregate seat-vote proportionality for different countries and years, they find that
nations using proportional representation systematically outperform nations
using single-member districts under plurality rule.[73] By the same token, the fit
between parties' seat and vote shares is tighter under proportional representation than under single-member districts.[74]

How much improvement in collective partisan alignment would the United
States see under proportional representation? Figure 6.3, borrowed from another study by Tamas, supplies a historical answer. The solid line indicates the
aggregate seat-vote proportionality of the U.S. House since 1900, with negative
(or positive) values indicating a pro-Democratic (or pro-Republican) bias. For
most of the last century plus, Democrats won disproportionately more seats than
votes, though the advantage has shifted to Republicans over the last generation.
Next, the large dotted line shows the disproportionality the U.S. House would
have exhibited had each state adopted proportional representation. I consider
this the reasonable best-case scenario—the most aggressive implementation of
proportional representation possible without constitutional change. From 1900
to about 1970, the U.S. House would still have been biased in a pro-Democratic
direction under state-level proportional representation. But this skew would
have largely disappeared over the last half-century, leaving behind excellent aggregate seat-vote proportionality. Lastly, as illustrated by the small dotted line,
the proportionality of the U.S. House would have been nearly perfect from 1900
to the present if the country *as a whole* had adopted proportional representation,
allocating seats to each party based on its share of the *national* vote. As I observed
in Chapter 2, however, this reform is outside this book's scope because it would
require a constitutional revolution. Within constitutional constraints, significant
but still contingent progress in proportionality is the most that can be achieved.

Significant progress in jurisdiction-wide, collective, *representational* alignment might also be expected under proportional representation. In this regime,
a party can thrive at any position in the ideological spectrum, provided that
enough voters are situated in the same ideological area. More to the point, *multiple* parties can succeed at *multiple* ideological locations, capturing among them
most of the electorate's policy preferences.[75] Under these conditions, the ideal

---

[73] *See, e.g.*, Pippa Norris, Electoral Engineering: Voting Rules and Political Behavior 88
(2004); Jay K. Dow, *Party-System Extremism in Majoritarian and Proportional Electoral Systems*, 41
Brit. J. Pol. Sci. 341, 348 (2011).

[74] *See, e.g.*, Norris, *supra* note 73, at 89.

[75] *See, e.g.*, Gary W. Cox, *Centripetal and Centrifugal Incentives in Electoral Systems*, 34 Am. J. Pol.
Sci. 903, 919–22 (1990) (using formal modeling to argue that parties tend to disperse ideologically
under proportional representation); Jay K. Dow, *Party-System Extremism in Majoritarian and
Proportional Electoral Systems*, 41 Brit. J. Pol. Sci. 341, 350–57 (2011) (confirming Cox's hypothesis
with empirical data).

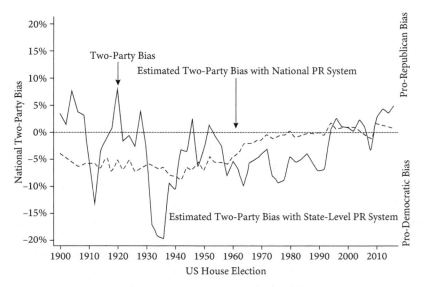

FIGURE 6.3 U.S. HOUSE DISPROPORTIONALITY UNDER STATUS QUO, STATE-LEVEL, AND NATIONAL-LEVEL PROPORTIONAL REPRESENTATION

Figure 6.3 is reproduced with permission from Bernard Tamas, *American Disproportionality: A Historical Analysis of Partisan Bias in Elections to the U.S. House of Representatives*, 18 ELECTION L.J. 47, 58 (2019), Copyright © 2019 by Mary Ann Liebert, Inc.

points of these diverse parties' legislators should better correspond to voters' views than the liberal and conservative monoliths of America's polarized parties. This logic, too, turns out to be sound. Switzerland notably uses the same districts to elect its two legislative chambers, but under party-list proportional representation for the lower house and plurality rule for the upper house. Collective representational alignment is far better in the lower house than in the upper one. In fact, on issues on which legislators and voters both vote (the latter in referenda), there's an almost perfect match between lower house legislators' and their constituents' stances.[76]

This result generalizes to a large set of Western democracies. The more proportional their electoral systems are, the more congruent legislators' ideologies are, in aggregate, with those of voters.[77] Proportional representation systems

[76] *See* David Stadelmann et al., *Mapping the Theory of Political Representation to the Empirics: An Investigation for Proportional and Majoritarian Rules*, 48 J. COMP. ECON. 548, 554–59 (2020).

[77] *See, e.g.*, JONATHAN RODDEN, WHY CITIES LOSE: THE DEEP ROOTS OF THE URBAN-RURAL POLITICAL DIVIDE 235–40 (2019); Branislav Dolny & Pavol Babos, *Voter-Representative Congruence in Europe: A Loss of Institutional Influence?*, 38 W. EUR. POL. 1274, 1289–93 (2015); Matt Golder & Jacek Stramski, *Ideological Congruence and Electoral Institutions*, 54 AM. J. POL. SCI. 90, 103–04 (2010).

thus "produce legislatures that accurately reflect the ideological *preferences* of citizens and not just their *votes*."[78] The result also holds for the sole American state to have tried a form of proportional representation. From 1870 to 1980, Illinois relied on state house districts with three members each, elected through cumulative voting. Under this policy, each voter had three votes, which she could allocate among candidates as she saw fit. During this period, the Illinois state house was much less polarized than the Illinois state senate, elected through single-member districts under plurality rule. In the lower chamber, but not in the upper one, the Democratic and the Republican parties were big ideological tents spanning the views of most voters.[79]

Unfortunately, scholars have barely begun to study whether *policy* alignment is better under proportional representation.[80] (This is a tough nut to crack because policy agendas vary from one country to the next and cross-national data on voters' policy preferences rarely exists.) Academics are also divided as to whether electoral systems influence the congruence between voters and *governing coalitions* in legislatures. An earlier literature mostly found that governing coalitions are more aligned under proportional representation,[81] while more recent works conclude that this kind of congruence is about the same under any electoral system.[82] Accordingly, the aligning benefits of proportional representation shouldn't be exaggerated. These gains do extend to collective partisan and representational alignment, which is no mean feat. But it remains unclear if enacted policies are more congruent with voters' views under proportional representation (and the recent analyses of governing coalitions arguably support the null hypothesis here).

* * *

Political parties are vitally important entities, the very building blocks of mass democracy. Nevertheless, alignment within parties has no democratic value. Parties are distinct from the polity itself, and intraparty congruence can

---

[78] Golder & Stramski, *supra* note 77, at 104.

[79] *See* Greg D. Adams, *Legislative Effects of Single-Member vs. Multi-Member Districts*, 40 AM. J. POL. SCI. 129, 140–41 (1996).

[80] The only such study of which I'm aware is Benjamin Ferland, *Electoral Systems and Policy Congruence*, 69 POL. STUD. 344 (2020), which only addresses levels of government spending.

[81] For one of the last hurrahs of this earlier literature, see G. Bingham Powell, Jr., *Representation in Context: Election Laws and Ideological Congruence Between Citizens and Governments*, 11 PERSP. POL. 9 (2013).

[82] *See, e.g.*, Benjamin Ferland, *Revisiting the Ideological Congruence Controversy*, 55 EUR. J. POL. RSCH. 358, 363 (2016) (noting "a new empirical consensus" that "levels of citizen-government congruence are similar under majoritarian and PR systems"); Mat Golder & Gabriella Lloyd, *Re-Evaluating the Relationship Between Electoral Rules and Ideological Congruence*, 53 EUR. J. POL. RSCH. 200, 204 (2014) ("[T]here is little compelling evidence . . . that governments in proportional democracies represent their citizens any better than governments in majoritarian democracies.").

undermine the polity-level alignment that really does matter, democratically speaking. Parties can be regulated in many ways, but only some of these rules have aligning implications. Rules about how parties choose their general election nominees generally don't have such effects. Alignment therefore shouldn't be a factor in the debate between more inclusive and more exclusive primaries. Ballot access restrictions can influence alignment both by changing the likelihood of minor party spoilers and by creating centrifugal or centripetal incentives for the major parties. But these impacts are relatively minor and hinge on the use of a plurality winner rule. Finally, plurality rule itself is quite misaligning compared to alternative electoral systems. Other single-winner systems mostly or fully prevent misalignment from minor party spoilers. More dramatically, the election of multiple winners per district using proportional representation leads to better partisan and representational—though maybe not policy—alignment.

I noted above that how votes are aggregated and then converted into legislative seats is a potent driver of alignment. Proportional representation is one mechanism for translating votes into seats. But the relevant method for single-member districts under plurality rule—and the subject of the next chapter—is redistricting. District lines determine which voters (backing which parties) are placed in which districts. These decisions have a huge impact on the partisan composition of the legislature, easily making the difference between a fairly constituted and a highly biased chamber. In turn, the partisan composition of the legislature powerfully affects its representational alignment. And since legislatures, well, legislate, representational alignment is closely tied to policy alignment. The next chapter empirically substantiates these propositions. It demonstrates that redistricting is probably the single lever movable under current law with the most sway (positive and negative) over alignment.

7

Redistricting

Introduction

Joseph Stalin once (supposedly) said he "consider[ed] it completely unimportant who . . . will vote, or how."[1] "[W]hat is extraordinarily important," on the other hand, is "who will *count* the votes, and how."[2] American elections are obviously freer and fairer than their Soviet counterparts. Still, designers of legislative districts in the United States might voice a sentiment quite similar to Stalin's. It's less significant how voters choose to cast their ballots. But it's absolutely critical how voters are assigned to districts. Those assignments determine whether individual districts are competitive or safe. The aggregation of individual districts then shapes the partisan makeup of the legislature. In a polarized era, that partisan makeup drives the legislature's ideological balance. And in the last step of this sequence, that ideological balance impacts the policies the government enacts, including how well they reflect popular preferences.

In this book's terminology, this means redistricting has the capacity to influence jurisdiction-wide partisan, representational, and policy alignment. Starting with partisan alignment, I presented data in Chapter 3 on the efficiency gaps of congressional and state legislative plans over the last several decades. The details of the efficiency gap can be bracketed for the moment, but what's relevant here is that it's one way of capturing the relationship between the partisan compositions of the legislature and of the electorate. That is, the efficiency gap is a quantitative measure of partisan alignment. Still more notably, as an empirical matter, some district plans give rise to large efficiency gaps while other maps result in small ones. This variation suggests that some plans should be assessed quite negatively, maybe even struck down, because of how severely they distort the legislature's partisan makeup relative to the electorate's partisan preferences. Conversely, other maps should be applauded, maybe even upheld against other kinds of challenges, thanks to their faithful translations of popular votes into legislative seats.

I opined earlier in the book that partisan alignment is less important than representational alignment (since the latter involves policy positions, not just party

---

[1] *Joseph Stalin 1879-1953*, OxFORD REFERENCE, https://www.oxfordreference.com/view/10.1093/acref/9780191843730.001.0001/q-oro-ed5-00010383 (last visited Feb. 1, 2024_).

[2] *Id.* (emphasis added).

Aligning Election Law. Nicholas O. Stephanopoulos, Oxford University Press. © Nicholas O. Stephanopoulos 2024.
DOI: 10.1093/9780197662182.003.0007

affiliations), which itself is less important than policy alignment (since the latter involves policy outcomes, not just policy positions). Discussions of redistricting commonly focus on its partisan consequences. But those conspicuous partisan effects have representational and policy implications, too. Specifically, district plans with pro-Democratic (or pro-Republican) efficiency gaps produce legislatures with more liberal (or conservative) median members. And the larger a plan's efficiency gap is (in absolute terms), the less congruent state policy is with the desires of the state public. The case for looking skeptically at plans with sizable efficiency gaps, and approvingly at maps with slight ones, is therefore stronger than those statistics alone would indicate. In this context, partisan, representational, and policy alignment march in lockstep.

A potential concern about fixating on plans' efficiency gaps is that these (and other similar) scores might be caused by factors other than intentional gerrymandering. Even in the absence of a partisan purpose, the argument might go, the combination of nonpartisan criteria like compactness with the geographic distribution of Democratic and Republican voters tends to favor one or the other party. One response to this concern is simply to ask anyone attacking a district plan to show that an unbiased (or less biased) map *could* be crafted. If so, then the enacted plan's skew is plausibly attributable to its own line-drawing choices as opposed to exogenous forces. More stringently, a computer algorithm could be used to generate a representative sample of maps that ignore partisanship while matching or beating the enacted plan on every nonpartisan criterion. If the enacted plan is more biased than most or all of these simulated maps, that's a strong indication that its skew is deliberate, not accidental.

Litigation against a misaligning plan, then, is easy to imagine. Its thrust would be that the plan exhibits a large partisan bias, maybe a skew bigger than would be expected given random, nonpartisan redistricting. And in fact, suits along these lines have proliferated in recent years. However, litigation isn't the only way to achieve fairer maps that do a better job aligning governmental outputs with popular preferences. One alternative is structural reform: removing redistricting authority from self-interested legislators and transferring it to commissions with no incentive to gerrymander. Studies find that, especially in the latest cycle, commissions enacted much less biased plans than did politicians. Another option (which can be paired with structural reform) is limiting the discretion of mapmakers through traditional criteria relating to district form and/or anti-partisanship criteria targeting partisan intent and/or partisan effect. There's some evidence that traditional criteria curb the worst line-drawing abuses. There's even more reason to think that anti-partisanship criteria are aligning (in the relatively few states that have adopted them).

This introduction has exclusively addressed jurisdiction-wide alignment so far. That's the more significant kind of alignment that's affected by redistricting, in my view. But district maps are obviously composed of individual districts, which raises the question of whether redistricting can also influence district-specific alignment. A substantial literature finds that it can. In particular, compliance with traditional criteria like compactness, respect for political subdivisions, and respect for communities of interest is linked to better district-specific representational alignment. The converse is true as well: Districts that disregard these requirements tend to have legislators whose ideologies are a worse fit for those of their constituents. Accordingly, districts that abide by traditional criteria are preferable from an alignment perspective to districts that flout these requirements. At least, this preference holds whenever compliance with traditional criteria can be attained without sacrificing performance on the more vital measures of jurisdiction-wide alignment.

What explains the connection between districts that adhere to traditional criteria and improved representational congruence at the district level? The dynamic is essentially informational. On one side of the voter-representative relationship, constituents find it easier to learn about their legislator when a district's boundaries are coherent and cognizable. Constituents are also more able to mobilize politically against their legislator in this circumstance if she embraces positions they oppose. On the other side of the relationship, a representative receives a clearer signal of voters' preferences when a district is comprised of a more homogeneous population. A representative is also more deterred from deviating from voters' views in this scenario since the odds of effective electoral retribution are higher. The underlying point is that the design of individual districts has informational repercussions for both constituents and legislators. These effects, in turn, can either bolster or undermine district-specific representation.

District Plans

A theme of the last two chapters was that many electoral regulations often believed to be aligning or misaligning actually have little impact on alignment. Recall the findings in Chapter 5 about the highest-profile contemporary voting restrictions, photo identification requirements for voting. They appear to cause next to no change in partisan, representational, or policy alignment. A corollary to this theme was that even policies that *do* statistically significantly influence alignment tend to do so only to a moderate substantive extent. To take an example from Chapter 6, instant-runoff voting mostly prevents misalignment due to non-Condorcet winners prevailing in elections. But non-Condorcet winners take office infrequently even under plurality rule, and instant-runoff voting doesn't seem to make representation or policy more congruent with public opinion.

In light of all these null or modest results, the aligning implications of redistricting are staggering. I reported in Chapter 3 that the *average* state legislative plan has produced an efficiency gap of around 6 percent over the last half-century. This figure means the advantaged party won 6 percentage points more state legislative seats, on average, than it would have under a map that yielded no jurisdiction-wide, collective, partisan misalignment at all.[3] Moreover, averages inherently hide the peaks and valleys of a distribution. The *most* biased state legislative plans of the last fifty years awarded the favored party more than *20 percentage points* more seats relative to a benchmark of perfect partisan alignment.[4] Some recent work of mine confirms that a skew of this magnitude is feasible today in several states. When a computer algorithm is instructed to gerrymander as aggressively as possible on a party's behalf—while still complying with nonpartisan criteria at least as well as the enacted state legislative plan—the algorithm creates an average of 13 percentage points more seats for the specified party relative to a party-blind baseline.[5] Going from a gerrymander for one party to a gerrymander for the other thus swings an average of 25 percent of a chamber's seats from one to the other party's column.[6]

These effects on partisan alignment plainly dwarf those of most of the electoral regulations examined in the last two chapters. The reason is that the mechanism through which redistricting influences the parties' legislative representation is so much more potent. Remember from Chapter 5 that voting restrictions (or expansions) impact partisan alignment by (1) decreasing (or increasing) voter turnout among (2) eligible voters who disproportionately back a certain party. At least in modern times, it's difficult for any voting policy either to change turnout dramatically or to do so particularly for one party's supporters. Similarly, the links between partisan alignment and the party regulations considered in Chapter 6 depend on unusual configurations of candidates. Ballot access restrictions only promote partisan alignment in the rare event that they exclude a minor party candidate who would have been a spoiler had she been allowed onto the general election ballot. Partisan alignment is also only furthered by alternatives to

---

[3] I only reported chamber-wide statistics for the House of Representatives in Chapter 3. The average *individual* congressional plan with at least seven districts (for which these calculations are more reliable) has similarly produced an efficiency gap of around 7 percent over the last half-century.

[4] The most biased congressional plans of the last fifty years (again with at least seven districts) reached an efficiency gap of *30 percent*.

[5] *See* Jowei Chen & Nicholas O. Stephanopoulos, *Democracy's Denominator*, 109 CALIF. L. REV. 1011, 1049 (2021).

[6] *See id.*

plurality rule if, uncommonly, plurality rule would permit a non-Condorcet winner to prevail but the other electoral systems wouldn't.[7]

In contrast, redistricting directly determines how votes are aggregated and then converted into legislative seats. To impact partisan alignment, unlike voting regulations, it doesn't have to change who votes or for whom. Nor, unlike party regulations, does its efficacy depend on certain candidate configurations. Instead, redistricting takes the set of voters in a jurisdiction and subdivides that set into one of an essentially infinite number of permutations. The selected permutation fixes the partisan makeup of each district: toward which party it leans and how competitive it is. In turn, when the partisan makeups of all districts are considered together, they generate the partisan profile of the legislative chamber. For the very same set of voters, the chamber's partisan profile can be dramatically different. It all depends on which permutation of districts is chosen.

In redistricting parlance, district boundaries influence partisan alignment through the techniques of cracking and packing. As I noted in Chapter 3, cracking refers to dispersing the targeted party's supporters among multiple districts, in all of which their candidates of choice lose by relatively narrow margins. Packing means concentrating the targeted party's backers in a few districts, in all of which their preferred candidates win by enormous margins. Essentially all contemporary gerrymanders rely on some combination of cracking and packing to manipulate the parties' shares of legislative seats. Historically, gerrymanders also overpopulated the targeted party's districts and underpopulated those favoring the line-drawing party. However, this misaligning tool has been unavailable since the Supreme Court announced the one-person, one-vote rule in the 1960s.[8]

To illustrate how cracking and packing can affect partisan alignment, suppose a state has 1,000 persons, all of whom are voters, 500 of whom support Party A, and 500 of whom back Party B. Say also that the state must be divided into ten equipopulous districts, and that when Party A is responsible for redistricting, it creates eight districts with 56 Party A voters and 44 Party B voters as well as two districts with 26 Party A voters and 74 Party B voters. In this scenario, the former eight districts are examples of cracking; they scatter Party B voters such that their candidates of choice are reliably (but not overwhelmingly) defeated. And the latter two districts are packed because they include so many Party B voters that their preferred candidates prevail by nearly 50 percentage points. Together,

---

[7] To round out the electoral regulations discussed in the last two chapters, there's no plausible mechanism through which primary type can affect partisan alignment. Even the impact of primary type on *representational* alignment hinges on assumptions about voter participation and voter knowledge that turn out generally not to hold.

[8] The adoption of the one-person, one-vote rule led to significant increases in policy alignment, especially in states whose legislative districts had previously been more malapportioned. *See* DEVIN CAUGHEY & CHRISTOPHER WARSHAW, DYNAMIC DEMOCRACY: PUBLIC OPINION, ELECTIONS, AND POLICYMAKING IN THE AMERICAN STATES 139–40 (2022).

the cracking and packing result in Party A claiming eight of ten seats even though it's favored by just half the electorate. That is, the cracking and packing result in gaping misalignment between voters' partisan preferences and legislators' party affiliations.

I explained in Chapter 3 that the efficiency gap follows directly from the recognition that partisan gerrymandering operates through cracking and packing. Both cracking and packing give rise to votes that are wasted in the sense that they don't contribute to a candidate's election. All votes cast for a losing candidate are wasted, as are votes for a winning candidate above the threshold required for victory. The efficiency gap simply totals each party's wasted votes, across all the districts in a plan, subtracts one sum from the other, and divides this difference by the number of votes cast in the election. The percentage that's produced by this calculation indicates which party is advantaged (and which is disadvantaged) by all the cracking and packing in a plan, and to what extent. The percentage also helpfully reveals how much larger (or smaller) a party's seat share is than it would have been under a zero-efficiency-gap map that equally wasted both parties' votes.[9]

It's worth flagging that the efficiency gap isn't the only measure of partisan misalignment attributable to redistricting. An older metric, partisan asymmetry, asks how different the parties' seat shares would be if, hypothetically, each party received the same share of the statewide vote. Actual election results are uniformly adjusted to estimate what would happen in that counterfactual election.[10] Another venerable measure, the mean-median difference, subtracts a party's mean vote share, across all a plan's districts, from its median vote share. The idea is that a party benefits from a plan if the party's performance in the critical median district exceeds its average statewide performance.[11] And more recently, scholars have proposed the declination, which first plots districts in order by vote share, then draws lines between the 50 percent point and each party's mean vote share in the districts it wins, and finally computes the angle between these lines. A neutral map has no reason to treat the 50 percent point as special, and so shouldn't exhibit a large angle between the lines. A map contorted by cracking and packing, on the other hand, should feature a sharp disjunction between the cracked districts favoring one party and the packed districts favoring the other.[12]

---

[9] *See generally* Nicholas O. Stephanopoulos & Eric M. McGhee, *Partisan Gerrymandering and the Efficiency Gap*, 82 U. CHI. L. REV. 831 (2015).

[10] *See generally* Bernard Grofman & Gary King, *The Future of Partisan Symmetry as a Judicial Test for Partisan Gerrymandering After LULAC v. Perry*, 6 ELECTION L.J. 2 (2007).

[11] *See generally* Michael D. McDonald & Robin E. Best, *Unfair Partisan Gerrymanders in Politics and Law: A Diagnostic Applied to Six Cases*, 14 ELECTION L.J. 312 (2015).

[12] *See generally* Gregory S. Warrington, *Quantifying Gerrymandering Using the Vote Distribution*, 17 ELECTION L.J. 39 (2018).

Academics, myself included, have made claims about the pros and cons of these metrics.[13] But that debate can be set aside here. In competitive states where gerrymandering can plausibly shift control of a legislative chamber from one party to the other, all the measures are highly correlated with one another.[14] Across all states, factor analysis shows that a single latent variable accounts for the bulk of the variance in the metrics.[15] A second latent variable that distinguishes the efficiency gap and the declination from partisan asymmetry and the mean-median difference, on the other hand, captures only a small share of the variance in the data.[16] And the two measures that are denominated in seat shares, the efficiency gap and partisan asymmetry, have nearly identical distributions.[17] In competitive states, then, these metrics are not just highly correlated, they also agree on how many more (or fewer) seats a party holds compared to a benchmark of perfect partisan alignment.

It would be bad enough if certain district plans were merely misaligning in partisan terms. In the redistricting context, though, partisan bias is closely linked to representational misalignment. At the state legislative level, there's an essentially linear relationship between plans' efficiency gaps and the ideal points of chambers' median members. A more pro-Democratic (or pro-Republican) efficiency gap is associated with a more liberal (or conservative) median legislator.[18] At the congressional level, likewise, states whose electorates are roughly evenly divided in their partisan loyalties tend to have delegations with quite liberal (or conservative) median representatives if the states' plans have large pro-Democratic (or pro-Republican) efficiency gaps. "[S]witching from a pro-Democratic to a pro-Republican [gerrymander]—while keeping constant the partisan preferences of the electorate—shifts the [ideological] median [of the congressional delegation] by about . . . 2 standard deviations, in a conservative direction."[19]

---

[13] See, e.g., Jonathan N. Katz et al., *Theoretical Foundations and Empirical Evaluations of Partisan Fairness in District-Based Democracies*, 114 AM. POL. SCI. REV. 164 (2020); Nicholas O. Stephanopoulos & Eric M. McGhee, *The Measure of a Metric: The Debate over Quantifying Partisan Gerrymandering*, 70 STAN. L. REV. 1503 (2018); Gregory S. Warrington, *A Comparison of Partisan-Gerrymandering Measures*, 18 ELECTION L.J. 262 (2019).

[14] See Stephanopoulos & McGhee, *supra* note 13, at 1563–64.

[15] See id. at 1556.

[16] See id.

[17] See Warrington, *supra* note 13, at 270.

[18] See CAUGHEY & WARSHAW, *supra* note 8, at 143–44; Devin Caughey et al., *Partisan Gerrymandering and the Political Process: Effects on Roll-Call Voting and State Policies*, 16 ELECTION L.J. 453, 464 (2017).

[19] Nicholas O. Stephanopoulos, *The Causes and Consequences of Gerrymandering*, 59 WM. & MARY L. REV. 2115, 2141 (2018); *see also* Stephanopoulos & McGhee, *supra* note 13, at 1567 (finding that, in competitive states, changes in the efficiency gap, partisan asymmetry, and the mean-median difference all significantly affect the average ideal points of congressional delegations); Kai Hao Yang & Alexander K, Zentefis, Gerrymandering and the Limits of Representative Democracy (Mar. 2022) (showing theoretically that partisan bias can greatly influence the ideological composition of a legislature).

The reason for this tight connection between partisan and representational misalignment is plain: legislative polarization. In modern American politics, almost all Democratic legislators are liberals and almost all Republican legislators are conservatives. Very few representatives are ideological moderates. Consequently, when a biased plan skews the *partisan* composition of a legislative chamber, it necessarily tilts the *ideological* makeup of the chamber, too. In the case of a Democratic gerrymander, the additional Democrats elected to the chamber are typically liberals who push the body to the left. The same is true, in reverse and to an even greater degree,[20] for a Republican gerrymander. Thanks to legislative polarization, the extra Republicans who take office tend to be staunch conservatives who make the chamber significantly more right-wing through their presence.

Of course, the votes legislators cast aren't just expressions of ideological preferences. They're also binding views as to whether particular bills should be passed. Bills that receive enough legislative support—as well as the approval of the executive—become law, at which point they concretely affect people's lives. You might hypothesize, then, that representational misalignment due to redistricting should translate into policy misalignment. Ideologically skewed legislatures should enact laws that are out of kilter with popular policy preferences. This expectation turns out to be accurate. A more pro-Democratic (or pro-Republican) efficiency gap isn't only associated with a more liberal (or conservative) median state legislator. It's tied to more liberal (or conservative) state policy, too. In fact, "a one standard deviation change in the efficiency gap has a larger effect on state policy than a change in the party of the governor."[21]

This suggestive finding has been explicitly extended to both majoritarian and collective policy alignment. To reiterate from Chapter 3, majoritarian policy alignment denotes whether a policy outcome is congruent with the median respondent's preference, while collective policy alignment is usually operationalized as the share of respondents who agree with a policy outcome. Figure 7.1, drawn from Devin Caughey and Christopher Warshaw's book on state democracy, plots majoritarian policy alignment (which the authors call "Congruence") against the absolute efficiency gap on the left, and collective policy alignment ("Agreement") against the absolute efficiency gap on the right. Both charts reveal a clear negative relationship. That is, when state legislative plans are highly biased in partisan terms, state policy is less congruent with the views of the median respondent and fewer respondents agree with state policy.

---

[20] *See* Caughey et al., *supra* note 18, at 464 (showing that Republican gerrymanders at the state legislative level move chambers' ideological medians in a conservative direction more than Democratic gerrymanders do so in a liberal direction); Stephanopoulos, *supra* note 19, at 2143 (same at the congressional level).

[21] Caughey et al., *supra* note 18, at 455; *see also* CAUGHEY & WARSHAW, *supra* note 8, at 145.

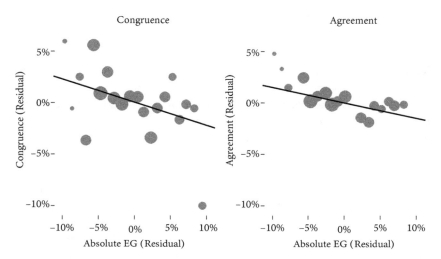

FIGURE 7.1 POLICY ALIGNMENT VERSUS PARTISAN ALIGNMENT IN STATE
LEGISLATURES

Figure 7.1 is reproduced with permission from DEVIN CAUGHEY & CHRISTOPHER WARSHAW,
DYNAMIC DEMOCRACY: PUBLIC OPINION, ELECTIONS, AND POLICYMAKING IN THE AMERICAN
STATES 145 (2022). Copyright © 2022 by University of Chicago Press.

By the same token, plans that give rise to better partisan alignment also yield a
closer fit between public policy and public opinion.[22]

Based on this discussion, the contours of a challenge (legal or political) to a
district map that exhibits a large partisan skew should be evident. The crux of
the argument would be that substantial partisan misalignment (as indicated by
measures like the efficiency gap) is itself democratically objectionable—and that
the democratic injury is compounded when partisan misalignment metastasizes
into representational and policy misalignment. In court, as I pointed out in
Chapter 4, a large partisan skew alone could suffice to render a plan presumptively invalid, if the model of the one-person, one-vote cases was followed.
Less aggressively, under the templates of sliding-scale scrutiny or disparate impact doctrine, a large partisan skew might shift the focus to the jurisdiction's
justifications for the misalignment produced by its map. Did the jurisdiction
pursue nonpartisan goals like respect for traditional criteria or compliance
with the Voting Rights Act? If so, could these objectives have been comparably
achieved by a less biased plan? Questions of this kind would become crucial if

---

[22] See CAUGHEY & WARSHAW, *supra* note 8, at 145.

the legal inquiry included not just a first stage about the extent of misalignment but also a second stage about the reasons for it.[23]

As I said in Chapter 4, I'm not interested in working out every legal or political issue about the implementation of alignment here. But I do want to address two potential concerns about the proposition that district maps with large partisan skews should be struck down or, at least, carefully scrutinized. I defer one of these until the next section: the possibility that partisan misalignment might be attributable to a combination of nonpartisan aims and political geography—not partisan intent. The other worry is specific to congressional plans and stems from the fact that they don't stand on their own bottoms. Rather, each congressional map elects a congressional delegation that's then a component of the House of Representatives. This relationship of a part to a whole makes it possible for the nullification of a particular state's biased congressional plan to *worsen* the bias of the entire House. The bias of the entire House and that of a given state's congressional map move in opposite directions when the House is skewed in one direction and the map is tilted in the other (before being negated). Under these conditions, when the map is invalidated, a partial offset against the House's countervailing bias is eliminated, thereby making that bias bigger.[24]

At present, this perverse dynamic is indeed a problem. Thanks to a lamentable Supreme Court decision (to which I return in Chapter 11),[25] there's currently no federal constitutional bar to congressional gerrymandering. Nor does any congressional statute limit the practice. However, several (but far from all) states restrict congressional gerrymandering under their *state* constitutions. This legal patchwork, under which congressional plans can be distorted for partisan gain in some states but not in others, sets the stage for state-specific anti-gerrymandering efforts to be counterproductive nationally. And that's exactly what happened in the most recent redistricting cycle. The House as a whole was slightly skewed in Republicans' favor after all states preliminarily drew their congressional districts in 2021–22. State courts in Maryland and New York then struck down those states' pro-Democratic gerrymanders, forcing their replacement with less biased maps. As a result, partisan alignment improved in Maryland's and New York's congressional delegations, but it deteriorated at the level that matters more—that of the entire House. The entire House is now substantially (no longer slightly) skewed in a Republican direction, making it

---

[23] This paragraph addresses misalignment being used as a sword against a biased plan. As a shield, the aligning impact of an unbiased plan could be used to defend that plan against attack on other legal or political grounds.

[24] For a discussion of this dynamic, see Aaron Goldzimer & Nicholas Stephanopoulos, *The Novel Strategy Blue States Can Use to Solve Partisan Gerrymandering by 2024*, SLATE, May 6, 2022, https://slate.com/news-and-politics/2022/05/new-york-democrats-partisan-gerrymandering-2024.html.

[25] *See* Rucho v. Common Cause, 139 S. Ct. 2484 (2019).

likely that federal representation and policy will be more conservative than most Americans want for the rest of the decade.[26]

Obviously, if a legal patchwork is the difficulty, a uniform legal quilt is the solution. If *all* states were subject to the *same* anti-gerrymandering rules for their congressional plans, then reducing the bias of a particular map wouldn't threaten to exacerbate the bias of the House as a whole. That map would have a low bias—and so would every other map, and so would the entire legislative chamber whose membership is determined by the sum of all the maps. In the federal litigation that preceded the regrettable Supreme Court decision, the plaintiffs tried to achieve this state of affairs by proposing a federal constitutional standard that would have applied to all congressional plans. Under this test, congressional maps would have been unlawful if (1) they were designed with partisan intent, (2) they gave rise to large and durable partisan misalignment (as demonstrated by measures like the efficiency gap), and (3) there was no legitimate, nonpartisan justification for this misalignment.[27] Alas, this proposal now amounts to a road not taken. But had the Court gone down this route, a properly aligned House would have been the destination.

Fortunately, federal constitutional law isn't the only—or even the best—way from here to there. *Congress* could also weave a uniform legal quilt by legislating the same anti-gerrymandering rules for all states' congressional plans. Congress could do so by requiring all states to use independent commissions to craft their congressional districts. I discuss this sort of structural reform later in this chapter. Additionally or alternatively, Congress could codify anti-gerrymandering criteria along the lines of the plaintiffs' proposal in the federal constitutional litigation. These criteria could proscribe partisan intent and/or partisan effect, in qualitative and/or quantitative terms. Interestingly, the House passed bills in 2019, 2021, and 2022 (all of which foundered on the Senate filibuster) that employed a mix of these strategies. The earlier two bills would have mandated the use of commissions *and* banned partisan intent and effect in general terms.[28] The last bill in the sequence dropped the commission requirement but added numerical teeth to the partisan effect prohibition, presumptively precluding maps with an efficiency gap above 7 percent or one congressional seat (whichever is greater).[29] All these approaches would have avoided the perverse dynamic by which a less biased plan in one state can cause a more biased House as a whole.

---

[26] *See* Goldzimer & Stephanopoulos, *supra* note 24 (discussing these developments).

[27] *See Rucho* 139 S. Ct. at 2516–17 (Kagan, J., dissenting) (describing this test).

[28] *See* For the People Act of 2019, H.R. 1, 116th Cong. §§ 2400–15 (2019); For the People Act of 2021, H.R. 1, 117th Cong. §§ 2400–15 (2021).

[29] *See* Freedom to Vote: John R. Lewis Act, H.R. 5746, 117th Cong. § 5003 (2022).

Political Geography

Turning to the other concern about striking down a district plan solely because of its large partisan skew, again, it's that this misalignment might be the product of nonpartisan criteria being applied against the backdrop of a certain political geography. If it so happens that, because of how Democratic and Republican voters are spatially distributed, maps drawn on the basis of nonpartisan criteria typically or necessarily favor a particular party, a variety of conclusions could follow, none of them conducive to nullifying an enacted plan about as biased in the same direction. First, partisan intent might be absent here. After all, if the enacted plan did aim for partisan gain, you'd expect it to be more tilted in the line-drawing party's favor than hypothetical nonpartisan maps—but, in this scenario, it isn't.[30] Second, there might be a compelling justification for the enacted plan's bias. That justification, of course, would be adherence to the nonpartisan criteria whose application makes the hypothetical maps comparably skewed. And third, the enacted plan might not be the underlying cause of the partisan misalignment. Instead, that misalignment should arguably be traced to exogenous factors beyond the plan's control.

In the popular media, this political geography concern has been fed by commentators' intuitions about the spatial patterns of Democratic and Republican voters. Democrats are too concentrated in cities, some pundits think, while Republicans are more efficiently distributed in suburbs, exurbs, and rural areas.[31] In the academy, a 2013 article by Jowei Chen and Jonathan Rodden most famously contends that political geography gives Republicans a "natural" advantage in the conversion of votes to seats.[32] Chen and Rodden use a computer algorithm to randomly generate—without considering partisanship—contiguous, compact, and equipopulous state legislative districts for twenty states.[33] The scholars then calculate the partisan asymmetry of each simulated map: the divergence between the parties' seat shares if they each hypothetically received half the statewide vote.[34] Chen and Rodden find that, in about four-fifths of the states they examine, Republicans usually win more than half the seats (and Democrats fewer) with half the statewide vote.[35] This result seems to confirm that, in most states, nonpartisan redistricting inherently favors Republicans.[36]

---

[30] Note that I wouldn't consider the absence of partisan *intent* to be much of a defense against a charge that a district plan has a large partisan *effect*.

[31] *See, e.g.*, BILL BISHOP, THE BIG SORT: WHY THE CLUSTERING OF LIKE-MINDED AMERICA IS TEARING US APART (2009).

[32] *See* Jowei Chen & Jonathan Rodden, *Unintentional Gerrymandering: Political Geography and Electoral Bias in Legislatures*, 8 Q.J. POL. SCI. 239 (2013).

[33] *See id.* at 260.

[34] *See id.* at 260–61.

[35] *See id.* at 263.

[36] *See also, e.g.*, JONATHAN A. RODDEN, WHY CITIES LOSE: THE DEEP ROOTS OF THE URBAN-RURAL POLITICAL DIVIDE 165–97 (2019) (conducting another redistricting simulation analysis and

There are reasons to question this conclusion. Chen and Rodden don't incorporate important nonpartisan criteria like respect for political subdivisions and compliance with the Voting Rights Act. If these requirements were included, the partisan properties of the simulated maps might shift.[37] The scholars' algorithm also doesn't produce simulated maps that are *representative* of the vast universe of possible maps that satisfy the selected parameters. Representative samples of maps (which other algorithms are capable of creating) might be more pro-Democratic or pro-Republican than Chen and Rodden's simulation sets.[38] And the 2000 election, the only one the scholars analyze, might be idiosyncratic. It certainly doesn't capture the parties' current geographic coalitions, more than twenty years later.[39]

Nevertheless, say that Chen and Rodden are right. That is, say that, for a given state, a cutting-edge algorithm that incorporates all applicable nonpartisan criteria typically generates maps biased in Republicans' favor, according to recent election results. And suppose that the enacted plan for this state is skewed in a Republican direction, too. What then? One tactic a (legal or political) opponent of the plan could attempt is to design a map that matches or beats the plan on every nonpartisan criterion but gives rise to no (or significantly less) partisan misalignment. If such a map could be drawn, it might suggest the enacted plan was crafted with partisan intent. After all, the plan's authors could have adopted—but chose not to—a much less biased district configuration. The existence of the alternative map might further undermine any defense that the enacted plan's skew is justified or caused by legitimate nonpartisan factors. How can those factors be held responsible, the rebuttal would go, when they're perfectly compatible with a much more neutral map?

This approach is persuasive enough that it has been used successfully in litigation. In a challenge to Wisconsin's highly pro-Republican 2010s state house plan, the plaintiffs submitted a "Demonstration Plan" that satisfied nonpartisan criteria as well as the enacted plan but was nearly unbiased.[40] This evidence

also showing that Republican voters tend to live in more competitive areas, especially in more competitive states); Nicholas Eubank & Jonathan Rodden, *Who Is My Neighbor? The Spatial Efficiency of Partisanship*, 7 STAT. & PUB. POL'Y 87, 94 (2020) (confirming the finding that Republican voters tend to live in more competitive areas).

[37] *See, e.g.,* Richard J. Powell et al., *Partisan Gerrymandering, Clustering, or Both? A New Approach to a Persistent Question*, 19 ELECTION L.J. 79, 92 (2020) (conducting an analysis much like Chen and Rodden's, but using additional criteria, a different algorithm, and more recent data, and concluding that "Republicans are advantaged only slightly due to the geographic distribution of partisans").

[38] *See, e.g.,* Benjamin Fifield et al., *The Essential Role of Empirical Validation in Legislative Redistricting Simulation*, 7 STAT. & PUB. POL'Y 52, 62, 65–66 (2020) (showing that Chen and Rodden's algorithm produces unrepresentative maps).

[39] More generally, the impact of political geography may vary from one electoral level to another (depending on how district magnitude relates to the sizes of partisan clusters) and from one election to the next (depending on partisan trends in different areas).

[40] *See* Whitford v. Gill, 218 F. Supp. 3d 837, 859 (W.D. Wis. 2016), *vacated*, 138 S. Ct. 1916 (2018).

helped convince the trial court that Wisconsin's "political geography cannot explain the burden that [the enacted plan] imposes on Democratic voters."[41] However, the inferences that supposedly follow from an alternative map are contestable. As to partisan intent, a jurisdiction could plausibly argue that little light is shed on its motives by its not enacting a plan of which it wasn't aware when redistricting occurred—and which *did* consider partisanship in order to reduce partisan skew. As to justification and causation, an unbiased alternative map only establishes that the application of nonpartisan criteria in a certain political geographic context doesn't *necessarily* lead to partisan misalignment. That map is mute as to whether the combination of nonpartisan requirements and the spatial distribution of voters *usually* benefits a particular party.

Because of these difficulties, an opponent of a skewed plan might also try to use Chen and Rodden's method—only, unlike these scholars, to show that the plan exhibits a *larger* bias than would be expected under nonpartisan redistricting. A computer algorithm would be deployed to produce a representative sample of simulated maps that ignore partisanship and perform at least as well as the enacted plan on all nonpartisan dimensions. The opponent's hope would be that the enacted plan is more skewed than most or all of these simulated maps. If it is, then a much stronger inference of partisan intent would arise. Why else than a desire for partisan gain would the enacted plan lead to worse partisan misalignment than the simulated maps that accomplish all the jurisdiction's nonpartisan goals? An enacted plan that's more biased than most or all simulations also falsifies claims that the plan's skew is justified or caused by valid nonpartisan factors. In the typical case, maybe even in every case, maps equally shaped by those factors—but not by partisan greed—yield less partisan misalignment.

Due to the force of this evidence, most plaintiffs have presented ensembles of algorithm-generated maps in recent partisan gerrymandering suits. These litigants have thus generally sought to make two statistical showings: first, that an enacted plan is highly biased according to measures like the efficiency gap; and second, that this skew is larger than would be anticipated under nonpartisan redistricting. Consider, for instance, a high-profile challenge to a North Carolina congressional plan in the 2010s. The plaintiffs demonstrated that the plan "produced the fourth-largest average efficiency gap of the 136 plans" used by states with at least seven congressional districts since 1972.[42] As illustrated by Figure 7.2, the plaintiffs further proved that the plan was more biased than all simulated maps created by an algorithm without using election results and matching or beating the plan in terms of all nonpartisan criteria. In the plot of

---

[41] *Id.* at 926.
[42] Common Cause v. Rucho, 318 F. Supp. 3d 777, 887 (M.D.N.C. 2018), *rev'd*, 139 S. Ct. 2484 (2019).

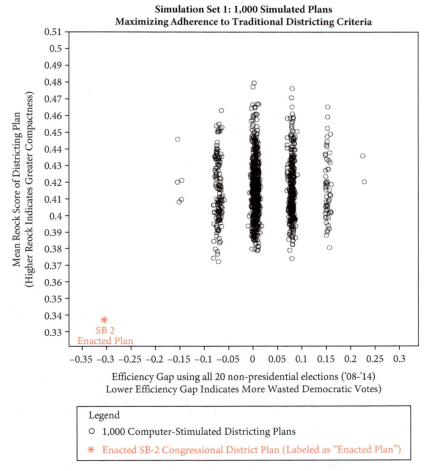

Simulation Set 1: 1,000 Simulated Plans
Maximizing Adherence to Traditional Districting Criteria

Efficiency Gap using all 20 non-presidential elections ('08-'14)
Lower Efficiency Gap Indicates More Wasted Democratic Votes)

Legend
○ 1,000 Computer-Stimulated Districting Plans
✳ Enacted SB-2 Congressional District Plan (Labeled as "Enacted Plan")

FIGURE 7.2 AVERAGE DISTRICT COMPACTNESS AND EFFICIENCY GAPS FOR 2016
NORTH CAROLINA PLAN AND 1,000 SIMULATED MAPS

Figure 7.2 is reproduced with permission from Expert Report of Jowei Chen at 32, Common Cause
v. Rucho, 318 F. Supp. 3d 777, 887 (M.D.N.C. 2018), rev'd, 139 S. Ct. 2484 (2019) (No. 1:16-CV-
1026). Copyright © 2018 by Jowei Chen.

average district compactness versus the efficiency gap, the plan is a stark outlier
compared to the simulated maps. Its districts are more misshapen and its pro-
Republican bias is 30 percentage points greater than most (and at least 15 percentage points greater than all) of the simulations.

To be sure, this North Carolina case is the one in which the Supreme Court ultimately held that partisan gerrymandering claims are nonjusticiable in federal

court.[43] But in her dissent, Justice Kagan fully embraced the logic of using redistricting simulations to probe if an enacted plan's skew is attributable to partisan or nonpartisan factors. "[T]he assemblage of maps, reflecting the characteristics and judgments of the State itself, creates a neutral baseline from which to assess whether partisanship has run amok."[44] Ensembles of algorithm-generated maps also continue to be mainstays of partisan gerrymandering litigation in *state* court.[45] And most relevant here, not even the Supreme Court majority asserted that nonpartisan criteria or political geography accounted for the bias of the disputed North Carolina plan. All the Justices thus seem (implicitly) to understand that not all partisan misalignment has an innocent explanation—and that, using modern empirical techniques, it's now possible to *tell* whether the reason for a plan's skew is benign or nefarious.

Litigation Alternatives

The discussion to this point hasn't been limited to litigation. You can imagine politicians, journalists, and activists citing the partisan bias of a district plan. You can also imagine these actors referring to algorithm-generated maps that probe whether partisan or nonpartisan factors drive a plan's skew. Still, it's undeniable that (outside of scholarship) this kind of information most often appears in suits brought under federal or state constitutional provisions. I now turn to strategies other than such suits for promoting alignment through redistricting. One option is structural reform, by which I mean taking away the power to draw district lines from politicians and giving it to multimember commissions. Another possibility is subjecting mapmakers (whoever they are) to tighter constraints. These constraints can curb gerrymandering indirectly, by requiring districts to abide by nonpartisan rules, or directly, by forbidding partisan intent and/or effect.[46]

Starting with structural reform, multimember commissions design state legislative maps in fifteen states[47] and congressional maps in ten states.[48] These institutions fall into three categories (which also correspond roughly to the order

---

[43] *See* Rucho v. Common Cause, 139 S. Ct. 2484 (2019).

[44] *Id.* at 2520 (Kagan, J., dissenting).

[45] For example, the same North Carolina plan that was upheld by the Supreme Court in *Rucho* was struck down by a state court in subsequent state constitutional litigation—which relied heavily on redistricting simulations. *See* Harper v. Lewis, No. 19 CVS 012667 (N.C. Super. Ct. Oct. 28, 2019).

[46] Such redistricting criteria obviously overlap with litigation as an anti-gerrymandering strategy since they're often enforced through lawsuits.

[47] *See Redistricting Commissions: State Legislative Plans*, Nat'l Conf. St. Legis. (Dec. 10, 2021), https://www.ncsl.org/research/redistricting/2009-redistricting-commissions-table.aspx.

[48] *See Redistricting Commissions: Congressional Plans*, Nat'l Conf. St. Legis. (Dec. 10, 2021), https://www.ncsl.org/research/redistricting/redistricting-commissions-congressional-plans.aspx.

in which they were established).[49] First, *politician* commissions are comprised of officeholders like the governor and the secretary of state. In use in states including Arkansas and Ohio, these bodies often have unbalanced partisan makeups. Second, *bipartisan* commissions have equal numbers of members from each party (typically appointed by legislative leaders) who then select a tiebreaking chair. Used by states like New Jersey and Washington, these entities aim to balance partisan forces rather than to exclude them entirely. And third, *independent* commissions are staffed by ordinary citizens chosen (in part) by lottery. Pioneered by California and Michigan, these institutions are relatively insulated from political pressures (though legislative leaders get to strike candidates from the applicant pool and commissioners are then picked using partisan quotas). The 2019 and 2021 federal bills I mentioned above would both have imposed this model on all states for congressional redistricting.[50]

A reasonable hypothesis is that commissions enact less biased plans than do politicians. In particular, bipartisan and independent commissions (which account for most of these bodies) have no incentive to try to benefit one party over the other. Half or more of a bipartisan commission's members might be expected to object to a gerrymander, and an even larger fraction of independent commissioners might see their job as avoiding—not engaging in—line-drawing for partisan advantage. At least in the current cycle, this surmise is correct. Drawn from a recent study by Warshaw and his coauthors, Figure 7.3 shows how the type of redistricting authority affects the predicted efficiency gap for congressional and state legislative maps adopted in 2021–22. Unsurprisingly, at both electoral levels, plans ratified by Democratic (or Republican) state governments have statistically significant pro-Democratic (or pro-Republican) skews.[51] Maps designed by commissions, in contrast, are much less biased. Both for Congress and for state legislatures, their average efficiency gaps are close to zero and statistically indistinguishable from perfect partisan alignment.[52]

The story is murkier—though still positive overall—for previous cycles. For the period from 1972 to 2012, I find that commission usage significantly reduces the absolute efficiency gap of congressional plans if the measure is calculated

---

[49] *See generally* Bruce E. Cain, *Redistricting Commissions: A Better Political Buffer?*, 121 YALE L.J. 1808 (2012).

[50] *See* For the People Act of 2019, H.R. 1, 116th Cong. §§ 2400–15 (2019); For the People Act of 2021, H.R. 1, 117th Cong. §§ 2400–15 (2021).

[51] *See* Christopher Warshaw et al., *Districts for a New Decade–Partisan Outcomes and Racial Representation in the 2021-22 Redistricting Cycle*, 52 PUBLIUS: J. FEDERALISM 428, 440 (2022); *see also, e.g.*, Stephanopoulos, *supra* note 19, at 2134 (showing that, in previous cycles too, Democratic (or Republican) control of the redistricting process typically led to a pro-Democratic (or pro-Republican) skew).

[52] *See* Warshaw et al., *supra* note 51, at 440; *see also id.* at 441–42 (finding that commission-drawn congressional plans roughly match the usual efficiency gaps of nonpartisan algorithm-generated maps).

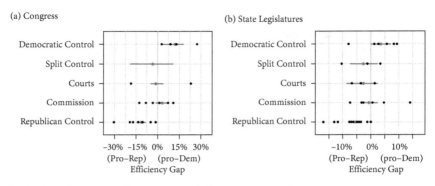

FIGURE 7.3 IMPACT OF REDISTRICTING AUTHORITY ON PREDICTED
EFFICIENCY GAP

Figure 7.3 is reproduced with permission from Christopher Warshaw et al., *Districts for a New Decade - Partisan Outcomes and Racial Representation in the 2021-22 Redistricting Cycle*, 52 PUBLIUS: J. FEDERALISM 428, 440 (2022). Copyright © 2022 by Oxford University Press.

using presidential election results.[53] But there's no discernible impact if it's computed with congressional election results, and commission usage doesn't seem to affect the absolute bias of state house maps.[54] Caughey and Warshaw confirm my conclusion about the lack of a relationship between commission usage and the absolute efficiency gap of state house maps, extending it to a slightly longer period (the balance of the 2010s) as well as to state senate plans.[55] However, these scholars also demonstrate that, when a commission is in place in a state, parties no longer gain a redistricting edge from winning control of an additional branch of the state government.[56] "As designed, commissions do seem to break the dominant party's ability to draw districts more favorable to themselves."[57]

Why are commissions more clearly aligning today than in the past? It's only speculation, but it might be because of the intense spotlight that now shines on

[53] *See* Nicholas O. Stephanopoulos, *Arizona and Anti-Reform*, 2015 U. CHI. LEGAL F. 477, 501; *see also* Stephanopoulos, *supra* note 19, at 2134 (commission usage doesn't significantly move the efficiency gap in either party's direction at the congressional and state house levels); Nicholas O. Stephanopoulos et al., *The Realities of Electoral Reform*, 68 VAND. L. REV. 761, 815 (2015) (commission usage significantly improves the representational alignment of the median state house member).

[54] *See* Stephanopoulos, *supra* note 51, at 501; *see also* Thad Kousser et al., *Reform and Representation: A New Method Applied to Recent Electoral Changes*, 6 POL. SCI. RSCH. & METHODS 809, 822 (2018) (California's adoption of a commission didn't improve the district-level representational alignment of members of Congress).

[55] *See* CAUGHEY & WARSHAW, *supra* note 8, at 149–50.

[56] *See id.*

[57] *Id.* at 150.

district maps' partisan effects. Thanks to high-profile partisan gerrymandering cases, there's more familiarity today with quantitative measures of partisan bias and redistricting simulations. Websites also now exist that can instantly calculate a proposed plan's skew[58] and compare it to an ensemble of algorithm-generated maps.[59] And with the House of Representatives frequently shifting from one party's control to the other's in recent years, it's obvious that commissions' choices can influence the national balance of power. In this informational and political environment, commissions might be especially attentive to the danger of accidentally stumbling into biased plans. Some commissions might even pro-actively consult election results, and compute draft maps' skews, to avoid falling into this trap.[60]

In any event, commissions *are* clearly aligning today, enacting plans that, on average, exhibit close to perfect partisan alignment. The upshot is that commissions should be adopted as quickly and widely as possible. Congressional action along the lines of the 2019 and 2021 bills is particularly promising because it would establish, in one blow, a commission for congressional redistricting in every state. Similarly, commissions' aligning benefits should be a defense against legal or political attacks on them. In court, commissions are sometimes alleged to violate the freedom of association[61] or the supposedly plenary authority of state legislatures.[62] In politics, commissions' critics (usually incumbent politicians) claim that they're bureaucratic bodies unaccountable to the people for their decisions.[63] A riposte to all these charges should be that commissions markedly improve democracy by giving rise to legislatures whose partisan compositions—and, consequently, ideological makeups and policy outputs—better reflect the will of the electorate.

Structural reform is one alternative to anti-gerrymandering litigation; tighter constraints on mapmakers (be they politicians, commissions, or courts) are an-other. For generations, many states have adhered to "traditional" redistricting criteria like compactness, respect for political subdivisions, and respect for

---

[58] *See* PLANSCORE, https://planscore.org (last visited Feb. 1, 2024).

[59] *See 50-State Redistricting Simulations*, ALARM PROJECT (Feb. 8, 2022), https://alarm-redist.git hub.io/fifty-states/.

[60] *See, e.g.*, Lisa Handley, Report to the Michigan Independent Citizens Redistricting Commission 28–33 (2021) (discussing and calculating several measures of partisan bias for maps drafted by the Michigan commission). Of course, if political geography is often biased in one or another party's favor, it becomes more important to affirmatively instruct a commission to pursue partisan fairness. Without an overt direction like this, a commission risks unintentionally benefiting the party advantaged by the jurisdiction's political geography.

[61] *See, e.g.*, Daunt v. Benson, 956 F.3d 396 (6th Cir. 2020).

[62] *See, e.g.*, Ariz. St. Legis. v. Ariz. Indep. Redist. Comm'n, 576 U.S. 787 (2015).

[63] *See, e.g.*, Fred Lucas, *What Happened in These States When Unelected Bureaucrats Took Over Redistricting*, DAILY SIGNAL (Dec. 22, 2021), https://www.dailysignal.com/2021/12/22/what-happe ned-in-these-states-when-unelected-bureaucrats-took-over-redistricting/.

communities of interest.[64] These criteria don't directly try to stop the pursuit of partisan gain. But they might do so indirectly by requiring line-drawers to achieve nonpartisan objectives whose attainment is incompatible with as large a partisan edge. Over the last few years, a handful of states have also implemented criteria that facially prohibit partisan intent and/or partisan effect. Florida's constitution, for example, provides that no plan "shall be drawn with the intent to favor or disfavor a political party."[65] Michigan's constitution states that "districts shall not provide a disproportionate advantage to any political party," as "determined using accepted measures of partisan fairness."[66] The 2019, 2021, and 2022 federal bills, too, would have banned congressional maps that "have been drawn with the intent or have the effect of materially favoring or disfavoring any political party" (to quote the last bill in this series).[67] As noted earlier, that bill would have presumptively invalidated any plan above a certain efficiency gap threshold as well.[68]

There's some evidence that the application of traditional criteria reduces the partisan bias of district plans. I find that, in the 2000s, states obligated to respect the boundaries of communities of interest had state legislative maps with lower levels of partisan asymmetry.[69] Another study examines in more detail the redistricting experiences of six states in that cycle. It also concludes that traditional criteria, especially respect for political subdivisions, significantly limited the discretion of mapmakers and prevented them from aggressively gerrymandering.[70] However, these analyses are both specific to a single period and lack controls or other methods more probative of causation. Their results are thus best seen as suggestive and awaiting confirmation from more rigorous research.

As for criteria explicitly targeting partisanship, they're so novel that scholars haven't yet investigated their effects.[71] Preliminarily, though, they seem quite potent. Under Florida's prohibition of partisan intent, the state supreme court

---

[64] See *Redistricting Criteria*, NAT'L CONF. ST. LEGIS (July 16, 2021), https://www.ncsl.org/research/redistricting/redistricting-criteria.aspx.

[65] FLA. CONST. art. III, §§ 20(a), 21(a).

[66] MICH. CONST. art. IV, § 6(13)(d).

[67] Freedom to Vote: John R. Lewis Act, H.R. 5746, 117th Cong. § 5003(c)(1) (2022).

[68] See *id.* § 5003(c)(3).

[69] See Nicholas O. Stephanopoulos, *Redistricting and the Territorial Community*, 160 U. PA. L. REV. 1379, 1462 (2012); *cf.* Nicholas O. Stephanopoulos, *Spatial Diversity*, 125 HARV. L. REV. 1905, 1966 (2012) (finding a curvilinear relationship between "spatial diversity" (a proxy for respect for communities of interest) and partisan asymmetry for congressional plans in the 2000s).

[70] See JONATHAN WINBURN, THE REALITIES OF REDISTRICTING: FOLLOWING THE RULES AND LIMITING GERRYMANDERING IN STATE LEGISLATIVE REDISTRICTING (2009).

[71] For a study of mine investigating earlier criteria targeting partisanship on an ad hoc basis, see Nicholas O. Stephanopoulos, *The Consequences of Consequentialist Criteria*, 3 U.C. IRVINE L. REV. 669 (2013).

struck down numerous congressional and state senate districts in the 2010s.[72] The remedial plans adopted after these decisions were significantly less biased than their predecessors.[73] Likewise, in the 2020s, Michigan's commission complied with the state's partisan fairness requirement by calculating several measures of partisan skew for its draft maps and seeking to minimize their values.[74] The plans the commission ultimately enacted were models of partisan alignment, especially relative to the gerrymandered maps they replaced.[75] And at the federal level, a pair of researchers considered what consequences the 2022 bill's efficiency gap threshold would have had for congressional plans across the country. That threshold would have led to the presumptive invalidation of most maps designed by politicians but few maps drawn by other actors.[76] The bill's impact would therefore have been sweeping yet focused on the nation's more objectionable plans.

The first takeaway about promoting alignment through redistricting criteria, then, is that more study is necessary. Better analyses of traditional criteria should be on the scholarly agenda, as should be *any* analyses of the new anti-partisanship criteria. The other point is that, provisionally, measures that attack partisanship frontally appear to be more aligning than measures that do so obliquely. The Florida and Michigan cases sketched in the previous paragraph are striking successes in terms of reducing district maps' biases. So would have been the 2022 bill—nationwide—had Congress passed it. In the many years in which they've been used, conversely, traditional criteria have not typically produced such triumphs. Now that technology makes it possible to comply with traditional criteria while still sharply skewing a plan in a party's favor,[77] there's even less reason to expect these requirements to be efficacious going forward.

[72] *See* League of Women Voters of Fla. v. Detzner, 172 So. 3d 363 (Fla. 2015); In re Senate Joint Resolution of Legis. Apportionment 1176, 83 So. 3d 597 (Fla. 2012). However, Florida's prohibition of partisan intent has been toothless, to date, in the current redistricting cycle.

[73] *Compare, e.g., Florida 2016-2020 Redistricting Plan*, PLANSCORE, https://planscore.org/florida/#!2016-plan-ushouse-eg (last visited Feb. 1, 2024), *with Florida 2012-2014 Redistricting Plan*, PLANSCORE, https://planscore.org/florida/#!2014-plan-ushouse-eg (last visited Feb. 1, 2024).

[74] *See* Handley, *supra* note 60, at 28–33.

[75] *Compare, e.g., Michigan Congressional Draft—Chestnut*, PLANSCORE (Nov. 2, 2021), https://planscore.org/plan.html?20211102T180623.315151618Z, *with Michigan 2012-2020 Redistricting Plan*, PLANSCORE, https://planscore.org/michigan/#!2020-plan-ushouse-eg (last visited Feb. 1, 2024).

[76] *See* Peter Miller & Anna Harris, *Sen. Manchin's Freedom to Vote Act Would Help Stop Gerrymandering, Our Research Finds*, WASH. POST, Jan. 10, 2022.

[77] *See* Chen & Stephanopoulos, *supra* note 5, at 1049 (showing that party-conscious algorithms can gerrymander effectively in either party's favor while matching or beating the enacted plan's performance on all nonpartisan criteria).

Individual Districts

Everything I've said so far in this chapter has pertained to district plans in their entirety, not to individual districts. Whole district plans give rise to jurisdiction-wide partisan misalignment that can be quantified by measures like the efficiency gap. The partisan biases of whole district plans can be compared to those of maps generated randomly by algorithms. Whole district plans might be less skewed if they're crafted by commissions or pursuant to certain criteria. And there's a reason for this emphasis. The primary way in which redistricting affects alignment is by determining how votes are aggregated and then converted into legislative seats. District plans in their entirety specify how this aggregation takes place—which votes are combined with which other votes in which districts. Individual districts, on the other hand, don't set the terms of this aggregation. They're the *result* of the aggregation rather than its blueprint.

Nevertheless, individual districts might influence alignment through another channel. Depending on how they're constructed, individual districts might induce legislators to take policy positions more congruent with the policy preferences of their constituents.[78] This boost in district-specific representational alignment, if repeated across multiple districts, could even add up to better representational alignment at the jurisdictional level. This dynamic, a sizable literature shows, isn't merely hypothetical. Legislators are ideologically closer to their constituents in districts that abide by traditional criteria like compactness, respect for political subdivisions, and respect for communities of interest.[79] When a whole district map is drawn to satisfy (rather than to spurn) these requirements, the result is a less polarized, more representationally aligned legislature.

At the district level, one study finds that respondents in more compact House districts report being ideologically more proximate to their representatives.[80] This effect is even larger for respondents whose partisanship diverges from that

---

[78] This improvement in representational alignment might apply—might even *especially* apply—to issues of local concern not well captured by the standard left-right ideological dimension.

[79] The evidence is mixed as to whether more *competitive* districts lead to better district-specific representational alignment. On the one hand, legislators from more competitive districts don't cast votes that are more congruent with the preferences of their constituents. *See, e.g.,* Kousser et al., *supra* note 54, at 824; John G. Matsusaka, When Do Legislators Follow Constituent Opinion? Evidence from Matched Roll-Call and Referendum Votes 18 (Feb. 2021). On the other, voters in more competitive districts *perceive* greater ideological alignment with their representatives. *See* Daniel C. Bowen, *Boundaries, Redistricting Criteria, and Representation in the U.S. House of Representatives*, 42 Am. Pol. Rsch. 856, 878 (2014). And House members from more competitive districts are less responsive to the views of out-of-district donors (and so presumably more responsive to the views of their own constituents). *See* Brandice Canes-Wrone & Kenneth M. Miller, *Out-of-District Donors and Representation in the U.S. House*, 47 Legis. Stud. Q. 361, 378–80 (2022). Given this ambiguity, I don't further consider competition as a tool for promoting district-specific representational alignment.

[80] *See* Bowen, *supra* note 79, at 876.

of their House members.[81] Another study reaches the same conclusion for House districts that more closely follow the boundaries of zip codes, which are reasonable proxies for communities of interest. In these districts, the perceived ideological distance between respondents and their representatives tends to be smaller.[82] Other studies examine media markets for newspapers[83] and television stations,[84] which often correspond to political subdivisions and communities of interest. House members from districts that are more congruent with media markets compile more moderate voting records[85] and cast votes that more aligned with their constituents' views.[86] Still other studies use districts' demographic, socioeconomic, or ideological homogeneity as a measure of compliance with traditional criteria. Legislators from more homogenous districts are less ideologically extreme[87] and more responsive to the characteristics[88] and preferences[89] of their constituents.

An implication of this work is that jurisdiction-wide representational alignment should also be better when districts are more mindful of traditional criteria. Individual legislators who more closely reflect their constituents' views should cumulate into a legislature that looks more like the electorate, too. The strongest support for this proposition comes from one of the studies that focus on district homogeneity. As displayed in Figure 7.4, Nolan McCarty and his coauthors plot the relationship between state senator ideology and the ideology of the median respondent in each district for districts that are (1) more ideologically homogeneous, (2) middling in their ideological variation, and (3) more ideologically heterogeneous. The scholars include separate best-fit lines for Democratic and Republican state senators. The key finding is that the gap between the Democratic and Republican best-fit lines is significantly narrower in the first panel (for more homogenous districts) than in the third (for more heterogeneous districts). That is, the distribution of state senator ideology is considerably less polarized and more similar to the distribution of respondent ideology

[81] See id. at 876–78; see also Stephanopoulos et al., supra note 53, at 813 (finding that the use of compactness criteria improves the district-specific representational alignment of state house members).
[82] See John A. Curiel & Tyler Steelman, Redistricting out Representation: Democratic Harms in Splitting Zip Codes, 17 ELECTION L.J. 328, 343 (2018).
[83] See James M. Snyder Jr. & David Stromberg, Press Coverage and Political Accountability, 118 J. POL. ECON. 355 (2010).
[84] See Patrick Balles et al., Television Market Size and Political Accountability in the US House of Representatives (May 2022).
[85] See Snyder & Stromberg, supra note 83, at 399.
[86] See Balles et al., supra note 84, at 16.
[87] See Nolan McCarty et al., Geography, Uncertainty, and Polarization, 7 POL. SCI. RSCH. & METHODS 775, 787–88 (2019).
[88] See Stephanopoulos, Spatial Diversity, supra note 69, at 1944–46.
[89] See Elisabeth R. Gerber & Jeffrey B. Lewis, Beyond the Median: Voter Preferences, District Heterogeneity, and Political Representation, 112 J. POL. ECON. 1364, 1376 (2004).

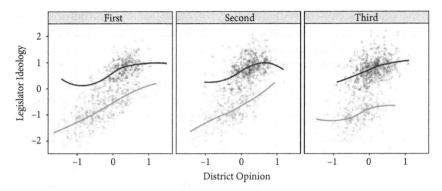

FIGURE 7.4 STATE SENATOR VERSUS DISTRICT IDEOLOGY BY IDEOLOGICAL
HOMOGENEITY TERCILE

Figure 7.4 is reproduced with permission from Nolan McCarty et al., *Geography, Uncertainty, and Polarization*, 7 POL. SCI. RSCH. & METHODS 775, 788 (2019). Copyright © 2019 by Cambridge University Press.

in more homogeneous districts.[90] If these districts are the product of traditional criteria being applied, as the scholars suggest, then these requirements are indeed linked to improved jurisdiction-wide representational alignment.[91]

But what accounts for this connection? Why is a legislator in a district that adheres to traditional criteria more likely to behave in a manner consistent with district opinion? Start from the perspective of voters in this kind of district. The district is apt to make geographic and political sense to them. It may follow the boundaries of entities that are important and familiar to voters, like neighborhoods, cities, and counties. These entities may be served by the same newspaper and television station, ensuring that voters are exposed to common information about developments in the district. And the district may be compact, so voters live relatively close to one another, and homogeneous, so voters are demographically and socioeconomically similar. In this sort of environment, voters should be more informed about their representative. The representative's votes, speeches, scandals, and so on should reach them more readily thanks to their shared media sources and interpersonal ties. By the same token, voters should find it easier to organize for or against their representative. The costs of

[90] *See* McCarty et al., *supra* note 87, at 788.
[91] *See also* Snyder & Stromberg, *supra* note 83, at 397 (showing that House members are less polarized when their districts better correspond to media markets); Stephanopoulos, *Spatial Diversity*, *supra* note 69, at 1948 (same when House districts are less spatially diverse).

political mobilization should be lower where voters obtain the same information and belong to the same community.[92]

Numerous studies document exactly these effects. As to voter knowledge, voters are more likely to recall House candidates' names in districts that are more compact[93] and more congruent with political subdivisions,[94] with zip codes,[95] and with media markets.[96] Voters are also more likely to state accurately how their House members voted on bills,[97] and to have read newspaper coverage about their House members,[98] in districts that better correspond to media markets. As to voter mobilization, voters are more apt to contact their House members in districts that are more compact[99] and more congruent with political subdivisions,[100] with zip codes,[101] and with media markets.[102] Voters also turn out at higher rates in House districts that are more homogeneous[103] and more congruent with media markets.[104] There's robust empirical support, then, for the view that the electorate is more informed and engaged when traditional criteria are more scrupulously heeded.

Now consider a legislator faced with an electorate like this. She has a substantial incentive to take positions that reflect the views of her constituents. She can expect more of those constituents to know her stances than if her district didn't abide by traditional criteria. She can also expect voters to organize more effectively against her if they don't approve of her positions—to reach out to her and to go to the polls. When voters cast ballots in districts more congruent with media markets, moreover, they do so in larger numbers for challengers.[105] The surest way for the legislator to avoid this potential threat is simply to act the way most of her constituents want her to act. The fact of her district-specific representational alignment will reach more voters than in a different kind of district less

---

[92] *See generally* Bernard Grofman, *Would Vince Lombardi Have Been Right if He Had Said: "When It Comes to Redistricting, Race Isn't Everything, It's the* Only *Thing"?,* 14 CARDOZO L. REV. 1237, 1262–63 (1993) (discussing the benefits that flow for voters when districts are "cognizable").

[93] *See, e.g.,* Bowen, *supra* note 79, at 882.

[94] *See, e.g.,* Jonathan Winburn & Michael W. Wagner, *Redistricting's Influence on Political Information, Turnout, and Voting Behavior,* 63 POL. RSCH. Q. 373, 379 (2010).

[95] *See, e.g.,* Curiel & Steelman, *supra* note 79, at 341.

[96] *See, e.g.,* Snyder & Stromberg, *supra* note 83, at 373.

[97] *See, e.g.,* Daniel Lipinski, *The Effect of Messages Communicated by Members of Congress: The Impact of Publicizing Votes,* 26 LEGIS. STUD. Q. 81, 92 (2001).

[98] *See, e.g.,* Snyder & Stromberg, *supra* note 83, at 369, 373.

[99] *See, e.g.,* Bowen, *supra* note 79, at 882.

[100] *See, e.g., id.*

[101] *See, e.g.,* Curiel & Steelman, *supra* note 82, at 342.

[102] *See, e.g.,* Timothy S. Prinz, *Media Markets and Candidate Awareness in House Elections, 1978-1990,* 12 POL. COMM. 305, 310 (1995).

[103] *See, e.g.,* Stephanopoulos, *Spatial Diversity, supra* note 69, at 1943.

[104] *See, e.g.,* Snyder & Stromberg, *supra* note 83, at 382.

[105] *See, e.g.,* James E. Campbell et al., *Television Markets and Congressional Elections,* 9 LEGIS. STUD. Q. 665, 673–74 (1984).

respectful of traditional criteria. That knowledge might dissuade the legislator's constituents from exercising their greater capacity to mobilize against her.

The legislator's desire to stay in office is thus one potential driver here. Another reason why compliance with traditional criteria could be linked to better representational congruence at the district level is the likelihood (noted by McCarty and his coauthors) that more compliant districts are also more ideologically homogeneous. Think of the plight of a representative in an ideologically *heterogeneous* district who would like to align her stances with those of her constituents, on normative rather than electoral grounds. Confronted by voters with dramatically different preferences, the representative receives conflicting signals instead of a single clear message how she should act. Whatever positions the representative ultimately takes, she must disappoint large fractions of her constituents. In contrast, life is much easier for a legislator in an ideologically homogeneous district who aspires to district-specific representational alignment. She does receive a single (or at least a more consistent) signal from voters. She's also able to satisfy more of her constituents when she takes stands. Alignment is a plausible goal for her, not an impossible dream.[106]

What this means, legally and politically, is that districts that follow traditional criteria are preferable to districts that don't. Because districts that follow traditional criteria promote district-specific (and even jurisdiction-wide) representational alignment, mapmakers should try to create these districts and courts should uphold them when they're challenged on other bases. On the other hand, mapmakers should refrain from crafting districts that flout traditional criteria and courts should appraise these districts warily due to their misaligning effects. The point is that the design of individual districts—not just of district plans in their entirety—has implications for alignment. Legal and political actors alike should take these implications into account.

Could there be tension between adhering to traditional criteria and minimizing whole district plans' partisan biases? There certainly could be. To reiterate, this is Chen and Rodden's argument: If traditional criteria are applied against the backdrop of contemporary American political geography, the result is usually a district map with a pro-Republican skew. To the extent Chen and Rodden are correct, traditional criteria should be sacrificed in favor of district plans that, in their entirety, give rise to jurisdiction-wide partisan alignment.

---

[106] *See generally* BRUCE E. CAIN, THE REAPPORTIONMENT PUZZLE 63 (1984) (noting that if a district "is very heterogeneous, then it may be very hard for one representative to represent all factions well," while if a district "is homogeneous, there is less internal reason for multiple representation").

The aligning (and misaligning) power of vote aggregation far exceeds that of traditional criteria. So a map that's unbiased but scornful of traditional criteria is much more aligning than a highly skewed map that dutifully conforms to these requirements. But as I explained above, Chen and Rodden's contention may be overstated. Quite often, especially with the aid of modern technology, it may be possible to draw district plans that both exhibit small partisan skews and comply with traditional criteria reasonably well. Where this approach is feasible, it's obviously the first-best option. It enables vote aggregation to drive jurisdiction-wide alignment at the same time that traditional criteria advance alignment at the district level.

* * *

In a system of single-member districts, there may be no electoral policy with as much aligning—and misaligning—potential as the configuration of district boundaries. District maps determine how votes are aggregated and then converted into legislative seats. If district maps produce jurisdiction-wide partisan misalignment, that distortion extends to representation and policy. District maps also generally don't need to produce jurisdiction-wide partisan misalignment. In most cases, the application of traditional criteria in a given political geographic context is compatible with unbiased plans. Accordingly, for courts concerned about alignment, there are few targets riper than highly skewed maps. Courts, however, aren't the only relevant actors here. Misalignment from redistricting can also be curbed by the adoption of independent commissions and the use of criteria barring lines from being drawn with partisan intent and/or partisan effect. And vote aggregation isn't the only mechanism through which redistricting affects alignment. When individual districts are designed pursuant to traditional criteria, voters know more about, and can mobilize more easily against, their legislators, who are thus induced to provide more congruent representation. For judicial and nonjudicial actors alike, then, the aligning ideal is an unbiased plan composed of districts conforming to traditional criteria.

In this chapter, I occasionally referred to the Voting Rights Act (VRA) as a nonpartisan requirement whose satisfaction might lead to misalignment. The VRA is that but it's also so much more: the crucial statutory commitment to ending racial vote denial, racial vote dilution, and the relegation of minority members to second-class political status. The VRA therefore warrants more careful examination, which it receives in the next chapter. I first consider to what extent VRA compliance does skew district maps. The answer hinges on the makeup of the districts that are created to abide by the VRA. A trade-off exists between alignment and minority representation only if these districts are unnecessarily packed with minority voters. I then address the aligning impact of the VRA as a whole—not just its application to redistricting. By finally incorporating minority members into the American political community, it significantly improved collective alignment. This boost was especially dramatic in the South, the region that had most systematically excluded minority members prior to the VRA's enactment.

8

The Voting Rights Act

Introduction

The Voting Rights Act (VRA) is the monumental 1965 law that restored democracy to the South after an absence of almost a century. The VRA aims to realize a set of values, all involving the political role of racial minorities. One of these is minority participation: the ability of minority members to vote without impediment from policies that intentionally or disparately hinder their exercise of the franchise. Another objective of the VRA is minority representation: the election of candidates favored by minority members (who often are, but need not be, minorities themselves). The VRA further aspires to bring about policy outcomes that are responsive to minority policy preferences.

These statutory goals are plainly important. Over the many decades in which they failed to be achieved, southern jurisdictions, in particular, could hardly claim to be democratic. But the VRA's ambitions are also plainly distinct from alignment. I observed in Chapter 1 that greater *overall* participation might lead to, but isn't the same thing as, closer alignment. The same is necessarily true for greater *minority* participation—more political involvement by a subset of the public. With respect to representation and policy, they're key facets of alignment. But not when they're tied to the preferences of minority members rather than all persons. In that case, they constitute group-specific representational or policy alignment. Group-specific alignment, I've reiterated throughout the book, is different from population-level alignment.

Not only are the VRA's values distinct from alignment, but many scholars believe that one of those values—minority representation—conflicts with alignment. When voting is racially polarized, the election of minority-favored candidates generally requires the creation of districts with large minority populations. Of course, the minority voters in those minority-heavy districts have to come from somewhere. The districts adjacent to the new minority-heavy districts are that somewhere. Those nearby districts are drained of their minority voters, making them Whiter and more likely to elect Republicans and conservatives. In the aggregate, this dynamic produces more minority representation along with more representation for Republicans and conservatives. If enough new districts electing Republicans and conservatives are formed, then jurisdiction-wide misalignment is the price of more minority representation. Or at least so the argument goes.

Aligning Election Law. Nicholas O. Stephanopoulos, Oxford University Press. © Nicholas O. Stephanopoulos 2024.
DOI: 10.1093/9780197662182.003.0008

Despite its prevalence, though, this claim is at least overstated and maybe even wrong. For one thing, the claim relies heavily on the experience of the 1990s, when many more districts electing Black-preferred candidates were created at the same time that conservative Republicans captured the House of Representatives as well as several state legislatures. But the 1990s are just one redistricting cycle. Even if that decade's maps did exchange some alignment for more minority representation, it hardly means this trade-off is inevitable. The more careful empirical work about the developments of the 1990s also shows that the rises in minority representation and conservative Republican representation were unrelated. Conservative Republicans actually did better in states that added fewer (or no) Black opportunity districts. If anything, the formation of those districts moved the ideological midpoints of congressional delegations to the left.

Moreover, the view that minority representation and alignment are inversely related overlooks factors that can attenuate or even reverse this supposed connection. One of these factors is the partisanship of the redistricting authority. A Republican line-drawer might concentrate minority voters in a few districts, thereby tilting numerous other districts (and the map as a whole) to the right. But a Democratic line-drawer has no reason to adopt this strategy. Instead, she can design minority opportunity districts with bare majorities (or even effective pluralities) of minority voters. Sure enough, empirically, the purported trade-off between minority representation and alignment disappears in plans enacted by Democrats. Another complicating factor is the partisanship of White voters located close to minority voters. If these White voters are moderately Republican, then a line-drawer might have to choose between a minority opportunity district and a Republican district, on the one hand, and two Democratic districts electing minority-nonpreferred candidates, on the other. But if the nearby White voters are heavily Republican—as in much of the modern South—then this trade-off again disappears. In this circumstance, the configuration that includes a minority opportunity district is also the option that maximizes Democratic representation.

So, fortunately, minority representation and alignment aren't (or don't have to be) at war with each other. What about the VRA's original objective (according to some, its only proper objective[1]) of minority participation? As a conceptual matter, the most plausible hypothesis is that greater minority participation results in closer alignment. When minority members are excluded from the political process, as in the pre-VRA South, the median actual voter may be quite different from the median eligible voter. In the case of a majority-minority jurisdiction, the median actual voter could even be a White conservative while the

---

[1] *See, e.g.,* Holder v. Hall, 512 U.S. 874, 914–45 (1994) (opinion of Thomas, J.) (arguing that the VRA doesn't protect against racial vote dilution).

median eligible voter is a minority liberal. Assuming the median actual voter's preferences help shape governmental outputs, the potential for rampant misalignment with the median eligible voter's views is obvious. But when minority members participate fully in the political process, the gap between the median actual voter and the median eligible voter shrinks. If turnout is equal across racial groups, there's no racial difference at all between the median actual voter and the median eligible voter. Assuming again a link between governmental outputs and the median actual voter's preferences, those outputs should now better reflect the median eligible voter's views.

Empirical evidence confirms that greater minority participation yields closer alignment. In the South, state policy outcomes became more congruent with the preferences of African American respondents after the VRA's enactment while remaining equally congruent with White respondents' views. These findings necessarily mean that population-level policy alignment improved as well. At the local level, heavily Black (especially majority-Black) jurisdictions subject to more stringent VRA enforcement saw the increased adoption of employment, education, and welfare policies that particularly benefited African Americans. Positing that African Americans favored these policies, this work also indicates better policy alignment thanks to the VRA. And in Congress, House members from heavily Black districts more protected by the VRA took more liberal positions on civil rights issues. Again supposing Black constituents supported these stances, the VRA brought about tighter representational alignment, too.

The VRA's Values

The core operative provision of the VRA is Section 2, which creates a cause of action for racial discrimination in voting. Prior to the Supreme Court's 2013 decision in *Shelby County v. Holder*,[2] Section 5 also prevented certain (mostly southern) jurisdictions from changing any electoral regulations unless they could show that the changes wouldn't worsen the electoral position of minority members. Both Section 2 and Section 5 prohibit what election lawyers call racial vote denial: restricting voting in ways that disparately harm minority members. Section 2 specifies that it's violated if minority "members have less opportunity than other members of the electorate to participate in the political process."[3] Similarly, measures are retrogressive under Section 5 if they "deny[] ... the right

---

[2] 570 U.S. 529, 540 (2013).
[3] 52 U.S.C. § 10301(b) (2018); *see generally* Nicholas O. Stephanopoulos, *Disparate Impact, Unified Law*, 128 YALE L.J. 1566 (2019) (discussing racial vote denial law).

to vote on account of race or color."[4] Both Section 2 and Section 5 further forbid what's known as racial vote dilution: reducing the number of minority-preferred officeholders by enacting electoral policies (like deviously drawn districts) that disfavor minority candidates of choice. A Section 2 violation is established if minority "members have less opportunity than other members of the electorate . . . to elect representatives of their choice."[5] Likewise, retrogression under Section 5 encompasses provisions "abridging" (a synonym for diluting) the franchise on racial grounds.[6]

The value that's undermined by racial vote denial is minority participation—more precisely, minority participation *commensurate to* White participation. Necessarily, an electoral policy that disparately prevents minority members from voting results in unequal minority and White participation.[7] On the other hand, minority representation is the value that underpins the theory of racial vote dilution. I've explained elsewhere that the elaborate body of precedent the Supreme Court has constructed under Section 2 aims for neither *maximal* nor *proportional* minority representation, but rather the extent of minority representation that's possible given the size, geographic distribution, political cohesion, and turnout of a minority population, up to a ceiling of proportionality.[8] One more value of the VRA is governmental responsiveness to the preferences of minority members. According to the Senate report that accompanied Section 2's revision in 1982, "a significant lack of responsiveness on the part of elected officials to the particularized needs of the members of the minority group" cuts in favor of liability.[9]

Like many of the VRA's proponents, I care deeply about minority participation, minority representation, and governmental responsiveness to minority concerns. It's vital for the political process to incorporate fully members of racial and ethnic minority groups—especially historically disadvantaged groups targeted by centuries of discrimination. My argument here, then, isn't that the VRA's values are unimportant. It's just that those weighty values are conceptually different from alignment. Matching the outputs of the government to the preferences of the *entire* public isn't the same as involving, representing, or responding to the views of, *minority* members.

Start with minority participation. In Chapter 1, I made the uncontroversial point that participation by all persons (minority members or not) is distinct

[4] 52 U.S.C. § 10304(a) (2018).
[5] *Id.* § 10301(b).
[6] *Id.* § 10304(a).
[7] *See, e.g.,* Brnovich v. Democratic Nat'l Comm., 141 S. Ct. 2321, 2339 (2021) ("disparity in impact" suggests "that a system is not equally open or that it does not give everyone an equal opportunity to vote").
[8] *See* Nicholas O. Stephanopoulos, *Race, Place, and Power,* 68 STAN. L. REV. 1323, 1337 (2016).
[9] S. REP. No. 97–417, at 29 (1982).

from alignment. Participation refers primarily to voting (in the political context) and secondarily to activities like contacting officeholders, organizing events, and donating money to candidates. All these elements of political involvement self-evidently differ from congruence between governmental outputs and popular preferences. This logic necessarily applies to minority as well as to overall participation. Just like the political involvement of the entire public, the engagement of minority members in politics is commendable, desirable—and not equivalent to alignment. The political engagement of minority members could help *lead* to alignment, but it's not the thing itself. A potential means to an end is still a means.

Turn next to minority representation and responsiveness to minority concerns. Representation and responsiveness *are* (or, at least, resemble) essential aspects of alignment. Representation—the identities of, and positions taken by, elected officials—is one of the governmental outputs that, I contend, should be congruent with popular preferences. Similarly, responsiveness is the rate at which governmental outputs vary given changes in popular preferences: a concept adjacent to whether governmental outputs correspond to popular preferences. Crucially, however, representation and responsiveness lose their connection to alignment as soon as *minority* is appended to them. Minority representation indicates how well minority members are represented, not whether elected officials' stances reflect the views of all their constituents. Likewise, a government responsive to minority concerns need not react with alacrity when the needs and interests of the general public shift. At various points in the book, I've distinguished group-specific alignment—alignment with the views of the wealthy, or the defenders of the status quo, or the members of a particular party—from population-level alignment. Minority representation and responsiveness to minority concerns are essentially two more versions of group-specific alignment. They may be deeply appealing in their own right, but they're not synonymous with the broader kind of alignment that's my interest here.

So the VRA's values are separate from the democratic principle that animates this project. This raises the question of how the former are related to the latter. One possibility is that the realization of the VRA's values conflicts with the achievement of alignment—that is, that compliance with the VRA is misaligning. As the next section discusses, this is precisely the link that, according to the conventional wisdom, exists between minority representation and alignment. It could also be that the VRA's values are orthogonal to alignment, that compliance with the VRA is compatible with (and not conducive to either) better or worse congruence between governmental outputs and popular preferences. This is the actual relationship between minority representation and alignment, I maintain in the next section based on extensive empirical evidence. The last option, of course, is that the VRA's values affirmatively promote alignment, that enforcement of the statute is aligning. Greater minority participation, I argue in the chapter's final section, indeed contributes to closer alignment by shrinking the gap between the median actual voter and the median eligible voter.[10]

A Tragic Choice?

Many scholars think there's a trade-off between the election of minority-preferred candidates (which I've been calling minority representation) and the satisfaction of minority members' policy preferences (which the literature terms minority substantive representation). The explanation for this widespread agreement is the dynamic I noted above by which minority opportunity districts are created by draining adjacent districts of their minority voters. The usual view is that the benefit in minority substantive representation from the creation of the minority opportunity districts is more than offset by the cost due to the adjacent districts being won by conservative Republicans hostile to minority interests. A leading election law casebook thus identifies a "tension between descriptive and substantive representation" for minority members.[11] Adam Cox and Richard Holden describe the "rough consensus" that "drawing districts that contain a majority of minority voters . . . hurts the Democratic Party more broadly."[12] Even the Supreme Court has commented that jurisdictions have to make "a political choice of whether substantive or descriptive representation [for minority members] is preferable."[13]

Those who make this trade-off claim (also known as the "perverse effects" thesis[14]) typically address the election of minority-preferred candidates versus minority substantive representation. The reasoning behind the claim, though, applies to alignment almost as squarely as to minority substantive representation.[15] Again, the main idea is that designing more minority opportunity districts

---

[10] I don't comment on the relationship between governmental responsiveness to minority concerns and alignment because (1) responsiveness is a secondary VRA value, the basis of neither racial vote denial nor racial vote dilution claims; (2) there's little, if any, literature on this relationship; and (3) it's likely (though not necessary) that a government responsive to minority concerns is also responsive to the needs and interests of the entire public.

[11] ELECTION LAW: CASES AND MATERIALS 235 (Daniel Hays Lowenstein et al. eds., 7th ed. 2022). Full disclosure: I'm one of this casebook's editors. In light of the below discussion, perhaps this passage in the casebook should be revised.

[12] Adam B. Cox & Richard T. Holden, *Reconsidering Racial and Partisan Gerrymandering*, 78 U. CHI. L. REV. 553, 555 (2011).

[13] Georgia v. Ashcroft, 539 U.S. 461, 483 (2003); *see also id.* (suggesting that "having fewer minority representatives" leads to "greater overall representation of a minority group by increasing the number of representatives sympathetic to the interests of minority voters").

[14] *See, e.g.,* Joseph Simons & Daniel J. Mallinson, *Party Control and Perverse Effects in Majority-Minority Districting: Replication Challenges When Using DW-NOMINATE*, 6 STAT. POL. & POL'Y 19 (2015).

[15] Almost, but not quite, as squarely because it's possible to imagine a pro-Democratic or pro-liberal status quo becoming better aligned thanks to the creation of more minority opportunity districts. In this scenario, these districts would improve alignment but worsen minority substantive representation (which previously benefited from the pro-Democratic or pro-liberal bias).

entails drawing more Republican districts, too. Drawing more Republican districts inevitably pushes measures of jurisdiction-wide partisan alignment in a Republican direction, and can easily produce pro-Republican misalignment. Moreover, in an era of extreme legislative polarization, almost all Democratic representatives are liberals and almost all Republican representatives are conservatives. So if additional minority opportunity districts cause partisan misalignment favoring Republicans, they're also likely to lead to representational misalignment favoring conservatives. Lastly, since legislators' job is to legislate, pro-conservative representational misalignment is apt to turn into pro-conservative policy misalignment as well.

Exponents of the perverse effects thesis rely on both (what they take to be) the innate logic of their position and studies focusing on the 1990s. The 1990s were the first redistricting cycle after Section 2 was amended in 1982 to make clear the provision could be violated by racial vote dilution even in the absence of any showing of discriminatory intent. In the wake of this statutory revision, states crafted about twice as many majority-Black congressional districts (thirty-two compared to seventeen)[16] as well as dozens more state legislative Black opportunity districts.[17] Of course, the 1990s were also the decade that saw Republicans achieve their greatest electoral success in legislative elections since before the New Deal. The House of Representatives flipped to Republican control after the 1994 election (for the first time in more than forty years), and the Republican share of southern state legislators surged from less than 30 percent almost to parity.[18]

Certain studies purport to link these rises in minority and Republican representation in the 1990s. The creation of new minority opportunity districts allegedly cost Democrats five to ten congressional seats they would have won under the previous decade's maps.[19] At the state legislative level, Democratic losses from bolstering minority representation are said to have been two to sixteen seats in each of ten southern state houses.[20] Other studies blame the additional minority opportunity districts of the 1990s for adverse shifts in the views

---

[16] *See, e.g.,* CHRISTIAN R. GROSE, CONGRESS IN BLACK AND WHITE: RACE AND REPRESENTATION IN WASHINGTON AND AT HOME 67 (2011).

[17] *See, e.g.,* Stephanopoulos, *supra* note 8, at 1369.

[18] *See, e.g.,* William D. Hicks et al., *Revisiting Majority-Minority Districts and Black Representation,* 71 POL. RSCH. Q. 408, 410 (2018).

[19] *See, e.g.,* DAVID T. CANON, RACE, REDISTRICTING, AND REPRESENTATION: THE UNINTENDED CONSEQUENCES OF BLACK MAJORITY DISTRICTS 74, 257 (1999); Kevin A. Hill, *Does the Creation of Majority Black Districts Aid Republicans? An Analysis of the 1992 Congressional Elections in Eight Southern States,* 57 J. POL. 384, 398–99 (1995).

[20] *See* David Lublin & D. Stephen Voss, *Racial Redistricting and Realignment in Southern State Legislatures,* 44 AM. J. POL. SCI. 792, 802 (2000); *see also* Charles S. Bullock III et al., *The Election of African American State Legislators in the Modern South,* 45 LEGIS. STUD. Q. 581, 593–98 (2020) (making similar claims about a longer period).

of pivotal legislators, such that they were less likely to support bills backed by minority legislators. In the House, the civil rights position of the median member moved substantially to the right after the Republican wave election of 1994.[21] In the South Carolina Senate, the fraction of bills on which the median member voted consistently with most Black members fell by almost 10 percentage points after the chamber's districts were redrawn in 1992.[22]

These findings have persuaded many scholars, but they ultimately fail to establish a negative relationship between the election of minority-preferred candidates and alignment (or, for that matter, minority substantive representation). First, the district plans enacted in the 1990s were just that: a few dozen maps designed at a single point in time and almost certainly unrepresentative of the near-infinite universe of maps that could have been drawn. Even if it were the case, then, that minority representation and alignment were inversely related in the plans of the 1990s, this doesn't mean the two values are necessarily at odds. A generation ago, it might have been possible to craft *other* maps—for example, ones that didn't pack minority voters to the same extent—that avoided any trade-off between minority representation and alignment.[23] And if that wasn't possible then, it might be doable now. Many relevant variables have changed significantly since the 1990s: the sizes of minority populations (larger today), their residential segregation (lower), their turnout (higher), the partisanship of White voters (more pro-Republican), and so on.[24] These shifts could well have broken whatever link existed between minority representation and alignment three decades ago.

Second, the most rigorous work about the plans of the 1990s concludes that their new minority opportunity districts actually didn't reduce—and may even have increased—Democratic and liberal representation. Ebonya Washington compares states covered by Section 5 (which accounted for essentially the entire rise in minority representation in the 1990s) to uncovered states. Over the decade, the proportion of Democratic congressional seats declined *less* in the covered than in the uncovered states.[25] The civil rights position and overall

---

[21] *See* GROSE, *supra* note 16, at 67; *see also, e.g.,* Charles Cameron et al., *Do Majority-Minority Districts Maximize Substantive Black Representation in Congress?*, 90 AM. POL. SCI. REV. 794, 795 (1996) ("[A] trade-off does exist between maximizing the number of black representatives in Congress and maximizing the number of votes in favor of minority-sponsored legislation.").

[22] *See* David Epstein et al., *Estimating the Effect of Redistricting on Minority Substantive Representation,* 23 J.L. ECON. & ORG. 499, 510–11 (2007).

[23] *See, e.g.,* Kenneth W. Shotts, *Racial Redistricting's Alleged Perverse Effects: Theory, Data, and "Reality",* 65 J. POL. 238, 240 (2003) (arguing that the enacted plans of the 1990s are "an unfair standard to use when assessing electoral outcomes after racial redistricting").

[24] For data on some of these shifts, see Stephanopoulos, *supra* note 8, at 1348, 1358, 1369–71, 1387–88.

[25] *See* Ebonya Washington, *Do Majority-Black Districts Limit Blacks' Representation? The Case of the 1990 Redistricting,* 55 J.L. & ECON. 251, 267 (2012).

liberalism of the average House member also stayed flat in the covered states while moving rightward in the uncovered states.[26] Analogously, in a pair of articles, Kenneth Shotts analyzes how the share of majority-minority districts in a state's congressional map affects the fraction of House members who are ideologically to the left of the overall House median. One piece finds that states that created more majority-minority districts in the 1990s had *more* representatives to the left of the House median.[27] The other article detects no significant relationship over the 1990s and 2000s between minority representation and the fraction of House members more liberal than the House median—still not the negative relationship posited by the perverse effects thesis.[28]

Third, Shotts's look at two decades, not just the 1990s, invites consideration of a longer time period. Simon Jackman examines the correlation between minority representation and partisan alignment from 1972 to 2016 in an expert report he filed in the case in which the Supreme Court eventually held that partisan gerrymandering claims are nonjusticiable. In that litigation, North Carolina asserted that its congressional plan's enormous pro-Republican bias was attributable to the state's effort to comply with the VRA. Jackman rebuts this claim by showing, in the charts reproduced as Figure 8.1, that there's no connection at the congressional level between minority representation and partisan skew. The charts plot the efficiency gaps of congressional maps against the shares of states' House members who are Black and Hispanic, respectively. In each chart, the loess curve that best fits the points around it is mostly flat. That is, the efficiency gap moves in neither a Democratic nor a Republican direction as Black or Hispanic representation rises or falls.[29]

Fourth, since even Jackman's report could be criticized for analyzing only *enacted* plans—not representative samples of *all* lawful maps—a coauthor and I use a computer algorithm to generate randomly large numbers of race-conscious and race-blind state house maps for about twenty states.[30] The race-conscious maps include as many minority opportunity districts as states' enacted plans. The race-blind maps are produced by omitting race as a parameter (so, unsurprisingly, they contain fewer minority opportunity districts than states' enacted plans). All the computer-generated maps ignore partisanship and

---

[26] *See id.*

[27] *See* Kenneth W. Shotts, *Does Racial Redistricting Cause Conservative Policy Outcomes? Policy Preferences of Southern Representatives in the 1980s and 1990s*, 65 J. POL. 216, 221 (2003).

[28] *See* Carlos A. Sanchez-Martinez & Kenneth W. Shotts, *Assessing Robustness of Findings About Racial Redistricting's Effect on Southern House Delegations*, 6 STAT. POL. & POL'Y 97, 110 (2015); *see also* Simons & Mallinson, *supra* note 14, at 31 (also detecting no significant relationship).

[29] *See* Rebuttal Report of Simon Jackman at 11–12, Common Cause v. Rucho, No. 1:16-CV-1026 (M.D.N.C. Apr. 17, 2017).

[30] *See* Jowei Chen & Nicholas O. Stephanopoulos, *The Race-Blind Future of Voting Rights*, 130 YALE L.J. 862, 888–903, 932–34 (2021).

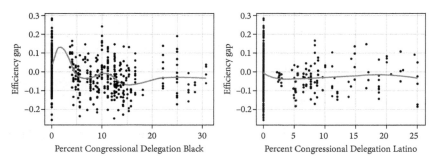

FIGURE 8.1 EFFICIENCY GAP VERSUS MINORITY REPRESENTATION IN
CONGRESSIONAL PLANS

Figure 8.1 is reproduced with permission from Rebuttal Report of Simon Jackman at 11–12,
Common Cause v. Rucho, No. 1:16-CV-1026 (M.D.N.C. Apr. 17, 2017). Copyright © 2017 by Simon
Jackman.

perform at least as well as states' enacted plans in terms of nonracial and nonpartisan criteria. When partisanship is brought back into the picture, it turns out
the race-conscious and the race-blind maps have very similar partisan profiles.[31]
The race-conscious maps (with their larger volumes of minority opportunity
districts) *aren't* more favorable for Republicans, as the perverse effects thesis
would predict. In fact, in the handful of deep southern states where there's an
appreciable partisan difference between the race-conscious and the race-blind
maps, it's *Democrats* who benefit from more minority opportunity districts.[32]
This is exactly the opposite result from that anticipated by the perverse effects
thesis.

Fifth, you might wonder what explains these findings. What's wrong with the
reasoning that Republicans and conservatives must be advantaged (jurisdiction-
wide) by the creation of more minority opportunity districts? One flaw in this
logic is that it neglects the partisanship of the redistricting authority. Of course,
a Republican mapmaker obliged by the VRA to design minority opportunity districts has an incentive to make these districts as heavily minority and
Democratic as possible. That way, the maximum number of Democratic votes is
wasted in these districts, leaving fewer Democratic votes to be distributed across
all other districts. However, a nonpartisan mapmaker (like a commission, a
court, or even a divided state government) has no reason to follow this approach.
A nonpartisan mapmaker can draw minority opportunity districts with smaller
minority and Democratic populations—especially where such districts are consistent with the application of traditional criteria—thereby squandering fewer

[31] *See id.* at 936–37.
[32] *See id.*

Democratic votes.[33] And a Democratic mapmaker can exploit this strategy even more aggressively, crafting minority opportunity districts with the smallest minority and Democratic populations necessary to ensure the election of minority-preferred, Democratic candidates. These products of Democratic gerrymanders might flout traditional criteria and have minority populations well below 50 percent.[34]

I confirm this hypothesis that the partisanship of the redistricting authority modulates the relationship between minority representation and alignment in a pair of articles. The dependent variables in the first piece are the share of Democratic state house seats and the ideology of the median state house member.[35] The outcome of interest in the second piece is the efficiency gap—jurisdiction-wide partisan alignment—at the congressional and state house levels.[36] In both articles, my method is to model the dependent variable as a function of minority seat share interacted with the actor responsible for redistricting (as well as various controls). And in both articles, the conclusion is clear: Consistent with the perverse effects thesis, when Republicans are in charge of redistricting, the share of Democratic state house seats falls, the ideology of the median state house member becomes more conservative, and the efficiency gap grows more pro-Republican, as minority representation rises. But all these consequences are attenuated when a nonpartisan mapmaker designs the districts. And they disappear entirely when the redistricting authority is Democratic. At the congressional level, a plan's predicted efficiency gap becomes increasingly *pro-Democratic* as minority representation rises, presumably because Democratic mapmakers efficiently allocate minority voters to capture more total seats.[37]

Lastly, one more reason why the perverse effects thesis falters is that it makes a simplistic assumption about the partisanship of White voters. The thesis implicitly requires White voters to be moderately Republican. (In election law parlance, racial polarization in voting must be significant but not overwhelming.[38]) Say White voters are, in fact, moderately Republican and a mapmaker has to

---

[33] Notably, the redistricting algorithm my coauthor and I use in the article discussed above is nonpartisan. That lack of partisanship, combined with the algorithm's attentiveness to traditional criteria, may help explain the similar partisan profiles of the race-conscious and the race-blind maps. *See id.* at 943–44.

[34] *See, e.g.,* Cox & Holden, *supra* note 12, at 572–79 (discussing how Democratic and Republican strategies under the VRA's constraints might vary); Kenneth W. Shotts, *The Effect of Majority-Minority Mandates on Partisan Gerrymandering*, 45 Am. J. Pol. Sci. 120, 121 (2001) (same); Stephanopoulos, *supra* note 8, at 1384–85 (same).

[35] *See* Stephanopoulos, *supra* note 8, at 1388–93.

[36] *See* Nicholas O. Stephanopoulos, *The Causes and Consequences of Gerrymandering*, 59 Wm. & Mary L. Rev. 2115, 2136–38 (2018).

[37] *See id.* at 2137–38; Stephanopoulos, *supra* note 8, 1389–93.

[38] The perverse effects thesis further assumes that minority voters are heavily Democratic and that they are, in fact, a numerical minority. These assumptions are usually more accurate than the partisanship of White voters.

draw two districts. The mapmaker might plausibly have to choose between (1) creating two Democratic districts, in each of which minority voters are numerous enough to guarantee the election of the Democratic candidate but *not* to elect their own candidate of choice, and (2) creating one minority opportunity (and Democratic) district with a larger minority population and one Republican district with a smaller minority population. It's this choice, when it can't be avoided, that poses the trade-off between minority representation and other values. But this choice *can* be avoided—often quite easily—when White voters in regions where minority opportunity districts can be crafted are anything but moderately Republican. Suppose these voters are mostly Democratic. Then altering districts' minority compositions doesn't affect their partisan leanings. Democrats win districts in these areas whether they're racially diverse or homogenous. Or posit that White voters are mostly (not moderately) Republican. Then it's difficult, maybe even impossible, for a mapmaker to design a Democratic district that isn't also a minority opportunity district. Any Democratic district is highly likely to contain enough minority voters to elect their preferred candidate, simply because most Democrats here are minority voters. In this scenario, minority representation makes possible—it doesn't conflict with—Democratic representation.[39]

My coauthored article with Jowei Chen starts to show empirically the important role played by the partisanship of White voters. We divide the states in our study into two categories based on whether White voters are more or less Republican (i.e., whether racial polarization in voting is higher or lower). In neither set of states do we find a negative relationship between minority representation and Democratic representation. As just suggested, though, in the higher-polarization states we determine that Democrats win more state house seats when districts are drawn race-consciously than race-blindly, such that more rather than fewer minority opportunity districts are created.[40] In a separate paper, Chen probes the impact of White voters' partisanship on an intrastate as well as an interstate level. He first freezes each minority opportunity district in the South and uses a race-blind computer algorithm to generate randomly all the other districts in each congressional map. He then unfreezes the minority opportunity districts and allows the algorithm to produce maps in their entirety. Comparing the two sets of simulations, existing minority opportunity districts benefit Republicans where nearby White voters are moderately Republican. In areas like central North Carolina and southeastern Virginia, freezing a minority

---

[39] For similar discussions, see Jowei Chen, Black Electoral Geography and Congressional Districting: The Effect of Racial Redistricting on Partisan Gerrymandering 10–11 (July 2016), and Chen & Stephanopoulos, *supra* note 30, at 930–31.

[40] *See* Chen & Stephanopoulos, *supra* note 30, at 937–39.

opportunity district results in more Republican districts overall compared to fully race-blind redistricting. But as implied by the above discussion, this pattern reverses where nearby White voters are mostly Republican. In rural swathes of Alabama, Georgia, Louisiana, Mississippi, and South Carolina, freezing a minority opportunity district yields more *Democratic* districts overall. Indeed, the frozen district is often the only Democratic district in the state—and would commonly flip to Republican control under fully race-blind redistricting.[41]

This may seem like an overly elaborate rebuttal of the perverse effects thesis. I think it's necessary, however, because of both the thesis's widespread acceptance and how unfortunate it would be if the thesis held. If minority representation and alignment were necessarily at odds, then we'd be confronted by a "tragic choice," in Guido Calabresi and Philip Bobbitt's terminology, a "conflict[] ... laid bare between ... humanistic moral values which prize life and well-bring."[42] We'd have to decide whether we care more about the election of minority-preferred candidates—one of the main goals of the VRA, the crown jewel of the civil rights movement—or governmental outputs that are congruent with popular preferences—a fundamental democratic principle.[43] But because minority representation and alignment can be simultaneously achieved, thankfully, we don't have to opt for one or the other of these objectives. A mapmaker can design more minority opportunity districts without thereby biasing governmental outputs in a Republican and conservative (or a Democratic and liberal) direction. True, a mapmaker can also force a trade-off between minority representation and alignment by excessively packing minority voters into minority opportunity districts. But in that case, the fault lies with the mapmaker, not with the aim of minority representation.[44]

Complements

Minority representation is the only VRA value that has frequently been linked to alignment. Minority representation, though, isn't the only VRA value. As I observed earlier, the VRA's original aspiration—the goal that motivated

---

[41] *See* Chen, *supra* note 39, at 12–13, 20–23.

[42] GUIDO CALABRESI & PHILIP BOBBITT, TRAGIC CHOICES: THE CONFLICTS SOCIETY CONFRONTS IN THE ALLOCATION OF TRAGICALLY SCARCE RESOURCES 18 (1978).

[43] Interestingly, when prompted to make something like this choice, most minority subjects prefer Democratic control of a legislature to more minority opportunity districts. *See* Albert H. Fang, How Racial Minorities Evaluate Trade-offs Between Descriptive and Partisan Representation 3 (June 10, 2019).

[44] It's worth noting that this whole section takes for granted the use of single-member districts in which victory requires a plurality of the vote. Under other electoral systems, like several forms of proportional representation, there's no conflict in principle or in practice between minority representation and alignment.

the law's architects in 1965 and prompted the first wave of VRA litigation and enforcement—was minority participation.[45] So how, if at all, might minority participation and alignment be related? Is there reason to think that minority members' more active involvement in politics could cause governmental outputs to become more or less congruent with popular preferences?

Yes, there is a basis for expecting greater minority participation to lead to closer alignment, especially under typical American political conditions. Consider a stylized picture of the pre-VRA South. African Americans were effectively excluded from the political process. Disenfranchised Blacks also had quite different policy preferences from most Whites: more supportive of redistribution, much more favorable toward civil rights, in a word, more liberal. In this environment, the median actual voter was always a White voter, and usually a conservative. Of course, one of this book's themes is that governmental outputs don't necessarily correspond to the wishes of the median actual voter. To the extent governmental outputs did match the views of the median actual voter in the pre-VRA South, though, significant, even staggering, misalignment with the preferences of the whole eligible electorate would have been the likely result. This point is clearest with respect to majority-Black jurisdictions, where the median eligible voter was a Black liberal. Here, governmental outputs congruent with the wishes of the median actual voter—probably a White conservative— would have been sharply at odds with the views of the median eligible voter. But the point also holds for at least some majority-White jurisdictions. Yes, if the median eligible voter in these areas was right of center and so were governmental outputs, there would have been no problem in terms of *majoritarian* alignment. But *collective* alignment—the fit between governmental outputs and *all* relevant persons' preferences—could still have been poor. Systematically ignoring the wishes of a large minority community is a blueprint for collective misalignment.

Turn next to the South after the VRA's enactment. Political participation by African Americans is now comparable to that of Whites. In particular, Black turnout now hovers close to White turnout, with the higher of the two varying by state, year, and whether White Hispanics are included in calculations of White turnout.[46] As a result, there's no longer a meaningful racial difference between the median actual voter and the median eligible voter. In majority-Black (or majority-White) jurisdictions, the median actual voter is almost certain to be Black (or White). Assuming again (unrealistically) that the median actual voter's views drive governmental outputs, this striking increase in Black political participation gives rise to an unambiguous prediction for majority-Black jurisdictions.

---

[45] As I also mentioned above, governmental responsiveness to minority concerns is still another VRA value, but one I bracket here for several reasons. *See supra* note 10.

[46] *See generally* BERNARD L. FRAGA, THE TURNOUT GAP: RACE, ETHNICITY, AND POLITICAL INEQUALITY IN A DIVERSIFYING AMERICA (2018).

The fit between what the government does and what the median eligible voter wants should be stronger now that the median eligible voter is (racially and likely ideologically) the same as the median actual voter. The situation is murkier for majority-White jurisdictions where the median actual voter could have been—and could continue to be—a White conservative. In these areas, majoritarian alignment might be largely unchanged by the VRA's incorporation of African Americans into the political process. Even here, though, it's plausible that collective alignment might have improved. It's one thing for the state to disregard the preferences of a disenfranchised minority; it's quite another for it to flout the wishes of a group whose political participation is commensurate to its numerical size.

This analysis should call to mind my discussion in Chapter 5 of the conditions under which voting regulations can substantially affect alignment. First, a voting expansion must enable or induce a considerable number of people to vote who otherwise wouldn't have cast ballots. Second, this population of new voters must have different partisan and/or ideological views from the pool of existing voters. Only if both conditions are satisfied can a voting expansion materially alter the composition of—not merely enlarge—the actual electorate.[47] Well, the VRA is a quintessential voting expansion, the most impactful such policy since the Nineteenth Amendment enfranchised women in 1920. Thanks to the VRA, tens of millions more African Americans, Hispanics, and other minority members are able to register and vote. And these new entrants into the political process indeed have distinctive partisan (more Democratic) and ideological (more liberal) preferences. So under Chapter 5's framework, too, the VRA has the potential to bolster alignment significantly through the channel of greater political participation.

Potential, however, can remain unfulfilled. I've already alluded to one reason why more minority participation might not lead to closer alignment (at least not in majority-White jurisdictions): racial polarization in partisanship and ideology. A related complication is that White voters' attitudes might not stay fixed in the face of more active c involvement by minority members. Instead, moderate and liberal White voters could become more conservative and White voters who were previously Democrats could start pulling the lever for Republican candidates. This "backlash" effect has been extensively documented.[48] To the

---

[47] See also Benjamin Highton, Voter Registration and Turnout in the United States, 2 PERSP. POL. 507, 510 (2004) (identifying these conditions as well).

[48] See, e.g., Desmond Ang, Do 40-Year-Old Facts Still Matter? Long-Run Effects of Federal Oversight Under the Voting Rights Act, 11 AM. ECON. J: APPLIED ECON. 1, 20–25, 31–34 (2019) (finding that Democratic vote share dropped in areas covered by Section 5 of the VRA due to White voters becoming more Republican); Richard H. Pildes, Why the Center Does Not Hold: The Causes of Hyperpolarized Democracy in America, 99 CALIF. L. REV. 273, 287–97 (2011) (discussing how the VRA caused greater polarization in American politics).

extent it holds, it produces even more extreme polarization between White and minority voters' partisan and ideological views. In these circumstances, satisfactory collective alignment could be still harder to achieve. When the electorate is split into two hostile camps—a White, conservative, Republican bloc and a minority, liberal, and Democratic grouping—any governmental output that pleases one side is likely to upset the other. Stark political division lowers the odds of mutually acceptable compromise.

Reasoning without data, then, suggests several possible relationships between minority participation and alignment. Which of these conceivable links is most corroborated by the available evidence? In my view, the happy story in which minority participation fuels closer alignment enjoys the most empirical support. But I concede that my judgment is provisional because the relevant literature is relatively sparse. Few studies of the VRA directly measure alignment so it's often necessary to make (plausible but contestable) inferences about how some other variable is tied to it. Similarly, few VRA studies distinguish between the mechanisms of minority participation and minority representation, again requiring leaps of faith (of varying difficulty) that minority participation is, in fact, the driver.

Starting with policy alignment at the state level, I mentioned in Chapter 5 the most compelling finding that minority participation improves this form of congruence. Devin Caughey and Christopher Warshaw track collective policy alignment (which they call "Agreement") and majoritarian policy alignment ("Congruence") with the preferences of Black and non-Black respondents in the South and the non-South from 1940 to 2020. As Figure 8.2 displays, collective and majoritarian policy alignment with the views of southern Blacks rose steadily for several decades after the VRA's enactment. Policy alignment with the views of southern Whites held roughly steady over this period.[49] Since Blacks and Whites comprised the vast majority of southern states' populations in this era, *overall* policy alignment with *all* persons' preferences necessarily increased. Moreover, this aligning trend was likely attributable mostly to greater minority participation (not to greater minority representation). As I noted above, the 1990s were the redistricting cycle when many more districts were created in the South where minority voters could elect their preferred candidates. Most of the gains in Black-specific and population-level policy alignment in the South, however, materialized prior to the 1990s, when greater minority participation was the VRA's main impact. Since the 1990s, Black-specific and population-level policy

---

[49] *See* DEVIN CAUGHEY & CHRISTOPHER WARSHAW, DYNAMIC DEMOCRACY: PUBLIC OPINION, ELECTIONS, AND POLICYMAKING IN THE AMERICAN STATES 134–35 (2022).

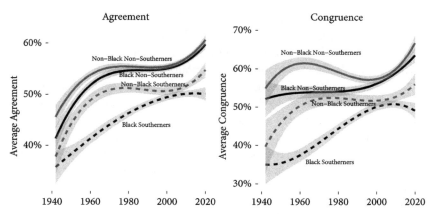

FIGURE 8.2 COLLECTIVE AND MAJORITARIAN POLICY ALIGNMENT WITH BLACK AND NON-BLACK RESPONDENTS' PREFERENCES IN THE SOUTH AND THE NON-SOUTH

Figure 8.2 is reproduced with permission from DEVIN CAUGHEY & CHRISTOPHER WARSHAW, DYNAMIC DEMOCRACY: PUBLIC OPINION, ELECTIONS, AND POLICYMAKING IN THE AMERICAN STATES 135 (2022). Copyright © 2022 by University of Chicago Press.

alignment in the South have stayed about the same (or even, more recently, declined somewhat).[50]

Next, with respect to policy alignment at the local level, a number of studies examine policy outcomes in counties formerly covered by Section 5. All these works use essentially the same methodology, comparing covered counties to similar uncovered counties, particularly along state borders between covered and uncovered states and within partially covered states. The consistent result of this scholarship is that Section 5 caused both enacted policies and socioeconomic conditions to improve for African Americans in covered counties. Section 5 was responsible for local governments hiring more Black employees,[51] increasing capital[52] and welfare[53] spending, receiving more state

---

[50] The recent decline in Black-specific policy alignment is probably attributable to Republicans capturing full control of southern state governments and enacting conservative policies disfavored by liberal Black respondents. *See id.* at 213. In addition, the fact that the trends in alignment in the non-South are more ambiguous suggests that the VRA—whose impact has always been greatest in the South—is responsible for the rise in southern alignment.

[51] *See, e.g.,* Abhay Aneja & Carlos Fernando Avenacio-Leon, *The Effect of Political Power on Labor Market Inequality: Evidence from the 1965 Voting Rights Act* 3 (Washington Ctr. for Equitable Growth, Working Paper No. 101620, 2020).

[52] *See* Andrea Bernini et al., *Race, Representation and Local Governments in the US South: the Effect of the Voting Rights Act* 34 (CEPR, Working Paper No. 12774, 2019).

[53] *See* Thomas A. Husted & Lawrence W. Kenny, *The Effect of the Expansion of the Voting Franchise on the Size of Government,* 105 J. POL. ECON. 54, 76 (1997).

funding,[54] reducing student-teacher ratios,[55] and arresting fewer Black individuals.[56] Section 5 further led to a smaller wage gap between Black and White employees,[57] more years of education and higher lifetime earnings for Black individuals,[58] and even lower rates of political violence.[59]

As interesting as these findings are, they don't explicitly establish that greater minority participation yielded closer alignment in counties formerly covered by Section 5. *Explicitly* no, but *implicitly* yes. To distinguish between the mechanisms of minority participation and minority representation, one study compares counties using at-large elections (which don't require redistricting) to counties using single-member districts (which do). Another study compares cities with stronger mayors (less affected by redistricting) to cities with stronger councils (more affected). Both pieces identify comparable or even larger effects on policy outcomes in covered jurisdictions where minority participation must have been the main or sole driver.[60] Analogously, several studies ask whether policy outcomes shifted more in ways that benefited African Americans in counties with larger Black populations. These works uniformly conclude the answer is yes, especially in counties with outright Black majorities.[61] As long as Black residents preferred these favorable policy changes—a reasonable assumption—policy alignment likely improved in these covered, heavily Black areas. Better policy alignment is the probable result when the wishes of a sizable (sometimes a majority) group are more closely heeded.

Moving to representational alignment, two studies investigate how Section 5 coverage influenced the civil rights records of members of the House of Representatives. One study operationalizes civil rights records using the second ideological dimension underlying all votes taken by House members. (The first ideological

---

[54] See Elizabeth U. Cascio & Ebonya Washington, *Valuing the Vote: The Redistribution of Voting Rights and State Funds following the Voting Rights Act of 1965*, 2014 Q.J. ECON. 379, 403.

[55] See id. at 422.

[56] See Giovanni Facchini et al., *The Franchise, Policing, and Race: Evidence from Arrests Data and the Voting Rights Act* 20 (Orlando Bravo Ctr. for Econ. Rsch., Working Paper No. 2020-018, 2020). *But see* Nicholas Eubank & Adriane Fresh, *Enfranchisement and Incarceration After the 1965 Voting Rights Act*, 116 AM. POL. SCI. REV. 791, 793 (2022) (finding that incarceration increased more in states (as opposed to counties) covered by Section 5).

[57] See, e.g., Aneja & Avenacio-Leon, *supra* note 51, at 3.

[58] See Daniel B. Jones & Ying Shi, *Reducing Racial Inequality in Access to the Ballot Reduces Racial Inequality in Children's Later-Life Outcomes* 3 (Inst. of Labor Econ., Working Paper No. 15095, 2022).

[59] See Jean Lacroix, *Ballots Instead of Bullets? The Effect of the Voting Rights Act on Political Violence* 1, 4 (Ctr. Emile Bernhxeim, Working Paper No. 20/007, 2020).

[60] See Aneja & Avenacio-Leon, *supra* note 51, at 31 (mayor-council versus council-manager systems); Bernini et al., *supra* note 52, at 33 (at-large versus single-member-district elections); *see also* Aneja & Avenacio-Leon, *supra* note 51, at 4 (agreeing that "the weight of the evidence favors" "a shift in a locality's 'median voter'" as the mechanism here, not "increasing the presence of black elected officials").

[61] See Aneja & Avenacio-Leon, *supra* note 51, at 30–31; Cascio & Washington, *supra* note 54, at 401; Eubank & Fresh, *supra* note 56, at 793; Facchini et al., *supra* note 56, at 20.

dimension, in contrast, captures House members' positions on economic issues.) The other study relies exclusively on House members' votes on civil rights bills. Both pieces determine that House members who represented covered districts took more liberal stances on civil rights matters than similarly situated legislators from uncovered districts.[62] The impact of coverage was substantial: a likelihood more than 10 percentage points higher of voting to expand civil rights.[63] And the impact was greater in fully than in partially covered districts, confirming that coverage was responsible for the heightened support for civil rights.[64]

Like the work on how Section 5 shifted policy outcomes in covered counties, these studies of House members' civil rights records don't directly address the relationship between minority participation and alignment. Again, though, these pieces certainly hint at a link. First, minority participation (not minority representation) must be the causal mechanism because the studies control for variables like districts' Black population shares and whether districts were represented by Black legislators.[65] Districts usually had to be *altered* to elect Black-preferred candidates, but districts are kept constant in the analyses, to the extent possible, except for their coverage status. Second, like the work on policy outcomes in covered counties, this scholarship looks at whether House members were stronger backers of civil rights in covered districts with larger Black populations. Indeed they were; coverage made legislators more than 20 percentage points more likely to vote for civil rights in majority-Black districts, compared to less than 10 percentage points more likely in districts with small Black populations.[66] Assuming (reasonably) once more that most Black constituents favored pro-civil rights positions, these findings mean that representational alignment was probably better in covered, heavily Black districts. In these areas, House members were more apt to vote for civil rights, just like many (sometimes most) of their constituents wanted.[67]

In theory, then, it's uncertain how the VRA's value of minority participation is connected to alignment, especially in majority-White jurisdictions. In practice, however, greater minority participation promotes closer alignment, even in majority-White jurisdictions. Policy alignment surged in the majority-White South after the VRA enfranchised African Americans. Policy alignment also rose in counties covered by Section 5, as did representational alignment in covered congressional districts. Moreover, these coverage effects held for majority-White areas, though they were more pronounced for places with Black majorities. Consequently,

---

[62] *See* Aneja & Avenacio-Leon, *supra* note 51, at 14–15; Sophie Schuit & Jon C. Rogowski, *Race, Representation, and the Voting Rights Act*, 61 Am. J. Pol. Sci. 513, 519 (2017).

[63] *See* Schuit & Rogowski, *supra* note 62, at 519.

[64] *See id.* at 521.

[65] *See* Aneja & Avenacio-Leon, *supra* note 51, at 45; Schuit & Rogowski, *supra* note 62, at 519.

[66] *See* Schuit & Rogowski, *supra* note 62, at 522–24.

[67] *See id.* at 523–24 ("As votes from historically marginalized groups increased in importance, legislators were more responsive to these groups' interests.").

not only is there no trade-off, no tragic choice, between minority participation and alignment, but these values appear to be complementary. At least in modern American history, as minority members have become more politically involved, governmental outputs have grown more congruent with popular preferences. For those (like me) who prize both minority participation and alignment, this is essentially the best-case scenario: the VRA's original aspiration turning out to further a vital democratic principle.

* * *

The VRA hopes to realize several values: minority participation, minority representation, and, to a lesser extent, governmental responsiveness to minority concerns. These are deeply resonant values but they're also plainly distinct from alignment. This distinctness makes it possible for the pursuit of the VRA's goals to facilitate, to be irrelevant to, or to impede the quest for alignment. A common claim is that the VRA's aim of greater minority representation does conflict with closer alignment. But this perverse effects thesis is refuted both by historical data about the district plans that states did enact and by computer simulations of the maps they could have drawn. The thesis also errs by ignoring the partisanship of the redistricting authority and the varying behavior of White voters. As for the VRA's objective of greater minority participation, scholars haven't previously tied it to alignment and ex ante reasoning suggests several possible relationships. Of these potential links, one is most supported by the available empirical evidence: the happy story where minority members' more active political involvement isn't misaligning, or neutral in its aligning impact, but rather affirmatively aligning.

I've now covered four of the five subfields of election law: voting, political parties, redistricting, and the VRA. The remaining subfield is money in politics and it's the subject of the next chapter. My core argument is that the advancement of alignment is a democratically compelling, doctrinally available defense for certain—but not all—campaign finance regulations attacked on First Amendment grounds. I first show that the Supreme Court hasn't rejected alignment as a valid justification for restrictions of money in politics. The Court *has* dismissed several other interests (broad notions of anticorruption, anti-distortion, and all forms of equality), but these aren't equivalent to alignment. I then demonstrate that unchecked campaign funding can be powerfully misaligning. Maybe the most striking finding is that elected officials have essentially the same ideological distribution as individual donors, which looks nothing like the pattern of preferences in the electorate as a whole. Lastly, I maintain that some common campaign finance regulations are aligning (and so could be defended on this basis) while others aren't. Limits on the contributions of individual donors, a highly polarized group, do lead to closer alignment. But caps on the donations of political action committees and political parties don't because these entities tend to give more to moderate candidates.

9

Campaign Finance

Introduction

In this book's vocabulary of swords and shields, we haven't yet seen alignment operating as an effective defense for a controversial category of electoral regulation. Misalignment is a powerful *sword* against gerrymandered district plans because they cause partisan, representational, and policy noncongruence at the jurisdictional level. Alignment is also a *poor* defense for many regulations of political parties—like specifications of primary type and restrictions on ballot access—because these measures don't induce significantly closer congruence.[1] To this point, though, there hasn't been a good example of alignment serving as a sturdy shield for electoral policies commonly challenged on other bases.

Campaign finance provides that elusive example. There's compelling evidence that certain regulations of money in politics lead to better representational alignment: officeholders with policy positions more reflective of their constituents' views. These laws therefore could (and should) be justified on the ground that they promote alignment, a state interest of the highest importance. Conversely, other campaign finance regulations appear not to affect, or even to worsen, representational alignment. So interestingly, the implications of alignment are heterogeneous in this context. It might be a sturdy shield for some provisions limiting, supplying, or disclosing money in politics. But the shield might turn brittle—or even into a sword—when used to try to rationalize other aspects of the campaign finance ecosystem.

I intentionally mentioned only representational alignment in the previous paragraph. Some limited evidence also suggests that money in politics (and its regulations) influence policy alignment, and I discuss these studies below. More abundant evidence indicates that campaign finance (and campaign finance laws) sway voters' decisions at the polls. You could thus imagine a form of partisan misalignment comparing voters' *actual* choices among candidates to the choices they *would* have made under different patterns of campaign funding. However, I don't attempt to defend any policies about money in politics on the ground that they reduce this kind of partisan misalignment. For one thing, the right

---

[1] To round out this high-level summary of the last few chapters, misalignment is a *blunt* sword against most voting restrictions because they usually don't much worsen partisan (or any other kind of) congruence.

Aligning Election Law. Nicholas O. Stephanopoulos, Oxford University Press. © Nicholas O. Stephanopoulos 2024.
DOI: 10.1093/9780197662182.003.0009

benchmark for measuring partisan misalignment, conceived this way, is unclear. Is it voters' choices if each candidate received and spent the same amount? Or if candidates' resources were commensurate to their popularity? Or if candidates didn't solicit or disburse any money at all? Additionally, this book doesn't fixate on the current Supreme Court's pronouncements, but it's still notable that the Court has categorically rejected any state interest in lessening this type of partisan misalignment. There's supposedly no "compelling governmental interest in preventing the corrosive and distorting effects of immense aggregations of wealth" on voters' decisions at the polls.[2]

The Court has dismissed other rationales for campaign finance regulation, too. These spurned interests include broader conceptions of corruption involving the undue influence of campaign funders as well as all notions of equality. Again, my aim here is to explore how alignment would work as a legal and political principle, even if this operation would conflict with existing doctrine. That said, it's useful in practice (if unnecessary to my argument) that representational and policy misalignment aren't equivalent to any of the interests the Court has rebuffed. With respect to distortion, it's only changes in *voters'* preferences due to money in politics that, according to the Court, can't be a basis for regulating that pool of funding. The Court has never said that changes in *officeholders'* preferences—of the sort that give rise to representational and policy misalignment—can't be a basis for regulating money in politics. With respect to undue influence corruption, the clout of campaign funders is, at most, one means among many through which misalignment is generated. The clout of campaign funders isn't even necessarily misaligning since, in some times and places, campaign funders and voters have similar ideological profiles. And as to equality, the egalitarian goal the Court has most emphatically rejected is parity among candidates' resources. But parity among candidates' resources is entirely unrelated to whether prevailing candidates heed or flout their constituents' wishes.

So alignment is appealing from a democratic perspective and available as a state interest from a doctrinal standpoint. The key remaining question is whether, empirically, money in politics is misaligning and policies limiting, supplying, or disclosing campaign funding are aligning. As intimated above, the answer varies by the category of the funder and of the regulation. Start with the three main groups of funders of American elections: individuals, political action committees (PACs), and political parties. Campaign funding from individuals, whether in the form of contributions or expenditures, is misaligning. Individual funders are much more ideologically polarized than the electorate as a whole. Individual funders also allocate their resources primarily on the basis of

---

[2]   Citizens United v. FEC, 558 U.S. 310, 348 (2010) (internal quotation marks omitted).

candidates' ideological proximity to them. As a result, the more individual funding a candidate receives, the more ideologically extreme—and misaligned with her constituents—that politician tends to be. In contrast, campaign funding from PACs and parties is usually aligning. The business and trade PACs that dominate the PAC sector give most generously to relatively moderate candidates. So do parties, albeit due to their desire to win as many seats as possible, not sincere centrism. Consequently, the more PAC or party funding a candidate receives, the more ideologically moderate—and aligned with her constituents—that politician tends to be.

These findings strongly imply that restrictions on individual funders should be aligning while curbs on PACs and parties should be misaligning. Sure enough, that's exactly what the empirical literature concludes. Individuals necessarily give less money to candidates when individual contribution limits are lower. In turn, candidates receive less of their total funding from individuals. Deprived of some of these dollars from ideological extremists, candidates migrate toward the ideological center, the home of the median voter. On the other hand, PACs and parties give less money to candidates when *their* contributions are capped at lower levels. Under these conditions, PAC and party donations make up smaller proportions of candidates' war chests. Unable to benefit as much from these ideologically moderate funding sources, candidates shift toward the ideological fringes, where large pools of money still await. The upshot is that restrictions on individual funders can be justified on the ground that they promote alignment. Curbs on PACs and parties, however, can't be defended on this basis, and if anything may be suspect because of their misaligning impact.

Ceilings on individuals', PACs', and parties' campaign funding are the most familiar regulations of money in politics. But they don't comprise the entirety of this policy universe. Other campaign finance laws include public financing, disclosure requirements, and (slightly further afield) lobbying regulations. Just as funding ceilings have heterogeneous effects on alignment, so do different kinds of public financing. Systems that obligate candidates to obtain some number of private contributions to quality for public funds are misaligning because of their reliance on ideologically extreme individual donors. In contrast, multiple-match and voucher approaches may be aligning (though the jury is still out) because they expand the donor pool and make it more representative of the electorate. As for disclosure requirements and lobbying regulations, their implications for alignment are only starting to be studied. Some early evidence, however, hints that both these rules cause enacted state policy to correspond more closely to public opinion.

Politicians, Not Voters

A good government group called Voters Not Politicians led the successful 2018 campaign for an independent redistricting commission in Michigan.[3] With respect to district design, prioritizing voters' over politicians' interests is exactly the right strategy. In the campaign finance context, though, I think that group's name has it backward. In my view, we should be highly attentive to how money in politics influences politicians: the ways in which it leads officeholders to take positions more or less congruent with the views of their constituents. But I *don't* believe we should focus on how money in politics affects the partisan or ideological preferences of voters themselves. At least for the purposes of analyzing and justifying campaign finance regulations, the mantra should be pursuing alignment (and avoiding misalignment) through politicians, not voters.[4]

To be sure, campaign spending does impact voters. More than 90 percent of winning House candidates, and more than 70 percent of Senate victors, raise and spend more money than their opponents.[5] (Though it's notoriously tricky to prove that greater resources *contribute* to success, not flow to stronger candidates more likely to prevail in the first place.[6]) The activity to which the largest share of campaign dollars is devoted—campaign advertising—also sways voters' choices among candidates. Persuasion through advertising is particularly prevalent in down-ballot races between lower-profile candidates about whom voters know less.[7] And when the enactment or repeal of campaign finance regulations changes the distribution of campaign spending, electoral consequences follow. For example, after the Supreme Court held in *Citizens United v. FEC*[8] that bans on corporate campaign expenditures are unconstitutional, Republican candidates did better at all levels thanks to the deployment of previously unavailable funds.[9]

Based on findings like these, one could claim that money in politics causes a novel type of partisan misalignment. The idea would be to compare the election results that *did* occur, given *actual* patterns of campaign spending, with the election results that *would* have materialized, given *hypothetical* campaign spending

---

[3] *See Redistricting*, VOTERS NOT POLITICIANS, https://votersnotpoliticians.com/redistricting/ (last visited Feb. 1, 2024).

[4] *Cf.* Anna Harvey & Taylor Mattia, *Does Money Have a Conservative Bias? Estimating the Causal Impact of* Citizens United *on State Legislative Preferences*, 191 PUB. CHOICE 417, 419 (2019) (distinguishing between "the electoral and preference effects" of campaign finance changes).

[5] *See, e.g., Did Money Win?*, CTR. FOR RESPONSIVE POL. (Apr. 1, 2021), https://www.opensecrets.org/elections-overview/winning-vs-spending.

[6] *See, e.g.,* Alan S. Gerber, *Does Campaign Spending Work?: Field Experiments Provide Evidence and Suggest New Theory*, 47 AM. BEHAV. SCI. 541 (2004).

[7] *See, e.g.,* John Sides et al., *The Effect of Television Advertising in United States Elections*, 116 AM. POL. SCI. REV. 702, 712–14 (2022).

[8] 558 U.S. 310 (2010).

[9] *See, e.g.,* Tilman Klumpp et al., *The Business of American Democracy:* Citizens United, *Independent Spending, and Elections*, 59 J.L. & ECON. 1 (2016).

patterns. The gap between these two sets of election results would then constitute the partisan misalignment attributable to the factor that produced the divergence between the actual and the hypothetical campaign spending patterns. To illustrate, scholars estimate that *Citizens United*'s invalidation of corporate spending bans led to Republican state legislative candidates winning about 4 percentage points more votes in subsequent elections.[10] This 4-percentage-point difference could therefore be seen as the extent of the partisan misalignment between the real world after *Citizens United*, with its unlimited corporate expenditures, and the counterfactual scenario where corporate spending remained prohibited.

My primary objection to this conception of partisan misalignment is its reliance on a hotly contested benchmark, namely, how voters would have behaved in a different campaign spending environment. There's simply no consensus—not even among campaign finance reformers—about the characteristics of the "right" campaign spending environment. Some reformers think all candidates should have equal resources; this impulse motivates "clean money" public financing programs that allocate equal funds to all qualifying candidates. Other reformers want as little campaign spending as possible; this was the mindset of the architects of the 1974 Federal Election Campaign Act Amendments (FECA) with their stringent limits on campaign contributions *and* expenditures.[11] Still other reformers envision political actors spending money in proportion to their ex ante popularity with voters (prior to the disbursement of any sums). The Supreme Court echoed these advocates in the 1990 case of *Austin v. Michigan Chamber of Commerce*,[12] the apex of the Court's receptivity to campaign finance regulation. "[E]xpenditures [should] reflect actual public support for the political ideas espoused by [campaign spenders]," the Court commented.[13] It's troubling if there's "little or no correlation" between expenditures and "the public's support for [campaign spenders'] political ideas."[14]

All these baselines are normatively plausible. That's why each has been endorsed at times by leading legal and political figures. But all these baselines are substantively different. A regime of *equal* candidate spending isn't the same as one of *minimal* candidate spending, which isn't the same as one of candidate spending commensurate to candidate *popularity*. And not only are the baselines different, but so, presumably, is voter behavior in each setting. Since campaign spending influences voter behavior, voters should be expected to make one set of choices when candidates expend the same resources, other choices

---

[10] *See* Nour Abdul-Razzak et al., *After Citizens United: How Outside Spending Shapes American Democracy*, 67 ELECTORAL STUD. Article 102190, at 8 (2020).

[11] *See* Buckley v. Valeo, 424 U.S. 1, 12–13 (1976) (describing FECA's "major contribution and expenditure limitations").

[12] 494 U.S. 652 (1990).

[13] *Id.* at 660 (addressing corporate spenders).

[14] *Id.* (addressing corporate spenders).

when candidates spend next to nothing, and still other choices when popular candidates spend more and unpopular candidates spend less. This divergence in voter behavior among plausible baselines cripples any effort to evaluate the partisan misalignment of the electoral status quo. To make that assessment, again, actual election results have to be compared to hypothetical election results under an alternative distribution of campaign spending. But the hypothetical results *vary* based on *which* alternative distribution is used for the analysis. The actual results must thus be compared to multiple sets of hypothetical results, yielding multiple answers to the question of how misaligned the electoral status quo is in partisan terms. Multiple answers, in this context, might as well be no answers at all.

To make this critique more concrete, return to the post-*Citizens United* world in which Republican state legislative candidates win about 4 percentage points more votes than they did prior to the decision. Is this 4-percentage-point difference an appropriate measure of the partisan misalignment of the electoral status quo? Not even close. The 4-percentage-point difference is the gap between the electoral status quo and the situation immediately before *Citizens United* nullified corporate spending bans. But no reformer would say that situation was entitled to any normative respect. The world just before *Citizens United* was still one in which candidates (and other political actors) spent huge and unequal sums uncorrelated to their ex ante popularity with voters. A proper analysis of *Citizens United*'s impact on partisan misalignment would therefore start, but hardly end, with the situation immediately before the decision. The analysis would also need to estimate the election results that would have hypothetically arisen if candidates' (and other political actors') expenditures were equalized, minimized, or linked to their appeal to voters. These hypothetical results would constitute the baselines with which both the electoral status quo and the world just before *Citizens United* would be compared. But to reiterate, these hypothetical results would *differ* from one baseline to another. The partisan makeup of the electorate would look one way given equal campaign spending, another way given minimal spending, and still another given spending proportional to popularity. So once more, any attempt to calculate the partisan misalignment of the electoral status quo would founder on the lack of agreement about the right benchmark for comparison.

Note that this objection doesn't apply to the forms of partisan misalignment I discussed earlier in the book. Certain ballot access rules and electoral systems can cause the candidate favored by a majority of voters over any opponent to fail to be elected. In this case, the baseline to which the election outcome should be compared is unitary and obvious: the expressed will of the actual electorate. Similarly, gerrymandered district maps can produce legislatures whose partisan compositions are sharply different from voters' partisan preferences. Here, too, the normative benchmark is singular and intuitive: by whom voters across the jurisdiction, in fact, want to be represented. Lastly, in the voting context, I recommended a baseline of the choices that eligible voters would have made among candidates.[15] This baseline bears some resemblance to the ones I've addressed in this chapter in that it's also hypothetical. It thus can't be observed directly and instead must be estimated using statistical techniques. Crucially, though, the baseline of eligible voters' partisan views is just *one* reference point. It isn't an *array* of counterfactual scenarios, each leading to a different conclusion about the degree of partisan misalignment. Campaign finance stands alone, then, in requiring multiple, likely conflicting analyses to evaluate partisan skew.

I mentioned above that the absence of an agreed-upon benchmark is my main reason for not defending any regulations of money in politics on the ground that they promote partisan alignment. My secondary reason is that the contemporary Supreme Court has made clear that, in its opinion, the pursuit of partisan alignment isn't a compelling state interest that can justify campaign finance laws. Now, a good deal of this book is in tension (or even outright conflict) with the current Court's rulings. In Chapter 11, in fact, I dub the Roberts Court the anti-alignment Court and condemn the many ways in which it has declined to further, or affirmatively undermined, this vital democratic value. Accordingly, I put relatively little weight on whether a given argument is doctrinally available or precluded by the Court's precedents. Relatively little weight, however, isn't no weight at all. It's at least practically relevant, to lawyers, litigants, and jurisdictions, whether they're making a claim that's consistent with existing doctrine or that would require its reversal. For courts and scholars, too, concerns about stare decisis arise when a position is advanced that can't be reconciled with current law. For these reasons, I dwell at some length in this section and the next on the compatibility of different kinds of alignment with the Court's campaign finance jurisprudence.

Unusually, the Court first recognized, before then rejecting, a state interest in avoiding the manipulation of voters' preferences through heavy and unbalanced campaign spending. In *Austin*, the Court didn't just endorse a baseline of campaign spending commensurate to public support for spenders' political ideas. The Court also held that jurisdictions can regulate campaign spending to prevent deviation from this baseline. They can "aim[] at a different type of corruption in the political arena: the corrosive and distorting effects of immense aggregations of wealth."[16] True, on its face, this key sentence doesn't specify that it's the distortion of *voters'* (not officeholders') choices about which the

---

[15] To be precise, I advocated this baseline for all voting policies other than voting qualifications. For voting qualifications, I advocated a baseline of the choices that *all* people would have made among candidates.

[16] *Austin*, 494 U.S. at 660.

Court was concerned. Immediately after acknowledging the anti-distortion interest, though, the Court added that "wealth can unfairly influence *elections*."[17] It's voters, of course, who cast ballots in elections and whose decisions can be swayed by campaign spending. The Court further warned of "the threat that huge [fortunes] . . . will be used to influence unfairly *the outcome of elections*."[18] Again, it's voters whose behavior (potentially altered by campaign spending) determines election outcomes.[19]

Austin's regime stood for two decades. It was then decisively toppled in 2010 by *Citizens United*. In *Citizens United*, the Court explicitly stated that a jurisdiction's goal of avoiding the distortion of voters' preferences by campaign spending "cannot support" campaign finance regulations.[20] The Court also harshly criticized *Austin's* baseline of campaign spending tied to public support for spenders' political views. That baseline is "irrelevant for purposes of the First Amendment," according to the Court.[21] Under the First Amendment, there can supposedly be no baseline establishing an aspirational distribution of political speech.[22] Following *Citizens United*, then, it's indisputable that jurisdictions can't defend policies about money in politics on the ground that they better align voters' actual choices with the choices they would have made in a different campaign spending environment. The contemporary Court simply refuses to accept that any hypothetical campaign spending environment has any normative or legal significance. Jurisdictions can either accept this reality and abandon any interest in the promotion of partisan alignment—or hope in vain that the Court responsible for *Citizens United* will renounce its own handiwork.

Conceptual Distinctiveness

At present, as a doctrinal matter, the pursuit of *partisan* alignment can't justify campaign finance regulations. What about a jurisdiction's desire to improve *representational* or *policy* alignment? Are these aims equivalent to the anti-distortion interest the Court validated in *Austin* and then repudiated in *Citizens United*? No, they're not, for the fundamental reason that these forms of alignment involve the

---

[17] *Id.* (emphasis added).

[18] *Id.* at 669 (emphasis added).

[19] For scholars sharing this understanding of *Austin's* anti-distortion interest, see, for example, Richard Briffault, *On Dejudicializing American Campaign Finance Law*, 27 GA. ST. U. L. REV. 887, 922 (2011) ("*Austin* was rooted in concern to protect the political equality of voters from corporate war chests."), and Julian N. Eule, *Promoting Speaker Diversity:* Austin *and* Metro Broadcasting, 1990 SUP. CT. REV. 105, 109 (*Austin's* theory was that "corporations spoke too loudly and wielded too much influence on the electorate").

[20] Citizens United v. FEC, 558 U.S. 310, 349 (2010).

[21] *Id.* at 351.

[22] *See id.* at 349–51.

effects of campaign funding on politicians, not voters. These forms of alignment therefore lack the key feature of the anti-distortion interest that's now doctrinally precluded. To see the point, consider how money in politics can lead to representational or policy misalignment. Candidates whose sincere views are more congruent with the preferences of voters can be induced to take less congruent positions in order to secure (what they deem to be) sufficient campaign funding. Call this process *adaptation*. Or candidates whose views are poorly aligned with the preferences of voters, to begin with, can benefit financially and maybe electorally from flows of campaign resources that are abundant precisely because of these politicians' misaligned stances. Call this process *selection*.[23] Through both adaptation and selection, representational misalignment can ensue as a result of money in politics. And as noncongruent officeholders take actions that have the force of law, representational misalignment can metastasize into policy misalignment, too.

Crucially (and unlike *Austin*-style distortion), these dynamics don't depend on the impact of campaign spending on voters. It's irrelevant whether large or uneven expenditures "influence unfairly the outcome of elections."[24] What matters instead is whether politicians behave differently, in ways less consistent with voters' preferences, because of the donations they receive or the funds that are spent on their behalf.[25] By the same token (and again unlike *Austin*-style distortion), representational and policy misalignment are measured without any reliance on a hypothetical benchmark of voters' views in a different campaign spending environment. To evaluate these kinds of noncongruence, voters' views are simply taken as they are and then compared to representational and policy outputs. If campaign spending doesn't change voters' minds, then their static preferences are the baseline for comparison. If money in politics does persuade voters, then their updated attitudes are the touchpoint for assessing representation and policy. Either way, there's no need for any counterfactual analysis, any contemplation of what voters would have done in a different campaign finance world.

To be sure, you could imagine types of distortion other than the one the Court recognized in *Austin* and then rejected in *Citizens United*. For instance, you could define a political system in which representation and policy reflect voters' views as a pure, unadulterated state. Then any divergence from this state—that is, any

---

[23] These are the same mechanisms I discussed in more general terms in Chapter 2. *See also, e.g.,* Harvey & Mattia, *supra* note 4, at 419 (also distinguishing between "the electoral and preference effects" of campaign funding).

[24] *Austin*, 494 U.S. at 669.

[25] *See* Lawrence Lessig, *What an Originalist Would Understand "Corruption" to Mean*, 102 CALIF. L. REV. 1, 15 (2014) (also distinguishing between "two paradigms—regulating speech that corrupts government officials (constitutional) and regulating speech said to corrupt citizens (unconstitutional)").

representational or policy misalignment—would constitute distortion.[26] But the availability of such conceptual moves makes no legal difference. Doctrinally, distortion doesn't encompass every sort of skew that could possibly be conceived. Rather, it refers to the specific phenomenon the Court has described in its campaign finance decisions: the shifting of voters' (not officeholders') preferences, due to heavy and unbalanced campaign spending (not giving), relative to a hypothetical (not actual) benchmark. Whatever might be the case for other varieties of distortion, *this* phenomenon isn't tantamount to representational or policy misalignment.[27]

The prevention of (a particular form of) distortion is one state interest the Court has spurned in the campaign finance context. Another is avoiding what's known as "undue influence"[28] corruption: campaign funders with too much sway over the actions of elected officials. Like the anti-distortion interest, the avoidance of undue influence corruption was initially found compelling by the Court before subsequently being dismissed. In a 2000 case, the Court acknowledged "the broader threat from politicians too compliant with the wishes of large contributors."[29] In a 2003 case, the Court further warned of "the danger that officeholders will decide issues . . . according to the wishes of those who have made large financial contributions."[30] More recently, however, the Court's understanding of the corruption that campaign finance regulations can legitimately try to stop has sharply contracted. In *Citizens United*, the Court stated that the anti-corruption "interest [is] limited to *quid pro quo* corruption"[31]—the deliberate trade of "dollars for political favors."[32] In the 2014 case of *McCutcheon v. FEC*, a plurality of the Court confirmed that "Congress may target only a specific type of corruption—'*quid pro quo*' corruption."[33]

It would be very helpful for proponents of alignment if quid pro quo corruption was synonymous with representational or policy misalignment. In that case, the prevention of these kinds of noncongruence would be the same as the lone anti-corruption interest the Court continues to accept. Unfortunately, this shoe just doesn't fit. Quid pro quo corruption refers to a transaction in which money

---

[26] *Cf.* Richard L. Hasen, *Fixing Washington*, 126 HARV. L. REV. 550, 572 (2012) (book review) (claiming that the "idea that campaign money distorts policy outcomes sounds very much like the language used by the Supreme Court in *Austin v. Michigan Chamber of Commerce*").

[27] *Cf.* Richard L. Hasen, *Is "Dependence Corruption" Distinct from a Political Equality Argument for Campaign Finance Laws? A Reply to Professor Lessig*, 12 ELECTION L.J. 305, 311 (2013) (ultimately conceding that an interest akin to representational alignment "differs in some particulars from the . . . argument in *Austin*").

[28] Interestingly, the phrase "undue influence" dates back to *Buckley v. Valeo*, 424 U.S. 1, 70 (1976), even though *Buckley* is usually associated with the narrower notion of quid pro quo corruption.

[29] Nixon v. Shrink Mo. Gov't PAC, 528 U.S. 377, 389 (2000).

[30] McConnell v. FEC, 540 U.S. 93, 153 (2003).

[31] Citizens United v. FEC, 558 U.S. 310, 359 (2010).

[32] FEC v. NCPAC, 470 U.S. 480, 497 (1985).

[33] McCutcheon v. FEC, 572 U.S. 185, 207 (2014) (plurality opinion).

(or some other asset) is intentionally exchanged for an officeholder's vote (or some other official action).[34] This concept is obviously different from representation or policy that fails to reflect popular preferences. Quid pro corruption focuses on whether there was a meeting of the minds—a mutual desire to trade campaign resources for an official act—between a funder and an officeholder. In contrast, representational and policy misalignment are unrelated to the motives that might explain governmental outputs. They're determined exclusively by those outputs' correspondence (or lack thereof) with voters' views. Moreover, the official act that's half of a corrupt quid pro quo exchange may or may not be contrary to public opinion. If it isn't, then quid pro quo corruption isn't even a driver of misalignment. If the official act does flout popular preferences, then quid pro corruption is just one of the many factors that can cause misalignment. To make a point that will repeat throughout this section, a misaligning *mechanism* isn't misalignment *itself.*

Given that representational and policy misalignment are distinct from quid pro quo corruption, do they converge instead with undue influence corruption? If so, that would be bad news for advocates of alignment because it would mean the pursuit of this democratic value is doctrinally barred in the realm of money in politics. I have to concede that misalignment is *linked* to undue influence corruption. To say that officeholders are "too compliant with" their campaign funders' preferences,[35] or too inclined to "decide issues . . . according to [those] wishes,"[36] is essentially to say that officeholders' and funders' positions are aligned. As long as funders and voters hold divergent views—a proposition I assess in the next section—officeholders who are aligned with the former must be misaligned with the latter.[37] Because of this connection between misalignment and undue influence corruption, I cited the Court's undue influence cases in Chapter 4 as evidence of the Court implicitly recognizing the appeal of alignment. If a future Court ever made this recognition explicit, it would likely rely heavily on these decisions.

But despite these parallels, representational and policy misalignment aren't identical to undue influence corruption. First, even if campaign funders' excessive sway over officeholders is the only driver of misalignment, it remains just that: the driver, not the actual outcome. To reiterate, a means that leads to misalignment is different from the end of misalignment itself. Second, campaign

---

[34] *See, e.g.,* Thomas F. Burke, *The Concept of Corruption in Campaign Finance Law,* 14 Const. Comment. 127, 130 (1997) (defining quid pro quo corruption); Yasmin Dawood, *Classifying Corruption,* 9 Duke J. Const. L. & Pub. Pol'y 103, 122 (2014) (same).

[35] Nixon v. Shrink Mo. Gov't PAC, 528 U.S. 377, 389 (2000).

[36] McConnell v. FEC, 540 U.S. 93, 153 (2003).

[37] *See, e.g.,* Dawood, *supra* note 34, at 125 ("The wrong of undue influence . . . is that elected officials are disproportionately responsive to the wishes of large donors as compared to other constituents.").

funders' undue influence over officeholders obviously isn't the only driver of misalignment. Within the campaign finance field, as I discuss later in this chapter, policies like public financing, disclosure requirements, and lobbying regulations all have significant aligning or misaligning effects. These policies don't directly apply to campaign funders and the extent to which they can use their resources to bolster their favored candidates. And outside the world of money in politics, there exist many, many more forces that push in aligning or misaligning directions. Much of this book, beyond this chapter, is devoted to identifying and analyzing these forces: voting restrictions and expansions, regulations of primary type and ballot access, the choice among electoral systems, partisan gerrymandering, the Voting Rights Act, labor law, legislative procedure, and so on.

Third, campaign funders' undue influence over officeholders doesn't necessarily cause misalignment. If funders and voters have the same policy preferences, then representation and policy that correspond to the views of funders also match those of voters.[38] At present, as described in the next section, funders and voters typically adhere to quite different ideologies. However, there was much more ideological convergence between funders and voters in earlier eras. And conceptually, the fact that undue influence corruption doesn't yield misalignment in all circumstances further demonstrates that these notions are distinct. Lastly, at least in my judgment, alignment is a clearer term than undue influence and one that's easier to operationalize. The Court's phrase doesn't tell us how much influence funders are *due*, nor does it help with the measurement of funders' (or voters') sway over politicians. On the other hand, representational and policy alignment plainly call for the comparison of voters' policy preferences with officeholders' positions and enacted policy outcomes. Both the inputs and the outputs in this formulation can be quantified and then examined in tandem.[39]

Beyond preventing distortion and undue influence corruption, there's one more objective the Court has ruled off-limits in the campaign finance context: pursuing any form of equality. In the foundational 1976 case of *Buckley v. Valeo*,[40] the Court considered equality justifications for federal spending limits on candidates and on individuals. The Court denounced the justifications in both settings, declaring in perhaps the field's best-known line that "the concept that government may restrict the speech of some elements of our society in order to

---

[38] *See, e.g.*, LAWRENCE LESSIG, REPUBLIC, LOST: HOW MONEY CORRUPTS CONGRESS—AND A PLAN TO STOP IT 243 (2011) ("[I]t is conceivable—assuming many contingencies—that a dependence upon 'contributors' could in effect be the same as a dependence upon voters.").

[39] *Cf.* David A. Strauss, *Corruption, Equality, and Campaign Finance Reform*, 94 COLUM. L. REV. 1369, 1386 (1994) (commenting that "[a]n ounce of administrability is worth a pound of theoretical perfection" in the campaign finance context).

[40] 424 U.S. 1 (1976).

enhance the relative voice of others is wholly foreign to the First Amendment."[41] The Court maintained its position on candidate equality in several subsequent cases. In one of these, faced with a "trigger" provision that allocated matching funds to publicly financed candidates if their opponents spent heavily, the Court commented that "it is not legitimate for the government to attempt to equalize electoral opportunities in this manner."[42] The Court also stuck to its guns on equalizing non-candidate spending in *Citizens United*. Quoting *Buckley*, it reaffirmed that "the Government has [no] interest 'in equalizing the relative ability of individuals and groups to influence the outcome of elections.' "[43]

From these decisions (as well as the academic literature), we can glean three types of equality. The first is equality of candidate resources, referred to by Richard Hasen and Daniel Lowenstein as equality of *outputs*. This sort of equality is present when candidates have the same amount of money to spend in their campaigns, but is absent when one candidate enjoys a financial advantage over her opponent.[44] The second, only hinted at in the doctrine but developed more fully by scholars like Yasmin Dawood and Kathleen Sullivan, is equality of *representation*. This variant exists when each voter is represented equally, but not when "elected officials are disproportionately responsive" to some of their constituents.[45] And the third is equality of voter influence over the political process, dubbed equality of *inputs* by Hasen and Lowenstein. Voters have equal influence (from a financial perspective) when they can each donate and spend the same amount of money. But they lack it when certain voters are able to deploy greater resources than others.[46]

Are any of these kinds of equality interchangeable with representational or policy alignment? If so, alignment would be an illegitimate interest under the Court's precedents, but I think the answer is no. To begin with, equality of candidate resources (that is, output equality) is simply an unrelated concept. A candidate may disburse just as much money as her opponent during a campaign, but then flout her constituents' preferences once in office. Conversely, a candidate may outspend her opponent (or be outspent), but then abide by voters' wishes after being elected. There's no logical link between a candidate's relative spending and her subsequent representational or policy alignment. In fact, there's not even much of a correlation between these variables. Even if equal spending produces

---

[41] *Id.* at 48–49.

[42] Ariz. Free Enter. Club's Freedom Club PAC v. Bennett, 564 U.S. 721, 750 (2011); *see also, e.g.,* Davis v. FEC, 554 U.S. 724, 742 (2008) ("The argument that a candidate's speech may be restricted in order to 'level electoral opportunities' has ominous implications....").

[43] Citizens United v. FEC, 558 U.S. 310, 350 (2010) (quoting *Buckley*, 424 U.S. at 48).

[44] *See* Hasen, *supra* note 27, at 312; Daniel Hays Lowenstein, *A Patternless Mosaic: Campaign Finance and the First Amendment After* Austin, 21 Cap. U. L. Rev. 381, 394 (1992).

[45] Dawood, *supra* note 34, at 125; *see also* Kathleen M. Sullivan, *Political Money and Freedom of Speech*, 30 U.C. Davis L. Rev. 663, 678 (1997).

[46] *See* Hasen, *supra* note 27, at 312; Lowenstein, *supra* note 44, at 393.

more competitive races, candidates who squeak into office are only barely more aligned with their constituents than candidates who prevail in landslides.[47] In addition, as I show later in this chapter, the effect of public financing systems that equalize candidate resources has been to *increase* misalignment, not to reduce it.

Next, equality of representation actually conflicts with majoritarian alignment. As a reminder, majoritarian alignment refers to the congruence of governmental outputs with the views of the median voter. As long as voters diverge in their opinions, such congruence can be achieved only if there's *noncongruence* with the views of voters at all other points in the distribution. Alignment with the median requires misalignment with all other locations. This conclusion also holds for collective alignment—minimizing the sum of the distances between governmental outputs and all voters' preferences. Unlike majoritarian alignment, collective alignment does take into account the views of all voters, not just voters at the midpoint of the distribution. But even collective representational alignment doesn't demand that all voters be represented *equally*. Instead, it asks that aggregate representational *inequality* be as low as possible. Again assuming heterogeneity in voter opinion, aggregate representational inequality can never be zero. Some voters' preferences must always be closer to officeholders' positions, while other voters' preferences must always be farther. All voters can never stand on equal representational footing.[48]

Finally, equality in the resources that voters can bring to bear in campaigns (i.e., input equality) is essentially the mirror image of undue influence corruption.[49] Undue influence corruption captures the state of affairs in which some campaign funders give or spend much more money than other individuals or entities, enabling them to overly sway officeholders' actions. Conversely, input equality denotes the absence of undue influence, a campaign finance ecosystem in which all individuals or entities can give or spend the same sums and there are no big funders enjoying excessive clout because of their big money. Because input equality is so closely tied to undue influence, all the points I made above about the latter also apply to the former. To wit: Input equality is *related* to representational and policy alignment, in that when voters can deploy the same campaign resources, representation and policy are likely to be more congruent with voters' preferences. Representation and policy are responsive to the distribution

---

[47] *See, e.g.,* Anthony Fowler & Andrew B. Hall, *Long-Term Consequences of Election Results,* 47 BRIT. J. POL. SCI. 351, 358 (2015).

[48] The implication of this analysis, of course, is that equality of representation is an unattainable ideal, at least if representation is understood as the distance between officeholders' and voters' policy positions. Additionally, equality of *representation* is obviously different from equality of *enacted policy.* So even if equality of representation was identical to collective *representational* alignment, it wouldn't be the same as collective *policy* alignment.

[49] *See* Hasen, *supra* note 27, at 312 (equating the prevention of undue influence corruption with "equality of *political inputs*").

of campaign funding, so when that distribution is more egalitarian, alignment is apt to improve.

However, input equality isn't *identical* to representational or policy correspondence. One, even if input equality is necessary and sufficient to achieve alignment, it's still only the means to that end, not the end itself. Once more, an aligning mechanism shouldn't be confused with actual alignment.[50] Two, input equality plainly isn't necessary and sufficient to achieve alignment. Alignment has many drivers, some inside the domain of money in politics, others outside. Input equality is no more and no less than one aligning factor out of a constellation of such variables. Three, under the right conditions, input *inequality* can promote alignment. Suppose a jurisdiction randomly selects half its voters and awards each lucky beneficiary the same sum to give or spend in the next election. Say the jurisdiction also bars its other voters from any financial participation in that election. The inequality in campaign funding couldn't be starker in this scenario. Yet these unequal inputs would still have an aligning impact because their distribution would mirror the one that would result if all voters (not just half) were subsidized. And four, the terminology of alignment seems more useful than that of input equality. Notably, input equality doesn't even hint at what value(s) might be vindicated if all voters could wield the same campaign resources. In contrast, alignment explicitly connects voters' side of the equation—popular preferences—to particular governmental outputs.

To be clear, my argument here isn't that the current Supreme Court—the anti-alignment Court of Chapter 11—could realistically hold that the pursuit of alignment is an available and compelling justification for campaign finance regulation. Justices that have deemed invalid state interests in avoiding distortion and undue influence corruption and seeking any form of equality would likely have few qualms shutting the door on alignment as well. My claim, then, is oriented toward the future rather than the present. A *differently* constituted Court, one not ideologically opposed to campaign finance regulation but still respectful of stare decisis, might find it helpful that alignment is conceptually distinct from the rationales for regulation the current Court has rejected. That distinctiveness would enable a future Court to uphold campaign finance laws that, in fact, promote alignment without disturbing any of its precedents. Decisions like *Buckley*, *Citizens United*, and *McCutcheon* stand only for the proposition that certain state interests are out of bounds in the campaign finance context. These rulings don't (and couldn't) preclude regulations of money in politics from being sustained on other grounds never contemplated by the cases.

---

[50] *Cf.* Ariz. Free Enter. Club's Freedom Club PAC v. Bennett, 564 U.S. 721, 783 (2011) (Kagan, J., dissenting) ("No special rule of automatic invalidation applies to statutes having some connection to equality....").

Campaign Funders

I just noted that a future Court could uphold campaign finance laws that, *in fact*, promote alignment. "In fact" is the critical phrase in this sentence (hence its italicization). For any regulation of money in politics to survive judicial review, the measure's connection to alignment couldn't just be asserted. That link, rather, would have to be established using reliable empirical evidence. Moreover, precisely because the advancement of alignment is distinct from other, more familiar interests, the burden of proof would be particularly heavy here. During its pro-regulatory heyday in the early 2000s, the Court sensibly stated that "[t]he quantum of empirical evidence needed to satisfy heightened judicial scrutiny . . . will vary up or down with the novelty and plausibility of the justification raised."[51] Under this sliding-scale approach, the furtherance of alignment may or may not be plausible, but it's certainly a new rationale for campaign finance regulation. So the necessary quantum of empirical support would be substantial.[52]

I assemble the evidence that some policies about money in politics promote alignment in this section and the two that follow. Here, I focus on the aligning or misaligning effects of different sources of campaign funding when they're *not* significantly curtailed.[53] Individual funders, it turns out, exert a misaligning influence because they tend to be ideologically extreme and to give or spend money on the basis of candidates' ideological proximity to them. On the other hand, the resources of most PACs are aligning because they're more likely to be deployed on behalf of moderate candidates (due to a combination of genuine centrism and desire for access). Political party funds are aligning for the same reason: more of these dollars flow to moderate candidates (due to parties' objective of winning as many races as they can). These findings suggest that restrictions on individual funders should improve alignment, while curbs on PACs and parties should be misaligning. The next section confirms that expectation, and the concluding section addresses some additional campaign finance laws.

Individuals who contribute money to candidates—individual donors—are the logical funders with whom to start because they account for a supermajority of candidates' total receipts. In the 2020 election, for example, House candidates received 68 percent of their funds from individual donors and Senate candidates

---

[51] Nixon v. Shrink Mo. Gov't PAC, 528 U.S. 377, 391 (2000); *see also* Renata Strause & Daniel P. Tokaji, *Between Access and Influence: Building a Record for the Next Court*, 9 Duke J. Const. L. & Pub. Pol'y 211, 214 (2014) ("A strong record is essential both to document the interests served by legislation, and to show that it is appropriately tailored.").

[52] This analysis also applies outside the courts. Before nonjudicial actors try to regulate money in politics, they should have good reason to think their policies will actually be aligning.

[53] For a similar survey of different sources of campaign funding (focusing on individuals), see Richard H. Pildes, *Participation and Polarization*, 22 U. Pa. J. Const. L. 341, 358–92 (2020).

a whopping 86 percent.[54] The most striking thing about individual donors is how different they are from their peers who don't give money to candidates. With respect to demographics, several surveys show that individuals who contribute to federal candidates are "overwhelmingly wealthy, highly educated, male, and white."[55] To illustrate, in the 2016 election, respondents with annual incomes above $150,000 were more than four times more likely to donate at least $100 than respondents earning less than $30,000 per year. Respondents with post-graduate degrees were more than four times more likely to give this much than respondents with less than a high school education. And respondents over sixty-five were more than three times more likely than respondents under thirty.[56]

With respect to ideology, likewise, study after study concludes that individual donors hold more extreme views than voters.[57] While the ideological distribution of the electorate is normal, with a single peak in the moderate middle, the ideological distribution of individual donors is starkly bimodal, with one peak in the liberal left and another in the conservative right. This result is robust to multiple analytic approaches. It holds for individual donors to congressional candidates,[58] individual donors to *all* candidates over the last fifty years,[59] and individual donors in all fifty states.[60] It also holds when individual donors' ideologies are estimated not through survey responses but rather through the identities of the candidates to whom they choose to contribute.[61] Individual donors are more extreme than non-donating voters, too, when their views are

---

[54] See *House and Senate Financial Activity from January 1, 2019 Through December 31, 2020*, FED. ELECTION COMM'N (Mar. 23, 2021), https://www.fec.gov/resources/campaign-finance-statist ics/2020/tables/congressional/ConCand1_2020_24m.pdf; *see also, e.g.*, Michael Jay Barber, Online Supplemental Materials: Ideological Donors, Contribution Limits, and the Polarization of American Legislatures 13 (Aug. 6, 2015) (showing that state legislative candidates have also received a plurality of their contributions from individual donors since the mid-1990s).

[55] PETER L. FRANCIA ET AL., THE FINANCIERS OF CONGRESSIONAL ELECTIONS: INVESTORS, IDEOLOGUES, AND INTIMATES 16 (2003); *see also, e.g.*, INST. FOR POL., DEMOCRACY & THE INTERNET, SMALL DONORS AND ONLINE GIVING: A STUDY OF DONORS TO THE 2004 PRESIDENTIAL CAMPAIGNS 12 (2006); Seth J. Hill & Gregory A. Huber, *Representativeness and Motivations of the Contemporary Donorate: Results from Merged Survey and Administrative Records*, 39 POL. BEHAVIOR 3, 9–10 (2017).

[56] See *5 Facts About U.S. Political Donations*, PEW RSCH. CTR. (May 17, 2017), https://www.pewr esearch.org/fact-tank/2017/05/17/5-facts-about-u-s-political-donations/.

[57] I also cited this evidence in Chapter 4 when I discussed groups (like individual donors) that enjoy unusually good representational alignment.

[58] See, e.g., Joseph Bafumi & Michael C. Herron, *Leapfrog Representation and Extremism: A Study of American Voters and Their Members in Congress*, 104 AM. POL. SCI. REV. 519, 537 (2010); Jesse H. Rhodes & Brian F. Schaffner, Economic Inequality and Representation in the U.S. House: A New Approach Using Population-Level Data 34 (Apr. 7, 2013).

[59] See Michael Barber, Ideological Donors, Contribution Limits, and the Polarization of State Legislatures 15 (Sept. 4, 2013).

[60] See *id.* at 16.

[61] See, e.g., Adam Bonica, *Avenues of Influence: On the Political Expenditures of Corporations and Their Directors and Executives*, 18 BUS. POL. 367, 385 (2016); Adam Bonica et al., *Why Hasn't Democracy Slowed Rising Inequality?*, 27 J. ECON. PERSPECTIVES 103, 115 (2013).

disaggregated by domain. Democratic donors are especially liberal on social issues, Republican donors are especially conservative on economic issues, and both parties' donors are especially supportive of free trade and immigration.[62]

The polarized ideologies of individual donors would matter less if they gave money for non-ideological reasons (like personal relationships or obtaining access to politicians). In that case, the *recipients* of the contributions wouldn't have a financial incentive to take ideologically extreme positions. But surveys conducted by numerous scholars all find that the most common explanation offered by individual donors for their contributions is candidates' ideological proximity to them. As Michael Barber puts it in a study of individual donors to Senate candidates, "ideological considerations are more likely to be rated as extremely important by donors than access-related motivations or motivations related to personal connections to the candidate."[63] In addition, many studies determine that the more ideologically extreme candidates are, the more money they raise from individual donors.[64] Individual donors' survey responses are therefore more than mere words. Their replies are corroborated by their actual pattern of contributing more heavily to candidates who share their polarized views.

In combination, individual donors' abundant resources, extreme ideologies, and ideological giving lead to glaring representational misalignment in their favor. Joseph Bafumi and Michael Herron use the voting records of members of Congress and the survey responses of individual donors to plot their ideologies in a common policy space. Adam Bonica relies on data about who gives and receives all disclosed campaign contributions to do the same. Both studies conclude that the ideological distributions of individual donors and of members of Congress are more or less identical. Both distributions are starkly bimodal, again in marked contrast to the normal distribution of the electorate in its entirety.[65] Similarly, Barber uses roll call votes and survey responses to estimate the ideologies of senators, individual donors, voters from each party, and all voters. The average senator is very ideologically distant from her state's median voter (who's represented only slightly better than a voter chosen at random). The average senator is substantially more aligned with the median voter from her

---

[62] *See* David Broockman & Neil Malhotra, What Do Donors Want? Heterogeneity by Party and Policy Domain 6 (Nov. 30, 2018).

[63] Michael Barber, Access Versus Ideology: Why PACs and Individuals Contribute to Campaigns 8 (Dec. 3, 2013); *see also, e.g.,* Michael Barber et al., *Campaign Contributions and Donors' Policy Agreement with Presidential Candidates,* 49 Pres. Stud. Q. 770, 781 (2019); Wesley Y. Joe et al., Do Small Donors Improve Representation? Some Answers from Recent Gubernatorial and State Legislative Elections 22 (Aug. 28, 2008).

[64] *See, e.g.,* Tyler Culberson et al., *Small Donors in Congressional Elections,* 47 Am. Pol. Rsch. 970, 986 (2019); Michael J. Ensley, *Individual Campaign Contributions and Candidate Ideology,* 138 Pub. Choice 221, 227 (2009); Walter J. Stone & Elizabeth N. Simas, *Candidate Valence and Ideological Positions in U.S. House Elections,* 54 Am. J. Pol. Sci. 371, 381 (2010).

[65] *See* Bafumi & Herron, *supra* note 58, at 522–26; Bonica, *supra* note 61, at 385.

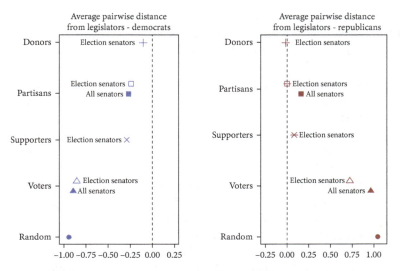

FIGURE 9.1 REPRESENTATIONAL ALIGNMENT BETWEEN SENATORS, INDIVIDUAL DONORS, AND VOTERS

Figure 9.1 is reproduced with permission from Michael J. Barber, *Representing the Preferences of Donors, Partisans, and Voters in the U.S. Senate*, 80 PUB. OP. Q. 225, 237 (2016). Copyright © 2016 by Oxford University Press.

own party. But "[a]mong both Republicans and Democrats, the average ideological congruence between senators and *donors* is nearly perfect."[66] Figure 9.1 reproduces Barber's chart displaying these findings.

Barber's analysis hints at a causal (not just a correlational) relationship between individual contributions and representational misalignment. Since senators represent their individual donors better than their constituents or even their co-partisans, the sway of that funding apparently exceeds the electoral incentive to appeal to the median voter as well as the partisan urge to please fellow party members. Additional evidence of causation comes from a series of studies that examine the impact of individual donor opinion on legislative behavior, controlling for variables like district opinion, co-partisan opinion, and party affiliation. These studies uniformly show that individual donor opinion is a statistically significant driver—in fact, one that usually outweighs "*both* district opinion and the preferences of partisans in the district."[67] Notably, individual

[66] Michael J. Barber, *Representing the Preferences of Donors, Partisans, and Voters in the U.S. Senate*, 80 PUB. OP. Q. 225, 238 (2016) (emphasis added).
[67] Brandice Canes-Wrone & Kenneth M. Miller, *Out-of-District Donors and Representation in the U.S. House*, 47 LEGIS. STUD. Q. 361, 373 (2022); *see also, e.g.,* Anne E. Baker, *Getting Short-Changed? The Impact of Outside Money on District Representation*, 97 SOC. SCI. Q. 1096, 1103–04 (2016);

donor opinion influences legislative behavior through both mechanisms cited earlier, adaptation and selection. Via adaptation, officeholders change their positions to match more closely the views of individual donors, in order to keep those funds flowing. Via selection, politicians whose true preferences better reflect those of individual donors receive more money and, maybe for that reason, win more votes. Thanks to both channels, individual donor opinion is a potent misaligning force.

This wraps up the basic argument about individual donors. Before turning to other sources of campaign funding, though, a few more points are worth flagging. First, not all individual donors are alike. Specifically, out-of-state donors more focused on national politics are more ideologically polarized than in-state donors more concerned about local issues.[68] Individual donors who contribute not just to candidates but also to ideological or single-issue PACs are more extreme, too, than all other individual donors.[69] As a result, it makes a difference for representational alignment *which* individual donors give money to candidates. Dollars from out-of-state donors and concurrent donors to ideological PACs are more misaligning than other kinds of individual contributions.[70]

Second, individual contributions (of all sorts) are more misaligning today than they were in earlier eras. Individual donors are now a larger source of candidate funding than they were in the past. At the congressional level, for instance, the fraction of candidates' resources coming from individual contributions has increased from below 50 percent in the 1980s to above 70 percent in recent elections.[71] Individual donors are also more likely now to self-identify as liberal or conservative. The share of ideological donors has risen from about 40 percent in the 1980s to more than 60 percent lately.[72] These trends of more ideological donors supplying more of candidates' funds imply growing representational misalignment due to individual contributions. And in fact, that's exactly what

Brandice Canes-Wrone & Nathan Gibson, *Does Money Buy Congressional Love? Individual Donors and Legislative Voting*, 46 CONG. & PRES. 1, 14 (2019); Rhodes & Schaffner, *supra* note 58, at 36–38.

[68] *See* Anne E. Baker, *The Partisan and Policy Motivations of Political Donors Seeking Surrogate Representation in House Elections*, 42 POL. BEHAVIOR 1035, 1043–44 (2020).
[69] *See* Jacob M. Grumbach, *Interest Group Activists and the Polarization of State Legislatures*, 45 LEGIS. STUD. Q. 5, 14–16 (2020).
[70] *See, e.g.*, Baker, *supra* note 68, at 1106; Canes-Wrone & Miller, *supra* note 67, at 376; Grumbach, *supra* note 69, at 23–24.
[71] *See* Michael Barber & Nolan McCarty, *Causes and Consequences of Polarization*, in NEGOTIATING AGREEMENT IN POLITICS: REPORT OF THE TASK FORCE ON NEGOTIATING AGREEMENT IN POLITICS 19, 31 (Jane Mansbridge & Cathie Jo Martin eds., 2013); *see also* Barber, *supra* note 54, at 13 (showing state legislative candidates, too, receiving a larger share of their funds from individual donors over time).
[72] *See* Raymond J. La Raja & David L. Wiltse, *Don't Blame Donors for Ideological Polarization of Political Parties: Ideological Change and Stability Among Political Contributors, 1972-2008*, 40 AM. POL. RESEARCH 501, 510 (2011).

a study by Brandice Canes-Wrone and Nathan Gibson demonstrates. In the 1988–92 period, individual donor opinion didn't have a statistically significant effect on senators' roll call votes (while overall state opinion did).[73] By the 2006–14 period, however, the familiar modern pattern appears in which individual donor opinion drives senators' positions and overall state opinion fades in comparison.[74]

Lastly, individual *spenders* ideologically resemble individual *donors*. By individual spenders I mean (the very few) people who spend directly to influence elections and (the more numerous) people who give money to non-candidate entities that can then make unlimited campaign expenditures. In the 2000s, 527 organizations (named for the section of the Internal Revenue Code that authorizes them) were the most important of these entities. According to Nolan McCarty and his coauthors, "[a]lmost all of the large contributors [to 527 organizations] [were] extremists."[75] Since *Citizens United*, the main non-candidate entities that can raise and spend unlimited sums have been Super PACs (which are required to disclose their donors) and dark money groups (which aren't). Of those who contribute to candidate-specific Super PACs, the vast majority also give to the candidates supported by those groups.[76] So in this context, individual spenders tend to be the very same people as individual donors. Of those who contribute both to candidates and to another major set of Super PACs, the Super PACs back more extreme candidates than do these funders with their direct donations.[77] So here, the same funders exert *more* misaligning influence as individual spenders than as individual donors. And as for dark money groups, while their very darkness precludes most analysis of their contributors,[78] the groups systematically "back[] more extreme candidates than do party organizations or access-seeking interest groups."[79] That is, the groups

[73] *See* Brandice Canes-Wrone & Nathan Gibson, *Developments in Congressional Responsiveness to Donor Opinion*, *in* CAN AMERICA GOVERN ITSELF? 69, 79 (Frances E. Lee ed., 2019).

[74] *See id.* at 80.

[75] NOLAN MCCARTY ET AL., POLARIZED AMERICA: THE DANCE OF IDEOLOGY AND UNEQUAL RICHES 156 (2006).

[76] *See Double-Duty Donors, Part II: Large Numbers of Wealthy Donors Hit Legal Limit on Giving to Candidates, Turn to Presidential Super PACs in Continuing Trend*, CTR. FOR RESPONSIVE POL. (Feb. 21, 2012), http://www.opensecrets.org/news/2012/02/double-duty-donors-part-ii-large-nu.html. Unfortunately, this study only covered contributions to candidate-specific Super PACs in 2011. More research is needed on donors to the entire array of Super PACs over a longer period.

[77] *See* Stan Oklobdzija, I'll Be Disclosed by Christmas: What 'Pop-Up PACs' Can Teach Us About Disclosure and Dark Money 8 (Dec. 16, 2019) (examining Super PACs that postpone disclosing their donors until just after an election).

[78] *But see* Stan Oklobdzija, *Public Positions, Private Giving: Dark Money and Political Donors in the Digital Age*, RSCH. & POL., Jan.–Mar. 2019 (exploiting a rarely available list of a dark money group's donors to study their ideologies).

[79] Stan Oklobdzija, Partisans, PACs or Purists: Where Does Dark Money Fall in the Interest Group Typology 4 (Aug. 1, 2020).

behave just like the individual spenders who, in all likelihood, finance their operations.[80]

I began this discussion with individual donors because they provide candidates with most of their resources. At both the federal and state levels, candidates' second-biggest funders are conventional PACs that, unlike Super PACs, are permitted to contribute to candidates.[81] PACs have an unsavory reputation in some reformist circles due to their association with powerful commercial interests. Ideologically, though, most PACs exhibit centrist preferences that could scarcely be more different from the polarized views of most individual funders. Barber and Bonica each use the ideologies of the candidates to whom PACs contribute to estimate the groups' own ideologies. The resulting distributions are normal, unimodal, and centered in the middle of the ideological spectrum in every case: for PACs that donated to state legislative candidates from 1996 to 2012,[82] for PACs that donated to federal candidates in 2012 (as depicted in Figure 9.2),[83] and for PACs that donated to any candidate over the 1980–2010 period.[84]

You might object that most PACs aren't *centrist* but rather *nonideological*—happy to give to Democrats and Republicans, liberals and conservatives, as long as their contributions get them access to the policymaking process. There's some force to this point. PACs are more likely than individual donors to give to candidates from both parties[85] and to incumbents instead of challengers.[86] The variance of the ideologies of the candidates to whom PACs contribute is also relatively high and so indicative of less ideological giving.[87] However, Bonica[88] and McCarty and his coauthors[89] each show that this variance *isn't* as high as it would be if PACs were actually insensitive to candidates' views. Accordingly, as Bonica puts it, "the vast majority of PACs incorporate ideological proximity into their contribution decisions," and "the majority of PACs locating in the center are better described as centrist than nonideological."[90] These centrist PACs are access-oriented, too, but they're not exclusively access-oriented.

---

[80]   *See* Oklobdzija, *supra* note 78, at 6 (determining that individuals supplied the vast majority of one dark money group's resources).

[81]   *See* Barber, *supra* note 54, at 13; Barber & McCarty, *supra* note 71, at 31.

[82]   *See* Barber, *supra* note 59, at 18–21.

[83]   *See* Barber, *supra* note 63, at 10–11.

[84]   *See* Adam Bonica, *Ideology and Interests in the Political Marketplace*, 57 AM. J. POL. SCI. 294, 301 (2013).

[85]   *See, e.g.,* Barber, *supra* note 63, at 12.

[86]   *See, e.g., id.* at 15.

[87]   *See, e.g., id.* at 13.

[88]   *See* Bonica, *supra* note 84, at 302.

[89]   *See* MCCARTY ET AL., *supra* note 75, at 148–50.

[90]   Bonica, *supra* note 84, at 302.

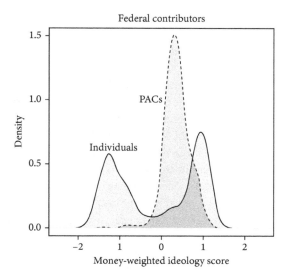

FIGURE 9.2 IDEOLOGIES OF PACs AND INDIVIDUALS DONATING TO FEDERAL
CANDIDATES

Figure 9.2 is reproduced with permission from Michael Barber, Access Versus Ideology: Why PACs
and Individuals Contribute to Campaigns 11 (Dec. 3, 2013). Copyright © 2013 by Michael Barber.

The corollary of most PACs being ideologically moderate is that moderate
politicians should receive more money from them (and extreme politicians less).
That's precisely what happens. At the congressional level, a centrist candidate
collects about $50,000 to $70,000 more from PACs than a typical Democrat or
Republican, and roughly $100,000 to $180,000 more than an extreme Democrat
or Republican.[91] At the state legislative level, likewise, moderate candidates take
in around $12,000 more from PACs than very liberal candidates, and close to
$7,000 more than very conservative candidates.[92] As a result, the dynamics of
adaptation and selection work the opposite way for most PACs than they do for
most individual funders—to induce better, not worse, representational alignment. Officeholders have a financial incentive to shift their positions toward the
center in order to elicit more PAC contributions. Politicians whose views are
genuinely moderate to begin with also benefit from greater PAC support, which
may translate into greater electoral success, too. These effects explain why the activities of most PACs, unlike those of most individual funders, are aligning.

---

[91] See id. at 306, 308.
[92] See Andrew B. Hall, How the Public Funding of Elections Increases Candidate Polarization
20–21 (Aug. 13, 2014); see also Michael J. Barber, Ideological Donors, Contribution Limits, and the
Polarization of American Legislatures, 78 J. POL. 296, 308 (2016).

I was careful to repeat the phrase, "most PACs," in the preceding paragraphs. Most PACs (both numerically and in dollars donated) are business or trade organizations.[93] These groups are indeed ideologically moderate, with a slight skew to the center-right.[94] Labor PACs, however, are liberal, not centrist; they give almost exclusively to liberal Democratic candidates.[95] And ideological or single-issue PACs (focusing on abortion, taxes, the environment, and the like) are highly polarized, resembling individual donors in their contribution strategies.[96] It's therefore not the case that all PAC money is aligning. This conclusion holds only for the large majority of PACs that are business or trade organizations.[97] An additional qualification is that the fraction of candidates' resources coming from PACs has fallen in recent years. This drop has been especially steep at the congressional level: from more than 40 percent in the 1980s to less than 20 percent today.[98] So while PAC dollars continue to exert an aligning influence, they push less strongly in that direction than a few decades ago.

Political parties are the final major source of candidates' funds.[99] Outside the realm of money in politics, parties perform many functions other than donating to candidates. In this campaign finance context, though, the behavior of parties is quite similar to that of most PACs. So this aspect of party behavior can be covered briskly. First, parties, like most PACs, give more heavily to moderate candidates and less generously to extreme candidates. Figure 9.3, drawn from work by Raymond La Raja and Brian Schaffner, plots the proportions of state party contributions that are made to state legislative candidates of different ideologies. This curve peaks in the middle of the ideological spectrum, corresponding to policy centrism. Conversely, the shares of party contributions that are made to liberal or conservative candidates, on the left or right of the ideological spectrum, decline dramatically.[100]

Second, just as moderate politicians receive more donations from PACs, so too do they get more money from parties. La Raja and Schaffner find that state

[93] See, e.g., Business-Labor-Ideology Split in PAC & Individual Donations to Candidates, Parties, Super PACs and Outside Spending Groups, CTR. FOR RESPONSIVE POL., https://www.opensecrets.org/elections-overview/business-labor-ideology-split?cycle = 2020 (last visited Feb. 1, 2024) (showing that, in the 2020 cycle, business PACs provided 64 percent of total PAC contributions, compared to 12 percent for labor PACs and 23 percent for ideological PACs).

[94] See, e.g., Michael Jay Barber, Buying Representation: The Incentives, Ideology, and Influence of Campaign Contributors in American Politics 12 (Sept. 2014).

[95] See, e.g., Bonica, supra note 84, at 306.

[96] See, e.g., Barber, supra note 94, at 12.

[97] See Connor Halloran Phillips, Interest Group Strategy and State Legislative Polarization 24 (Sept. 26, 2022) (finding that labor PAC contributions make state legislators more liberal while ideological PAC contributions make them more polarized).

[98] See Barber, supra note 54, at 13; Barber & McCarty, supra note 71, at 31.

[99] See RAYMOND J. LA RAJA & BRIAN F. SCHAFFNER, CAMPAIGN FINANCE AND POLITICAL POLARIZATION: WHEN PURISTS PREVAIL 64 (2015); Barber & McCarty, supra note 71, at 31.

[100] See LA RAJA & SCHAFFNER, supra note 99, at 71.

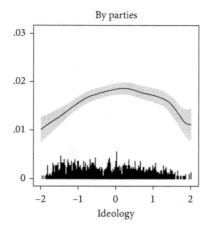

FIGURE 9.3 PROPORTIONS OF STATE PARTY CONTRIBUTIONS TO STATE LEGISLATIVE
CANDIDATES OF VARYING IDEOLOGIES
Figure 9.3 is reproduced with permission from RAYMOND J. LA RAJA & BRIAN F. SCHAFFNER,
CAMPAIGN FINANCE AND POLITICAL POLARIZATION: WHEN PURISTS PREVAIL 71 (2015). Copyright
© 2015 by University of Michigan Press.

legislators with centrist ideologies obtain about 8 percent of their campaign resources from state parties.[101] On the other hand, state party contributions comprise only around 4 percent of the total receipts of conservative state legislators,
and an even lower 2 percent of the war chests of liberal state legislators.[102] Parties
are thus a substantial (if not exactly overflowing) source of funding for moderate
politicians. But party financial support for extreme politicians is negligible, especially compared to the dollars from individual donors that are showered on
these actors.

Lastly, the same caveats that apply to PACs as an aligning force apply to parties
in this capacity, too. Like PACs, parties don't give to moderate candidates solely
out of sincere centrism. Instead, "party insiders are chiefly interested in winning," so "their priority is to invest in candidates who will be most competitive
in a general election—candidates whose views are closest to those of the median
voter."[103] And party contributions typically account for even smaller fractions
of candidates' resources than do PAC contributions. At the congressional level,
for example, candidates have received less than 10 percent of their total receipts
from parties since the 1980s—at all times, less than half of what they've taken in
from PACs (and less than one-quarter of what they've gotten from individual

---

[101] *See id.* at 82 (discussing only states without limits on party fundraising and contributing).
[102] *See id.* (same).
[103] *Id.* at 23.

donors).[104] A funding pool this comparatively small is plainly limited in how much alignment it can induce. The fewer party dollars are available to moderate candidates, the less incentive officeholders have to stake out centrist positions, and the smaller an edge true centrists enjoy in the first place.

Curbs on Campaign Funders

The last section set the stage for this part's examination of the key question (from the standpoint of alignment): If the government restricts the activities of campaign funders like individuals, PACs, and parties, what are the aligning implications? An intuitive (and, it turns out, correct) hypothesis is that when the government constrains *misaligning* sources of campaign funding, representational alignment improves as a result, while when the government curbs *aligning* sources of campaign funding, the consequence is representation that less accurately reflects constituent opinion. Consider the mechanism of adaptation. When less misaligning (or aligning) money can be obtained from a particular funding source, because of governmental regulation of that source, officeholders have less reason to shift their stances in that misaligning (or aligning) direction. This logic also holds for the mechanism of selection. When governmental policy means that fewer misaligning (or aligning) funds flow to candidates with certain ideologies, candidates who genuinely hold those views are less financially and electorally advantaged. In other words, the same dynamics that lead to better or worse alignment when campaign funding is *unchecked* have the opposite effects when the funding spigot is tightened or closed.

Beginning again with individual donors—the quintessential misaligning funding sources in modern American politics—Barber documents each step of how limits on them promote representational alignment. First, individual contributions to candidates tend to be smaller when caps on these donations are lower. As states vary from no cap at all to the most restrictive cap in the country, the average contribution to state legislative candidates falls from about $400 to $100.[105] Second, more individual donors hit the contribution ceiling when that ceiling is lower. The share of individual donors giving the maximum legal amount to state legislative candidates rises from roughly 3 percent when this maximum is at its peak to around 13 percent when this maximum reaches its national nadir.[106] Third, candidates raise smaller amounts from individual donors

---

[104] *See* Barber & McCarty, *supra* note 71, at 31; *see also* LA RAJA & SCHAFFNER, *supra* note 99, at 64 (showing that state legislative candidates also receive less than 10 percent of their resources from parties in most states).

[105] *See* Barber, *supra* note 59, at 32.

[106] *See id.* at 33.

when individual contribution limits are tighter. State legislative candidates' average receipts from individual donors drop from approximately $8,000 to $4,000 as states go from no cap on individual giving to the lowest cap in America.[107]

And fourth, in the culmination of this sequence, officeholders are more ideologically moderate—and more aligned with their constituents—when individual contribution limits have more bite. Adopting individual contribution limits (of any magnitude) where they didn't previously exist, especially in states with more professional legislatures, makes Democratic state legislators significantly less liberal and Republican state legislators significantly less conservative. These moderating effects are quite large: on the order of twice the within-state ideological variance of Democratic or Republican state legislators.[108] Lowering (as opposed to initially adopting) individual contribution limits is aligning as well. Halving these limits, for instance, causes the ideologies of Democratic (or Republican) state legislators to move by about one-third (or one-tenth) of their within-state ideological variance in a conservative (or liberal) direction.[109]

These findings make a powerful legal case for upholding caps on individual contributions. Alignment is a compelling democratic value, it's conceptually distinct from the state interests the Supreme Court has rejected in the campaign finance domain—and it's meaningfully furthered by restrictions on individual donations. I noted above that the empirical bar is higher for a novel rationale for campaign finance regulation like the advancement of alignment. The evidence I've summarized plainly clears this hurdle. When their activities aren't constrained, individual donors are, in fact, a potent misaligning force. By the same token, when individual donors' giving *is* curbed, substantially better representational alignment is indeed the result. Consequently, future courts unbound by the current Court's hostility to campaign finance laws should have few qualms sustaining individual contribution limits. And nonjudicial actors should be even quicker to enact these highly aligning policies.

What about limits on individual campaign *expenditures*? There's little scholarship about direct caps on individual spending because such caps have been unconstitutional ever since *Buckley* more than forty years ago.[110] There's also little work about restrictions on how much individuals can give to non-candidate entities like 527 organizations, Super PACs, and dark money groups that can

---

[107] *See id.* at 34.

[108] *See id.* at 37–38.

[109] *See id.; see also* Nicholas O. Stephanopoulos et al., *The Realities of Electoral Reform*, 68 VAND. L. REV. 761, 812 (2015) (also finding that individual contribution limits improve the representational alignment of Democratic and Republican state legislators). *But see* DEVIN CAUGHEY & CHRISTOPHER WARSHAW, DYNAMIC DEMOCRACY: PUBLIC OPINION, ELECTIONS, AND POLICYMAKING IN THE AMERICAN STATES 156, 158–59 (2022) (finding that individual contribution limits don't improve state *policy* alignment).

[110] *See* Buckley v. Valeo, 424 U.S. 1, 39–51 (1976).

engage in unlimited spending. Such restrictions have been unlawful since shortly after *Citizens United*.[111] In a pair of recent articles, however, Anna Harvey uses *Buckley* and *Citizens United* as exogenous events to study the impact on representational alignment of the policies that were struck down thanks to those decisions. After *Buckley*, state ceilings on campaign spending could no longer be enforced. In states that had such ceilings before *Buckley*, and that also held concurrent federal and state elections, the ideologies of members of Congress shifted to the right in the wake of the Court's intervention. Representational misalignment in a conservative direction thus likely increased after campaign spenders were unshackled.[112] The story was much the same after *Citizens United* enabled individuals to give freely to Super PACs and other non-candidate entities. The ideologies of state legislators in states affected by the Court's new rule swung to the right, probably indicating growing representational misalignment in conservatives' favor.[113]

These articles aren't as definitive as I'd like. The *Buckley* study relies on spillovers from state-level spending—not actual spending on congressional elections—to evaluate changes in congressional representation.[114] And the *Citizens United* study can't distinguish between the individual spending unleashed by the decision and the new outlays of corporations and unions.[115] Still, this suggestive evidence should be combined with the sizable literature, discussed in the previous section, establishing that individual spenders resemble individual donors in their ideological extremity. As a whole, this body of work is quite convincing that individual spenders are a driver of representational misalignment, even if it can't (yet) nail down the corollary that limits on individual spenders are aligning. If and when this proof materializes, it will mean that curbs on individual donors and on individual spenders should enjoy the same legal status in the eyes of future courts willing to acknowledge alignment as a weighty state interest. Both policies should be permissible because both induce better representational alignment.[116] *Buckley*'s distinction between

---

[111]   *See* Speechnow.org v. FEC, 599 F.3d 686 (D.C. Cir. 2010) (effectively authorizing the creation of Super PACs by invalidating limits on their campaign expenditures).

[112]   *See* Anna Harvey, *Is Campaign Spending a Cause or an Effect? Reexamining the Empirical Foundations of* Buckley v. Valeo *(1976)*, 27 SUP. CT. ECON. REV. 67, 95 (2019).

[113]   *See* Harvey & Mattia, *supra* note 4, at 427–29.

[114]   *See* Harvey, *supra* note 112, at 89, 93.

[115]   However, by all accounts, individual spending post-*Citizens United* dwarfs corporate and union spending. *See, e.g.*, Bonica, *supra* note 61, at 370–74. That's why I don't separately consider limits on corporate and union expenditures in this chapter. These expenditures are comparatively small enough (even now that they're unrestricted) that they likely don't have large effects on alignment.

[116]   Note that, on a per-dollar basis, contribution limits are likely more aligning than expenditure limits because money given directly to a candidate is more valuable (and so more potentially misaligning) than money spent independently to support a candidate. *See, e.g.*, Richard L. Hasen, *Three Wrong Progressive Approaches (and One Right One) to Campaign Finance Reform*, 8 HARV.

individual contribution limits (usually valid) and individual expenditure limits (categorically unconstitutional) would therefore crumble. That distinction follows from the Court's skepticism that individual spending leads to *quid pro quo corruption*.[117] Even if that skepticism is warranted (count me among those who doubt it[118]), it can't justify treating individual contributions and individual expenditures differently when *alignment* is the rationale for regulation.[119]

Turning from individual funders to PACs, Barber again provides a step-by-step guide to how restrictions on their donations influence alignment.[120] The effects of PAC contribution limits mirror those of individual contribution limits, only this time they result in worse (not better) representational alignment because most PACs' donations are aligning (not misaligning). First, PACs' contributions to candidates tend to be smaller when caps on these donations are lower. As states vary from no cap at all to the most stringent cap in the country, the average PAC contribution to state legislative candidates falls from about $1,000 to $150.[121] Second, more PACs hit the contribution ceiling when that ceiling is lower. The fraction of PACs giving the largest possible donation to state legislative candidates rises from roughly 1 percent under the highest PAC contribution limit in the nation to around 25 percent under the lowest limit.[122] Third, candidates raise smaller amounts from PACs when curbs on PACs' donations are stricter. State legislative candidates' average receipts from PACs drop from approximately $8,000 to $1,000 as states go from no cap on PAC giving to the lowest cap in America.[123]

Lastly, and most importantly, officeholders are more ideologically extreme—and less aligned with their constituents—when PAC contribution limits have sharper teeth. Adopting PAC contribution limits (of any size) where they

---

L. & Pol'y Rev. 21, 33 (2014) (observing that "$20 million in a Super PAC supporting Member of Congress X is less bad (but still bad) than $20 million in Member X's campaign account").

[117] *See* Buckley v. Valeo, 424 U.S. 1, 45–48 (1976).

[118] *See, e.g.*, Bruce E. Cain, *Is "Dependence Corruption" the Solution to America's Campaign Finance Problems?*, 102 Calif. L. Rev. 37, 43 (2014) (a candidate doesn't "feel any less obligated to a large independent spender than to a large contributor"); David Cole, *First Amendment Antitrust: The End of Laissez-Faire in Campaign Finance*, 9 Yale L. & Pol'y Rev. 236, 272 (1991) ("expenditures are just as corrupting as contributions").

[119] Going deeper into the doctrinal weeds, the Court subjects expenditure limits to strict scrutiny but contribution limits to less demanding "exacting" scrutiny. So it's logically possible (if practically unlikely) that evidence about the aligning impact of expenditure limits would be insufficient to uphold them under a more stringent standard of review—even though analogous evidence about how contribution limits promote alignment *would* suffice to save them under a more lenient standard.

[120] I don't address PAC *expenditure* limits because (1) conventional PACs typically don't engage in much independent spending; and (2) such spending has never been legally restricted. For the same reasons, I don't comment on *party* expenditure limits later in this section.

[121] *See* Barber, *supra* note 59, at 32.

[122] *See id.* at 33.

[123] *See id.* at 34.

didn't previously exist, especially in states with less professional legislatures, makes Democratic state legislators significantly more liberal and Republican state legislators significantly more conservative. These centrifugal impacts are substantial: on the order of half or all the within-state ideological variance of Democratic or Republican state legislators, respectively.[124] Lowering (rather than initially adopting) PAC contribution limits is misaligning, too. Halving these limits, for example, causes the ideologies of Democratic (or Republican) state legislators to shift by about one-twentieth (or one-sixth) of their within-state ideological variance in a liberal (or conservative) direction.[125]

The upshot of this analysis is that PAC contribution limits—unlike individual contribution limits—can't be defended against First Amendment challenges on the ground that they improve representational alignment. Even future courts ready to recognize this defense, in principle, should conclude, in practice, that most PACs' donations are aligning and that restrictions on these donations are misaligning.[126] To be sure, PAC contribution limits could potentially be justified on *other* bases. In particular, it might be the case that PACs' donations, when unchecked, often form quids that are corruptly exchanged for quos from grateful officeholders. If so, the prevention of quid pro quo corruption would be a persuasive rationale for PAC contribution limits.[127] But this possibility is irrelevant to this chapter's argument. Even if restraints on PACs' donations further other goals, they don't promote (in fact, they hinder) the achievement of alignment between elected officials and their constituents.

Political parties are the final campaign funders whose contributions are subject to different degrees of governmental regulation. Since parties' donations (like most PACs') are aligning, you might expect curbs on these donations to lead to worse representational misalignment. And you'd be right. La Raja and Schaffner show that when states restrict parties' contributions to state legislative candidates, these candidates receive less of their funding from parties and more from ideologically extreme individual donors. The decline in party support is sharpest for challengers, dropping from about 20 percent of total receipts when party donations are unlimited to less than 15 percent when they're capped.[128]

---

[124] *See id.* at 37–38.

[125] *See id.*; *cf.* Stephanopoulos et al., *supra* note 109, at 812 (finding that PAC contribution limits worsen the representational alignment of Democratic but not Republican state legislators).

[126] To repeat a point from the last section, not all PACs' donations are aligning; specifically, donations from labor PACs and ideological PACs are misaligning. *See* Phillips, *supra* note 97, at 24. It's therefore likely that *limits* on labor PACs' and ideological PACs' contributions would result in *better* representational alignment. However, this proposition hasn't been empirically established. Regulatory distinctions between different kinds of PACs might also conflict with the principle that "the First Amendment generally prohibits the suppression of political speech based on the speaker's identity." Citizens United v. FEC, 558 U.S. 310, 350 (2010).

[127] *See, e.g.,* Buckley v. Valeo, 424 U.S. 1, 35–36 (1976) (upholding PAC contribution limits on this basis).

[128] *See* LA RAJA & SCHAFFNER, *supra* note 99, at 80.

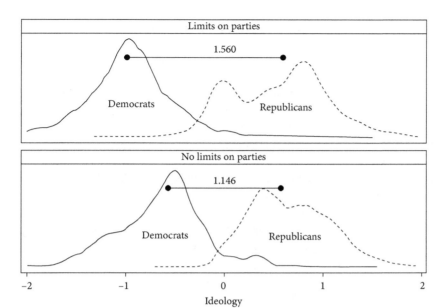

FIGURE 9.4 IDEOLOGICAL DISTRIBUTIONS OF STATE LEGISLATORS IN STATES WITH AND WITHOUT PARTY CONTRIBUTION LIMITS

Figure 9.4 is reproduced with permission from RAYMOND J. LA RAJA & BRIAN F. SCHAFFNER, CAMPAIGN FINANCE AND POLITICAL POLARIZATION: WHEN PURISTS PREVAIL 99 (2015). Copyright © 2015 by University of Michigan Press.

La Raja and Schaffner further demonstrate that it's ideologically moderate candidates who are most disadvantaged by party contribution limits. The share of their funding coming from parties falls from around 8 percent without limits to roughly 3 percent with limits. In contrast, very liberal candidates obtain about the same (very low) party backing with or without limits, and very conservative candidates actually get slightly more of their resources from parties when party giving is constrained.[129]

The predictable consequence of party contribution limits financially disadvantaging centrists is that they prompt officeholders to move toward the ideological fringes. That is, they result in greater legislative polarization and worse representational misalignment. Figure 9.4, borrowed from La Raja and Schaffner, displays the ideological distributions of Democratic and Republican state legislators in more professional state legislatures when party contribution limits do exist (top panel) and don't exist (bottom panel). With these restrictions

[129] See id. at 82.

in place, the ideological distance between the median Democratic and the median Republican representative (a common measure of legislative polarization)
is about 1.6 units on a scale from -2 to + 2. This is a considerably larger ideological gap, indicative of considerably worse collective representation, than
the roughly 1.1-unit gap that arises when party donations are unlimited.[130]
Moreover, this correlational finding persists when a more rigorous multivariate
analysis is undertaken. "States that limit what parties can raise and spend appear
to experience more polarization than those that do not have such limits."[131]

Through the lens of alignment, then, party contribution limits stand on the
same legal and political footing as PAC contribution limits. They too can't be
defended against First Amendment claims on the ground that they improve
representational alignment—not even before future courts inclined to take
this defense seriously. The simple fact is that party contribution limits make
the problem of misalignment worse, not better. For the same reason, nonjudicial actors seeking to promote alignment should consider relaxing or repealing
(not tightening or enacting) these restrictions. As elaborated in the next section,
nonjudicial actors could even think about channeling *public* funds to parties, to
supply them with more resources that they would then direct to more moderate,
better aligned candidates.

Other Regulations

Campaign finance reformers sometimes talk about ceilings and floors, leveling
down money in politics and leveling it up.[132] In this vocabulary, the policies
I covered above are obviously ceilings: caps on the contributions or expenditures
of individuals, PACs, or parties. On the other hand, the archetype of a campaign
finance floor is public financing: the provision of public funds to candidates (either directly or via individuals or parties). Interestingly, there's no single answer
to the question of how public financing influences alignment. Public financing
can be misaligning when it's conditioned on the activities of ideologically
polarized individual donors. But it can also be aligning when it makes the individual donor pool more representative of the electorate or when it uses parties,
not individuals, as intermediaries. In addition to public financing, I address two
other campaign finance regulations here: requirements that contributions and/
or expenditures be disclosed and rules about the lobbying of elected officials.

---

[130] *See id.* at 99.

[131] *Id.* at 103. *But see* Michael J. Malbin & Charles R. Hunt, Party Contribution Limits and
Polarization 5–6 (June 2017) (disagreeing with La Raja and Schaffner's conclusions).

[132] *See, e.g.,* Jonathan Bernstein, *For Floors, Not Ceilings, in Campaign Finance,* WASH. POST, Apr.
13, 2012.

Some emerging evidence suggests that both these regulations lead to a closer match between enacted policy and public opinion.

The version of public financing whose aligning impact has been most thoroughly studied is the so-called "clean money" system. Under this system, in use in Arizona, Connecticut, and Maine, state legislative candidates who obtain a certain number of small contributions from individual donors then receive public grants that fund the rest of their campaigns. Publicly funded candidates must also abide by spending limits and accept no further donations (from individuals, PACs, or parties).[133] Despite its popularity with reformers, clean money turns out to be misaligning for two reasons. It makes public funding contingent on candidates' ability to raise money from ideologically extreme individual donors. And it eliminates most contributions from ideologically moderate funding sources, namely, PACs and parties. Andrew Hall finds that the ideological divergence between Democrats and Republicans representing highly competitive state legislative districts jumps after clean money is instituted. In "treated" states that adopt clean money, that divergence grows from 1.2 to 1.5 units on a 4-unit scale, while in "control" states that don't change to public financing, the ideological gap between Democratic and Republican state legislators stays roughly constant.[134] More recently, Mitchell Kilborn and Arjun Vishwanath confirm this finding and extend it to publicly financed (as opposed to all) candidates in clean money states. Both candidates who accept public funds from the outset and candidates who later switch from private to public financing are more ideologically polarized than privately financed candidates.[135]

However, the misaligning effect of clean money might be fixable. Suppose that, to qualify for public funds, candidates had to obtain at least some number of small donations from registered Democrats, registered Republicans, and registered independents. Then candidates couldn't become eligible for public financing solely by appealing to ideologically extreme individuals from their own party. Instead, candidates would have to convince independents and even supporters of the opposing party to give to them—which would likely induce candidates to take more moderate, better aligned stances. Or say that after public funds were disbursed to candidates, PAC and party contributions could continue while individual contributions couldn't. Then aligning funding sources would remain available after the triggering of public financing, but misaligning

---

[133] *See, e.g.,* Hall, *supra* 92, at 4–5.

[134] *See id.* at 18–19.

[135] *See* Mitchell Kilborn & Arjun Vishwanath, *Public Money Talks Too: How Public Campaign Financing Degrades Representation*, 66 AM. J. POL. SCI. 730, 738–40 (2022); *see also* Seth E. Masket & Michael G. Miller, *Does Public Election Funding Create More Extreme Legislators? Evidence from Arizona and Maine*, 15 ST. POL. & POL'Y Q. 1, 9–12 (2014) (finding that clean money polarizes Republican state legislators in Arizona); *cf.* Stephanopoulos et al., *supra* note 109, at 812 (finding that public financing generally worsens district-level representational alignment).

sources wouldn't, again probably resulting in representation more consistent with constituent opinion. To be sure, these are just hypotheses about policies that have never been tried. But they're reasonable hypotheses based on the same dynamics that explain why other campaign finance regulations are aligning or misaligning. Jurisdictions drawn by the allure of clean money—replacing most private campaign funds, and the problems they cause, with public resources—should certainly consider these tweaks.

Next, two forms of public financing turbocharge individual donations to candidates with public dollars. Multiple-match programs, used by cities including New York City, San Francisco, and Washington, D.C., disburse public funds to candidates in specified multiples of individual contributions. In New York City, for instance, individual donations up to $175 to city council candidates are matched eight-to-one by the government. As under clean money, publicly funded candidates in multiple-match systems must comply with spending limits, but they're not barred from receiving contributions from PACs or parties.[136] The other policy in this category is Seattle's unique Democracy Vouchers program. Each registered voter in the city is sent four $25 vouchers prior to each municipal election. The recipient can then distribute this publicly supplied money as she sees fit to candidates for city council, city attorney, and mayor.[137]

Unfortunately, scholars haven't yet studied the representational implications of multiple-match or vouchers. But these types of public financing do clearly change the pool of individual donors, making it more reflective of the electorate as a whole. With respect to multiple-match, Elizabeth Genn and her coauthors compare donors to city council candidates in New York City (the jurisdiction with the longest experience with this policy) to donors to state house candidates running in the same areas (who are ineligible for public financing). Donors to city council candidates are poorer (with almost the same poverty rate as the city overall), more racially diverse (with almost the same non-White proportion), and less educated (with almost the same share not completing high school). Multiple-match thus attracts a more representative group of donors than conventional private financing.[138] Jennifer Heerwig and Brian McCabe conduct a similar analysis for Seattle's vouchers, comparing voucher users to cash donors, actual voters, and registered voters. Remarkably, by the third election with

---

[136] See, e.g., Michael J. Malbin et al., Small Donors, Big Democracy: New York City's Matching Funds as a Model for the Nation and States, 11 ELECTION L.J. 3, 5–7 (2012); Matching Funds Program, NEW YORK CITY CAMPAIGN FINANCE BD., https://www.nyccfb.info/program (last visited Feb. 1, 2024).

[137] See, e.g., Democracy Voucher Program, SEATTLE, https://www.seattle.gov/democracyvoucher (last visited Feb. 1, 2024).

[138] See ELISABETH GENN ET AL., DONOR DIVERSITY THROUGH PUBLIC MATCHING FUNDS 14 (2012); see also CATHERINE HINCKLEY KELLEY ET AL., DEMOCRATIZING THE DISTRICT: D.C's FAIR ELECTIONS PROGRAM IN 2020, at 16–17 (2021) (finding that donors became more geographically, racially, and socioeconomically diverse after Washington, D.C. adopted multiple-match); OPEN

vouchers, poor city residents were "slightly *over*represented among voucher users compared to registered voters," residents over sixty were "roughly equal as a share of both voucher users and registered voters," and "people of color were as likely to vote as to use a voucher."[139] That is, voucher users were nearly identical demographically and socioeconomically to the broader electorate.

To reiterate, these studies are merely suggestive because they don't analyze the *ideologies* of individual donors or officeholders in multiple-match or voucher systems. So we can't say for sure that donors become less ideologically extreme when these policies are enacted or that politicians take positions closer to those of their constituents. While still unproven, though, these effects are at least plausible. Recall the causal sequence through which individual donors induce representational misalignment under regular private financing: (1) Individual donors are demographically and socioeconomically distinct from the electorate as a whole; (2) they're also more ideologically extreme than most voters; (3) they make contributions to candidates on the basis of ideological proximity; (4) politicians therefore either shift their stances toward the ideological fringes to raise more money (adaptation) or benefit financially from holding more extreme views in the first place (selection). Multiple-match and voucher systems falsify the initial premise of this sequence. Under these policies, individual donors *aren't* demographically and socioeconomically distinct from the electorate as a whole (or, at least, are much less distinct in these ways). In turn, the negation of the first premise makes the second premise less likely to hold. People's ideologies are closely related to their demographic and socioeconomic characteristics. So a donor pool with the same demographic and socioeconomic makeup as the broader electorate probably has a more centrist ideological distribution than an older, Whiter, richer donor pool. And if the second premise ceases to apply, then the whole causal sequence collapses. Politicians have no financial reason to cater to the ideological extremes if individual donors in multiple-match and voucher systems are more moderate. To the contrary, politicians have the opposite incentive: to migrate toward the ideological center that is now the region where they can raise more money.

& Accountable Elections Comm'n, Report on Open and Accountable Elections: 2020 Election Cycle 17 (2021) (same for Portland, Oregon).

[139] Jennifer A. Heerwig & Brian J. McCabe, Broadening Donor Participation in Local Elections: Results from the Seattle Democracy Voucher Program in 2021, at 7–8 (2022) (emphasis added); *see also* Brian J. McCabe & Jennifer A. Heerwig, *Diversifying the Donor Pool: How Did Seattle's Democracy Vouchers Program Reshape Participation in Municipal Campaign Finance?*, 18 Election L.J. 323, 336 (2019) ("[T]he Democracy Voucher program successfully . . . shifted the donor pool in a more egalitarian direction."). *But see* Chenoa Yorgason, Campaign Finance Vouchers Do Not Reduce Donor Inequality 13, 16 (July 8, 2021) (disagreeing with Heerwig and McCabe's conclusions).

The last major type of public financing steers public funds to parties—not candidates or individuals. Around ten states currently subscribe to this approach. Typically, each taxpayer checks a box on her tax return indicating if she wants some amount of public money (ranging from $1 to $25) to go to a party (and, if so, which party). Parties can then use these public dollars without limitation in some states, or for specified purposes like conventions or voter registration drives in other states. No matter how these programs are structured, they're not particularly well-funded. In no state, that is, do parties receive enough public money to cover the campaign expenditures of all or even most of their candidates.[140] Abroad, however, the public financing of parties is more prevalent and generous. More than a hundred countries directly provide public funds to parties, often based on their votes received in, or legislative seats held after, recent elections. Under many of these systems, the resources that parties obtain from the state constitute the bulk of all campaign spending.[141]

To my knowledge, there's no work on how the public financing of parties is related to alignment. This is likely because, in America at least, these programs are relatively old, underfunded, and not the priority of most reformers. A handful of academics, though, do continue to push for this variant of public financing. Some law professors argue that publicly financed parties would efficiently distribute funds among candidates[142] and counteract a trend toward political fragmentation.[143] More relevant here, La Raja and Schaffner, the scholars who most thoroughly document the aligning impact of party money, advocate "public subsidies to political parties" because they would "dilute the negative impact of both ideological and rent-seeking donors."[144] This policy prescription seems well worth trying. Since parties are relatively centrist actors in the campaign finance ecosystem, significantly boosting their resources through ample public financing would likely exert a centripetal influence on candidates hoping to benefit from their contributions. At the same time, increasing the sway of this aligning funding source would likely reduce the pull of misaligning sources like individual donors. Of course, this is more speculation about another policy that has never been attempted in America. But again, the logic behind the proposal

---

[140] *See, e.g., Public Financing of Campaigns: Overview*, Nat'l Conf. St. Legis. (Feb. 8, 2019), https://www.ncsl.org/research/elections-and-campaigns/public-financing-of-campaigns-overv iew.aspx.

[141] *See, e.g.*, Org. Econ. Coop. & Dev., Financing Democracy: Funding of Political Parties and Election Campaigns and the Risk of Policy Capture (2016); *Public Funding of Parties*, ACE: The Electoral Knowledge Network, https://aceproject.org/epic-en/CDTable?view = country&question = PC12 (last visited Feb. 1, 2024).

[142] *See* Daniel Hays Lowenstein, *On Campaign Finance Reform: The Root of All Evil Is Deeply Rooted*, 18 Hofstra L. Rev. 301, 351–55 (1989).

[143] *See* Richard H. Pildes, *Romanticizing Democracy, Political Fragmentation, and the Decline of American Government*, 124 Yale L.J. 804, 842–45 (2014).

[144] La Raja & Schaffner, *supra* note 99, at 139.

is sound, and the experiences of many other nations demonstrate that publicly financed parties can work in practice.

The final two categories of regulations I consider here involve neither ceilings nor floors on money in politics. Disclosure requirements mandate that candidates, PACs, parties, and other political actors make public their contributions and/or expenditures. These laws may compel regulated entities to disclose aggregate giving and/or spending, to itemize certain types of contributions and/or expenditures, and to file reports with the government at certain intervals.[145] And lobbying regulations apply to efforts to influence officeholders through means other than campaign finance: quintessentially meetings at which gifts or entertainment may be provided, information may be supplied, and legislation or other policy issues may be discussed. Lobbying regulations may include narrow or broad definitions of lobbying, requirements that lobbyists register with the government, requirements that certain lobbying activities be disclosed, prohibitions on certain lobbying activities (like gifts or entertainment), and specifications of conflicts of interest.[146]

In one of the few campaign finance studies to directly examine policy (as opposed to representational) alignment, Patrick Flavin finds that states with stricter disclosure requirements enact sets of policies that are more congruent with public opinion. Moving from an especially lax to an especially stringent disclosure regime is associated with a "quite large" boost in policy alignment "[f]rom a substantive standpoint."[147] Flavin doesn't comment on the reasons for this result, but a likely explanation is that officeholders are deterred from adopting policies that reflect the ideologically extreme views of their funders when this funding is highly visible to the public. It's evidently one thing to make policy that pleases funders when this funding stays hidden—but quite another to follow funders' policy preferences over voters' when funders' giving and spending are clear for all to see. In the latter case, elected officials may fear electoral retribution from informed and unhappy voters if they embrace misaligned policies. So instead, politicians may be more willing to enact laws that disappoint their funders but correspond more closely to the will of the electorate.

With respect to lobbying, considerable evidence indicates that it can drive misalignment. Per Figure 9.5, Alex Garlick shows that, in both Congress and three state legislatures, the greater the number of ideological interest groups that lobby representatives on a given bill, the more polarized voting on that

---

[145] See, e.g., Disclosure and Reporting Requirements, NAT'L CONF. ST. LEGIS. (July 17, 2015), https://www.ncsl.org/research/elections-and-campaigns/disclosure-and-reporting-requirements.aspx.

[146] See, e.g., Lobbyist Regulation, NAT'L CONF. ST. LEGIS., https://www.ncsl.org/research/ethics/lobbyist-regulation.aspx (last visited Feb. 1, 2024).

[147] Patrick Flavin, State Campaign Finance Laws and the Equality of Political Representation, 13 ELECTION L.J. 362, 370–71 (2014).

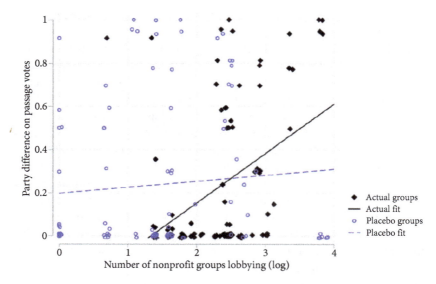

FIGURE 9.5 PARTY DIFFERENCE IN SUPPORT FOR A BILL VERSUS VOLUME OF
IDEOLOGICAL GROUPS LOBBYING ON A BILL

Figure 9.5 is reproduced with permission from Alex Garlick, *Interest Group Lobbying and Partisan Polarization in the United States: 1999-2016*, 10 POL. SCI. RSCH. & METHODS 488, 500 (2022). Copyright © 2022 by Cambridge University Press.

bill tends to be. That is, more lobbying by ideological interest groups is linked to worse representational misalignment. (In contrast, more lobbying by business or governmental groups has no effect on polarization or alignment.)[148] Additionally, Alexander Hertel-Fernandez and Theda Skocpol zero in on maybe the most lavishly funded ideological interest group in the country: Americans for Prosperity (AFP), the Koch brothers' main institutional vehicle for lobbying and grass-roots activism. In states where AFP had a paid director in the 2010s, the probability of new restrictions on public-sector union bargaining rights was almost 30 percentage points higher.[149] As the strength of AFP and its Koch-backed sister organizations varied across states from lowest to highest, the likelihood of a state expanding Medicaid

---

[148] *See* Alex Garlick, *Interest Group Lobbying and Partisan Polarization in the United States: 1999-2016*, 10 POL. SCI. RSCH. & METHODS 488, 495–96 (2022).

[149] *See* Theda Skocpol & Alexander Hertel-Fernandez, *The Koch Network and Republican Party Extremism*, 14 PERSPECTIVES ON POL. 681, 694 (2016).

fell by fully 70 percentage points.[150] Moreover, these AFP policy objectives were almost universally unpopular. AFP lobbying and grass-roots activism thus "pull[ed] government policy away from the preferences held by most Americans and toward those of a smaller group of business, activists, and donors."[151]

Since lobbying is often a misaligning force, lobbying regulations should improve alignment. Flavin demonstrates in another study that they do indeed. States with stricter rules about lobbying enact sets of policies that are more congruent with public opinion. This increase in policy alignment is quite large, greater than the impact (positive or negative) of any other variable in Flavin's analysis.[152] Accordingly, lobbying regulations belong in the same analytical category as disclosure requirements, publicly financed parties, multiple-match and voucher systems of public financing, and (from the last section) restrictions on individual contributions and expenditures. All these policies do (or are quite likely to) promote alignment, and so should be upheld by future courts and endorsed by policymakers for that reason. On the other hand, clean money public financing (addressed in this section) and caps on PAC and party donations (covered above) are birds of a different feather. These measures widen the gap between governmental outputs and popular preferences, and so can't be defended in legal or political fora on aligning grounds.

* * *

Campaign finance is the only area examined by this book where, I argue, partisan alignment is an inapplicable aim. This is primarily because of intense disagreement about the right hypothetical benchmark with which to compare actual election outcomes, and secondarily because of Supreme Court decisions deeming partisan alignment an illegitimate state interest in this context. The Court has also rejected several other rationales for campaign finance regulation: preventing the distortion of election outcomes, avoiding undue influence corruption, and pursuing any kind of equality. However, the promotion of representational or policy alignment is conceptually distinct from all these precluded interests. At most, some of these interests may be aligning mechanisms, not alignment itself. Turning from theory to practice, the essential fact is that,

---

[150] See Alexander Hertel-Fernandez et al., *Business Associations, Conservative Networks, and the Ongoing Republican War over Medicaid Expansion*, 41 J. HEALTH POL., POL'Y & L. 239, 254 (2016).

[151] ALEXANDER HERTEL-FERNANDEZ, STATE CAPTURE: HOW CONSERVATIVE ACTIVISTS, BIG BUSINESSES, AND WEALTHY DONORS RESHAPED THE AMERICAN STATES—AND THE NATION 254 (2019).

[152] See Patrick Flavin, *Lobbying Regulations and Political Equality in the American States*, 43 AM. POL. RSCH. 304, 316–17 (2015).

in modern American politics, some sources of campaign funding tend to worsen, while others tend to improve, representational and policy alignment. Individuals above all, as well as ideological organizations and labor unions, are usually misaligning campaign funders. On the other hand, the resources of business groups and political parties exert an aligning influence for the most part. This typology of campaign funders determines which campaign finance laws are aligning—and so could be justified on this basis in legal or political debates—and which ones aren't. Measures that restrict ideologically extreme individual funders, make the individual donor pool more representative of the entire electorate, or subsidize comparatively centrist parties, lead to better alignment. But policies that cap the contributions of relatively moderate PACs or parties, or that link public financing to the choices of polarized individual donors, are misaligning.

To this election law specialist, regulations of the electoral process are the most intuitive way to make governmental outputs more (or less) congruent with popular preferences. That's why this chapter, and the four before it, focused on different election law subfields: voting, political parties, redistricting, the Voting Rights Act, and, here, campaign finance. But there are any number of *nonelectoral* levers the government might also be able to pull to improve alignment. Policies about activities other than elections might be aligning, too, due to dynamics other than the electoral ones I've canvassed so far. The next chapter considers some of these ways in which alignment might be advanced through nonelectoral means. Legislature procedure is one promising candidate. The elimination of countermajoritarian obstacles in the legislative process unsurprisingly makes it easier for majority preferences to prevail. Media regulation is another potentially impactful tool. When media coverage makes an issue more salient, public policy in that area tends to better reflect public opinion. Labor law is one more intriguing mechanism. There's substantial evidence that when unions are stronger thanks to pro-labor policies, what the government does is more consistent with what the people want. Lastly, one of the main drivers of legislative polarization—and hence representational misalignment—appears to be growing economic inequality. Fiscal measures that would result in a more egalitarian resource distribution, then, would likely yield more congruent representation as well.

10

Nonelectoral Domains

Introduction

In his pioneering *Harvard Law Review* foreword, Daryl Levinson argues against the siloization of public law. "[P]olitical process theory and voting rights jurisprudence"—both aspects of election law—"are typically viewed as their own enterprises, disconnected from the separation of powers, federalism," and other public law domains.[1] But all these fields "might be usefully understood as different . . . tools for accomplishing the same basic task of redistributing and balancing power."[2] "[T]he electoral process" that's the subject of election law "is just one channel of political influence among many . . . and is not always the most important in predicting which interests will ultimately prevail."[3] So "[i]f the democratic ideal" for which election law strives "is to equalize political power, then the reach of the law of democracy will inevitably exceed its grasp."[4] At least, election law's reach will exceed its grasp unless it's analyzed together with—not apart from—the rest of public law.

Levinson's interest is power generally while I focus here on how the exercise of governmental power can lead to alignment (or not). With this minor caveat, Levinson's insight is entirely applicable to this book's project. Election law has some capacity to make governmental outputs more (or less) congruent with popular preferences. But election law isn't the only field with this potential. To fully grasp how legal mechanisms can further (or hinder) alignment, then, it's necessary to go beyond election law and to consider public law as a whole. Moreover, the same factors that make alignment legally and politically attractive in the election law context also give it appeal across all of public law. The constitutional text, the intent of the Constitution's drafters, Supreme Court (especially Warren Court) precedent, the democracy principle of state constitutions—all the strands of argument I surveyed in Chapter 4—are hardly limited to election law. To the contrary, they suggest that alignment is a legal and political metavalue, available as a sword or shield whether the issue is elections or anything else the government regulates.

---

[1] Daryl J. Levinson, *Foreword: Looking for Power in Public Law*, 130 HARV. L. REV. 31, 37 (2016).
[2] *Id.* at 113.
[3] *Id.* at 128.
[4] *Id.*

Aligning Election Law. Nicholas O. Stephanopoulos, Oxford University Press. © Nicholas O. Stephanopoulos 2024.
DOI: 10.1093/9780197662182.003.0010

Accordingly, in this chapter, I discuss a number of nonelectoral areas in which law or policy could be aligning. Each area I cover is the topic of at least some empirical literature finding that certain governmental interventions promote alignment. But there could well be other nonelectoral approaches, not addressed here, that are aligning as well. The scholarship on advancing alignment through means other than elections is still in its infancy, so future research could identify additional aligning options. Furthermore, I restrict my examination in this chapter to measures the *government* could take. I defer any inquiry into *private* aligning activity until Chapter 12. And as I've mentioned previously, this book deals only with subconstitutional changes to our legal and political order. Changes that would require constitutional amendment—most notably, reforming or abolishing the U.S. Senate—could be highly aligning but are beyond this project's scope.

The lawmaking process may be the most intuitive nonelectoral domain with implications for alignment. Elections, well, elect candidates to office. Once in office, these legislators and executives enact policies. It stands to reason that the procedures these elected officials use to enact policies help determine the substance of the policies that are adopted. The substance of the policies that are adopted, in turn, helps determine the extent of policy alignment with public opinion. This series of links has been documented most thoroughly with respect to the legislative process. Legislative committees whose members are approved by the whole chamber (not just a particular party) result in the passage of more moderate, better aligned bills. So do mechanisms that weaken the agenda control of the majority party, like the discharge petition in the U.S. House of Representatives that enables a vote on a bill over the objection of the House Speaker. So, too, do majoritarian rules for ending debate (in contrast to the three-fifths threshold for halting a U.S. Senate filibuster) and for overriding a veto (in contrast to the two-thirds threshold in our federal system).

The lawmaking process conceptually follows elections. In contrast, voter knowledge conceptually precedes them. Voters can be more or less informed about candidates' positions, incumbents' records, and the details of political issues. More informed voters are more capable of voting for more ideologically proximate candidates and rewarding (or punishing) incumbents for their aligned (or misaligned) records. Unfortunately, voter knowledge is a function of many variables that are beyond the government's easy reach: education, political interest, social interaction, and the like. At least one major driver of voter knowledge, however, can be influenced by the state: the intensity and accuracy of media coverage. Numerous studies find that when the media covers an issue more vigorously, making that issue more salient for voters, policy congruence with respect to that issue is higher. The question then becomes how to foster more and better media coverage. The First Amendment, with its commitment to freedom of the press, is one answer, especially in comparative perspective. Subsidies enabling more journalists to cover political issues (especially at the state and local levels) could also be effective. The Federal Communications Commission's (FCC's) fairness doctrine, which formerly required broadcasters to present issues of public importance in a balanced manner, could be revived as well.

Stick with the three-stage model in which alignment is affected by (1) voter knowledge, (2) elections, and (3) the lawmaking process. Labor unions—the subject of labor law—are active at each of these stages. Union members are better informed about political issues than are nonmembers. Union members also turn out to vote at higher rates than do nonmembers. And unions try to sway lawmakers directly (not just electorally) through lobbying and grass-roots activism. Thanks to these efforts—which, critically, are on behalf of large masses of low- and middle-income workers—greater union density leads to better population-level alignment and less group-specific misalignment in favor of the rich. By the same token, policies that contribute to greater union density are aligning too. Of these, the most important is the agency shop, under which union members *and* nonmembers in a unionized workplace pay fees to cover the costs of collective bargaining.

Of course, unions are far from the only politically active organizations. To the extent groups advancing the interests of corporations and the wealthy influence public policy (without moving public opinion), policy misalignment is the obvious result. Interestingly, though, economic inequality isn't just a *product* of misalignment; it's also a *cause*. Over the last century, trends in economic inequality have almost perfectly foreshadowed trends in legislative polarization. When Americans' incomes have been more equal (as in the middle of the twentieth century), Congress has been less polarized. When income inequality has been higher (as in the Gilded Age and today), Congress has been more sharply divided by party and ideology. To reiterate a point I've made before, legislative polarization is synonymous with representational misalignment as long as the distribution of public opinion is roughly normal. This equivalence means that measures that would reduce economic inequality—like higher taxes and greater redistribution—would also be aligning. By reducing economic inequality, these steps would dampen legislative polarization, which in turn would bolster representational alignment.

Applicability

My rationale for discussing nonelectoral domains in this chapter is the same as Levinson's for addressing all of public law. Nonelectoral law and policy can affect alignment. In some cases, they can have *more* of an impact on alignment than election law and policy. Examining only how governmental regulations of elections drive alignment, then, would entail ignoring an array of comparably effective governmental interventions in other areas. Doing so would highlight some aligning (and misaligning) channels while leaving others obscured. Put differently, the stark misalignment that characterizes modern American politics has many causes: some related to elections, others to nonelectoral governmental activity, and still others to nongovernmental activity. If only electoral tools are available, then there's only so much progress we can make toward a more aligned political order. Adding nonelectoral, but still governmental, actions to our toolkit makes more improvement possible. And as I explain in Chapter 12, if nongovernmental actions are included in our menu of options, too, even more headway can be made.

The functional case for considering nonelectoral domains therefore seems ironclad. But what about the legal case? Do standard modes of legal argument support the recognition of alignment as a value across all of public law? I believe so. Recall that, in Chapter 4, I cited four types of evidence indicating that alignment is a cognizable legal principle in the election law context: the federal constitutional text, the intent of the federal Constitution's drafters, the state constitutional commitment to democracy, and Supreme Court precedent. Much of this material is just as compelling beyond as within the sphere of election law. Consider federal constitutional provisions like the Preamble, the Guarantee Clause, the Privileges or Immunities Clause, and the Equal Protection Clause. None of these provisions is limited (or even overtly pertains) to elections. Or take the many statements by James Madison, John Bingham, and other constitutional architects that "public opinion must be obeyed by the government"[5] and that a popular majority has the "absolute, unquestioned, unchallenged right . . . to control [the] entire political power."[6] Again, these paeans to alignment are entirely nonelectoral and so fully applicable outside the election law context. Likewise, according to Jessica Bulman-Pozen and Miriam Seifter, the democracy principle of state constitutional law comprises popular sovereignty, majority rule, and political equality.[7] These tenets can guide not just the organization of elections but also the operation of the whole political system.[8]

---

[5] 14 THE PAPERS OF JAMES MADISON 170 (Robert A. Rutland et al. eds., 1983).

[6] CONG. GLOBE, 39TH CONG., 2D SESS. 450 (1867).

[7] *See* Jessica Bulman-Pozen & Miriam Seifter, *The Democracy Principle in State Constitutions*, 119 MICH. L. REV. 859, 864 (2021).

[8] For an example of another scholar identifying democracy as an overarching constitutional value, see Jack M. Balkin, *Republicanism and the Constitution of Opportunity*, 94 TEX. L. REV. 1427, 1428 (2016) (labeling "republicanism, or representative democracy" as one of "a small number of underlying principles that are not directly stated but that we infer from constitutional text and structure").

As for Supreme Court precedent, it's true that, in Chapter 4, I only covered cases involving electoral issues like voting, political parties, redistricting, and campaign finance. These quintessential election law cases might not be thought relevant to the recognition of alignment in nonelectoral domains. However, as Aziz Huq observes, "there has been an explosion of 'democracy talk' by the Justices" in recent years, "especially in cases concerning the structure and functioning of the federal government."[9] In disputes about federalism, the separation of powers, and administrative law, the Court has repeatedly invoked democratic values to justify its rulings. These decisions haven't always referred to alignment itself, but they've lauded, and reasoned on the basis of, related concepts. These decisions have thus laid a precedential foundation for deploying alignment (or something similar to it) across all of public law.

In the federalism context, for example, concern about state-level policy misalignment underpins the anti-commandeering doctrine, which forbids the federal government from ordering states to take particular actions. As the Court wrote in the 1992 case of *New York v. United States*, "[w]here Congress encourages state regulation rather than compelling it, state governments remain responsive to the local electorate's preferences."[10] In the absence of federal commandeering, that is, state-level policy alignment can be expected to arise. When the federal government does issue commands to states, on the other hand, "elected state officials cannot regulate in accordance with the views of the local electorate."[11] Instead, state governments must obey the federal directives even when they're at odds with the wishes of state voters. It was precisely to avoid this clash between federally mandated state policy and state public opinion that the Court crafted the anti-commandeering doctrine in *New York* and other cases.[12]

Analogously, one reason why the Court is skeptical of limits on the President's removal power is the Court's worry that (essentially) unremovable agency officials will adopt policies that flout voters' preferences. According to the Court, in the 2020 case of *Seila Law LLC v. CFPB*, when the President can remove

---

[9] Aziz Z. Huq, *The Counterdemocratic Difficulty*, 117 Nw. U. L. Rev. 1099, 1102 n.10 (2023). In earlier periods, the promotion of alignment was also a rationale cited by the Court for protecting political speech. *See, e.g.*, Stromberg v. California, 283 U.S. 359, 369 (1931) ("The maintenance of the opportunity for free political discussion [serves] the end that government may be responsive to the will of the people . . . ."). Additionally, the first prong of *Carolene Products*'s footnote four can be read as advocating heightened judicial scrutiny for misaligning "legislation which restricts those political processes which can ordinarily be expected to bring about" alignment. United States v. Carolene Prods. Co., 304 U.S. 144, 152 n.4 (1938).

[10] 505 U.S. 144, 168 (1992).

[11] *Id.* at 169.

[12] *See, e.g.*, Printz v. United States, 521 U.S. 898, 930 (1997) (arguing that, when states are commandeered, "they are . . . put in the position of taking the blame for [the federally mandated policy's] burdensomeness and for its defects"); FERC v. Mississippi, 456 U.S. 742, 787 (1982) (O'Connor, J., concurring in the judgment in part and dissenting in part) (arguing that, thanks to commandeering, state "representatives are no longer responsive to local needs").

high-ranking officials at will, their "authority remains subject to the ongoing supervision and control of the elected President."[13] The President, in turn, remains
"directly accountable to the people through regular elections," in which the
President can be punished (or rewarded) for unpopular (or popular) decisions
made by the President's removable subordinates.[14] In contrast, "a single individual accountable to no one," "neither elected by the people nor meaningfully
controlled (through the threat of removal) by someone who is," may be more
likely to promulgate policies that are noncongruent with voters' views.[15] With
"no boss or electorate looking over her shoulder," an official effectively free from
removal "may dictate and enforce policy for a vital segment of the economy affecting millions of Americans."[16]

This fear of the executive branch defying public opinion motivates the
nondelegation doctrine and the major questions doctrine, too, both of which aim
to force Congress (rather than agencies) to make policy choices. Legislation that
manages to win the approval of both chambers of Congress and the President
is apt to "embody a wide social consensus," Justice Gorsuch wrote in the 2022
case of *West Virginia v. EPA*.[17] Such legislation fulfills "our Republic's promise
that the people ... should have a meaningful say in the laws that govern them."[18]
However, when an agency resolves important issues without clear congressional guidance, its actions "often bear the support only of the party currently in
power."[19] Even worse, "[p]owerful special interests ... are sometimes uniquely
able to influence the agendas of administrative agencies."[20] When these forces
drive agency activity, policy misalignment "flourish[es]" while the wishes of the
public are "left to ever-shifting winds."[21]

I don't necessarily agree with the Court's logic in these cases. In fact, I've previously argued that the democratic benefits that accrue from barring federal

---

[13]   140 S. Ct. 2183, 2203 (2020).
[14]   *Id.*
[15]   *Id.*
[16]   *Id.* at 2204; *see also, e.g.,* Free Enter. Fund v. Pub. Co. Account. Oversight Bd., 561 U.S. 477, 497
(2010) (arguing that, when the President's removal power is limited, "the public cannot determine
on whom the blame or the punishment of a pernicious measure ... ought really to fall" (internal quotation marks omitted)); Morrison v. Olson, 487 U.S. 654, 711 (1988) (Scalia, J., dissenting) (arguing
that limits on the President's removal power erode "the political check that the people will replace
those in the political branches ... who are guilty of abuse").
[17]   142 S. Ct. 2587, 2618 (2022) (Gorsuch, J., concurring).
[18]   *Id.* at 2624.
[19]   *Id.* at 2618.
[20]   *Id.* (internal quotation marks omitted).
[21]   *Id.; see also, e.g.,* Gundy v. United States, 139 S. Ct. 2116, 2134 (2019) (Gorsuch, J., dissenting)
(arguing that, when the nondelegation doctrine is violated, "legislation ... risk[s] becoming nothing
more than the will of the current President," and so no longer "the product of widespread social consensus"); Indus. Union Dep't v. Am. Petrol. Inst., 448 U.S. 607, 685 (1980) (Rehnquist, J., concurring
in the judgment) (arguing that the nondelegation doctrine "ensures ... that important choices of
social policy are made by Congress, the branch of our Government most responsive to the popular
will").

commandeering, granting the President an unrestricted removal power, and enforcing the non-delegation and major questions doctrines are trivial.[22] But the issue here isn't whether the Court is empirically *correct* in its assertions about how federalism, the separation of powers, and administrative law can promote democratic values. The point, rather, is that the Court commonly *makes* these assertions. That is, the Court commonly alludes to, and relies on, concepts closely linked to alignment in its rulings in nonelectoral domains. Accordingly, to the extent precedent supports the recognition of alignment in the election law context, it does so as well across the rest of public law. If anything, the relevant nonelectoral case law might be *more* compelling, at this historical juncture, because it's mostly the handiwork of the modern (not the Warren) Court.

There's no legal bar, then, to considering how nonelectoral law and policy can affect alignment. But a practical problem does loom large. The literature on the aligning implications of nonelectoral law and policy is quite thin. It's much less developed than, say, the voluminous work establishing the misaligning impact of partisan gerrymandering or the benefits of certain campaign finance regulations for representational alignment. In this chapter, I therefore cite studies that don't directly analyze alignment, as long as their methods make possible reasonable inferences about alignment. I also have less confidence than I'd like that I've identified the nonelectoral domains that most significantly influence alignment. In the absence of much relevant scholarship, it remains possible that other legal and policy options are highly aligning (or misaligning), but these effects have not yet been empirically demonstrated.

One more prefatory note: Several aspects of the federal Constitution are likely drivers of misalignment. Because small states tend to be conservative, the U.S. Senate, which represents all states equally, skews policy in a right-wing direction.[23] Because the U.S. House is composed of delegations from all the states, the chamber can't be elected using proportional representation on a nationwide basis, meaning that the aligning advantages of that system can't be realized.[24] As is well-known, the Electoral College periodically produces misfires—instances of stark misalignment—between the winner of the nationwide popular vote and the person who actually becomes President.[25] Even the Constitution's commitments to federalism (as opposed to a unitary federal government) and the separation of powers (as opposed to the fusion of legislative and executive powers in a parliament) have been associated with misalignment by comparative

[22] *See generally* Nicholas O. Stephanopoulos, *Accountability Claims in Constitutional Law*, 112 Nw. U. L. Rev. 989 (2018).
[23] *See, e.g.,* Richard Johnson & Lisa L. Miller, *The Conservative Policy Bias of U.S. Senate Malapportionment*, 23 PS: Pol. Sci. & Pol. 10, 12–15 (2023).
[24] *See, e.g.,* Bernard Tamas, *American Disproportionality: A Historical Analysis of Partisan Bias in Elections to the U.S. House of Representatives*, 18 Election L.J. 47, 57–59 (2019).
[25] *See, e.g.,* Robert M. Alexander, Representation and the Electoral College 94 (2019).

studies.[26] However, I say no more about these potentially misaligning features of our constitutional order for the simple reason that they would require constitutional amendments to be changed. Constitutional amendments of any kind are implausible under contemporary political conditions—and amendments that would revise the basic structure of our government are essentially unimaginable. So instead, I limit myself to laws and policies that could be enacted without a constitutional revolution. Fortunately, this set of subconstitutional (and nonelectoral) measures that could improve alignment is far from empty.

Lawmaking Process

The political process can be roughly but usefully divided into three stages: a pre-electoral period in which voters acquire information (or not) about issues, candidates, and parties; elections themselves, the subject of the rest of this book; and a post-electoral period in which elected officials enact laws and otherwise make policy. It should be obvious that the configuration of this post-electoral lawmaking process can have major effects on alignment. It should also be obvious that the lawmaking process has many dimensions: its level of professionalism, the existence of term limits for its participants, the particular hurdles a bill must surmount to become law, the unitary or plural nature of the executive branch, and the availability of direct democracy. There are other facets of the lawmaking process, too, but the ones I just named have been empirically tied to alignment, and so are a suitable focus for this discussion.

Beginning with legislative professionalism, state legislatures vary widely in the salaries, staff, and other facilities they provide to legislators. Legislators in more professional state legislatures might be expected to have a greater capacity to discern public opinion (thanks to their more abundant resources) as well as a stronger incentive to abide by it (to keep their more desirable positions). These legislators could also benefit from more assistance in drafting, and more time to pass, legislation that reflects popular preferences. And in fact, that's exactly what the evidence shows. "[M]embers of professionalized legislatures have higher awareness of their constituency's preferences than members from citizen legislatures."[27] These legislators make fewer errors in their "perception of their districts' preferences on immigration, guns, gay rights, reproductive rights,

---

[26] *See, e.g.,* Kathrin Thomas, Conditions of Positional Policy Congruence 19 (June 28–30, 2012) (federalism); Christopher Wlezien & Stuart N. Soroka, *Political Institutions and the Opinion-Policy Link*, 35 W. Eur. Pol. 1407, 1419–20 (2012) (federalism); Christopher Wlezien & Stuart N. Soroka, Public Opinion and Public Policy 13 (Dec. 22, 2021) (separation of powers).

[27] Zoe Nemerever & Daniel Butler, *The Source of the Legislative Professionalism Advantage: Attracting More Knowledgeable Candidates*, 20 St. Pol. & Pol'y Q. 416, 418 (2020).

welfare, and universal healthcare."[28] In part because of this better grasp of constituency opinion, more professional legislatures enact more aligned policies. "[L]egislative professionalization has a strong, robust, and positive effect on [policy] congruence," making it significantly more likely that state public policy matches the majority of state public opinion.[29]

Next, term limits might be thought to lead to worse alignment. Elected officials barred from running for reelection could be less motivated to learn, or heed, the preferences of constituents whose approval they no longer need. Since term limits result in more turnover of elected officials, parties could also be more active in candidate recruitment. In finding candidates to contest offices whose current holders can't run again, parties might prioritize partisan loyalty over other traits. Again, these suppositions are confirmed by the available evidence. With respect to state executive branch officials, one study finds that term limits attenuate the connection between public opinion and public policy. "[W]ithout a strong electoral incentive, term-limited elected administrators do not consistently promote citizens' interests . . . ."[30] Similarly, with respect to state legislators, another study concludes that term limits exacerbate legislative polarization and hence representational misalignment. "[T]erm limits increase party polarization by reducing legislators' electoral incentives and diminishing the value of elective office, in turn increasing the role of parties in recruiting and supporting legislative candidates."[31]

Legislative professionalism and term limits are undeniably important, but they're somewhat removed from what I consider to be the core of the lawmaking process: the gauntlet a bill must run to become law. This gauntlet has four phases

---

[28] *Id.*

[29] Jeffrey R. Lax & Justin H. Phillips, *The Democratic Deficit in the States*, 56 AM. J. POL. SCI. 148, 165 (2012); *see also* Scott J. LaCombe, *Measuring Institutional Design in U.S. States*, 102 SOC. SCI. Q. 1511, 1526 (2021) (finding that a composite variable that includes legislative professionalism "has a positive and significant relationship with policy congruence"); Cherie Maestas, *Professional Legislatures and Ambitious Politicians: Policy Responsiveness of State Institutions*, 25 LEGIS. STUD. Q. 663, 675 (2000) ("[L]egislatures that are more professionalized do, in fact, produce policy that is more congruent with statewide public opinion."); Susan M. Miller, *Administering Representation: The Role of Elected Administrators in Translating Citizens' Preferences into Public Policy*, 23 J. PUB. ADMIN. RSCH. & THEORY 865, 886 (2013) (confirming Lax and Phillips's results).

[30] Miller, *supra* note 29, at 881.

[31] Michael P. Olson & Jon C. Rogowski, *Legislative Term Limits and Polarization*, 82 J. POL. 572, 572 (2020); *see also* Andrew C.W. Myers, How Declining Electoral Incentives Drive Ideological Polarization: Evidence from State Legislative Term Limits 8 (Sept. 15, 2022) (confirming Olson and Rogowski's results and extending them to state legislative candidates). Interestingly, Lax and Phillips find that term limits *improve* the congruence of state public policy with state public opinion. *See* Lax & Phillips, *supra* note 29, at 162. However, as John Matsusaka observes, this is probably because "having the [voter] initiative process is almost a necessary and sufficient condition for having term limits, and most states adopted term limits through the initiative process." John G. Matsusaka, *Popular Control of Public Policy: A Quantitative Approach*, 5 Q.J. POL. SCI. 133, 151 (2010). Accordingly, "the term limits coefficient is likely to be a strong proxy for the initiative process," not an independent driver of state policy alignment. *Id.*

in most American jurisdictions. First, a bill must make it from a legislative committee to the chamber floor. Second, on the chamber floor, the bill must receive a vote. Third, the bill must exceed the necessary threshold of support to win this vote. And fourth, the bill must also secure the approval of the other chamber and the executive. At each of these phases, the relevant rules can be structured in different ways, more or less conducive to the achievement of policy alignment. The central hypothesis the literature has tested is that rules that empower the majority *party* are misaligning because they enable that party to pull policy outcomes in the preferred direction of most of its members. In contrast, rules that empower the majority of the *entire chamber* are aligning because they increase the influence of the chamber median, which is likely to be closer to the center of public opinion than either party median.

Regrettably, this literature has tested this hypothesis using a proxy for policy alignment instead of the concept itself. This proxy is the majority roll rate: the proportion of all votes in a legislative chamber that succeed despite the opposition of a majority of the members of the majority party. Majority rolls are presumed to be cases of better policy alignment than votes in which the majority party gets its way because of the usual way in which majority rolls take place: moderate members of the majority party defecting and joining a mostly united minority party to pass legislation over the objections of more extreme members of the majority party. As Molly Jackman observes, "[m]ajority rolls occur when the [majority] party is divided, typically with moderate members— including the median legislator in the chamber—supporting the bill and more extreme members opposing it."[32] Majority rolls thus likely "limit the extent to which the growing polarization of party leaders affects the extremity of legislative outcomes, as long as the median legislator's preferences are relatively moderate."[33]

Returning to the four phases of the legislative process, several kinds of committee rules advantage the majority party in state legislatures: granting the majority party the right to appoint committee members,[34] not requiring chamber-wide votes to confirm the majority party's committee appointments, allowing committees not to hear, or not to report to the chamber floor, bills referred to them, and not permitting a discharge procedure through which bills

---

[32] Molly C. Jackman, *Parties, Median Legislators, and Agenda Setting: How Legislative Institutions Matter*, 76 J. POL. 259, 260 (2014).

[33] *Id.* at 271; *see also, e.g.,* Michael Kistner & Boris Shor, Agenda Control in the States: Parties, Interests Groups, and Majority Rolls 23 (Apr. 8, 2022) ("Much of this legislation—which is ultimately passed via a coalition of legislators from both parties [in majority rolls]—is likely centrist in ideological terms."). Note, however, that better alignment via more majority rolls could come at the cost of greater legislative disorder due to diminished agenda control by the majority party.

[34] Committee appointments by seniority are the infrequent alternative to majority party committee appointments. *See* Sarah F. Anzia & Molly C. Jackman, *Legislative Organization and the Second Face of Power: Evidence from U.S. State Legislatures,* 75 J. POL. 210, 215 (2013).

can advance to the floor despite their lack of committee approval.[35] In both a solo article and a piece coauthored with Sarah Anzia, Jackman finds that all these majority-party-advantaging committee rules lower the majority roll rate and so probably worsen policy misalignment. Figure 10.1, reproduced from Jackman's solo article, indicates the impact of a floor vote on committee appointments as well as a discharge procedure. Not requiring a floor vote on committee appointments reduces the majority roll rate by about 5 percentage points, while not permitting a discharge procedure cuts that rate by roughly 3 percentage points.[36]

Proceeding (like a fortunate bill) from committee to the chamber floor, the majority party in state legislatures often, but not always, has the power to decide whether, and in which order, votes are held. This power can be wielded by either the majority leader or a majority-party-controlled calendaring or rules committee. Where the majority party lacks the power to set the agenda, the order of votes is determined by either a fixed formula or a seniority-based committee. Even where the majority party does possess the agenda-setting power, that authority can be undercut if the full chamber can oust the bill scheduler or force a vote over the bill scheduler's opposition. Again, Jackman alone, and Anzia and Jackman together, show that most of the floor rules that benefit the majority party lower the majority roll rate. As Figure 10.1 illustrates, this likely misaligning effect holds for not allowing a floor vote on the bill scheduler (though this impact fails to rise to statistical significance in a multivariate analysis) and for not permitting the full chamber to force a vote.[37] Per Anzia and Jackman's joint work, this likely misaligning effect applies as well to conferring the agenda-setting power to the majority leader or a majority-party-controlled committee.[38]

Receiving a vote is one thing; winning it is another. The most notable obstacle to winning a vote is a supermajority requirement like the three-fifths threshold for stopping a U.S. Senate filibuster. Because few state legislatures have

[35] In the U.S. House of Representatives, a discharge procedure exists but is used very rarely. In 2002, it was deployed to pass the Bipartisan Campaign Reform Act—a package of campaign finance measures that was both popular itself and aligning in its impact on subsequent legislation. *See* Dan Nowicki, *How A Little-Used Procedural Maneuver Led to John McCain's Greatest Legislative Triumph*, ARIZONA REPUBLIC, May 9, 2018.

[36] *See* Jackman, *supra* note 32, at 265; *see also* Anzia & Jackman, *supra* note 34, at 218–19 (finding that the majority roll rate is reduced by committees' right not to schedule hearings, their right not to report bills to the chamber floor, and the appointment of their members without a floor vote); *cf.* Robert J. McGrath & Josh M. Ryan, *Party Effects in State Legislative Committees*, 44 LEGIS. STUD. Q. 553, 569–71 (2019) (finding that majority parties with appointment power over committees systematically stack committees in their favor in partisan and ideological terms).

[37] *See* Jackman, *supra* note 32, at 267.

[38] *See* Anzia & Jackman, *supra* note 34 , at 221; *see also* Jesse M. Crosson, *Stalemate in the States: Agenda Control Rules and Policy Output in American Legislatures*, 44 LEGIS. STUD. Q. 3, 28 (2019) ("[W]hen legislative parties are empowered to set a chamber's voting calendar and thereby exercise negative agenda control, significantly less policy change occurs.").

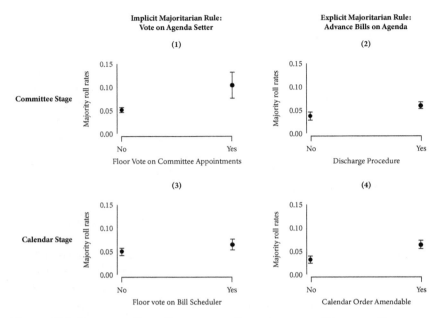

FIGURE 10.1 IMPACT OF STATE LEGISLATIVE COMMITTEE AND CALENDAR RULES ON MAJORITY ROLL RATE

Figure 10.1 is reproduced with permission from Molly C. Jackman, *Parties, Median Legislators, and Agenda Setting: How Legislative Institutions Matter*, 76 J. POL. 259, 265 (2014). Copyright © 2014 by University of Chicago Press.

supermajority requirements, there are no studies examining their impact on the majority roll rate (let alone policy alignment). There are also no such studies of the Senate because it's a single chamber as to which it's difficult to establish causation. However, scholars have identified all bills that passed the U.S. House, that received majority but not supermajority support in the Senate, and that presumably would have been signed into law by the President.[39] Many of these bills—civil rights provisions in the first half of the twentieth century, campaign finance and lobbying disclosure proposals in the early 1990s, election, immigration, and labor reforms in recent years—were quite popular with the public, meaning that the Senate filibuster caused policy misalignment in these cases.[40] On the

---

[39] *See* SARAH A. BINDER & STEVEN S. SMITH, POLITICS OR PRINCIPLE? FILIBUSTERING IN THE UNITED STATES SENATE 135 (2001) (covering the period from 1789 to 1994); Alex Tausanovitch & Sam Berger, *The Impact of the Filibuster on Federal Policymaking*, CTR. AM. PROGRESS (Dec. 5, 2019), https://www.americanprogress.org/article/impact-filibuster-federal-policymaking/ (covering the period from 1993 to 2018).

[40] *See, e.g.*, BINDER & SMITH, *supra* note 39, at 154 ("Most civil rights legislation considered during the twentieth century appears to have been supported by popular majorities and yet was successfully bottled up by filibusters ....").

other hand, other bills thwarted by the Senate filibuster were opposed by most people: the permanent elimination of the estate tax, protections for corporations against liability, a national ban on abortion, and so on.[41] Accordingly, a reasonable conclusion about the Senate filibuster is that it's often, but not necessarily, misaligning, and that its consequences depend on whether the fifty-first or sixtieth senator happens to be closer to the center of public opinion.[42]

The last challenge faced by a bill that's passed by one chamber (maybe pursuant to a supermajority requirement) is securing the approval of the other chamber and the executive. Comparative studies find that having another chamber in the first place is linked to a lower likelihood of national policy being consistent with national public opinion.[43] This probability falls from about 70 percent under unicameralism to below 60 percent under bicameralism.[44] As the authors of the leading article comment, "the checks and balances present in bicameral systems might make it more difficult for governments to provide the policies that the public wants."[45] A similar dynamic explains why higher thresholds for overriding gubernatorial vetoes are tied to more policy stasis—and so more policy misalignment when the public prefers policy change. Higher override thresholds make it harder for state legislatures to enact laws over the objections of governors. Higher override thresholds therefore produce larger "gridlock intervals": ideological ranges within which no bills can become law because they're opposed by the governor and/or the pivotal legislators needed to overcome a gubernatorial veto.[46] Larger gridlock intervals aren't always misaligning, but they are when the public disfavors "conservatism and incrementalism [and] privileging the status quo."[47]

The gubernatorial veto is one aspect of the executive branch. One more is whether the executive branch is unitary or plural. The federal executive branch

---

[41] See, e.g., Polls: Hiking Estate Tax Less Popular Than Taxing Mega Wealth, Income, THE HILL (Feb. 15, 2019), https://thehill.com/hilltv/what-americas-thinking/430224-polls-increasing-inhe ritance-taxes-is-less-popular-than-taxing/ (finding only 31 percent support for eliminating the estate tax).

[42] See, e.g., BINDER & SMITH, supra note 39, at 154 (agreeing that "[t]here is no necessary correspondence between the Senate's decision rule and the fit of the Senate outcome to popular will"); see also Jonathan S. Gould et al., Democratizing the Senate from Within, 13 J. LEG. ANALYSIS 502, 517–28 (2021) (showing how the ideology of the pivotal senator varies under the status quo, under a regime with no filibuster, and if senators representing a popular majority could end debate).

[43] See Anne Rasmussen et al., The Opinion-Policy Nexus in Europe and the Role of Political Institutions, 58 EUR. J. POL. RSCH. 412, 425 (2019); Thomas, supra note 26, at 19; cf. Jim Battista et al., Policy Representation in the State Legislatures 31 (Apr. 24, 2015) (constructing a model of American state legislatures under which "eliminating Bicameralism . . . lead[s] to the largest improvement in representation").

[44] See Rasmussen et al., supra note 43, at 426.

[45] See id. at 425–26.

[46] See Robert J. McGrath et al., Gubernatorial Veto Powers and the Size of Legislative Coalitions, 40 LEGIS. STUD. Q. 571, 577 (2015).

[47] Id. at 589.

is unitary, of course, with the President alone at its head. However, states vary widely in whether, and to what extent, they elect executive branch officials other than the governor with authority over specific substantive fields. Christopher Berry and Jacob Gersen theorize that plural executives should "produce political outcomes closer to public preferences" because "they make elections more effective mechanisms for selecting and controlling officials."[48] An executive with responsibility over a single area only has to try to compile a strong record in that one domain, and can subsequently be evaluated by voters based only on that one-dimensional record. More recently, Susan Miller empirically confirms Berry and Gersen's hypothesis. Across states, the presence of a policy-specific elected official is associated with a higher likelihood of state public policy matching the majority of state public opinion (in the field administered by the official).[49] "[D]iffusing executive authority to independently elected administrators" thus leads to "enhanced policy congruence, particularly when the administrators' electoral connection is strong" in that they're not term-limited.[50]

Plural executives straddle the boundary between electoral and nonelectoral policy in that their plurality is unrelated to elections but they improve alignment because they're elected. Direct democracy is a final aligning tool that also blurs this boundary, being nonelectoral in that it enacts policy but electoral in that it does so via a popular vote. According to a review of the literature on direct democracy, "the [voter] initiative process makes [state] policy more congruent with [state] majority opinion."[51] Over a large set of issues, policy congruence is about 10 percentage points higher in states that allow voter initiatives than in states that bar them, and this differential remains significant in a multivariate analysis.[52] How come? The direct explanation is fairly intuitive. A policy that's adopted through a voter initiative must have been backed by a majority of the voters who cast a ballot on that measure. But there are potentially important indirect channels as well. One is that legislators might be motivated to enact congruent policies (or not to enact noncongruent policies) in order to avoid voter initiatives that would undo their work.[53] Another indirect route through which direct democracy is aligning, recently uncovered by political scientists, is its provision to legislators of "inimitable insight [and] policy-specific information

[48] Christopher R. Berry & Jacob E. Gersen, *The Unbundled Executive*, 75 U. CHI. L. REV. 1385, 1387, 1394 (2008).

[49] *See* Miller, *supra* note 29, at 881–87.

[50] *Id.* at 866.

[51] John G. Matsusaka, *Public Policy and the Initiative and Referendum: A Survey with Some New Evidence*, 174 PUB. CHOICE 107, 109 (2018).

[52] *See* Matsusaka, *supra* note 31, at 145, 147–52; *see also* LaCombe, *supra* note 29, at 1526 (finding that a composite variable that includes the availability of direct democracy "has a positive and significant relationship with policy congruence").

[53] *See, e.g.,* Matsusaka, *supra* note 51, at 118.

about the preferences of [legislators'] median constituent[s]."[54] After processing this information, "lawmakers [are] less likely to shirk and vote against their constituencies."[55]

In sum, the lawmaking process offers a reassuring proof of concept that, for the purpose of promoting alignment, it's worthwhile to look beyond election law to the rest of public law. Had this inquiry been restricted to election law, it would have overlooked a whole suite of aligning options: increasing legislative professionalism, eliminating term limits, requiring committees to report bills to the chamber floor, requiring votes on bills that make it to the floor, allowing bills to pass by simple majorities, allowing vetoes to be overridden by simple majorities, downsizing from two legislative chambers to one, dividing executive power among multiple elected officials, enabling direct democracy, and so on. All these possibilities are subconstitutional in that they could be adopted by state and local governments (and, in some cases, the federal government) without federal constitutional amendments. And in combination, these measures are likely at least as conducive to the achievement of alignment as the electoral reforms that were the preoccupation of the last five chapters.[56]

Media Coverage

In the rough model of politics I sketched out above, the lawmaking process unfolds after elections are over. What happens *before* elections are held is that voters acquire information about issues, candidates, and parties. Crucially, better informed voters are more able to engage in spatial voting: voting for the candidate or party whose ideological position is closer to their own.[57] Better informed voters have greater capacity to determine both their own stances and the views of candidates or parties. These determinations are the predicate for identifying

[54] Joshua Huder et al., *Shirking the Initiative? The Effects of Statewide Ballot Measures on Congressional Roll Call Behavior*, 39 Am. Pol. Rsch. 582, 601 (2011).

[55] *Id.*; *see also* Vladimir Kogan, *When Voters Pull the Trigger: Can Direct Democracy Restrain Legislative Excesses?*, 41 Legis. Stud. Q. 297, 307–15 (2016) (finding that, after a conservative overhaul of collective bargaining was soundly rejected in an Ohio referendum, the voting records of Republican members of the Ohio legislature shifted to the left).

[56] An important point is that reforms of the lawmaking process and of elections *interact* with one another. Reforms of the lawmaking process like the ones described here are likely to be most aligning when elections are structured to give rise to reasonable representational alignment. In that case, these reforms of the lawmaking process should help translate representational alignment into policy alignment.

[57] *See, e.g.*, Stephen A. Jessee, *Partisan Bias, Political Information, and Spatial Voting in the 2008 Presidential Election*, 72 J. Pol. 327, 338 (2010) (finding that "more informed voters seem to discriminate more precisely based on their policy views relative to the positions taken by candidates"). Of course, even if better informed voters are more able to engage in spatial voting, they may still choose to vote on a different basis, like partisanship.

which candidate or party is ideologically more proximate. In turn, as I explained in Chapter 2, spatial voting is an important driver of alignment. Spatial voting directly enables voters to *select* more aligned officeholders. Spatial voting also indirectly incentivizes elected officials to *adapt*, to shift their positions toward those of voters, in order to boost their odds of reelection when they next face voters' judgment.

If more voter information makes possible better spatial voting, which itself is aligning, the next issue is how to improve voter information. Unfortunately, many of the factors linked to greater voter knowledge are beyond the government's near-term reach. Scholars find that more rather than less educated, wealthier rather than poorer, male rather than female, and White rather than minority individuals tend to be more knowledgeable about politics.[58] These are demographic and socioeconomic characteristics the government is powerless to change in the short run (or at all). However, there's another determinant of voter information that's somewhat more amenable to governmental intervention: media coverage. Studies show that people who consume more traditional news media[59] and even social media[60] are more politically knowledgeable. This evidence suggests that, if the volume and quality of media coverage could be increased, better spatial voting would ensue, as would, ultimately, better alignment.

I'll turn shortly to ideas for boosting the volume and quality of media coverage. Before doing so, though, I survey the limited but promising literature that connects media coverage to alignment (or to related democratic values). First, in their groundbreaking study of policy congruence at the state level, Jeffrey Lax and Justin Phillips investigate the association between the salience of an issue— which they operationalize as the extent of newspaper coverage of that issue—and the fit between public policy and public opinion on that issue. They find that issue salience is a statistically significant driver of policy congruence. In their model, decreasing newspaper coverage of an issue from its actual to the minimum observed level reduces the likelihood of policy congruence on that issue from 48 percent to 26 percent. Conversely, increasing newspaper coverage from its true to the maximum observed level makes policy congruence 8 percentage points more likely, 56 percent versus 48 percent.[61]

---

[58] *See, e.g.*, MICHAEL X. DELLI CARPINI & SCOTT KEETER, WHAT AMERICANS KNOW ABOUT POLITICS AND WHY IT MATTERS 56–74 (1996); Ilya Somin, *Political Ignorance and the Countermajoritarian Difficulty: A New Perspective on the Central Obsession of Constitutional Theory*, 89 IOWA L. REV. 1287, 1354–63 (2004).

[59] *See, e.g.*, Claes H. de Vreese & Hajo Boomgaarden, *News, Political Knowledge and Participation: The Differential Effects of News Media Exposure on Political Knowledge and Participation*, 41 ACTA POLITICA 317 (2006).

[60] *See, e.g.*, Drina Intyaswati et al., *Social Media as an Information Source of Political Learning in Online Education*, 11 SAGE OPEN (2021).

[61] *See* Lax & Phillips, *supra* note 29, at 162–63; *see also id.* at 161 (finding that greater issue salience makes state public policy more *responsive* to public opinion); Andrew C. W. Myers, A Pressing

Second, Christopher Williams and Martijn Schoonvelde examine whether media coverage conditions the so-called thermostatic relationship between governmental outputs and popular preferences. According to the thermostatic model, the more the government does in a given area at a given point in time, the less people subsequently want it to do, and vice versa. Williams and Schoonvelde show that when media attention is nearly absent, the thermostatic model breaks down in that the amount of federal spending in an area at t1 has no effect on whether the public favors more or less spending in that area at t2. In contrast, when media coverage is more intense, the thermostatic model operates as expected in that net public opinion at t2 is negatively responsive to public policy at t1.[62] Williams and Schoonvelde therefore conclude that "[m]edia coverage" is "a necessary, but not a sufficient, condition for public responsiveness to occur."[63] In other words, "it takes three to tango"—the government, the people, and enough media attention to adequately inform the people.[64]

And third, Steven Rogers analyzes how the presence of more or fewer journalists covering state legislatures affects the electoral penalty that state legislators incur for compiling voting records at odds with their constituents' preferences. As Figure 10.2 displays, if there are only five journalists covering a state legislature (a low bar that half the states still fail to meet), a state legislator pays a small electoral price for even stark representational misalignment. Her predicted vote share decreases by only about a percentage point as her ideological distance from her mean constituent increases by up to three standard deviations from its observed value. On the other hand, if there are forty journalists covering a state legislature (as in the largest states), the electoral downside of extreme representational misalignment is significantly steeper. In that case, a state legislator's predicted vote share falls by more than 3 percentage points as she moves from her actual ideological distance from her mean constituent to a gap three standard deviations wider.[65] As Rogers puts it, "these findings suggest that voters are better

Concern? How Newspaper Coverage Affects Accountability in State Legislatures 23 (Sept. 21, 2023) (finding that greater newspaper coverage reduces state legislative polarization and thus increases representational alignment).

[62] *See* Christopher J. Williams & Martijn Schoonvelde, *It Takes Three: How Mass Media Coverage Conditions Public Responsiveness to Policy Outputs in the United States*, 99 Soc. Sci. Q. 1627, 1633–34 (2018).

[63] *Id.* at 1634.

[64] *Id.*; *see also* Fabian G. Neuner et al., *Mass Media as a Source of Public Responsiveness*, 24 Int'l J. Press/Pol. 269 (2019) (empirically confirming each of the intermediate steps through which media coverage conditions the thermostatic relationship, such as people identifying and responding to changes in media coverage).

[65] *See* Steven Rogers, *Electoral Accountability for State Legislative Roll Calls and Ideological Representation*, 111 Am. Pol. Sci. Rev. 555, 561–62 (2017).

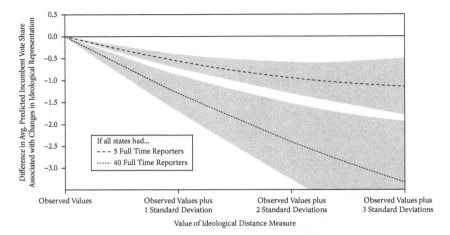

FIGURE 10.2 IMPACT OF REPRESENTATIONAL MISALIGNMENT ON STATE LEGISLATOR
VOTE SHARE UNDER DIFFERENT LEVELS OF MEDIA COVERAGE

Figure 10.2 is reproduced with permission from Steven Rogers, *Electoral Accountability for State
Legislative Roll Calls and Ideological Representation*, 111 AM. POL. SCI. REV. 555, 562 (2017).
Copyright © 2017 by Cambridge University Press.

equipped to hold their representatives accountable when the fourth estate pays
attention to state legislators."[66]

More media coverage is credibly tied, then, to better alignment itself, to
stronger thermostatic responsiveness of public opinion to public policy, and to
increased electoral accountability for misaligned officeholders. How can more
media coverage be attained? This isn't the place for detailed prescriptions about
the media sector but a few points are worth stressing. One is that America's robust commitment to a free press, reflected in constitutional rules like the media's
immunity in many cases from libel or defamation suits,[67] is itself beneficial.
A comparative study of the thermostatic model finds that, in countries with more
limits on the freedom of the press, public preferences about the volume of governmental welfare spending are unrelated to the actual scale of such spending.
However, in countries with fewer limits on press freedom, the thermostatic
model revives and people favor more (or less) welfare spending when the government spends less (or more) in that area.[68] The United States protects the
freedom of the press more zealously than most (though not as avidly as some)

[66] *Id.* at 561; *see also* Myers, *supra* note 61, at 13–14 (finding a smaller electoral penalty for extreme
state legislators subjected to less newspaper coverage).
[67] *See, e.g.,* New York Times Co. v. Sullivan, 376 U.S. 254 (1964).
[68] *See* Dan Hiaeshutter-Rice et al., *Freedom of the Press and Public Responsiveness*, 19 PERSP. POL.
479, 484–85 (2021).

other nations.[69] The implication of this study is that it should maintain, if not enhance, these safeguards.

A *free* press, of course, could still be a *poor* press, one that lacks the resources to report effectively on many issues. So another idea to increase media coverage is to subsidize the press, to supply it with the money and manpower it needs to do its job well. The United States has little experience with direct press subsidies (though it has exempted the media from certain taxes, labor laws, and inter-state commerce restrictions).[70] But direct press subsidies are common in other Western democracies, where they flow to newspapers, magazines, and television and radio broadcasters.[71] These funds often come with strings attached: creating a certain share of new content, devoting a certain share of coverage to public interest programming, restricting advertising, and so on.[72] Such conditions are also allowed in the United States as long as they don't discriminate on the basis of viewpoint.[73] Nondiscriminatory conditions paired with direct press subsidies, then, promise not just more but also better media coverage—coverage that addresses more issues and addresses them fairly and accurately. None of the studies I cited above distinguishes between more and better coverage, but it stands to reason that higher reporting volume *and* quality are more aligning than higher volume alone.

Lastly, it might not be necessary to attach nondiscriminatory conditions to the carrot of direct press subsidies. For almost forty years, the FCC simply required broadcasters to comply with the fairness doctrine, under which they had to "give adequate coverage to public issues" and "coverage [had to] be fair in that it accurately reflect[ed] the opposing views."[74] In a famous 1969 case, the Supreme Court upheld the fairness doctrine against a First Amendment challenge, in part because it helped to educate the public about the subject matter of democracy. According to the Court, the fairness doctrine didn't undermine but rather advanced "the First Amendment goal of producing an informed public capable of conducting its own affairs."[75] It's true that the fairness doctrine has been defunct

---

[69] *See, e.g., World Press Freedom Index*, REPORTERS WITHOUT BORDERS (2022), https://rsf.org/en/index (ranking the United States forty-second out of 180 countries in press freedom).

[70] *See, e.g.,* Joshua P. Darr, *Government Subsidies to Save Local News*, NIEMENLAB (Dec. 2021), https://www.niemanlab.org/2021/12/government-subsidies-to-save-local-news/. The United States also has many public broadcasters, of which the best-known are NPR and PBS. *See, e.g., Public Broadcasting Fact Sheet*, PEW RSCH. CTR. (June 29, 2021), https://www.pewresearch.org/journalism/fact-sheet/public-broadcasting/.

[71] *See, e.g.,* Paul Clemens Murschetz, Government Subsidies to News Media: Theories and Practices 4–16 (June 2022).

[72] *See, e.g., id.* at 4.

[73] *See, e.g.,* Bd. of Regents of Univ. of Wis. System v. Southworth, 529 U.S. 217, 234 (2000) (holding that a system of subsidies that "respects the principle of viewpoint neutrality . . . must be found consistent with the First Amendment").

[74] Red Lion Broad. Co. v. FCC, 395 U.S. 367, 377 (1969); *see also generally* STEVEN J. SIMMONS, THE FAIRNESS DOCTRINE AND THE MEDIA (2022).

[75] *Red Lion*, 395 U.S. at 392.

(since 1987) for almost as long as it was in operation (1949–87). It's also true that modern First Amendment doctrine focuses more on the rights of speakers and less on how speech affects the audience's capacity for self-government.[76] Nevertheless, the 1969 precedent is still good law, the congressional statute authorizing the fairness doctrine has never been repealed, and all it would take to restore the policy is an FCC action reversing its revocation. That's an easier lift than the adoption of many other potentially aligning measures.

Labor Law

The model of politics I've been using here is overly simple for several reasons, one of which is that it separates stages that interest groups with policy objectives might seek to influence simultaneously. These groups might aim to provide information to voters to prompt them to see issues, candidates, and parties through the groups' preferred prisms.[77] The groups might also try to mobilize voters when elections are held, persuading them to go to the polls and to vote consistently with the groups' preferences. And the groups might make efforts to sway policymakers through lobbying, campaign funding, and grass-roots activism. In all these ways, the groups might hope to increase the likelihood of the enactment of their favored policies.

Many groups that employ these strategies have goals that the public as a whole doesn't share. Think of groups advancing the interests of corporations, wealthy individuals, or various social or cultural activists. When these groups manage to shape public policy (without concurrently changing public opinion), policy misalignment is the necessary result. But one group that uses these techniques— organized labor—stands out for its mass membership, its focus on economic issues, and its advocacy for low- and middle-income workers. As labor scholars Kate Andrias and Benjamin Sachs write, unions are nearly unique in that "they aggregate the political resources and political power of people who, acting as individuals, are disempowered relative to wealthy individuals and institutions."[78] This characterization of unions suggests that their activities, unlike those of many other groups, should be aligning. Are they?

Before answering, let me document the impact of unions at each of the three stages of my rough model of politics. First, union membership is linked to significantly greater political knowledge, especially among less educated individuals. In a multivariate model, a union member with up to a high school diploma answers

---

[76] See generally, e.g., Citizens United v. FEC, 558 U.S. 310 (2010).
[77] See generally Nicholas O. Stephanopoulos, Quasi Campaign Finance, 70 DUKE L.J. 333 (2020).
[78] Kate Andrias & Benjamin I. Sachs, Constructing Countervailing Power: Law and Organizing in an Era of Political Inequality, 130 YALE L.J. 546, 552 (2021).

about two more questions about politics correctly than a nonunion member with this much education. This improvement reduces the knowledge gap with college graduates by approximately one-third. It's also comparable to the advantage in political knowledge that middle-income, White, and male individuals have, respectively, over low-income, non-White, and female individuals.[79] Moreover, "among the prominent correlates of political knowledge, including[] race, gender, education, [and] interest in politics," union membership is one of the few "that can be influenced by policymakers . . . via legislation that empowers or weakens organized labor."[80]

Second, unions don't just educate their members, they also induce them to vote. Controlling for other demographic and socioeconomic characteristics, union membership leads to about a 7-percentage-point increase in the likelihood of voting. This boost is even larger for low- and middle-income union members, whose lack of affluence would otherwise be a driver of lower turnout.[81] And when union members vote, they pull the lever for Democratic candidates at unexpectedly high rates. Again controlling for other demographic and socioeconomic factors, union membership raises the probability of voting for Democratic candidates by more than 10 percentage points.[82] Union membership is thus a more potent determinant of vote choice than all but a few variables (like race or religion, which, unlike union membership, policymakers are powerless to change).

And third, unions continuously seek to sway elected officials by lobbying them, funding their campaigns, and pressuring them through constituent contacts, rallies, advertising, and other channels.[83] Of course, unions are hardly alone in wielding these tools to shape the lawmaking process. What's distinctive about unions, though, is that their activities help policymakers more accurately perceive constituent opinion. The higher union membership is in a congressional district (and so, presumably, the more contact unions have with a U.S.

[79] *See* David Macdonald, *How Labor Unions Increase Political Knowledge: Evidence from the United States* 43 POL. BEHAVIOR 1, 11–12 (2021).

[80] *Id.* at 19; *see also, e.g.,* Michael Becher & Daniel Stegmueller, *Reducing Unequal Representation: The Impact of Labor Unions on Legislative Responsiveness in the U.S. Congress,* 19 PERSP. POL. 92, 105 n.6 (2020) (noting the positive "union effects on political information").

[81] *See* Jan E. Leighley & Jonathan Nagler, *Unions, Voter Turnout, and Class Bias in the U.S. Electorate, 1964-2004,* 69 J. POL. 430, 436–37 (2007); *see also, e.g.,* JAKE ROSENFELD, WHAT UNIONS NO LONGER DO 170 (2014) (finding that union membership leads to a 5-percentage-point increase in the likelihood of voting).

[82] *See, e.g.,* Richard B. Freeman, *What Do Unions Do . . . to Voting?* 30 (Nat'l Bureau of Econ. Rsch., Working Paper No. 9992, 2003); Nate Silver, *The Effects of Union Membership on Democratic Voting,* FIVETHIRTYEIGHT (Feb. 26, 2011), https://fivethirtyeight.com/features/the-effects-of-union-mem bership-on-democratic-voting/.

[83] *See, e.g.,* Becher & Stegmueller, *supra* note 80, at 94 (noting "[t]he ability of unions to increase the rate of political [outreach]—including contacting officials, attending rallies, [and] making donations").

House member's office), the lower the error rate of House staffers is in estimating constituent support for repeal of the Affordable Care Act, gun control, infrastructure spending, and so on. In contrast, as corporate contacts with House members' offices increase, and as corporate contributions to House members rise, House staffers make more and more mistakes about the content of constituent opinion.[84]

Accordingly, higher union membership affects all three stages of my simple model of politics. It results in greater political knowledge, a larger and more Democratic electorate, and policymakers who are better informed about constituent opinion. These findings make the ultimate impact of higher union membership on alignment an unsurprising denouement. Higher union membership improves representational alignment by causing officeholders to be roughly equally responsive to the policy preferences of their rich and poor constituents. Michael Becher and Daniel Stegmueller provide the most convincing demonstration of this relationship. They determine the responsiveness of U.S. House members' voting records to the views of their high- and low-income constituents as union membership varies by district from very low to very high. As Figure 10.3 shows, at most levels of union membership, House members are more responsive to the desires of the wealthy. But when district union density is about a standard deviation above its national mean, House members become as responsive to the poor as to the rich. And when district union density reaches its national apex, House members are actually *more* responsive to the poor than to the rich (though this difference isn't quite statistically significant).[85]

If higher union membership is aligning, policies that lower union membership should be misaligning. Of these policies, the most prominent in modern American politics are so-called "right-to-work" laws, which prohibit employers and unions from negotiating contracts under which employees must either be union members or contribute to the costs of union representation. The enactment of right-to-work laws leads to roughly a 4-percentage-point decline in union membership within five years[86]—a huge drop given that the national unionization rate currently hovers around 10 percent.[87] Right-to-work laws also

[84] *See* Alexander Hertel-Fernandez et al., *Legislative Staff and Representation in Congress*, 113 AM. POL. SCI. REV. 1, 12–13 (2019).

[85] *See* Becher & Stegmueller, *supra* note 80, at 99–102; *see also* Christopher Ellis, *Social Context and Economic Biases in Representation*, 75 J. POL. 773, 783 (2013) (finding that "a district's union strength is strongly associated with more equal key vote representation [in Congress]"); Patrick Flavin, *Labor Union Strength and the Equality of Political Representation*, 48 BRIT. J. POL. SCI. 1075, 1076 (2016) (finding that "states with higher levels of union membership weigh citizens' opinions more equally in the policy-making process").

[86] *See* Nicole Fortin et al., *Right-to-Work Laws, Unionization, and Wage Setting* 18 (Nat'l Bureau of Econ. Rsch., Working Paper No. 30098, 2022).

[87] *See* News Release, Bureau of Labor Statistics (Jan. 19, 2023), https://www.bls.gov/news.release/pdf/union2.pdf.

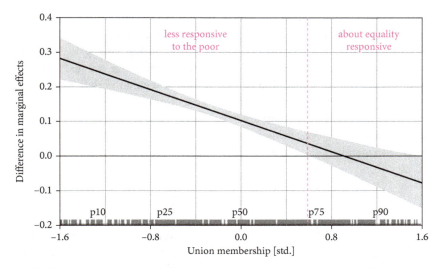

FIGURE 10.3 DIFFERENCE IN U.S. HOUSE MEMBER RESPONSIVENESS TO RICH AND POOR CONSTITUENTS BY DISTRICT UNION DENSITY

Figure 10.3 is reproduced with permission from Michael Becher & Daniel Stegmueller, *Reducing Unequal Representation: The Impact of Labor Unions on Legislative Responsiveness in the U.S. Congress*, 19 PERSP. POL. 92, 102 (2020). Copyright © 2020 by Cambridge University Press.

have implications for all three stages of my model of politics. They result in fewer workers being contacted (and potentially educated about politics) by organizers, a smaller and less Democratic electorate, and less union money funding candidates' campaigns.[88] Ultimately, right-to-work laws cause state policies to shift sharply in a conservative direction. This move to the right holds whether state policies are aggregated into ideological indices or considered individually.[89] And this rightward move in public policy occurs without a parallel rightward move in public opinion. Consequently, right-to-work laws significantly worsen policy alignment in states where they're adopted.

The upshot is that unions shouldn't be seen as merely economic entities whose effects are limited to the terms and conditions they negotiate for their members. Unions are also important political actors that—when empowered by large memberships—improve the alignment of the whole system of government. So what are some ways to increase union density in the United States? Obvious

[88] *See* James Feigenbaum et al., *From the Bargaining Table to the Ballot Box: Political Effects of Right to Work Laws* 11–19 (Nat'l Bureau of Econ. Rsch., Working Paper No. 24259, 2018).

[89] *See id.* at 21–23; *see also* DEVIN CAUGHEY & CHRISTOPHER WARSHAW, DYNAMIC DEMOCRACY: PUBLIC OPINION, ELECTIONS, AND POLICYMAKING IN THE AMERICAN STATES 156 (2022) ("Disempowering labor unions does seem to cause more conservative policymaking . . . .").

places to start are repealing right-to-work laws at the state level (as Michigan recently did) or forbidding these laws federally (as the Wagner Act did in the 1930s and 1940s). Other sensible proposals include authorizing agricultural and domestic workers to unionize, allowing workers to unionize not just by voting but also by signing membership cards, and guaranteeing the right to unionize for public sector workers.[90] None of these steps would be easy. American labor law is famously ossified, having barely changed at the federal level in seventy-five years.[91] But if it could rise from its slumber, the benefits wouldn't be restricted to new union members. They would extend, rather, to American democracy itself.

Economic Inequality

Unions are some of the groups that are active at each of the stages of my rough model of politics. But they're far from the only, or even the most important, such groups. In fact, at each stage, unions and other mass-membership organizations are vastly outgunned by groups pursuing the interests of businesses and wealthy individuals. Pre-electorally, the groups connected to the billionaire Koch brothers are the biggest spenders on what I've previously called "quasi campaign finance": communications with voters about public policies (instead of candidates for office).[92] During elections, business-linked donors give more than ten times more money to federal candidates than do labor-linked donors.[93] Post-electorally as well, businesses spend more than thirty times more money lobbying the federal government than do unions and public interest organizations.[94] These statistics bring to mind E. E. Schattschneider's famous line about why the outcomes of the pluralist interplay of different groups are skewed in favor of moneyed interests. "The flaw in the pluralist heaven is that the heavenly chorus sings with a strong upper-class accent."[95]

---

[90] See, e.g., Heidi Shierholz et al., *Latest Data Release on Unionization Is a Wake-Up Call to Lawmakers*, ECON. POL'Y INST. (Jan. 20, 2022), https://www.epi.org/publication/latest-data-release-on-unionization-is-a-wake-up-call-to-lawmakers/.

[91] See, e.g., Cynthia L. Estlund, *The Ossification of American Labor Law*, 102 COLUM. L. REV. 1527 (2002).

[92] See, e.g., Alexander Hertel-Fernandez et al., *When Political Mega-Donors Join Forces: How the Koch Network and the Democracy Alliance Influence Organized U.S. Politics on the Right and Left*, 32 STUD. AM. POL. DEV. 127, 144 (2018).

[93] See, e.g., *Business-Labor-Ideology Split in PAC & Individual Donations to Candidates, Parties, Super PACs and Outside Spending Groups*, CTR. FOR RESPONSIVE POL. (Mar. 6, 2023), https://www.opensecrets.org/elections-overview/business-labor-ideology-split.

[94] See, e.g., Lee Drutman, *How Corporate Lobbyists Conquered American Democracy*, THE ATLANTIC (Apr. 20, 2015), https://www.theatlantic.com/business/archive/2015/04/how-corporate-lobbyists-conquered-american-democracy/390822/.

[95] E. E. SCHATTSCHNEIDER, THE SEMISOVEREIGN PEOPLE: A REALIST'S VIEW OF DEMOCRACY IN AMERICA 34–35 (1975).

There's an obvious relationship, then, between economic inequality and policy misalignment. Economic inequality necessarily means that the businesses and wealthy individuals at the top of the economic distribution command enormous resources. When these actors expend some of these resources on politics, they influence what the government does. To the extent this impact is confined to what the government does—not what the people want it to do—policy misalignment is the inevitable result. Public policy moves in the direction sought by the economic elite while public opinion doesn't (at least, not to the same degree).

I documented this obvious relationship between economic inequality and policy misalignment in Chapter 3. When the policy preferences of the rich diverge from those of other income groups, the federal government is more likely to heed the desires of the rich.[96] Here, though, I want to highlight a different, subtler mechanism through which economic inequality leads to misalignment. This mechanism yields representational (not policy) misalignment, and it operates through the intermediary of legislative polarization. Economic inequality, it turns out, is very highly correlated with the ideological distance between the median Democratic legislator and the median Republican legislator. Nolan McCarty and his coauthors first identified this correlation more than a decade ago. In the chart reproduced in Figure 10.4, which "has achieved something of a celebrity . . . status among social scientists,"[97] they showed that the Gini coefficient (a standard measure of income inequality) tracked congressional polarization nearly perfectly between about 1950 and 2010.[98] Other scholars have since extended this finding in several ways. The correlation between income inequality and congressional polarization is even stronger using other, better measures of income inequality.[99] States with greater income inequality have more polarized U.S. senators.[100] States with greater income inequality also have more polarized state legislatures.[101] And comparatively, countries with greater income inequality have more polarized national legislatures, too.[102]

---

[96] See generally, e.g., MARTIN GILENS, AFFLUENCE AND INFLUENCE: ECONOMIC INEQUALITY AND POLITICAL POWER IN AMERICA (2012).

[97] Dan Alexander & Asya Magazinnik, Income Inequality and Electoral Theories of Polarization 4 (Feb. 6, 2022).

[98] See Michael Barber & Nolan McCarty, Causes and Consequences of Polarization, in NEGOTIATING AGREEMENT IN POLITICS: REPORT OF THE TASK FORCE ON NEGOTIATING AGREEMENT IN POLITICS 19, 30 (Jane Mansbridge & Cathie Jo Martin eds., 2013) (displaying an updated version of this chart); see also NOLAN MCCARTY ET AL., POLARIZED AMERICA: THE DANCE OF IDEOLOGY AND UNEQUAL RICHES 6 (2008) (displaying the original version).

[99] See John V. Duca & Jason L. Saving, Income Inequality and Political Polarization: Time Series Evidence over Nine Decades, 62 REV. INCOME & WEALTH 445, 447 (2015).

[100] See James C. Garand, Income Inequality, Party Polarization, and Roll-Call Voting in the U.S. Senate, 72 J. POL. 1109, 1121–23 (2010).

[101] See John Voorheis et al., Unequal Incomes, Ideology and Gridlock: How Rising Inequality Increases Political Polarization 13–17 (Aug. 21, 2015).

[102] See Noam Lupu & Zach Warner, Why Are the Affluent Better Represented Around the World, 61 EUR. J. POL. RSCH. 67, 75–78 (2022) (examining collective representational alignment directly).

FIGURE 10.4 INCOME INEQUALITY AND CONGRESSIONAL POLARIZATION OVER TIME

Figure 10.4 is reproduced with permission from Michael Barber & Nolan McCarty, *Causes and Consequences of Polarization, in* NEGOTIATING AGREEMENT IN POLITICS: REPORT OF THE TASK FORCE ON NEGOTIATING AGREEMENT IN POLITICS 19, 30 (Jane Mansbridge & Cathie Jo Martin eds., 2013). Copyright © 2013 by American Political Science Association.

Why are legislatures more ideologically polarized in more economically un-equal jurisdictions? The story seems to proceed in two parts. First, at the level of the mass public, greater income inequality increases the political salience of financial status. Poorer people become more focused on redistributing resources, and richer people on stopping such transfers. The connection between people's income and their partisanship and ideology therefore tightens.[103] Second, at the level of the legislature, politicians have an incentive to follow the lead of their constituents. In the United States, Democratic legislators stand to gain the votes and dollars of Democrats and liberals by advocating redistribution. Republican legislators similarly stand to benefit from Republican and conservative votes and dollars by opposing it. Legislators' positions thus both diverge by party and grow more sensitive to their constituents' resources.[104] Put another way, greater income inequality makes financial status the axis around which more of politics revolves. This axis initially divides the mass public and then polarizes the legislature as well.[105]

---

[103] *See, e.g.,* MCCARTY ET AL., *supra* note 98, at 82–88; Garand, *supra* note 100, at 1119–21.

[104] *See, e.g.,* MCCARTY ET AL., *supra* note 98, at 36–44; Garand, *supra* note 100, at 1121–26.

[105] Interestingly, while still a significant driver of voting behavior, income differentiated Democratic from Republican voters no more (or even less) than variables like race, gender, education, age, and religion in the most recent presidential election (2020). *See National Exit Poll for Presidential Results*, CBS NEWS (Dec. 14, 2020), https://www.cbsnews.com/elections/2020/united-states/president/exit-poll/.

In turn, legislative polarization necessarily implies collective representational misalignment *if* one condition is satisfied. The ideological distribution of the population must be less bimodal—more normal—than that of the legislature. And so it is. I presented abundant evidence in Chapter 3 that, to this day, most people are moderates and relatively few are extremists.[106] How can this be, given the result I just cited that greater income inequality increases the correlation between people's income and their partisanship and ideology? The explanation, of course, is that most people have moderate incomes. Even in an era in which financial status is a more vital political axis, moderate incomes aren't linked to rigid partisanship or fringe ideology. To the contrary, they're associated with the opposite political behavior: less loyal attachment to either major party and more centrist policy positions.[107] That's why greater income inequality doesn't produce a population as polarized as the legislature. Greater income inequality primarily polarizes the rich and the poor—but the rich and the poor are outnumbered by the broad middle class.

The causal chain should now be clear between greater income inequality, then legislative polarization, and ultimately representational misalignment. But my interest here is finding nonelectoral ways to lessen—not to exacerbate—misalignment. This causal chain should have that aligning capacity if its first step is *lower* income inequality. A more *equal* economic distribution would presumably result in legislative *depolarization*, which itself would promote *better* representational alignment. The question then becomes how to bring down income inequality from the heights it has reached in recent years. And the intuitive answer is redistribution: higher taxes on the wealthy combined with expanded benefits for those at lower levels in the income distribution. These expanded benefits could include access to better education, healthcare, and housing, a higher minimum wage, more generous unemployment insurance, more tax credits for poorer workers, and many other policies.[108] To be sure, these redistributive measures would be at least as hard to enact as the labor reforms I flagged in the previous section. A hallmark of a political system that revolves around financial status is that the rich (and the party they dominate) furiously oppose redistribution. But the practicality of these ideas isn't my present concern. It's their ability to align that's my focus here. And in this respect, the case is strong that redistribution would

---

[106] *See generally, e.g.,* Anthony Fowler et al., *Moderates,* 117 Am. Pol. Sci. Rev. 643 (2023).

[107] *See, e.g.,* McCarty et al., *supra* note 98, at 82–88; Garand, *supra* note 100, at 1119–21.

[108] *See generally, e.g.,* Haas Institute for a Fair and Inclusive Society, Responding to Rising Inequality: Policy Interventions to Ensure Opportunity for All (2014) (focusing on federal reforms); Megan E. Hatch & Elizabeth Rigby, *Laboratories of (In)equality? Redistributive Policy and Income Inequality in the American States,* 43 Pol'y Stud. J. 163 (2015) (focusing on state reforms).

lead to representation that better reflects what voters want from their elected officials.

* * *

There's nothing that limits the applicability of the democratic value of alignment to the electoral context. The constitutional text, the Framers' original intent, Supreme Court precedent, state constitutional law—all these forms of reasoning support the recognition of alignment as a compelling principle across all of public law. However, while a large literature probes the aligning implications of electoral regulations, much less work addresses the impact of nonelectoral rules on alignment. From this small set of studies, a number of policies stand out as potentially aligning: Changes to the legislative process that empower the *chamber* majority (and disempower the majority *party*). Other tweaks to the structure of government like increasing legislative professionalism, eliminating term limits, dividing executive authority, and allowing direct democracy. Actions that raise the intensity and quality of media coverage, thereby better informing voters about issues, candidates, and parties. Laws that boost union membership and so create a counterweight to the political power of corporations and wealthy individuals. And redistribution from these moneyed interests to people at the bottom and middle of the income distribution, which is simultaneously depolarizing and aligning. To be clear, this is just a partial list. There could be many more steps (not yet confirmed by empirical analysis) the government could take to bolster alignment. But even this incomplete tally is enough to make my point, which is that alignment can be furthered meaningfully through nonelectoral means.

The plethora of aligning and misaligning policies—both electoral and nonelectoral—creates an opportunity for the courts. They could significantly improve American democracy by stringently examining misaligning measures while deferentially reviewing aligning regulations when they're challenged on other grounds. As I explained in Chapter 4, one Supreme Court, the Warren Court, took advantage of this opportunity, promoting alignment throughout its election law jurisprudence. Unfortunately, as I argue in the next chapter, today's Supreme Court, the Roberts Court, bears no resemblance to its mid-twentieth-century predecessor. When confronted with misaligning laws like partisan gerrymanders and certain voting restrictions, this Court has universally sustained them. This might seem like judicial restraint, except that when the Court has faced aligning laws, it has often struck them down. Invalidation has been the fate of one campaign finance regulation after another, as well as one of the pillars of the Voting Rights Act, maybe the most aligning statute in American history. This dismal record is why I label the Roberts Court the anti-alignment Court—the modern Court most hostile to the pursuit of alignment by judicial and nonjudicial actors alike.

11

The Anti-Alignment Court

Introduction

My claim in this chapter is that over the nearly two decades during which Chief Justice John Roberts has led the Supreme Court, it has undermined the democratic value of alignment at nearly every turn. Over and over, the Court has declined to intervene when plaintiffs have challenged misaligning electoral practices. Even worse, the Court has repeatedly exercised its power of judicial review to nullify aligning electoral laws enacted by other actors. This record is the opposite of the pro-alignment jurisprudence of earlier Courts, especially the Warren Court. This record is also unnecessary given all the modalities of interpretation—constitutional text, drafters' intent, judicial precedent—that support the recognition of alignment as a legal goal. And as long as the Court retains its current composition, this record means it won't be an aligning force in American governance. To the contrary, the Court will be more apt to fan the flames of misalignment than to try to douse them.

Unsurprisingly, I'm far from the only scholar to notice (or to decry) the Roberts Court's streak of antidemocratic decisions. In a high-profile *Harvard Law Review* foreword, Michael Klarman writes that "today's Republican Justices seem insensitive, or even hostile, to [a] conception of the Court's constitutional role" under which "judicial intervention can foster democracy rather than subvert it."[1] In a major lecture, Pamela Karlan similarly concludes that "this is a countermajoritarian Court," whose "decisions regarding the political process have exacerbated the countermajoritarian drift in our politics."[2] Aziz Huq further explains how, "[s]ince John Roberts was appointed to the office of Chief Justice . . . the Supreme Court has elaborated several lines of doctrine that have enabled or accelerated democratic backsliding."[3] Even sitting federal judges[4] and prominent conservative

---

[1] Michael J. Klarman, *Foreword: The Degradation of American Democracy—and the Court*, 134 HARV. L. REV. 1, 178–79 (2020).

[2] Pamela S. Karlan, *The New Countermajoritarian Difficulty*, 109 CALIF. L. REV. 2323, 2344, 2354 (2021).

[3] Aziz Z. Huq, *The Supreme Court and the Dynamics of Democratic Backsliding*, 699 ANNALS AM. ACAD. POL. & SOC. SCI. 50, 54 (2022).

[4] *See* Lynn Adelman, *The Roberts Court's Assault on Democracy*, 14 HARV. L. & POL'Y REV. 131, 131 (2019) ("[T]he Court's hard right majority is actively participating in undermining American democracy.").

Aligning Election Law. Nicholas O. Stephanopoulos, Oxford University Press. © Nicholas O. Stephanopoulos 2024. DOI: 10.1093/9780197662182.003.0011

academics[5] now air critiques along these lines.

My contribution in this chapter, then, isn't the identification of the Roberts Court's antidemocratic record. Instead, it's the *taxonomization* of that record: the development of a classification scheme using the terminology of alignment and the assignment of cases to the proper conceptual category. The first axis along which the Court's rulings can be sorted is obvious: whether they promote the achievement of alignment (pro-alignment) or frustrate that aim (anti-alignment). The other key axis is whether the Court upholds the challenged electoral practice (passive) or strikes it down (active). Combine these two dimensions and four possibilities emerge. The Court can either improve or worsen alignment by either wielding or refusing to exercise its power of judicial review.

In this simple schematic, the passive anti-alignment quadrant is full of Roberts Court decisions. For example, partisan gerrymandering can be more misaligning than any other contemporary electoral policy. Yet this Court has upheld a series of extreme partisan gerrymanders. And the Court ultimately ruled that partisan gerrymandering is categorically nonjusticiable—entirely unregulable by the federal courts. Likewise, some (though not all) voting restrictions foster misalignment by driving a wedge between the median actual voter and the median person who would have voted in the absence of the restrictions. Yet this Court has never invalidated a voting limit. Photo ID requirements for voting, purges of voter rolls, tight deadlines for absentee voting, curbs on assisting absentee voters—the Court has sustained all these measures and more.

Roberts Court decisions also cram the active anti-alignment quadrant. The Voting Rights Act (VRA) dramatically boosted alignment, especially in the South, by enabling millions of minority citizens to vote. Yet this Court nullified the VRA provision, Section 5, most responsible for this widespread enfranchisement. Many campaign finance regulations are aligning as well: caps on individual contributions and expenditures, some public financing systems, disclosure requirements, and so on. Yet this Court has been relentless in its crusade against limits on money in politics. The Court has struck down one campaign finance rule after another, thereby opening the floodgates to distortive electoral giving and spending.

In contrast, both pro-alignment quadrants are mostly empty. Rulings invalidating severe partisan gerrymanders or misaligning voting restrictions would go in the active pro-alignment quadrant. But the Roberts Court has issued no such rulings. Similarly, the passive pro-alignment quadrant is where cases would go that uphold aligning redistricting policies or validate campaign

---

[5] *See* William Baude, *The Real Enemies of Democracy*, 109 Calif. L. Rev. 2407, 2415 (2021) ("[T]he Court is not going to fix the democratic imperfections in the Constitution . . . .").

finance regulations. This region isn't completely vacant since this Court hasn't nullified all checks on partisan gerrymandering or the whole edifice of campaign finance law. But the few tendrils in this zone are pitiable compared to the luxuriant growths in the active anti-alignment quadrant, where decisions abound attacking voting rights protections and limits on money in politics. That, in brief, is why I call the Roberts Court the anti-alignment Court.[6] Its jurisprudence isn't quite maximally opposed to alignment. But its anti-alignment rulings, both passive and active, far outnumber their counterparts on the pro-alignment side of the ledger.

Taxonomy

Commentary on the Supreme Court often probes the extent to which the Court's decisions are textualist, originalist, consistent with historical practice, consistent with precedent, and the like.[7] In the same vein, we can ask to what degree the Court's decisions promote or undermine democracy. More specifically (and more in line with this book's thesis), we can ask to what degree the Court's decisions promote or undermine the democratic value of alignment. Posing this question amounts to treating alignment as a factor akin to more familiar modalities of interpretation like text, history, and precedent. Just as a ruling of the Court can heed or flout the constitutional text, the record of historical activity, or the body of judicial doctrine, so too can a Court ruling strengthen or weaken the connection between governmental outputs and popular preferences. In other words, a Court ruling can be classified as pro-alignment or anti-alignment.

This single analytical dimension might be sufficient for certain purposes. But I want to add to it one more axis capturing whether a Court ruling is passive or active: that is, whether the Court sustains or strikes down the challenged electoral regulation. Deeming legislation unconstitutional (especially if enacted by Congress), Justice Holmes once said, "is the gravest and most delicate duty that this Court is called on to perform."[8] So it's sensible to distinguish between cases where the Court affirmatively acts—invalidates laws that would otherwise remain operative—and cases where the Court refrains from exercising its

---

[6] In earlier work, for essentially the same reasons, I labeled the Roberts Court the anti-*Carolene* Court, scornful of the famous prescription in *United States v. Carolene Products Co.*, 304 U.S. 144, 152 n.4 (1938), that the Court nullify "legislation which restricts those political processes which can ordinarily be expected to bring about repeal of undesirable legislation." *See* Nicholas O. Stephanopoulos, *The Anti-*Carolene *Court*, 2019 Sup. Ct. Rev. 111.

[7] *See, e.g.*, William Baude, *Is Originalism Our Law?*, 115 Colum. L. Rev. 2349 (2015) (arguing that most Court decisions are originalist); David A. Strauss, *Common Law Constitutional Interpretation*, 63 U. Chi. L. Rev. 877 (1996) (arguing that most Court decisions reason based on precedent).

[8] Blodgett v. Holden, 275 U.S. 142, 148 (1927) (Holmes, J., concurring).

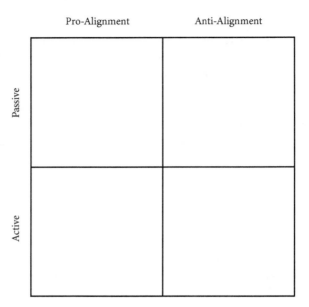

FIGURE 11.1   MATRIX OF ELECTION LAW CASES (EMPTY)

power of judicial review for any number of reasons. Moreover, I've emphasized throughout this book that alignment can be wielded, legally and politically, as a sword or as a shield. In this vocabulary, active Court decisions are like sword thrusts and passive ones like shield deployments. (Although the Court, of course, can reject or accept laws on many grounds other than their consequences for alignment.)

As Figure 11.1 indicates, these two dimensions, each with two possible values, can be combined to form a matrix with four total quadrants.[9] Starting with the passive pro-alignment quadrant, it includes cases where the Court confronts electoral policies that, as an empirical matter, improve alignment and upholds them. By declining to intervene here—by deciding that the aligning policies are constitutional—the Court boosts alignment compared to the counterfactual where it nullified these policies. Next, in cases in the active pro-alignment quadrant, the Court faces measures that are empirically misaligning and strikes them down. Here, judicial intervention is the means through which alignment is enhanced. Had the Court sat on its hands instead, worse alignment would have ensued thanks to the perpetuation of the misaligning measures.

---

[9] For a similar taxonomy, albeit in the terminology of *Carolene Products* rather than alignment, see Stephanopoulos, *supra* note 6, at 117–23.

On the other side of the matrix, the passive anti-alignment quadrant comprises cases where the Court is presented with misaligning electoral practices and allows them to remain in effect. The Court has the opportunity to bolster alignment here. But the Court squanders this chance by holding its fire, by doing nothing where doing something would have excised a distortive regulation from the election code. Lastly, in cases in the active anti-alignment quadrant, the Court considers challenges to aligning laws and rules in favor of these challenges. These are the most disturbing anti-alignment decisions of all. Here, if the Court had simply desisted from exercising its power of judicial review, it would have brought about better alignment relative to the counterfactual of judicial intervention. By quashing the aligning outputs of the political process, the Court is directly responsible for damaging American democracy.

In the sections below, I assign rulings of the Roberts Court to these four quadrants. I begin with the anti-alignment quadrants because they encompass many more of this Court's election law cases. I also focus on the Court's highest-profile decisions though I cite less prominent cases too. In discussing these rulings, I go beyond merely categorizing them by flagging passages where the Court seems to acknowledge (and usually to express disinterest in) their implications for alignment. I further identify areas where anti-alignment decisions haven't yet been issued but are looming just over the horizon. And while I perform this exercise only for the Roberts Court—the anti-alignment Court—I could similarly criticize a number of Rehnquist Court and Burger Court cases.

Passive Anti-Alignment Rulings

I place rulings in the passive anti-alignment quadrant, again, if the Court upholds misaligning electoral policies. Severe partisan gerrymandering, I explained in Chapter 7, is the quintessential misaligning electoral policy in modern American politics. Aggressive partisan gerrymanders necessarily give rise to partisan misalignment: more seats for the line-drawing party than it deserves given its support from the electorate. In turn, partisan misalignment leads to representational misalignment—legislators whose positions don't faithfully reflect the views of their constituents—because of the ideological polarization of today's politicians. And because legislators' positions become law if sufficiently widespread, representational misalignment ultimately breeds policy misalignment: regulations of people's lives that people don't actually want.

The alignment-based argument for the judicial nullification of extreme partisan gerrymanders is therefore ironclad. But the Roberts Court has acted exactly to the contrary.[10] First, in a 2006 case, the Court upheld a Texas congressional plan whose partisan intent and effect were undisputed. "The legislature does seem to have decided to redistrict with the sole purpose of achieving a Republican congressional majority," the Court's plurality opinion conceded.[11] And the plan did "result[] in the majority Republican Party capturing a larger share of the seats."[12] Nevertheless, the Court couldn't think of a workable standard for resolving partisan gerrymandering claims, and sustained the plan for that reason.[13]

Next, in a 2018 case, the Roberts Court greenlit a Wisconsin state legislative plan whose nearly unprecedented partisan misalignment was the centerpiece of the trial record. That plan, the district court found, had the fifth-largest average efficiency gap of all state house maps since 1972.[14] However, the Court stated that even if partisan gerrymandering is severe—and even if no nonjudicial actor is likely to help— it's not the Court's job to lend a hand. Noting the plaintiffs' argument that "this Court *can* address the problem of partisan gerrymandering because it *must*," the Court responded that "[s]uch invitations must be answered with care."[15] The Court further held that even evidence of glaring misalignment doesn't confer standing to individuals to bring partisan gerrymandering claims. Such misalignment isn't "an individual and personal injury of the kind required for Article III standing."[16] Rather, such misalignment implicates "group political interests."[17] "But this Court is not responsible for vindicating generalized partisan preferences."[18]

A year later, in *Rucho v. Common Cause*, the Roberts Court considered two more partisan gerrymanders. In Maryland, Democrats awarded themselves seven of eight congressional districts,[19] and in North Carolina, Republicans crafted a congressional plan with the fourth-worst average efficiency gap since 1972.[20] The Court recognized the democratic harms wreaked by these and other biased maps. (As Justice Kagan quipped in dissent, "really, how could it not?"[21])

---

[10] To the cases I discuss below, you could add *Abbott v. Perez*, 138 S. Ct. 2305 (2018), in which the Court upheld Texas's highly biased district plans against charges that they were tainted by intentional racial discrimination.

[11] League of United Latin Am. Citizens v. Perry, 548 U.S. 399, 417 (2006) (plurality opinion).

[12] *Id.* at 419.

[13] *See id.* at 423.

[14] *See* Whitford v. Gill, 218 F. Supp. 3d 837, 861 (W.D. Wis. 2016), *vacated*, 138 S. Ct. 1916 (2018).

[15] Gill v. Whitford, 138 S. Ct. 1916, 1929 (2018). I note that I helped litigate this case.

[16] *Id.* at 1931.

[17] *Id.* at 1933.

[18] *Id.*

[19] *See* Rucho v. Common Cause, 139 S. Ct. 2484, 2493 (2019). I note that I also helped litigate the North Carolina case.

[20] *See* Common Cause v. Rucho, 318 F. Supp. 3d 777, 887 (M.D.N.C. 2018), *vacated*, 139 S. Ct. 2484 (2019).

[21] *Rucho*, 139 S. Ct. at 2512 (Kagan, J., dissenting).

"Excessive partisanship in districting," the Court observed, "leads to results that reasonably seem unjust."[22] "[G]errymandering is 'incompatible with democratic principles,'" the Court continued.[23] In fact, "partisan gerrymanders violate the core principle of [our] republican government . . . namely, that the voters should choose their representatives, not the other way around."[24] Accordingly, the Court emphasized that it "does not condone excessive partisan gerrymandering," nor does it fail to hear "complaints about districting."[25]

Given the Court's appreciation of the democratic injuries inflicted by extreme partisan gerrymandering, you might have thought the Court's next move would have been to strike down the Maryland and North Carolina plans. That certainly would have been the next move of a pro-alignment Court. But the Roberts Court is the anti-alignment Court, and it followed each acknowledgement of the antidemocratic nature of partisan gerrymandering with a declaration that this fact in no way calls for judicial intervention. "[G]errymandering is incompatible with democratic principles"—but that "does not mean that the solution lies with the federal judiciary."[26] "[G]errymanders violate the core principle of our republican government"—but "[t]hat seems like an objection more properly grounded in the Guarantee Clause," which "does not provide the basis for a justiciable claim."[27] Some contend that "this Court *can* address the problem of partisan gerrymandering because it *must*"—but "[t]hat is not the test of our authority under the Constitution."[28]

These passages are among the clearest expressions of the passive antialignment perspective ever to appear in the *United States Reports*. They capture the position that absolutely no connection does or should exist between an electoral policy causing misalignment and the Court interceding to invalidate that policy. Misalignment simply isn't the Court's problem to solve. In fact, when misalignment is the crux of plaintiffs' objections to a category of electoral measures, the right judicial response, in this Court's view, is to stop providing a forum for those objections. Of course, that's precisely what the Court did in *Rucho* by deeming partisan gerrymandering claims nonjusticiable under the federal Constitution.

Turning from partisan gerrymanders to voting restrictions, these limits can be—but aren't necessarily—misaligning. As I discussed in Chapter 5, measures that make voting more difficult lead to misalignment if (1) they prevent a substantial number of people from voting who would have cast ballots in the

---

[22]   *Id.* at 2506.

[23]   *Id.* (quoting Ariz. St. Legis. v. Ariz. Indep. Redist. Comm'n, 576 U.S. 787, 791 (2015)).

[24]   *Id.* (internal quotation marks omitted).

[25]   *Id.* at 2507.

[26]   *Id.* at 2506 (internal quotation marks omitted).

[27]   *Id.* (internal quotation marks and alterations omitted).

[28]   *Id.* at 2507 (internal quotation marks omitted).

absence of the measures; and (2) these people have distinctive partisan and/ or policy preferences. Under this framework, many modern voting restrictions aren't highly misaligning because they stop relatively few people from voting and/or these people aren't very different from those who do cast ballots. Even if the *impact* of many modern voting restrictions isn't highly distortive, however, the *intent* underlying them usually is. The vast majority of these laws are enacted by unified Republican governments, often just after taking power, especially in states with large minority populations.[29] Moreover, these laws' architects some-times admit—even boast of—their aim of suppressing the turnout of Democratic voters.[30]

Confronted by policies whose motives are misaligning, but whose effects are more ambiguous, a pro-alignment Court would at least review them care-fully. Such a Court might not nullify every voting restriction it considered, but it would be ready to pull the trigger if there was evidence that misaligning intent had, as hoped, led to misaligning impact. The Roberts Court, on the other hand, has never struck down a voting limit. In three merits decisions, and several more shadow docket rulings,[31] it has upheld every measure it has faced burdening voting. In these cases, the Court has also made clear that the potential for mis-alignment is extraneous to its analysis. Even if a voting restriction was shown to shift the actual electorate away from the eligible electorate, that is, the Court would still approve the measure.

The Roberts Court's first merits decision about a voting limit, in the 2008 case of *Crawford v. Marion County Elections Board*, remains its most important.[32] In *Crawford*, the Court rejected a constitutional challenge to Indiana's photo ID requirement for voting. A plurality held that this requirement was justified by the state's interest in preventing in-person voter-impersonation fraud, even though "[t]he record contains no evidence of any such fraud actually occurring in Indiana at any time in its history."[33] More relevant here, the plurality also conceded that one of the statute's goals was partisan misalignment. "It is fair to infer that partisan considerations"—advantaging Republicans by reducing

---

[29] *See, e.g.*, Keith G. Bentele & Erin E. O'Brien, *Jim Crow 2.0? Why States Consider and Adopt Restrictive Voter Access Policies*, 11 PERSP. POL. 1088 (2013); Daniel R. Biggers & Michael J. Hanmer, *Understanding the Adoption of Voter Identification Laws in the United States*, 45 AM. POL. RSCH. 560 (2017).

[30] *See, e.g.*, Michael Wines, *Some Republicans Acknowledge Leveraging State Voter ID Laws for Political Gain*, N.Y. TIMES, Sept. 20, 2016, at A15.

[31] I discuss the merits decisions below. For some of the shadow docket rulings, see, for example, *Democratic National Committee v. Wisconsin State Legislature*, 141 S. Ct. 28 (2020) (upholding Wisconsin's tight deadline for the return of absentee ballots); *Andino v. Middleton*, 141 S. Ct. 9 (2020) (upholding South Carolina's witness requirement for absentee ballots); and *Purcell v. Gonzalez*, 549 U.S. 1 (2006) (upholding Arizona's identification requirement for voting and proof-of-citizenship requirement for registering to vote).

[32] 553 U.S. 181 (2008).

[33] *Id.* at 194 (plurality opinion).

Democratic turnout—"may have played a significant role in the decision to enact [the statute]."[34] But this misaligning purpose was legally immaterial, in the plurality's opinion. As long as a voting restriction is "supported by valid neutral justifications" like stopping fraud, "those justifications should not be disregarded simply because partisan interests may have provided one motivation for the votes of individual legislators."[35] In other words, a misaligning purpose doesn't condemn, or even heighten judicial scrutiny of, a voting limit as long as a jurisdiction can identify some other legitimate objective that the policy serves.

Crawford was a constitutional case; the Roberts Court's next merits decision about a voting restriction came in a 2018 case under the National Voter Registration Act (NVRA). In that case, the Court ruled that Ohio's removal of more than a million individuals from its voter registration list, because the state (likely erroneously) thought they had moved, didn't violate the NVRA.[36] In her dissent, Justice Sotomayor pointed out that this large-scale purge of the voter roll was probably misaligning. The purge "disproportionately affected minority, low-income, disabled, and veteran voters," who were "particularly vulnerable to unwarranted removal."[37] The purge thus "marginalized their influence in the political process" and undercut the democratic principle that "all individuals, regardless of race, income, or status, [be able] to exercise their right to vote."[38] As in *Crawford*, the Court's response to this evidence of potential misalignment was indifference. "Justice Sotomayor's dissent says nothing about what is relevant in this case," the Court replied.[39] The notion that misalignment might have some bearing on the disposition of a case about a voting limit was "misconceived."[40]

The Roberts Court's last merits decision about voting restrictions, in 2021, involved claims under the Constitution and Section 2 of the VRA. In that decision, the Court upheld both Arizona's refusal to count ballots cast in the wrong precinct and its ban on third parties assisting voters with mail-in ballots.[41] Again, as Justice Kagan observed in dissent, there was data suggesting that these policies are misaligning. The discarding of wrong-precinct ballots, in particular, "results in Hispanic and African American voters' ballots being thrown out at a statistically higher rate than those of whites."[42] This disparate disenfranchisement of minority voters "can affect election outcomes" when races are close (a

[34] *Id.* at 203.
[35] *Id.* at 204.
[36] *See* Husted v. A. Philip Randolph Inst., 138 S. Ct. 1833, 1841–48 (2018).
[37] *Id.* at 1864 (Sotomayor, J., dissenting).
[38] *Id.* at 1865.
[39] *Id.* at 1848 (majority opinion).
[40] *Id.*
[41] *See* Brnovich v. Democratic Nat'l Comm., 141 S. Ct. 2321, 2343–50 (2021).
[42] *Id.* at 2366 (Kagan, J., dissenting).

common occurrence in Arizona).[43] "If you were a minority vote suppressor in Arizona ... you would want that rule in your bag of tricks."[44] But again, the Court was unmoved by this risk of misalignment. The Court characterized the racial disparities caused by Arizona's laws as "small in absolute terms."[45] The Court also announced that these disparities must be considered alongside several other factors, none of which have much to do with misalignment.[46] "[T]he mere fact there is some disparity in impact does not necessarily mean" a voting limit is unlawful.[47]

To reiterate, these cases about voting restrictions are less compelling examples of the Roberts Court's passive anti-alignment approach than are the partisan gerrymandering cases. That's because the evidence is equivocal that Indiana's photo ID requirement for voting, Ohio's voter roll purge, Arizona's discarding of wrong-precinct ballots, and other modern voting limits are actually misaligning. The fairest conclusion about these cases thus isn't that this Court *has* significantly worsened alignment by declining to invalidate burdens on voting. Instead, it's that the cases' reasoning reveals that the Court plausibly *would* worsen alignment by failing to intervene if, in the future, the Court was faced with a voting burden that was, in fact, highly misaligning.

Active Anti-Alignment Rulings

A plausible defense for the Roberts Court's passive anti-alignment rulings is that they reflect judicial restraint, not hostility to the democratic value of alignment. Maybe this Court puts a thumb on the scale against exercising its power of judicial review. Maybe the Court's default inclination is to let the chips fall wherever the political process chooses. Even if this defense is conceivable for cases in the passive anti-alignment quadrant, however, it crumbles for cases in the active anti-alignment quadrant. In these cases—of which there are many already, and maybe more forthcoming—the Court doesn't restrain itself, doesn't exhibit reluctance to wield its power to strike down legislation, doesn't defer to the outputs of the political process. To the contrary, the Court affirmatively intercedes to thwart the aligning efforts of nonjudicial actors. The ensuing misalignment is the fault of the Court alone, and of the Court's activity rather than passivity.

---

[43] *Id.* at 2368.
[44] *Id.*
[45] *Id.* at 2344 (majority opinion).
[46] *See id.* at 2338–41.
[47] *Id.* at 2339.

The Roberts Court's 2013 decision in *Shelby County v. Holder* may be its most notorious active anti-alignment ruling (though the competition is stiff).[48] In *Shelby County*, the Court effectively nullified Section 5 of the VRA, the crown jewel of the statute. For almost the preceding half-century, Section 5 had barred certain, mostly southern jurisdictions from altering their election laws unless they first proved that their changes wouldn't worsen the electoral position of minority voters. As I showed in Chapter 8, Section 5 strongly improved alignment during the decades it was in effect, primarily by increasing political participation by minority voters. At the state level, the alignment of enacted policies with the preferences of voters (especially minority voters) surged in the South.[49] In covered counties, policy alignment rose as well, particularly in heavily minority areas where minority-preferred measures were increasingly adopted.[50] In covered districts with large minority populations, too, Section 5 was responsible for better representational alignment in that legislators were more likely to take the pro-civil rights stances favored by their constituents.[51]

The Roberts Court nevertheless decided that the formula that determined which jurisdictions were subject to Section 5 was unconstitutional. The Court acknowledged the democratic gains that had occurred in covered areas (albeit without using the language of alignment). "[T]here have been improvements on the ground."[52] "[O]ur nation has made great strides."[53] The Court further attributed much of this progress to Section 5. "There is no doubt that these improvements are in large part *because of* the Voting Rights Act."[54] "The Act has proved immensely successful at redressing racial discrimination and integrating the voting process."[55] But in a perplexing twist, the Court condemned the VRA's coverage formula simply because it relied on information from the 1960s and 1970s—"decades-old data and eradicated practices."[56] The Court's preference for a formula based on "current data reflecting current needs" therefore took priority over the continued operation of arguably the most aligning statute in American history.[57] Just because "Congress could have updated the coverage formula . . .

---

[48]   570 U.S. 529 (2013).

[49]   *See* Devin Caughey & Christopher Warshaw, Dynamic Democracy: Public Opinion, Elections, and Policymaking in the American States 134–35 (2022).

[50]   *See, e.g.*, Elizabeth U. Cascio & Ebonya Washington, *Valuing the Vote: The Redistribution of Voting Rights and State Funds following the Voting Rights Act of 1965*, 2014 Q.J. Econ. 379, 395–423.

[51]   *See, e.g.*, Sophie Schuit & Jon C. Rogowski, *Race, Representation, and the Voting Rights Act*, 61 Am. J. Pol. Sci. 513, 519–24 (2017).

[52]   *Shelby Cnty.*, 570 U.S. at 550.

[53]   *Id.* at 549.

[54]   *Id.* at 548.

[55]   *Id.*

[56]   *Id.* at 551.

[57]   *Id.* at 553.

but did not do so," the Court neutered the law that had brought genuine democracy, for the first time since Reconstruction, to the South.[58]

I mentioned that *Shelby County* has competitors for the title of the Roberts Court's most infamous active anti-alignment ruling. These rivals are the cases, including *Citizens United v. FEC*, in which this Court has invalidated one campaign finance regulation after another.[59] Some rules about money in politics, I documented in Chapter 9, promote alignment. Limits on individuals' contributions to candidates, for instance, are aligning because individual donors tend to hold extreme ideological positions. These extreme views significantly sway politicians when this pool of funding is regulated less or not at all.[60] Limits on individuals' campaign expenditures, likewise, boost alignment because individual spenders are essentially the same people (with the same polarized ideologies) as individual donors.[61] And disclosure requirements appear to be aligning (though the evidence is thinner) because politicians are more reluctant to enact policies favored by their funders but opposed by the public when campaign giving and spending are plain for all to see.[62]

Given this evidence, a pro-alignment Court would uphold at least these campaign finance regulations. But the Roberts Court has often done the opposite. To avoid repetition, I'll just flag three of this Court's decisions in the main text, though the full list of the Court's nullifications of rules about money in politics is quite a bit longer.[63] First, in a 2014 case, the Court struck down the aggregate federal limit on how much money individual donors can give, in total, to candidates for federal office per election cycle.[64] The Court thereby enabled wealthy (and usually ideologically extreme) individual donors to exert even more influence over politicians. This would be bad enough from a pro-alignment perspective. Adding salt to the wound, however, was the plurality's ironic peroration *in favor of* alignment (which I also quoted in Chapter 4). "[P]olitical responsiveness," the plurality opined, is "at the heart of the democratic process."[65] Indeed,

---

[58]   *Id.* at 557.

[59]   558 U.S. 310 (2010).

[60]   *See, e.g.*, Michael Barber, Ideological Donors, Contribution Limits, and the Polarization of State Legislatures 37–38 (Sept. 4, 2013).

[61]   *See, e.g.*, Anna Harvey, *Is Campaign Spending a Cause or an Effect? Reexamining the Empirical Foundations of* Buckley v. Valeo *(1976)*, 27 SUP. CT. ECON. REV. 67, 95 (2019).

[62]   *See, e.g.*, Patrick Flavin, *State Campaign Finance Laws and the Equality of Political Representation*, 13 ELECTION L.J. 362, 370–71 (2014).

[63]   For additional Roberts Court rulings striking down campaign finance regulations, see, for example, *FEC v. Cruz*, 142 S. Ct. 1638 (2022) (invalidating a federal statutory provision limiting the use of post-election contributions to repay candidates for personal loans to their campaigns); *Arizona Free Enterprise Club's Freedom Club PAC v. Bennett*, 564 U.S. 721 (2011) (invalidating a key portion of Arizona's public financing system); and *Randall v. Sorrell*, 548 U.S. 230 (2006) (invalidating Vermont's contribution and expenditure limits).

[64]   *See* McCutcheon v. FEC, 572 U.S. 185, 203–27 (2014) (plurality opinion).

[65]   *Id.* at 227.

"responsiveness is key to the very concept of self-governance through elected officials."[66] So it is, but the plurality was in no position to say these words. Its invalidation of the aggregate federal limit on campaign contributions *undermined* responsiveness (and alignment) by increasing the clout of ideologically unrepresentative individual donors. If the plurality really wanted a more responsive (and better aligned) political system, it should have left this law alone.

Second, in *Citizens United*, the Roberts Court held that the federal ban on campaign expenditures by corporations and unions was unconstitutional.[67] *Citizens United* itself had mixed effects on alignment. On the one hand, some corporations and almost all unions support politicians who espouse noncentrist positions.[68] On the other hand, most corporations (accounting for most corporate campaign funding) prefer more moderate politicians.[69] Liberating the former set of entities to make unlimited campaign expenditures was thus misaligning, while freeing the latter set had the opposite impact. Even if *Citizens United*'s direct consequences for alignment were ambiguous, though, its indirect implications were plainly misaligning. Just two months after *Citizens United*, in a decision that cited *Citizens United* more than twenty times, the D.C. Circuit ruled that all funders, including individuals, can make unlimited contributions to Super PACs, which in turn can make unlimited campaign expenditures.[70] This decision triggered a massive increase in the money ultimately disbursed by individuals on electoral spending.[71] These individual funders of Super PACs (like individual donors to candidates) tend to be ideologically extreme,[72] and Super PAC expenditures (like campaign contributions) substantially sway politicians.[73] At just one remove, then, *Citizens United* was responsible for considerable misalignment. It led straight to the lower-court ruling that unleashed Super PACs into our politics.

And third, in a 2021 case, the Roberts Court nullified a California regulation requiring charities to disclose their major donors to the state attorney general.[74] The charity bringing this suit was the Americans for Prosperity Foundation: one

---

[66] *Id.*

[67] *See* 558 U.S. 310, 336–66 (2010).

[68] *See, e.g.,* Adam Bonica, *Ideology and Interests in the Political Marketplace*, 57 AM. J. POL. SCI. 294, 306 (2013).

[69] *See, e.g.,* Michael Jay Barber, *Buying Representation: The Incentives, Ideology, and Influence of Campaign Contributors in American Politics* 12 (Sept. 2014).

[70] *See* SpeechNow.org v. FEC, 599 F.3d 686 (D.C. Cir. 2010).

[71] *See Total Outside Spending by Election Cycle, Excluding Party Committees*, CTR. FOR RESPONSIVE POL., https://www.opensecrets.org/outside-spending/by_cycle (last visited Feb. 1, 2024).

[72] *See, e.g., Double-Duty Donors, Part II: Large Numbers of Wealthy Donors Hit Legal Limit on Giving to Candidates, Turn to Presidential Super PACs in Continuing Trend*, CTR. FOR RESPONSIVE POL. (Feb. 21, 2012), http://www.opensecrets.org/news/2012/02/double-duty-donors-part-ii-large-nu.html.

[73] *See, e.g.,* Anna Harvey & Taylor Mattia, *Does Money Have a Conservative Bias? Estimating the Causal Impact of* Citizens United *on State Legislative Preferences*, 191 PUB. CHOICE 417, 427–29 (2019).

[74] *See* Americans for Prosperity Found. v. Bonta, 141 S. Ct. 2373, 2385–89 (2021).

of the many entities funded by the Koch brothers whose collective lobbying and grass-roots activism result in policy misalignment in a conservative direction.[75] Thanks to the Court's decision, the Americans for Prosperity Foundation was able to keep its donor list secret, from not only the public but even state officials trying to police charitable fraud. The Court's decision further hinted that conventional campaign finance disclosure requirements might be next on the chopping block. The Court borrowed its standard of "exacting scrutiny" from campaign finance cases.[76] The Court also applied that standard rigorously, in a manner that could doom rules that campaign contributions and expenditures be reported.[77] As Justice Alito exulted in his concurrence, "I agree that the exacting scrutiny standard drawn from our election-law jurisprudence has real teeth."[78] "It requires both narrow tailoring and consideration of alternative means of obtaining the sought-after information."[79]

This suggestion that the Roberts Court might, in the future, strike down campaign finance disclosure requirements brings me to my last set of active anti-alignment examples. These examples involve areas where this Court hasn't *yet* frustrated the aligning efforts of nonjudicial actors—but where, based on the Court's precedents and pronouncements, such frustration is possible, even probable, in the future. One such area is the congressional regulation of federal elections. Another is the regulation of federal elections by state actors other than the state legislature: the governor, election administrators, state courts, and the people themselves through direct democracy.

In 2021–22, Congress came tantalizingly close to passing the most ambitious package of electoral reforms in American history. The House of Representatives repeatedly approved omnibus election law bills, the last of which nearly prompted the Senate to forbid the filibuster for this category of legislation. As I discuss in the next chapter, most of these bills' elements are likely constitutional, even under the Roberts Court's jurisprudence. A few provisions, though, would be aligning if enacted yet could easily raise this Court's hackles.[80] The first election law bill approved by the House would have required all states to use independent commissions to design their congressional districts.[81] Independent

---

[75] *See, e.g.,* ALEXANDER HERTEL-FERNANDEZ, STATE CAPTURE: HOW CONSERVATIVE ACTIVISTS, BIG BUSINESSES, AND WEALTHY DONORS RESHAPED THE AMERICAN STATES—AND THE NATION 254 (2019).

[76] *See Americans for Prosperity Found.,* 141 S. Ct. at 2383 (plurality opinion).

[77] *See id.* at 2385–89 (majority opinion).

[78] *Id.* at 2391 (opinion of Alito, J.).

[79] *Id.*

[80] For discussion of more federally enacted electoral reforms to which the Roberts Court might object, see Stephanopoulos, *supra* note 6, at 155–57 (independent redistricting commissions for state legislative plans); *id.* at 157–59 (independent redistricting commissions with membership restrictions); and *id.* at 161–62 (automatic voter registration).

[81] *See* For the People Act of 2021, H.R. 1, 117th Cong. §§ 2411–15 (2021).

redistricting commissions, I explained in Chapter 7, reduce or eliminate the misalignment that arises due to partisan gerrymandering. Both that bill and the one that almost sparked a revolution in Senate procedure would also have barred states from disenfranchising ex-felons and enforcing photo ID requirements for voting.[82] Per Chapter 5, these voting restrictions tend to have equivocal effects on alignment but blatant misaligning motives. And the bill that ultimately died in the Senate would have specified a new coverage formula for the VRA, under which jurisdictions would be covered by Section 5 if they incurred enough voting rights violations over the preceding twenty-five years.[83] Section 5, again, was highly aligning in the decades in which it operated.

The flaw the Roberts Court might discern in a mandate that states use independent redistricting commissions is its directive nature. "[T]he Federal Government may not compel the States to implement . . . federal regulatory programs," the Rehnquist Court once held.[84] For its part, the Roberts Court extended the anti-commandeering doctrine to federal prohibitions (not just obligations) of state action.[85] Under this doctrine, it's potentially troubling that the first House bill provided that "each State *shall* establish a nonpartisan agency in the legislative branch."[86] In turn, this agency "*shall* establish an independent redistricting commission,"[87] which "*shall* . . . establish[] single-member congressional districts using [specified] criteria."[88] All these *shall*s could be seen as federal orders to the states: binding rules as to how (and by whom) their congressional districts must be drawn. As conservative critics alleged at the time, these provisions "would likely run into the Supreme Court's doctrine against federal 'commandeering,'"[89] and "would surely invite legal challenge as a violation of the anti-commandeering doctrine."[90]

Next, the Roberts Court might object on the basis of the Qualifications Clause to both bills' bans on disenfranchising ex-felons and enforcing photo ID requirements for voting. The Qualifications Clause can be read as authorizing states alone to determine "the Qualifications requisite for [their] Electors" in state legislative and congressional elections.[91] This Court seemed to endorse

---

[82] *See id.* §§ 1401–09, 1903; Freedom to Vote: John R. Lewis Act, H.R. 5746, 117th Cong. §§ 1701–09, 1801 (2022).

[83] *See* H.R. 5746 § 9004.

[84] Printz v. United States, 521 US 898, 925 (1997).

[85] *See* Murphy v. NCAA, 138 S. Ct. 1461, 1478–79 (2018).

[86] H.R. 1 § 2414(a)(1) (emphasis added).

[87] *Id.* § 2411(a)(1) (emphasis added).

[88] *Id.* § 2403(a) (emphasis added).

[89] Walter Olson, *House Passes Political-Omnibus Bill H.R. 1*, CATO AT LIBERTY (Mar 11, 2019), https://perma.cc/2RQM-TP2R.

[90] Ilya Shapiro & Nathan Harvey, *What Left-Wing Populism Looks Like*, NAT'L REV. (Mar 7, 2019), https://perma.cc/8T9U-JCCZ.

[91] U.S. CONST. art. I, § 2.

this reading in the 2013 case of *Arizona v. Inter Tribal Council of Arizona*, in which the Court stated that, because of the Qualifications Clause, "Congress [may] regulate *how* federal elections are held, but not *who* may vote in them."[92] The argument against the congressional negation of state policies denying the franchise to ex-felons and limiting the franchise to individuals with photo IDs, then, is that these policies supposedly establish voting qualifications. In other words, these policies supposedly hold that not having been convicted of a felony and possessing a photo ID are qualifications for voting. If the policies really do amount to voting qualifications—and if voting qualifications really can be set by states alone, not by Congress—then Congress could lack the authority to override the policies.

Lastly, the trouble with an updated coverage formula for the VRA, from the Roberts Court's perspective, is that it would only solve one of the two constitutional problems the Court identified in *Shelby County*. Yes, an updated formula would be based on "current data reflecting current needs," as the Court insisted.[93] But an updated formula would do nothing to alleviate the Court's other concern: that racial discrimination in voting might no longer be severe enough anywhere in America to justify Section 5's preclearance regime. Only "exceptional conditions can justify" a requirement that certain jurisdictions preclear election law changes before being allowed to implement them, the Court stated in *Shelby County*.[94] But exceptional conditions might no longer exist, in the Court's view, since "things have changed dramatically" since Section 5's enactment in 1965.[95] Because of this purported change, the Court expressed sympathy for the argument that Section 5 itself, not just its coverage formula, is now unconstitutional. That argument, the Court said in a line that could haunt any attempt to revive Section 5, has "a good deal of force."[96]

The last few examples were cases where *Congress* might pass an aligning electoral law and the Roberts Court, in an active anti-alignment ruling, might invalidate it. The final group of scenarios I'll cover involve state actors other than the state legislature promoting alignment and this Court possibly obstructing their efforts. There are many ways in which nonlegislative state actors can take (and, historically, have taken) aligning steps. To name just a handful: Governors can veto misaligning measures approved by the state legislature (like partisan gerrymanders and some voting restrictions). Election administrators can run elections pursuant to policies that increase voter participation, and potentially improve alignment, beyond the levels contemplated by the state legislature. State

---

[92]   570 U.S. 1, 16 (2013).
[93]   Shelby Cnty. v. Holder, 570 U.S. 529, 553 (2013).
[94]   *Id.* at 535 (internal quotation marks omitted).
[95]   *Id.* at 547.
[96]   *Id.*

courts can strike down misaligning state laws (again, like partisan gerrymanders and some voting restrictions) because of their violations of state constitutions. And the people themselves can harness direct democracy to boost alignment, for instance, by creating independent redistricting commissions and adopting certain campaign finance rules.

Why could these aligning acts by nonlegislative state actors—if they apply to federal elections—draw the ire of the Roberts Court? Because of what's known as the "independent state legislature" (ISL) theory, a theory that purports to forbid regulations of federal elections adopted by nonlegislative state actors to the extent they conflict with the wishes of the state legislature. The ISL theory is derived from the text of two constitutional provisions: the Elections Clause of Article I, Section 4 and the Electors Clause of Article II, Section 1. Both provisions state that "the Legislature thereof" can regulate federal elections: the "Times, Places and Manner of holding [congressional] Elections,"[97] according to the Elections Clause, and the "Manner" in which presidential electors are appointed,[98] according to the Electors Clause. Based on these provisions, proponents of the ISL theory contend that the state legislature is the *only* state actor that can make rules about federal elections. Rules about federal elections promulgated by nonlegislative state actors are therefore unconstitutional, at least to the extent they contravene the state legislature's preferences.

In other periods, the ISL theory would be nothing more than an academic curiosity. In our era of the Roberts Court, though, this highly misaligning doctrine has begun to win the Court's partial support. In the 2015 case of *Arizona State Legislature v. Arizona Independent Redistricting Commission*, Chief Justice Roberts wrote a dissent (joined by three more Justices) in which he argued that Arizona's independent redistricting commission was unconstitutional under the ISL theory.[99] "In Arizona," he asserted, "redistricting is not carried out by the legislature."[100] Rather, "as the result of a ballot initiative" that itself circumvented the legislature, "an unelected body called the Independent Redistricting Commission draws the lines."[101] While this opinion was a dissent, two of the Justices in the majority in *Arizona State Legislature*, Justice Ginsburg and Justice Kennedy, were subsequently replaced by Justices more receptive to the ISL theory, respectively, Justice Barrett and Justice Kavanaugh. In a 2020 case, Justice Kavanaugh notably joined an opinion by Justice Gorsuch that fully embraced the ISL theory. "[S]tate legislatures—not federal judges, *not state judges, not state governors, not other state officials*—bear primary responsibility for setting

[97] U.S. CONST. art. I, § 4.
[98] *Id.* art. II, § 1.
[99] 576 U.S. 787 (2015).
[100] *Id.* at 826 (Roberts, C.J., dissenting).
[101] *Id.*

election rules," averred Justice Gorsuch.[102] He then cited one of the textual sources of the ISL theory: the Elections Clause of Article I, Section 4.[103]

Still more significantly, in the 2023 case of *Moore v. Harper*, Chief Justice Roberts authored a majority opinion that, for the first time, recognized a weak form of the ISL theory.[104] The backdrop was that the North Carolina Supreme Court had held that a highly biased (and legislatively enacted) congressional plan was an unlawful partisan gerrymander under the state constitution. State legislative leaders then asserted that this state court decision violated the federal Constitution by infringing the state legislature's essentially plenary authority over congressional elections. In *Moore*, the Supreme Court rejected the strongest versions of the ISL theory (along with the petitioners' challenge). The Elections Clause, the Court ruled, doesn't "vest[] state legislatures with exclusive and independent authority when setting the rules governing federal elections."[105] But the Court nevertheless endorsed a more modest ISL doctrine under which state court decisions under state law about federal elections may, if they're too outlandish, be unconstitutional. "[S]tate courts may not so exceed the bounds of ordinary judicial review," the Court decreed, "as to unconstitutionally intrude upon the role specifically reserved to state legislatures by [the Elections Clause]."[106]

To be sure, the Roberts Court has not yet concluded that any state court ruling actually violates this weak form of the ISL theory. And it's possible, as Justice Thomas predicted in his dissent in *Moore*, that this framework will be "a forgiving standard in practice," under which most ISL claims will be "quickly resolved with generic statements of deference to the state courts."[107] In addition, my discussion of what the Court might do if Congress approved sweeping electoral reforms was doubly speculative. First, Congress would have to pass those reforms, and second, to nullify some of them, the Court would have to follow its precedents to their logical endpoints. Consequently, I put less weight on the scenarios in which the Court *could* hand down active anti-alignment rulings in the *future*. Instead, I prioritize cases in which the Court *did* make active anti-alignment rulings in the *past*. As the first half of this section illustrates, there are more than enough cases in the latter category—*Shelby County, Citizens United,*

---

[102] Democratic Nat'l Comm. v. Wis. State Legis., 141 S. Ct. 28, 29 (2020) (Gorsuch, J., concurring in denial of application to vacate stay).

[103] *See id.*

[104] 143 S. Ct. 2065 (2023). This weak form of the ISL theory also appeared in the Court's per curiam opinion in *Bush v. Palm Beach County Canvassing Board*, 531 U.S. 70 (2000), and in Chief Justice Rehnquist's concurrence in *Bush v. Gore*, 531 U. S. 98 (2000).

[105] *Moore*, 143 S. Ct. at 2083.

[106] *Id.* at 2090.

[107] *Id.* at 2106 (Thomas, J., dissenting).

several of the Court's other campaign finance decisions—to fill the active anti-alignment quadrant on their own.

The (Almost) Empty Sets

If the two anti-alignment quadrants are crammed with one Roberts Court ruling after another, the two pro-alignment quadrants are mostly, though not entirely, empty. Start with the active pro-alignment quadrant. This is where cases go if they lead to better alignment by invalidating misaligning electoral practices like partisan gerrymanders and certain voting restrictions. To repeat, this Court has never struck down a gerrymandered district map on the ground that it sought or attained partisan advantage. Nor will the Court do so, given its holding in *Rucho* that partisan gerrymandering is nonjusticiable. The Court also has never nullified any measure impeding voting. Under the Constitution, the NVRA, and the VRA, the Court's conclusion about every voting limit it has encountered has been that the policy passes legal muster.

However, the Roberts Court *has* repeatedly invalidated portions of partisan gerrymanders for reasons *unrelated* to partisan gerrymandering. In a series of *racial* gerrymandering cases, this Court determined that particular districts in Alabama's state legislative plans,[108] Virginia's state house plan,[109] North Carolina's congressional[110] and state legislative[111] plans, and Wisconsin's state house plan,[112] were likely unlawful because they were designed for predominantly racial purposes and didn't satisfy strict scrutiny. All these maps were highly biased in a Republican direction, and all of them had to be redrawn, in part, because of the Court's rulings. The Court further held that Alabama diluted the electoral influence of African American voters, thereby violating Section 2 of the VRA, by enacting a congressional plan that included one rather than two districts in which Black voters could elect their preferred candidates.[113] This plan also exhibited a pro-Republican skew, and it too had to be reshaped due to the Court's decision.

These cases are why the active pro-alignment quadrant isn't completely bare.[114] But they should be discounted as examples of the Roberts Court intervening to promote alignment for two reasons. First, the legal theories of

---

[108] *See* Ala. Legis. Black Caucus v. Alabama, 575 U.S. 257 (2015).
[109] *See* Bethune-Hill v. Va. State Bd. of Elections, 580 U.S. 788 (2017).
[110] *See* Cooper v. Harris, 581 U.S. 285 (2017).
[111] *See* North Carolina v. Covington, 138 S. Ct. 2548 (2018).
[112] *See* Wis. Legis. v. Wis. Elections Comm'n, 595 U.S. 398 (2022).
[113] *See* Allen v. Milligan, 143 S. Ct. 1487 (2023).
[114] To this short list, you could perhaps add *Frank v. Walker*, 574 U.S. 929 (2014), in which the Supreme Court vacated an appellate court stay that had prevented a district court injunction prohibiting Wisconsin from enforcing its photo ID requirement for voting from going into effect. But photo ID requirements don't appear to be highly misaligning, and in any event, the Court's

racial gerrymandering and racial vote dilution are distinct from the concept of misalignment. Again, racial gerrymandering means relying on race when crafting districts to a predominant and unjustified degree. Individual districts can be racially gerrymandered (or not) whether a map as a whole is tilted in one, or another, or neither party's favor. Similarly, racial vote dilution means that a *racial* group's legislative representation has been reduced relative to some benchmark. Its presence (or absence) doesn't entail the diminished (or enhanced) representation of any *partisan* group. Racial gerrymandering and racial vote dilution therefore aren't proxies for misalignment. They're separate theories that aim to prevent and remedy other injuries inflicted by redistricting.

Second, precisely because of these conceptual differences, rulings in favor of plaintiffs on racial gerrymandering or racial vote dilution grounds aren't necessarily aligning. When districts stricken as racial gerrymanders are part of a partisan gerrymander, mapmakers can respond by designing new districts that no longer weigh race so heavily—but are just as biased in partisan terms.[115] That's what happened in the wake of the 2017 case of *Cooper v. Harris*, probably the Roberts Court's most prominent racial gerrymandering decision. North Carolina Republicans reacted to the Court's nullification of two congressional districts by drawing new lines without considering race at all, but flaunting their intent to "'give a partisan advantage to 10 Republicans and 3 Democrats.'"[116] The remedial plan they enacted was the very one at issue in *Rucho*: the congressional map with the fourth-worst average efficiency gap since 1972.[117]

Likewise, the view that plaintiffs' victories in racial vote dilution cases are *misaligning*—because they skew plans to the right—is so widespread that it has its own name: the perverse effects thesis. In Chapter 8, I argued at length that the perverse effects thesis is usually incorrect. In general, it's possible to create more minority opportunity districts without thereby tilting maps so that they benefit Republicans and conservatives. But under either the perverse effects thesis (obviously), or my refutation of it, there's no basis for expecting successful racial vote dilution claims typically to *improve* alignment. At worst (under the perverse effects thesis), these wins systematically push plans to the right. At best (given

---

shadow docket action was based entirely on the proximity of the next election—not any substantive unease about Wisconsin's policy.

[115] At least, mapmakers can so respond when a single party still controls the redistricting process. Alone among the Roberts Court's racial gerrymandering cases, *Bethune-Hill* was aligning because, after it was decided, Virginia had divided rather than unified Republican government. A special master was thus assigned to redraw the stricken districts.

[116] *Rucho v. Common Cause*, 139 S. Ct. 2484, 2510 (2019) (Kagan, J., dissenting).

[117] Similarly, after the Supreme Court invalidated portions of one Wisconsin state house plan on racial gerrymandering grounds, an even more biased map crafted by the Republican legislature was ultimately adopted. *See* Johnson v. Wis. Elections Comm'n, 401 Wis. 2d 198 (2022).

what I understand to be the empirical reality), the wins have inconsistent, highly contingent implications for alignment.[118]

Accordingly, I give the Roberts Court some credit—but not much—for these redistricting rulings. These rulings' reasoning had nothing to do with alignment. And even though the rulings invalidated parts of biased maps, they often yielded remedial plans no fairer than the gerrymanders they replaced. My verdict on this Court's record in the final quadrant, comprising passive pro-alignment cases, is equally tepid. From one perspective, the Court has declined several invitations to block aligning federal and state actions. But from another, these invitations asked the Court to overturn generations of precedent and to destabilize pillars of our electoral system. The Court deserves only faint praise for turning down these opportunities to exacerbate the misalignment that already pervades American politics.

I've already mentioned the Roberts Court's passive pro-alignment decisions involving the ISL theory. In *Arizona State Legislature* and *Moore*, respectively, the Court upheld Arizona's independent redistricting commission and North Carolina's state court decision striking down a partisan gerrymander against ISL challenges. In *Arizona State Legislature*, the Court not only upheld Arizona's commission but also made clear that it did so, in part, because of the commission's ability to avoid the misalignment that stems from partisan gerrymandering. "The people of Arizona turned to the initiative to curb the practice of gerrymandering," declared the Court in the final paragraph of its opinion.[119] "In so acting, Arizona voters sought to restore the core principle of republican government, namely, that the voters should choose their representatives, not the other way around."[120] Unfortunately, as I also explained above, *Arizona State Legislature* might sit on thin legal ice. Chief Justice Roberts had four votes in that case to nullify Arizona's commission on the basis of the ISL theory, and his stance could have the support of six Justices today. Analogously, *Moore* repudiated the strongest versions of the ISL theory but affirmatively recognized a weak form. Under this weak form, aligning state court decisions under state law about federal elections are unconstitutional if they seem too eccentric to federal courts.

Another passive pro-alignment decision of the Roberts Court concerned redistricting, too, but was unrelated to the ISL theory. In a 2016 case, the Court unanimously held that the one-person, one-vote rule doesn't require

---

[118] In the unusual context of *Milligan* itself, though, the Roberts Court's decision was aligning. That's because the second Black opportunity district that had to be created thanks to the Court's ruling could only be formed by sacrificing a Republican district, thus making Alabama's congressional plan as a whole less biased in a Republican direction.

[119] Ariz. St. Legis. v. Ariz. Indep. Redist. Comm'n, 576 U.S. 787, 824 (2015).

[120] *Id.* (internal quotation marks omitted).

jurisdictions to equalize districts' numbers of adult citizens.[121] Had the Court forced jurisdictions to change their apportionment base from persons to adult citizens, district plans already skewed in a Republican direction would have become more pro-Republican still.[122] The Court's maintenance of the apportionment status quo prevented this further distortion. However, the advantage that Republicans stand to gain from equalizing districts' adult citizens, instead of their persons, is quite limited in most states: on the order of just 1 percentage point more seats.[123] The Court also didn't announce that states *can't* equalize districts' adult citizens; it merely said they're not *obligated* to do so. The Court's decision thus didn't avert very much misalignment. And the misalignment it did avert could occur anyway if states try to switch their apportionment base voluntarily.

The Roberts Court's final major set of passive pro-alignment rulings addressed campaign finance regulations.[124] In *Citizens United*, the Court upheld federal statutory requirements that funders of independent campaign expenditures state their responsibility for campaign ads and publicly disclose their spending.[125] These requirements, the Court correctly observed, promote representational alignment by "provid[ing] . . . citizens with the information needed to hold . . . elected officials accountable for their positions."[126] In a 2011 case, the Court also strongly suggested that most public financing systems are constitutional. "We do not today call into question the wisdom" of these policies, some of which are aligning, the Court stated.[127] "[G]overnments may engage in public financing of election campaigns," and "doing so can further significant governmental interests."[128] And in a 2014 case, a plurality similarly implied that the "base" federal contribution limits, which restrict how much money donors can give directly to federal candidates, are valid. "[W]e have previously upheld" these highly aligning regulations "as serving . . . permissible objective[s]," the plurality pointed out.[129] "[W]e leave the base limits undisturbed," the plurality went on, and they "remain the primary means of regulating campaign contributions."[130]

---

[121] *See* Evenwel v. Abbott, 578 U.S. 54, 63–75 (2016).

[122] *See* Jowei Chen & Nicholas O. Stephanopoulos, *Democracy's Denominator*, 109 Calif. L. Rev. 1011, 1039–40 (2021).

[123] *See id.*

[124] A couple less significant rulings in this category are *Harris v. Arizona Independent Redistricting Commission*, 578 U.S. 253 (2016) (upholding a reasonably fair state legislative plan against a one-person, one-vote challenge); and *Washington State Grange v. Washington State Republican Party*, 552 U.S. 442 (2008) (upholding a top-two primary system, which may slightly improve alignment, against a First Amendment challenge).

[125] *See* Citizens United v. FEC, 558 U.S. 310, 366–72 (2010).

[126] *Id.* at 370.

[127] Ariz. Free Enter. Club's Freedom Club PAC v. Bennett, 564 U.S. 721, 753 (2011).

[128] *Id.* at 754 (internal quotation marks and alterations omitted).

[129] McCutcheon v. FEC, 572 U.S. 185, 192–93 (2014) (plurality opinion).

[130] *Id.* at 209.

Again, though, a crucial caveat must be affixed to these otherwise encouraging decisions. All of them could plausibly be overturned in the years ahead. I described in the previous section a 2021 case in which the Roberts Court invalidated a disclosure requirement outside the campaign finance context.[131] The logic of that ruling, I noted, could be extended to mandates that campaign contributions and expenditures be reported without much difficulty. Likewise, in the 2011 case in which this Court hinted that *other* public financing systems are lawful, the Court struck down the public financing policy it actually faced.[132] The Court's decision, Justice Kagan also cautioned in dissent, does in fact threaten other public financing regimes because "*[a]ny* system of public financing . . . imposes a similar burden on privately funded candidates" as the policy the Court rejected.[133] In the 2014 case in which a plurality seemed to affirm the legality of the base federal contribution limits, too, the Court nullified the aggregate federal contribution limit.[134] And once more, Justice Breyer warned in dissent that the Court's approach "is flatly inconsistent with the broader definition of corruption upon which" the constitutionality of conventional contribution limits depends.[135]

There are some dogs that didn't bark, then, in the Roberts Court's election law jurisprudence—some situations in which this Court properly stood on the sidelines instead of stepping in to stop the aligning efforts of nonjudicial actors. But there aren't many of these silent dogs: just a handful, compared to the much greater volume of cases in which the Court did hand down anti-alignment rulings. These dogs were also supposed to stay mute according to long-standing precedents. For them to have made a racket, the Court would have had to renounce several of its earlier decisions. And in the years to come, the Court may well spurn these prior cases. If it does so, the noiseless dogs of the passive pro-alignment quadrant will become the newest, loudest members of the active anti-alignment zone.

⋆ ⋆ ⋆

Earlier in this chapter I displayed an empty two-by-two matrix. One dimension indicated whether a judicial ruling is aligning (pro-alignment) or misaligning (anti-alignment). The other axis denoted whether a court upholds a challenged electoral practice (passive) or invalidates it (active). I present another version of this matrix below, this time with the quadrants filled in with the election law

---

[131] *See* Americans for Prosperity Found. v. Bonta, 141 S. Ct. 2373 (2021).
[132] *See Bennett*, 564 U.S. at 734–55.
[133] *Id.* at 770 (Kagan, J., dissenting).
[134] *See McCutcheon*, 572 U.S. at 196–227 (plurality opinion).
[135] *Id.* at 244 (Breyer, J., dissenting).

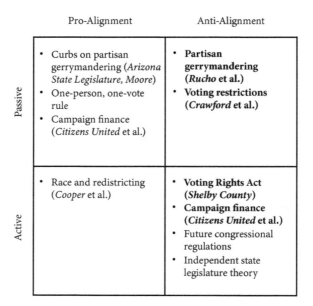

	Pro-Alignment	Anti-Alignment
Passive	• Curbs on partisan gerrymandering (*Arizona State Legislature, Moore*) • One-person, one-vote rule • Campaign finance (*Citizens United* et al.)	• **Partisan gerrymandering (*Rucho* et al.)** • **Voting restrictions (*Crawford* et al.)**
Active	• Race and redistricting (*Cooper* et al.)	• **Voting Rights Act (*Shelby County*)** • **Campaign finance (*Citizens United* et al.)** • Future congressional regulations • Independent state legislature theory

FIGURE 11.2 MATRIX OF ELECTION LAW CASES (FILLED)

cases of the Roberts Court. Lines of doctrine are bolded if they're good examples of the judicial behavior identified by a given quadrant. They're left in Roman typeface if they're less compelling for some reason—because they anticipate future decisions, are at high risk of reversal, or have limited implications for alignment. And I flag by name a few prominent cases that exemplify certain kinds of judicial behavior.

The takeaways from this now-completed matrix (Figure 11.2) should be familiar by this point. The passive anti-alignment quadrant is full of Roberts Court rulings: in particular, partisan gerrymandering cases like *Rucho* and voting restriction cases like *Crawford*. The active anti-alignment quadrant also brims with this Court's jurisprudence. That's where you'll now find *Shelby County* discarding the core of the VRA and *Citizens United* and many other decisions nullifying campaign finance regulations. Additionally, it's where you may soon find the Court rejecting new congressional electoral reforms and overturning state court rulings under the ISL theory. In contrast, the two pro-alignment quadrants are much lonelier places. They include only a few race-and-redistricting cases (mostly not, in fact, aligning) and a hodgepodge of decisions that certain aligning policies can stay in place (for now, though maybe not for good). This record is what earns the Roberts Court the sobriquet of the anti-alignment Court. For almost two decades, it has undermined this vital democratic value far more often than it has furthered it.[136]

If the federal courts are now a skeptical, even hostile, forum for proponents of alignment, where can these advocates go instead? The aligning alternatives to federal litigation are the subject of the next chapter. One of these alternatives is new congressional legislation. Even though there are some congressional actions at which the Roberts Court would likely look askance, there remains a great deal that Congress can do to improve alignment. State-level efforts are also possibilities. There are few limits on the aligning laws that state legislatures can enact. If state legislatures instead enact misaligning laws, state courts can (subject to the ISL theory) strike them down. And in many states, voters themselves can adopt aligning policies, or abandon misaligning ones, through direct democracy. Some final options are nonlegal and nongovernmental. On their own, constituents can simply contact their elected officials more frequently—a step that has been shown to boost alignment. In addition, an entrepreneurial institution could estimate and report public opinion at a granular level—another strategy with significant aligning potential.

[136] In previous work I've speculated that partisanship helps explain the Roberts Court's record in election law cases. *See* Stephanopoulos, *supra* note 6, at 178 ("Running like a red thread through the Roberts Court's anti-*Carolene* decisions is perceived, and actual, partisan advantage."). Putting this point in terms of alignment, in its passive anti-alignment rulings, this Court has generally declined to disturb policies that resulted in pro-Republican, pro-conservative misalignment. And in its active anti-alignment rulings, the Court has usually pushed misalignment in the same pro-Republican, pro-conservative direction through its interventions. In other words, the Court's anti-alignment decisions haven't been random or neutral in their partisan or ideological effects. Rather, they've largely accrued to the benefit of the Court's preferred party and ideology.

12

Aligning Alternatives

Introduction

To some lawyers and scholars—especially those for whom the Warren Court exemplified the aligning role the Supreme Court can play in American governance—the previous chapter may have read like the counsel of despair. Chief Justice Warren once wrote that the Court must "carefully scrutinize[]" electoral regulations to ensure that "the institutions of state government are structured so as to represent fairly all the people."[1] If a Court (like the Roberts Court) refuses to closely examine potentially misaligning rules, who else can possibly promote alignment? Politicians, in particular, seem to be implausible saviors. Politicians are the self-interested schemers who often *distort* "the institutions of state government" so they're *not* "structured so as to represent fairly all the people." So how can politicians further alignment if the Court abandons this democratic project?

In fact, politicians and other figures outside the federal judiciary have the legal ability to take many aligning measures. More surprisingly, these actors also have the political will to do so in certain (though far from all) circumstances. The double-barreled thesis of this chapter is thus that, legally and politically, there are serious aligning alternatives to the federal courts. Legally, other actors *can* significantly advance alignment. And politically, other actors sometimes *do* significantly advance alignment. Of course, it would be better for the federal courts to work in tandem—not at cross-purposes—with other actors in the pursuit of a more aligned system of governance. But even in the face of federal judicial indifference, or outright opposition, the aligning game is far from over. The right response to the anti-alignment record of the Roberts Court, then, isn't despair. It's determination. Determination to think creatively about how other actors can improve alignment. And determination to push for these aligning steps, consistently and forcefully, until they become reality.

Beginning with the federal government, Congress has vast authority to regulate elections at all levels. Critically, this power doesn't flow from a single constitutional source. Instead, it stems from an array of provisions, which, together, form a multilayered foundation for congressional electoral supervision. Think

---

[1] Kramer v. Union Free Sch. Dist. No. 15, 395 U.S. 621, 627–28 (1969).

Aligning Election Law. Nicholas O. Stephanopoulos, Oxford University Press. © Nicholas O. Stephanopoulos 2024.
DOI: 10.1093/9780197662182.003.0012

first of a horizontal plane representing all elections in America. The Elections Clause authorizes Congress to make laws about the portion of this plane corresponding to congressional elections. The Electors Clause confers the same power over presidential elections. And the Guarantee Clause enables Congress to regulate state and local elections to safeguard their republicanism. Next imagine a series of additional levels under the top one, each denoting another basis for congressional action applicable to all elections. The Fourteenth Amendment's Enforcement Clause authorizes Congress to prevent or remedy most constitutional election law violations. The Enforcement Clauses of the Fifteenth and other Amendments empower Congress to target racial and other forms of voting discrimination. Through the Commerce Clause, Congress can reach money and commercial products in politics. Through the Spending Clause, Congress can induce states to enact electoral policies of their own. And at the bottom of this multilayered foundation lies the Necessary and Proper Clause, expanding the scope of every provision above it.

Not only does Congress possess sweeping authority over elections, it has also repeatedly exercised this power in aligning ways. In earlier eras, Congress forced states to switch from at-large to districted congressional elections, protected African Americans from voting discrimination in the First and Second Reconstructions, and extensively regulated campaign finance. In our own time, Congress came within a couple votes of enacting an extraordinary set of aligning measures in 2021–22. Among (many) other things, the bills that almost passed would have mandated independent redistricting commissions, ended most voter suppression efforts, revived Section 5 of the Voting Rights Act (VRA), facilitated voting and voter registration, and created a new system of public financing for campaigns. These bills' existence and near-passage show that many politicians are willing to support a range of highly aligning policies. These bills' major provisions are also likely constitutional, even under the jurisprudence of the Roberts Court. The key to their validity, again, is the multilayered foundation that undergirds them. Thanks to this robust edifice, even if this Court were to hold that some clause doesn't authorize some action, several other clauses would still support the disputed step.

Turning to the states, there are virtually no aligning measures that are beyond their power to adopt. State legislatures are the default regulators of state and federal elections in our system. Unless preempted by federal law, they have the discretion to enact the electoral regulations of their choice. Governors, administrators, voters via direct democracy, and state courts can also take all actions authorized by state law with respect to state elections. These include gubernatorial vetoes, administrative regulations, voter initiatives, and judicial decisions. In the recent past, there was some dispute as to whether nonlegislative state actors enjoy the same freedom with respect to federal elections. However, the Supreme Court dispelled the cloud cast by the independent state legislature (ISL) theory over gubernatorial, administrative, direct democratic, and most state judicial acts pertaining to federal elections. The weak form of the ISL theory recognized by the Court potentially bars only highly novel state court rulings applicable to federal elections.

The real issue at the state level, then, is political will—not legal ability—to adopt aligning policies. Regrettably, elected officials who believe they benefit from misaligning rules rarely support the revision or rescission of those rules. But the converse also holds: Politicians who think they're disadvantaged by existing misalignment often back aligning measures, seeing in them the promise of both personal and democratic gain. In addition, voters tend to be less self-interested than politicians and more receptive to proposals that boost alignment. Direct democracy is thus a viable way to circumvent elected officials in some jurisdictions, to enact aligning reforms despite their opposition. And state judges commonly have different constituencies and incentives from state politicians. State judges are responsible for enforcing state constitutions, too, most of which endorse a democracy principle that's very similar to alignment.

Lastly, aligning public policy can be complemented by aligning private activity: steps taken by individuals and private entities, without the force of law, to enhance alignment. One such channel aims to change the informational environment of politicians. There's evidence that, when politicians are contacted by a representative slice of their constituents, or told what their constituents think about certain issues, politicians cast votes that are more consistent with their constituents' views. Another channel emphasizes the information available to voters. When voters read nonpartisan guides summarizing candidates' positions, or use interactive tools that compare voters' to candidates' stances, voters are better able to vote spatially—for more ideologically proximate candidates. One more channel relies on private action that parallels aligning campaign finance regulation. Private groups can make publicly mandated disclosure more potent. Private organizing can also deter some campaign funding by Super PACs and corporations, both potentially misaligning sources of money in politics.

Horizontal Federal Authority

The elected branches of the federal government are the obvious aligning alternative to the federal courts. Congress can pass, and the President can sign, electoral legislation that promotes alignment.[2] To grasp the full electoral authority of the

---

[2] Congress and the President can also promote alignment through means other than legislation. *See generally* Nicholas O. Stephanopoulos, *The New Pro-Majoritarian Powers*, 109 CALIF. L. REV. 2358 (2021) (discussing each congressional chamber's power to judge its members' elections as well

federal elected branches, the crucial point is the sheer number of relevant constitutional provisions: almost a dozen in total. Because of this unusual efflorescence
of constitutional text, parsing any single clause in isolation is unproductive. Each
clause must always be understood as a piece of a larger jigsaw puzzle, a thread
in a broader tapestry. It's the assembled puzzle, the woven tapestry, that defines
the whole scope of federal electoral power. The volume of germane provisions
also makes redundancy and reinforcement the touchstones of legal analysis in
this area. Frequently, when Congress legislates about elections, its authority to
do so stems from multiple clauses simultaneously. Together, these clauses form a
sturdier basis for congressional intervention than any provision standing alone.
They fill in one another's gaps, offer distinct but overlapping rationales for intervention, and confirm that congressional action is a feature (not a breach) of the
constitutional design.[3]

Additionally, the sheer number of electoral clauses means that my commentary on each provision is necessarily abbreviated. I capture the state of current
doctrine on each clause. But I don't trace the evolution of this doctrine. Nor do
I address its consistency with the original meaning at the time of each provision's
enactment. And nor do I speculate how the law might continue to evolve under
the guidance of the Roberts Court. To avoid a dry recitation of precedents, I also
focus less on what the cases say and more on how they fit together. I argue that
they create a multilayered foundation for congressional electoral authority—
extending horizontally to grant Congress power over most electoral matters, and
reaching vertically to provide it with multiple bases for most measures it passes.

The logical place to start is the Elections Clause of Article I: the Constitution's
clearest articulation of (a part of) Congress's electoral authority. The Clause
empowers Congress to "make or alter . . . Regulations" of "[t]he Times, Places and
Manner of . . . Elections for Senators and Representatives."[4] The provision thus
applies to congressional elections but not to presidential, state, or local races.
The provision also doesn't define its key terms—the times, places, and manner
of elections—leaving it to the courts to supply their content. Stepping into the
breach, the courts have construed this language exceptionally broadly.[5] Under

---

as presidential enforcement of the Guarantee Clause). I bracket these nonlegislative means here because they're less general and more obscure than legislation.

[3] For another scholar stressing the multiplicity of constitutional provisions empowering Congress
to regulate elections, see Franita Tolson, *The Spectrum of Congressional Authority Over Elections*,
99 B.U. L. Rev. 317, 326–27 (2019) (arguing that the combination of the Elections Clause with the
Fourteenth and Fifteenth Amendments "should inform the level of deference that the Court uses to
analyze congressional acts").

[4] U.S. Const. art. I, § 4.

[5] For another scholar agreeing with this characterization, see Samuel Issacharoff, Comment,
Beyond the Discrimination Model on Voting, 127 Harv. L. Rev. 95, 111 (2013) (explaining how the
Supreme Court has "put the Elections Clause on a higher rung of full federal power than even the
Commerce Clause").

the Clause, "Congress has plenary and paramount jurisdiction over the whole subject" of congressional elections, declared the Supreme Court in an 1879 case.[6] This power "may be exercised as and when Congress sees fit," and "so far as it extends and conflicts with the regulations of the State, necessarily supersedes them."[7] The Court added in a 1932 case that the Clause's "comprehensive words embrace authority to provide a complete code for congressional elections."[8] Even the Roberts Court agreed, in a 2013 case, that "[t]he Clause's substantive scope is broad."[9]

Consistent with these pronouncements, the Court has held that Congress can legislate about almost every conceivable aspect of congressional elections. Congress can make it a crime for private, nongovernmental actors to interfere with voting in congressional races.[10] Congress can regulate congressional general as well as primary elections.[11] Congress can make rules for elections in which congressional and non-congressional candidates are on the ballot—and that apply to both types of races.[12] Congress can order states to administer congressional elections in certain ways, notwithstanding the usual ban on commandeering.[13] As the Court put it in 1932, in its best-known summary of the Election Clause's scope, Congress can reach "not only [the] times and places" of congressional races, but also their "notices, registration, supervision of voting, protection of voters, prevention of fraud and corrupt practices, counting of votes, duties of inspectors and canvassers, and making and publication of election returns."[14]

Maybe most controversially,[15] Congress can even regulate who votes (not just how voting is conducted) in congressional elections. In 1970, Congress passed a law that, among other things, lowered the minimum voting age in congressional elections from twenty-one to eighteen.[16] In the Court's subsequent decision in

---

[6]   *Ex parte* Siebold, 100 U.S. 371, 388 (1879).

[7]   *Id.* at 384.

[8]   Smiley v. Holm, 285 U.S. 355, 366 (1932).

[9]   Arizona v. Inter Tribal Council of Ariz., Inc., 570 U.S. 1, 8 (2013).

[10]   *See, e.g., Ex parte* Yarbrough (*The Ku-Klux Cases*), 110 U.S. 651, 666 (1884).

[11]   *See, e.g.,* United States v. Classic, 313 U.S. 299, 317 (1941).

[12]   *See, e.g., The Ku-Klux Cases*, 110 U.S. at 662.

[13]   *See, e.g.,* Branch v. Smith, 538 U.S. 254, 280 (2003) (plurality opinion).

[14]   Smiley v. Holm, 285 U.S. 355, 366 (1932).

[15]   The controversy stems from Article I's statement that voters in U.S. House elections "shall have the Qualifications requisite" for voters in state house elections. U.S. CONST. art. I, § 2. Arguably, this clause's more specific language means that the Elections Clause's more general reference to the "manner" of elections can't encompass the setting of qualifications for voting in congressional races. In dicta in *Arizona v. Inter Tribal Council*, a majority of the Court embraced this view, opining that "the Elections Clause empowers Congress to regulate *how* federal elections are held, but not *who* may vote in them." 570 U.S. 1, 16 (2013). But this was merely dicta, and as Richard Hasen has noted, *Mitchell* "remains good law unless overruled by the Court." Richard L. Hasen, *Too Plain for Argument: The Uncertain Congressional Power to Require Parties to Choose Presidential Nominees Through Direct and Equal Primaries*, 102 NW. U. L. REV. 2009, 2018 (2008).

[16]   *See* Voting Rights Act Amendments of 1970, Pub. L. No. 91-285, §§ 301–05, 84 Stat. 314, 318–19 (1970).

Oregon v. Mitchell,[17] four Justices would have struck down this provision and another four would have upheld it on a broader equal protection theory.[18] But in his controlling opinion for the Court, Justice Black sustained it squarely on Elections Clause grounds. "[T]he powers of Congress to regulate congressional elections[] includ[e] the age and other qualifications of the voters," he wrote.[19] "Congress has ultimate supervisory power over congressional elections."[20] Since *Mitchell*, Congress has both required states to allow former residents who have moved abroad to vote in congressional elections[21] and made American citizenship a prerequisite for voting for Congress.[22] Thanks to *Mitchell*, neither of these congressionally imposed voting qualifications has ever been challenged.[23]

Stepping back from these cases, we can start to see the structure of Congress's electoral authority emerging. Remember the horizontal plane I described at the outset, encompassing every possible electoral topic and level. The Elections Clause doesn't fill this plane. It doesn't give Congress plenary power over every electoral issue. But it does demarcate a portion of the plane—that involving congressional elections—in which Congress enjoys essentially complete control. The Clause also confers to Congress some electoral power outside this portion. As noted above, Congress can regulate non-congressional elections under the provision, to the extent they're held concurrently with (and can't be disentangled from) congressional elections.

Recall the vertical dimension I mentioned earlier, too, registering different legal rationales for congressional electoral action. The Elections Clause doesn't occupy all of this dimension either. In fact, it supplies just a single basis for Congress to regulate elections: that under a particular constitutional provision, Congress explicitly has the authority to set or change the times, places, and manner of congressional elections.[24] As you'll see below, this justification for congressional intervention is usually underpinned by several more, each corresponding to a distinct legal theory. The sources of congressional power thus often stack up, forming a pillar stronger than the sum of its parts.

---

[17] 400 U.S. 112 (1970).
[18] *See id.* at 117–18 (opinion of Black, J.) (describing the Justices' votes).
[19] *Id.* at 122.
[20] *Id.* at 124.
[21] *See* 52 U.S.C. §§ 20301–11 (2018).
[22] *See* 18 U.S.C. § 611 (2018).
[23] *See also* Tashjian v. Republican Party of Conn., 479 U.S. 208, 229 (1986) (confirming *Mitchell's* "conclusion that these provisions [of Article I] do not require a perfect symmetry of voter qualifications in state and federal legislative elections").
[24] This is just a paraphrase of the Election Clause's text. The deeper rationale for the provision's allocation of electoral power to Congress is that some institution must be able to regulate congressional elections, and Congress is a more trustworthy grantee for this power than are the states. *See, e.g.*, THE FEDERALIST No. 59 (Alexander Hamilton) ("[A]n exclusive power of regulating elections for the national government, in the hands of the State legislatures, would leave the existence of the Union entirely at their mercy.").

You may have noticed that, in my discussion of the Elections Clause, I carefully referred to *congressional* rather than *federal* elections. I did so because *presidential* elections are federal elections, as well, but are outside the heartland of Congress's Elections Clause authority. Congress's power to regulate presidential elections derives, instead, from the Electors Clause of Article II.[25] This provision states that "Congress may determine the Time of ch[oo]sing the Electors" (presidential electors, of course, being the individuals who officially select the President under the Constitution's complicated Electoral College system).[26]

As a textual matter, the Electors Clause is plainly narrower than the Elections Clause. It only authorizes Congress to set the time of presidential elections. It's silent about the places, and more importantly the manner, of these races. Nevertheless, the courts have construed the Electors Clause coextensively with the Elections Clause, holding that the former endows Congress with the same authority over presidential elections that the latter grants it over congressional races.[27] In a 1934 case, for instance, the Supreme Court ruled that Congress has the "power to pass appropriate legislation to safeguard [a presidential] election . . . . from impairment or destruction."[28] "[T]he choice of means to that end presents a question primarily addressed to the judgment of Congress."[29] In *Mitchell*, similarly, Justice Black's controlling opinion announced that "it is the prerogative of Congress to oversee the conduct of presidential and vice-presidential elections."[30] This prerogative is identical in the presidential and congressional contexts: "It cannot be seriously contended that Congress has less power over the conduct of presidential elections than it has over congressional elections."[31]

Unsurprisingly, given these views, the Court has held that Congress can mandate the disclosure of campaign contributions and expenditures,[32] restrict campaign donations, and institute a system of public financing for presidential elections.[33] As at the congressional level, the Court has also ruled that Congress can change the qualifications for voting in presidential elections. The 1970 law that lowered the congressional voting age to eighteen did the same

---

[25] As discussed below, this power also derives from the Necessary and Proper Clause.

[26] U.S. CONST. art. II, § 1.

[27] For scholars echoing this view, see Dan T. Coenen & Edward J. Larson, *Congressional Power over Presidential Elections: Lessons from the Past and Reforms for the Future*, 43 WM. & MARY L. REV. 851, 891 (2002) ("[T]he [presidential electoral] power is fully coextensive with Congress's sweeping authority to regulate in any way the 'Manner' of House and Senate elections.").

[28] Burroughs v. United States, 290 U.S. 534, 545 (1934).

[29] *Id.* at 547.

[30] Oregon v. Mitchell, 400 U.S. 112, 124 (1970) (opinion of Black, J.).

[31] *Id.; see also* U.S. Term Limits, Inc. v. Thornton, 514 U.S. 779, 894 (1995) (Thomas, J., dissenting) ("[T]he treatment of congressional elections in Article I parallels the treatment of Presidential elections in Article II.").

[32] *See Burroughs*, 290 U.S. at 548.

[33] *See* Buckley v. Valeo, 424 U.S. 1, 90 (1976).

for the presidential voting age.[34] The statute further abrogated state residency requirements for voting for President, directed states to allow voters to register for presidential elections until thirty days before election day, and established that voters can vote absentee for President as long as they request their ballots at least seven days before the election.[35] All these measures were upheld in *Mitchell*—the ones unrelated to age by an 8–1 vote.[36] As Justice Black elaborated, "[e]ssential to the survival and to the growth of our national government is its power to fill its elective offices and to insure that the officials who fill those offices are as responsive as possible to the will of the people whom they represent."[37]

Returning to the dimensions of congressional electoral authority, the Electors Clause delimits an additional region in the horizontal plane: that involving presidential elections. Within this region, Congress possesses the same power as in the zone for congressional elections, which is to say almost complete control. On the vertical axis of rationales for congressional electoral action, the Clause also provides another justification: that a specific constitutional provision authorizes Congress to fix certain aspects of presidential elections.[38] But this basis is best understood as paralleling, not supplementing, the reason for congressional intervention supplied by the Elections Clause. In other words, a given electoral regulation can be grounded in either the Elections Clause (if it relates to congressional elections) or the Electors Clause (if it covers presidential elections) but not both provisions.[39]

What about a regulation of *state* or *local* elections? Congress can't impose one under the Elections Clause or the Electors Clause (except to the extent the rule is intertwined with regulations of federal elections). Rather, Congress's broadest source of power to legislate about non-federal elections is the Guarantee Clause of Article IV. "The United States shall guarantee to every State in this Union a Republican Form of Government," the Clause reads.[40] States' elections (indeed, their entire systems of government) must thus be republican. If and when they become unrepublican, the federal government is authorized to step in and restore democracy at the state or local level.[41]

[34] *See* Voting Rights Act Amendments of 1970, Pub. L. No. 91-285, §§ 301–05, 84 Stat. 314, 318–19 (1970).

[35] *See* § 202, 84 Stat. at 316–17.

[36] *See Mitchell*, 400 U.S. at 118–19 (opinion of Black, J.) (describing the Justices' votes).

[37] *Id.* at 134.

[38] As with the Elections Clause, the deeper non-textual rationale for authorizing Congress to legislate about presidential elections is that the federal government must ultimately be able to regulate the elections that constitute it. To quote Justice Black again, "under its broad authority to create and maintain a national government," Congress must have "power under the Constitution to regulate federal elections." *Mitchell*, 400 U.S. at 134 (opinion of Black, J.).

[39] With the caveat that a presidential electoral regulation could be based on both the Electors Clause and Congress's Elections Clause power to reach mixed elections.

[40] U.S. CONST. art. IV, § 4.

[41] Why just at the state or local (and not at any) electoral level? Because a state's federal elections determine its representatives (congressional members and presidential electors) in the government

Republicanism, of course, is a hotly contested concept.[42] As I explained in Chapter 4, though, scholars have arrived at a rough consensus that, at least as an originalist matter, the essence of republicanism is popular sovereignty: government by and for the people, in whom all political power is ultimately vested. In turn, popular sovereignty is typically operationalized through majority rule, which itself is largely equivalent to majoritarian alignment. Under the Guarantee Clause, then, Congress can regulate non-federal elections (at least) to prevent and remedy majoritarian misalignment. Majoritarian misalignment, this book has shown, can occur for many reasons: voter suppression, malapportionment, partisan gerrymandering, unchecked campaign funding, and so on. All these practices (or absences of practices) can impede a popular majority from electing its preferred candidates, receiving its preferred representation, and enacting its preferred policies. All these choices, that is, can undermine the value of popular sovereignty that constitutes the core of the Clause. And when this tenet is threatened, it's clear from the Clause's text that Congress is empowered to act. Congress is the legislature of the United States. Under the Clause, it's the United States that's the guarantor of republicanism in every state.

Critically, any congressional judgment that intervention is necessary to safeguard popular sovereignty can't be second-guessed by the courts. The Supreme Court hasn't said much about the Guarantee Clause. But the one holding it has reiterated for almost two centuries is that issues arising under the Clause are nonjusticiable, incapable of judicial resolution. This is the case when a plaintiff invokes the Clause to argue that some state law is unrepublican and thus unconstitutional.[43] More relevant here, it's also the case when Congress legislates pursuant to the Clause: No litigant can allege that the statute exceeds Congress's authority to guarantee a republican form of government. As the Court put it in a foundational 1849 decision, "Congress must necessarily decide . . . whether [a state government] is republican or not."[44] "And its decision is binding, on every other department of the government, and could not be questioned in a judicial

---

of a different sovereign: the United States. These elections don't select the officials who actually govern the state itself. No matter how deficient a state's federal elections, then, it's hard to say the state has fallen below the threshold of republicanism if its non-federal elections still top this bar. See, e.g., Gabriel J. Chin, *Justifying a Revised Voting Rights Act: The Guarantee Clause and the Problem of Minority Rule*, 94 B.U. L. REV. 1551, 1586 (2014) ("The Guarantee Clause benefits the states, not the federal government, so some other rationale will have to be found to the extent that [congressional legislation] applies to purely federal elections.").

[42] This is precisely why some scholars argue that suits alleging unrepublican practices should remain nonjusticiable. See, e.g., Richard L. Hasen, *Leaving the Empty Vessel of 'Republicanism' Unfilled: An Argument for the Continued Non-Justiciability of Guarantee Clause Cases* 10–19 (Loyola L. Sch. Pub. L. & Legal Theory Working Paper No. 2003-10, 2003).

[43] See, e.g., Pac. States Tel. & Tel. Co. v. Oregon, 223 U.S. 118 (1912).

[44] Luther v. Borden, 48 U.S. (7 How.) 1, 42 (1849).

tribunal."[45] Or as the Court affirmed in an 1871 case, "[t]he action of Congress upon the subject cannot be inquired into."[46] "[T]he judicial is bound to follow the action of the political department of the government, and is concluded by it."[47]

This 1871 case involved the Reconstruction Acts that Congress passed after the Civil War to prevent the former Confederate states from disenfranchising African Americans and to prescribe detailed rules for these states' elections. Notably, these landmark statutes weren't enacted under the Fourteenth or Fifteenth Amendments (which hadn't yet been ratified). Instead, Congress approved these laws pursuant to its Guarantee Clause power. The first of the laws stated that "peace and good order" had to be congressionally enforced until "republican State government can be legally established."[48] The Supreme Court also recognized that Congress's "authority was derived from the obligation of the United States to guarantee to every State in the Union a republican form of government."[49] Consequently, the Clause isn't some obsolete constitutional oddity, a "sleeping giant" (in Senator Charles Sumner's words[50]) that has never awoken. To the contrary, in one of the most fateful periods in American history, Congress based several of its most controversial actions squarely on the Clause. At least during Reconstruction, as Sumner observed, the Clause "c[a]m[e] forward with a giant's power."[51]

Revisiting the dimensions of congressional electoral authority, the Guarantee Clause occupies the rest of the horizontal plane: the area corresponding to state and local elections. The entire plane is therefore filled, meaning that Congress is empowered to regulate congressional, presidential, and non-federal elections alike. On the vertical axis of rationales for congressional electoral action, the Clause supplies one more parallel justification for legislation: the need to prevent or remedy states' lapses into unrepublicanism. Again, Congress can generally cite this reason instead of, but not as well as, the Elections Clause or the Electors Clause when it addresses electoral issues.

---

[45] Id.

[46] White v. Hart, 80 U.S. (13 Wall.) 646, 649 (1871).

[47] Id.; see also Ohio ex rel. Davis v. Hildebrant, 241 U.S. 565, 570 (1916) (noting that it's Congress "upon whom the Constitution has conferred the exclusive authority to uphold the guaranty of a republican form of government").

[48] An Act to Provide for the More Efficient Government of the Rebel States, § 1, 14 Stat. 428, 428 (1867).

[49] Texas v. White, 74 U.S. (7 Wall.) 700, 727 (1868).

[50] See WILLIAM M. WIECEK, THE GUARANTEE CLAUSE OF THE U.S. CONSTITUTION 290 (1972).

[51] Id. Outside of Reconstruction, Congress also frequently invoked the Guarantee Clause in the context of the admission of new states. See generally Charles O. Lerche, Jr., The Guarantee of a Republican Form of Government and the Admission of New States, 11 J. POL. 578 (1949).

Vertical Federal Authority

I turn next to a series of constitutional amendments (starting with the Fourteenth) that bear some resemblance to the Guarantee Clause. Like the Clause, these amendments authorize Congress to avoid or cure certain evils. These evils, though, are distinct from the unrepublican rule that's the Clause's concern. Whether congressional action is consistent with the amendments is also a justiciable issue. And the amendments aren't limited to certain types of elections but rather enable Congress to reach federal, state, and local races. The amendments thus begin to form layers below the horizontal plane that was the subject of the previous section: rationales that Congress can offer for electoral legislation in addition (not as opposed) to its Elections Clause, Electors Clause, or Guarantee Clause powers.

The provisions of the Fourteenth Amendment that are relevant here are the Equal Protection Clause of Section 1 and the Enforcement Clause of Section 5. The former prohibits each state from "deny[ing] to any person within its jurisdiction the equal protection of the laws,"[52] while the latter states that "Congress shall have power to enforce, by appropriate legislation, the provisions of this article."[53] Historically, the courts were highly deferential toward Congress's exercises of its Fourteenth Amendment enforcement authority. As long as the courts could "perceive a basis upon which the Congress might resolve the conflict as it did," they would uphold the challenged legislation.[54] In a 1997 case, however, the Supreme Court changed the operative standard to require "a congruence and proportionality between the injury to be prevented or remedied and the means adopted to that end."[55] So there must now be a closer fit between the policy chosen by Congress and the underlying constitutional harm.

It's well understood that "congruence and proportionality" is a more demanding test—one more likely to result in the invalidation of a congressional statute—than rational basis review. But scholars haven't fully grasped just how many "injur[ies] to be prevented or remedied" there are in the electoral context. In fact, much of election law revolves around causes of action that stem from different kinds of violations of the Equal Protection Clause. All these transgressions are evils that Congress can try to avoid or cure through its Fourteenth Amendment enforcement power.

---

[52] U.S. Const. amend. XIV, § 1.

[53] Id. § 5.

[54] Katzenbach v. Morgan, 384 U.S. 641, 653 (1966); see also, e.g., Ex parte Virginia, 100 U.S. 339, 345–46 (1879) ("Whatever legislation is appropriate . . . is brought within the domain of congressional power.").

[55] City of Boerne v. Flores, 521 U.S. 507, 520 (1997).

Consider burdens on the right to vote ranging from mere inconvenience to outright disenfranchisement. It's under the Equal Protection Clause that the courts have established a system of sliding-scale scrutiny that adjusts the rigor of judicial review based on the severity of the burden.[56] Or take the principle, announced in *Bush v. Gore*, that ballots can't be treated differently in one part of a state than in another. This is also an equal protection doctrine.[57] The Equal Protection Clause is the source, as well, of the theories of racial vote dilution (intentionally reducing the electoral influence of minority voters)[58] and racial gerrymandering (drawing districts with a predominant racial motive).[59] While it has now been deemed nonjusticiable,[60] severe partisan gerrymandering is unconstitutional, too, because it offends the equal protection norm of treating each party's voters symmetrically.[61]

That the congruence-and-proportionality standard is relatively more restrictive, then, matters less in the electoral domain than in most other areas. There are simply so many potential violations of the Equal Protection Clause— spanning franchise burdens, unequal ballot treatment, racial vote dilution, racial gerrymandering, partisan gerrymandering, and more—that Congress can seek to prevent or remedy. Put another way, the sphere of arguably unconstitutional conduct is unusually large in the electoral realm. So even if the congruence-and-proportionality standard doesn't allow Congress to venture far beyond this sphere, what Congress can lawfully regulate is still quite a lot.

Updating the matrix of congressional electoral authority, the Fourteenth Amendment doesn't fill any more space in the horizontal plane. That is, it doesn't empower Congress with respect to any particular category of electoral topics or levels. But on the vertical axis of rationales for congressional electoral action, the Fourteenth Amendment does provide the first justification that can supplement, not just parallel, the reasons I have covered so far. When Congress legislates to avoid or cure breaches of the Equal Protection Clause, it can do so while also invoking its authority under the Elections Clause, the Electors Clause, or the Guarantee Clause. The same statute can be grounded in both Congress's power over a certain class of elections and its ability to enforce the Fourteenth Amendment.

The next group of pertinent amendments (the Fifteenth, Nineteenth, Twenty-Fourth, and Twenty-Sixth) can be considered as a group thanks to their shared

---

[56] *See, e.g.*, Burdick v. Takushi, 504 U.S. 428, 434 (1992). Sliding-scale scrutiny also applies to burdens on candidates' access to the ballot, *see, e.g., id.*, and on parties' ability to manage their internal affairs, *see, e.g.*, Wash. State Grange v. Wash. State Republican Party, 552 U.S. 442, 451–52 (2008).

[57] *See* Bush v. Gore, 531 U.S. 98, 104 (2000).

[58] *See, e.g.*, Rogers v. Lodge, 458 U.S. 613, 617 (1982).

[59] *See, e.g.*, Shaw v. Reno, 509 U.S. 630, 649 (1993).

[60] *See* Rucho v. Common Cause, 139 S. Ct. 2484 (2019).

[61] *See* Davis v. Bandemer, 478 U.S. 109, 143 (1986) (plurality opinion).

structure. They all stipulate, using nearly identical language, that the right of citizens of the United States to vote shall not be denied or abridged on a certain basis. This forbidden basis is "race, color, or previous condition of servitude" in the Fifteenth Amendment,[62] "sex" in the Nineteenth Amendment,[63] "failure to pay any poll tax or other tax" in the Twenty-Fourth Amendment (for federal elections only),[64] and "age" in the Twenty-Sixth Amendment (for citizens eighteen or older).[65] All four amendments also describe Congress's enforcement authority in almost the same terms (which themselves are almost the same as the Fourteenth Amendment's Enforcement Clause). Under each provision, "Congress shall have power to enforce this article by appropriate legislation."[66]

The Supreme Court has only commented on Congress's enforcement authority under the Fifteenth Amendment. According to the Court, for a measure to be lawful, Congress must reasonably think the step will serve the goal of stopping racial discrimination in voting. "Congress may use any rational means to effectuate the constitutional prohibition of racial discrimination in voting," the Court held in an important 1966 case.[67] Notably, the Roberts Court implicitly affirmed this view in the 2013 case of *Shelby County v. Holder*,[68] which otherwise marked the nadir of the Court's conception of Congress's Fifteenth Amendment enforcement power. Over and over, the Court called it "irrational" for Congress to subject certain jurisdictions to a preclearance requirement before they could change their election laws, based on a formula that relied on data from the 1960s and 1970s.[69] Not once in *Shelby County* did the Court hint that the formula's flaw was its lack of congruence and proportionality with the underlying evil of racial discrimination in voting.

Most likely, highly deferential rational basis review would also apply to exercises of Congress's enforcement authority under the Nineteenth, Twenty-Fourth, and Twenty-Sixth Amendments. It would certainly be odd if Congress had less power under these strikingly similar provisions than under the Fifteenth Amendment.[70] This is speculation, though, since the Court has never addressed Congress's ability to fight voting discrimination on the basis of sex, wealth, or age. Another note of caution is that Justices have sometimes suggested (albeit without the Court ever holding) that only intentional racial discrimination in

---

[62] U.S. CONST. amend. XV, § 1.
[63] U.S. CONST. amend. XIX, § 1.
[64] U.S. CONST. amend. XXIV, § 1.
[65] U.S. CONST. amend. XXVI, § 1.
[66] *Id.* amend. XV, § 2; *id.* amend. XIX, § 2; *id.* amend. XXIV, § 2; *id.* amend. XXVI, § 2.
[67] South Carolina v. Katzenbach, 383 U.S. 301, 324 (1966).
[68] 570 U.S. 529 (2013).
[69] *See, e.g., id.* at 554, 556.
[70] *See, e.g.,* Akhil Reed Amar, *The Lawfulness of Section 5—and Thus of Section 5*, 126 HARV. L. REV. F. 109, 119 (2013) ("[E]very one of these amendments has contained express language suggesting that Congress should have a considerable choice of means in discharging its powers....").

voting violates the Fifteenth Amendment.[71] If this dismissal of disparate impact liability became law, it, too, would presumably extend to the Nineteenth, Twenty-Fourth, and Twenty-Sixth Amendments. In that case, the standard of review might remain highly deferential, but the sphere of arguably unconstitutional conduct that Congress could target would contract. Congress would then need a rational basis for thinking that a given policy would reduce purposeful voting discrimination on account of race, sex, wealth, or age.

But this rational basis might be available surprisingly often. In one of the cases in which the Court intimated that the Fifteenth Amendment only bars intentional racial discrimination in voting, the Court evaluated the VRA provision, Section 5, that formerly prevented certain jurisdictions from revising their election laws in ways that diminished the influence of minority voters. Although this was a disparate impact provision, the Court upheld it, explaining that it was "an appropriate method of promoting the purposes of the Fifteenth Amendment."[72] "Congress could rationally have concluded that, because electoral changes by jurisdictions with a demonstrable history of intentional racial discrimination in voting create the risk of purposeful discrimination, it was proper to prohibit changes that have a discriminatory impact."[73] The Court recently reiterated this reasoning in a case in which it "reject[ed the defendant's] argument that § 2 [of the VRA]," another disparate impact provision, "is unconstitutional under the Fifteenth Amendment."[74] Under this logic, Congress could also attack electoral practices that differentially burden women compared to men, the poor relative to the rich, and the young versus the old. Again, Congress could reasonably believe that these practices' disparate impacts indicate the presence of at least some deliberate voting discrimination, which Congress is unquestionably authorized to thwart.

Like the Fourteenth Amendment, the Fifteenth, Nineteenth, Twenty-Fourth, and Twenty-Sixth Amendments don't claim any more ground in the horizontal plane of congressional electoral power. They don't enable Congress to legislate about specific electoral topics or levels. But also like the Fourteenth Amendment, the Fifteenth, Nineteenth, Twenty-Fourth, and Twenty-Sixth Amendments add to the vertical axis of rationales for congressional electoral action. They supply another justification (actually, four more justifications) for Congress to regulate elections: that Congress is trying to stop voting discrimination on the basis of race, sex, wealth, or age. These reasons can be cited alongside all the ones discussed already. So Congress can root its electoral interventions not just in the Elections Clause, the Electors Clause, or the Guarantee Clause, and not just in its

---

[71] *See, e.g.*, City of Mobile v. Bolden, 446 U.S. 55, 62 (1980) (plurality opinion).
[72] City of Rome v. United States, 446 U.S. 156, 177 (1980).
[73] *Id.*
[74] Allen v. Milligan, 143 S. Ct. 1487, 1516 (2023).

effort to prevent or remedy equal protection violations, but also in its resolve to end voting discrimination.

This leaves a number of provisions—the Commerce Clause, the Spending Clause, and the Necessary and Proper Clause—that aren't primarily about elections but still have significant applications in the electoral context. Starting with the Commerce Clause, it has been construed to authorize Congress to regulate activities that have "substantial effects" on interstate commerce.[75] In an earlier time, this formulation could perhaps have endowed Congress with essentially plenary power over elections. After all, elections, well, elect candidates to office, who then implement policies about taxation, health care, immigration, and a host of other issues. These policies plainly have substantial effects on the national economy.[76] But this line of argument is now foreclosed. In more recent cases, the Supreme Court has clarified that Congress can only address commercial activities under the Commerce Clause.[77] Many aspects of elections, however, are quintessentially noncommercial. In particular, casting a ballot isn't just a noneconomic act on its face; it's forbidden from being made an economic transaction by the federal ban on vote buying.[78]

Other parts of the electoral process, though, are commercial in nature and so regulable under the Commerce Clause. For example, jurisdictions purchase voting machines that voters then use to cast their ballots. These machines are conventional items of commerce that cross state lines and comprise a national market. So Congress can pass laws about them, say, requiring them to be accessible to disabled people or secure against hacking.[79] Likewise, campaign finance is, as its name confirms, financial. When donors make contributions to candidates, or people or organizations spend independently to express their own electoral views, they necessarily engage in economic transactions with substantial interstate effects. Congress can thus legislate about all money in politics, at all electoral levels, pursuant to its Commerce Clause authority.[80]

Apropos of money, the Spending Clause enables Congress to offer funds to the states with strings attached: conditions the states must satisfy to receive the federal dollars. These conditions can be any measures that aren't themselves

---

[75] *See, e.g.*, Wickard v. Filburn, 317 U.S. 111, 125 (1942).

[76] *See, e.g.*, Coenen & Larson, *supra* note 27, at 879 (agreeing that, "[i]n an earlier era, proponents of [electoral] reform ... would have raced to embrace the Commerce Clause").

[77] *See, e.g.*, United States v. Morrison, 529 U.S. 598, 611 (2000).

[78] *See* 18 U.S.C. § 597 (2018).

[79] *See, e.g.*, Stephanie Philips, *The Risks of Computerized Election Fraud: When Will Congress Rectify a 38-Year-Old Problem?*, 57 ALA. L. REV. 1123, 1159 (2006) (agreeing that, "even under the recent, restrictive interpretations of Congress's Commerce Clause power ... Congress does have the authority to regulate voting systems sold to states").

[80] *See, e.g.*, Marlene Arnold Nicholson, *Campaign Financing and Equal Protection*, 26 STAN. L. REV. 815, 824 (1974) ("Should Congress decide to reform state campaign financing practice, the commerce clause is probably the safest grant of authority upon which to rely.").

unconstitutional—even measures that Congress wouldn't have the right to impose directly.[81] But the conditions must be related to the purpose of the funds; Congress can't require the states to do one thing to receive money earmarked for another, completely different thing.[82] The overall terms of Congress's proposals to the states also can't be unduly coercive. The states, that is, must be genuinely free to turn down the federal dollars, along with the obligations that come with them.[83]

Under its Spending Clause power, then, Congress could affix all kinds of electoral conditions to funds offered to the states to administer their elections. These funds would presumably have the aim of making elections freer and fairer—a better instrument for accurately registering the will of the people. So any requirement that also served this goal would be related to the funds' purpose. Moreover, it's improbable that electoral legislation could run afoul of the prohibition on overly coercive federal programs. At present, the states manage to run their elections without any consistent federal subsidization. So if Congress did suddenly make federal money available, it would hardly be a stretch for the states to say no, if they didn't like the attached strings. By rejecting the congressional proposal, the states would simply be opting to maintain the status quo.

Lastly, the Necessary and Proper Clause allows Congress to adopt policies that aren't explicitly authorized by its enumerated powers but that advance these powers' ends. Congress's chosen measures must merely be "convenient" or "useful" or "conducive" to accomplishing goals recognized by other constitutional clauses.[84] "[T]he statute [need only] constitute[] a means that is rationally related to the implementation of a constitutionally enumerated power."[85] However, the steps taken by Congress can't "undermine the structure of government established by the Constitution" or amount to a new "great substantive and independent power."[86] If they do, no matter how necessary the congressional policies may be, they aren't proper ways of achieving constitutional objectives.

In the electoral domain, the Necessary and Proper Clause has often been invoked to justify congressional regulations of presidential elections.[87] Remember that the only constitutional provision that mentions presidential elections, the Electors Clause, is textually quite meager. The Necessary and Proper Clause has compensated for this sparse language in three different ways. Most obviously, congressional regulations of presidential elections are "convenient" or "useful" or "conducive" to the exercise of Congress's Electors Clause authority to set the time for choosing electors. Second, congressional legislation

---

[81]   See, e.g., South Dakota v. Dole, 483 U.S. 203, 207 (1987).

[82]   See, e.g., id.

[83]   See, e.g., Nat'l Fed. Indep. Bus. v. Sebelius, 567 U.S. 519, 581 (2012).

[84]   United States v. Comstock, 560 U.S. 126, 133–34 (2010) (internal quotation marks omitted).

[85]   Id. at 134.

[86]   Sebelius, 567 U.S. at 559 (internal quotation marks omitted).

[87]   See, e.g., Burroughs v. United States, 290 U.S. 534, 545–48 (1934).

about presidential elections is rationally related to Congress's expansive power over congressional elections. In particular, Congress's efforts to safeguard the integrity of congressional elections would be frustrated if fraudsters could claim they were only trying to subvert concurrently held presidential elections.[88] And third, the Supreme Court has held that Congress implicitly has the authority to "preserve the departments and institutions of the general government from impairment or destruction, whether threatened by force or by corruption."[89] Congressional rules for presidential elections further this unenumerated end, rendering them "a question primarily addressed to the judgment of Congress."[90]

In the matrix of congressional electoral power, the Commerce Clause and the Spending Clause function just like the Fourteenth, Fifteenth, Nineteenth, Twenty-Fourth, and Twenty-Sixth Amendments. They don't occupy any more of the horizontal plane since they don't enable Congress to regulate any particular electoral topics or levels. But they do add notches to the vertical axis since they provide further rationales for congressional electoral action: namely, that Congress is legislating about economic aspects of elections that have substantial effects on interstate commerce, or that Congress is linking electoral conditions to electoral funds that it's offering to the states.

In contrast, the Necessary and Proper Clause doesn't have a distinct place of its own in either the horizontal or the vertical dimension. Instead, it operates as a sort of supplement for all the other provisions, expanding their coverage to include not just explicitly authorized means but also all other measures that relate to the provisions' purposes. This enhancement applies in the horizontal plane to the Elections Clause, the Electors Clause, and the Guarantee Clause, allowing each provision to spread beyond its apparent boundaries. The boost applies to the clauses that comprise the vertical axis, too, widening and deepening each justification for congressional electoral regulation.

* * *

I realize that this discussion of planes, axes, and other spatial concepts may be confusing. For visually oriented readers, I therefore present Figure 12.1, which shows graphically how all the pieces of Congress's electoral authority fit together. The horizontal plane on top represents the universe of American elections and indicates which provision enables Congress to regulate which category of elections. Again, this universe is divided among the Elections Clause for congressional elections, the Electors Clause for presidential elections, and

---

[88] *See, e.g.*, Richard Primus & Cameron O. Kistler, *The Support-or-Advocacy Clauses*, 89 FORDHAM L. REV. 145, 167 n.119 (2020).

[89] *Burroughs*, 290 U.S. at 545.

[90] *Id.* at 547.

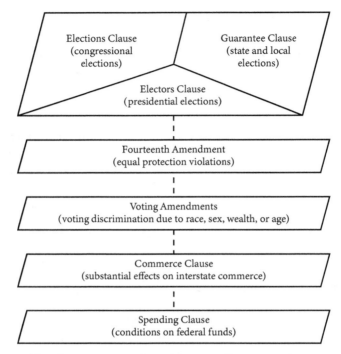

FIGURE 12.1 THE DIMENSIONS OF CONGRESSIONAL ELECTORAL AUTHORITY

Figure 12.1 is reproduced with permission from Nicholas O. Stephanopoulos, *The Sweep of the Electoral Power*, 36 CONST. COMMENT. 1, 72 (2021). Copyright © 2021 by University of Minnesota Law School.

the Guarantee Clause for state and local elections. All the levels below that top plane then correspond to complementary legal reasons—capable of being asserted concurrently—for congressional electoral action. Once more, these are preventing or remedying equal protection violations under the Fourteenth Amendment; fighting voting discrimination due to race, sex, wealth, and age under the Fifteenth, Nineteenth, Twenty-Fourth, and Twenty-Sixth Amendments; addressing economic aspects of elections with substantial effects on interstate commerce under the Commerce Clause; and tying electoral conditions to electoral funds under the Spending Clause. Finally, all the borders in the diagram are somewhat indistinct because of the Necessary and Proper Clause. As just explained, it extends the reach of each enumerated power to additional means related to the power's function. Like cement, the Clause thus fills the spaces between the other provisions, bonding them into an even firmer foundation for federal legislation.

Federal Policies

Congress has the *legal* authority, then, to enact electoral laws that promote alignment. But has Congress demonstrated—and does it continue to possess—the *political* will to pass aligning legislation? Historically, the answer is yes. On several occasions, Congress has approved landmark statutes that significantly improved the alignment of the American system of governance. To name some of these milestones, in the Apportionment Act of 1842, Congress prohibited states from selecting their members of the U.S. House of Representatives through at-large elections. Instead, Congress required states to use single-member districts to choose their House members.[91] Single-member districts aren't without their problems. As I explained in Chapter 7, they're vulnerable to both partisan gerrymandering, a major driver of jurisdiction-wide misalignment, and disregard for traditional line-drawing criteria, which fosters district-specific misalignment. Still, single-member districts are much less misaligning than at-large elections, whose hallmark is that they enable a cohesive majority to sweep *every* legislative seat.[92] Especially when the majority that wins all the seats is a narrow one, the extent of collective misalignment is staggering, exceeding that of even the worst gerrymanders of single-member districts.

During the First and Second Reconstructions, Congress also enacted a series of laws targeting racial discrimination in voting. In the aftermath of the Civil War, the Reconstruction Acts and the Enforcement Acts forbade race-based disenfranchisement and enforced this ban through aggressive measures including the federal takeover of state and local election administration.[93] In the 1960s, the VRA was the crown jewel of the civil rights movement. Its core provisions nullified discriminatory voting rules, imposed a preclearance requirement on recalcitrant southern jurisdictions, and created a nationwide cause of action for racial discrimination in voting.[94] I showed in Chapter 8 that the VRA boosted alignment by increasing minority participation, and didn't undermine alignment (as some critics allege) by increasing minority representation. The same conclusions apply to the Reconstruction Acts and the Enforcement Acts of the years after the Civil War. By incorporating African Americans as full members of southern states' political communities, these statutes made possible aligned

---

[91] *See* An Act for the Apportionment of Representatives Among the Several States According to the Sixth Census, 5 Stat. 491 (1842).

[92] *See, e.g.*, ERIK J. ENGSTROM, PARTISAN GERRYMANDERING AND THE CONSTRUCTION OF AMERICAN DEMOCRACY 25 (2013) (showing that the plurality party won every House seat in 95 percent of congressional general ticket elections between 1800 and 1840).

[93] *See* Nicholas O. Stephanopoulos, *The Sweep of the Electoral Power*, 36 CONST. COMMENT. 1, 35–36 (2021) (describing these statutes in detail).

[94] *See* Voting Rights Act of 1965, Pub. L. No. 89-110, 79 Stat. 437 (1965).

political systems for the first time in these states' histories.[95] One of the many tragedies of the end of Reconstruction is that it snuffed out the flame of alignment that burned, all too briefly, in the South.

As a last example of aligning congressional action, consider the Federal Election Campaign Act Amendments of 1974 (FECA), Congress's most extensive regulations of money in politics. Among other things, FECA limited campaign contributions from individuals to federal candidates. It capped expenditures in federal campaigns by individuals and groups.[96] It mandated the disclosure of federal campaign giving and spending above certain thresholds. And it offered voluntary public financing to presidential candidates in primary and general elections.[97] Each of these steps, I argued in Chapter 9, likely advances representational alignment. Curbs on the contributions and expenditures of individuals, who tend to be highly ideologically polarized, are especially aligning. The disclosure of campaign funding also appears to be aligning, though the available evidence is slimmer. And while no study is on point, FECA's public financing scheme for presidential general elections plausibly furthers alignment, too, since it doesn't rely on the decisions of polarized individuals to donate to candidates.[98]

I want to emphasize here that the politicians who conceived of, drafted, and voted for these aligning policies didn't only have democratic motives. They also wanted to benefit their political parties and their own careers. In 1842, Whigs had been the victims of state governments under Democratic control that switched from single-member districts to at-large elections in order to wipe out Whig representation in the House. By prohibiting at-large elections, Whigs thought they would win more House seats.[99] After the Civil War, almost all African Americans in the South supported Republicans, who thereby stood to gain by ensuring that Blacks could vote, run for office, and otherwise participate in politics.[100] The situation was the same in the 1960s, except that Democrats replaced Republicans

---

[95] See, e.g., XI WANG, THE TRIAL OF DEMOCRACY: BLACK SUFFRAGE AND NORTHERN REPUBLICANS, 1860-1910, at 63 (1997) (quoting a proponent of the First Enforcement Act who stated that, thanks to the law, "the whole people, and not [] a part of them only," would have "the right and the means to cooperate in the management of their common affairs").

[96] Of course, this provision never went into effect thanks to the Supreme Court's decision in Buckley v. Valeo, 424 U.S. 1 (1976).

[97] See Federal Election Campaign Act Amendments of 1974, Pub. L. No. 93-443, 88 Stat. 1263 (1974).

[98] See, e.g., Julian E. Zelizer, Seeds of Cynicism: The Struggle over Campaign Finance, 1956-1974, 14 J. POL'Y HIST. 73, 74 (2002) (noting that the coalition that pushed for FECA's adoption "believed that representative government could be improved" through campaign finance reform).

[99] See, e.g., ENGSTROM, supra note 92, at 43–51.

[100] See, e.g., Vikram David Amar & Alan Brownstein, The Hybrid Nature of Political Rights, 50 STAN. L. REV. 915, 943 (1998).

as the authors, and putative beneficiaries, of ambitious voting rights legisla-tion.[101] And in the Watergate era, Republicans outraised Democrats and were tarnished by President Nixon's campaign finance scandals. Through FECA, Democrats hoped to achieve funding parity and to signal that they (unlike their rivals) weren't in bed with big money.[102]

Should we think less of Congress's aligning electoral laws because they were passed with mixed motives—for the sake of democracy and political advan-tage? I don't believe so. Members of Congress nearly always act, at least in part, on the basis of perceived political advantage. Were we to insist on applauding only legislation approved for entirely apolitical reasons, we'd quickly find we'd have very little to cheer. Moreover, aligning electoral laws passed with mixed motives are still aligning. The tighter fit between governmental outputs and popular preferences remains even though it wasn't the sole objective of the laws' proponents. Writing about the first Reconstruction, historian Xi Wang observes that Republicans "linked principle and expedience together when they [legislated about] issues of black suffrage and federal enforcement."[103] In my view (and Wang's), this is no rebuke. Alignment doesn't lose its luster just be-cause it's entwined with, and pursued through, ordinary politics.

Historically, then, many members of Congress backed aligning electoral measures at key junctures. What about today? The developments of 2021–22 in-dicate that many members of Congress remain willing to vote for policies that would significantly improve the alignment of the American political system. In this period, the House repeatedly passed omnibus election law bills containing numerous aligning provisions (and many more provisions promoting other democratic values).[104] Most of these bills also enjoyed majority support in the Senate, though none managed to attract the sixty votes necessary to break a fili-buster. In the showdown over the last of these bills, forty-eight senators actually voted to end the filibuster, for good, for electoral legislation. Just two votes—on a procedural issue, not the substance of the bill—therefore prevented the most ex-pansive set of electoral reforms in American history from becoming law.[105]

---

[101] The situation was actually more complex in the 1960s, in that while the VRA may have won Democrats the votes of newly enfranchised African Americans, it also likely cost them the support of many White voters. That's why President Johnson is rumored to have said, around the time of the VRA's passage, "we just delivered the South to the Republican Party for a long time to come." Ari Berman, Give Us the Ballot: The Modern Struggle for Voting Rights in America 38 (2015).

[102] See, e.g., Richard L. Hasen, The Nine Lives of Buckley v. Valeo, in First Amendment Stories 345, 350 (Richard W. Garnett & Andrew Koppelman eds., 2010).

[103] Wang, supra note 95, at xxiv.

[104] See For the People Act of 2021, H.R. 1, 117th Cong. (2021); Freedom to Vote: John R. Lewis Act, H.R. 5746, 117th Cong. (2022); John R. Lewis Voting Rights Advancement Act of 2021, H.R. 4, 117th Cong. (2021).

[105] See, e.g., Mike DeBonis, Manchin, Sinema Join with GOP in Rejecting Attempt to Change Filibuster Rules, Effectively Killing Democratic Voting Bill, Wash. Post, Jan. 19, 2022.

Driving the events of 2021–22 was the usual mix of disinterested and self-interested motives. Democrats had unified control of the federal government in this biennium. Scanning the political landscape, they discerned misalignment that was both severe in absolute terms and favorable to Republicans and conservatives as a directional matter. (Recall that these were the principal findings of my empirical survey of contemporary American politics in Chapter 3.) Democrats thus found themselves in a position analogous to Whigs in 1842, Republicans after the Civil War, and their own predecessors in the Civil Rights and Watergate eras. Like these parties, at these historical moments, Democrats in 2021–22 wielded the power of the federal government despite bearing the brunt of the period's misalignment.[106] And like these parties, Democrats in 2021–22 identified, and tried to exploit, an opportunity to advance both democratic values and their own political prospects. Had any of the omnibus election law bills been enacted, governmental outputs would have become considerably more congruent with popular preferences. Governmental outputs would have become considerably more congruent with Democratic and progressive preferences, too, since these are the views with which representation and policy are typically misaligned at present.

I mentioned several of the aligning measures of the 2021–22 bills in the previous chapter. The first bill approved by the House would have compelled all states to use independent commissions to craft their congressional districts.[107] Both that bill and the one that almost evaded the Senate filibuster would have barred states from disenfranchising ex-felons and enforcing photo ID requirements for voting.[108] The bill that ultimately died in the Senate would have specified a new coverage formula for Section 5 of the VRA based on the volume of voting rights violations over the preceding twenty-five years.[109] And the list of aligning provisions goes on. The final 2022 bill would have set a quantitative partisan bias threshold that congressional district plans couldn't exceed.[110] Both that bill and the initial House bill would have allowed eligible individuals to register to vote both on election day and during early voting.[111] Both bills would have tightened campaign finance disclosure requirements, eliminating dark money, extending disclaimer rules to online media, and obligating politically

---

[106] To be precise, Democrats controlled Congress but not the presidency when FECA was enacted in 1974.

[107] *See* H.R. 1 §§ 2411–15.

[108] *See id.* §§ 1401–09, 1903; H.R. 5746 §§ 1701–09, 1801. Again, these voting restrictions tend to have equivocal effects on alignment but blatant misaligning motives.

[109] *See* H.R. 5746 § 9004.

[110] *See id.* § 5003(c).

[111] *See* H.R. 1 § 1031; H.R. 5746 § 1031.

active nonprofits to reveal their donors.[112] And both bills would have instituted a voucher system of public financing for congressional candidates.[113]

My main point here is that all these aligning policies aren't the dreams of quixotic reformers. Rather, they're measures that were included in high-priority bills that were backed by a majority of House members, forty-nine or fifty senators, and the President of the United States in 2021–22. Even though these bills were unable to overcome the Senate filibuster, they still establish the political plausibility, today, of step after aligning step. But I also want to address the *legality* (not just the *viability*) of these provisions in this section. I noted in the previous chapter that the Roberts Court might have qualms, in particular, about the mandate to use redistricting commissions, the override of state laws disenfranchising ex-felons and requiring a photo ID to vote, and the new coverage formula for Section 5. Despite these reservations, I think each of these policies ultimately should and would be upheld, even by this Court. The reason, not surprisingly, is the multilayered legal foundation that undergirds every congressional electoral regulation.[114]

Beginning with the mandate to use redistricting commissions, there's no doubt that Congress can legislate about the design of congressional districts. Congress has done so since the 1842 Apportionment Act on the basis of the Elections Clause, congressional redistricting being a central aspect of the "Manner of . . . Elections for . . . Representatives."[115] Congress can also require the use of commissions under its authority to enforce the Fourteenth and Fifteenth Amendments. When self-interested politicians draw district lines, they often engage in malapportionment, partisan gerrymandering, racial gerrymandering, and racial vote dilution: all violations of the Reconstruction Amendments.[116] Commissions that sideline politicians in favor of more neutral mapmakers are therefore at least a reasonable, and most likely a congruent and proportional, response to this high risk of unconstitutional activity. As for the charge that a *mandate* to use commissions impermissibly commandeers states, the Supreme Court has held that Congress *can* issue orders to states under the Elections Clause.

---

[112] *See* H.R. 1 §§ 4001–4902; H.R. 5746 §§ 6001–6202.

[113] *See* H.R. 1 §§ 5101–04; H.R. 5746 §§ 8102–05.

[114] For an extended argument that even more aggressive congressional actions are constitutional, see Stephanopoulos, *supra* note 93, at 72–84.

[115] U.S. Const. art. I, § 4; *see also, e.g.,* An Act for the Apportionment of Representatives to Congress Among the Several States According to the Ninth Census, § 2, 17 Stat. 28, 28 (1872) (imposing an equal population requirement for congressional districts for the first time); An Act Making an Apportionment of Representatives in Congress Among the Several States Under the Twelfth Census, § 3, 31 Stat. 733, 734 (1901) (same for a compactness requirement).

[116] Notably, even while holding that partisan gerrymandering is *nonjusticiable,* the Supreme Court confirmed in *Rucho v. Common Cause* that "*unconstitutional*" partisan gerrymandering does exist. 139 S. Ct. 2484, 2499 (2019) (emphasis added).

Specifically, Congress can dictate "the manner in which a State is to fulfill its pre-existing constitutional obligations" to administer congressional elections.[117]

Moreover, even if the anti-commandeering doctrine did apply to exercises of the Elections Clause (and the Enforcement Clauses of the Fourteenth and Fifteenth Amendments), it could easily be satisfied. Congress could simply offer states a choice: *Either* establish your own redistricting commission *or* have the federal government set it up for you. A statutory choice isn't a federal command, and so can't amount to unlawful commandeering.[118] It's also plain that Congress could itself create redistricting commissions for states unwilling to adopt them. Congress could draw all congressional district lines directly if it wished, these boundaries again being part of the manner of congressional elections.[119] This greater power necessarily includes the lesser power of delegating congressional redistricting to newly instituted federal commissions.

Next, the override of state voting restrictions (like disenfranchising ex-felons and requiring a photo ID to vote) could be justified on several grounds. Like the mandate to use redistricting commissions, the override of state voting limits involves the manner of congressional elections.[120] This brings the override within the ambit of the Elections Clause. Because Congress has equivalent authority under the Elections Clause and the Electors Clause, the override is equally valid with respect to presidential elections. It's true that not having a felony conviction could be seen as a qualification for voting. Possession of a photo ID, though, isn't a plausible voting qualification. It's better understood as a way to enforce actual qualifications like age, residency, and citizenship.[121] And even if lack of a felony conviction is a voting qualification, under Justice Black's controlling opinion in *Mitchell*, this doesn't exempt state laws disenfranchising ex-felons from Congress's reach under the Elections Clause and the Electors Clause. Lack of a felony conviction is no different than age, residency, and citizenship requirements for voting in federal elections—all voting qualifications that Congress has repeatedly regulated.

---

[117] Branch v. Smith, 538 U.S. 254, 280 (2003) (plurality opinion); *see also, e.g.,* Justin Weinstein-Tull, *Election Law Federalism*, 114 MICH. L. REV. 747, 782 (2016) ("Congress may enact election legislation that forces a state to take action it might not otherwise take, without violating the anticommandeering doctrine.").

[118] *See, e.g.,* New York v. United States, 505 U.S. 144, 167 (1992) (recognizing "Congress' power to offer States the choice of regulating that activity according to federal standards or having state law pre-empted by federal regulation").

[119] *See, e.g.,* Oregon v. Mitchell, 400 U.S. 112, 121 (1970) (opinion of Black, J.) (observing that Congress possesses "the power to lay out or alter the boundaries of the congressional districts").

[120] *See, e.g.,* Smiley v. Holm, 285 U.S. 355, 366 (1932) (noting that, under the Elections Clause, Congress can address the "supervision of voting," the "protection of voters," and the "prevention of fraud and corrupt practices").

[121] *See, e.g.,* Crawford v. Marion Cnty. Election Bd., 553 U.S. 181, 193 (2008) (remarking that "photo identification is one effective method of establishing a voter's qualification to vote").

What if the Roberts Court overruled Justice Black's opinion in *Mitchell*? This move would have no bearing on the lawfulness of the override of state photo ID requirements for voting since, again, these rules aren't voting qualifications. However, the move would necessitate a basis other than the Elections Clause and the Electors Clause for the override of state ex-felon disenfranchisement provisions. This basis could be found in the Enforcement Clause of the Fifteenth Amendment.[122] In numerous states, ex-felons were deprived of the franchise in the late nineteenth and early twentieth centuries as elements of larger efforts to intentionally prevent African Americans from voting.[123] Even in states without Jim Crow histories of voter suppression, the disenfranchisement of ex-felons disproportionately excludes minority members from the electorate.[124] So the rational basis for the congressional enfranchisement of ex-felons is either obvious (that these individuals were barred from voting for invidious reasons) or the same as in prior cases (that the disparate impact of ex-felons' disenfranchisement suggests a racially discriminatory motive). Either way, the predicate for the use of Congress's Fifteenth Amendment enforcement authority is satisfied.

The last measure I identified in the previous chapter as potentially problematic, in the eyes of the Roberts Court, is a new coverage formula for Section 5. A new coverage formula, relying on recent rather than decades-old data, *would* plainly resolve the Court's primary concern in *Shelby County*. A formula incorporating "current data reflecting current needs" could no longer be tarred as "irrational" because of its alleged obsolescence.[125] To strike down a preclearance regime based on an updated formula, then, the Court would have to hold outright that preclearance itself is an unreasonable policy given modern levels of racial discrimination in voting. The Court might well be reluctant to

---

[122] With respect to any voting qualification other than the disenfranchisement of ex-felons, Congress's power to annul the restriction would be bolstered by the Fourteenth Amendment. As noted above, one of the many equal protection doctrines pertaining to election law creates a system of sliding-scale scrutiny for burdens on voting. State voting qualifications often levy substantial burdens on the franchise without advancing legitimate state interests. So Congress could invoke its Fourteenth Amendment enforcement authority to attack these qualifications, arguing that its intervention is congruent and proportional to the restrictions' violations of the Equal Protection Clause. However, this approach is inapplicable to the disenfranchisement of ex-felons. In *Richardson v. Ramirez*, 418 U.S. 24, 54 (1974), the Supreme Court held that, because Section 2 of the Fourteenth Amendment bars any state's congressional representation from being reduced on the ground that the state has disenfranchised citizens "for participation in rebellion, or other crime," U.S. CONST. amend. XIV, § 2, such disenfranchisement can't contravene the Equal Protection Clause of Section 1. If the exclusion of ex-felons can't breach the Equal Protection Clause, then Congress also can't try to prevent or remedy this exclusion through its enforcement power. There simply isn't an underlying equal protection problem for Congress to avoid or cure.

[123] *See, e.g.,* George Brooks, *Felon Disenfranchisement: Law, History, Policy, and Politics,* 32 FORDHAM URB. L.J. 851, 854–59 (2005).

[124] *See, e.g., State-by-State Data,* SENT'G PROJECT, https://www.sentencingproject.org/the-facts/#map (last visited Feb. 1, 2024) (showing the Black-white and Hispanic-White disparities in incarceration in each state).

[125] Shelby Cnty. v. Holder, 570 U.S. 529, 553, 556 (2013).

issue such a controversial verdict—to decree that the evils of racial vote denial and racial vote dilution have been sufficiently cured that preclearance is now an irrational exercise of Congress's Fifteenth Amendment enforcement power. Since *Shelby County*, the Court has said that "no one suggests that discrimination in voting has been extirpated or that the threat has been eliminated."[126] The Court has also referred to "Alabama's extensive history of repugnant racial and voting-related discrimination."[127] These statements would seem empty if, in its next breath, the Court were to declare that racial discrimination in voting is, in fact, a thing of the past.

And even if the Court took this leap, it wouldn't reach its desired destination—the invalidity of Section 5—unless it engaged in more interpretive gymnastics. Many election law changes that could be denied preclearance pertain to congressional and presidential elections. So Congress could regulate these changes under the Elections Clause and the Electors Clause, respectively, unless the Court were to rewrite its doctrine about these provisions.[128] Election law changes that don't involve federal elections necessarily implicate state or local elections. Under the Guarantee Clause, Congress has the authority to legislate about these elections when it decides that doing so would help to safeguard republican rule. A congressional determination along these lines would certainly be plausible here given that few practices are as unrepublican, as inconsistent with the value of popular sovereignty, as racial discrimination in voting. Such a congressional determination would also be categorically nonjusticiable, unless the Court were to reverse almost two centuries of precedent by holding that congressional judgments about state and local republicanism actually are reviewable.[129]

This leaves only aligning measures in the 2021–22 bills that I didn't flag in the previous chapter because the case for their constitutionality is so strong. A quantitative partisan bias ceiling for congressional district plans is a garden-variety regulation of the manner of congressional elections. It strongly resembles other congressional redistricting criteria that Congress has enacted over the years under the Elections Clause, including compactness, contiguity, equal population, and the requirement that each district be represented by a single member.[130] The same point applies to election day and same-day registration for federal elections. These policies are in the heartland of Congress's Elections

---

[126] Brnovich v. Democratic Nat'l Comm., 141 S. Ct. 2321, 2343 (2021).

[127] Allen v. Milligan, 143 S. Ct. 1487, 1506 (2023) (internal quotation marks omitted).

[128] *See, e.g.*, Franita Tolson, *Reinventing Sovereignty?: Federalism as a Constraint on the Voting Rights Act*, 65 Vand. L. Rev. 1195, 1198 (2012) ("The Elections Clause, when combined with [other provisions], provides ample constitutional justification for the VRA.").

[129] *See, e.g.*, Amar, *supra* note 70, at 114 (observing that Congress "retain[s] the same broad power under the Republican Guarantee Clause to ensure electoral integrity within individual states" through a preclearance regime).

[130] *See, e.g.* Stephanopoulos, *supra* note 93, at 77 & n.420 (describing these criteria).

Clause power, legally indistinguishable from prior regulations of voter registration for federal elections.[131] As for campaign finance reforms like more extensive disclosure and public financing for congressional elections, no one questions Congress's authority to take these steps under the Elections Clause and the Commerce Clause. The First Amendment issues are only slightly more serious here. Even in *Citizens United*, the high water mark of campaign finance deregulation, only one Justice asserted that certain disclosure rules are unlawful.[132] Similarly, the Roberts Court denied cert, without any public dissent, in a challenge to Seattle's voucher system of public financing—the model for the recent federal proposal.[133]

To conclude this discussion, I'll note I'm in good company in stressing the multilayered legal foundation for the aligning provisions in the 2021–22 bills. The final 2022 bill began by setting forth, in unusual detail, "findings of general constitutional authority."[134] These findings described Congress's "broad authority to regulate the time, place, and manner of congressional elections under the Elections Clause."[135] They added that Congress "has both the authority and responsibility . . . . to enforce the Guarantee Clause."[136] This section continued that Congress "has broad authority . . . to legislate to enforce the provisions of the Fourteenth Amendment, including its protections of the right to vote and the democratic process."[137] The section further referred to Congress's "authority to legislate to eliminate racial discrimination in voting and the democratic process pursuant to both" the Fourteenth and Fifteenth Amendments.[138] Cited as well were Congress's "power[s] to protect the right to vote from denial or abridgment on account of sex, age, or ability to pay a poll tax or other tax pursuant to the Nineteenth, Twenty-Fourth, and Twenty-Sixth Amendments."[139] Were a bill like this to become law, then, its constitutional defense wouldn't be limited to one or another clause. Instead, the full extent of Congress's horizontal and vertical authority over elections would be invoked, making clear that multiple bases exist for each electoral regulation.

---

[131] *See, e.g.*, National Voter Registration Act of 1993, 52 U.S.C. §§ 20501–11 (2018).

[132] *See* Citizens United v. FEC, 558 U.S. 310, 480–85 (2010) (Thomas, J., concurring in part and dissenting in part).

[133] *See* Elster v. City of Seattle, 140 S. Ct. 2564 (2020).

[134] Freedom to Vote: John R. Lewis Act, H.R. 5746, 117th Cong. § 3 (2022).

[135] *Id.* § 3(1).

[136] *Id.* § 3(2).

[137] *Id.* § 3(3)(A).

[138] *Id.* § 3(4)(A).

[139] *Id.* § 3(5)(A).

State Policies

Turning to aligning measures adopted by states, my legal and political claims are stronger still than with respect to federal legislation. Legally, in the absence of federal preemption, state actors have essentially plenary authority to regulate federal, state, and local elections. The Supreme Court recently eliminated any doubt about the power of nonlegislative state actors to regulate federal elections (with the minor exception of state courts enforcing state laws in outlandish ways). Politically, the multiplicity of states, and of state actors capable of promoting alignment, combine with the lower threshold for policymaking at the state level to generate many more opportunities for aligning action. These opportunities arise continuously in the states—not only, as in Washington, at extraordinary moments like Reconstruction, the Civil Rights Era, and Watergate.

In our system of government, state actors are the default regulators of elections. As I argued above, Congress *may* legislate about many aspects of federal, state, and local elections. But for these elections to occur in the first place, state actors *must* make rules for, and then administer, them. Without state action there can be no elections. Accordingly, the Supreme Court has long recognized that "States retain broad autonomy in structuring their governments."[140] States "have broad powers to determine the conditions under which the right of suffrage may be exercised."[141] Each state also "has the power to prescribe the qualifications of its officers and the manner in which they shall be chosen."[142] "Redistricting," too, "is primarily the duty and responsibility of the State."[143]

Importantly, several kinds of state actors can exercise this default authority to regulate elections. State legislatures, of course, can pass electoral bills. Governors can (generally[144]) sign these bills into law or veto them. Other executive branch officials can promulgate electoral rules (and must actually run elections). In states with direct democracy, voters themselves can propose and then approve initiatives about electoral matters. And state courts can decide cases about electoral issues under state constitutional and statutory provisions. As Miriam Seifter writes, "state institutions offer crucial *democratic opportunity*"—"the opportunity for popular majorities to rule on equal terms" with respect to both electoral regulations and other policy areas.[145]

For a time, as detailed in the previous chapter, some judges and scholars maintained that nonlegislative state actors are barred from regulating federal

---

[140] Shelby Cnty. v. Holder, 570 U.S. 529, 543 (2013).

[141] Carrington v. Rash, 380 U.S. 89, 91 (1965) (internal quotation marks omitted).

[142] Boyd v. Nebraska *ex rel.* Thayer, 143 U.S. 135, 161 (1892).

[143] Perry v. Perez, 565 U.S. 388, 392 (2012) (internal quotation marks omitted).

[144] In some states, governors lack the power to veto district plans. *See, e.g.,* FIONA KNIAZ & KRISTOFFER SHIELDS, REDISTRICTING: THE ROAD TO REFORM 13 (2021).

[145] Miriam Seifter, *State Institutions and Democratic Opportunity*, 72 DUKE L.J. 275, 280 (2022).

elections, at least to the extent their regulations conflict with state legislatures' preferences. But in *Moore v. Harper*, the Supreme Court rejected these strong forms of the ISL theory. The Court reaffirmed its earlier holdings that state legislatures' preferences with respect to federal elections can be overridden by gubernatorial vetoes, popular referenda, and voter initiatives transferring regulatory powers to nonlegislative bodies (like redistricting commissions).[146] The Court also ruled that the ISL theory "does not insulate state legislatures from the ordinary exercise of state judicial review."[147] Rather, the only limit imposed by the ISL theory is that "state courts may not transgress the ordinary bounds of judicial review" by capriciously construing or applying state laws.[148]

The legality of most state-level aligning action is therefore clear. What about its political plausibility? Unfortunately, state actors are often loath to take steps that advance alignment. In particular, when a single party fully controls a state government—and benefits from misalignment in its partisan and ideological direction—that party has few political incentives to support aligning measures. Aligning measures would make governmental outputs *less* congruent with the party's desires. To choose to back aligning measures, the party would have to prioritize the quality of democracy over its own self-interest. That prioritization is foreign to most parties in most circumstances.

However, state governments are complex and variable, and the actors who comprise them have incentives that cut in favor of aligning action with some regularity. To make this point, I'll use redistricting as a case study. Redistricting occurs (at least) every decade and so is on the state policy agenda more frequently than other electoral topics. Redistricting is also unusually easy to link to partisan alignment thanks to the availability of quantitative measures of partisan bias for district plans. In the redistricting context, then, state-level aligning action is uncommon but hardly exceptional. It's undertaken, at times, by state legislatures (even under conditions of unified government), by governors (especially under divided government), by redistricting commissions, by voters through direct democracy, and by state courts enforcing state constitutions. This array of viable options demonstrates that aligning progress is often (though certainly not always) possible through state policymaking channels.

Starting with state legislatures, divided government is the scenario in which they most frequently enact unbiased district maps: maps that lead to excellent partisan alignment. When the legislature and the governorship are controlled by different parties, or when the legislature itself is under split control, the votes are generally lacking to pass aggressive gerrymanders that result in severe partisan

[146] *See* 143 S. Ct. 2065, 2081–83 (2023).
[147] *Id.* at 2081.
[148] *Id.* at 2089.

misalignment. That's why I found, in an earlier empirical study, that divided government is associated with a reduction in the absolute magnitude of the efficiency gap (relative to unified government) for both state legislative and congressional plans.[149] Under divided government, typically, no single actor has the power to force through a plan that's highly skewed in that actor's favor.

Under unified government, on the other hand, a single party does wield this power but doesn't always exploit it. A party might value safe seats for its incumbents more than a map that awards the party more seats won by slimmer margins. In 2001, for instance, California Democrats fully controlled the state government yet enacted almost perfectly neutral state legislative and congressional plans.[150] These plans, though, exhibited extremely low levels of competition.[151] Alternatively, a party might feel obligated by popular pressure to take aligning action. In 2018, to illustrate, Ohio Republicans wanted to stop a voter initiative that would have removed redistricting entirely from the control of the elected branches. So they placed on the ballot (and voters then endorsed) an alternative measure that created rigorous partisan fairness requirements for district maps but also allowed politicians to continue to play a role in redistricting.[152] Or there might be tension between a party's legislative and gubernatorial wings, which plays out in aligning ways. In 2011, for example, the Democratic governor of New York agreed to approve the Democratic legislature's plans only if the legislature put on the ballot a proposal establishing a redistricting commission. This proposal passed in 2014, endowing New York with a new commission bound by a strict partisan fairness rule.[153]

Speaking of governors, while this New York experience is anomalous, they commonly further alignment under divided government by vetoing, or threatening to veto, biased plans.[154] In the most recent redistricting cycle, governors vetoed maps in Kansas, Kentucky, Louisiana, Maryland, Pennsylvania, and Wisconsin. Some of these vetoes were overridden by legislative supermajorities, but the vetoes held in the purple states of Pennsylvania and Wisconsin, eventually leading to the adoption of fairer court-drawn plans.[155] In other situations,

---

[149] See Nicholas O. Stephanopoulos, *Arizona and Anti-Reform*, 2015 U. CHI. LEGAL F. 477, 507.

[150] See, e.g., *California 2002-2010 Redistricting Plan*, PLANSCORE, https://planscore.org/california/#!2002-plan-ushouse-eg (last visited Feb. 1, 2024) (showing a 0 percent average efficiency gap for California's 2000s congressional plan).

[151] See, e.g., Eric McGhee, *Reflections on "Redistricting and Legislative Partisanship"*, 1 CAL. J. POL. & POL'Y 1, 3–4 (2009).

[152] See, e.g., *Ohio*, ALL ABOUT REDISTRICTING, https://redistricting.lls.edu/state/ohio/ (last visited Feb. 1, 2024) (describing Ohio's redistricting process in the wake of this referendum).

[153] See, e.g., *New York*, ALL ABOUT REDISTRICTING, https://redistricting.lls.edu/state/new-york (last visited Feb. 1, 2024) (describing New York's redistricting process in the wake of this referendum).

[154] See also Miriam Seifter, *Saving Democracy, State by State?*, 110 CALIF. L. REV. 2069, 2083 (2022) ("State governors . . . have been vetoing some of the most problematic . . . bills offered up by countermajoritarian legislatures.").

[155] See the state-by-state summaries of redistricting in the 2020 cycle at ALL ABOUT REDISTRICTING, https://redistricting.lls.edu/ (last visited Feb. 1, 2024).

governors don't need to use their veto pens because the prospect of a veto is sufficient to prompt negotiation and, ultimately, agreement with the legislature. I noted above that, in my earlier study, I discerned a link between divided government and a smaller absolute efficiency gap for state legislative and congressional maps.[156] The cases in this divided government category are precisely those where a governor and a legislature from different parties managed to make a deal.

Next, as I showed in Chapter 7, states in which commissions design districts enjoy better partisan alignment. In the last redistricting cycle, commission-drawn plans at both the state legislative and congressional levels had average efficiency gaps near zero, statistically indistinguishable from perfect partisan alignment.[157] Historically, too, parties were unable to tilt maps in their favor by winning control of an additional branch of the state government in states where commissions, not the elected branches, were responsible for redistricting.[158] These benefits accrue because independent and bipartisan commissions are comprised, respectively, of ordinary citizens chosen at random and equal numbers of politicians from each major party. In institutions structured in these ways, majorities in support of gerrymanders can rarely be assembled. Moreover, commissions weren't just an element of the initial election law bill passed by the U.S. House in 2021. They've also been created by more and more states through state-level channels. In advance of the last redistricting cycle alone, Colorado, Michigan, New York, and Virginia all transferred authority over redistricting to newly instituted commissions.[159]

Direct democracy is the main state-level channel through which commissions have been adopted.[160] Focusing on the four new commissions in the last redistricting cycle, Colorado's, New York's, and Virginia's were enacted through referenda following legislative referrals. That is, state legislatures first placed the measures on the ballot, and voters then approved them at the polls.[161] On the other hand, Michigan's new commission was the product of a voter initiative. Voters, not politicians, drafted the proposal, gathered enough signatures to put it on the ballot, and then backed it by a large margin.[162] Direct democracy can also be harnessed to pass aligning redistricting reforms other than commissions. As

[156] See supra note 149 and accompanying text.
[157] See Christopher Warshaw et al., Districts for a New Decade—Partisan Outcomes and Racial Representation in the 2021-22 Redistricting Cycle, 52 PUBLIUS: J. FEDERALISM 428, 440 (2022).
[158] See DEVIN CAUGHEY & CHRISTOPHER WARSHAW, DYNAMIC DEMOCRACY: PUBLIC OPINION, ELECTIONS, AND POLICYMAKING IN THE AMERICAN STATES 149–50 (2022).
[159] See Creation of Redistricting Commissions, NAT'L CONF. ST. LEGIS (Dec. 10, 2021), https://www.ncsl.org/redistricting-and-census/creation-of-redistricting-commissions.
[160] See also Seifter, supra note 145, at 296–97 ("[T]he vote for or against an initiative operates statewide. It cannot be gerrymandered or fall prey to the biases of political geography.").
[161] See Creation of Redistricting Commissions, supra note 159.
[162] See id.

I observed earlier, a 2018 referendum in Ohio resulted in the imposition of strict partisan fairness rules for state legislative and congressional plans.[163] Likewise, a 2018 voter initiative in Missouri endorsed a quantitative efficiency gap ceiling for state legislative maps.[164] Direct democracy regularly (though not necessarily[165]) succeeds in the redistricting context because voters tend to be supportive of efforts to fight gerrymandering. These efforts poll well—even among partisans whose preferred party is advantaged by the status quo—and have compiled an impressive electoral record in recent years.

State courts are the last state actors who can promote alignment through their redistricting moves.[166] State courts can strike down biased plans as violative of state constitutional provisions protecting equality, free speech, and fair elections. State courts almost never did so prior to the last redistricting cycle. In that cycle, though, state courts nullified gerrymanders in Alaska, Maryland, New York, North Carolina, Ohio, and Wisconsin. Several more suits along these lines are still pending as of this book's writing.[167] State courts can also craft neutral maps in the first instance when other state actors deadlock. In the last redistricting cycle, court-drawn (like commission-drawn) state legislative and congressional plans had average efficiency gaps near zero, statistically indistinguishable from perfect partisan alignment.[168] Historically as well, court-drawn state legislative plans were associated with a reduction in the absolute magnitude of the efficiency gap.[169]

Why are some state courts willing to make these aligning redistricting moves? There are legal and political explanations. Legally, as I discussed in Chapter 4, most state constitutions are committed to the democracy principle, an amalgam of popular sovereignty, majority rule, and political equality that's analogous to the concept of alignment. Thanks to the democracy principle, the legal resources are usually there for state courts inclined to invalidate gerrymanders. There are usually state constitutional provisions and precedents interpreting these provisions with which gerrymanders are incompatible.[170] Politically, state

---

[163] *See supra* note 152 and accompanying text.

[164] *See 2018 Ballot Measures*, Mo. Sec'y of State, https://www.sos.mo.gov/elections/petitions/2018BallotMeasures (last visited Feb. 1, 2024).

[165] *See* Nicholas O. Stephanopoulos, *Reforming Redistricting: Why Popular Initiatives to Establish Redistricting Commissions Succeed or Fail*, 23 J.L. & Pol. 331 (2007) (showing that most redistricting initiatives historically failed).

[166] *See also* Jessica Bulman-Pozen & Miriam Seifter, *Countering the New Election Subversion: The Democracy Principle and the Role of State Courts*, 2022 Wis. L. Rev. 1337, 1339 ("[S]tate court application of the democracy principle can mitigate several impending threats to elections . . . .").

[167] *See* Yurij Rudensky, *Status of Partisan Gerrymandering Litigation in State Courts*, Brennan Ctr. for Justice (Dec. 18, 2023), https://www.brennancenter.org/our-work/research-reports/status-partisan-gerrymandering-litigation-state-courts.

[168] *See* Warshaw et al., *supra* note 157, at 440.

[169] *See* Stephanopoulos, *supra* note 149, at 507.

[170] *See generally* Jessica Bulman-Pozen & Miriam Seifter, *The Democracy Principle in State Constitutions*, 119 Mich. L. Rev. 859 (2021).

supreme court justices are almost always elected statewide, not from districts. This means that the forces that distort districted elections—gerrymandering and political geography—are generally inapplicable to state supreme court elections. As a result, state supreme court justices with their statewide constituencies have no direct interest in preserving skewed district configurations. In fact, they may have the opposite interest if they affiliate with a party different from the one benefited by gerrymandering.[171]

To be sure, most or all of these state-level routes to alignment may be blocked in a particular state. Consider Texas. Its Republican legislature and Republican governor have no political incentive to end its pro-Republican gerrymandering. Texas's state supreme court justices don't personally profit from gerrymandering but, as nine Republicans, are content to condone the practice. Texas has no redistricting commission. Nor does Texas permit any form of direct democracy through which incumbent officeholders might be circumvented. And many states resemble Texas in having unified government, a state supreme court sympathetic to that government, no redistricting commission, and/or no direct democracy. My argument, then, isn't that state-level aligning action is always an available alternative to federal litigation or legislation. I only claim that several kinds of state actors legally can take aligning steps, and politically wish to take these steps on some, but far from all, occasions.

Private Actions

All the aligning strategies I've covered, to this point, have been *governmental* strategies: ways to use the powers of the federal government, and of state governments, to further alignment. This emphasis is understandable. Alignment refers to the congruence of governmental outputs with popular preferences. Public policy is the most intuitive method for changing governmental outputs, making it more likely they will reflect people's views. People's views can also be influenced by public policy, potentially shifting so they better correspond to governmental outputs.

However, it should be plain from Chapter 9—the chapter on campaign finance—that the drivers of alignment aren't exclusively governmental. Campaign contributions and expenditures are *private* actions. They're financial transactions made by private parties of their own volition, uncompelled by the government. Yet campaign giving and spending, especially when undertaken by ideologically polarized individuals, are a major contributor to representational misalignment. This example suggests that, just as certain private actions

---

[171] *See* Seifter, *supra* note 145, at 296.

are misaligning, other private actions might make governmental outputs more congruent with popular preferences. This section corroborates this suggestion, identifying three separate channels through which private actions can be aligning. The first of these channels operates on the informational environment of politicians; the second on the informational environment of voters; and the third on the campaign finance ecosystem. There could be other kinds of aligning private actions, too, but these three, at least, are validated by existing evidence.

Beginning with politicians, their stark representational misalignment was a theme of Chapter 3. In modern American politics, elected officials at all levels tend to be ideologically extreme relative to their constituents. In a groundbreaking study, David Broockman and Christopher Skovron find that state legislative candidates' and officeholders' *perceptions* of their constituents' policy preferences are also extreme. In particular, across ten issues, Republican politicians overstate their constituents' conservatism by anywhere from around 10 to more than 40 percentage points.[172] More relevant here, Broockman and Skovron further show that these misperceptions of public opinion correlate with partisan differences in constituents' contact with their representatives. Of the constituents who reach out to Republican legislators, notably, 12 percentage points more are Republicans compared to a hypothetical baseline in which all constituents are equally likely to call, write, or visit.[173] In earlier periods, on the other hand, these partisan differences in constituents' contact with their representatives didn't exist. Nor, in these eras, did politicians systematically err in their estimates of public opinion.[174]

An implication of Broockman and Skovron's work is that, if politicians were again (as in prior times) contacted by a representative sample of their constituents, their perceptions of public opinion would become more accurate. In turn, if politicians' perceptions of public opinion were sharper, their policy positions might more faithfully mirror their constituents' policy views. At least, in this scenario, politicians with misaligned positions would sense that lack of congruence—not, as at present, think their stances *do* match public attitudes they've erroneously appraised. This, then, is the first form of aligning private activity: constituents reaching out to politicians in large, but more importantly in representative, numbers. Extensive contact whose rate doesn't vary by constituents' partisanship or ideology has the potential to better inform

---

[172] *See* David E. Broockman & Christopher Skovron, *Bias in Perceptions of Public Opinion Among Political Elites*, 112 AM. POL. SCI. REV. 542, 553 (2018).

[173] *See id.* at 558.

[174] *See id.* at 559; see also Alexander Hertel-Fernandez et al., *Legislative Staff and Representation in Congress*, 113 AM. POL. SCI. REV. 1, 12–13 (2019) (finding that many congressional staffers also misperceive constituent opinion and that these errors are related to contact from conservative, corporate-based (rather than liberal, mass-based) groups).

politicians about public opinion, and thereby to improve representational alignment.[175]

A pair of creative experiments offer some support for the effectiveness of this approach. Scholars randomly assigned certain state legislators to be the targets of emails and phone calls from activists who backed an antismoking bill in New Hampshire and an antibullying bill in Michigan. In both cases, the targeted representatives were significantly (10 to 20 percentage points) more likely to vote for the bills.[176] These results hint that if contact with legislators was consistent across the partisan and ideological spectrum, not confined to activists with distinctive demands, then legislators might cast votes broadly reflective of their constituents' preferences. In this event, legislators would be pushed and pulled by different sets of constituents, these pressures varying in proportion to the numbers of constituents holding different views. Optimistically, the outcome of all the countervailing forces would be representation in rough equilibrium with constituents' desires.

This aligning mechanism is plausible but quite complex. It relies on politicians correctly *inferring* their constituents' policy preferences when they're contacted by representative samples of their constituents. But what if politicians didn't have to infer their constituents' views? What if they could simply be *told* what their constituents think, according to issue-specific surveys of public opinion? In another intriguing experiment, Daniel Butler and David Nickerson conducted a large poll of New Mexico registered voters, enabling them to calculate support by state house district for a pending fiscal proposal.[177] These scholars then conveyed the results of the poll to some but not other state house members. Among the legislators informed about their constituents' preferences, their votes on the fiscal proposal were highly responsive to public opinion. The more strongly their constituents backed the measure, the more likely the legislators were to vote for it. Conversely, among the legislators denied this data, there was no correlation at all between their votes and their constituents' attitudes toward the bill.[178]

Butler and Nickerson's experiment raises another aligning possibility: Instead of indirectly educating politicians about public opinion by contacting them at a uniform rate, private actors could directly inform politicians by providing the results of issue-specific surveys. Historically, the expense of generating this

---

[175] *See, e.g.,* Broockman & Skovron, *supra* note 172, at 561 (noting that their findings "suggest[] that any biases in representation that may result from misperceptions of public opinion could be feasible to correct").

[176] *See* Daniel E. Bergan, *Does Grassroots Lobbying Work? A Field Experiment Measuring the Effects of an E-Mail Lobbying Campaign on Legislative Behavior*, 37 AM. POL. RSCH. 327, 342 (2009); Daniel E. Bergan & Richard T. Cole, *Call Your Legislator: A Field Experimental Study of the Impact of a Constituency Mobilization Campaign on Legislative Voting*, 37 POL. BEHAVIOR 27, 28 (2015).

[177] *See* Daniel M. Butler & David W. Nickerson, *Can Learning Constituency Opinion Affect How Legislators Vote? Results from a Field Experiment*, 6 Q.J. POL. SCI. 55, 58–63 (2011).

[178] *See id.* at 67–71.

data would have been prohibitive. Each constituency would have required its own poll, each poll costing (at least) several thousand dollars. Over the last two decades, however, political scientists have honed a technique, multilevel regression and poststratification (MRP), that allows public opinion at many lower levels to be estimated accurately from a single survey at a higher level.[179] A single national poll with a couple thousand respondents can be used to produce credible opinion estimates for all fifty states.[180] A large national poll, like the Cooperative Election Study run annually by a consortium of universities, can give rise to solid opinion estimates for all states, congressional and state legislative districts, and bigger municipalities.[181] A state poll can yield good opinion estimates for essentially all substate entities.

A university, nonprofit group, or other private actor, then, could generalize Butler and Nickerson's method by creating a "constituency preference lookup" website making available MRP-derived opinion estimates by constituency, issue, and date.[182] The administrator of this website would apply MRP to all suitable national and state polls on a rolling basis as the polls came in. The results of this analysis would be disseminated through an easy-to-use lookup feature. An elected official or candidate (or other interested party) could simply specify her constituency and then see estimates of residents' views on a host of issues. If the website caught on, write Christopher Elmendorf and Abby Wood in a discussion of the idea, "a quick lookup of constituency preference might become virtually automatic for legislators prior to casting potentially controversial roll call votes."[183] "And as use of the website [became] second nature, candidates, legislators, and local party officials [w]ould develop more accurate perceptions of district-level opinion."[184] From these more accurate perceptions, better representational alignment would hopefully ensue. That's what happened in Butler and Nickerson's experiment, and it's a reasonable hypothesis that their findings would extend to other times and places.

Moving from politicians' to voters' informational environments, lack of knowledge about candidates' policy positions can prevent even otherwise inclined voters from voting spatially. Picture a voter who would like to cast a ballot for the candidate whose policy stances most closely resemble her own, but who's unaware of most or all candidates' views on most or all issues. This voter

---

[179] *See, e.g.,* Jeffrey R. Lax & Justin H. Phillips, *How Should We Estimate Public Opinion in the States,* 53 AM. J. POL. SCI. 107 (2009).

[180] *See, e.g., id.* at 116–20.

[181] *See, e.g.,* Chris Tausanovitch & Christopher Warshaw, *Measuring Constituent Policy Preferences in Congress, State Legislatures, and Cities,* 75 J. POL. 330 (2013).

[182] Christopher S. Elmendorf & Abby K. Wood, *Elite Political Ignorance: Law, Data, and the Representation of (Mis)perceived Electorates,* 52 U.C. DAVIS L. REV. 571, 576 (2018).

[183] *Id.* at 630.

[184] *Id.*

is missing the necessary information to vote spatially. She can try to use rough proxies for candidates' policy positions like the parties to which they belong. But party affiliation doesn't distinguish between moderates and extremists within the same party, and is unavailable anyway in the many local elections in which voting is nonpartisan. Alternatively, this voter can abandon any attempt at spatial voting and cast her ballot on some other basis, like incumbency, charisma, media attention, or the state of the economy. In this case, the powerful aligning engine of spatial voting sputters to a halt.[185]

I argued in Chapter 10 that the government can take steps to better inform voters and thereby facilitate spatial voting. Specifically, the government can promote more and deeper media coverage of politics through financial subsidies and regulations like the Federal Communications Commission's fairness doctrine. But private actors—my focus here—can also improve voters' knowledge about candidates' policy stances in at least two ways. First, private actors can compile and distribute voter guides that summarize candidates' views on salient issues, often through graphics like tables or checklists. Historically, newspapers and organizations like the League of Women Voters have commonly published such guides.[186] Second, reflecting advances in technology, private actors can create websites that ask people a few questions about their own policy positions and then show them spatial maps indicating how ideologically close or far candidates are from them. Outside academia, Vote Smart's "Vote Easy" resource is a good example of this sort of site (for federal elections).[187]

While these efforts may seem laudable but ineffectual, evidence is mounting that they actually work. In one in a series of experiments by Cheryl Boudreau, Christopher Elmendorf, and Scott MacKenzie, the authors find that the majority of subjects asked if they would like more information before declaring their vote choice in a mayoral election respond favorably. Most of these subjects also prefer the direct information about candidates' policy stances supplied by a voter guide to the proxies offered by parties' endorsements.[188] More significantly, in other experiments in this series, Boudreau and her collaborators determine that subjects exposed to voter guides or spatial maps are more able to engage in spatial voting, in that the relationship tightens between their policy views and those

---

[185] *See, e.g.,* Stephen A. Jessee, *Partisan Bias, Political Information, and Spatial Voting in the 2008 Presidential Election,* 72 J. POL. 327, 335 (2010) ("Less informed voters . . . may lack the basic political knowledge to make decisions based on candidates' actual policy positions . . . .").

[186] *See, e.g., Voter Guides,* LEAGUE OF WOMEN VOTERS, https://www.lwv.org/tag/voter-guides (last visited Feb. 1, 2024).

[187] *See VoteEasy,* VOTE SMART, https://justfacts.votesmart.org/about/voteeasy/ (last visited Feb. 1, 2024).

[188] *See* Cheryl Boudreau et al., *The Civic Option? Using Experiments to Estimate the Effects of Consuming Information in Local Elections,* J. EXP. POL. SCI. 1, 9 (2022).

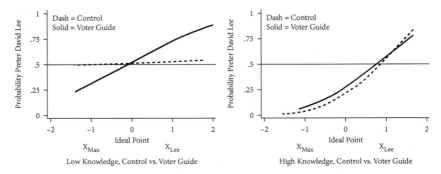

FIGURE 12.2 PREDICTED LIKELIHOODS OF SUBJECTS PREFERRING MORE
CONSERVATIVE CANDIDATE BY SUBJECT KNOWLEDGE AND EXPOSURE TO
VOTER GUIDE

Figure 12.2 is reproduced with permission from Cheryl Boudreau et al., *Informing Electorates via
Election Law: An Experimental Study of Partisan Endorsements and Nonpartisan Voter Guides in
Local Elections*, 14 ELECTION L.J. 2, 18 (2015). Copyright © 2015 by Mary Ann Liebert, Inc.

of their preferred candidates. Moreover, this effect is much stronger for subjects
who begin with less knowledge about local politics.[189]

Figure 12.2 presents the results of the first experiment by Boudreau and her
team, involving a San Francisco Board of Supervisors election and a voter guide
as a treatment. In the control group of low-knowledge subjects, there's essentially no correlation between a subject's ideology and the likelihood that she
favors the more liberal candidate (Eric Mar) or the more conservative candidate
(David Lee). But in the treated group of low-knowledge subjects, a strong link
materializes between subject ideology and vote choice, as a more liberal (or conservative) subject is now much more apt to prefer Mar (or Lee). In the control
and treated groups of high-knowledge subjects, on the other hand, there's little
difference in how subject ideology and vote choice are related. In both cases,
a more liberal (or conservative) subject is much more likely to favor Mar (or
Lee).[190] The upshot is that high-knowledge voters can vote spatially without
receiving additional information. But for the aligning engine of spatial voting
to function for low-knowledge voters, they need more data about candidates'
policy positions—and can obtain it from private actors.

---

[189] *See* Cheryl Boudreau et al., *Informing Electorates via Election Law: An Experimental Study
of Partisan Endorsements and Nonpartisan Voter Guides in Local Elections*, 14 ELECTION L.J.
2, 15–19 (2015) [Boudreau et al., *Informing Electorates*]; Cheryl Boudreau et al., *Roadmaps to
Representation: An Experimental Study of How Voter Education Tools Affect Citizen Decision Making*,
41 POL. BEHAVIOR. 1001, 1015–20 (2019).
[190] *See* Boudreau et al., *Informing Electorates, supra* note 189, at 15–19.

Campaign finance is the last channel I discuss through which private actors can bolster alignment. As I explained in Chapter 9, certain governmental regulations of money in politics are aligning, including the mandatory disclosure of campaign funding, limits on Super PACs, and curbs on corporations with ideologically extreme preferences. Interestingly, private actors have options at their disposal that can supplement, or even partly substitute for, these governmental rules. Start with disclosure. Private actors can take the voluminous data about campaign giving and spending reported to the Federal Elections Commission (FEC) and state regulators and make it available in a much more accessible format. In fact, that's exactly what the Center for Responsive Politics does for federal,[191] and the National Institute on Money in Politics does for state,[192] campaign funding data. Almost everyone relies on these groups' work rather than the clunky websites of the FEC and state regulators. These groups' work thus makes disclosure more aligning than it otherwise would be. If campaign funding data could only be found on governmental websites, then fewer journalists, rival campaigns, and ordinary people would find it, and disclosure would be less effective in every respect.[193]

With respect to Super PACs, private actors can take advantage of private law to deter these groups' generally misaligning spending. In particular, opposing candidates can enter into a contract stipulating that their race should be decided without Super PAC (or other outside) spending and, critically, enforcing this agreement by obligating each candidate to pay a hefty penalty if any covered group does make expenditures on her behalf. While this notion of "contracting around *Citizens United*," as Ganesh Sitaraman puts it,[194] may seem farfetched, Scott Brown and Elizabeth Warren did just that in their 2012 U.S. Senate race in Massachusetts. They signed the so-called People's Pledge, under which each campaign committed to contributing to charity 50 percent of any outside group's spending in support of that campaign. Strikingly, the People's Pledge held. There was virtually no third-party spending in the Brown-Warren race after the agreement was reached, and on the few occasions when outside groups did make

---

[191] *See* CTR. FOR RESPONSIVE POL., https://www.opensecrets.org/ (last visited Feb. 1, 2024).

[192] *See* NAT'L INST. FOR MONEY IN POL., https://www.followthemoney.org/ (last visited Feb. 1, 2024).

[193] *See, e.g.,* Robert Yablon, *Campaign Finance Reform Without Law,* 103 IOWA L. REV. 185, 223 (2017) ("By translating raw disclosure reports and data into more usable forms, with search functionalities, charts, and more, these groups help to promote public oversight of the electoral process."). Additionally, private actors can induce disclosure in situations where it's not legally compelled, for instance, by pressuring corporations to provide more information about their campaign funding. As Yablon notes, "[a] majority of major corporations now disclose more about their political expenditures than the law requires," often thanks to "agreements [they] have reached with shareholder groups, which routinely bring resolutions seeking greater transparency." *Id.* at 222.

[194] *See* Ganesh Sitaraman, *Contracting Around* Citizens United, 114 COLUM. L. REV. 755 (2014).

expenditures on Brown's behalf, his campaign duly paid the penalty.[195] Since the Brown-Warren race, candidates have entered into similar arrangements a few more times, and contemplated doing so even more frequently.[196]

And as for corporations, both shareholders and other private actors can dissuade them from deploying their treasuries to influence elections.[197] Shareholders can file resolutions urging corporations to refrain from campaign giving and spending or, at least, to supply campaign funding only if certain criteria are satisfied. Consumers and other concerned parties can boycott corporations that make campaign contributions or expenditures or, less aggressively, negatively publicize these corporate outlays. And again, these tactics aren't merely the fancies of academics; instead, they're increasingly adopted by activists on the ground. Roberto Tallarita shows that shareholder proposals regarding corporate campaign spending comprise the single largest category of "social" proposals over the last decade. These proposals now also tend to receive more votes from shareholders than in earlier times.[198] Likewise, Robert Yablon highlights several successful boycotts of corporations that intervened financially in campaigns. For instance, Target was, well, the target of backlash after it spent on behalf of a controversial gubernatorial candidate, and the firm ultimately apologized and changed its campaign spending policy.[199] Thanks to these and other efforts, most public companies abide by protocols that constrain their campaign funding, and "the amount of money they inject into the system is only a fraction of what it could be.[200]

To be clear, I don't think aligning private actions can fully replace aligning public policy. They can't reach (or can barely reach) major drivers of misalignment like partisan gerrymandering and campaign funding by ideologically extreme individuals (as opposed to Super PACs and corporations). Aligning private actions also face vexing collective action problems: Why should *you* reach out to your representative, or read a voter guide, or boycott a corporation, when the aligning benefits will accrue to the entire polity? Accordingly, my point here is only that private actions can move the alignment needle to some degree. Public policy has to be part (probably most) of the solution, too. Nor do I make any claim to comprehensiveness about the three categories of aligning private actions I've identified here. Some data suggests the aligning potential of measures within each category. But this evidence is preliminary, and future studies

---

[195] *See id.* at 757–58.
[196] *See id.* at 758–59; *see also* Yablon, *supra* note 193, at 217 (describing an agreement between Hillary Clinton and Rick Lazio not to rely on soft money in their 2000 U.S. Senate race in New York).
[197] Of course, such dissuasion is only aligning with respect to the subset of corporations with ideologically extreme preferences.
[198] *See* Roberto Tallarita, *Stockholder Politics*, 73 HASTINGS L.J. 1697, 1714, 1725 (2022).
[199] *See* Yablon, *supra* note 193, at 211–12.
[200] *Id.* at 210.

might undercut it or, more optimistically, spot more ways in which private actors can contribute to an aligned political system.

* * *

The Roberts Court's refusal to play an aligning role means that, if alignment is to be furthered, it must be actors other than the federal judiciary who do the furthering. Fortuitously, there's no shortage of other actors with the legal ability and, sometimes, the political will to take aligning measures. At the federal level, Congress has sweeping regulatory authority over elections both horizontally (across different types of elections) and vertically (on different substantive grounds). Congress has also repeatedly used this vast power to promote alignment, and almost did so again through the omnibus election law bills of 2021–22. At the state level, the ISL theory now poses few, if any, problems for aligning efforts undertaken by nonlegislative state actors with respect to federal elections. All these actors—governors, other executive officials, the people via direct democracy, state courts—and state legislatures, too, advance alignment on certain occasions, at least in the redistricting context. Finally, private actors have some capacity to boost alignment on their own, independent of public policy. These private aligning channels operate on the informational environment of politicians, the informational environment of voters, and the campaign finance ecosystem. In sum, these aligning alternatives to federal litigation make clear that our anti-alignment Court doesn't condemn us to an anti-alignment fate.

Conclusion

Wisconsin Revisited

I began this book with a snapshot of Wisconsin's political system over the last decade. I conclude this project by revisiting Wisconsin and using it to illustrate many of the themes of the preceding chapters. Why Wisconsin? In part because I'm familiar with its recent political history having litigated cases about its district plans in the 2010s and 2020s. Also partly because Wisconsin has been the site of so much election law litigation of late: over not just redistricting[1] but voting restrictions,[2] the impact of the coronavirus pandemic on voting,[3] and the Voting Rights Act, too.[4] And why a particular state, rather than the federal government, as a concluding case study? Because a good deal of misalignment at the federal level is the product of hardwired constitutional features: the malapportioned Senate, the Electoral College with its penchant for wrong-winner outcomes, the House with its fifty state delegations, and so on. All these features are beyond this book's scope because they're unchangeable without constitutional amendments. But all these features are irrelevant to a state-level polity like that of Wisconsin.

Reprise

In Chapter 1, then, I described the rights-structure debate that dominates modern election law. On one side are the balancers: the many judges and few academics who believe that cases should be adjudicated by weighing burdens on individual rights against countervailing state interests. In the other camp are the structuralists: the many scholars who want cases to be decided based on their implications for structural democratic values, specifically competition or participation. My main point was that both the balancers and the structuralists are blind to alignment. To the balancers, the absence of alignment isn't a burden on any cognizable right, and so doesn't need to be weighed against any justificatory state interest. To the structuralists, alignment is a different democratic value

---

[1] *See, e.g.*, Gill v. Whitford, 138 S. Ct. 1916 (2018).
[2] *See, e.g.*, Luft v. Evers, 963 F.3d 665 (7th Cir. 2020).
[3] *See, e.g.*, Democratic Nat'l Comm. v. Wis. St. Legis., 141 S. Ct. 28 (2020).
[4] *See, e.g.*, Wis. Legis. v. Wis. Elections Comm'n, 595 U.S. 398 (2022).

Aligning Election Law. Nicholas O. Stephanopoulos, Oxford University Press. © Nicholas O. Stephanopoulos 2024.
DOI: 10.1093/9780197662182.003.0013

from competition or participation. In fact, alignment isn't even much furthered by highly competitive or participatory elections.

Wisconsin nicely demonstrates the balancers' and the structuralists' insensitivity to alignment. As I'll discuss in a moment, misalignment is rife in Wisconsin. But the Supreme Court, the pioneer and leading practitioner of rights-interests balancing, deemed this fact immaterial in a 2018 case. Distortion of the Wisconsin "legislature's overall composition and policymaking" doesn't even "present[] an individual and personal injury of the kind required for . . . standing"—let alone trigger heightened scrutiny or establish liability.[5] As balancer-in-chief, "[t]he Court's . . . role is to vindicate . . . individual rights," not to combat misalignment.[6] Unlike the balancers, the structuralists would at least be interested in Wisconsin's democratic record. But competitive structuralists would focus on the closeness and contestedness of Wisconsin elections, and they would be pleased by what they found (in statewide races). Similarly, participatory structuralists would emphasize voter turnout in Wisconsin, which is high by American standards. Neither competitive nor participatory structuralists would notice the misalignment that mars Wisconsin's political system.

Next, in Chapters 2 and 3, I respectively addressed the theory and the empirics of alignment. Conceptually, there are three key axes that identify different facets of alignment. One is the political unit within which alignment is analyzed: a specific district or an entire jurisdiction. Another is the method through which popular preferences are summarized: majoritarian or collective. And the third axis is the type of governmental output: party affiliation, representation, or policy. Alignment, I further argued, is more compelling as a democratic value when it's sought with respect to people's overall ideologies, not their views on each individual issue. Analogously, misalignment is more troubling when it's durable than when it quickly fades away. So understood, alignment is no stranger to democratic theory (as some have claimed). To the contrary, it overlaps with central tenets of the delegate model of representation, pluralism, and deliberative democracy. Nor does alignment fall victim to the social choice critique that most people's policy preferences are unstable and unstructured. At least in the modern era, most people's policy preferences are adequately captured by a single ideological dimension that's quite consistent over time.

Empirically, I showed that misalignment of every kind is rampant in contemporary American politics. At both the federal and state levels, for example, just over half of respondents, on average, agree with the government's enacted policy on any given issue. So there's usually collective policy misalignment with the views of almost half the population. Likewise, elected officials of all

---

[5] *Gill*, 138 S. Ct. at 1931 (internal quotation marks omitted).
[6] *Id.* at 1933.

stripes—federal, state, and local; legislative and executive—are ideologically polarized. Since the ideological distribution of the public is roughly normal, collective representational misalignment is nearly universal. Just about everywhere you look, officeholders are more extreme than their constituents. And because of partisan gerrymandering above all (though political geography and happenstance play roles too), many district plans exhibit high levels of collective partisan misalignment. This bias means that the partisan compositions of legislatures often diverge sharply from the partisan preferences of voters. This bias also feeds the representational and policy misalignment I just described.

Wisconsin shines little light on the theoretical commentary of Chapter 2. But it exemplifies the empirical patterns of misalignment presented in Chapter 3. As to policy misalignment, it was most glaring during Wisconsin's period of unified Republican government from 2011 to 2019. This era saw the adoption of one archconservative policy after another, on issues including taxes, unions, guns, abortion, and the environment, even though the state's electorate was almost perfectly divided.[7] As to representational misalignment, Wisconsin's legislature has long been one of the most ideologically polarized in the country.[8] This representational skew in favor of the ideological extremes has been compounded since 2013 by a pronounced tilt to the right.[9] In recent years, that is, Wisconsin's legislature has been both more polarized and more conservative than the state's population. And as to partisan misalignment, Wisconsin's state legislative plans have been exceptionally biased in Republicans' favor in the 2010s and 2020s.[10] Republicans have routinely won legislative supermajorities, sometimes after receiving fewer votes statewide than Democrats. This legacy of the "great gerrymander of 2012" has now distorted Wisconsin's political system for more than a decade.[11]

In Chapter 4, I contended that conventional legal materials support (even if they don't compel) the constitutionalization of alignment. Alignment overlaps considerably with the concepts of popular sovereignty, promised to each state by the Guarantee Clause, and equality, codified by the Equal Protection Clause. Constitutional drafters like James Madison and John Bingham defended their

---

[7] According to the aggregate measure of state policy ideology introduced in Devin Caughey & Christopher Warshaw, *The Dynamics of State Policy Liberalism, 1936-2014*, 60 AM. J. POL. SCI. 899 (2016), Wisconsin experienced the biggest right-wing policy shift in its history from 2010 to 2014.

[8] *See* Boris Shor & Nolan McCarty, *The Ideological Mapping of American Legislatures*, 105 AM. POL. SCI. REV. 530, 546 (2011).

[9] *See* Devin Caughey et al., *Partisan Gerrymandering and the Political Process: Effects on Roll-Call Voting and State Policies*, 16 ELECTION L.J. 453, 463 (2017).

[10] *See Wisconsin's 2012-2020 State House Redistricting Plan*, PLANSCORE, https://planscore.org/wisconsin/#!2020-plan-statehouse-eg (last visited Feb. 1, 2024); *Wisconsin's 2012-2020 State Senate Redistricting Plan*, PLANSCORE, https://planscore.org/wisconsin/#!2020-plan-statesenate-eg (last visited Feb. 1, 2024).

[11] Sam Wang, *The Great Gerrymander of 2012*, N.Y. TIMES, Feb. 2, 2013, at SR1.

handiwork on the ground that it would lead to a government bound by the will of the people. In one decision after another, the Warren Court recognized alignment as a constitutional and normative value of the highest order. And in state constitutions, alignment is at the core of the democracy principle that's itself the foundation of state constitutional law. I further explained that alignment could be legally instantiated in two ways: as a sword and as a shield. As a sword, it would be used to challenge misaligning electoral practices. As a shield, its function would be to defend aligning electoral policies disputed on other bases.

Wisconsin's constitution demonstrates how state charters often endorse alignment more overtly than does the federal Constitution. All parts of Wisconsin's government "deriv[e] their just powers from the consent of the governed," the constitution declares in its first article.[12] Majoritarianism, the charter continues, is the operative rule for both popular elections and legislative votes.[13] Through popular elections—including for several executive positions, for judges, and to recall officeholders with poor records—Wisconsin acknowledges that "the people are the source of all political power, and to them should their officers and rulers be responsible."[14] Relying on these and other provisions, the state supreme court extended the franchise to Black residents in 1866, four years before the Fifteenth Amendment had to be ratified to achieve this goal at the federal level.[15] In 1892, the court struck down state legislative maps that "violate[d] and destroy[ed] one of the highest and most sacred rights and privileges of the people," namely, "equal representation in the legislature."[16] The court thus anticipated the federal reapportionment revolution that occurred seventy years later. The court even sought to "prevent the legislature from gerrymandering,"[17] an aim the Roberts Court has now foresworn for federal law.

In Chapter 5, I started exploring how particular election law subfields implicate alignment. For regulations of the voting process, I argued, the baseline for evaluating alignment can't be the preferences of actual voters. That's because actual voters are themselves the product of voting regulations: the people who are able to cast ballots thanks to, or in spite of, these rules. In this context, the views of the population operated on by voting regulations—typically, the pool of eligible voters—provide a more sensible benchmark. I also showed that most modern voting regulations don't significantly influence alignment. Voting

---

[12] Wis. Const. art. I, § 1.

[13] See, e.g., id. art. III, § 7; art. XII, §§ 1–2; art. XIII, §§ 7–8, 12.

[14] JOURNAL OF THE CONVENTION TO FORM A CONSTITUTION FOR THE STATE OF WISCONSIN 106–08 (1847).

[15] See Gillespie v. Palmer, 20 Wis. 544 (1866).

[16] State ex rel. Att'y Gen. v. Cunningham, 51 N.W. 724, 729 (1892).

[17] Id. at 730. In a recent case, moreover, Wisconsin's state supreme court invalidated highly biased state legislative plans because of their large numbers of noncontiguous districts. See Clarke v. Wis. Elections Comm'n, 998 N.W.2d 370 (Wis. 2023).

expansions like automatic voter registration and convenience voting aren't especially aligning. Nor are voting restrictions like curbs on convenience voting and photo ID requirements for voting too misaligning. The reason is that these policies tend to affect relatively small numbers of people, whose partisan and policy preferences are relatively similar to those of unaffected people. Put another way, for most Americans today, the main drivers of voting are cognitive—knowing and caring about elections—not institutional.

Between 2011 and 2014, Wisconsin's unified Republican government enacted a series of voting restrictions. These included a photo ID requirement for voting, a proof-of-citizenship requirement for college students registering to vote, a cutback to early voting locations and hours, and a ban on certain modes of sending absentee ballots.[18] The motive for these curbs was unquestionably partisan: "suppress[ing] Democratic votes to gain a partisan advantage," in the words of a federal district court.[19] But it's much less clear whether the policies actually caused substantial misalignment. The best available studies find that voting restrictions of these types have negligible partisan impacts. Wisconsin also remains a narrowly divided swing state in the wake of the Republican campaign to limit voting, just as it was before. This experience therefore highlights one of this book's more counterintuitive lessons. Even highly informed political elites are often wrong about the consequences of electoral reforms. Specifically, many voting restrictions that are widely *thought* to be misaligning end up leaving few discernible traces.

In Chapter 6, I discussed regulations of political parties (including the electoral systems within which parties compete). I made the theoretical point that intraparty alignment—congruence of party outputs with party members' preferences—has little democratic appeal. Parties are important parts of any polity but they're not the polity itself, the entity within which alignment does matter, democratically speaking. Intraparty alignment can also threaten the more familiar forms of alignment if a party that's internally aligned, but misaligned with the population as a whole, wins control of the levers of government. I further surveyed the empirical evidence about the effects of party regulations. Like voting regulations, regulations of how parties choose their general election nominees impact alignment only at the margins. Restrictions on minor party ballot access can sometimes prevent stark misalignment, if an excluded party would have been a spoiler had it made the ballot. But this scenario is both infrequent and only possible under a plurality winner rule. Alternatives to plurality rule, lastly, have considerable aligning potential. Single-winner alternatives like

---

[18] *See* One Wisconsin Inst., Inc. v. Thomsen, 198 F. Supp. 3d 896, 906–07 (W.D. Wis. 2016), *rev'd*, 963 F.3d 665 (7th Cir. 2020).

[19] *Id.* at 927.

pairwise voting can eliminate the risk of minor party spoilers. More ambitiously, multiple-winner systems of proportional representation promise better partisan and representational alignment.

Wisconsin helps to refute the common claim that more inclusive primaries breed more moderate officeholders. The state invented the open primary at the dawn of the twentieth century.[20] In 1981, Wisconsin went all the way to the Supreme Court to defend this system against the national Democratic Party's attempt to close it to non-Democrats.[21] Yet as I mentioned above, Wisconsin has one of the most ideologically polarized legislatures in the country, bereft of almost any moderate members.[22] Wisconsin's recent presidential elections also illustrate how generous minor party ballot access can be misaligning. In four of six elections since 2000, a minor party candidate's vote share exceeded the winning candidate's margin of victory.[23] So the winning candidate might not have been the Condorcet winner in some of these races. And this prospect of minor party spoilers could have been avoided had Wisconsin used pairwise voting (or another alternative to plurality rule) in presidential elections. Even the bias and polarization of Wisconsin's legislature could have been mitigated by a multiple-winner system of proportional representation.

In Chapter 7, I addressed redistricting, particularly the practice of partisan gerrymandering. There's likely no practice in modern American politics as consistently misaligning as gerrymandering. Many district plans exhibit large partisan biases. These biases frequently metastasize into severe representational and policy misalignment. These biases also tend to be unnecessary in that much fairer maps are usually possible given jurisdictions' political geographies and nonpartisan line-drawing criteria. Litigation against highly skewed plans, then, is the legal upshot of my approach. But there are political upshots, too. Evidence is mounting that independent redistricting commissions and explicit partisan fairness requirements reduce plans' partisan tilts. So jurisdictions should transfer redistricting authority to commissions and codify fairness criteria. And while district *maps* and the *jurisdiction-wide* misalignment they often generate are rightfully the priority of reformers, *individual* districts also warrant some attention because of the *district-specific* misalignment they can yield. Individual districts that flout traditional line-drawing requirements are linked to legislative representation that's less congruent with constituent opinion. So jurisdictions

---

[20] *See, e.g., Wisconsin Primary History*, WisPolitics (Sept. 9, 2019), https://www.wispolitics.com/2019/wisconsin-primary-history/.

[21] *See* Democratic Party of U.S. v. Wisconsin ex rel. La Follette, 450 U.S. 107 (1981).

[22] *See supra* note 8 and accompanying text.

[23] *See United States Presidential Elections in Wisconsin*, Wikipedia, https://en.wikipedia.org/wiki/United_States_presidential_elections_in_Wisconsin (last visited Feb. 1, 2024).

should enact traditional criteria and, as importantly, mapmakers should heed and courts should enforce them.

Wisconsin is the contemporary poster child for ruthless gerrymandering. Its 2010s state house plan wasn't just the Roberts Court's impetus to disclaim any interest in the structural democratic value of alignment. Over its lifetime, that plan also exhibited the worst efficiency gap in the entire nation.[24] Not to be outdone, as of this writing, Wisconsin's 2020s state house plan has again been the most biased in America.[25] Moreover, as detailed earlier, these record-setting skews haven't been confined to the partisan context. Instead, they've penetrated the domains of representation and policy, rendering them both much more conservative than most Wisconsinites would like. And nor has the misalignment attributable to redistricting in Wisconsin been limited to the jurisdiction-wide variety. The state's 2010s and 2020s state house districts have blithely disregarded county boundaries, broken up cities, and even joined noncontiguous communities.[26] These districts have thus fostered less congruent district-specific representation to go along with pervasive jurisdiction-wide misalignment.

In Chapter 8, I analyzed how the Voting Rights Act (VRA) relates to the pursuit of alignment. The VRA's objectives of minority participation, minority representation, and policy responsiveness to minority concerns are conceptually distinct from alignment. At most, participation, representation, and responsiveness are democratic values that are correlated with, not equivalent to, alignment. And when these values are sought for *minority* members, they become wholly unlike alignment with the preferences of the *entire* population. Zeroing in on the VRA's aspiration of minority representation, some allege that this goal conflicts with the promotion of alignment. But this critique assumes that minority opportunity districts drawn to comply with the VRA must be inefficiently packed with Democratic voters. Minority opportunity districts *can*—but don't *have to*—be heavily Democratic. When they're designed carefully so they don't needlessly waste Democratic votes, the tension between minority representation and alignment disappears. As for the VRA's original aim of minority participation, it has an uncomplicated positive association with alignment. In theory and in practice, enabling more minority members to vote, especially in heavily minority areas, results in a better fit between governmental outputs and popular preferences.

Wisconsin's redistricting travails over the last two cycles demonstrate that minority representation and partisan alignment aren't necessarily connected. In

[24] *See 2020 State House District Maps*, PLANSCORE, https://planscore.org/#!2020-statehouse (last visited Feb. 1, 2024).

[25] *See 2022 State House District Maps*, PLANSCORE, https://planscore.org/#!2022-statehouse (last visited Feb. 1, 2024). However, this plan was invalidated in *Clarke v. Wis. Elections Comm'n*, 998 N.W.2d 370 (Wis. 2023).

[26] *See, e.g.*, David A. Leib & Scott Bauer, *Lawsuit Targets Wisconsin Legislative Districts Resembling Swiss Cheese*, A.P. NEWS, Aug. 13, 2013.

2012, a federal district court held that Wisconsin's state house plan violated the VRA by cracking the Latino community in Milwaukee.[27] When this violation was remedied, thereby boosting Latino representation, the plan's partisan bias was entirely unaffected. The plan was previously, and remained, exceptionally skewed in Republicans' favor. Because of this severe tilt, this plan was challenged later in the decade as a partisan gerrymander. In this litigation, the plaintiffs presented an alternative map that included the same number of minority opportunity districts as the enacted plan but was almost perfectly neutral in partisan terms.[28] This map established that minority representation could be kept constant in the Wisconsin legislature even while partisan misalignment was drastically reduced. And in 2022, the Supreme Court concluded that the VRA didn't require creating a seventh Black opportunity district in Milwaukee.[29] When the state supreme court duly adopted a state house plan with six Black opportunity districts, the plan's partisan bias barely changed.[30] Just as adding a Latino opportunity district was compatible with maintaining a huge pro-Republican skew in 2012, so was subtracting a Black opportunity district ten years afterward.

In Chapter 9, I covered the last election law subfield, the regulation of campaign finance. I conceded that the prevention of partisan misalignment isn't a valid rationale for limits on money in politics. This is primarily because of the lack of any agreement about the "right" campaign spending baseline, relative to which the status quo could be evaluated. However, I argued that the advancement of representational alignment is both a compelling and a doctrinally available justification for campaign finance regulation. This interest doesn't suffer from a baseline problem. Nor is it precluded by Supreme Court decisions rejecting the avoidance of undue influence corruption, distortion, and inequality—all separate concepts from misalignment—as reasons for restricting money in politics. Turning to the empirics, the aligning impacts of campaign finance policies hinge on the ideological profiles of the funders they affect. Individual funders tend to be ideologically extreme. So measures that curb their giving and spending diminish their sway over officeholders and thus improve representational alignment. In contrast, political action committees (PACs) and political parties are usually more moderate (even if their moderation is often strategic, not sincere). So caps on their campaign funding weaken a centripetal force in American

---

[27] See Baldus v. Members of Wis. Gov't Accountability Bd., 849 F. Supp. 2d 840, 854–58 (E.D. Wis. 2012).

[28] See Whitford v. Gill, 218 F. Supp. 3d 837, 924 (W.D. Wis. 2016), vacated, 138 S. Ct. 1916 (2018); see also Jowei Chen, The Impact of Political Geography on Wisconsin Redistricting: An Analysis of Wisconsin's Act 43 Assembly Districting Plan, 16 ELECTION L.J. 443, 448–52 (2017) (finding that randomly generated Wisconsin state house maps that preserved all of the enacted plan's minority opportunity districts tended to be far less biased than the enacted plan).

[29] See Wis. Legis. v. Wis. Elections Comm'n, 595 U.S. 398, 403–06 (2022).

[30] See Johnson v. Wis. Elections Comm'n, 401 Wis. 2d 198 (2022).

politics and induce politicians to move toward the ideological poles. The point is that alignment isn't a monolith in the campaign finance context. Its prescriptions vary widely based on how rules constrain or empower different categories of funders.

Wisconsin's campaign finance regulations do less than they constitutionally could to further representational alignment. Compared to other states, Wisconsin's limits on individual contributions to statewide candidates are quite lax. These ceilings are currently set at $20,000 per election, while the national median is only about $4,000.[31] Thanks to these high caps, ideologically polarized individual donors are able to give profusely to statewide candidates and so, potentially, to skew the representation they provide if elected. Unlike multiple other states, Wisconsin also restricts PAC contributions to candidates, especially stringently at the state legislative level.[32] Business and trade organizations whose donations could exert a moderating influence are therefore barred from supplying as much money as they might otherwise choose. Further, in a 2015 decision, the state supreme court held that outside groups can freely coordinate their activities with candidates, and don't need to report these activities, if the activities are confined to issue advocacy.[33] Wisconsin's campaign finance disclosure regime thus has a gaping hole, diminishing its aligning benefits. Lastly, the state offers no public financing to candidates at any electoral level.[34] So Wisconsin eludes the misalignment that some public financing systems can bring about, but only by eschewing the closer representational congruence promised by other approaches.

In Chapter 10, I considered how alignment can be promoted through *non*electoral means. As a legal and political objective, alignment may be most intuitive in the electoral context. But its appeal hardly vanishes as we cross from election law to other public law domains. In fact, the same resources that make alignment a plausible constitutional value for elections apply equally to nonelectoral processes. So *which* nonelectoral processes have the most aligning potential? Preliminarily, four enjoy at least some empirical support. One, legislative procedures that enhance the agenda-setting authority of *chamber* majorities—as opposed to majority *parties*—appear to improve policy alignment. Two, interventions that result in more and deeper media coverage of

[31] *See Campaign Contribution Limits: Overview*, NAT'L CONF. ST. LEGIS. (Oct. 4, 2019), https://www.ncsl.org/elections-and-campaigns/campaign-contribution-limits-overview; *State Limits on Contributions to Candidates, 2023-2024 Election Cycle*, NAT'L CONF. ST. LEGIS. (May 2023), https://documents.ncsl.org/wwwncsl/Elections/Contribution-Limits-to-Candidates-2023-2024.pdf.
[32] *See State Limits on Contributions to Candidates, 2023-2024 Election Cycle, supra* note 31. However, Wisconsin doesn't limit state party contributions to candidates, and its caps on individual contributions to state legislative (as opposed to statewide) candidates are unremarkable. *See id.*
[33] *See* State ex rel. Two Unnamed Petitioners v. Peterson, 866 N.W.2d 165 (Wis. 2015).
[34] *See Public Financing of Campaigns: Overview*, NAT'L CONF. ST. LEGIS. (Feb. 6, 2023), https://www.ncsl.org/elections-and-campaigns/public-financing-of-campaigns-overview.

politics seem to boost representational alignment by enabling more voters to engage in accurate spatial voting. Three, measures that increase union density may be aligning for several reasons: because union members are more politically informed, because they vote at higher rates, and because union organizations are effective lobbyists for popular policies. And four, the near-perfect correlation between economic inequality and legislative polarization suggests that, if our society became less materially unequal, our legislatures would be less polarized and more reflective of popular preferences.

In Wisconsin, these nonelectoral forces interestingly push in different directions. On the one hand, the majority party in the Wisconsin legislature (in recent years, the Republican party) has a firm grip on the legislative agenda. As a federal district court found, "given the legislative practice and custom of Wisconsin, legislative action is controlled, as a practical matter, solely by the majority caucus."[35] As a result, the majority party is rarely rolled and policies opposed by most majority party legislators are rarely enacted—even if they're supported by the public. Additionally, Wisconsin's unified Republican government in the 2010s first limited collective bargaining by public employees and then approved a "right-to-work" law forbidding the agency shop. Union membership in Wisconsin consequently declined from about 13 percent in 2011 to roughly 7 percent in 2022.[36] On the other hand, Wisconsin has an unusually large number of journalists covering its state legislature: thirty as of 2022, a total exceeded only by five much bigger states.[37] Wisconsin also has a low level of income inequality compared to other states (albeit a high level by historical or international standards).[38] This mixed picture could be the outcome of Republican officeholders using the most accessible nonelectoral tools to skew the political system in their favor. Unions can be brought to heel through straightforward legislation, and legislative agenda control doesn't even require passing a bill. In contrast, neither journalistic coverage nor income inequality can be manipulated as easily by elected officials.

In Chapter 11, I portrayed the Roberts Court as the anti-alignment Court, undermining this democratic value at every turn. I introduced two dimensions along which a Court decision can be classified: whether it upholds an electoral regulation (passive) or strikes it down (active); and whether a decision improves alignment (pro-alignment) or worsens it (anti-alignment). In the simple matrix

---

[35] Whitford v. Gill, 218 F. Supp. 3d 837, 882 (W.D. Wis. 2016), *vacated*, 138 S. Ct. 1916 (2018).

[36] See *Union Membership Historical Table for Wisconsin*, U.S. BUREAU OF LABOR STAT., https://www.bls.gov/regions/midwest/data/unionmembershiphistorical_wisconsin_table.htm (last visited Feb. 1, 2024).

[37] See *U.S. Statehouse Reporters by State*, PEW RSCH. CTR. (Apr. 5, 2022), https://www.pewresearch.org/journalism/interactives/u-s-statehouse-reporters-by-state/.

[38] See *Income Inequality by State*, WORLD POPULATION REV. (July 2023), https://worldpopulationreview.com/state-rankings/income-inequality-by-state.

that arises from combining these dimensions, the two anti-alignment quadrants are filled with Roberts Court rulings. The passive anti-alignment quadrant includes cases refusing to invalidate extreme partisan gerrymanders and potentially distortive voting restrictions. The active anti-alignment quadrant is the site of cases nullifying a pillar of the VRA as well as one campaign finance rule after another. By comparison, the two pro-alignment quadrants are nearly (though not entirely) empty. They contain only a few cases declining to espouse even more misaligning positions and holding that certain partisan gerrymanders were unlawful for reasons unrelated to their gerrymandering. The Roberts Court, then, isn't quite a *maximally* anti-alignment Court. But it's close enough for the epithet to fit.

For a single mid-sized state, Wisconsin accounts for a disproportionate share of the Roberts Court's election law decisions. In turn, a disproportionate share—maybe all—of these decisions have been misaligning. I've already mentioned the 2018 ruling in which this Court upheld Wisconsin's state house plan against a partisan gerrymandering claim despite this plan's massive pro-Republican bias.[39] This is a paradigmatic passive anti-alignment case. Also arguably in this quadrant (depending on the exact empirics) are the Court's decisions not to hear a challenge to Wisconsin's photo ID requirement for voting,[40] to greenlight Wisconsin's election day deadline for *voters* to *send* absentee ballots,[41] and to okay the state's same deadline for *it* to *receive* these votes.[42] In still other rulings, the Court exercised its power of judicial review to negate policies that increased alignment in Wisconsin. In a 2007 case, the Court determined that Wisconsin Right to Life, a conservative advocacy group funded by wealthy right-wing donors, couldn't be lawfully barred from spending money on issue advocacy.[43] In a 2022 case, the Court concluded that a state house plan designed by Wisconsin's governor overly prioritized race, leading to that plan's replacement by a more skewed map crafted by the Republican legislature.[44] Together, these decisions show the Roberts Court sometimes sitting on the sidelines, sometimes entering the field of Wisconsin politics—and just about always aggravating misalignment through its actions.

Finally, in Chapter 12, I explained that not all roads to better alignment are blocked by the anti-alignment Court. At the federal level, Congress has nearly plenary authority to enact aligning electoral laws. This power extends horizontally to cover elections of every kind (federal, state, and local) and vertically to

[39] *See* Gill v. Whitford, 138 S. Ct. 1916 (2018).
[40] *See* Frank v. Walker, 575 U.S. 913 (2015).
[41] *See* Republican Nat'l Comm. v. Democratic Nat'l Comm., 140 S. Ct. 1205 (2020).
[42] *See* Democratic Nat'l Comm. v. Wis. St. Legis., 141 S. Ct. 28 (2020).
[43] *See* FEC v. Wis. Right to Life, Inc., 551 U.S. 449 (2007).
[44] *See* Wis. Legis. v. Wis. Elections Comm'n, 595 U.S. 398 (2022).

provide multiple constitutional bases for any congressional legislation. This power also has not lain dormant historically, and was almost deployed again in 2021–22 to revolutionize American elections. At the state level, an array of actors can take aligning measures: state legislatures, governors, election administrators, state courts, and voters via direct democracy. Most doubts about the legality of nonlegislative state actors regulating federal elections were also removed by a recent Supreme Court ruling. True, state actors don't always have the incentive (as opposed to the ability) to advance alignment, but they do often enough that their contributions can't be ignored. And alignment can be furthered not just by the government but by the people, acting on their own, as well. Private parties can inform politicians what their constituents really think about policies. Private parties can provide the materials voters need to vote spatially. And private parties can supplement, and to some extent replace, public regulations of campaign finance.

Had Congress passed an omnibus election law bill in 2021–22, Wisconsin's federal elections would have been transformed. In one stroke, the state would have been obliged to abandon many of its misaligning electoral policies. For instance, an independent commission would have crafted Wisconsin's congressional map pursuant to an explicit partisan fairness requirement.[45] Given these institutional and procedural safeguards, the map almost certainly wouldn't have exhibited (as the actual plan did) the worst partisan misalignment in America in the 2022 election.[46] Similarly, most of the potentially distortive voting restrictions that Wisconsin adopted in the 2010s would have been overridden. The state would have had to stop disenfranchising eligible voters lacking photo IDs, requiring college students to prove their citizenship to register to vote, and curbing early and absentee voting. And while the omnibus legislation wouldn't have disturbed Wisconsin's own campaign finance rules (for state and local elections), it would have brought unprecedented transparency and public funding to federal elections in the state. Better representational alignment would likely have ensued as voters learned more about the flows of campaign dollars and used vouchers to give more campaign dollars themselves.

Of course, Congress didn't ultimately approve an omnibus election law bill in 2021–22. Yet even without new congressional legislation, state actors in Wisconsin have recently taken some aligning measures, in the redistricting context, and may soon make even more progress. Wisconsinites elected a Democratic governor in 2018 (and reelected him in 2022). In 2021, he vetoed the gerrymandered state legislative and congressional maps passed by the

---

[45] That is, if the initial House bill requiring independent redistricting commissions had been enacted.

[46] See 2022 Congressional District Maps, PLANSCORE, https://planscore.org/#!2022-ushouse (last visited Feb. 1, 2024).

Republican legislature. He then submitted his own substantially less biased maps to the state supreme court, which had become responsible for redistricting after the elected branches deadlocked. The court initially selected the governor's maps over the legislature's because of their better compliance with traditional criteria.[47] More impactfully, in 2023, Wisconsinites replaced a conservative state supreme court justice with a liberal, giving rise to a 4–3 liberal majority. The reshaped court held that Wisconsin's state legislative plans violated the state constitution because of their many noncontiguous districts.[48] In the wake of this ruling, the legislature agreed to the adoption of the governor's proposed remedial maps, thereby finally eliminating the vestiges of the great gerrymander of 2012.[49] And perhaps most surprisingly, faced with the imminent judicial termination of gerrymandering in Wisconsin, the leader of the Republican legislature proposed an independent redistricting commission.[50] A commission, if the elected branches could agree on its contours, would be an even better solution to gerrymandering than litigation.

American Microcosm

Wisconsin is a microcosm of America, then, with respect to alignment. In Wisconsin, as in America, misalignment is ubiquitous. In Wisconsin, as in America, the lack of fit between governmental outputs and popular preferences is a grave legal and political problem. In Wisconsin, as in America, the Roberts Court exacerbates the situation instead of trying to fix it. In Wisconsin, as in America, Congress could be the solution if it could only vault all the hurdles of federal lawmaking. And in Wisconsin, as in America, state actors may not be the saviors we pine for, but they're the saviors we've got. Today—not in some notional future with a different Congress or a different Court—state actors can, and sometimes do, take steps to bolster our democracy.

---

[47] *See* Johnson v. Wis. Elections Comm'n, 971 N.W.2d 402 (Wis. 2022), *rev'd in part*, 595 U.S. 398 (2022). After an intervening U.S. Supreme Court decision, the Wisconsin Supreme Court adopted the legislature's state legislative plans. *See* Johnson v. Wis. Elections Comm'n, 972 N.W.2d 559 (Wis. 2022).

[48] *See* Clarke v. Wis. Elections Comm'n, 998 N.W.2d 370 (Wis. 2023).

[49] *See* Anjali Huynh, *New Wisconsin Legislative Maps Diminish G.O.P. Advantage*, N.Y. TIMES, Feb. 19, 2024, at A13.

[50] *See* Robin Vos, *Take Yes for an Answer and Resolve Redistricting Chaos*, LA CROSSE TRIBUNE, Sept. 21, 2023.

Index

For the benefit of digital users, indexed terms that span two pages (e.g., 52–53) may, on occasion, appear on only one of those pages.

Figures are indicated by italic *f* following the page number.

www.ingramcontent.com/pod-product-compliance
Lightning Source LLC
Chambersburg PA
CBHW062200050725
29174CB00003B/44